MARKETING
CHANNELS

SECOND EDITION

THE PPC MARKETING SERIES

Louis E. Boone, Consulting Editor

Louis E. Boone, The University of Tulsa
CLASSICS IN CONSUMER BEHAVIOR

Louis E. Boone, The University of Tulsa
James C. Johnson, St. Cloud State University
MARKETING CHANNELS, Second Edition

James C. Johnson, St. Cloud State University
READINGS IN CONTEMPORARY PHYSICAL DISTRIBUTION,
 Second Edition

James C. Johnson, St. Cloud State University
Donald F. Wood, San Francisco State University
CONTEMPORARY PHYSICAL DISTRIBUTION

Stephen K. Keiser, University of Delaware
Max E. Lupul, California State University, Northridge
MARKETING INTERACTION: A DECISION GAME

Howard A. Thompson, Eastern Kentucky University
THE GREAT WRITINGS IN MARKETING

MARKETING CHANNELS

SECOND EDITION

Louis E. Boone
The University of Tulsa

James C. Johnson
St. Cloud State University

Tulsa, Oklahoma

Manufactured in the United States of America.

Library of Congress Catalog Card Number 76-57506

ISBN 0-87814-026-3

Foreword

AMERICA'S MOST COLORFUL WRITER on channels, Mark Twain, commented on the constant vigilance and study required to maintain familiarity with the flows of the Mississippi River:

> Imagine . . . a piece of river twelve or thirteen hundred miles long, whose channel was shifting every day! . . . The first thing a pilot did when he reached New Orleans or St. Louis was to take his final and elaborate report to the (pilots') association parlors and hang it up there. . . . In those parlors a crowd was always gathered together, discussing changes in the channel, and the moment there was a fresh arrival, everybody stopped talking until this witness had told the newest news and settled the latest uncertainty.[1]

The analogies between Twain's Mississippi and contemporary marketing are obvious. He noted the ways in which the channel kept changing, the constant development of new paths, and interestingly enough, the apparent long-run tendency toward a shortening of the river's historic irregular and complex route. Twain outlined the fervid debate about both the feasibility of controlling the channel and the best means for achieving that objective. To push the simile even farther, he quoted Edward Atkinson (who incidentally has since come into some fame as a pioneer marketing writer) as arguing: ". . . the best form of outlet is a single deep channel,"[2] but he also noted that there was no unanimity concerning Atkinson's proposition.

Many similar turbulences appear in contemporary marketing flows. Some paths, such as franchising, that once received rather moderate usage have recently assumed increased significance. Even more dramatically, new institutions, such as retail furniture warehouses and catalog showrooms, have now become part of the marketing pattern. The location of much channel activity has shifted, moving at least in part from the city center to the periphery. Yet all of these changes have been accompanied by eddies and backflows. Downtown rehabilitation and the development of pedestrian malls provide at least some reaction to the current centrifical tendency. The spectacular growth of bantam

1. *Life on the Mississippi*, Harper's 1911 edition, pp. 135–36.
2. *Life* . . . , p. 510.

superettes (an interesting contradiction in terms) suggests that all marketing activity will not flow through gigantic outlets. Nevertheless, prediction of the way the channel will go tomorrow remains a perplexing problem. Moreover, not only are marketing channels changing, but our methods of studying those changes and our value systems for appraising their merits are also in a state of evolution.

As Twain pointed out, such a situation calls for information and a system of lights and markers. Professors Boone and Johnson have assembled an excellent informative set of guidelights to help meet that need. The papers included in this volume deal with the changes in the channel components themselves, the changes in the components' relationships with each other, the feasibility and desirability of various degrees and methods of internal and external channel control, the emerging social criteria for channel evaluation, and the probable directions of future change. Most of the articles included here are quite recent; they come from a variety of sources, and they all illustrate the fascination inherent in analyses of channel problems. Instructors, students, and marketers alike should find this book a useful guide to deeper understanding of channel forces and patterns.

Stanley C. Hollander
Michigan State University

Preface

THE STUDY OF marketing channels, as a separate aspect of marketing, has dramatically come of age during the past five years. New courses in *Marketing Channels* have appeared and some universities have broadened—or added to—their retailing offerings to courses in *Marketing Institutions*. But text materials have not kept pace with these developments. Professor David L. Appel recognized the paucity of teaching materials when he referred to marketing channels as ". . . one of the key remaining 'gaps' in the marketing literature."[1]

The purpose of the Second Edition of *Marketing Channels* is to present a truly *readable* approach to the subject of marketing channels and institutions. The presentation of channel theory is always followed by actual examples of business applications. To achieve this objective, selections were chosen from a wide variety of sources. Included in the text are articles from such publications as the *Journal of Marketing, Journal of Retailing, Sales and Marketing Management, Business Horizons, Fortune, MSU Business Topics, Wall Street Journal, Journal of Business Research,* and the *Marquette Business Review*. Selection of each article was made on the combined bases of fundamental contributions, ability to stimulate reader involvement, and skill in presentation of ideas and concepts. All of the selections have been previously screened by students for both fundamental contributions and readability. In order to emphasize *current* business applications of channel concepts, most of the business publication articles have been published in 1975 and 1976.

The book contains eleven chapters. Chapter One introduces the subject of marketing channels. An overview of this dynamic area of marketing is presented featuring selections that were written over a 55-year time span. A marketing classic written in 1921 by Paul Wesley Ivey notes three basic channel problems that manufacturers experience. It is followed by a 1976 article posing solutions to these quandaries.

Chapters Two and Three are devoted to analyses of the major marketing institutions: retailing and whoesaling. The role of retailing and wholesaling in the marketing channel is examined; some major prob-

1. *Journal of Marketing*, Vol. 36 (April 1972), p. 102.

lems facing these institutions are analyzed; and possible future developments and directions are discussed.

Chapter Four deals with sources of conflict in marketing channels and methods of obtaining cooperation among channel members. Chapter Five is devoted to the subjects of channel leadership and control and explores the development of vertical marketing systems in the United States.

The unique problems and opportunities in channels for industrial products are the subjects of Chapter Six. Franchising—the reasons behind its rapid growth during the 1960s and 1970s and its current and future problems—is examined in Chapter Seven. Chapter Eight broadens the horizons of marketing channels by considering international channels. The Japanese distribution system—often characterized as "long," complex, and relatively inefficient—serves as a case study in this chapter.

The legal issues involved in channel management are becoming increasingly more complicated and important. Chapter Nine presents an overview of the primary legal considerations facing marketers in the channel area.

A number of interfaces between channel activities and the area of societal responsibility are examined in Chapter Ten. Included are such subjects as ecology and the channel implications of recycling products, door-to-door selling, open dating, and unit pricing. The final chapter is devoted to an analysis of important emerging trends in marketing channels. Considered here are such subjects as the catalog showroom, direct sales, mail order marketing, cooperative advertising, instore servicing, and the growth of independent retailers in the food industry.

We believe that *Marketing Channels* will serve several market targets. Professors teaching courses in Marketing Channels and Marketing Institutions will find this book especially relevant for their classes. The text should also be useful as a supplement for courses in retailing and physical distribution. In this capacity, the book should enable the student to obtain a broader conception of how these specific courses fit into a marketing channel. In addition, marketing practitioners should find this book informative and helpful in solving their current channel problems.

Acceptance of the first edition of *Marketing Channels* has been gratifying. The second edition is significantly strengthened by the suggestions of a large number of marketing colleagues who are listed in the Acknowledgements page. We would also like to thank all of the authors and publishers for allowing us to reprint their works in this text. Special thanks is due to Professor Bert Rosenbloom for suggesting that we include the classic Paul Wesley Ivey article.

Tulsa, Oklahoma   Louis E. Boone
St. Cloud, Minnesota   James C. Johnson
January 1977

Acknowledgments

We gratefully acknowledge the suggestions of the following marketing scholars in the development of the Second Edition of *Marketing Channels*:

Boris W. Becker
Oregon State University

Frederick J. Beier
University of Minnesota

Louis P. Bucklin
University of California, Berkeley

Richard M. Clewett
Northwestern University

James A. Constantin
University of Oklahoma

C. Samuel Craig
Cornell University

Ronald C. Curhan
Boston University

Samuel M. Gillespie
Texas A&M University

Myron Goble
Shippensburg State College

Joseph P. Guiltinan
University of Massachusetts

Joseph F. Hair, Jr.
Louisiana State University

Stanley C. Hollander
Michigan State University

Bert C. McCammon, Jr.
University of Oklahoma

Anthony F. McGann
University of Wyoming

Patrick E. Murphy
Marquette University

Jacob Naor
University of Maine-Orono

Robin T. Peterson
New Mexico State University

Larry J. Rosenberg
New York University

Bert Rosenbloom
Drexel University

Philip B. Schary
Oregon State University

William L. Shanklin
Kent State University

Stanley F. Stasch
Loyola University

Louis W. Stern
Northwestern University

Brian Sternthal
Northwestern University

Shelby D. Hunt
University of Wisconsin-Madison

David L. Kurtz
Eastern Michigan University

Richard S. Lopata
SAM Associates, Inc.

Robert E. Stevens
Oral Roberts University

Robert E. Weigand
University of Illinois at Chicago
Circle

Contents

Chapter 1

Introduction

MARKETING CHANNELS PERFORM an integral role as components of the firm's marketing strategy. By delivering products and title to them to consumers at the right place, at the right time, and in the right amounts, marketing channels also perform a service to society by generating time, place, and ownership utility.

The importance of marketing channels can be seen almost daily in business magazines and professional journals. A 1976 *Wall Street Journal* article discussed the battle between Polaroid and Kodak in the instant-photography field. It was noted:

> In trying to blunt Kodak's entry, however, Polaroid is wrestling with several problems, including its bad relations with dealers. In part, the trouble has arisen because self-developing pictures eliminate the processing business for dealers. But it's also because discount stores, intent on building traffic, heavily advertise Polaroid products at cutrate prices, leaving little profit for dealers. "I carry Polaroid only because I have to to meet customer demand," snaps one dealer in a typical comment.[1]

Because of this friction between Polaroid and the traditional camera retailers, Kodak products are given significantly more shelf space and attention than the Polaroid cameras. Polaroid is taking several actions designed to improve its rapport with channel members. A new "partnership" program was initiated under which dealers who exceed their sales quotas earn large year-end bonuses. In April, 1976, a 24-hour toll-free phone service was installed. Dealers are encouraged to use this service to receive answers about photo questions, to place orders, and to check on the status of previously ordered shipments.[2]

A casual look at the hundreds of marketing channels in everyday use is sufficient to convince the observer that there is no such thing as a "best" marketing channel. "Best" for Avon may be direct from man-

1. William H. Carley, "Polaroid Seen Wary, Worried as it Girds for Kodak Arrival in Instant-Photo Field," *The Wall Street Journal* (April 16, 1976), p. 4. See also "Slow Deliveries Dog the Kodak 'Instant,'" *Business Week* (July 26, 1976), p. 43.
2. *Ibid.*

1

ufacturer to consumer through a sales force of almost 700,000 sales-women.[3] The "best" channel for frozen foods may be from food processor to agent middleman to merchant wholesaler to supermarkets and other retail grocers to consumer. Instead of searching for a "best" channel for all products, the business firm must analyze alternative channels to determine the optimum channel (or channels) for its products.

The Wilkinson Sword Company has traditionally used independent brokers in marketing its products. When Wilkinson recently introduced a new type of shaving blade (a convenience good), the firm took action to develop an intensive distribution system. To accomplish this objective, Wilkinson contracted with Colgate-Palmolive to market the Wilkinson blades through Colgate's extensive sales force and established channels for convenience type products. The results of the improved channel are revealed in improved blade sales. During the first eighteen months of the cooperative operation, Wilkinson's blade sales increased by ninety percent.

John Paige, vice-president of sales for the Bic Pen Corporation, credits Bic's marketing channels for the success of their low-priced pens. When discussing the reasons for the success of the Bic Banana pen, he stated ". . . where we have the edge is in our distribution."[4] The Bic marketing channel includes approximately 200,000 retail stores and more than 12,000 commercial dealer outlets.

The first selection in this chapter by Professors Cox and Schutte presents a lucid discussion of the challenges and opportunities involved in channel management. Marketing channels are defined and the article stresses the importance of coordinating channel activities with the other ingredients of the marketing mix in order to contribute to the objective of profitably satisfying chosen consumer segments.

The next article by Joseph P. Guiltinan presents a fascinating look at channel evolution. Guiltinan suggests a five-stage model explaining the observed evolutionary pattern.

The third selection deserves the label *marketing classic*. The article, first published in 1921, carefully and systematically presents the manufacturers' problems in dealing with channel members. Unfortunately, the problems discussed by Ivey more than a half-century ago have not been solved; in fact, they have intensified in magnitude.

The fourth article illustrates the concept of scrambled merchandising by discussing the unique channel chosen by the Hanes Corporation to market their "L'eggs" pantyhose.

3. "Troubled Avon Tries a Face-Lifting," *Business Week* (May 11, 1974), pp. 98–106.

4. "A Zany Campaign to Sell the Bic Banana," *Business Week* (May 27, 1972), p. 76. See also Ronald G. Shaw, "Brand Dominance in Mass Market," *Marketing Times* (September–October, 1974), pp. 22–25.

The last article in this chapter examines one solution to the channel coordination problems mentioned previously in the article by Professor Ivey. It discusses how the Helene Curtis Company insures that wholesalers are not the *ultimate* customer for their products.

1.1 A LOOK AT CHANNEL MANAGEMENT

Reavis Cox and Thomas F. Schutte

"Contrary to many textbooks, a channel of distribution is not a static network."

A LOOK AT CHANNEL MANAGEMENT

A strange anomaly in marketing today is the extent to which both managers and students who accept the idea that marketing efforts should be customer-oriented overlook the fact that, if efforts so oriented are to be successful, managers must use effective marketing channels. Conventional textbooks speak of the four P's as constituting the variables which management has under its control in working with marketing problems—product, place, price, and promotion. They discuss in great detail some of the things managers can do under these headings, but they offer little more than vague descriptions of the numbers and kinds of agencies through which these things must be done. Only a small number of specialized students—and most of these only in very recent years—have come to grips with what is involved if these agencies are to be organized into combinations and sequences that will do well the whole job of connecting production and consumption. This is a major but largely neglected problem in management. Some of the managers themselves are beginning to see dimly what is required, but they have made little progress in formalizing their ideas into rules or procedures.

The purpose of this paper . . . is to stimulate a rethinking of the role of management as applied to the channel. Emphasis will be placed upon the problems of the firm rather than the academic discipline of marketing in general. What we hope to do is to help managers, as well as students, develop new perspectives in channel management by providing:

1. Some examples of managerial problems raised by channels.
2. An operational definition of channel management.

Reprinted by permission from the authors and publisher. Reavis Cox and Thomas F. Schutte, "A Look at Channel Management," *Marketing Involvement in Society and The Economy*, edited by Philip R. McDonald (Chicago: American Marketing Association, 1970), pp. 99–105.

3. A look at some characteristics of managerial thinking about channels.

4. Some suggestions for rethinking the channel concept and its application to management.

EXAMPLES OF DISTRIBUTION PROBLEMS

The scope and magnitude of channel problems may be obscured both by the way marketing or distribution is defined and by the ways in which distribution programs are developed and carried into effect. It is interesting to note how often firms visualize their problems, not as problems in distribution, but as problems in selling, advertising, sales promotion, pricing, product management, or even manufacturing. A good way to see what we mean is to look at some examples of confusion which were selected by the authors without any attempt to be systematic or thorough.

1. A well-known pharmaceutical manufacturer assigns the responsibility for what it calls customer trade relations to its public relations department. The management of finished goods, inventories, warehouses, and physical distribution is a responsibility of the manufacturing department. Customer requests, servicing, returns, and allowances are divided between marketing and finance without a clear assignment to either group. No one is formally responsible for seeing to it that these scattered activities add up to a coordinated overall program. Can one be surprised that the central management is beginning to wonder whether its organization does not automatically produce underachievement in distribution?

2. A leading manufacturer of toiletry products distributes exclusively through drug wholesalers and drug chains. In response to spending heavily for promotion, advertising, and personal selling, it built up a strong consumer demand for one of its lines. Nearly two-thirds of the potential market for the sorts of goods constituting this line is bought by consumers through nondrug trades, and this proportion is increasing. Members of these trades wanted the product, but the company, dominated by principles derived from other products, would not change its distribution policy. Consequently, sales of the line have been falling for two years as the company refuses to see that products must be sold where consumers expect to find them not where sellers like to put them.

3. A large trucking company receives as many as 300,000 garments in one day from local manufacturers. Through a program of prompt, efficient handling and shipping, the firm can put garments on hangers in the receiving rooms of retailers, over a large geographic area, within 24

hours of receipt. The chairman of the board of the trucking company laments, "We get the garment quickly to the stores, on hangers, and ready to move to the sales floors. Then we discover that they sit around for days or even weeks waiting for someone to attach price tags." One part of a marketing system was done well, but the system, as a whole, faltered.

4. The idea that the economy offers an opportunity for someone to set up a gigantic distributor of automotive parts for competing manufacturers is relatively new. Until the creation of such a firm, the thousands of manufacturers, producing even more thousands of products, marketed them through a multitude of selling organizations. Customers for these parts, primarily garages and service stations, were constantly badgered by a plethora of salesmen representing manufacturers. Not only was the selling costly, but the complexity of the enormous number of automobiles, the number of parts needed for one vehicle, and the models to be served were all such that parts service centers required an intelligence system, effective inventory control, and sharp reductions in selling costs. But the need was not visualized until the new distributing firm recognized the need for analyzing the entire distribution system, brought it to the consciousness of parts users, and provided a service to meet it.

5. A furniture retailer currently receives many goods from manufacturers that require repair and refinishing. It employs two full-time men to do this work. The president of the retail operation justifies the presence of the two workers because they cost less than he would have to pay for the work involved and the loss of sales incurred in shipping the damaged goods back to the supplier. This retailer is looking for a manufacturer who will help him eliminate the need for having two full-time men. He believes a less costly system is possible. Some supplier that does its homework in looking at the entire channel may find this retailer to be a good, profitable account.

6. A well-known manufacturer of consumer paper products introduced a "giant economy box" of one product. Thanks to heavy promotion, consumers wanted it. So the retailers stocked it, but many supermarkets did so reluctantly because they had to stock it on the floor. They lacked shelf space for it. Thus, the manufacturer was vulnerable to competition from others who could satisfy the consumers' demand without penalizing the retailers. The extensive marketing research done by the producer during product development found a consumer need but failed to recognize that the retailer also had needs to be satisfied.

One could go on and on with such illustrations of the failure of businessmen to recognize the true nature of the channel problems, but these examples are sufficient for our purposes.

WHAT THE CHANNEL OF DISTRIBUTION IS

For present purposes, a channel of distribution may be defined as an organized network of agencies and institutions which, in combination, perform all the activities required to link producers with users and users with producers in order to accomplish the marketing task. From the point of view of the seller, the channel permits him to find and supply users of his goods. From the point of view of the buyer, the channel finds and delivers to him the want-satisfying goods he seeks. Some intangible services also require the use of channels to connect suppliers with users.

Contrary to many textbooks, a channel of distribution is not a static network. Not only are new channels created for new products as they appear, but also new channels often are developed for existing products. For example, a manufacturer of proprietary drugs may restrict his distribution of a suntan lotion to drug stores and the agencies that serve them until his penetration of the drug store market is optimized, at which time he may revise his distribution system to include variety chains and supermarkets. Likewise, the same proprietary drug manufacturer may decide to modify his policy of distributing exclusively through wholesalers because chain stores that will not buy through wholesalers now hold more of the market than do independent drug stores.

It should be noted that a new channel of distribution normally is created because both buyers and sellers need it in order to fulfill their joint marketing task as effectively as possible. For example, Smith, Kline and French Laboratories rely on over 400 drug wholesalers and over 35,000 drug stores to perform the services required if products such as Contac, Sea and Ski, and Love are to reach and satisfy consumers. On the other hand, the Drug House, Inc., one of the country's largest drug wholesalers of proprietary and ethical products, expects SKF to perform a number of services that will facilitate its servicing of individual drug stores; for example, putting inner-packs of six units each in the shipping cases.

Hartz Mountain, Inc., a producer of proprietary health care products for small animals, distributes through numerous rack jobbers to many thousands of pet shops and supermarkets. It does so because these jobbers provide, more cheaply than anyone else, the services of weekly stocking, dusting, and rehabilitation of goods on the shelves. Furthermore, the rack jobber provides the financial service of reimbursing the central offices with their due net profits without any previous billing to the chain and with subsequent dollar pay-out by the chain.

CONVENTIONAL THINKING ABOUT CHANNELS

Although the management of marketing channels has not received the formal attention it deserves from businessmen, a number of ways in which managements tend to view the problem may be discerned. Some of these are not really conscious formulations but rather what we may call "*as if* propositions." That is, the managers behave *as if* the channel is a certain kind of structure without spelling out their assumptions in detail. At least six such propositions can be stated.

1. Channels are determined by the characteristics of the product. A seller of goods following this rule holds that the shape and design of the channel that distributes his products are determined by their characteristics. Thus, goods of high unit-value can absorb high costs but require protection against loss or theft; perishability imposes a need for refrigeration and quick handling; large size or heavy weight calls for special materials handling equipment; and so on. The best channel in this view is the one that minimizes the cost imposed by the products' characteristics. This orientation may cause a seller to become so preoccupied with his product that he loses sight of other needs felt by the intermediate traders and ultimate users.

2. The channel stops at the loading platform. Some businessmen seem to see distribution as ending (rather than beginning) when the goods have been shipped. In essence, this notion sees distribution as an activity consisting of loading the product onto a common or contract carrier at the shipper's dock. What happens thereafter is the buyer's responsibility. The concept, thus badly stated, may be oversimplified in many cases; but it would be interesting to know how many firms see marketing in effect as a process of getting customers to take goods physically as near to the manufacturing plant as possible and to assume responsibilities for them from that point on.

3. The channel is primarily, if not exclusively, an agency for the physical distribution of goods. The literature and traditions of marketing are such that one can easily come to view distribution as physical distribution alone and thus overlook all the other tasks that must be performed by channels. Such a view is really an extension of the loading-platform thesis; but it opens the way to a consideration of choices as to where the seller's loading platform shall be located. Physical distribution is an important component part of the distribution process but viewing it as the distribution process is still a very narrow concept. Too often, sellers who overemphasize physical distribution tend to look upon their channel problem as being that of locating warehouses or selecting a viable form of transportation system for their products.

4. There is no provision within firms for the management of channels.

This may be called the vacant-chair thesis. Of the many possible conventions followed in channel management, this is one of the most important. It can be stated simply: Nobody serves or is expected to serve as manager of the firm's channels because the firm has no manager of marketing. If the company is well organized functionally, the various aspects of marketing will be handled by a number of officers—the purchasing agent, the customer relations manager, the traffic manager, the sales manager, the warehouse manager, and so on. But there will be no one man who coordinates the relations of the firm with all the agencies that form its marketing channel.

This view carries some significant consequences with it. In the absence of a channel manager one must ask: Who designs the distribution system for new products? Who reviews the needs and resources for existing products in order to make certain that required adjustments are made in the channel system? Who speaks for the company in dialogues with members of the channel?

Somehow or other, management gets questions answered; but the officers who answer them remain unidentified, and the chair of the distribution manager seems to remain vacant.

5. *The manufacturer constructs and manages the channel.* This concept can be called the dominant force thesis. It sees the manufacturer as both the architect and the captain of the channel. His is the dominant force. Textbooks commonly look at the distribution function almost as if the manufacturer presents all the stimuli and the distributive agencies (whether wholesalers, agents, or retailers) merely respond to what he does.

The fact that some manufacturers seem to act according to the dominant force theory may cause strain and conflict within the channel. The chairman of the board of the Rawlings Corporation says of the relationship between manufacturers and retailers, "I have been surprised and appalled at the *bad feelings, complete misunderstanding, and even distrust that exist between the manufacturers and the retailer.*"[1] He explains his concept of the relationships between the two by offering an analogy:

> The situation reminds us a little of the climax of a "Western." Two cowboys silently face each other in the middle of a hushed Front Street, each waiting for the other to draw.
> Each of our "heroes" feels that the other has done him dirt. The manufacturer is telling himself that the dealer hasn't been loyal, while the dealer firmly believes that the manufacturer has gotten just what he deserves.
> So they stand there and stand there—each waiting for the other to draw.

1. R. D. Brown, "Selling Through—Not to—Retailers," in Malcolm P. McNair and Mira Berman, eds., *Marketing Through Retailers* (New York: American Management Association, 1967), p. 59.

Meanwhile back on the ranch, nobody is minding the cows and someone else is selling the beefsteak.[2]

6. *Nobody manages the channel.*   Earlier in the paper we defined a channel as an organized network of agencies. But who organizes and manages the channel as a whole? One answer is that nobody does. The channel works as free competition is said to work in that the play of market forces attracts people to the performance of needed services and drives them to cooperate with one another in the absence of formal management. Somehow or other, the distribution task is accomplished even though no agency has any authority to command others.

Some students deplore this situation. They ask how a channel manager can be created, apparently assuming that formal management would improve the efficiency of the distribution system. A few writers seem to think that in practice channel systems, even though they usually do not have formally recognized managers sometimes do have *de facto* managers or captains. They achieve their position by virtue of their firm's having market power and the will to lead.

RETHINKING THE CONCEPT OF CHANNEL MANAGEMENT

We can now consider some suggestions as to how the marketing manager can develop a better understanding by his firm of the channel problems it faces. The central principle to be followed is that the firm must think not solely in terms of its own operation within the channel but rather in terms of relationships of its own operations to the operation of all other agencies within the channel. It also must keep in mind the fact that effectiveness in its own activities is not enough.

Somehow, matters must be worked out so that everything done by everybody in the channel adds up to effectiveness at the point where the final user chooses it over the offerings made to him by competing channels.

THINKING IN TERMS OF SYSTEMS

Systems analysis is in danger of becoming a superficial "buzz word" in the study of marketing today, but there is real merit in applying the concept to channel management. It must be admitted that, very often, little rationale is apparent in a firm's distribution system. The utility of systems analysis may be demonstrated if we look upon it as being helpful in the following sorts of studies:

2. *Ibid.,* p. 60.

a. A description of existing structure of a firm's channel or channels.

b. An assessment of needs and responses of each agency in the actual or desired channel for each product.

c. An evaluation of each specific channel and the flows it embodies from the joint or comon viewpoint of *all* the agencies concerned.

d. A consideration of modifications and adjustments that might be made in the channels for given products.

The Existing Structure.   All too often, a seller of goods views his channel relationship as one between himself and his immediate customer, or alternatively, as one between himself and the final user of his product, without regard to intermediate buyers. The first task in assessing a channel management system is to develop a critical-path description of the agencies perfoming the various channel services for given products. This assessment can often be made most effectively by considering the work done by the channel members as being that of conducting a number of "flows," i.e., the physical flow of the good, the flow of ownership, the flow of information, and so on.

The importance of this orientation has been stressed by one well known channel theorist, Professor Ralph Breyer. In an interview with one of the authors, he emphasized what he thought to be the most critical problems in distribution today. One of these was "the channel overview" problem. Here, he noted:

> One must examine the channel from a total-channel point of view—not just the manufacturer's, or the wholesaler's, or the retailer's. Without this commitment to the study and management of channels as a whole, little progress can be made toward the optimizing of distribution. It is entirely *wrong* to view a channel from the standpoint of the manufacturer only or to think that what is good for the manufacturer is good for the channel.

A simplistic version of a channel from the viewpoint of the manufacturer can be seen in Figure 1. A similar simplistic version from this viewpoint of the wholesaler can be seen in Figure 2. In Figure 1, the channel is for one product or line produced by one manufacturer. In Figure 2, the channel is for competing products made by several manufacturers but handled by one wholesaler. The charts are familiar enough but they ordinarily are used with little imagination. It takes little insight to see that the ideas of manufacturer and wholesaler as to what constitutes "effective" operation of a "good" channel can differ sharply. Anyone who sets himself up to be the channel leader or captain will need to keep this fact in mind.

Just recently, a Madison Avenue creative enthusiast has advocated that manufacturers take a more adventuresome approach to couponing

Fig. 1 A simplistic structure of a trade channel from the viewpoint of a manufacturer.

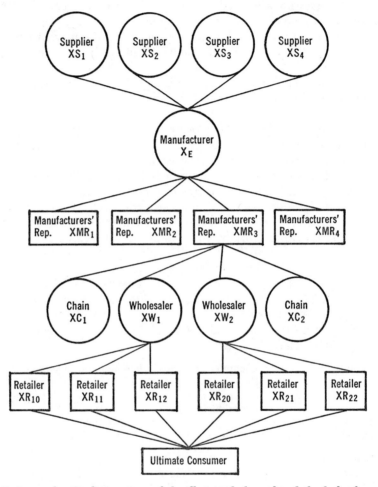

Owing to the simplistic nature of the illustrated channel and the lack of space, the identification of the physical ownership, information, and money flows was omitted.

ads.[3] He advocates the "wild" use of all shapes and sizes of the con-sumer "cents-off" tear-out coupons placed in print media. Uniformity of coupons it terms of the familiar rectangular approach would go by the wayside. Instead, a cents-off coupon for dog food would be shaped like a French Poodle or a cents-off coupon for wet soup would be

3. Stephen Baker, "Wild Shapes, Sizes Are Today's Look in Coupons," *Adver-tising Age* (August 4, 1969).

FIG. 2 A simplistic structure of a trade channel from the viewpoint of a wholesaler.

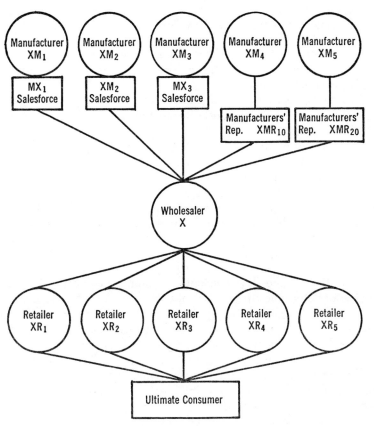

Owing to the simplistic nature of the illustrated channel and the lack of space, the identification of the physical ownership, information, and money flows was omitted.

shaped like a bowl of soup. While such new adventures may be eye catching and even appealing to consumers, we wonder if the Madison Avenue creative genius has ever appraised the consequences of the new shapes from the standpoint of the retailers who redeem the coupons. Imagine the stacking, sorting, cataloging, and storing problems faced by retailers and redemption centers! Here is where some application of Figure 1 and Figure 2 might be helpful to manufacturers.

In trying to sort out the tasks performed by each agency in a channel, much less simplistic approaches are required. One of these is to use what has been called the "flow" approach. This elaborates the structures charted in Figures 1 and 2 by visualizing what happens in a channel not as one flow but as a group of several interrelated flows. In a book on channel management being prepared by the present authors, channels are viewed as conducting four flows:

1. *The physical flow of the goods*, i.e., a sequence of agencies or (more precisely) facilities through which the goods move for transportation, storage, sorting, and so on.

2. *The flow of ownership or control*, i.e., a sequence of agencies through which moves the authority to decide what shall be done with the goods.

3. *The flow of information*, i.e., a sequence of agencies through which users tell producers and distributors what they want, while producers and distributors simultaneously tell users what they have to sell and try to persuade users to buy it.

4. *The flow of money*, i.e., a sequence of agencies through which capital is assembled and brought into the marketing process and an overlapping sequence of agencies through which buyers pay sellers for what they buy.

Application of the flow concept to channel management makes it possible to determine the precise role of each agency or facility in the channel of distribution. Discrepancies in the effectiveness with which agencies perform specific activities may be observed. For example, one firm has developed a critical-path appraisal of its physical distribution system. In doing so it has found that its three public warehouses were handling in a dissimilar manner the customers' original orders, the shipping orders, bills of lading, and the informational feedback to the sales (carbons of various order papers). As a result, customers were receiving inconsistent and often poor service.

Assessing the Needs and Responses of Each Firm Within the Channel.
One of the saddest shortcomings in channel management is the seller's frequent failure to consider the marketing needs and responses of his customers. How often does a seller objectively determine what his customers need in each of the flows? The manufacturer, if he makes any guess at all, is likely to decide intuitively what the customers want to do, or even can do, relative to each of the flows. There is nothing unusual about a firm that thinks one or two reports by salesmen will tell what its wholesalers are thinking.

Very unusual is a carefully designed, thorough, and systematic effort to find out the facts. An example is what one company calls its "Dealer Forum":

I write from some experience. In the Office Machines Division we created a Dealer Forum, and this proved very effective. We rotated our members on this Dealer Forum every two years. The meetings were held with the top management of the Division, including the manufacturing, engineering, financial, and marketing heads, as well as the general manager. Many fine programs came out of the Dealer Forum, and it was so successful . . . we . . . are going to adopt the same type of program with our sporting goods retailers.[4]

In a recent informal study, a drug manufacturer found that one of its advertising agencies not only failed to understand the nature of the management system for the total channel but did not really understand the role of its detail men. The agency was aiming its promotional pieces at the doctors without realizing that these pieces must also meet the needs and wishes of the detail men. For many of the pieces, there was no opportunity to test their effectiveness with doctors because the detail men never used them. The moral to be drawn from this simple illustration is that knowing the needs and responses of channel members is just as important as knowing the needs and responses of ultimate consumers.

Evaluation of the Channels As a Whole.   As Professor Breyer's comments suggested earlier, what is good for the manufacturer or any other seller is not necessarily good for all other sellers and buyers within the channel. Once the needs and responses of all the components within the trade channel have been assessed, it becomes possible to evaluate the viability of the present channel system. Here, numerous questions might serve as a guideline in evaluation. Such questions as the following might be raised: Are there discrepancies in the performance of the flows among members of the channel? Are there alternative firms or agencies that might be more effective than those now used in carrying the product through the channel and to the ultimate consumer? What will be the impact on the channel structure and the requisite channel flows if new agencies or firms are added to the channel? Are there conventional ways of acting that inhibit the marketing effectiveness of sellers and buyers within the channel?

Possible Modifications and Adjustments of the Channel.   After evaluation of a channel system comes the problem of making whatever modifications or adjustments seem to be needed. The appropriate guideline should be: "Observe the consequences of any change upon all agencies in the entire structure." Also, it should be emphasized that modifications or adjustments ought to occur *only after* the preceding three steps in the systems procedure have been taken.

4. Brown, op. cit., p. 60.

THE MANAGERIAL RESPONSIBILITY FOR CHANNELS

Despite the fact that every businessman and every consumer needs effectiveness in the operations of every complete channel of which he is a member, formal management of the system can rarely be established by any method other than vertical integration. However, one tremendous service can be performed by each member of a non-integrated channel. This is to make someone in its corporate hierarchy responsible for doing what can be done to achieve full channel efficiency. Thus, the channel function would become just as distinct an operating assignment as sales, advertising, or promotion.

The responsibilities of the channels manager should be stated broadly as opposed to, say, the narrow view of those who want to make physical distribution a managerial task.

The responsibilities should include at least the following:

1. *Systems management.*
   a. Reviewing the existing structure of specific flows (ownership, physical movement, information, and money).
   b. Developing an inventory of the needs of each agency within the channel.
   c. Modifying and adjusting the channel to meet the needs for change.
2. *Channel relations.*
   a. Informing channel members of marketing programs and changes in any facet of marketing and non-marketing programs.
   b. Receiving information and questions from trade customers relative to any facet of marketing and non-marketing programs.
3. *Internal coordination of distribution, as affected by:*
   a. Manufacturing.
   b. Finance.
   c. Marketing.

The above list of responsibilities is not definite. It nevertheless provides a start towards the development of a well-organized channel management function within the firm. It thus offers business management an opportunity to make a significant contribution to the strengthening of what is unquestionably one of the least managed areas of marketing today.

QUESTIONS FOR DISCUSSION

1. What is a marketing channel?
2. Compare and contrast marketing channels with physical distribution.

3. Why are marketing channels such an important aspect of a firm's marketing mix?

4. "There are too many middlemen in most channels of distribution." Why do middlemen exist between the manufacturer and the ultimate consumer? Why might more than one level of middlemen exist?

5. Discuss some of the "conventional" thinking about channels and note potential fallacies in the logic of each proposition.

6. Cox and Schutte state, "There is no provision within firms for the management of channels." Discuss this statement fully.

7. Why should a channel be thought of as a system?

8. The article states, "The moral to be drawn . . . is that knowing the needs and responses of channel members is just as important as knowing the needs and responses of ultimate consumers." Discuss fully.

1.2 PLANNED AND EVOLUTIONARY CHANGES IN DISTRIBUTION CHANNELS

Joseph P. Guiltinan

". . . It is important to remember that distributive innovations are developed by individuals and/or firms, often with several unsuccessful, abortive attempts."

Although much of the marketing channel literature has focused on one or more facets of change in channel structure, this literature has not been synthesized to develop a better understanding of the process of channel evolution. The lack of an accepted theory of channel evolution is reflected in the disparity among predictions of leading scholars in the field. While Davidson[1] sees a faster rate of change in distributive institutions in the future, Bucklin[2] envisions a slower rate of change. Similarly, consensus is lacking on the direction and implications of future evolutionary trends.

The purposes of this article are to explore the scope and significance of channel evolution and to review existing explanations for this phenomenon. The review suggests that these explanations inadequately explain channel evolution in advanced economies where channel management and planning occur. Instead, a five-stage model incorporating these traditional modes of analysis is proposed. Although this comprehensive theory does not completely specify the order of all evolutionary changes, it facilitates the development of hypotheses on the rate, direction, and consequences of future changes in distribution channels.

SCOPE OF CHANNEL EVOLUTION

Our primary concern is not with the initial development of channel systems, but rather with the forces that determine subsequent changes.

Reprinted by permission from the author and publisher. Joseph P. Guiltinan, "Planned and Evolutionary Changes in Distribution Channels," *Journal of Retailing* (Summer, 1974), pp. 79–91ff.

1. William Davidson, "Changes in Distributive Institutions," *Journal of Marketing*, 32 (January 1970), p. 7.

2. Louis Bucklin, *Competition and Evolution in the Distributive Trades* (Englewood Cliffs, N.J.: Prentice-Hall, Inc., 1972), p. 169.

The forces that shape and reshape specific channel forms are complex. More specifically, we are concerned with understanding the determinants of structural change in the channel, including changes in the number, functions, type, and relationship among channel intermediaries. Further, our concern with evolution encompasses both the "macro" and "micro" levels—evolution of channels by line of trade and evolution of a given firm's channels.

In terms of societal and macroeconomic significance, channel evolution is most important at aggregate levels. Patterns of competition by line-of-trade, levels of economic concentration, and the general level of quality and availability of goods and services are significantly affected by major evolutionary changes in the dominant distributive mode of a given line-of-trade. The initial impact of mail-order houses, supermarkets, franchising, and other distribution innovations offers ample proof of this impact.[3]

Throughout this article it is important to remember that distributive innovations are developed by individuals and/or firms, often with several unsuccessful, abortive attempts. It is after one or more institutions have refined the innovation that such changes are adopted by other channels in a given line of trade.

In order to gain a more complete understanding of this process we shall examine channel evolution in the context of four kinds of forces traditionally considered in channel theory.

1. Constraints on Evolutionary Behavior
2. Institutional Changes
3. Allocation of Functions
4. Relationships Among Channel Members

Then, we shall suggest an alternative perspective which attempts to integrate the foregoing streams of inquiry in terms of channel objectives and strategies.

FORCES INFLUENCING EVOLUTION

Constraints on Evolutionary Behavior. Some theorists have indicated that channel structure is constrained by organizational factors and by product-related aspects of marketing policy. Michman suggests that channel structure is a function of factors such as product life cycle, progressive physical distribution systems, and effective communication networks.[4] Aspinwall saw the development of promotional and channel strategy as linked to the characteristics of goods.[5]

3. Same reference as footnote 2. See also references 8, 11, 17.
4. Ronald Michman, "Channel Development and Innovation," *Marquette Business Review*, XV (Spring 1971), pp. 45–49.
5. Leo Aspinwall, "The Characteristics of Goods and Parallel Systems Theories,"

Both Buckin[6] and Tillman[7] have suggested that the next key constraint in channel evolution is financial. The ability to generate sufficient capital to innovate and to develop strong distribution systems—particularly in retailing—will be limited to some extent to the "conglomerchants"—large-scale, multiline retailing empires.

McCammon offers several suggestions concerning barriers to evolutionary change, including institutional solidarity in resistance to change, organizational rigidity leading to incremental responses to innovation, and the anti-innovation entrepreneurial values of small business managers.[8] Citing the work of Silk and Stern,[9] he notes that institutional innovation has typically come from outside of the established power structure, especially in retailing. Therefore, in order to produce innovation, channel evolution processes must deal with rigidity in institutions, in the allocation of functions, in relationships among members, and in policies.

CHANGES IN DISTRIBUTIVE INSTITUTIONS

Probably the most obvious kind of change and evolution in a distribution system is the development of the institutions which comprise it. Institutional change—particularly in retailing—has received a significant amount of attention in the literature, as scholars attempted to explain the forces leading to changes in retail structure, strategies and policies.

McNair's "Wheel of Retailing" concept pioneered such efforts. His hypothesis suggested that innovative retailers originate as low margin, low price operations, first challenging their mature competitors—comprised of higher margin, service and facilities oriented merchandisers—and later, gradually emulating them, thus providing the opportunity for still newer low-margin retail methods to evolve.[10]

McNair has received some support from Hollander on the validity of

---

in Eugene Kelley and William Lazer, eds., *Managerial Marketing* (Homewood, Ill.: Richard D. Irwin, Inc., 1958), pp. 434–50.

6. Louis Bucklin, loc. cit.

7. Rollie Tillman, "Rise of the Conglomerchant," *Harvard Business Review*, 49 (November–December, 1971), pp. 44–57.

8. Bert C. McCammon, "Alternate Explanations of Institutional Change and Channel Evolution," Stephen Greyser, ed., *Toward Scientific Marketing* (Chicago: American Marketing Association, 1964), pp. 477–90.

9. Alvin Silk and Louis W. Stern, "The Changing Nature of Innovation in Marketing—A Study of Selected Business Leaders 1852–1958," *Business History Review* (Fall 1963), pp. 182–99.

10. Malcolm McNair, "Significant Trends and Developments in the Postwar Period," A. B. Smith, ed., *Competitive Distribution in a Free, High-Level Economy and its Implications for the University* (Pittsburgh: University of Pittsburgh Press, 1958).

this concept as a rough description of domestic patterns of change.[11] A further descriptive notion, presented by Hall *et al.* and elaborated by Hollander is the "retail accordion" concept which reflects the apparent cyclical pattern in which domination by general-line,wide-assortment retailers alternates with domination by specialized, narrow-line merchants.[12]

Gist, attempting to develop a more generalized conceptualization of these theses, suggests that retail evolution can be viewed as a dialectic process in which synthesized combinations of established and innovative forms of retailing tend to emerge and change at a relatively stable rate over time.[13]

Dreesman, also searching for a more fundamental explanation, suggests an economic ecology perspective. Thus, in viewing the phenomena described by McNair, he suggests that the propensity to trade up as the enterprise matures reflects impure and imperfect competition in retailing and forces average costs and margins in retailing to higher ceilings. Additionally, biological analogies of convergence, hypertrophy, and regression are advanced to show the response of retailing to market factors.[14]

Similarly, Thomas suggests a sociological analysis of the market. In particular he suggests that the "identity-sustaining function of shopping" along with wealth distribution permits the prediction of successful retail innovations. Retailers respond by emphasizing price and convenience in periods in which shopping is not a major identity-sustaining function, while department stores flourish when this is a major function.[15]

Bucklin in an extremely complete analysis of retail and wholesale evolution suggested that retail evolution was related to the development of retail market structures through four stages: periodic, permanent, fragmented, and vertically integrated markets. Apparently, the cyclical movements described by the accordion theory can be directly related to environmental changes such as level and extent of demand, money supply, supply technology, and the managerial skills of entrepreneurs.[16]

11. Stanley Hollander, "The Wheel of Retailing," *Journal of Marketing*, 24 (July 1960), pp. 37–42.

12. Margaret Hall, John Knapp, and Christopher Winsten, *Distribution in Great Britain and North America* (London: Oxford University Press, 1961), and Stanley Hollander, "Notes on the Retail Accordion," *Journal of Retailing*, 42 (Summer 1966), pp. 29–40.

13. Ronald Gist, *Marketing and Society* (New York: Holt, Rinehart and Winston, Inc., 1971), pp. 370–71.

14. A. C. R. Dreesman, "Patterns of Evolution in Retailing," *Journal of Retailing*, 44 (Spring 1968), pp. 64–81.

15. R. E. Thomas, "Changes in the Distribution Systems of Western Industrialized Economics," *British Journal of Marketing*, 4 (Summer 1970), pp. 62–69.

16. Same reference as footnote 2, p. 70.

Similar points of view have been expressed by Moyer[17] and Tillman[18] to describe two separate trends toward large-scale retailing. While scalar economics and access to capital are critical to these trends, both are secondary to the demographic and lifestyle changes that influence the market place.

To summarize, explanations for various institutional change processes do not provide a precise set of circumstances for predicting when an institutional change will occur, but indicate that change seems to result from competing efforts to meet the changing shopping needs of one or more market segments.

The significance of institutional change in analyzing channel evolution is critical. As Davidson has suggested, ". . . in the long run, the nature of channels is determined from the 'bottom up' rather than from the 'top down.'"[19]

For a given line of trade, then, the retail-customer interface is important in that changes in institutions are tied to gaps in the retail availability-customer need matchup. Such changes, should they occur, are also likely to provide pressure for changes in activities and relationships among members of the channel.

CHANGES IN ALLOCATION OF FUNCTIONS

Finding the institutional approach too narrow, Dommermuth and Anderson prefer to define the channel as a unique system of functional performances. They argue that the efficient performance of functions (such as transportation, promotion, inventory, and transaction) is the *raison d'etre* of the channel. Consequently, the evolution of the channel is more usefully analyzed in terms of changes in the performance of a function—by improved management by the institution performing it and/or by the reallocation of functions among institutions.[20]

The most rigorous analyses of channel evolution have been based on this functional perspective of the channel.

Stigler's model of evolution viewed the channel as following a single basic evolutionary path: delegation of functions at low levels of output followed by reintegration at higher levels of output where the necessary scalar economies for various functions were achieved.[21] While this was

17. M. S. Moyer, "The Roots of Large Scale Retailing," *Journal of Marketing*, 26 (October, 1962), pp. 55–59.
18. Same reference as footnote 7.
19. William Davidson, "Distribution Breakthrough," Lee Adler, ed., *Plotting Marketing Strategy* (New York: Simon and Schuster, 1967), p. 283.
20. William Dommermuth and R. Clifton Anderson, "Distribution Systems— Firms, Functions, and Efficiencies," *Business Topics*, 17 (Spring, 1969), pp. 51–56.
21. George Stigler, "The Division of Labor is Limited by the Extent of the Market," *Journal of Political Economy*, LIX (June 1951), pp. 185–93.

a useful concept for channels in which evolution is rather quick, it was not developed precisely enough for analyzing the smaller changes that are significant in slower evolutionary situations.

Such issues are considered by Bucklin who suggests that channels approach a normative channel structure as increasingly lower cost combinations of the functional acts required for a given array of services are substituted for one another.[22] In this case, then, the normative channel is the set of institutions that evolves in the long run under "reasonably" competitive circumstances. Since technology and consumer buying patterns are always changing, however, the normative channel is always changing. Thus, evolution would appear to be a continuous process.

Also employing a static model, Baligh and Richartz examined partial equilibrium conditions for the entire vertical marketing system.[23] Their conditions for equilibrium suggest that not only the activities of member units, but also the relationship among these units are necessary to define an equilibrium structure. Thus in equilibrium

> Every firm performs a function.
> No firm within the structure finds it profitable to change relationships.
> No firm outside the structure finds it profitable to alter the existing relationships.

The structure that maximizes total profits and monetary value of consumer utilities is the optimal vertical marketing structure.

Consequently, the allocation of functions *and* the relationships among members are both significant factors in evolving distribution structures which are optimal. The importance of functional change in understanding changes in relationships among members has also been substantiated empirically.

McKeon found the stability observed at the macro-wholesale level to be misleading. When analyzed by line-of-trade a great deal of structural change is evident over time with much reallocation of functions and many changes in relationships between manufacturers and wholesalers. Such changes indeed appear to reflect changes in the "time-space-quantity-vanity gap between the assortments of sellers and buyers."[24]

Similar findings regarding inter-institutional reallocation between wholesalers and retailers are reported by Bucklin,[25] while McCammon

22. Louis Bucklin, *A Theory of Distribution Channel Structure* (Berkeley: Institute of Business and Economic Research, 1966).

23. Helmy Baligh and Leon Richartz, *Vertical Market Structures* (Boston: Allyn and Bacon, Inc., 1967).

24. James McKeon, "Conflicting Patterns of Structural Change in Wholesaling," *Economic and Business Bulletin*, 24 (Winter 1972), pp. 37–53.

25. Same reference as footnote 2, pp. 68–71 and 194–201.

and Bates indicated comparable processes helped fuel the growth of contractual marketing systems.[26]

To summarize, channels evolve as new functional activity alignments become necessary. And, as was the case with institutions, such changes result from market-determined forces—competitors' actions and the changing mix of services desired by consumers.

Analyzing institutional change enabled us to assess the evolutionary role played by components of the channel structure. Analyzing the functional allocation process provided an assessment of the role played by sequenced activities in evolving structures. In both cases, we also noted the changing relationships among activity-performing components.

RELATIONSHIPS AMONG CHANNEL MEMBERS

Just as institutions and the allocation and performance of functions may change, the relationships that exist among members may change. Two key relational dimensions to consider are the locus of channel control and the level of conflict in the channel.

Conflict is inherent in all but the equilibrium structure. Only in equilibrium is the division of rewards and duties optimal for the entire channel.[27] Yet, if Bucklin and Baligh and Richartz are correct, the normative channel continually changes due to changes in market forces and technology. Conflict can arise due to the perception of one or more members of the channel that their goals are not being fully realized.[28] As market forces and technology create new demands on the channel, conflict serves as a manifestation of the need for continued evolution. It arises out of disagreement among channel members with decisions on channel policy and functions made at the locus of channel control.

Channel control indicates the ability of one channel member to determine marketing policies of another channel member.[29] Channel control derives from economic power (oligopolistic or oligopsonistic) and from whatever power can be generated through a firm's position in the

26. Bert C. McCammon and Albert D. Bates, "The Emergence and Growth of Contractually Integrated Channels in the American Economy" in Peter D. Bennett, ed., *Marketing and Economic Development* (Chicago: American Marketing Association, 1965), pp. 496–515.

27. Same reference as footnote 23, pp. 8–11.

28. Louis W. Stern and James Heskett, "Conflict Management in Interorganizational Relations: A Conceptional Framework," L. W. Stern, ed., *Distribution Channels: Behavioral Dimensions* (Boston: Houghton-Mifflin, 1969), pp. 288–305.

29. Louis W. Stern, "Potential Conflict Management Mechanisms in Distribution Channels: An Interorganizational Analysis," Donald N. Thompson, ed., *Contractual Marketing System* (Lexington, Mass.: Heath, Lexington Books, 1971), pp. 11–40.

channel.[30] Further, control is fostered by a host of other demand-and-cost-related determinants, such as market knowledge, homogeneity of supply and demand, stability of demand, and product development and promotion costs.[31]

Seemingly, then, market-determined forces influence the locus and effectiveness of channel control, just as they influenced institutional change and functional reallocation. Changes in channel control can (and have) led to changes in institutions, functional allocation, channel policies and objectives, and changes in the control over scarce resources.[32]

CHANNEL OBJECTIVES AND STRATEGIES

The paramount role played by market forces in influencing channel evolution is evident in all of the foregoing factors. Both consumers and competitors stimulate innovation and change. McCammon is not greatly oversimplifying when he suggests that many of the structural changes in distribution can be explained by a simple challenge and response model.[33]

Nevertheless, while pressures for institutional change, for changes in functional allocation, or for changes in relationships may arise from market forces, few channels still react to such pressure for change automatically. Each of the changes in distribution recently forecast by Davidson involves strategic managerial decisions, not merely tactical reaction.[34] Similarly, the analyses of specific structural changes presented by McCammon and Bates,[35] by Sturdivant,[36] and by Oxenfeldt and Kelly[37] also suggest the development of planned strategies to deal with institutional, functional, or relational change.

30. Robert Little, "The Marketing Channel: Who Should Lead This Extracorporate Organization?" *Journal of Marketing*, 34 (January 1970), pp. 31–38.

31. Louis Bucklin, "The Locus of Channel Control," Robert King, ed., *Marketing and the New Science of Planning* (Chicago: American Marketing Association, 1969), pp. 146–47.

32. See for instance David Wilemon, "Power and Negotiation Strategies in Marketing Channels," *Southern Journal of Business*, 7 (February 1972), pp. 71–81; and Dov Izraeli, "The Cyclical Evolution of Marketing Channels," *European Journal of Marketing*, 5 (Autumn 1971), pp. 137–44.

33. Same reference as footnote 8.

34. Same reference as footnote 1.

35. Same reference as footnote 26.

36. Fred Sturdivant, "Determinants of Vertical Integration," Stephen Greyser, ed., *Toward Scientific Marketing* (Chicago: American Marketing Association, 1964), pp. 477–90.

37. Alfred Oxenfeldt and Anthony Kelly, "Will Successful Franchise Systems Ultimately Become Wholly-Owned Chains?" *Journal of Retailing*, 44 (Winter 1968–1969), pp. 69–85.

This writer offers the thesis that most channels in this economy no longer change strictly on a natural evolutionary basis. It is suggested that changes in the structure of a given channel can be explained by changes in the strategic distribution objectives of key channel members. Such members may be strong channel captains or developers of a new product or other institutions with a major interest or stake in a given channel. Changes in these objectives stem from the pressures brought about through institutional obsolescence, inefficient functional performance, and/or conflict. Additionally, it is suggested that such objectives tend to follow a sequence over time through five stages (Exhibit 1).

STAGE 1 EARLY DEVELOPMENT

In this stage, channel objectives simply involve the development of *contacts and communication* with ultimate buyers. Channel structure is that which is "conventional" for a given type of product or line of trade, often involving agents or brokers or merchant wholesalers.

EXHIBIT 1

Stage	Primary Source of Influence on Policy	Illustrative Policies
Contactual/ Communication	Product characteristics	M-W-R channel Little channel direction
Coverage/ Capacity	Institutional effectiveness in reaching consumers	Intensive distribution Multiple brands
Control	Channel member relationships and marketing policies	Franchising Administered systems Exclusive distribution
Cost	Economic efficiency	Voluntaries, cooperatives
Cooperation/ Consolidation	Access to capital	Vertical integration

Many firms remain in these kinds of channels for prolonged periods of time because they are consistent with the perceived roles and objectives of some channel members.[38]

38. This point is illustrated by Philip McVey, "Are Channels of Distribution What the Textbooks Say?" *Journal of Marketing*, 24 (January 1960), pp. 61–65; and by Warren Wittreich, "Misunderstanding the Retailer," *Harvard Business Review*, 40 (May–June 1962), pp. 147–52 ff.

In other situations, however, such alignments become outmoded after a period of time due to the need for faster expansion, the need to improve market impact, or the need and ability to achieve scalar economies.

STAGES 2–4 DEVELOPMENT OF VERTICAL MARKETING NETWORKS

Firms that find initial alignments unsatisfactory will shift the channel objective—and as a consequence, the channel structure—as goals, resources, and opportunities change.

Each stage corresponds to a particular channel objective in this period of evolution. However, the three may occur in any sequence.

Typically, stage two will arise due to the need for expansion. Consequently, *coverage and/or capacity* will be the predominant channel goals. If the need for expansion is very pressing and capital is lacking, a franchise system may evolve at this time. Alternatively, more extensive use of retail outlets (possibly requiring scrambled merchandising and a multiple brand policy) is likely to result.

In either event, some delegation is likely to take place in the marketing policies of such channels as new institutions are selected. As coverage is gradually achieved, two additional problems may surface. Changes in the institutions selected may lead to high cost channels or to channels which employ undesirable marketing policies.

Stage three occurs, then, when the coverage objective is subordinated to a new objective such as *control*. This objective tends to become more significant once coverage has been achieved. It reflects a need for developing coordinated and internally consistent marketing policies and strategies within the channel—perhaps through the development of administered systems or, again, possibly via franchising agreements.

Having coped with institutional changes and policies as well as the need for internal policy consistency, stage four might reflect a shift to *cost* as the primary channel objective. That is, as markets grow to reach scalar economies for existing institutions and policies, certain functions may be repositioned to achieve more efficient allocation. Voluntaries and cooperatives as well as other contractual systems seem to reflect the attainment of this stage of development.

STAGE 5 COLLABORATIVE ALIGNMENTS

Regardless of the sequence of objectives in stages two through four, some channels will continue to experience conflict since optimal channel configuration is never reached.

In order to reduce or eliminate conflict, objectives of *cooperation and/ or consolidation* take primacy in stage five. Channels that reach this stage typically experience conflict situations which are not very amenable to solution by existing alternatives other than complete consolidation through vertical integration. Where this latter strategy is impractical due to financial or other constraints,[39] channel forms of a highly cooperative orientation will need to be developed—possibly by incorporating some of the mechanisms suggested by Stern[40] into contractual or administered systems.

IMPLICATIONS

The channel stage theory provides a basic framework for understanding the interaction among the complex forces that influence evolution in individual channels and, as a result, lead to changes in the dominant structure of entire lines of trade. Although the sequence of stages and the conditions for shifting between stages are not precisely postulated, the theory permits construction of hypotheses on the rate, direction, and consequences of future changes in channel structure and policy.

RATE OF CHANGE

Based on our foregoing analysis of change agents, two sets of factors can be identified which influence the rate of evolutionary change.

Factors favoring relatively fast rates of change include:

1. Rapid changes in consumer life styles, shopping patterns and attitudes toward shopping.
2. More intensive development of new services and types of products, and shorter product life cycles.
3. Less resistance to innovation through a decline in the importance of small retailers and in organizational rigidity.

Factors favoring relatively slow rates of evolution include:

1. Lack of access of many distributive institutions to capital markets.
2. Increased economic concentration leading to antitrust constraints and greater barriers to innovative entry.
3. As stage five is approached, the gap between the "normative" and existing channels is reduced, and so is the impetus for change.

Considering both sets of factors, it is hypothesized that barring a continued upheaval in the mix of services demanded by consumers, the

39. Same reference as footnotes 36 and 37.
40. Same reference as footnote 29.

movement toward the normative channel and economic concentration will predominate among those forces influencing the rate of change.

DIRECTION OF CHANGE

No uniform direction of change can be postulated for all distribution channels. However, our channel stage theory provides the basis for hypotheses on alternative directions.

    1. Channels will remain in stage one in those cases in which:

        a. few economies can be achieved by repositioning activities,
        b. the locus of control is weak or undefined, and/or
        c. retail institutions must be flexible in adjusting assortment and services to meet rapidly changing customer needs.

    2. Channels will be more likely to move through subsequent stages toward stage five to the extent that:

        a. many economies of scale are evident,
        b. the locus of control is well defined, and
        c. customer demands on retail institutions are relatively standardized.

    3. Channels experiencing extremely high conflict levels but unable to implement a stage five solution (for financial or organizational reasons) may become susceptible to dissolution, government intervention, or acquisition.

CONSEQUENCES OF CHANGE

McCammon and Bates have examined one effect of channel evolution, and suggest that as channels evolve through vertical marketing networks, competition involves rivalry between systems as well as rivalry among institutions.[41] Such competition is generally associated with the extensive use of private brands, centralized inventory control permitting wider assortments, economics of scale in advertising, and centralized price marking. When considered along with the trend toward economic concentration, this phenomena would be expected to lead to the following consequences:

    1. Less price competition due to fewer direct comparisons.
    2. Greater emphasis on nonprice dimensions such as service, quality, assortment in retail level competition.
    3. Increased planning in distribution and more complete utilization of computer-based mathematical models for inventory, price, assortment, transportation decisions.

41. Same reference as footnote 26.

4. Reduced rate of progress toward the "normative channel" for firms reaching stage five either because

    a. vertical integration may leave no mechanism to effect change, or because

    b. lack of conflict and lack of workable competition to induce change.

5. To the extent that channels remaining in stage one are more flexible in meeting changing consumer demands, they will regain much of the competitive edge lost due to the scalar economies accruing to more integrated channels.

A possible outcome of these trends, then, is the development of two types of distribution flows. One such flow would involve highly centralized and programmed systems for distributing relatively standardized products and services. A second, dynamic sector would deal with goods and services that are frequently changed to meet consumer need changes. Most new distribution systems and institutions will develop in the latter sector, especially for economically depressed areas, many service industries, and highly discretionary or personalized product categories. In these situations, consumer change is rapid, or few scalar economies exist, and/or entry is relatively easy. Such channels will exhibit little planning and a highly visible role for the consumer and other traditional evolutionary forces.

QUESTIONS FOR DISCUSSION

1. Discuss several factors that have influenced the development of marketing channel evolution.

2. Discuss fully the five-stage model suggested by the author.

3. Identify the four kinds of forces traditionally considered in channel theory. Discuss each force.

4. Explain the "wheel of retailing" hypothesis.

5. What is a vertical marketing network?

6. What factors determine the *rate* of change in channel evolution? Discuss the importance of each factor.

1.3 THE MANUFACTURER'S MARKETING PROBLEM

Paul Wesley Ivey

"After bending every effort to eliminate the jobber [wholesaler] and to force goods upon the retailer, the manufacturer's pride naturally revolted against making overtures to them. To the majority of manufacturers, however, this appeared the only way out of the difficulty."

Extensive readjustments have been made of the factors in the system of distribution. These changes have frequently involved considerable disorder, amounting at times almost to chaos. The usual course of distribution has been from the manufacturer to the jobber, from him to the retailer, and finally from the retailer to the consumer. Thus each marketing function was differentiated and performed by an independent organization. Hence, when within recent years manufacturers, jobbers, and retailers attempted to take over each other's functions, disorder naturally resulted. Integration of marketing functions meant the elimination of some old types of middlemen and the combining of their functions under new organizations. The struggle for survival has made the period of transition a bitter one and confusing in its significance even to the parties directly concerned.

This readjustment was brought about by the transformation of a seller's market into a buyer's market, and in the transition advertising was destined to play an important role. When advertising became known as a marketing force, manufacturers attempted to use it as a device to eliminate the jobber, and in some cases the retailer. It was believed that a consumer demand could be created by advertising which would make possible a permanent, steady outlet for the goods and enable a cheaper distribution of them. This plan necessitated the building up of a sales organization which was often a costly expansion, but the belief was prevalent that a cheaper selling expense would ultimately result.

Reprinted with permission from the March 1921 issue of FACTORY, a Morgan-Grampian publication. Paul Wesley Ivey, "The Manufacturer's Marketing Problem," *Administration* (March, 1921), pp. 341–347.

II

While the change in relationship between demand and supply was the underlying cause of market readjustments with their resulting disorder of mechanism, the immediate reasons for integration are found in certain practices of market functionaries. Manufacturers allege that jobbers refuse to push their goods and that the goods of competitors are given preference. Manufacturers naturally desire to increase their production as much as possible in order to utilize to the fullest extent the capabilities of their plants, thereby reducing unit costs, but this desirable result cannot be attained because the larger production has no market, and the jobber refuses to create a market. This forces the manufacturer to create his own market by advertising. The result is that he goes into the jobbing business.

The manufacturer also accuses the jobber of putting out his own private brands in competition with the brands of his clients. This competition cuts down the market for the manufacturer's product. After the manufacturer has established a reputation for his goods, this reputation is endangered by substitute brands sold by the jobber, who controls the channels of trade to the retailer. Thus hampered on every side and out of touch with the markets, and dependent for distribution on jobbers who could not be depended upon to push their goods, manufacturers have revolted and gone over the heads of both jobber and retailer.

In most cases it has been necessary for the manufacturer to eliminate the retailer as well as the jobber because the retailer has been controlled more or less absolutely by the jobber. This control was largely owing to the fact that the jobber had made personal friends with the retailer through long years of personal solicitation through his salesmen. Moreover, the jobber in many cases had extended credit to the retailer until the latter often lived only by sufferance of the former. Because of fear and gratitude on the part of the retailer, the jobber was thus enabled to hold control of the most important outlet for the manufacturer's goods. These conditions of distribution finally became unbearable for manufacturers, and when relief appeared in the form of advertising it was eagerly turned to by the manufacturers as the solution of their marketing problem. It was now believed that, on the one hand, the jobber could be eliminated from the marketing system, or be forced to carry the goods because of retailer-demand, while, on the other hand, retailers would be coerced into handling the advertised goods by reason of consumer-demand. Unfortunately for the manufacturer, such an easy victory was not to be won.

III

As against these charges, the jobber on his side lays the blame for the present market disorder largely at the door of the manufacturer. He affirms that the manufacturer attempted to eliminate the jobber even before the latter put out his own private brands, and in retaliation for the manufacturer's entrance into the jobbing business the jobber has gone into the manufacturing business or has assumed control of sources of supply. This entrance into manufacture has been necessary for the jobber, he says, because the manufacturer removed from him the handling of the manufacturer's brand, leaving the jobber with a retailer market but nothing of a specified character to satisfy its demand. In order to keep his organization intact, therefore, the jobber has been obliged to produce or procure his own brands, or to contract with others to produce the goods on which to put his label.

The jobber finds fault also with the retailer for the present market disorder, affirming that as the unit of retailing has increased in size there has been a greater tendency for retailers to go direct to manufacturers for goods on which they could secure the jobber's quantity discount. Jobbers claim this "cream of the business" for their own, and see no justification for the manufacturer's selling over their heads to the large retail stores. The manufacturer, on the other hand, replies that he is justified in selling to any store which is willing to buy in large quantities similar to those offered to jobbers.

Because of this narrowing of outlet for the jobber's goods, the latter has in many cases gone into the retail business. This has stiffened competition in retailing and caused cries of protestation from members of the retail trade. The jobber has replied that he must create a market for his goods by going into retailing, since the manufacturer has provided a market for himself by creating a consumer-demand, and because the retailer has sought to eliminate him by going over his head to the manufacturer. Such action on the part of the jobber made the problem more complicated.

IV

About the same time as jobbers began complaining that the retailers were seeking the jobbers' elimination, the retailers in their turn were complaining that the jobbers were seeking to eliminate them. This was being accomplished, said the retailers, by the jobbers' taking the "cream of their business," *i.e.*, by capturing the trade of large establishments, such as boarding-houses, hotels, public institutions, societies, clubs, etc. To this accusation the jobber replied that these buying units desired goods in large quantities such as were being sold to retailers, and that it was no more than right that these units should be supplied direct and given a quantity discount.

V

In the midst of all this confusion, the manufacturer had been advertising in the effort to create a market for his goods, but success had been uncertain because of the other factors in the marketing system. It is true that by means of advertising consumers were led to ask for the advertised goods in retail stores, but jobbers were coaching retailers to substitute the jobbers' brands for the advertised articles. Substitution proved to be surprisingly easy, and the longed for and eagerly sought after outlet for the manufacturer's goods proved to be a mirage. Something had to be done to remedy the situation. As cleverly distinctive trade-marks and convincing copy would not prevent the retailer from making substitutions, some other means of protection had to be found.

After bending every effort to eliminate the jobber and to force goods upon the retailer, the manufacturer's pride naturally revolted against making overtures to them. To the majority of manufacturers, however, this appeared the only way out of the difficulty.[1] The old channels of marketing must be used but some new way had to be devised to get the jobber and retailer to *co-operate* with the manufacturer in securing the largest possible distribution. If a fairly large distribution could be obtained, one large enough to enable the plant to continue production in the face of decreasing costs, that was all the manufacturer desired. And if some rapprochement with the jobber and retailer could accomplish this result, then that was the thing to do, and that was the thing the manufacturer proceeded to do.

A new turn in the readjustment of the factors of marketing was thus given by the manufacturer's return to the old channels of distribution. While so doing, however, the manufacturer has not relinquished his advertising. He still creates his consumer-demand, but he does not expect too much of it. He no longer looks upon consumer-demand as a force capable of over-turning established methods of marketing goods, but, rather, as a supplementary device enabling him to establish a permanent, stable, progressive trade when used in *conjunction* with present marketing facilities. Advertising is now viewed as a means of securing the co-operation of both the jobber and the retailer, rather than as a

1. Only a comparatively few manufacturers could create their own retail outlets.

means of eliminating either of them. As a consequence, the jobber and retailer, realizing their permanence, are acquiring a much healthier frame of mind towards the manufacturer's goods.

VI

The question arises, How has the manufacturer succeeded in thus se-curing the co-operation of the jobber in enlarging his distribution? This has been accomplished in the first place by dealing fairly with the jobber and giving the latter *all* of the manufacturer's goods. Assured of all of the manufacturer's business, the jobber undertakes to give it a broad outlet into retail channels. In the second place, assured of a large staple con-sumer-demand, the jobber is induced to handle the goods even though a smaller percentage of profit may be secured than is derivable from unadvertised brands. In the third place, the jobber is assured of a re-tailer-demand because of certain methods recently applied by the manufacturer to secure for his product the retailer's good-will. These methods took the following forms:

After satisfying the demands of the jobber and securing his whole-hearted co-operation in acquiring wide distribution, the manufacturer found he still had a retailer problem on his hands. The retailer in many instances had been opposed to handling nationally advertised merchan-dise because it carried a smaller percentage of profit than did jobber's brands. In such cases, even though there was a consumer-demand and the jobber was willing to handle and push the advertised manufacturer's goods, the retailer was enticed away to goods giving a larger profit by other jobbers to whose interest it was to handle them. This situation demanded an educational campaign for the benefit of the retailer con-ducted by the manufacturer, to whose interest it was to widen the out-let for his merchandise and make good the vast sums that had been ex-pended in the creation of the consumer-demand.

This effort of the manufacturer to get the co-operation of the retailer has taken many forms, but one of the first necessities of the case was to convince the retailer that a larger total profit could be made on advertised brands than on unadvertised, even though the advertised brands did not carry so large a profit per sale as did those unadvertised. This was often a most difficult proposition to prove to the retailer's sat-isfaction. An advertised article might only carry a gross profit of 25 per cent while the unadvertised brand perhaps carried a 40 per cent margin. To show that the selling of the higher-margin goods lost money to the retailer in the long run was the task of the manufacturer, and this he accomplished by proving that it *cost less to sell* the advertised goods. The manufacturer argued that his goods could be sold in larger quantities, in quicker time, and by cheaper salespeople, than could unadvertised goods, since the manufacturer's goods were already partially sold before the customer came into the store. Likewise he argued that the *prestige* of the store handling well-known goods was greater than that of a store handling less well-known brands. The fact that the demand for the advertised goods would be more stable was also insisted upon, as well as the ability of the jobber to give prompt and efficient service.

But the manufacturer did not stop here. He not only proved to the retailer that the latter could make more money by handling the advertised line, but he went even further—*he helped the retailer sell it.* In other words, the manufacturer held that his obligation to the retailer did not cease when the goods were produced and given to the jobber and when advertising copy had been placed in magazines and newspapers. In addition the manufacturer took upon himself the obligation of moving the goods off the shelves by teaching the retailer methods of salesmanship and advertising *within* the store. These co-operative selling methods have taken many forms, but the most common of them are found in dealer-literature, window displays, and demonstrations.

VII

Dealer-literature seeks to portray the selling points of the goods in the most concise and convincing manner, as well as to indicate its superiority over that of competitors. Human-interest copy, such as that describing processes of manufacture, origin of raw materials, meaning of designs, and history of development, arouses the enthusiasm of both retailer and salespeople. A statement of the tests to which the goods have been subjected tends to secure the confidence of the store in the goods; while comprehensive enumerations of ways in which the merchandise can meet the divergent needs of customers give salespeople interesting and logical material out of which convincing sales talks can be constructed. This effort to make retailers expert in the selling of their goods gives manufacturers an advantage which means more to them than even their consumer-demand. In the last analysis, the retailer is the key to the marketing system. Efforts of manufacturers within recent years indicate that they are at least aware of this all-important fact.

In the matter of window displays, some manufacturers provide at cost to the retailer a monthly service of window display. This high grade service has been prepared by experts. Each display is tested for its selling power before being sent from the factory. Invariably it represents a far greater value than it costs the retailer. Not only is such display designed from the standpoint of selling power but likewise from the standpoint of ease of installation. Each display can be quickly set up by unskilled salespeople. Furthermore, the display is arranged in parts so that it can be made to fit any window. Similar service for aiding the merchant is being provided by other manufacturers.

Besides these internal methods of moving advertised goods off the shelves, the factory sends demonstrators from time to time to prove to the store's customers that what is claimed in the advertising matter is true. These demonstrations, while valuable from the standpoint of securing new customers for the store and being an advertising feature, have added value in creating in the retailer and his salespeople renewed enthusiasm and confidence in the merchandise. When the latter are *sold* there is little difficulty in selling the street. The manufacturer is beginning to realize that he must *sell* the retailer and his salespeople the *idea* before he can hope to sell them the *actual* merchandise. And this holds true even though an order of the actual merchandise is already in the store. More goods will not be ordered unless the merchandise in stock moves quickly. The methods indicated above are designed to result in quick turnovers.

VIII

From all this it might appear that the manufacturer has met the retailer more than halfway in his attempt to increase the distribution of his product. However that may be, he seems willing to go still further. Many of the more progressive manufacturers are not merely satisfied with educating the retailer to sell more of *their goods*, but they are carrying out a plan of retailer education which aims to enable the retailer to sell more of *all goods*. Justification for this wider education comes from the growing belief that the more prosperous the retailer can be made, the better customer he becomes. The more prosperous he is the sooner he pays his bills, the more trade he draws, the more loyal he becomes.

The nature of this wider retailer education varies under different circumstances and with the needs of the various merchants, but usually covers better accounting methods, more efficient store arrangement, up-to-date advertising, business-building salesmanship, trade information on how to meet competition, specific questions of price-fixing, figuring turnover, etc.

Preceding paragraphs have shown that manufacturers are more and more abandoning *coercive* methods and are adopting *co-operative* means of increasing their distribution. Many of them have come to realize that they cannot perform the jobbing function so cheaply as the jobber, and that it is desirable to retain the jobber in their distributive scheme if he can be induced to push their goods. This desire of the manufacturers has been partially attained by helping the jobber to get a market for their merchandise and by assuring him 100 per cent of the output. On the other hand, the manufacturer has come to realize that he cannot hope to get distribution without the help and friendly co-operation of the retailer. Hence he is becoming more and more friendly to the retailer, taking upon himself some of the responsibility of getting the goods off the retailer's shelves. He thus proves to the retailer that quick turnover is not a mirage but a reality, and because of this tangible proof the retailer is much more attracted toward advertised goods, even though they bear a less percentage of profit than advertised manufacturers' brands.

The retailer seems to be the keystone in the marketing arch. A readjustment of stones has been made and some of them have been temporarily left out, but the falling arch has made necessary a quick new adjustment in which the retailer has been recognized as being in the most strategical position. A realization of this fact by retailers ought to go far toward voluntary co-operation on their part with the other functionaries in the marketing system.

It is apparently true that where co-operation is impossible integration is inevitable, and where integration is impossible co-operation is inevitable. In the majority of cases integration of marketing functions has been impossible and hence co-operation of market functionaries has resulted. Integration has been impossible in most lines for several reasons. For one thing, manufacturers lack capital to purchase or create their own retail stores. Moreover, they lack ability, capital, and experience to create their own jobbing department. Again, they could not secure wide distribution through small selling organizations. And finally, retailers and jobbers boycotted the manufacturer's products in territories where their own selling organizations could not penetrate. Where wide distribution can be secured for a product by eliminating the middleman and taking over his functions, integration is the logical development; but where the difficulties involved in the combining of functions are too great, wide distribution can be secured only by intelligent co-operation with the existing marketing mechanism. This co-operation is going on in the grocery and other lines where wide distribution is difficult to secure through a manufacturer's selling organization.

That close co-operation between the market functionaries will ultimately produce a few large integrated systems rather than numerous small independent organizations is a possible development of the situation. Co-operating with a merchant to the extent of moving his goods off the shelves and improving his general merchandising methods may possibly lead to a more intimate association wherein additional selling functions of the retailer will be taken over by the manufacturer until complete integration takes place between the merchant and the manu-facturer, or between the merchant and other stores with which the manufacturer has similar connections. Although drug manufacturers had apparent insuperable difficulties to overcome in securing their retail outlet, these have been overcome by a co-operative combination of stores in which the manufacturers are financially interested, while the stores in turn are financially interested in the business of the drug manufacturers. Here integration has absorbed a wide field of goods from a co-operative starting point. Similar tendencies are seen in other directions.

IX

This article has already indicated that integration became an important disturbing force when the supply of goods increased at a more rapid rate than the demand. It should be understood, however, that supply is not the actual amount of shoes, clothing, or furniture that is on the market at any one time, but rather the potential supply or productive capacity of manufacturing plants. In other words, the ability to produce goods in large amounts exists at the present time, while during the last century productive capacity existed between narrower limits. If produc-tive capacities are utilized to their fullest extent, costs per unit of prod-uct decline; if they are only partially utilized, costs are higher. To get into a more advantageous producing stage, an outlet for production must be secured.

The decreasing cost stage of production is sought by manufacturers not merely because it will return larger immediate profits. A more vital motive is present. Production under decreasing costs produces a cushion of profits which serves as an insurance fund for the profitable contin-uance of the business during periods of depression and in spite of vig-orous competition. For example, if the production cost of an article, including a fair profit, is 20 cents because of production under decreas-ing costs, while the production cost of a similar competing article is 24 cents because of less favorable production costs due to inadequate dis-tribution, the selling price will be fixed by the latter producer, and the article will sell for 24 cents. The first manufacturer could afford to sell the article for 20 cents if he was forced to do so, but under ordinary competition he may elect to keep his present production and sell his article for 24 cents, making an extra profit of 4 cents per article. This extra profit in the aggregate will serve as a cushion to ease up the shock of adverse business conditions, while if the market contracts he is able to lower his price to 20 cents and put his competitor out of business. It is this protection given them by decreasing costs that makes manufacturers struggle for wide distribution which will enable them to produce under the most favorable cost conditions. In some lines integration of marketing functions produces the desired result, while in other lines co-operation in its varying degrees of completeness makes a temporary enlargement of distribution possible. The struggle for business protection is at the root of the struggle for markets.

QUESTIONS FOR DISCUSSION

1. According to the article, what power does the manufacturer have over the retailer? What power does the retailer have over the manufacturer?

2. Based on this 1921 article, is the manufacturer, the wholesaler, or the retailer the channel captain? Defend your answer.

3. What action did the manufacturer take in an attempt to force the firm's products on wholesalers and retailers? Did it work? Why?

4. Was there any discussion of vertical integration in this article? Discuss.

5. Identify and explain the suggested co-operative techniques discussed in this article.

6. Ivey states, "It is apparently true that where co-operation is impossible integration is inevitable, and where integration is impossible co-operation is inevitable." Explain.

1.4 OUR L'EGGS FIT YOUR LEGS

Business Week

"L'eggs' toughest job, though, was to convince the supermarket and drugstore chain retailers . . . All we asked for was 2½ square feet of their store— that was less than anyone else. The key word, however, that sold retailers was 'consignment'."

At 8:00 a.m. every Monday through Friday, 29-year-old Joanne Miller climbs into a white Chevrolet van and drives around the Pocono Mountains countryside of upstate Pennsylvania delivering 4-in.-high white plastic eggs to local supermarkets and drugstores. Dressed in a red, white, and blue hot pants uniform, and wearing tinted glasses and knee-high boots, Mrs. Miller is hardly ever taken for the local Easter Bunny. Store people know her instead as "route girl" for a national pantyhose manufacturer—"L'eggs," a new division of the $176-million Hanes Corp., of Winston-Salem, N.C., which has kept the highly competitive, splintered hosiery industry on the run for the last 24 months.

Joanne Miller and 450 other "route girls" around the country are part of the strong brand image that "L'eggs" has built up in the two years it has been in operation. The elongated white plastic displays which Joanne sets up to hold the super-ostrich egg packages also promote the image. "L'eggs" heavy start-up investment and highly sophisticated distribution and control system was a substantial drain on Hanes's earning for the first 18 months, but it has recently turned a profit. With $35-million in sales for 1971, "L'eggs" has climbed into first place as the largest selling brand of hoisery in supermarkets and drugstores scattered throughout the country.

An extremely secretive business, the $1.84-billion hosiery industry is filled with hundreds of small-, medium-, and large-sized companies selling some 600 different brands of stockings and pantyhose. Burlington Industries, Kayser-Roth, and Hanes—the top three manufacturers— all have well-known brand names, but extensive private labeling by department stores, discount operations, and more recently, supermarket and drugstore retailers, has swollen the number of hosiery brands in the marketplace and reduced their individual visibility.

Reprinted by permission from *Business Week* (March 25, 1972), pp. 96–100.

NEW MARKET

The pantyhose boom in supermarkets started in early 1969 with the introduction of the Lady Brevoni brand by a leading manufacturer in West Germany. The pantyhose gave stores a margin of 40% on a low retail price of 79¢ and was shipped in ready-to-display cartons. "With that promotion, pantyhose became a commodity, not just a fashion item," a competitor notes. Says Ken Peskin, advertising manager of Supermarkets General Corp.: "Pantyhose has become a very big item for supermarkets. It's hardly a little rack in the corner anymore."

About the same time, Hanes Corp. hired 33-year-old David E. Harrold, a former marketing man at General Foods Corp., to research how it could sell a newly designed one-size line of pantyhose to the lucrative supermarket and drugstore outlets. Up until this time, Hanes had been selling hosiery to department store outlets only. Hanes paid $400,000 for market research—a high price in the normally conservative hosiery industry. Harrold concluded that women were not particularly impressed by strong price promotion of hosiery in supermarkets and drugstores. And many were disgusted by the lack of uniform quality control for many private labels. "For a while, I always bought medium-tall in the same brand for 79¢ a pair," says Pat Sasha, a New Jersey social worker. "One week they sagged and bagged, the next week I could hardly sit down they were so tight."

Harrold also found that while hosiery and health and beauty aid products were introduced into supermarket outlets at approximately the same time—10 to 12 years ago—supermarkets got only 12% of hosiery sales in 1968, while sales of the top 20 health and beauty aid products in the same outlets had grown to 50%. With this background, Hanes decided it would gamble on a program geared to building brand loyalty and with ads emphasizing quality rather than price. The new "L'eggs" hosiery, at $1.39 a pair, costs at least 30¢ more than most pantyhose sold in supermarkets and drugstores.

In fact, private labeling has kept other pantyhose prices on a continuous downhill spiral in the last few years. For example, A&P has had price promotions offering private label brands at 39¢ a pair, Waldbaum's at three for $1, and Pathmark, at 49¢ a pair. Hanes, however, will not budge on the price it charges for "L'eggs." Says Walter Pilcher, product brand manager for "L'Eggs": "In Detroit—the most discount-oriented city in the country—we have to police the retailers in order to maintain a fair-trade position. I have been called arrogant and stupid because we took our display out of one supermarket where the owner insisted on underpricing "L'eggs.""

Says Harrold, who is now a Hanes corporate vice-president: "We decided that to be successful, any new brand would have to establish a clear-cut identity—something on a par with Maxwell House Coffee or Tetley Tea."

"L'eggs'" subsequent hefty $10-million introductory advertising budget—double the amount spent by the total hosiery industry—neatly tied in its distinctive egg-shaped point-of-purchase display with newspaper and television ads using the slogan, "Our 'L'eggs' fit your legs." The company spent an additional $5-million on national consumer promotion, using introductory direct-mail coupons worth 25¢ or 35¢ off on each "L'eggs" purchase. "We used classic consumer marketing techniques to build this brand image," says Robert Odear, who recently took Harrold's place as marketing manager for "L'eggs." "Our advertising," he adds, "took into consideration the fact that consumer brand awareness of hosiery was virtually nonexistent in supermarkets and drugstores, and that brand permanency had to be reinforced to the consumer and to the trade as well."

CONSIGNMENT

"L'eggs'" toughest job, though, was to convince the supermarket and drugstore chain retailers. "We had to trade off a past reputation with department stores into the supermarkets," says Harrold. "All we asked for was 2½ sq. ft. of their store—that was less than everyone else." The key word, however, that sold retailers was "consignment." Typically, retailers buy inventory, but "L'eggs" is completely paid for by the manufacturer. The retailer makes no financial investment at all. Each store averages about $1,300 a year profit from a single "L'eggs" display, and he has no service costs since route girls do all the re-stocking and cleaning.

To overcome the out-of-stock and service problems that hurt other hosiery manufacturers, "L'eggs" opted for direct store delivery and hired an Atlanta-based management consulting firm, Executive Control Systems, to develop an information-gathering and control system. The ECS system that "L'eggs" now uses integrates all activities—from manufacturing to placement of the product in the store. When the first product assortment is provided on consignment, resupply is based on individual display units. The computerized control system coordinates manufacturings, warehouse distribution, retail inventory balance, sales and market analysis, billings and accounts. "With this system, we can optimize the route girl's workload and schedule her from week to week," says Joseph Neeley, director of administration for "L'eggs." Now selling in 75% of the major urban markets across the country, "L'eggs" expects to go completely national this year, although executives admit that New

York City, with its heavy auto and pedestrian traffic, presents distribution difficulties. "The thought of route girls parking and unloading on Manhattan streets causes my stomach to turn," says Odear.

Meanwhile, back on the road, Joanne Miller is busy fighting the Pocono's rainy, slippery roads, high winds ("It blows my 'L'eggs' away"), and the "cookie men, milkmen, and meat-men all trying to see store managers." But no matter what, she is always an enthusiastic salesgirl. "A few weeks ago it was down to about 5 degrees," says Joanne. "A woman stopped and asked me while I was unloading, 'What's so great about "L'eggs"?' Why, just look at the way they fit," answered Joanne, and obligingly rolled up her woolen slacks to display a baggy pair of gray long johns. "We both just stood there and roared," said Joanne. "It wasn't exactly a hard sell, but she bought a pair anyway."

QUESTIONS FOR DISCUSSION

1. Why did the Hanes Corporation decide on a new marketing channel for their pantyhose?

2. What is consignment selling? Why do retailers like it?

3. How important do you feel channel strategy was to Hanes Corporation in regard to their overall marketing mix for "L'eggs"?

1.5 BUILDING SOLID BRIDGES TO YOUR CUSTOMERS

Harvey Appelbaum

"We [Helene Curtis] are constantly striving to strengthen our wholesale dealer's bridge to its customers. It may be the dealer's bridge, but our success depends on its strength, on its ability to 'carry' our merchandise to the beauty salons and men's styling shops that are our dealer's customers."

There's your salesman—isn't he great? His shoes are as shiny as his car. His blue suit, his shirt, tie, and hair, even his sample bag and attaché case—all are perfect.

He's about to call on his distributor, fresh from your sales meeting. The adrenalin is still flowing from his "shot in the arm."

Aren't you proud? Your man's sample case is tightly packed, but everything's in order because he does his homework. All the quota sheets, IBM sheets, home office sheets, and account record sheets are made out in advance. The clock strikes nine as he opens the door for his nine-thirty appointment. He's there on "Lombardi time," early!

He says hello to everybody. He knows everyone's first name. Isn't he terrific? "Come on in," says the buyer. "Yes, sir" is your salesman's respectful reply.

Now comes the sales call, right out of the book, and it's a classic.

He's a pleasure to watch. He keeps his jacket on, tie tight to his collar, no smoking, no gum, never once saying, "You know." The buyer is relaxed and there's minimum small talk. The buyer has a problem, but your man is solving it before his very eyes, using it to lead right into his presentation.

If only you could tape the presentation. Not only does he get quota but 25% over it (after all, someone has to make up for that S.O.B. at the other end of the territory that never buys quota).

The quantity discount, the extra request, the trip for the buyer—he handles them as well as he handles the dealer salesman's P.M. program,

Reprinted by permission from the publisher. Harvey Appelbaum, "Building Solid Bridges To Your Customers," *Sales and Marketing Management* (February 23, 1976), pp. 27–31.

the free samples, and the free advertising material. Now his job is done and he's packing up, keeping the chitchat to a minimum because he's got a lot of other calls to make. He's got to do the same thing throughout his territory, and the way he's going, you know he will.

But what's the result?

Time passes. It's almost 60 days later and he's making his first trip back. Let's look in again.

Can this be the same salesman? His jacket's off, tie loose, cigarette dangling from his lips, and pleading words are coming from his mouth.

The buyer says, "It doesn't sell. My people can't sell it. They're not asking for it! It's too expensive. The deal's too big. I've got more in stock now than I started with. I'm not paying for it. I'm sending it back, freight collect!"

Welcome, readers, to the cold water—you never finished building your bridges to your customers. At Helene Curtis, we feel, as most companies do, that we have built and are maintaining a strong bridge to our own field force. The next step is building a longer bridge from a company's own salespeople to its wholesale dealers—it, too, needs to be a strong bridge.

Here's where our philosophy of "T.N.T." comes to bear. It may be hokey, but we devoutly believe in "Through (our wholesaler), Not To." We are also constantly striving to strengthen our wholesale dealer's bridge to its customers. It may be the dealer's bridge, but our success depends on its strength, on its ability to "carry" our merchandise to the beauty salons and men's styling shops that are our dealer's customers.

The sale that opened this article is only Step 1 of building bridges. In fact, a *complete* dealer sales call accounts for only 25% of our salespeople's time. The remainder of the time on this call should have been spent on *how* the product or promotion is going to be sold by the dealer to its customer and what the dealer is going to do to assure the flow of that merchandise across that bridge.

Our salesperson, after completing an agreement on a "how to sell" approach individualized for that dealer, makes an appointment for Step 2. He or she then presents the entire program to the dealer's salespeople at what we call a kick-off meeting. This is a sales meeting. Our people have received considerable training in conducting such a meeting in order to impart all possible product knowledge, sales techniques, motivation, and enthusiasm.

Because our salesperson has to stay in the real world when making recommendations, we have Step 3. This step is part of our philosophy, too, and it starts at the top. Our salespeople are assigned territories not by dollar volume or dealer count, but by dealer salespeople count—the number of salespeople our customers have. Our people spend 25% of their time actually selling to dealers and another 25% holding kick-off meetings. The balance of their time is spent working with their dealer's salespeople. We call it *detailing*, but it's really training—training the dealer's salespeople, trying to strengthen the bridge from wholesaler to retailer.

At Helene Curtis this calls for our district manager's making appointments with the dealer's salespeople in the coming month, usually at the dealership where they pick up their drop-offs, samples, sales literature, etc. Remember that I explained that this promotion is "car stocked" at kick-off meetings. Also, while riding in the dealer's salesperson's car, our district manager discusses the calls that will be made and the procedures to be followed in the salons and shops.

We prefer to have the dealer's salesperson write his "regular" orders first. Then we make our presentation with the dealer's salesperson observing. In this way, our order is a plus to the "regular" business, and by observation, he learns various sales techniques. During the first part of the day, with our person selling the promotion, the sales calls and techniques are discussed back in the car—it's like a one-on-one sales meeting. When the dealer's salesperson feels ready to try, he proceeds—with our backup help, if necessary, These calls and sales are later analyzed and critiqued.

Using this method, we find that by midday the dealer's salesperson is presenting the new promotion alone, and our district manager is handling other products and promotions. By the end of the day, the dealer salesperson is "expert" in the major promotion and better acquainted with other products that he or she might have missed in the past.

When deciding whom to detail with in each dealership, we give first priority to the dealer's new salespeople, who obviously need the most help. However, there are times when we deviate. In some dealerships there is the "lead" salesperson, someone that all the other salespeople follow. Sometimes we detail with that lead person for a day or two prior to the kick-off meeting. During this time, various techniques will be tried and the more successful ones presented at the kick-off meeting. If the lead salesperson is willing—and he usually is—we let him openly discuss the various sales techniques.

There are also times when the dealer's more experienced salespeople will get "stuck" on a product or promotion. After a day when our salesperson observes the first one or two presentations, we can make an adjustment or change the entire proposal to achieve a successful conclusion.

Finally, Step 4—follow up: replan, readjust, repromote, resell.

When our district managers follow those four steps, they have really "perpetuated" themselves in each dealership with each of the dealer's salespersons, thereby building a solid bridge to the ultimate customer.

In terms of cost we know that the extra business our district managers will write will never pay for their detailing days. However, when they develop an army of loyal followers, it pays off for us in the long run.

Do the shops and salons like it? Yes. They really like the opportunity to speak to a "factory" salesperson. The dealer's salespersons like it because we don't waste their valuable time. We do what has to be done. They sell more of our merchandise, use us to "crack" their more difficult customers, get a bigger share of their market, and earn more commissions.

As for the buyers, they have in a way made our district managers their sales managers for our products. Our dealers feel that, not only do we give the "everything" to market a product, we give of ourselves and our time, and they love it. That's one of the reasons they have made us No. 1 in the professional products industry.

There are other benefits for us. The most important is that our people are on the firing line, where the action is. To take advantage of this, our daily call reports are designed to have our people communicate various information that assists us in all our future marketing plans.

If you want to build bridges, build them in four steps. And start with T.N.T.—Through the wholesaler, Not To him.

QUESTIONS FOR DISCUSSION

1. The article discussed T.N.T. Explain this term and its importance to Helene Curtis Industries.

2. The article discusses the concept of "building bridges to your customers." Discuss fully the meaning of this statement.

3. Explain the four steps used to increase sales at Helene Curtis.

Chapter 2

Marketing Institutions: Retailing

THE TWO MAJOR MARKETING INSTITUTIONS—wholesaling and retailing—are the subjects of Chapters Two and Three. Although the simplest, most direct channel is from manufacturer to consumer or industrial user, less than five percent of the dollar value of all consumer goods move through this route. The presence of thousands of wholesalers and retailers indicates that these institutions are performing important marketing functions. These include convenient storage of goods near the consumer; reduced distribution costs through wholesalers and retailers representing a number of different manufacturers; performing a financing function for the consumer or manufacturer; and providing an information link between the manufacturer and consumer.

Retailing, sometimes called the last three feet of the marketing channel, consists of *all the activities involved in the sale of products and services to the ultimate consumer for his or her own use.* Retailing includes not only sales in retail stores, but also automatic vending machines, telephone and mail-order sales, and direct house-to-house solicitations by salespersons. As Table 2-1 indicates, nonstore retailing accounted for less than three percent of total 1972 retail sales of $459 billion.

Retail institutions evolve over time in response to changing market conditions and shifts in consumer demands. The general store, the retailing outpost in frontier America, gradually gave way to limited-line stores who specialized in grocery lines, hardware, drugs, and bakery products. The service food store declined in importance as self-service supermarkets emerged. As some stores appeared to shrink in size (convenience food stores), others (the *hyper-marché* or superstore) grew to gigantic proportions.

The first selection by Stanley C. Hollander presents a lucid description of Malcolm McNair's famous "Wheel-of-Retailing" theory of retail change. Briefly, the "wheel" theory states that retailers enter business by offering lower prices and limited services. Over time, however, the retailer feels the need to upgrade services. Since retail markups are a function of operating costs (including the costs of providing services)

TABLE 2-1   Retail Trade by Type of Operation

Type of Operation	Number of Establishments	Sales (billions)	Percentage of Total Sales
Building materials, hardware, garden supply, and mobile home dealers	83,842	23.8	5.2
General merchandise	56,245	65.1	14.2
Department stores	7,742	51.1	11.1
Variety stores	21,852	7.3	1.6
Other	26,651	6.7	1.5
Food stores	267,352	100.7	21.9
Automobile dealers	121,369	90.0	19.6
Gasoline service stations	226,459	33.7	7.3
Apparel and accessory stores	129,201	24.7	5.4
Furniture, home furnishings, and equipment stores	116,857	22.5	4.9
Eating and drinking places	359,524	36.9	8.0
Drugstores and proprietary stores	51,542	15.6	3.4
Other retailers*	338,359	34.4	7.5
Nonstore retailers	162,121	11.6	2.5
Mail-order houses	7,982	4.6	1.0
Automatic merchandising machine operators	12,845	3.0	0.7
Direct selling	141,294	4.0	0.9
Total retail trade	1,912,871	459.0	100.0

* Includes liquor, jewelry, and sporting goods stores, florists, etc.
Source: U. S. Bureau of the Census, Census of Retail Trade, 1972, Establishment and Firm Size (Washington, D. C.: U. S. Government Printing Office, 1976), pp. 1–8–1–36.

and turnover, prices eventually rise. As the prices increase, an environment is created conducive to new retailers entering the market and competing by offering lower prices and fewer services. The latter retailers eventually also become higher-priced merchants and new opportunities are thus created for another low-price retailer. Many examples of this theory are present in the form of chain stores, supermarkets, discount retailers, and early department stores. As Hollander points out, some exceptions to the "wheel" theory are also present—such as convenience food stores, suburban shopping centers, and vending machines—but the wheel pattern has been present often enough to serve as a general indicator of future retailing developments.

Professor Robert E. Stevens focuses on retail innovations in the second selection and develops a technological model to explain changes that occur in the retail sector.

In the final selection in Chapter Two, well-known writer and researcher Leo Bogart presents his conception (as well as those of twelve leaders in American retailing) of "The Future of Retailing." Bogart reviews the data from a forecasting study of executives in department store groups, in independent department stores, chains, and discount store organizations, as well as others knowledgeable in the retailing field and makes projections concerning the economic and social forces impacting on retailing operations. Bogart focuses on employment patterns, technological innovations, store operations, customer service predictions, and competitive trends that are just now beginning to emerge in retailing. The article is a stimulating preview of retailing in 1990.

2.1 THE WHEEL OF RETAILING

Stanley C. Hollander

"New types of retail institutions are often established by highly aggressive, cost-conscious entrepreneurs who make every penny count and who have no interest in unprofitable frills. But, . . ."

"The wheel of retailing" is the name Professor Malcolm P. McNair has suggested for a major hypothesis concerning patterns of retail development. This hypothesis holds that new types of retailers usually enter the market as low-status, low-margin, low-price operators. Gradually they acquire more elaborate establishments and facilities, with both increased investments and higher operating costs. Finally they mature as high-cost, high-price merchants, vulnerable to newer types who, in turn, go through the same pattern. Department-store merchants, who originally appeared as vigorous competitors to the smaller retailers and who have now become vulnerable to discount house and supermarket competition, are often cited as prime examples of the wheel pattern.[1]

Many examples of conformity to this pattern can be found. Nevertheless, we may ask: (1) Is this hypothesis valid for all retailing under all conditions? (2) How accurately does it describe total American retail development? (3) What factors cause wheel-pattern changes in retail institutions?

The following discussion assembles some of the slender empirical evidence available that might shed some light on these three questions. In attempting to answer the third question, a number of hypotheses should be considered that marketing students have advanced concerning the forces that have shaped retail development.

Reprinted by permission from Stanley C. Hollander, "The Wheel of Retailing," *Journal of Marketing*, Vol. 25 (July 1960), pp. 37–42, published by American Marketing Association.

1. M. P. McNair, "Significant Trends and Developments in the Postwar Period," in A. B. Smith (editor), *Competitive Distribution in a Free, High-Level Economy and Its Implications for the University* (Pittsburgh: University of Pittsburgh Press, 1958), pp. 1–25 at pp. 17–18.

TENTATIVE EXPLANATIONS OF THE WHEEL

A. RETAIL PERSONALITIES

New Types of retail institutions are often established by highly aggressive, cost-conscious entrepreneurs who make every penny count and who have no interest in unprofitable frills. But, as P. D. Converse has suggested, these men may relax their vigilance and control over costs as they acquire age and wealth. Their successors may be less competent. Either the innovators or their successors may be unwilling, or unable, to adjust to changing conditions. Consequently, according to this view, deterioration in management causes movement along the wheel.[2]

B. MISGUIDANCE

Hermann Levy has advanced the ingenious, if implausible, explanation that retail trade journals, seduced by profitable advertising from the store equipment and supply industry, coax merchants into superfluous "modernization" and into the installation of overly elaborate facilities.[3]

C. IMPERFECT COMPETITION

Although retail trade is often cited as the one type of business that approaches the Adam Smith concept of perfect competition, some economists have argued that retailing actually is a good example of imperfect competition. These economists believe that most retailers avoid direct price competition because of several forces, including resale price maintenance, trade association rules in some countries, and, most important, the fear of immediate retaliation. Contrariwise, the same retailers feel that service improvements, including improvements in location, are not susceptible to direct retaliation by competitors. Hence, through a ratchet process, merchants in any established branch of trade tend to provide increasingly elaborate services at increasingly higher margins.[4]

---

2. P. D. Converse, "Mediocrity in Retailing," *Journal of Marketing*, Vol. 23 (April, 1959), pp. 419–420.

3. Hermann Levy, *The Shops of Britain* (London: Kegan Paul, Trench, Trubner & Co., 1947), pp. 210–211.

4. D. L. Shawver, *The Development of Theories of Retail Price Determination* (Urbana: University of Illinois Press, 1956), p. 92.

D. EXCESS CAPACITY

McNair attributes much of the wheel effect to the development of excess capacity, as more and more dealers enter any branch of retail trade.[5] This hypothesis rests upon an imperfect competition assumption, since, under perfect competition excess capacity would simply reduce margins until the excess vendors were eliminated.

E. SECULAR TREND

J. B. Jefferys has pointed out that a general, but uneven, long-run increase in the British standard of living provided established merchants with profitable opportunities for trading up. Jefferys thus credits adjustments to changing and wealthier market segments as causing some movement along the wheel. At the same time, pockets of opportunity have remained for new, low-margin operations because of the uneven distribution of living-standard increases.[6]

F. ILLUSION

Professor B. Holdren has suggested in a recent letter that present tendencies toward scrambled merchandising may create totally illusory impressions of the wheel phenomenon. Store-wide average margins may increase as new, high-markup lines are added to the product mix, even though the margins charged on the original components of that mix remain unchanged.

DIFFICULTIES OF ANALYSIS

An examination of the actual development of retail institutions here and abroad does shed some light on both the wheel hypothesis and its various explanations. However, a number of significant difficulties hinder the process.

1. Statements concerning changes in retail margins and expenses are the central core of the wheel hypothesis. Yet valid information on historical retail expense rates is very scarce. Long-run changes in percentage margins probably do furnish fairly reliable clues to expense changes, but this is not true over short or intermediate periods. For example, 1957 furniture-store expense rates were about 5 percentage

5. Same reference as footnote 1.
6. J. B. Jefferys, *Retail Trading in Great Britain*, 1850–1950 (Cambridge: Cambridge University Press, 1954), various pages, especially p. 96.

points higher than their 1949–1951 average, yet gross margins actually declined slightly over the same period.[7]

2. Historical margin data are somewhat more plentiful, but these also have to be dredged up from fragmentary sources.[8]

3. Available series on both expenses and margins merely note changes in retailers' outlays and receipts. They do not indicate what caused those changes and they do not report changes in the costs borne by suppliers, consumers, or the community at large.

4. Margin data are usually published in averages that may, and frequently do, mask highly divergent tendencies.

5. A conceptual difficulty presents an even more serious problem than the paucity of statistics. When we talk about "types" of retailers, we think of classifications based upon ways of doing business and upon differences in price policy. Yet census categories and other systems for reporting retail statistics are usually based upon major differences in commodity lines. For example, the "pineboard" druggists who appeared in the 1930s are a "type" of retailing for our purposes. Those dealers had cruder fixtures, charged lower prices, carried smaller assortments, gave more attention to turnover, and had less interest in prescriptions than did conventional druggists. Yet census reports for drugstores necessarily included all of the pineboards that maintained any sort of prescription department.

Discount houses provide another example of an important, but amorphous, category not reflected in census classifications. The label "discount house" covers a variety of retailers. Some carry stocks, others do not. Some have conventional store facilities, whereas others operate in office buildings, lofts, and warehouses. Some feature electrical appliances and hard goods, while others emphasize soft goods. Some pose as wholesalers, and others are practically indistinguishable from all other popular priced retailers in their fields. Consequently discount dealers' operating figures are likely to be merged into the statistics reported for other appliance, hardware, or apparel merchants.

EXAMPLES OF CONFORMITY

BRITISH

British retailing provides several examples of conformity to the wheel pattern. The grocery trade has gone through several wheel-like evolu-

---

7. Cited in Fabian Linden, "Department Store Operations," *Conference Board Business Record*, Vol. 14 (October, 1958), pp. 410–414, at p. 411.

8. See Harold Barger, *Distribution's Place in the American Economy Since 1869* (Princeton: Princeton University Press, 1955).

tions, according to a detailed analysis made by F. G. Pennance and B. S. Yamey.[9] Established firms did initiate some changes and some margin reductions, so that the pattern is obscured by many cross currents. But the major changes seem to have been due to the appearance and then the maturation, first, of department-store food counters; then, of chain stores; and finally, of cut-price cash-and-carry stores. Now supermarkets seem to be carrying the pattern through another evolution.[10]

Jefferys also has noted a general long-run upgrading in both British department stores and chains.[11] Vague complaints in the co-operative press and a decline in consumer dividend rates suggest that wheel-like changes may have occurred in the British co-operative movement.[12]

AMERICAN

Very little is known about retail margins in this country before the Civil War. Our early retail history seems to have involved the appearance, first, of hawkers, walkers, and peddlers; then, of general stores; next, of specialty stores; and finally, of department stores. Each of these types apparently came in as a lower-margin, lower-price competitor to the established outlets, and thus was consistent with the wheel pattern. We do not know, however, whether there was simply a long-run decline in retail margins through successive improvements in retail efficiency from one type to another (contrary to the wheel pattern), or whether each of the early types was started on a low-margin basis, gradually "upgraded," and so provided room for the next entrant (in accordance with the pattern).

The trends toward increasing margins can be more easily discerned in many branches of retailing after the Civil War. Barger has described increases over the years 1869–1947 among important retail segments, including department stores, mail-order firms, variety stores, and jewelry dealers. He attributes much of the pre-World War I rise in department-store margins to the absorption of wholesaling functions. Changes in merchandise mix, such as the addition of soda fountains and cafeterias to variety stores and the upgrading of mail-order merchandise, seem to

9. F. G. Pennance and B. S. Yamey, "Competition in the Retail Grocery Trade, 1850–1939," *Economica*, Vol. 22 (March, 1955), pp. 303–317.

10. "La Methode Americaine," *Time*, Vol. 74 (November 16, 1959), pp. 105–106.

11. Same reference as footnote 6.

12. "Battle of the Dividend," *Co-operative Review*, Vol. 36 (August, 1956), p. 183; "Independent Commission's Report," *Co-operative Review*, Vol. 38 (April, 1958), pp. 84–89; "£52 Million Dividend in 1957," *Co-operative Review* (August, 1958), pp. 171–172.

have caused some of the other increases. Finally, he believes changes in customer services have been a major force in raising margins.[13] Fabian Linden has extended Barger's observations to note similar 1949–1957 margin increases for department stores, variety chains, and appliance dealers.[14]

Some other examples of at least partial conformity to the wheel pattern may be cited. Many observers feel that both discount-house services and margins have increased substantially in recent years.[15] One major discount-house operator has stated that he has been able to keep his average markup below 12%, in spite of considerable expansion in his facilities and commodity mix.[16] However, the concensus seems to be that this probably is an exception to the general rule.

A study of gasoline pricing has pointed out how many of the so-called "off-brand" outlets have changed from the "trackside" stations of pre-war days. The trackside dealers typically maintained unattractive and poorly equipped installations, at out-of-the-way locations where unbranded gasoline was sold on a price basis. Today many of them sell well-promoted regional and local brands, maintain attractive, efficient stations, and provide prompt and courteous service. Some still offer cut prices, but many have raised their prices and margins up to or above national brand levels.[17] Over time, many of the pineboard druggists also seem to have become converted to fairly conventional operations.[18]

NON-CONFORMING EXAMPLES

FOREIGN

In underdeveloped countries, the relatively small middle- and upper-income groups have formed the major markets for "modern" types of retailing. Supermarkets and other modern stores have been introduced in those countries largely at the top of the social and price scales, contrary to the wheel pattern.[19] Some nonconforming examples may also be

13. Same reference as footnote 8, p. 82.
14. See footnote 7.
15. D. A. Loehwing, "Resourceful Merchants," *Barron's*, Vol. 38 (November 17, 1958), p. 3.
16. S. Masters, quoted in "Three Concepts of Retail Service," *Stores*, Vol. 41 (July-August, 1959), pp. 18–21.
17. S. M. Livingston and T. Levitt, "Competition and Retail Gasoline Prices," *The Review of Economics and Statistics*, Vol. 41 (May, 1959), pp. 119–132 at p. 132.
18. Paul C. Olsen, *The Marketing of Drug Products* (New Brunswick: Rutgers University Press, 1948), pp. 130–132.
19. H. S. Hettinger, "Marketing in Persia," *Journal of Marketing*, Vol. 15 (Janu-

found in somewhat more industrialized environments. The vigorous price competition that developed among Japanese department stores during the first three decades of this century seems directly contrary to the wheel hypothesis.[20] B. S. Yamey's history of resale price maintenance also reports some price-cutting by traditional, well-established British merchants who departed from the wheel pattern in the 1880s and 1890s.[21] Unfortunately, our ignorance of foreign retail history hinders any judgment of the representativeness of these examples.

AMERICAN

Automatic merchandising, perhaps the most "modern" of all American retail institutions, departed from the wheel pattern by starting as a high-cost, high-margin, high-convenience type of retailing.[22] The department-store branch movement and the concomitant rise of planned shopping centers also has progressed directly contrary to the wheel pattern. The early department-store branches consisted of a few stores in exclusive suburbs and some equally high-fashion college and resort shops.

Only in relatively recent years have the branches been adjusted to the changing and more democratic characteristics of the contemporary dormitory suburbs. Suburban shopping centers, too, seem to have appeared first as "Manhasset Miracle Miles" and "Ardmores" before reaching out to the popular price customers. In fact, complaints are still heard that the regional shopping centers have displayed excessive resistance to the entry of really aggressive, low-margin outlets.[23] E. R. A. Seligman and R. A. Love's study of retail pricing in the 1930s suggests that pressures on prices and margins were generally by all types of retailers. The mass retailing institutions, such as the department and chain stores, that had existed as types for many decades were responsible for a goodly

ary, 1951), pp. 289–297; H. W. Boyd, Jr., R. M. Clewett, & R. L. Westfall, "The Marketing Structure of Venezuela," *Journal of Marketing*, Vol. 22 (April, 1958), pp. 391–397; D. A. Taylor, "Retailing in Brazil," *Journal of Marketing*, Vol. 24 (July, 1959), pp. 54–58; J. K. Galbraith and R. Holton, *Marketing Efficiency in Puerto Rico* (Cambridge: Harvard University Press, 1955), p. 35.

20. G. Fukami, "Japanese Department Stores," *Journal of Marketing*, Vol. 18 (July, 1953), pp. 41–49 at p. 42.

21. "The Origins of Resale Price Maintenance," *The Economic Journal*, Vol. 62 (September, 1952), pp. 522–545.

22. W. S. Fishman, "Sense Makes Dollars," *1959 Directory of Automatic Merchandising* (Chicago: National Automatic Merchandising Association, 1959), p. 52; M. V. Marshall, *Automatic Merchandising* (Boston: Graduate School of Business Administration, Harvard University, 1954), pp. 108–109, 122.

23. P. E. Smith, *Shopping Centers* (New York: National Retail Merchants' Association, 1956), pp. 11–12; M. L. Sweet, "Tenant-Selection Policies of Regional Shopping Centers," *Journal of Marketing*, Vol. 23 (April, 1959), pp. 399–404.

portion of the price cutting.[24] As McNair has pointed out, the wheel operated very slowly in the case of department stores.

Finally, Harold Barger has described the remarkable stability of over-all distributive margins during the years 1919–1947.[25] Some shifting of distributive work from wholesalers to retailers apparently effected their relative shares of the total margins during this period, but this is not the type of change contemplated by the wheel pattern. Of course, the stability Barger notes conceivably could have been the result of a perfectly smooth functioning of the pattern, with the entrance of low-margin innovators providing exactly the right balance for the upcreep of margins in the longer established types. But economic changes do not come in smooth and synchronized fashion, and Barger's data probably should indicate considerably wider oscillations if the wheel really set the mold for all retailing in the post-war period.

CONCLUSIONS

The number of non-conforming examples suggests that the wheel hypothesis is not valid for all retailing. The hypothesis, however, does seem to describe a fairly common pattern in industrialized, expanding economies. Moreover, the wheel is not simply an illusion created by scrambled merchandising, as Holdren suggests. Undoubtedly some of the recent "upcreep" in supermarket average margins is due to the addition of nonfood and other high margin lines. But in recent years the wheel pattern has also been characteristic of department-store retailing, a field that has been relatively unreceptive to new commodity groups.[26]

In some ways, Jefferys' secular trend explanation appears most reasonable. The tendency of many established retailers to reduce prices and margins during depressions suggests also that increases may be a result of generally prospering environments. This explanation helps to resolve an apparent paradox inherent in the wheel concept. Why should reasonably skilled businessmen make decisions that consistently lead their firms along seemingly profitable routes to positions of vulnerability? Jefferys sees movement along the wheel as the result of sensible, business-like decisions to change with prospering market segments and to leave the poorer customers to low-margin innovators. His explanation is supported by the fact that the vulnerability contemplated by the wheel hypothesis usually means only a loss of market share, not a loss

24. E. R. A. Seligman and R. A. Love, *Price Cutting and Price Maintenance* (New York: Harper & Brothers, 1932).

25. Same reference as footnote 8, pp. ix, x.

26. R. D. Entenberg, *The Changing Competitive Position of Department Stores in the United States by Merchandise Lines* (Pittsburgh: University of Pittsburgh Press, 1957), p. 52.

of absolute volume. At least in the United States, though, this explanation is partially contradicted by studies showing that prosperous consumers are especially prone to patronize discount houses. Also they are equally as likely to shop in supermarkets as are poorer consumers.[27]

The imperfect competition and excess capacity hypotheses also appear highly plausible. Considerably more investigation is needed before their validity can be appraised properly. The wheel pattern developed very slowly, and very recently in the department-store field. Yet market imperfections in that field probably were greater before the automobile gave the consumer shopping mobility. Major portions of the supermarket growth in food retailing and discount-house growth in appliance distribution occurred during periods of vastly expanding consumption, when excess capacity probably was at relatively low levels. At the moment there is little evidence to suggest any clear-cut correlation between the degree of market imperfection and the appearance of the wheel pattern. However, this lack may well be the result of the scarcity of empirical studies of retail competition.

Managerial deterioration certainly must explain some manifestations of the wheel, but not all. Empires rise and fall with changes in the quality of their leadership, and the same thing seems true in business. But the wheel hypothesis is a hypothesis concerning types of retailing and not merely individual firms. Consequently, the managerial-deterioration explanation holds true only if it is assumed that new people entering any established type of retailing as the heads of both old and new companies are consistently less competent than the first generation. Again, the fact that the wheel has operated very slowly in some fields suggests that several successive managerial generations can avoid wheel-like maturation and decay.

QUESTIONS FOR DISCUSSION

1. What is the "wheel of retailing" hypothesis?

2. Which explanation of this theory seems most plausible to you?

3. Outline retailing changes that you can think of in your home town that tend to support or invalidate the "wheel" theory.

4. Discuss briefly how an understanding of the "wheel" theory could be helpful to an established retailer.

5. Are there any exceptions to the "wheel of retailing" theory in the United States? Discuss.

27. R. Holton, *The Supply and Demand Structure of Food Retailing Services, A Case Study* (Cambridge: Harvard University Press, 1954).

2.2 RETAIL INNOVATIONS: A TECHNOLOGICAL MODEL OF CHANGE IN RETAILING

Robert E. Stevens

"Change is the essence of retailing. Indeed, it is almost redundant to use the words change and retailing in the same sentence."

Change is the essence of retailing. Indeed, it is almost redundant to use the words change and retailing in the same sentence. An examination of retailing in America reveals a process of continual change. This process involves an adaptation of retail institutions to changes in the environment or an adaptation of the environment to changes in retailing.

Retail innovations have been the subject of much of the marketing literature. Various writers have atempted to: (1) Explain why certain patterns of change have occurred,[1] (2) Explain why other businessmen have adopted a retail innovation,[2] (3) Use biological analogies to describe the process of change in retailing,[3] and (4) Depict change in retailing as a continuous cycle.[4] However, the nature of the changes that occur in retailing has never been adequately dealt with in the literature.

This paper presents a conceptual model of change in retailing based on the Shaw-Alderson model of technological change in marketing. This model can be used to explain why change occurs in retailing, how

Reprinted by permission of the author and publisher. Robert E. Stevens, "Retail Innovations: A Technological Model of Change in Retailing," *Marquette Business Review* (Spring, 1976).

1. M. P. McNair, "Significant Trends and Developments in the Postwar Period," in A. B. Smith's (editor) *Competitive Distribution in a Free, High, Level Economy and Its Implications for the University* (Pittsburgh: University of Pittsburgh Press, 1958), pp. 1–25. For an elaboration of McNair's work, see Stanley C. Hollander, "The Wheel of Retailing," *Journal of Marketing*, July, 1960, pp. 37–42.

2. Perry Bliss, "Schumpeter, the 'Big' Disturbance and Retailing," *Social Forces*, October, 1960, pp. 72–76.

3. A. C. R. Dreesman, "Patterns of Evolution in Retailing," *Journal of Retailing*, Spring, 1968, pp. 64–81.

4. Edward A. Brand, "The Retailing Cycle," *Management Perspectives in Retailing*, Second Edition, edited by Ronald R. Gist, John Wiley and Sons, Inc., New York, New York, 1971, pp. 28–30.

it occurs, and why change is accepted by consumers. Past evolution of some important aspects of retailing will be explained in terms of the model and the direction of future retail evolution will be predicted.

WHY CHANGE OCCURS IN RETAILING

Change is initiated in retailing, as in other fields of business enterprise, to create or take advantage of opportunities. The initiators of change are attempting to maximize their opportunities—opportunities for sales, profits, return on investment, prestige, etc.

Some innovations have been the result of attempts to adjust to changes in the environment—shopping centers are an example. Other innovations have been the result of a specific attempt to perform the retailing function in a new way—automated retailing. However, both types of innovations have been brought about by management's desire to maximize its opportunities.

THE NATURE OF RETAIL INNOVATIONS

A. W. Shaw, a pioneer in the development of marketing thought, said that one of the essential elements of any phase of business is the application of motion to matter.[5] He proceeded to describe the marketing process in terms of the motions or movements involved in market distribution.

Wroe Alderson extended the Shaw analysis by specifying three distinct types of movement in marketing—the movement of goods and services, the movement of information, and the movement of people. Alderson relates these movements to technological change in marketing by stating that:

> Technological change in marketing involves improvements in one or the other of these types of movements or it may involve a substitution of one type of movement for another to achieve greater economy or effectiveness in the total marketing process.[6]

This statement gives the basic elements of a model for explaining and predicting change in marketing. Application of this model to retailing provides an enlightened view of the nature of change in the field of retailing.

The innovations that occur in retailing, according to the model, are

5. A. W. Shaw, "Some Problems in Market Distribution," *Harvard Business Review*, Vol. 40, No. 4, July–August, 1962, pp. 113–122.

6. Wroe Alderson, *Dynamic Marketing Behavior*, Richard D. Irvin, Inc., Homewood, Illinois, 1965, p. 262.

the result of: (1) improving efficiency (and/or effectiveness) in performing the functions involved in moving goods, people, and information, and (2) substituting one type of movement for another (conceivably, some combination of 1 and 2 is also possible). The movements referred to are the actual physical movements involved in the distribution of goods and services. The movement of goods and services and the movement of people may be regarded as the primary activities while the movement of information serves to facilitate the other two types of movements. Information in this context, helps match people and goods and avoids mismatching.[7]

APPLICATION OF THE MODEL TO PAST RETAIL INNOVATIONS

The validity of the Shaw-Alderson model as applied to innovations in retailing can be demonstrated through an examination of retail evolution in the United States. The following table lists some of the major changes that have occurred in retailing in the last century. Column 1 specifies the movement or substitutions involved for each of these changes while Column 2 specifies the consumer benefit of the change.

As is clearly shown in this table, every major innovation in retailing has involved an improvement in performing one or the other types of movements, or it has involved the substitution of one type of movement for another.

Mail-order retailing, for example, involved substituting the movement of information and goods for the movement of people. The information about available goods was transmitted through the catalogs and brochures and in turn, the goods moved to the people through the mail. The consumer benefited through wider assortment and the convenience of home delivery.

The growth and success of the single-line (specialty) store involved the substitution of the movement of information and people for the movement of goods. Customers had to go to several stores to get what had previously been available at one store—the general store. The improved assortment of goods more than offset the consumer inconvenience and effort required to shop several stores.

The department store, as an innovation, substituted the movement of information and goods for the movement of people. The goods available through many single-line stores were brought under one roof. Consumers benefited through more convenience and a large assortment of different types of goods and services.

7. Ibid., pp. 262–263.

THE NATURE OF RETAIL INNOVATIONS AND
ACCOMPANYING CONSUMER BENEFITS

Retail Innovation	Movement Involved	Consumer Benefit
Mail-Order Retailing	Substituted Movement of Information and Goods For People	Assortment–Convenience
Specialty Stores	Substituted Movement of Information and People For Goods	Assortment
Department Stores	Substituted Movement of Information and Goods For People	Assortment–Convenience
Supermarkets	Improved Efficiency in Movement of Goods	Price
Chain Stores	Improved Efficiency in Movement of Goods	Price
Shopping Centers	Substituted Movement of Information and Goods For People	Assortment–Convenience
Discounting	Improved Efficiency in Movement of Goods	Price
In-Home Shopping?	Substitute Movement of Information and Goods For People	Convenience

Supermarkets and discount operations involved improvements in the movement of goods *inside* the retail store while the growth of chain stores involved increased efficiency in the movement of goods *outside* the store (and inside too when self-service was adopted). Alderson states that:

> One of the great advantages of chain operations in either field (groceries or drugs) is the chance to combine warehouses, retail stores, and the truck fleet connecting them into a fully integrated goods handling mechanism.[8]

The same description—goods handling mechanisms—also fits supermarkets and discount operations. The customer acts as an "order picker" and the turnover of goods is increased. The customer benefits through lower prices.

The suburban shopping center entailed substituting the movement of information and goods for the movement of people. This change in the locational pattern of retailing found acceptance because of increased consumer convenience.

8. Ibid., p. 266.

CONSUMER ACCEPTANCE OF
RETAIL INNOVATIONS

The consumer, of course, actually determines whether or not any innovation in retailing is successful. A careful analysis of past innovations reveals three basic consumer benefits or retail innovations—better assortments of goods and services, more convenience, or lower prices.

These consumer benefits should not be confused with patronage motives. Although a consumer may shop at a particular store for these benefits, the three consumer benefits explain why a retail innovation is accepted by consumers. A consumer may shop at a particular store because of the assortment, for example, but in this case the assortment helps her choose one store over another and not one innovation over another. The three consumer benefits have a much broader application than specific patronage motives.

One of these benefits must be increased with no decrease in the other two or an acceptable trade-off of benefits must be accomplished (i.e., less assortment but more convenience) for any change in retailing to gain consumer acceptance.

IN-HOME SHOPPING: A FUTURE INNOVATION

One of the purposes of a model is to enable the user to predict. Predicting with a high degree of accuracy requires valid models of the operating environment. One method of demonstrating the validity of a model is to see how well it explains past events. The Shaw-Alderson model does seem to offer logical explanations for past changes in the field of retailing. However, the predictive validity of a model can only be established through using the model to predict, and then assessing the accuracy of the prediction.

Barring an economic catastrophe (depression or hyperinflation), the next major change in retailing should involve in-home shopping. Improvements in the efficiency of moving information should enable retailers to substitute the movement of information and goods for the movement of people and bring the historical tendency for increased consumer convenience to its logical conclusion—in-home shopping.

Initially, shopping of this nature could involve the picture-phone or a combination of the television set and telephone. Ultimately, such a retail innovation could involve a home telecommunications system with routine purchase decisions—purchase of staple items—completely computerized. The exact nature of the innovation will, of course, be determined by the developments in communications, computer, and marketing technology.

SUMMARY

This paper has presented a conceptual model of retail innovations based on technological change in marketing. This model explains why change occurs, how it occurs, and why change is accepted by consumers. Thus, the conceptual model is complete. Maximization of opportunities causes businessmen to attempt to change the retail operating environment by improving the efficiency of movement or substituting one movement for another. Consumers accept the changes because of increased benefits or an acceptable trade-off of benefits.

QUESTIONS FOR DISCUSSION

1. According to this article, why does change take place in retailing? Discuss.

2. Discuss the Shaw-Alderson model as it relates to change in retailing.

3. What retailing innovation does Professor Stevens predict may be forthcoming? Discuss.

2.3 THE FUTURE OF RETAILING

Leo Bogart

Merchandising experts foresee interesting trends developing that most retailers will be acting on.

If we look back to the great changes in U.S. general merchandise retailing since the end of World War II, it is apparent that few people then could have predicted exactly what form the future would take. Nor can we make an accurate forecast now, as we look ahead the same time span to the year 2000.

Both in the practice of retailing and in its competitive structure, many of the significant changes that have taken place in the past few decades have been a by-product of the tremendous changes in our population: in where and how people have chosen to live, work, and buy.

In the next few decades, these trends will continue, but some of the most important new forces of change will be those wrought by the technological revolution—in the handling of information, in communication, in transportation, in packaging, in warehousing and inventory management, and in the serving of customer needs.

No one can foretell the future. But people who exercise leadership and power, in any field of endeavor, are in the best position to translate their own assumptions about the shape of the future into decisions and actions that in turn affect the course of events. Thus an understanding of expert opinions about the long-range future can present us with important information and guidance for the short run. That was the purpose of the research on which this article reports.

What are the points on which a substantial number of retailers feel that some immediate action must be taken? Consider:

1. Retailers must revive shrinking profits by the improvement of man/machine systems within the store.

2. They must take advantage of the steady trend toward a service-oriented society by offering more new and profitable services, by developing the boutique concept to personalize customer service within

the store, by developing branch stores as specialty shops, and by differentiating their own store images from those of their competitors. The department store concept of "one-stop shopping" may well give way to the "one-stop shopping center."

3. Department store managements must face up to a steady increase in the competition they face from discounters, from revitalized specialty stores, from food and drug chains, and from direct-to-customer warehouse furniture outlets. Increased competition suggests that there will be a reshuffling of the merchandise mix carried in each type of store—with some departments discontinued and others built up—so that stores may eventually classify themselves more by *what* they sell than by *how* they buy it, mark it up, or sell it. Some of the most significant influences on the future of retailing will continue to come from the basic changes in our society. Yet there appears to be in retailers' attitudes a note of fatalism with respect to the basic social issues that will determine the future of our city centers in the rest of this century and beyond.

The future of the downtown flagship department store, the vitality of central city shopping, the drama of vigorous competition through extensive consumer choice—all these depend on society's willingness to solve the problems of urban transportation, of personal security, and ultimately of poverty and racial conflict. These issues will affect the profits, practice, and competitive structure of American retailing far more than other problems that somehow seem more manageable and specific.

The emphasis on the immediate is reflected throughout our study in the short-run terms in which most retailers tend to think and act. The developments that lie immediately ahead excite the most interest.

The counterpart of this attitude is an unwillingness to spend much time now worrying about developments that lie far ahead. Even when these might have the most profound effects, they are considered as matters beyond the control of any individual retail management.

But are they beyond the influence of the retailing business as a whole? Perhaps this discussion can serve as a reminder that retailing has many tomorrows before it, and the shape they take is being determined partly by the actions that retailers take or fail to take now.

ECONOMIC FORCES

For a generation, retailers have built volume in a steadily expanding market, and they expect the expansion to continue through the rest of this century. In spite of wide publicity given to the recent decline in the U.S. birth rate, most retailers recognize that a declining birth rate will not lead to any decrease in the actual size of the population during this century.

The GNP of the future will reflect greater labor productivity as well as increased size of population. Two out of five retailers are optimistic enough to believe that productivity will double its present 1.8% annual rate of increase within the century, probably in the late 1980's.

There is a generally optimistic acceptance of the view of independent economists regarding the outlook for continuing increases in family income. Although today only one American family in four has an income of $15,000 or more, the Conference Board estimates that this proportion will rise to 60% in 1972 dollars by 1990. The typical retailer concurs, believing that by 1987 three out of five families will be at that income level. Retailers feel that this rise in income will upgrade the demand for quality and specialty merchandise and for broader assortments; it will require better customer service and better personnel. Four in five believe this development will have considerable impact, but only one in four believes that retailers have to start planning for it now.

One reason for the anticipation of a growth in income is the view (held by about two out of three retailers and by three out of five of the economists polled) that within the next decade a negative income tax or other form of federal income support program will have virtually eliminated poverty. A majority of retailers, however, believe that the elimination of poverty will by itself have comparatively little impact on retailing.

Consumer expenditures in the future will reflect not only increasing affluence, but changes exemplified by rising levels of education and higher aspirations. Today, about 33% of American males in the 30-to-34 age group have been to college. The Conference Board predicts that the proportion will be 38% by the year 1990.

Four out of five retailers and nine out of ten of the educational sociologists polled believe the proportion will be 50% by the year 2000, and 1989 is the year they usually name. However, retailers see comparatively little direct impact on their business.

Retailers are well aware that an increase in government expenditures will not be automatically translated into increased consumer spending. Four out of five of them (and nine of every ten professional economists who responded) believe that by the late 1980's government expenditures will reach 30% of total GNP, compared with the present proportion of 24%. But only about a third of the retailers think that this development would have considerable impact on the retail business.

Of greater impact would be a sharp extension of government controls over business, with more antitrust actions and limitations on corporate growth and diversification. Nine out of ten retailers believe this would have a major effect (presumably on plans for expansion and diversification) by the early 1980's. A third of the retailers believe that they must start planning for it now.

However, not many retailers (at first, two in ten; finally, three in ten) believe that as much as half of their time in the foreseeable future will have to be devoted to involvement in political or community activities as a result of government controls rather than to minding the store.

Also seen on the horizon for the 1980's (by nine out of ten economists and three out of four retailers) is the introduction of a pricing factor in most goods to cover the cost of disposing of them and of neutralizing their effect on the environment. While this might be expected to affect the cost of goods to the consumer as well as package design, most retailers believe that it will have little effect on their business.

SOCIAL FORCES

The developments mentioned so far represent economic forces extraneous to retailing that will govern the dimensions of the retail market. The character of retail business will also be significantly affected by other social trends on which projections are somewhat less certain.

Among both retailers and urban affairs experts, two in three believe that in the remainder of this century a solution will be found for teenage unemployment in urban ghettoes which might reduce the incidence of crime and drug addiction to about a third of their present levels.

The panelists have a lower level of confidence in their own judgment on this disturbing subject than on any other in our study; but they became more optimistic as they thought about the matter; and by the third questionnaire, three out of four thought a solution would be found.

Although two out of five recognize that the solution to this problem might have considerable impact on retailing, only one in twenty has the feeling that this is something retailers ought to be planning for right now. If this development occurs, retailers think it could lead to a reduction of shrinkages (the current euphemism for thefts), to a revival of downtown shopping, and to new sources of store personnel.

A revival of the central cities through massive government urban reconstruction and a return of the white middle class would have considerable impact on retail business, in the eyes of seven retailers out of ten. But only half of the retailers and few of the urban affairs specialists believe that this is likely to occur in this century.

Even those who believe it will happen think it will take at least twenty years to reverse the central cities' declining share of metropolitan population. If this happened, retailers comment that it could lead not only to the revitalization of the flagship downtown store, but to the development of more inner-city branch stores.

Also in the future is the probability that a massive infusion of public funds will revitalize mass transportation and reduce passenger car use by a fourth of the present level. Over half of the retailers, but two out of five of the urban affairs experts, believe that this will happen by the year 2000.

Retailers' optimism grew as they reflected on this subject, and in the final questionnaire two out of three concurred. Curiously, only half of those on the panel believe that such a development would have considerable impact on the future of retailing.

Retailers have learned to live with a constantly changing population of customers. An increase in the frequency with which people move their homes, from the present level of 18% a year to 25%, is generally expected to occur by 1985. However, two out of three retailers believe that this trend will have only moderate impact on retail business.

Actually, census data show that the proportion of people moving each year has remained roughly constant over the past decade. Greater population mobility would increase the demand for home furnishings and rentals; it could make stores more important as community centers; and it could make a unified, nationwide credit system more desirable.

EMPLOYMENT PATTERNS

Changes in work patterns could affect retailers in their dealings with both employees and customers. More than eight out of ten retailers (and two out of three industrial relations experts) believe that the four-day workweek will become standard by the late 1980's. Three out of five retailers believe this would have considerable impact.

Some observe that it could lead to 365-day, 24-hour-a-day openings for stores, thereby raising in-store labor costs; they also point out that it would expand the market for leisure merchandise. But few think that it calls for immediate planning.

Even less importance is attached to a decline in the average length of the workweek (now 38.3 hours). A projection of the historical decline in the number of average weekly work hours would indicate that a 32-hour workweek could not occur before 2010, but nine out of ten industrial relations experts and retailers agree that it will happen before the year 2000—probably by 1984. This could lead to an increase in store labor costs and encourage the extension of store opening hours.

For the first time in history, a majority (52%) of women age 18 to 64 are now employed. Although the Conference Board projects an extremely slow growth in the percentage of women working, four out of five retailers (and two out of three industrial relations experts) believe that the proportion will rise to 65% by about 1987.

Retailers comment that having more women in the labor force would upgrade women's fashions and encourage longer store opening hours. Only a bare majority of them, however, think this will have considerable impact on their business, and only one in four thinks it calls for immediate action.

The entry of more women into the labor force might well be a factor supporting the trend toward Sunday openings, which in the nearly unanimous opinion of the panel will be legal in 95% of the country by 1983 (compared with approximately 50% today). Some comment that this may add to the difficulty of recruiting good personnel, but only one in seven feels that retailers must do something about it right now.

Late store openings and the rise of the convenience store have also been associated with the rising proportion of women who work. Few retailers believe that as many as a third of all department stores will go in the direction of 24-hour openings, even for substores handling convenience-type merchandise. However, a majority do agree that such a development would have considerable impact on retail business if it ever occurred.

Retailers are also skeptical about the prospects of a reduction in store labor costs, which now represent 19% of all operating costs for department and specialty stores. Few believe this ratio can be reduced to 15%, even with an increased application of technology and a trend toward self-service, but two out of three agree that such a reduction would have considerable effect.

Employee turnover represents an important reason for high labor costs, but a majority of the retailers think it unlikely that the present rates could be reduced by as much as 20% through higher pay, improved working conditions, and better selection and training. In spite of the prevailing pessimism about the chances for improvement, a comparatively high proportion of the panelists believe that sweeping or considerable changes in operations or planning are now called for in this area.

TECHNOLOGICAL INNOVATIONS

Among the most portentous developments in technology is the spread of cable TV, which at least one retailer in three (a far higher proportion than for any other development) believes will have revolutionary impact, especially on promotion and sales methods. Nearly three out of four think that CATV will grow from its current penetration of 10% of U.S. households to 50% by the early 1990's; most believe that by that date virtually all homes on the cable will be able to automatically order merchandise which has been displayed.

New technology is also expected by many to have an important effect on the structure of retail business. A majority of retailers believe that in ten years better in-store use of computerized information will reverse the present trend for tactical decisions to be centralized in chain store operations (even though most retailers accept a trend toward centralized buying). Over two out of five believe that this is an area which demands attention right now.

A similar proportion of retailers think that there is an important need for immediate attention to the improvement of man/machine systems within the store to reduce sales transaction time and customer inconvenience and anxiety. Four out of five retailers foresee that pretesting procedures in this area can virtually eliminate human error by 1985. (However, only one discounter in four shows optimism on this point.)

Many customer service problems result from the lack of coordination among individual store credit cards and accounts. Two out of three panelists believe that by the year 1989 these will be eliminated through a centralized, nationwide credit and banking system. Three out of five agree that this would have considerable impact (it would reduce operating expense, but also reduce store loyalty).

However, very few believe that the prospect calls for any immediate action, even though more and more stores are accepting credit cards other than their house accounts.

A much higher proportion of retailers (nearly two out of five) want to start thinking now about the prospect that general buying facilities or cooperative central buying offices will account for a rising proportion of all general merchandise bought. Between 50% and 60% of general merchandise purchasing is now centralized in this way, and a majority of retailers think that this proportion could rise by 1986 to 75% of all general merchandise bought.

STORE OPERATIONS

In the short run, stores are likely to be affected by another important trend that almost all retailers believe is already under way and that three out of five think is having a considerable impact. This is the trend toward a shrinking of profit margins on most utilitarian items. Three out of five initially said it demands immediate action and planning, and as they thought about the subject, the proportion grew to three out of four. This development puts pressure on stores to tighten internal cost controls and to promote higher-margin products and services, while eliminating unprofitable items.

One way for department stores to control costs is to eliminate home delivery as a free service. Three out of four panelists believe that this will happen by 1981, but only one in four thinks it will have much effect on profit margins.

By about the same date, three out of four retailers believe that stores will have divested themselves of real estate and will lease their locations. On this point also, only one in four thinks this might have a considerable effect on profits.

Today, some 235,000 general merchandise store units (including specialty stores other than food and drug stores) handle nearly $100 billion of retail business. Will the changes in society and in the structure of retail business allow general merchants to handle the same volume as today with 25% fewer store units? A majority of retailers think not, and they also reject the possibility that there could be as much as a 20% decline in the number of items (now over 100,000) carried by the average ($25 million) store unit.

(A good many retailers believe that this subject deserves attention. A reduction in items could, of course, be effected by eliminating unprofitable departments rather than by reducing assortments across the board.)

At the same time, there is wide consensus that productivity, in terms of sales per square foot of selling space, will continue to increase. By 1985, most retailers think it will be 20% higher (in constant dollars) than the present average of $74 for stores grossing over $1 million. Retailers comment that although a greater yield would add to profits, it would also demand more flexibility in store layouts.

One reason for improved yield may be the growth of self-service racks and automatic vending. Eight out of ten retailers think that these methods will account for double the present volume of general merchandise sales before the end of the century (1990 is the typical date named). And seven out of ten rate this development as one that will have considerable impact, especially in shrinkage controls, on store layouts and fixtures, and on promotion.

By the mid-1980's, most retailers believe, at least 50% of all department store volume will be self-service, compared with the present 40%. By that date it is also expected that there will be a 50% increase in the proportion of merchandise items sold in standardized packaging units or in a modular form to permit simplified warehousing, handling, and inventory control.

The developments just mentioned do not, however, mean that there will be less floor space devoted to high-fashion merchandise than at present. Currently, some 55% is given over to fashion apparel and quality home furnishings. A majority of the panelists doubt that this proportion will decline by as much as a third before the end of the century.

Instead, the predominant view is that store space will be handled in a much more flexible fashion than at present. Two out of three of our experts believe that half of the space in all new store units will be designed as open or swing areas for more adaptive utilization. Two out of three also think this development will have considerable impact, and three out of five feel that merchants should go to work on the problem immediately.

As more and more department store branches are set up, will they continue to carry a full merchandise line, including housewares, furniture, and major appliances? Three out of four retailers agree that department store branches will more and more be set up as specialty stores to meet the competition from suburban discounters and from warehouse selling centers.

Seven out of ten consider this a major development, and a majority of all the panelists feel it deserves immediate attention. There is an interesting difference of opinion here, since those who anticipate this trend believe it is already at hand and will be manifested in the present decade, while one out of three does not believe it will happen in this century.

COMPETITIVE TRENDS

As cable TV comes along and as catalog stores, direct mail, and phone selling become more important, what proportion of the general merchandise business will continue to be done within the store itself?

A significant minority of retailers (almost half) believe that by the end of the century as much as a third of all general merchandise business will be done outside the store, perhaps as early as 1984. A number of those who hold this opinion believe that sweeping changes are called for right away in anticipation of this trend.

However, few believe that direct selling to the consumer by the manufacturer, with the help of stronger warranties, is likely to become an important element in the market for appliances, furniture, housewares, or home furnishings. Only one in five thinks this might account for as much as 25% of such sales by the year 2000.

A substantial majority of retailers, however, regard the new form of furniture warehouse retailer (like Levitz and Wickes) as an important threat to established stores. Nearly three out of four believe that the warehousers will quadruple their share of the furniture market (now $7.5 billion) by the mid-1980's. Four out of five consider this a development that will have considerable impact on retail business; seven out of ten (a much higher proportion than for any other prospective development) regard it as something that calls for an immediate response, perhaps by getting department stores into the furniture warehouse business themselves.

In 1972, discounters' sales accounted for 15% of the total general merchandise business (excluding groceries). The growth of this industry in the past two decades represents perhaps the most important retailing phenomenon of the century. Is this line of growth likely to continue?

Three out of five experts think the discounters' share will reach 25% before the year 2000, perhaps by 1986, but fewer than half believe that this competitive challenge requires considerable change in the present policies or plans of traditional department stores.

About half, however, believe there may be a reversal of the existing trend for both discounters and department stores to incorporate grocery departments as a means of building customer traffic. Those who hold this view believe that the trend has already been reversed and will take effect in this decade, but few retailers regard it as an important development for their business.

Two out of three believe that grocery, drug, and other specialty retailers are likely to represent an important new source of competition in the sale of general merchandise.

Most of our panelists believe that by 1980 new department store units will be located in geographical clusters, each within a few miles of other units of the same chain, and almost never located as single operational units. This development is considered to be close at hand, but a majority of the panelists do not consider it of great importance, perhaps because many feel it is already a well-established trend.

Also coming up in the short run, in the view of four out of five, is an increased emphasis on boutiques and specialty shops within department stores, to provide individualized service and to appeal to specific kinds of customers. About half of our panelists consider this development important, and an increasing proportion of them (seven out of ten on the final questionnaire) think that it calls for immediate action.

Another well-established trend, which nine out of ten retailers believe will accelerate in the next few years, is a renewed emphasis on the pleasurable or social aspects of shopping, the old tradition of excitement in the marketplace. This, retailers believe, will lead more stores to locate close to a variety of competitors in a single shopping complex as they move deeper into the suburbs. This trend could lead to ever-larger shopping centers, retailers comment, thus reviving the urban spirit in a suburban context.

However, only half of the panelists believe that entertainment, recreational, and cultural centers will be increasingly used by individual stores to promote customer traffic. This whole subject must be considered in relation to the widespread expectation of an expansion of general merchandise sales through cable TV, catalogs, or phone orders.

The expansion of chain and group retailing organizations has had its counterpart in the decline of small, independent specialty stores. Seven out of ten retailers see no prospect that the growth of franchising might reverse the present rate of small business failures.

At the same time, a thin majority believe that the surviving specialty stores will become stronger. On the first questionnaire, half thought that by the mid-1980's specialty stores could increase their present 40% share of the general merchandise market by as much as 20%. This proportion rose to three out of five by the third questionnaire.

Seven out of ten initially (and on reflection, nine out of ten) agree that the growth of small specialty stores will be deliberately fostered during the late 1970's by major stores seeking an atmosphere of competitive shopping excitement at their new surburban locations.

CUSTOMER SERVICES

In 1960, services represented 30% of all personal consumption expenditures exclusive of medical care, education, and religion. By 1970, the proportion had risen to 32%. By 1990, it will be 40%, in the opinion of nearly nine out of ten of both the retailers and the economists polled, and most retailers consider this to be a development of considerable importance for the expansion of store volume.

Seven out of ten merchants believe that, by the end of the 1980's, 20% of the sales volume of general merchandise stores will be generated by new, personalized customer services made possible by new information technology and visual display techniques. Four out of five consider this a development that will have a great impact on retailing.

New services may indeed represent potential new profits for retailers, but there is a question as to what the customer can legitimately expect in the way of traditional, merchandise-related store services.

Three out of four retailers believe that by the early 1980's significantly more consumers will be willing to pay a higher markup in order to get more personal service and a wider assortment of unique and individualized merchandise. Retailers say this change in consumer expectations will require each store to define its special niche more carefully.

A parallel and related trend is the rental or leasing of consumer durables like cars, appliances, and home furnishings. By 1986, such rentals will be up 50% from today's $635 million level, according to three out of four of our panelists. Two out of three consider this a matter of great importance, but only one in four believes there is anything that retailers should now be doing about it.

Today, 10% of all consumer goods sold in the United States are imported from foreign suppliers. Three retailers out of four, but only three out of five of the international economists polled, believe this proportion will double before the year 2000, probably by the end of the 1980's. As the study progressed, more of the retail panelists became convinced that the proportion of imports would rise, leading to greater internationalization of both buying and selling. However, few consider that this trend will significantly affect their businesses.

The growth of retailing chains has resulted in a steady increase in the importance of private labels, but most retailers feel that private-label merchandise can never be satisfactory for most consumers on many items. Only two in five retailers can see the day when it might account for as much as half of all general merchandise sales.

Whatever may be the importance of private labels as a means of establishing store identity, retailers will increasingly seek to individualize their store images or personalities to appeal to distinctive market segments (rather than to "everybody"). Three out of four retailers believe this tendency will be markedly evident by the end of the century, and a number commented that it might demand more creative advertising.

Nearly two in three immediately judged this to be something with which store managements should now be concerned, and the proportion increased to three out of four as the panelists thought about it.

There is also a widespread consensus that store advertising will in the immediate future make more pinpointed use of media to reach consumers in specific geographic areas or social strata. Most retailers feel that a third of their advertising will fall into this category by 1982, and a majority of them consider this subject important and something that deserves early attention. Only three out of ten, however, see any prospect for a substantial increase in advertising-to-sales ratios.

CONCLUSION

Retail business shows great confidence as it faces the future; it expects change but is also rather sure of its ability to live with that change successfully. Retailers do not see much likelihood that existing social and economic trends will be modified or reversed. On most issues, they show a fairly high degree of agreement with independent experts. However, even when retailers see the trends as unfavorable, they are unlikely to say that they demand immediate attention.

No business is more oriented to immediacy than retailing. Each day presents the merchant with new challenges and with a fresh set of consumer demands and competitive pressures. What makes his business so exciting is precisely the day-to-day changes that stimulate store traffic, the constant innovations in merchandising, the use of promotion to make each day's offerings and assortments in his store different from his competitor's.

In the years to come, retailers will be dealing with a customer who is better disposed to trade up, more strongly oriented to high fashion and good taste, more inclined to pick and choose, more sophisticated and skeptical, and more deeply concerned to get information about the merchandise he or she buys. Retailers expect to be selling to these customers in a more selective fashion, to sharpen the image of their stores, to appeal to specific kinds of consumers—specific as to where they live and specific as to how they live.

The increasing complexity of both retail business and its social environment will demand more sophistication and broader-gauge knowledge from retail management, and a tremendous expansion of the research and planning functions.

QUESTIONS FOR DISCUSSION

1. Identify the major economic and social forces that appear to have the greatest potential impact on future retail operations.

2. What changes are expected in the following areas during the final decades of the twentieth century:
   a. employment patterns in retailing
   b. technological innovations
   c. store operations
   d. competition
   e. customer services.

Chapter 3

Marketing Institutions: Wholesaling

THE SUBJECT OF THIS CHAPTER—wholesalers and wholesaling middlemen —are considerably less well-known to the general public than are retailers. Even though nearly 370,000 wholesaling establishments generated total sales of $695 billion in 1972, the general public rarely comes into contact with them and appears to possess a vaguely negative attitude toward this important marketing institution as the major culprit in rising prices.

But wholesaling middlemen—like their retailer counterparts—continue to exist only so long as they provide a needed service. These functions may include providing storage and breaking bulk into smaller units for sale to retail customers; provision of delivery services; market information to retail customers and to the manufacturer; and financing for either retailers or manufacturer.

What is wholesaling? It can be formally defined as *the activities of persons or firms selling to retailers and other wholesalers or to industrial users but who do not sell in significant amounts to ultimate consumers.* While the term *wholesaler* is usually applied to only those wholesaling middlemen who take title to the products that they handle, the broader term *wholesaling middlemen* is used to describe not only those middlemen who assume title to the goods that they handle, but also agents and brokers who perform important wholesaling activities but who do not take title to the goods.

In many industries, large-scale wholesaling middlemen are beginning to emerge as prominent channel members. An example is Cramer Electronics, a large wholesaler of electronic equipment. Large national wholesaling middlemen such as Cramer came into existence only within the past fifteen years. In 1966, these middlemen accounted for 8 percent of all sales to retailers. By the end of 1970 the percentage had grown to twenty. This growth is a reflection of the inability of the manufacturers to adequately cover the total market and the increased service that the independent wholesaling middlemen provide for their customers. Cramer credits service as the major reason for its sales growth. Cramer provides customers with 24- to 48-hour delivery service, as compared with 8 to 10 weeks for many component manufacturers. This reduction in turnaround between order time and its delivery allows Cramer's customers to significantly reduce their inventory of replacement parts, thereby also reducing their inventory carrying costs.[1]

The first selection in Chapter Three by Richard S. Lopata gives a broad, fast-paced overview of this marketing institution. A real contribution of this article is that it indicates, in a very positive manner, that the wholesaling industry is, for the most part, a strong and vibrant industry that is successfully facing the challenges of constant channel metamorphosis.

The second selection by James C. McKeon builds on the first by specifically outlining some of the structural changes that the wholesaling industry has experienced. Again, the reader will be impressed by the vitality and flexibility of this industry and its ability to adapt to the constantly changing needs of its customers.

1. "When The Other Guy Pauses—We Charge!" *Business Week* (February 6, 1971), p. 42.

3.1 FASTER PACE IN WHOLESALING

Richard S. Lopata

*Although the wholesaling industry represents a major
segment of the U.S. economy, it is little understood
as an area, poorly defined, and considered by many
to be dying or even dead.*

Although the wholesaling industry represents a major segment of the
U.S. economy, it is little understood as an area, poorly defined, and
considered by many to be dying or even dead. This paradox is reflected
directly in the general literature of management, which contains little
about wholesaling despite the fact that a majority of our large companies have a stake in it. Graduate schools of business also seem to neglect wholesaling; witness the fact that the number of courses they offer
which deal with it can be counted on the fingers of one hand. Business
schools, university extensions, the American Management Association,
and many other organizations very frequently sponsor seminars on manufacturing, for instance, and yet devote no attention to wholesaling.
Why? I suspect that for many people the answer to this question would
be, "Well, there's really nothing much *to* wholesaling these days—it's a
declining business function." Nothing could be more mistaken.

Today wholesaling is a big, growing industry that is changing rapidly
and significantly. In this article I want to put wholesaling in a better and
more realistic perspective, and especially to show how it is changing,
and must continue to change, in response to the challenges of our
present-day economy.

WHOLESALERS TODAY

First of all, who are the wholesalers? Today there are some 185,000 independent merchant wholesalers. Altogether they generated almost $220
billion in revenues in 1968. They are a highly diverse group—i.e., big,
small, profitable, unprofitable, satiated, hungry, smart, dumb, conserva-

tive, and change-seeking. E. B. Weiss has described the new whole-saling milieu as a "scrambled" world in which there are wholesalers who manufacture, wholesalers who retail, and wholesalers who are uncertain whether they are producers, wholesalers, jobbers, retailers, financiers, or whatever.

In a number of ways, the wholesaler feels the impact of constant changes and innovations in the whole marketplace. Technological advances, product line proliferation, changing retail structures, and social adjustments are only a few of the real problems that complicate his life. Each improved product passing through the wholesale level generates a new demand for investments in warehouse space, market analysis, and sales training, and for myriad adjustments in the wholesaler's information systems. Each major retailing shift designed to satisfy customer needs obliges him to adjust his selling patterns, to review the customer service levels, to study product assortments, and to revise his strategies.

He must also deal with the growing aspirations of his once-content employees, the changing values of the available labor pool, and the increasing demands of the community for social service. The typical wholesaler faces such challenges with each new day—often without the resources of the larger manufacturing organizations that sell to and through him. If one still regards today's wholesaler as that traditional, unsophisticated middleman of the past, he must wonder how the wholesaler has survived at all—let alone grown strong—in our complicated social and economic system.

In the course of professional contacts, and in studies and seminars conducted over the past two decades with thousands of wholesalers and their suppliers, my colleagues and I have drawn certain conclusions that may help to explain the survival and growth of today's independent wholesaler and to forecast his future.

FUNCTIONS & CHARACTERISTICS

An initial problem in discussing wholesaling is the matter of definition. Webster defines the wholesalers as "a merchant middleman who sells chiefly to retailers, other merchants, or industrial, institutional, and commercial users mainly for resale or business use." This is somewhat vague for my persent purposes, and I should like to narrow down the definition of the wholesaler. The wholesaler is one who:

1. Purchases goods from manufacturers for his own account (as distinguished from the agent, who typically does not purchase for his own account) and resells them to other businesses.

2. Operates one or more warehouses in which he receives and takes title to goods, stores them, and later reships them. (In some cases, he may have goods shipped directly by the manufacturer to the customer, so the goods do not actually pass through his warehouse. Still, a good part, and usually

all, of the goods which the wholesaler handles do, in fact, pass through his warehouse.)

The wholesaler's customer group varies according to his product mix. For example, there is one broad class of wholesalers who sell to retailers such diverse commodities as food, drugs, tobacco, hardware, dry goods, and appliances. Another class sells such items as food, paper products, medical goods and supplies, and so on, to restaurants and institutions. A third class sells building materials to builders and contractors. A fourth class sells manufacturing supplies such as tools, chemicals, abrasives, and so on, to manufacturers. In the complex automotive parts aftermarket, there are even warehouse distributors who sell only to other jobbers—i.e., wholesalers who sell to retail outlets.

Finally, we may classify wholesalers in terms of ownership. The wholesaling function can be performed by "manufacturers' branches" or by retail chains. The branches are captive wholesaling operations owned and operated by a manufacturer; this practice is common in electrical supplies (e.g., Westinghouse Electric Supply Company and General Electric Supply Company), and in plumbing (e.g., Crane Supply Company and Amstan-American Standard). Captive branch operations are also common among truck manufacturers, full-line farm-equipment manufacturers, and the large producers of major appliances. In the retail food field, A&P, Kroger, and other chains operate warehouse systems which do, in fact, perform a wholesaling function.

Here I shall be mainly concerned with the *merchant* wholesaler as described by the Department of Commerce. The merchant wholesaling house may be privately or publicly owned, but in either case it stands in the market as a distinctive, independent enterprise. According to the Department's definition, the merchant wholesaler is primarily engaged in buying and selling in the domestic market. More specifically, he buys and sells merchandise on his own account; sells principally to retailers or to industrial, commercial, or professional users; usually carries stocks; assembles in large lots and generally redistributes in small quantities, usually through salesmen; extends credit to customers; makes deliveries; services merchandise sold; and renders advice to the trade.

While the entire wholesaling category includes factory branches, petroleum bulk stations, merchandise agents, brokers, and so on, the merchant wholesaling category excludes such operations.

PERIOD OF GROWTH

In 1939, merchant wholesaler sales amounted to $23.6 billion, or 41% of all wholesaling as defined by the Department of Commerce. By 1963, the volume had increased almost sevenfold, to $157.4 billion, or 42% of total wholesaling activity. In the 1960's, however, the merchant wholesalers have *really* come on strong—in 1968 their sales were about $220 billion, as shown in Table 1.

TABLE 1   Sales of U.S. Merchant Wholesalers, 1954–1968.

| | Sales (in billions of dollars) | | | | Compounded annual growth rate | |
	1954	1958	1963	1968	1954–1963	1963–1968
Durable goods	$ 39.9	$ 50.9	$ 67.4	$ 98.1	6.0%	7.8%
Nondurable goods	43.2	49.7	61.6	86.6	4.0	7.0
Miscellaneous products	18.2	21.4	28.4	35.2	5.1	4.2
Total	$101.3	$122.0	$157.4	$219.9	5.0%	7.1%
GNP	$364.8	$447.3	$589.2	$860.6	5.5%	7.9%

Sources: U. S. Census of Business, *Wholesale Trade—Summary Statistics and Monthly Wholesale Trade Reports*; and Office of Business.

Economics, U. S. Department of Commerce, *Gross National Product or Expenditure*.

As one can see from this table, merchant wholesaling volume grew at an annual rate of 7.1% between 1963 and 1968; this compares favorably with the 7.9% growth rate of the gross national product for the same period. Growth in the two largest segments (durable and nondurable goods) was at least 7%, while the "Miscellaneous" category decreased to 4.2%. The decrease in this category may be due in part to the fact that farm products (a major segment) have been increasingly recategorized as part of the food manufacturing system. Table 1 also shows that from 1963 to 1968 the wholesaling volume increased very substantially.

Why this remarkable growth instead of the deterioration that some have predicted? Not all the credit can be given to a "new breed" of wholesaler, as has been suggested. Some credit—perhaps the lion's share —must go to manufacturers. In numerous commodity lines, manufacturers have evaluated distribution alternatives, tried them out, and later abandoned these attempts to "eliminate the middleman." They have learned, albeit at substantial tuition fees, that they can eliminate the middleman, but they cannot eliminate the economic *function* of wholesaling.

There are four good reasons why this is so:

1. The wholesaler has continuity in and intimacy with the market.

2. He has a more acute understanding of the costs of holding and handling inventory, in which, after all, he has a major capital commitment.

3. He can concentrate his managerial talent on localized marketing strategies without the distractions of manufacturing problems.

4. He has the important advantage of local entrepreneurship.

One hypothesis suggested to explain the rapid expansion of wholesaling is that independent wholesalers are growing in strength through the default of the manufacturers. That is, manufacturers, preoccupied with return on investment, prefer to allocate scarce resources to research and production rather than to distribution, which they know has historically delivered a much lower return. Manufacturers also frequently view entry into wholesaling as an added burden on their already beleaguered management teams. Finally, and more tangibly, there remains the fear of some manufacturers that the federal government may attack their expansion into distribution operations. A case in point is the vigorous government attack on paper manufacturers' acquisitions of paper distributing organizations.

For most manufacturers, experience proves the value of a strong, independent wholesale network. In many instances, such a network has resulted in the lowest possible total distribution cost—which is of course the manufacturers' real goal in this area.

Wholesalers have thus survived and even thrived in the modern economy. The types of wholesalers, of both durable and nondurable goods, have changed significantly and continue to change, as have the numbers of wholesalers engaged in handling particular commodity lines and combinations of lines. Let's look more closely at some of these shifts.

Table 2 shows the sales growth of merchant wholesalers in the nondurable goods area for the period 1954–1968. Unfortunately, the figures by themselves do not satisfactorily reflect certain important changes in the composition of the wholesaling group, although they do reflect some of the dynamics that have been at work. Comparing the compounded growth for the two periods, 1954–1963 and 1963–1968, gives one a rough indication of where some of the major changes have occurred:

Grocery wholesalers grew more rapidly in the 1963–1968 period than in 1954–1963 because of the strengthening of the voluntary and cooperative organizations that have so successfully withstood the inroads of the food chains.

The tobacco jobbers grew at a slower rate in 1963–1968, probably because many of them were absorbed into wholesale grocery operations during this period. An increase in direct-vending operations and the controversy surrounding the effects of smoking on health also contributed to this slowdown.

Of the categories shown, the dry-goods and apparel category increased at the lowest rate in 1954–1963 (2.5%) and the highest rate in 1963–1968 (7.7%). One explanation for this upward shift is that in the

TABLE 2   Sales of Selected Nondurable Goods by U.S. Merchant
           Wholesale Groups, 1954–1968.

	Sales (in billions of dollars)			Compounded annual growth rate	
	1954	1958	1963	1968	1954–1963	1963–1968
Groceries and related products	$22.2	$25.3	$30.9	$44.1	3.7%	7.4%
Beer, wine, distilled alcoholic beverages	5.7	6.6	8.2	11.1	4.1	6.3
Drugs, chemicals, allied Products	3.4	4.6	6.0	8.8	6.1	8.0
Tobacco, tobacco products	3.2	3.7	4.7	5.6	4.4	4.0
Dry goods, apparel	5.7	5.9	7.1	10.3	2.5	7.7
Paper and paper products	3.0	3.6	4.7	6.7	5.0	7.3
Total	$43.2	$49.7	$61.6	$86.6	4.0%	7.0%

Source, U. S. Census of Business, *Wholesale Trade—Summary Statistics and Monthly Wholesale Trade Reports.*

later period there were broadened opportunities in lower-cost imported items, accompanied by broadened consumer and retailer acceptance of such imports. Significantly, the wholesalers in this area acted aggressively in shifting from the domestic to the foreign sources to exploit the new opportunities and the changes in consumer buying habits.

DURABLE-GOODS WHOLESALERS

Table 3 shows us some noteworthy shifts in the durable-goods merchant wholesalers. For example, the growth rate of the "hardware, plumbing, and heating" category expanded in 1963–1968, while the "lumber, construction materials" category remained about the same. How could this have been, since both are closely related to construction activity? Part of the explanation for the low growth rate in construction materials is that the large building materials manufacturers increased their direct distribution to builders. Also, the chains (like Wickes and Sears) increased their share of the building-materials market, and the construction of single-family dwellings was sluggish. In contrast, the marked growth in hardware, plumbing, and heating is largely due to better exploitation of the industrial and home-improvement markets.

Some segments of wholesaling have followed changes in the marketplace, and some have even introduced improvements, while others have failed to respond to market shifts. As in other business forms, the wholesaler who survives and grows must remain flexible. He must be astute enough to cope with the encroachment of manufacturers, as the elec-

TABLE 3   Sales of Selected Durable Goods by U.S. Merchant
Wholesale Groups, 1954–1968.

	Sales (in billions of dollars)				Compounded annual growth rate	
	1954	*1958*	*1963*	*1968*	*1954– 1963*	*1963– 1968*
Auto equipment, motor vehicles	$ 4.0	$ 7.2	$10.3	$16.8	10.5%	10.1%
Electrical goods	6.3	8.0	9.9	15.0	5.1	8.6
Furniture, home furnishings	2.1	2.5	3.4	5.0	5.5	8.0
Hardware, plumbing and heating supplies	4.9	6.0	6.8	9.8	3.7	7.4
Lumber, construction materials	6.6	6.3	8.7	10.4	3.0	3.7
Machinery, equipment and supplies	9.4	12.4	16.9	25.4	6.5	8.4
Metals, minerals	4.2	5.6	7.9	11.0	7.4	7.0
Scrap, waste materials	2.4	2.9	3.5	4.7	4.3	6.1
Total	$39.9	$50.9	$67.4	$98.1	6.1%	7.8%

Source: U. S. Census of Business, *Wholesale Trade—Summary Statistics and Monthly Wholesale Trade Reports.*

trical distributors appear to have done. He must also cope with the encroachment of retailers. To this extent, the food wholesalers appear to have been more successful than have their building-materials counterparts.

The growth of wholesaling is a complex phenomenon; and, as my remarks thus far have indicated, a major source of this complexity is the great variety of conditions peculiar to each commodity. Nevertheless, the wholesaler has indeed foiled the prophets of doom of the 1940's. The percentages shown for the 1963–1968 period are substantially higher, in almost all cases, than the percentages for 1954–1963.

SOME COMING SHIFTS

On balance, then, the independent wholesaler remains a vital and significant part of our economic system. So long as there are men willing to take on the risks, problems, and specialized functions of handling and selling a changing variety of goods to changing markets, there will be a large, vital, and independently operated wholesaler-distributor sector in the U.S. economy.

The wholesaler's success will depend on his response to the manufacturers and retail chains that want to absorb his function and on his ability to adapt and apply new concepts and techniques. Just as the manufacturers' strategies change with technological, political, and social developments, so must those of the merchant wholesalers.

It is possible to identify some commodity wholesalers who will pass from the scene. Others will swiftly shift to new commodities. Some will build regional or national networks of warehouses along single commodity lines, as have the paper merchants, electrical supply companies, and automotive parts distributors. Others will form tighter wholesale-retail franchised groups, such as Super Valu, Ace Hardware, Butler Brothers, and Western Auto. Still others will become multicommodity super-marketing systems, with all the accoutrements of sophisticated marketing technology. As a matter of fact, such wholesalers as these already exist; a prime example is Foremost-McKesson, whose sales of over $1 billion in 1967 included the wholesaling of drugs, grocery products, liquor, and health and beauty aids.

CHANGE IN ATTITUDE

Many wholesalers have stopped regarding themselves as strictly warehousing or break bulk points in the distribution complex, and have begun to stimulate and respond to their markets on their own. This new marketing posture requires that the wholesaler dissect his available markets to determine which segments are potentially the most profitable and exploitable ones. In some instances, he has shifted selling emphasis from traditional markets to new ones. For example:

Many electrical and electronics distributors have directed a new sales effort in recent years to industrial and commercial markets, to supplement their established electrical-contractor market.

The progressive plumbing house has expanded its market from nearly complete reliance on master plumbers and craftsmen to include industrial accounts as well.

Many grocery wholesalers, both the voluntary food groups and those independents who still exist, have added a sales effort geared to the growing institutional market, including hotels, airlines, restaurants, hospitals, and schools.

Interestingly, the 1967 business census shows that merchant wholesaler sales for the first time are divided about equally between retailers (or resellers) and business and industrial users.

Market analysis is strongly influencing the type and variety of merchandise and commodity lines handled by the wholesaler. One effect is that the wholesaler is now increasingly sensitive in his selection of product lines, and tends to review and adjust his product range in response to the needs of his various market segments. At the same time, however, he is more cautious than before; he carefully weighs the cost of entry into new markets against the cost of satisfying new needs of established markets.

It is true that some independent wholesalers (as well as some manufacturers with captive wholesale networks) have inflated opinions as to the depth, breadth, and flexibility of their organizations. This is, after a few successes in adjusting their products to existing market segments, they tend to feel that they can serve *any* market segment. They take the highly optimistic stance that a *real* wholesaler can handle any product for any market, that "all it takes is some managerial skill."

But successful wholesaling is founded on the service satisfactions of proximity, broad product assortments, and rapid response to the needs of local retailers, contractors, and other customers. Wholesaling organizations by nature must count as their most important resource their intimate knowledge of the product and service requirements of a particular market segment. In the sense that manufacturers can best rely on their know-how for *producing* for selected markets, wholesalers can best rely on their know-how for *servicing* selected markets. Venturing beyond the available knowledge and skill requires significant investments of time and money, and instant success is by no means guaranteed.

The point to be emphasized here is that long-run truth must arise from short-run reality. The cost of multiple short-run adjustments to exotic market segments is real and high. A line of building materials *can* be added to the ordinary lines handled by a paper merchant, for example, but the attendant traumas militate against any significant increase in short-run profit.

BASIC TRENDS

This conglomerate-type expansion is not the most significant kind of change that is taking place in wholesaling patterns today. The more important developments lie closer to the traditional operations of wholesaling; and within the current swirl of changing patterns one can distinguish several major trends that are shaping the future of wholesale distribution.

INCREASED INTEGRATION

Historically, the goods-producing and distribution area of the economy has been separated into four distinct levels—manufacturing, wholesaling, retailing, and consuming. This structure of levels is becoming blurred. Because of wholesale-retail franchising, conglomeration, and joint venturing, *vertical* and *horizontal* marketing systems are emerging. In some of these systems the merchant wholesaler holds a pivotal position. Consider the following examples:

J. M. Jones Company of Champaign/Urbana, Illinois, is an IGA wholesale grocer. It dominates its Central Illinois grocery market through its *owned* and member stores. Indeed, the total national IGA wholesale network operates more stores than its competitor, A&P.

Allied Farm Equipment Company of Chicago, a basic distributor of short lines of farm equipment, manufactures over 200 items for its network of branches in the United States and Canada.

Midas International, which originated as an automotive warehouser-distributor, today both *buys* and *manufactures* items for its franchised network of over 500 Midas Muffler and Brake Shops.

Distronics Corporation is a joint venture of six plumbing and heating wholesalers which provides them with real-time, on-line, random-access computer services. At any distance up to 1,200 miles, a member wholesaler is able to make use of a central computer on a joint basis with his fellow venturers.

Additional examples can be found in drug, hardware, furniture, appliance, and other commodity groups. Most interestingly, and certainly significantly, these systems seem to have evolved through creative entrepreneurship rather than as a result of studied corporate effort. If this is true, then the trend is quite likely to continue as the merchant wholesaler (who is essentially an entrepreneur) becomes more sophisticated and searches for new opportunities.

MORE "AGGRESSIVE" SERVICE

As newer technologies develop, new marketing systems evolve, and more sophisticated financial concepts come into use, the merchant wholesalers are adjusting their service emphasis. For example:

Among industrial equipment and supply distributors, service and merchandising efforts are being tailored in the light of both OEM (i.e., original equipment manufacture) and MRO (maintenance and repair operations) activities. To provide better service for its industrial customers, Englewood Electric Supply Company of Chicago has shifted its emphasis from personal-contact sales to programmed reordering via Data Phone.

A number of wholesale druggists now handle the retail druggist's customer account records. This "service" is really a device to "tie" the retailer more closely to one wholesaler.

In the grocery field, credit extension used to be a prime function of the wholesaler. Today almost all wholesale grocery products flow into retail stores on a cash basis, for all intents and purposes. Here service has shifted from credit extension to merchandising support, inventory management counseling, and profit analysis on behalf of the retailer.

These changes suggest the vigor with which the wholesaler is search-

ing for competitive advantage and his willingness to break with traditional methods. Such action, I might say, is hardly in keeping with
the view of the wholesaler as a sterile anachronism.

PRICING AND CREDIT

The wholesaler has been critically reviewing pricing and credit policies,
and he has made numerous changes. First, he has examined his prices in
terms of the internal costs both to himself and to his customer. He has
found, for example, that pricing arrangements such as system contracting ordinarily result in lower cost and better service for the customer
than do older and more conventional pricing methods. Today's merchant wholesaler is likely to regard the improvement in service as a
decisive advantage of system contracting, even given the fact that the
selling price resulting from it may frequently be higher or lower than
the current price in the open market. In fact, a number of wholesaler-
distributors have been successful in switching customers from direct account buying by persuading them that "our price may be higher, from
time to time, but remember—your internal possession costs will be lower
because of our improved service."

He is also reviewing credit policies and revising them to take advantage of sophisticated financial methods. For example, a major electrical
and electronics distributor in Canada has revised his credit operations
and policies to emphasize two modern concepts: (a) a concept of accounts receivable management which includes the use of probability
assessments of trade-category risks, and (b) control by importance and
exception. This revision led him to reduce the term of credit from 60
days to 40 days, a step that released a substantial amount of capital
which he put to much more profitable use in building inventory and
exploring his markets.

Wholesalers will continue to experiment with new approaches to
pricing and credit. One evidence of this is that it is not unusual to find
a wholesaler applying only direct costs to a special sale as a means of
competitive pricing, ignoring traditional gross-margin requirements.
Also, it is not unusual to find a wholesaler requesting an "extra 5%" from
a supplier for a special deal and then giving the customer an extra 7%!
This trend reflects the restlessness and inquisitiveness of modern wholesaling management.

REGIONAL COVERAGE

One can cite numerous new approaches to regional coverage. Thus,
subsidiary branches and "twigs" with limited, fast-moving inventories,
but with ready access to the central warehouse, are sprouting all over

the map. This new pattern is well established among plumbing, heating, and cooling distributors, and wholesalers of electrical parts and equipment are adopting it as rapidly as they can identify which items move fastest and where. Indeed, the 1963 census showed that the branch-operating wholesalers, who represent about 7% of all merchant wholesalers, accounted for approximately 36% of total merchant wholesaler volume.

Of particular interest is a leapfrogging strategy of market penetration that some wholesalers are now following. Instead of an "oil slick" type of expansion, these wholesalers are trying "backfire" tactics: they are reaching out as far as 1,000 miles from headquarters to establish operations which hopefully will spread back to the home base. These new operations have been started both by missionary effort and through acquisition. This closing of distance is bound to increase as communication and physical-distribution techniques advance.

ORGANIZATIONAL FORM & SIZE

The trend toward larger corporate organizations through public financing, merger, and acquisition is pervading the economy, and it is particularly notable in the wholesaling area. The Bureau of the Census reports the following facts about the composition of the merchant wholesaling group:

	1958	1963
Sole proprietorships	31.0%	27.5%
Partnerships	15.3%	10.6%
Corporations	52.6%	61.3%
Cooperatives and other forms	1.1%	0.6%
Total number of merchant wholesalers	190,000	209,000

Furthermore, in 1958 Moody's *Industrial Manual* listed 70 wholesale distributors and jobbers; but by 1967 the listing had risen to 129, an increase of nearly 85% in only nine years.

These data indicate a definite shift from proprietorships and partnerships to the corporate form—the traditional, family-owned operations are declining in numbers, and the publicly held wholesaling corporations are increasing. There is every reason to expect this trend to continue, inasmuch as the formalized corporate structure enhances the ability to grow.

In our continued contact with wholesalers, my colleagues and I have also noted their mounting interest in setting values on their equity and their willingness to loosen their hold on ownership through public issues and employee stock plans. Tax laws have undoubtedly stimulated this open-mindedness, and in this sense have exerted a highly beneficial influence. Public ownership brings more capital resources and, at the same time, brings pressure on management to use more sophisticated management techniques. It also spurs a search for opportunities to auto-mate in such areas as information systems, materials handling, order selection and processing, and delivery operations.

The Census Bureau also reports that, according to sales volume figures, merchant wholesalers are growing in size. Between 1958 and 1963, there was a 7% increase in the number of merchant wholesale establishments with less than $1 million in annual sales, a 27% increase in establishments with $1 million to $5 million in sales, and a 41% increase in establish-ments with sales in excess of $5 million a year.

Still, of some 209,000 establishments owned by 185,000 merchant wholesalers in 1968, only about 1,400 were generating over $10 million in annual sales. A Dun & Bradstreet listing of wholesalers by location, sales, and employee size shows that approximately 4,000 merchant whole-salers presently generate more than $5 million in sales.

Evidently, the wholesaler-distribution is changing his corporate form and growing in size. This trend, along with other trends already noted, shows that wholesaling is responsive to its environment and that it can effectively adapt to the pressures for lower-cost distribution from both suppliers and customers.

THE CHALLENGES

The wholesalers must continue to interpret these pressures and respond and adapt to them. There is considerable evidence that the wholesalers realize this. They have, for example, converted their trade associations into centers for researching present and future problems of distribution and educating their members about them. They have also pooled their efforts in order to gain from their collective experience.

At the center of the pool is the National Association of Wholesalers, a federation of over 58 commodity-line organizations. It offers a compre-hensive education and development program for all types of wholesalers. Its leadership has both followed and been spurred on by the individual commodity associations.

The NAW and many of the member associations have developed dynamic leadership in their full-time staff and in the individual whole-sale houses. This leadership recognizes its own stake in pulling the in-dustry behind it, but it must battle ignorance, inefficiency, sloth, and the practices of certain kinds of marginal operators who undermine the advancement of the industry as a whole.[1]

1. See Louis E. Newman, "Diseases That Make Whole Industries Sick," HBR, March–April 1961, p. 87.

A second source of innovative leadership is the manufacturing sector. The wholesaler-distributor and his supplying manufacturer share a common goal: to reduce the cost of distribution with (a) obtaining sufficient profit for adequate return on investment and (b) paying for innovation necessary to ensure growth of the enterprise. The manufacturer, with his larger resources, has a strong motive for helping the wholesaler develop an operational network that can meet these challenges, and in fact many manufacturers have come forward to offer useful assistance. The wholesaler is basically an entrepreneurial personality, and frequently has plowed ahead on his own; but he is the first to acknowledge the important contribution that the manufacturing sector has made to improving financial, promotional, sales, and inventory management within wholesaling.

INVENTORY MANAGEMENT

Judging from various surveys and trade discussions, the wholesaler's major problem is inventory control and management. One might expect this, since inventory comprises the main part of a wholesaler's assets and the number of different items kept in stock can be very large indeed. Beyond that, however, our economy has annually generated a monumental number of new products, particularly in the past few years. As companies further increase their R&D expenditures on new-product development, the inventory problem of wholesalers will grow more and more acute.

Product proliferation is most apparent in the grocery area, where the number of new-product introductions has been matched, and even exceeded, by the number of modifications in the size and packaging of older product lines. Similar product expansions are taking place in the automotive parts, electronic equipment and components, building materials, plumbing, heating, air conditioning, electrical, industrial papers, and numerous other lines. Today, for example, the automotive distributor carries about 70,000 identifiable items, as compared with 40,000 only ten years ago. Each item must be identified, labeled, handled, stacked, controlled, picked, packed, shipped, and invoiced—a very considerable job.

The sheer number of inventoried items presents an immense and unending problem for individual wholesalers. How much of what should he carry in stock, and when? One of the wholesaler's reactions has been to demand that manufacturers reduce the size and variety of the lines they offer. Another is "cherry picking" of lines.

These reactions are based on the wholesaler's realization that a full and complete line is often not the most profitable one. The practice of carrying every item in a commodity line in stock at all times is fast disappearing, and the practice of maintaining only 80%–95% coverage is becoming increasingly common.

Manufacturers are also becoming increasingly sensitive to line profitability. American Standard, for example, recently reduced its line of brass fittings by more than 30%, much to the relief of many of its network members.

TABLE 4 Comparison of a Farm-Equipment Wholesaler's Sales, Grouped by Product Category, in 1963 and 1967.

Category	Annual Sales per line	Number of lines	1963 Total dollar volume	Percent of total sales	Number of lines	1967 Total dollar volume	Percent of total sales
C	$0–$49,000	23	$532,000	36%	23	$425,000	20%
B	$50,000–$199,000	5	$695,000	46%	8	$819,000	39%
A	$200,000 and over	1	$267,000	18%	3	$859,000	41%

To come to grips with the inventory management problem, some wholesalers are selecting items and setting stock levels according to patterns of item demand and item movement. One way of doing this is to group all items on an "ABC" basis for analysis. In an article in *Sales/Marketing Today*, William P. Hall describes the case of one farm-equipment wholesaler who started to apply the ABC concept to his inventory analysis in 1963.[2] By 1967 he had achieved a much more profitable stock configuration. Table 4 gives some of the relevant figures. Note that in 1963, B- and C-items accounted for 82% of his volume. His strategy was to shift concentration to A- and B-items by:

Dropping many supply items in the C-category and steering sales efforts toward the higher-priced lines, with larger dollar volume.

Aiming promotion and preseason selling campaigns directly at higher-value lines.

Retraining salesmen as equipment demonstrators, and discouraging them from merely "taking small orders."

By 1967, he had achieved significant results. Although the number of C-items (23) was the same in 1967 as it had been in 1963, the dollar volume in this category dropped from 36% to 20% over the four years. At the same time, the dollar volume of A-items grew from $267,000 in 1963 to a healthy $859,000 in 1967, when it represented 41% of sales. Sales of A- and B-items accounted for 80% of his total sales volume.

Another significant element of inventory management is inventory carrying cost. Studies indicate that the annual cost of possession ranges

2. "The ABC Principle in Management," November 1968, p. 15.

from 20% to 35% of the average cost of inventory. Thus a wholesaler with a $500,000 inventory should not ordinarily tolerate cost of $100,000 to $175,000, say, for carrying slow-moving or unsalable items. If he finds himself in this kind of situation, the wholesaler should remember that *turnover is the name of the game.* If his $500,000 inventory turns twice, his per-dollar carrying cost is 10¢ to 17.5¢. With ten turns, his per-dollar cost drops to 2¢ to 3.5¢.

As I have suggested, the wholesaler is beginning to obtain assistance and advice on new approaches to inventory control and management from his suppliers. To an increasing extent he expects to benefit from his suppliers' overall knowledge of market requirements. Some progressive manufacturers who recognize these needs are even conducting educational programs for the wholesalers who distribute their products. For example:

The UCON Refrigerants Division of Union Carbide has held many successful seminars for its network members over a period of some years. In 1968, Union Carbide researched, developed, and conducted extensive seminars in inventory management for its wholesalers. The two-day program included specially prepared materials, work sheets, checklists, and illustrations of inventory control systems that covered the entire typical inventory of a wholesaler, not just his inventory of refrigerant items.

Unfortunately, however, the wholesalers who really practice modern inventory management techniques and strategies are few in number. Although it is true that every wholesaler has some sort of inventory control system, integrated systems of selling, buying, and financing are still quite rare.

SALES MANAGEMENT

Wholesalers have been sales-oriented, traditionally, but as a group they have not really caught on yet to modern, professional, systematic techniques of selling and promotion. Much of their sales effort has been personal selling by individual salesmen. Some exceptional wholesaler-distributors are demonstrating real imagination in this area, of course: for instance, wholesale druggists are utilizing in-house telephone sales techniques to support the efforts of their more highly specialized personal salesmen. These personal salesmen limit their calls to key accounts, specialized customers, and prospects that show high potential. In fact, some drug wholesalers are taking 80% of their orders over the telephone.

Automatic reordering is another innovation that has been adopted to capture repeat sales and achieve lower costs. It is being used in electronics, plumbing, hospital supplies, and numerous other commodity lines. Since the automated approach frees salesmen from routine reordering tasks, it provides them with more time for specialized customer counseling and creative selling. In a number of cases, the use of "cash and carry" and catalog selling has substantially reduced the size of the wholesaler's sales force.

Wholesalers who operate multibranch companies are beginning to concentrate their big selling efforts on their customers' top management. They use their individual branches and twigs primarily to provide routine delivery service and to introduce product variations at the buyer level. This pattern indicates a trend toward divorcing the selling function from the product-handling function at the local level.

Personal salesmen in the wholesale area are also striving for deeper understanding of their customers' businesses. In particular, they are learning to help customers identify opportunities to reduce cost—for example:

An electronics distributor in Ann Arbor analyzed the stockkeeping methods of one of his industrial customers and recommended revised delivery schedules, prearranged items, packs suitable for assembly line use, and standardized item identification. The customer was able to reduce the possession costs on his stock by 15% of its average value.

Unfortunately—once again—most wholesale selling is still conducted on a highly personal basis by relatively untrained and unsophisticated salesmen who call only on well-established customers. Still, wholesalers recognize the need for more systematic and sophisticated sales efforts, a need which is being satisfied in part by the National Association of Wholesalers.

The NAW began conducting sales management seminars and workshops in 1947. Paul Courtney, Executive Vice President of NAW, estimates that in the past five years more than 1,250 wholesaler-distributor houses have participated in one or more of these, and another 4,500 have participated in other programs. Individual commodity associations have also established more specialized sales training programs to help wholesalers field systematic, technically sound selling forces.

Aggressive manufacturers who have important stakes in their distributor networks have also increased their efforts to provide wholesaler managers with educational support through their field representatives and, in some cases, through formal training programs.

PROMOTION MANAGEMENT

Manufacturers are also assisting their wholesalers with dealer shows, trade shows, advertising direct-mail promotion, and catalog preparation. Certain wholesalers, however, have rejected supplier assistance in this area in favor of proprietary programs that emphasize house identification. The wholesaler who elects this course is usually attempting to identify himself as *the* source for certain high-quality product lines, rather than as simply a "Brand X" wholesaler. This approach has been adopted by quite a number of wholesalers who deal in musical instruments and in the plumbing and heating and cooling lines. For example:

The David Wexler Company of Chicago is a well-known merchant of musical merchandise. A relatively unknown item gains prestige and an aura of special value just by being listed in its catalog—witness the fact that customers have testified, "If an item is found in the Wexler catalog, it must be good."

The wholesaler faces not only product expansion, but a concomitant *promotion* expansion on the part of his suppliers. He is thus placed in the position of a "promotional censor," who is literally forced to sift and screen the promotional items and concepts that are directed into his local market. He often bases such screening on a purely subjective set of criteria. Table 5 indicates that this censorship is very extensive. The figures in this table were developed from a survey of 400 wholesalers I conducted in 1966 in conjunction with the National Association of Wholesalers.

TABLE 5   Comparison of Wholesale Promotions Offered and Those Actually Accepted by 400 Wholesalers in 1966.

Commodity line	*Average number of promotions . . .*		Percent accepted
	offered to each wholesaler	*accepted by each wholesaler*	
Electrical	56	8	14.3%
Plumbing, heating and cooling	36	8	22.2
Drug	3,700	390	10.5
Food, candy, and tobacco	244	39	16.0

Despite what I shall call intense promotional efforts by the suppliers, these wholesalers screened out between 78% and 90% of all promotions offered to them. In fact, the highest number of offerings met the lowest percentage of acceptance. The wholesalers who participated in the survey indicated that they support a promotion if:

It is well structured to generate sales and profit.

It is offered by a supplier who has cultivated a good relationship with the wholesaler.

The supplier's salesman is properly trained and communicative.

The promotion incorporates sound forward planning.

It is "tailored," at least to some extent, to the individual wholesaler or his market.

It reflects recognition of the wholesaler's handling costs and promotion budget.

While most wholesalers are not promotionally sophisticated, they are becoming increasingly selective about promotions:

The progressive wholesaler usually develops an overall promotional strategy and then seeks out promotions that mesh well with this strategy in terms of timing and objectives.

He is learning how to *use* supplier promotion programs for his own advantage, and is no longer content merely to be used *by* the supplier in his promotion activity.

He is becoming more active in designing his own promotions.

Alert suppliers are nurturing and supporting such creativity on the part of the wholesaler; they find this cooperative approach less costly and more productive than the system of outright wholesaler censorship. By cooperating in this area, the supplier finds that he can sometimes ride along on the wholesaler's own promotion efforts at little or no additional cost to himself.

There are many dramatic examples of excellent sales and promotional programs conducted by wholesalers, particularly the larger corporate ones. Yet it appears that most wholesalers practice the basic functions of selling and promotion on a haphazard basis, with few controls and with insufficient energy. Their opportunities for upgrading such activities are enormous, and even the most elementary improvements can be highly profitable.

FINANCIAL PLANNING & MANAGEMENT

Because he is traditionally sales-oriented, the wholesaler has tended to leave finances to manage themselves. I have observed, though, that the old saw, "If it's good for sales, let's do it," appears to be giving way to "What's the profit impact?"

Many factors are pressuring the wholesaler into paying more attention to the principles of good financial management—increased competition, increasingly complex tax-reporting requirements, and his growing engagement with computerized information and control systems, to name a few. The manufacturer has long recognized that good information systems, good budgeting, and good accounting are fundamental to the control of his own complex operations; the wholesaler is beginning to recognize this as well.

The NAW has responded to this recognition with seminars on financial planning and management, and other trade associations are offering a number of outstanding programs for their memberships. The Central Supply Association (plumbing and heating products) has organized a five-day seminar for executives which covers thees topics:

The business executive in a changing world.
Corporate goals and objectives.
Long-range plans and policies.
Formal and informal organization.
Management information systems.
Management succession.
Communication networks.
Automation and the use of computers.
Management sciences, such as operations research.
The use of financial ratios.
Credit and financial management.

Manufacturers naturally recognize their own advantage in encouraging the managements of distributor networks to learn more about financial management. General Electric, Union Carbide, and Steelcase are only a few of the suppliers with training programs in this area.

PROFITS

Despite a lack of financial sophistication, wholesaling profits have been good in recent years, sometimes much better than the published figures reveal. During one series of seminars, my colleagues and I asked 80 wholesalers to calculate their rate of return, using their most accurate data and *eliminating assets related to nonbusiness activities*, which we suspected to be a distorting factor in many of the published financial reports. After such adjustments, the median rate was 17%, which is very close to the median reported by Dun & Bradstreet for all manufacturer groups. This experiment added substance to our belief.

For years wholesaling has been portrayed as the classic low-return, high-volume "sad sack" of the business world. This is inaccurate. Table 6 compares the rates of return on tangible net worth of selected manufacturers with those of their related wholesalers. The figures show that while the wholesaler's return is generally lower than the manufacturer's, in several cases it is actually a little higher.

Our experience leads us to believe that wholesalers are beginning to appreciate ROI concepts. In particular, most of them recognize two vital conditions for gaining ground in their businesses:

1. A rate of capital turnover that permits a relatively high level of activity with a relatively low capital base. (In practice, they frequently achieve this by reducing accounts receivable and inventory per dollar of sales. In their efforts to improve their capital turnover, wholesalers have begun to adopt such modern controls as cash-flow budgeting, a relatively recent development for this group.)

2. Good capital leverage based on a relatively high ratio of debt to equity. (Quite a number of wholesalers have overcome their native conservatism about debt, and are willing to take advantage of the services that investment banking offers them.)

TABLE 6   Profits of Selected U.S. Merchant-Wholesalers and Manufacturers, 1966 and 1967.

| | Net profit on tangible net worth[1] | | | |
| | Merchant wholesalers | | Manufacturers | |
1. Durable goods	1966	1967	1966	1967
Auto parts and accessories	7.56%	6.85%	14.60%	11.05%
Electrical parts and supplies	10.83	8.65	14.89	14.83
Furniture and home furnishings	8.20	8.90	10.94[2]	7.87[3]
Hardware	6.56	3.87	12.15[4]	9.51[5]
Plumbing and heating supplies	7.97	6.23	8.51	8.41
Lumber and building materials	6.84	6.73	9.76[6]	7.55[7]
Metals and minerals	10.30	8.33	9.90[8]	9.23[9]

1. Median percentages, after taxes.
2. Furniture.
3. Wood and upholstered household furniture.
4. Hardware and tools.
5. Cutlery, hand tools, and general hardware.
6. Average of concrete, gypsum, and plaster products and lumber.
7. Average of concrete, gypsum, and plaster products, and sawmills and planning mills.
8. Integrated iron and steel operations.
9. Iron and steel foundries.

| | Net profit on tangible net worth[1] | | | |
| | Merchant wholesalers | | Manufacturers | |
2. Nondurable goods	1966	1967	1966	1967
Groceries	7.83%	6.42%	10.53%[2]	11.25%[3]
Wine and liquors	7.68	7.40	10.38[4]	7.48[4]
Drugs and drug sundries	9.16	6.50	14.93	10.38
Chemical and allied products	12.93	7.43	10.01[5]	8.35[5]
Apparel and accessories	6.82	6.72	9.22	7.83
Paper	8.61	6.92	10.17	8.50

1. Median percentages, after taxes.
2. Fruits and vegetable canners.
3. Canned and preserved fruits, vegetables, and seafoods.
4. Malt liquors.
5. Average of agricultural and industrial chemicals.

Source: Dun & Bradstreet, Inc., *Key Business Ratios in 125 Lines*, 1966 and 1967.

On the other hand, we see ample evidence that the great majority of wholesalers are unsophisticated in financial matters. Too often they leave budgeting, financial analysis, and elementary planning to their bookkeeper or the local accounting firm. Indeed, such widespread financial ignorance lends support to the observation that wholesaling is a "wholesome" business in which money can be made in spite of the lack of management sophistication. This may once have been the case, but I doubt that it is so any longer—for wholesaling, or any other major area of our present economy.

CONCLUSION

Like the rest of the economy, wholesaling is in a state of rapid change. The dynamics of the business world have hit some commodity lines and some kinds of wholesalers harder than others, but I believe that all have been affected. It is difficult to assess the violence and rapidity of change in this industry because of certain factors that blur visibility. Low-volume operations, for example, and family- or privately-controlled operations account for a substantial portion of the wholesaling volume, and one cannot usually obtain reliable statistics about such operations. Also, of course, wholesale-distribution networks owned or controlled by manufacturers account for another sizable chunk of the volume, and one cannot always separate the progress of these operations from that of their parents.

Despite the poor visibility, however, one can see that a growing number of wholesale operations are using modern business techniques and concepts. Since wholesalers view themselves as entrepreneurs and as profit-oriented businessmen, there is reason to believe that they will not restrict their activities to wholesaling alone. Indeed, they appear quite willing to develop marketing systems, some of which include manufacturing and retailing operations, using their wholesale houses as operational focal points.

On the negative side, a number of wholesalers are still tied to traditional forms and methods of operations, accepting the newer management techniques only slowly if at all. So far, the less sophisticated wholesaler seems to be surviving; in so doing, he demonstrates the intense need in our economy for the continued services of this resilient enterpreneur. It is questionable, however, whether the future will continue to allow easy entry into wholesaling or permit the inefficiencies of naive management. In the light of continuing pressures for lower-cost distribution, more complex marketing systems, and advancing management technologies, the only courses open to the myopic wholesaler are to close shop, sell out, or shape up.

In general, however, wholesalers seem determined to participate in our expanding economy. To an increasing extent, they are educating themselves and demonstrating a willingness to invest in newer systems and techniques. They are seeking and listening to the counsel of their more sophisticated suppliers, and they are cooperating with them on common problems.

As wholesalers continue to build their management strength and learn to handle the risks inherent in change, I am confident that they will maintain pace with the economy, prosper within it, and add value to it. The outcome, hopefully, will be a much more effective and efficient distribution structure in our economy.

QUESTIONS FOR DISCUSSION

1. (a) What is a wholesaler?
   (b) What function does he perform?

2. Why has the wholesaling segment of a marketing channel, instead of dying (as has been predicted for years) actually been a growth industry?

3. Lopata refers to a change in wholesalers' attitudes. What has been this change?

4. What basic trends do you believe will take place in the wholesaling industry over the next twenty years?

5. How important is inventory control to a merchant wholesaler? Why?

6. Based on the discussion in this article, do you think a career in wholesaling would be challenging and mentally stimulating? Explain your answer.

3.2 CONFLICTING PATTERNS OF STRUCTURAL CHANGE IN WHOLESALING

James C. McKeon

This stability and fragmentation at the macro-wholesale level has masked the dynamic and turbulent structure at the micro-wholesale level. This article removes the facade of stability and analyzes the changes occurring between and among various kinds of business.

An economic system coordinates the activities of two groups: producing groups and consuming groups. The desires of these two groups are in conflict. The producing groups would like to make production choices and to have the consuming groups take possession of the goods produced directly at the time and site of production. The consuming groups, on the other hand, would like to direct production to their specific preferences and to have the economy bring the goods to them in consumable quantities at specific times, as their needs arise.

To provide a time-space-communications bridge between producer and consumer, institutions called economic intermediaries have come into existence. These intermediaries specialize in collecting, sorting, and dispersing processes which are necessities for any economic order beyond the primitive. Collecting is the process by which goods produced in small lots are brought together into large lots. Sorting is the process by which goods are (1) rearranged into smaller lots, each of which meets certain specifications of quality, size, and so on; or (2) rearranged into groupings suitable for users' needs. Dispersion, the final process, involves the movement of goods toward the ultimate consumer.

The structure of economic intermediaries is extremely complex. This is because time-space-communication activity requirements must be tailored to implement efficient interaction among different types of producing and consuming groups. The diversity of these requirements has led to a wide variety of intermediary specialists, even in static econo-

Reprinted by permission of the author and publisher from *Economic and Business Bulletin* (Winter 1972), pp. 37–48.

mies. In dynamic economies this diversity is even more complex because of the rapidly changing production technology and purchasing and consumption patterns. Furthermore, the efficient performance of collecting, sorting and dispersing often requires specialized skills and facilities operating at scales and locations different from those of production or consumption. The result of all these forces has been the development of an extremely complex structural arrangement of diverse intermediaries. These structural arrangements, together with sequences of producers, intermediaries, and consumers, are called distribution channels. The distribution channel is the key structural arrangement in marketing.

The producers, intermediaries, and consumers in a channel interact with each other. Therefore, changes at any level will affect all other channel levels. The changes lead to cooperation and competition among the channel members. Palamountain isolates three forms of distributive conflict: (1) horizontal competition among intermediaries of the same type; (2) intertype competition among intermediaries of different types of the same channel level; and (3) vertical conflict between channel members at different channel levels.[1] The first form, horizontal competition, is well researched in traditional economic analysis and is usually referred to as "competition." However, both intertype competition and vertical conflict among intermediaries are neglected in microeconomic theory. There are two kinds of intermediaries: wholesale and retail intermediaries. This paper focuses on intertype competition among wholesale intermediaries and vertical conflict encountered by wholesale intermediaries.

The general objective of this paper has been to contribute to the understanding of channel structure theory, which is essential to an understanding of the institutional structure, relationships among channel members, channel effectiveness, channel changes, and channel management.

It would be presumptuous to attempt any complete survey of channel structural theory and change within a single paper. Accordingly, it seeks to achieve the following specific objectives:

1. To develop a conceptual framework which can be used to explain, measure, and evaluate the structural changes at the wholesale level in the American economy.

2. To identify and measure these structural changes.

3. To identify, describe, and analyze the major forces responsible for these structural changes.

The Census of Business is the primary source of statistical data for the analysis of patterns of structural change in wholesaling. Other

---

1. Joseph C. Palamountain, *The Politics of Distribution*. Cambridge, Mass.: Harvard University Press, 1955.

sources of statistical data are the Census of Manufacturers, the Department of Agriculture, the Federal Trade Commission, and various trade associations. Data from these sources are used to identify, measure, and categorize the structural changes.

The sources of information regarding the conceptual framework and the forces responsible for the structural changes in wholesaling are a review of the literature dealing with changes in wholesaling and personal interviews, and correspondence with economists, government personnel, authors of wholesaling literature, and trade association personnel.

STRUCTURAL CHANGES AT
MICRO-WHOLESALE LEVEL

For years there have been predictions that wholesalers "will decline," "are declining," or "are dead." These predictions are not necessarily wrong. Their veracity depends on the qualifications one attaches to the word "wholesalers." There is a substantial amount of confusion concerning the differences in the concepts of wholesaling and retailing. There is even more confusion over the various meanings of the word "wholesalers." It might mean all wholesale establishments, all independent wholesale establishments, all independent wholesale establishments handling a particular kind of goods, or all independent wholesale establishments rendering a particular kind of service. Thus the conclusions reached concerning the rise or fall of wholesale trade will depend on the particular segment of wholesale trade being examined.

This paper uses the definitional and categorization systems employed by the Bureau of Census for the wholesale trade sector of our economy. The Census Bureau's measure of wholesale trade reflects all transactions including duplicate transactions at the wholesale level but understates the true volume of wholesale trade. This understatement comes about because approximately 50 percent of the total goods produced bypasses the total wholesale structure as defined by the Census Bureau. Nevertheless, the Bureau's measure is the best available measure of the wholesaling task.

An examination of wholesale trade at the micro-wholesale institutional level suggests that the structure has been relatively stable since 1929. The growth of wholesale trade volume has kept pace with the overall economy growth. The relative importance of the major types of operations have shifted but not to the extent one might expect with the growth of large-scale manufacturers and retailers. For example, merchant wholesalers have accounted for roughly two-fifths of the wholesale trade volume since 1929. No other type of operation accounts for

more than 20 percent of the trade. There is a trend for a greater proportion of sales to be concentrated in large multi-establishment firms; however, this trend is restricted primarily to the groups of wholesale
establishments of manufacturing firms. In addition, the wholesale institutional structure is highly fragmented in that there is a variety of types
of wholesale operations ranging from full-service merchant wholesalers
who perform all equalization functions to brokers who specialize in
buying or selling functions. Another aspect of this fragmentation is the
relatively large proportion of sales handled by small firms and establishments. This stability and fragmentation at the macro-wholesale level
has masked the dynamic and turbulent structure at the micro-wholesale
level. This paper removes the facade of stability and analyzes the
changes occurring between and among various kinds of business.

Wholesale institutional structure is far from stable.[2] One reason is
that not all types of operations handle all kinds of goods. For example,
assemblies specialize in farm products. Manufacturers' sales branches
and offices do not handle general line groceries, fish, fresh fruits and
vegetables, iron and steel scrap, and waste materials. Agents and brokers handle every kind of goods except general line groceries. On the
other hand, merchant wholesalers handle each of forty-two kinds of
goods.

Second, the proportion or share of wholesale trade handled by merchant wholesalers varies from a low of 14 percent of the motor vehicle
volume to a high of 100 percent of general line grocery volume. The
latter result is primarily a definitional phenomenon. The share of trade
handled by manufacturers' sales branches varies from a low of 1 percent
of printing and writing paper volume to a high of 62 percent of the
commercial machinery and equipment volume. For manufacturers' sales
offices the low and high shares respectively are 1 percent of meat volume
and 61 percent of the volume of chemicals. For agents and brokers, the
low and high respective shares are 2 percent of the tire volume and 37
percent of the apparel and electronic parts and equipment volume.

These data show conclusively that the importance of various types
of operation varies with each type of trade. This emanates from the fact
that for each trade the very nature of the wholesaling task differs. Thus
it is only natural that in trades where the stocking function is relatively
important, merchant wholesalers and/or manufacturers' sales branches
will be dominant forces. Conversely, in trades where the buying and
selling function is relatively important, agents and/or manufacturers'
sales offices are dominant forces.

These data also show that while merchant wholesalers' share of whole-

2. The Census Bureau assigns each wholesale establishment to a kind of business
classification according to the individual commodity or commodity group which is
the primary source (greater than 50 percent) of the establishment's receipts.

sale trade varies considerably from one kind of business to another, the merchant wholesaler is an important institution in every kind of business. The merchant wholesalers' minimum share of wholesale volume (14 percent of the motor vehicle volume) is greater than the minimum share of other types of operation. Similarly, the merchant wholesalers' maximum share of wholesale volume is far greater than the maximum share of other types of operation.

PATTERNS OF STRUCTURAL CHANGE

In some trades merchant wholesalers have grown at the expense of manufacturers' sales branches; in other trades the reverse is true. In still others, both merchant wholesalers' and manufacturers' branches have grown at the expense of manufacturers' sales offices and/or agents and brokers; in other trades the reverse is true. The nature of changes over time in the share of wholesale trade by type of operation is different for each trade. Nevertheless, these changes can be classified into a number of patterns of structural change. Four basic patterns have been identified. Table 1 presents descriptions of each pattern of structural change and decision rules to be used in distinguishing among these four patterns.

Each of thirty-five kinds of business was categorized. The time span used in this categorization was 1939 to 1963. In some cases where the data were not complete, the author estimated the pattern of structural change.

The results of this categorization are shown in Table 2. Two patterns of structural change account for twenty of the thirty-five kinds of business. In twelve trades the primary structural change involved a shift in importance to merchant wholesalers and away from manufacturers' sales branches. Merchant wholesalers of meat, plumbing fixtures, farm equipment, service-establishment equipment, iron and steel products, and tobacco products increased their share of wholesale trade substantially. These gains in importance of merchant wholesalers will surprise many marketing scholars. Only four kinds of business involved the reverse pattern change—a shift to manufacturers' sales branches and away from merchant wholesalers.

The second most popular pattern of structural change is Pattern 3b— a growing importance of the selling function relative to the inventory function. This pattern of change accounts for eight kinds of business as shown in Table 2. With the exception of apparel, both merchant wholesalers' and manufacturers' sales branches have experienced a decline in share. In the case of apparel, wholesalers have increased their share of wholesale trade from 40 to 42 percent, while the manufacturers' sales branches experienced a loss in share from 20 to 7 percent between 1939 and 1963. In all eight kinds of business, manufacturers' sales offices have increased their share of trade, especially the sales offices handling paints, chemicals, confectionery, printing and industrial paper and home furnishings.

TABLE 1   Description of Rules Used for Identifying Wholesaling Structural Changes

PATTERN 1   *Shift to alternative stocking operations.*

This type of structural change recognizes that merchant wholesalers' and manufacturers' sales branches perform similar wholesaling functions. The primary change is a shift from one type of stocking operation to another. There are two kinds of Pattern 1 changes which may be identified as follows:

a. Merchant wholesalers' share of trade increased over time while manufacturers' sales branches' share of trade declined.

b. Manufacturers' sales branches share of trade increased over time while merchant wholesalers' share declined.

PATTERN 2   *Shift to alternative selling operations.*

This type of structural change recognizes that manufacturers' sales offices and agents and brokers perform identical wholesaling functions. The primary structural change is a shift from one type of selling operation to another. The decision rules for identifying the two kinds of Pattern 2 change are as follows:

a. Agents' and brokers' share of trade increased over time while the share of manufacturers' sales offices declined.

b. Manufacturers' sales offices' share of trade increased over time while the share of agents and brokers declined.

PATTERN 3   *Shift in inventory function relative to selling function at wholesale level.*

The primary structural change is the growth or decline in the inventory function relative to the selling function. The decision rules to identify the changes are as follows:

a. Growing importance of the inventory function relative to the selling function exists when the combined share of wholesale sales accounted for by the merchant wholesalers and manufacturers' sales branches has increased over time.

b. Growing importance of the selling function relative to the stocking function exists when the combined share of the agents' and brokers' and manufacturers' sales offices has increased over time.

PATTERN 4 *Other structural changes.*

These changes are a special group and contain much of the food trades and scrap trades where manufacturers are not involved at the wholesale level. The structural changes between the independent wholesale operations primarily reflect shifts in importance of the ancillary wholesaling functions of assembling, financing, advising and counseling, breaking-bulk, and delivering, rather than stocking and selling functions.

TABLE 2   Patterns of Structural Change for Various Kinds of Business

PATTERN 1a

5014	Tires, tubes
5047	Meat, meat products
5063	Electrical supplies, apparatus
5074	Plumbing, heating equipment
5083	Farm and garden machinery
5086	Professional equipment
5087	Service-establishment equipment
5091P	Iron and steel products
5094	Tobacco, tobacco products
5096P	Stationery, office supplies
5097P	Household, office furniture
5098P	Construction materials

PATTERN 2a.

(None)

PATTERN 3a

5013	Automotive equipment
5988	Transportation equipment
5098P	Lumber, millwork and plywood

PATTERN 1b

| 5012 | Automobiles, other motor vehicles |
| 5022 | Drugs, proprietaries, sundries |

Note: "P" means "Part."

| 5072 | Hardware |
| 5082P | Commercial machinery, equipment |

PATTERN 2b.

| 5032 | Dry goods, piece goods, notions |

PATTERN 3b

5028	Paints, varnishes
5029	Other chemicals, allied products
5035	Apparel and accessories, hosiery, lingerie
5039	Footwear
5045	Confectionery
5096P	Printing, writing paper
5096P	Industrial, personal paper
5097P	Home furnishings

PATTERN 4

5042	General line groceries
5043	Dairy, dairy products
5044	Poultry, poultry products
5046	Fish, seafood
5048	Fresh fruits, vegetables
5093P	Iron, steel scrap
5093	Waste materials

In automotive equipment, lumber and millwork and transportation equipment trades, the primary structural change has been an increase in importance of inventory establishments versus selling establishments. In each of these trades, and especially in automotive equipment and lumber trades, wholesalers are of considerable importance.

Pattern 2, which involves a shift from one type of selling establishment to another, is of little importance. This does not mean that such shifts are not taking place. It means that only in the case of dry goods, piece goods, and notions has there been a primary shift in channel from agents and brokers to manufacturers' sales offices. There are no wholesale trades where the primary change has been a shift from manufacturers' sales offices to agents and brokers.

Type 4 pattern of structure change deals primarily with ancillary wholesaling functions as opposed to stocking and selling functions. The ancillary functions are assembling, financing, advising and counseling, breaking-bulk, and delivering. In the food trades and scrap trades, manufacturers do not generally have wholesale operations. Therefore, the structural changes involve shifts in importance between independent wholesale operations—between independent stocking and non-stocking operations or between different types of independent stocking and non-stocking operations. The changes in importance of each independent wholesale operation primarily reflect shifts in importance of the ancillary wholesaling functions.

CHANNEL STRUCTURAL SHIFTS

PATTERN 1

Structural Pattern 1a (merchant wholesalers' share of trade increasing over time while manufacturers' sales branches' share of trade has declined) is basically a shift from one type of stocking operation (manufacturers' sales branches) to another type of stocking operation (merchant wholesalers). The gains by merchant wholesalers in these trades, and especially because they are at the expense of manufacturers' sales branches, refute the claim that "the wholesaler is dead!" There appear to be two forces causing the increased importance of the merchant wholesalers: (1) their willingness to adjust to a changing supply and/or demand structure; and (2) competitive operating performance. The first force can be further divided into changes in the tasks performed, adjustment to industrial demand, and adjustment to retail demand.

Merchant wholesalers of meat, iron and steel products, and household and office furniture changed their basic tasks, and as a result, increased their share of wholesale sales in their respective channels. Meat wholesalers were originally butchers and retailers who shifted to wholesaling following, first, the concentration of slaughter in large packers located in terminal points, and second, the dominance of chains in the meat retailing. Meat wholesalers gained a dominant position in wholesaling through specialization by product and customer. Iron and steel wholesalers were once warehousing depots for small industrial users and emergency depots for large users. A need for post-production processing developed because the steel mills, under the pressure of mounting costs and competition from foreign steel mills and substitute products, were forced into longer rollings of standardized products. Steel wholesalers developed the service center concept to absorb this postproduction processing function. Furniture wholesalers developed the showroom concept to serve as a display area for small and large retailers. This showroom concept enabled retailers to stock only standard high-turnover items and thereby control their inventory costs.

Merchant wholesalers of electrical supplies and apparatus, plumbing and heating equipment, construction materials, and stationery and office supplies have adjusted to industrial demand by redirecting their selling efforts primarily to contractors and builders and changing their product line. One of the consequences of this customer specialization by electrical supplies and apparatus wholesalers was the dropping of electrical appliances in order to concentrate on products used by contractors and builders. The stationery wholesalers redirected their efforts from retail accounts to industrial and commercial accounts, requiring a broadening of their product line to include office equipment and furniture.

Wholesalers of tobacco, farm and garden machinery, and tires and tubes adjusted to demand at the retail level. The key to the success of tobacco wholesalers has been flexibility, mainly by broadening product lines to include candy and a myriad of other products. This broadening of product line is in keeping with the tendency for their retail customers to broaden their lines. Farm and garden machinery wholesalers seized the opportunity to serve florists, hardware dealers, and a new type of retailer—the garden supply dealers. This opportunity emanated from the demand of suburban families for power mowers, fertilizer, tillers, trimmers, and other lawn and garden care equipment. Tire wholesalers are often called "gypsies" of distribution because of their flexible trading activities. As their primary task (for example, the need for tire repair and service) declined, they had to adjust in order to survive. Wholesalers began to do a considerable amount of redistribution to other wholesalers in order to control the inventory problem created by the tremendous variety and sizes of tires. Furthermore, tire wholesalers entered into retailing in an effort to combat the complete channel integration by the tire manufacturers, the service stations, and large mass merchandisers.

Merchant wholesalers of professional equipment and service-establishment equipment have apparently been successful because of their comparable operating expenses with manufacturers' sales branches in their respective channels. As was pointed out, it is unusual for merchant wholesalers and sales branches to have comparable operating expenses. Cause and effect relationships are extremely difficult to identify in these two channels but the ability of merchant wholesalers to maintain competitive operating expenses probably has discouraged manufacturers from establishing their own branches.

Briefly, the thread that links the merchant wholesalers of the above twelve trades appears to be their willingness to adjust to a changing environment. The merchant wholesalers in these twelve trades have not been passive "ordertakers." They have become more sensitive to the needs of their customers and their trade channel system. They have recognized opportunities; even more important, they have taken the necessary steps to capitalize on these opportunities.

Structural Change Pattern 1b may be identified as follows: manufacturers' sales branches' share of trade increases over time, while merchant wholesalers' share declines.

Pattern 1b is like Pattern 1a in that they are both shifts from one type of stocking operation to another. However, Pattern 1b is the reverse of Pattern 1a. Pattern 1b is a shift of wholesale trade from merchant wholesalers to manufacturers' sales branches, whereas Pattern 1a is a shift from manufacturers' sales branches to merchant wholesalers. Pattern 1b changes constitute a definite move toward vertical integration on the part of manufacturers.

The conditions which encourage a great dominance by the manufacturers' sales branches are (1) a large increase in sales volume, especially if sales are concentrated among a limited number of manufacturers; (2) an increase in importance of after-service function; and (3) an increased unwillingness of the merchant wholesalers to provide the aggressive selling.

The motor vehicles and commercial machinery channels served as examples of an increased need for after-service coupled with a large growth in sales concentrated among few manufacturers. The auto manufacturers control their channel by advertising heavily to presell the consumer, and establishing exclusive dealer franchises to insure quality after-service. The computer and other commercial machinery manufacturers established branches to serve as parts depots and service centers to insure quality after-service. In some cases, these machinery manufacturers lease their equipment, thereby providing an additional reason for maintaining the equipment.

The drug and hardware trade channels are examples of traditional merchant wholesaler and retailer rigidity in accepting and adjusting to environmental change. The primary changes were the development of a large number of new products, the advent of scrambled merchandising, and the growth of large-scale retailers. The drug channel was affected by all the above developments and the hardware channel was affected primarily by the latter two developments at the retail level. The manufacturers' reaction in both channels to the wholesalers' failure to adjust was identical—the establishment of branches. To the credit of the wholesalers, they began to do something about their plight, although only after the sales branches had gained a substantial share of wholesale sales. In both channels, the initial reaction was specialization by product line. Some traditional general-line wholesalers shifted to a specialty-line operation, but it is believed that most of the "shift" from general-line to specialty-line wholesalers is the result of the establishment of new specialty-line wholesalers. Also, some general line wholesalers dropped some traditional services performed for their retail customers and added others. The added services were in the area of retail location analysis, forecasting, financing, and store layout. The wholesalers' latest strategies in the drug and hardware channels have been the establishment of wholesaler-sponsored and retailer-sponsored cooperatives.

PATTERN 2

None of the thirty-five kinds of business studied experienced a Pattern 2a structural change (agents' and brokers' share of trade increased over time while the share of manufacturers' sales offices declined). A Pattern 2b structural change (manufacturers' sales offices' share of trade increases over time while the share of agents and brokers declines) involves forward integration on the part of the manufacturer, in that the manufacturer has preempted the selling function traditionally performed by independents. Only one of the thirty-five kinds of business studied experienced a Pattern 2b change (5032: dry goods, piece goods, notions).

The following analysis is complicated because of several factors. First, the Census Bureau has combined the data for establishments handling dry goods, piece goods, and notions, even though the channels for each of these kinds of business are unique. By combining these data, the differences among the channels are masked. Second, the available information about the characteristics of the operations at each level for each channel is limited. Finally, there has been a considerable amount of vertical integration, both up and down, in this kind of business. As a result of this integration, the original categorization of establishments which were based on the performance of single functions has become outdated. Nevertheless, four developments can be identified, and to a certain extent, their impact on the channel structure can be measured.

First, the forward integration of the textile mills and the backward integration by the textile converters occurred in several steps. The first was the integration of spinning and weaving operations. The next step was the adoption of the selling function by the mills, which eventually led to the decline of the agent and broker. The third step in the vertical integration development which occurred after World War II was the integration of production functions (spinning and weaving) and the converting and finishing functions.

Second was the horizontal integration on the part of the vertically integrated operations. By broadening their product lines, the integrated firms reduced the risk of a loss of demand in a narrow range of products. The broadening of the product line also reduced the overhead costs per item and increased the demand for the product line.

Third, the development of man-made fibers has had the same impact as the trend toward horizontal integration. Man-made fiber channels are generally shorter than natural fiber channels because close liaison among the yarn producer, weaver, and user is required in developing a product with the desired characteristics. This requirement dictates the use of direct channels.

Fourth was the rise of the large-scale retailer and the consequential decline of the traditional, small-scale, dry goods stores. Generally, large-scale retailers such as department stores and limited price variety stores buy direct from manufacturers. The shift from gray goods to finished dry goods by agents and brokers only retarded their decline.

While the primary structural change was an increase in the share of wholesale sales of manufacturers' sales offices and a decline in the share of agents and brokers, there have been changes in the stocking operations. In particular, converters have declined in numbers and importance due to vertical integration, forward by the mills and backward by the converters. The growth of the large-scale retailers has hurt dry goods wholesalers whose survival depends on the survival of the small-scale retailers. Dry goods wholesalers have become specialty operations often involving franchise lines and private brands. Piece goods wholesalers have actually increased their number of establishments and share of wholesale sales. Mills and converters are employing a selective distribution policy in assigning a limited number of strategically located piece goods wholesalers. These wholesalers offer "immediate" replacement of fabric bolts to retailers. In this way, the mills and converters are insured an adequate selling effort.

The desires of the channel members to (1) achieve production economies and (2) overcome the risk and confusion in the market place have resulted in the substitution of coordinated manufacturing, converting, and merchandising channel structure for an uncoordinated, speculative channel structure.

Pattern 3a (that is, the combined share of wholesale sales accounted for by merchant wholesalers and manufacturers' sales branches has increased over time) reflects the growing importance of the stocking function relative to non-stocking functions.

The automotive and transportation equipment trades are both service trades so their tasks and, hence, their channel organizations reflect the nature of the demand for service. The demand for service in both trades can be translated to mean primarily ready availability of parts and repair service. The differences in channel organization reflect the differences in the characteristics of the availability of parts and repair service demanded. In both trades, the demand for service is diverse because of the range in the types and makes of vehicles, types of repair, degree of specialization by type of repair of the repair centers, and parts usage. The key to understanding the differences in the channel structure of the automotive and transportation channels is the differences in demand for parts and service availability. The demand for parts and service availability can be translated to mean that an owner of a vehicle can have his vehicle repaired wherever and whenever he desires. To supply such service, however, would cost considerably more than the owner would be willing to pay. The owner must therefore compromise his demands for immediate service. The result is a distribution channel which balances the need for immediate availability and the cost of delivering it. The degree of availability is determined by the temporal and spatial gap between the point of production and consumption. The motorist is considerably more demanding than the owners of aircraft, trains, or boats in that he requires closer temporal and spatial availability. However, close spatial availability is limited in the case of transportation equipment, for repairs can be made only at a limited number of locations; for aircraft at airfields, for trains at railroad yards, and for boats at dock facilities. There are no such limitations for repair facilities of automobiles. In a metropolitan area there may be only one repair center for each type of transportation equipment, but hundreds of repair centers for automotive equipment.

The channel structures reflect these differences in the demand for parts and service availability and the diversity of the demand for repair. The automotive parts and equipment channel has several wholesale levels made up of many widely dispersed, multiple unit, small-scale operations which redistribute their goods to each other in order to achieve close temporal and spatial availability at a reasonable cost. The transportation parts and equipment channel do not have to meet such stringent demands for close temporal and spatial availability of parts and repair service. The owners of aircraft, railroad, and marine equipment employ preventive maintenance methods to a greater extent than do automotive vehicle owners, and thus reduce the need for close temporal and spatial availability. As a result the channel for transportation equipment has only one wholesale level, and it is not composed of particularly small-scale operations.

In the lumber trade, the basic characteristics of lumber (bulky, heavy, quality variation, and so on) make it important to reduce the number of times lumber must be physically handled. Drop shippers, agents, and brokers sold lumber in carload lots and were historically the primary wholesale operations. The strength of these operations emanated from their knowledge of the market in terms of available buyers and sellers, grades of lumber, prices, credit ratings, and other information. As time passed, better grading systems and better and faster communications and transportation systems were developed. More important, mills were forced into a smaller size mix for a given product, thereby creating a greater need for cutting to size at the wholesale level. This need was served by merchant wholesalers with yards. In addition, wholesalers with yards have the advantage of selling both ways: direct mill or warehouse shipments.

In the 1940s entrepreneurs began to develop wood products, the first of them plywood. The new products matched the needs of the builders and consumers more precisely, thereby reducing the variety gap. Prior to the development of wood products to meet specific needs, manufacturers of lumber sales depended upon the aggressiveness of their retailers, for there was no opportunity for product differentiation or branding. With the development of plywood, manufacturers established a number of sales branches in order to achieve the necessary selling effort.

Concomitant with the development of plywood, manufacturers and mills began to integrate vertically into paper and pulp manufacturing. The integration into paper and pulp manufacturing sought to gain high utilization of the timber resources. Further integration into other trades and at wholesale and retail levels in the lumber trade followed. These integrated manufacturers increasingly assumed the responsibility of coordinating manufacturing, wholesaling, and retailing. The latest development has been the development of superdealers who perform both the wholesaling and retailing functions.

Briefly, the shift from commodity to product class accounted for most of the changes in channel structure of the lumber trade. Also, the development of large vertically integrated manufacturers and of super-dealers has changed the structure of the lumber trade from one of small-scale buyers and sellers to large-scale buyers and sellers.

Pattern 3b.   (The combined share of wholesale sales accounted for by agents and brokers and manufacturers' sales offices has increased over time.) This pattern has witnessed a shift of wholesale sales from stocking operation to non-stocking operations, primarily from manufacturers' sales branches to sales offices.

The analyses of apparel, footwear, home furnishings, confectionery, and paint were made difficult because a relatively large percentage of manufacturers' output is sold direct to retail, industrial, and commercial accounts, without the involvement of traditional wholesale operations. These direct sales are not included in the Bureau of the Census's measure of wholesale trade; the interpretation of changes at the wholesale level must therefore be done carefully. Another factor making the analysis difficult is the fact that the Census Bureau's classification of "agents and brokers" includes auctions, merchandise brokers, commission merchants, import agents, export agents, manufacturers' agents, selling agents, purchasing agents, and resident buyers. The data for each of these operations are combined, thus making the interpretation of changes difficult.

The increased risk of product perishability is the predominant factor which explains the increased importance of non-stocking wholesale operations in the apparel and footwear trades. The risk of product perishability has increased over time because of faster and more frequent fashion and style changes, which are the result of faster and more effective transportation and communications. With faster and more frequent fashion and style changes, the selling function of manufacturers' sales offices, manufacturers' agents and selling agents, and the purchasing and information functions of resident buyers has increased in importance.

The growth of large-scale retailers and the growth of large-scale purchases by small-scale retailers were also important factors in explaining the growth in importance of non-stocking operations in the apparel, footwear, confectionery, home furnishings, and paint trades. General merchandise stores such as department stores and discount houses were particularly important in the apparel, home furnishings, and paint trades. These large-scale retailers generally buy in large volume directly from the manufacturer or his representatives, or through resident buyers. Thus any growth in importance of these retailers would result in a growth in importance of non-stocking wholesale operations in the confectionery trade. Supermarkets generally buy direct from manufacturers or through a manufacturers' sales office or confectionary or food brokers.

Large-scale sales to small-scale retailers are economically feasible under certain conditions, for example when a retailer specializes in a particular style, type, or manufacturers' line, or when the product is sufficiently unique to warrant high prices. Small-scale apparel, footwear, paint, and confectionery retailers have become more specialized by price lines, type of product, and manufacturers' line.

An increased desire by manufacturers to gain greater channel control in order to reduce the product perishability risks is a factor in the apparel, footwear, and confectionery trades. The methods employed by manufacturers to reduce this risk are outright ownership of retail outlets and selective or exclusive distribution. These methods lead to direct sales or sales through sales offices or agents and brokers.

Merchant wholesalers in the apparel, footwear, confectionery, home furnishing, and paint trades are relegated to serving small retailers. The merchant wholesalers in these trades have managed to survive in spite of the trends toward vertical integration and direct sales to retailers because (1) small retailers with specialized knowledge still control a sizable share of retail sales; (2) the manufacturing level of these channels is highly fragmented; and (3) product line diversity in terms of styles, sizes, and colors is increasing.

The wholesale structures of the paper and chemical trades have been affected by the growth in direct sales between manufacturers and industrial customers. Many of these customers are very large and buy raw materials and supplies in corresponding large quantities, thus making direct sales economically feasible.

In the paper trade a number of new products and processes have been developed in folding boxes and other packaging materials and in construction paper products. The development of these products required close contact between sellers and buyers. Furthermore, long-term purchasing contracts are often required to offset the high development costs. These conditions favor direct sales. Similarly, chemical manufacturers have developed a number of new products, many of which are made to the buyer's specifications.

Merchant wholesalers declined in importance in both the paper and chemical trades. In general, they are relegated to servicing small customers. The greatest declines were in the industrial and personal paper trades because the manufacturers sold industrial paper direct to industrial accounts and personal paper to food store chains. In the printing and writing paper trade, the greater growth of printing paper versus writing paper had the effect of making the wholesaler less important, for he had primarily distributed writing paper. Wholesalers of chemicals are small-scale operations and are getting smaller on the average. The increased diversity of chemical products has created opportunities for wholesalers, but their lack of knowledge of chemistry has been a deterrent since World War I.

As in the case of consumer products, bypassing wholesale stocking operations does not eliminate the wholesaling functions of storage, assembly, and credit. The buyer or seller must assume these functions.

IMPORTANCE OF ANCILLARY FUNCTIONS AS OPPOSED TO STOCKING AND SELLING FUNCTIONS

Type 1 and 2 patterns of structural change do not involve functional shifts but deal with shifts in ownership concerning who shall perform a given function. Type 3 patterns of structural change deal with functional shifts without regard to ownership. All three types deal with only two wholesaling functions: namely, stocking and selling. Type 4 pattern of structural change deals with ancillary wholesaling functions as opposed to stocking and selling functions. The ancillary functions of assembling, financing, advising and counseling, breaking-bulk and delivering are more important in the Type 4 trades channels.

All food channels have been influenced by four major developments: (1) a shift in consumption from fresh to processed foods with built-in service; (2) a trend toward large-scale, specialized, and concentrated farming; (3) a trend toward large-scale processing; and (4) a trend toward large-scale retail operations. In the general line grocery trade, the development of corporate food chains in the 1920s, the development of the supermarket concept in the early 1930s and the adoption of the supermarket concept by the food chains led to a great emphasis on costs. The development of retailer buying groups and cash-and-carry wholesalers were examples of this emphasis on costs. These two developments, however, were limited because they failed to compete with the food chains on fronts other than merchandise cost. Not until the retailer-owned cooperatives and the voluntary group wholesalers were established did the independent retailers have a way to match both the cost and merchandising advantages of the food chains.

In the dairy, fruit, vegetable, and poultry trades, a distinction between fresh and manufactured products must be made. In general, the fresh product channels have been shortened, thereby eliminating the need for some traditional wholesale operations such as assemblers in shipping point markets and wholesalers, jobbers, and purveyors in terminal markets. The shortening of these fresh product channels has been brought about by (1) the backward and forward integration of shipping point producers, processors, and assemblers, and terminal market whole-salers, jobbers, and purveyors; (2) direct purchasing of large-scale re-tailers; and (3) the use of perishables as merchandising specials by the food chains. Merchant wholesalers in these fresh food products have been forced to shift their sales efforts from retailers to institutions and restaurants.

The shift in consumption to manufactured or processed products has had a stabilizing effect at the wholesale level. The processing reduces the perishability, thereby reducing the need for speed of movement and enabling storage by merchant wholesalers and manufacturers' sales branches.

A final development in food wholesaling which was encouraged by the growth of supermarket sales of nonfood products was the establish-ment of rack merchandisers. Supermarket managers can concentrate their efforts on their major lines by using rack merchandisers to handle the sundry items.

In the iron and scrap trade, drop shippers have been traditionally the predominant wholesale operation in that they served as the "sales-men," information sources, and financial supporters of the processors. Following the period of low scrap demand and prices in the late 1950s, the processors installed larger, more efficient equipment in order to achieve better quality control and lower costs. Since the processors can match the buyers' needs more precisely, there is less need for the drop shippers. The Census data for 1958 and 1963 confirm the move to larger processors and less dependence upon drop shippers to sell their output.

CONCLUSIONS

Several important conclusions may be deduced from this article. In all cases, the validity of the conclusions is limited by the fact that available data are inadequate in many respects. It is believed, however, that more and better data would not alter the basic character of the findings.

Wholesaling is a necessary and dynamic function in our economy. Change in channel structures is a permanent characteristic. The stability at the macro-wholesale level is misleading. At the micro-level, whole-saling is very dynamic. The channel structure depends upon the time-space-quantity-variety gap between the assortments of sellers and buy-ers. To the extent that this gap changes, the wholesaling task changes. The discrepancy of assortments may apply to any of the functions or flows of marketing. If a discrepancy develops and provides an economic advantage, pressure will appear for an established channel member or an outsider to fill the discrepancy. A discrepancy may occur at any point in the channel. Furthermore, a discrepancy can result from an endless number of and variety of factors. In an economy where social, economic, political, and technological changes are revolutionary, the marketing tasks to be performed and the channel structures change rapidly. The future growth of wholesaling can be expected to expand in a direct relationship with the long-run expansion of output in the economy.

A wholesaling operation can be eliminated as an entity, but someone must perform the wholesaling tasks and absorb the costs formerly done by the agency, assuming the wholesaling tasks are necessary. Just who assumes the tasks depends upon the relative size and financial strength of the channel members. If a new operation fails to perform an important function, failure is inevitable (for example, retailer buying groups and cash-and-carry wholesalers). Equalization tasks may even be passed onto the ultimate consumers. Part of the cost savings of supermarkets were the result of the consumer's willingness to assemble her own order, arrange for credit elsewhere, and deliver her own orders to her home.

Each type of wholesaling operation has a primary or critical role in the channel. If that critical role becomes obsolete with the passage of time, the particular operation will eventually disappear unless it assumes a needed role.

The critical focus of competition is that point at which the goods and services pass out of the market into the hands of some terminal buyer. Thus in the long run, the final consumer is the channel captain or administrator. In the short run, the channel captain may operate at any level, may be an established firm, or may even be an innovator outside the established power structure. Regardless of who the short-run channel captain is, if his leadership is not in agreement with the demands of the final buyers, his role as channel captain will be short-lived.

Voluntary cooperation, selective and exclusive distribution policies, and franchising are examples of an extension of a firm's organization. Recognizing that the final consumer is the long-run channel captain leads to a further conclusion that this recognition is equivalent to applying the marketing concept to the extension-of-the-organization system concept of channels. For maximization of long-term profits and consumer satisfaction, the channel must act as a unit.

The end result of the manufacturers' selective and exclusive distribution policies and franchising had led, and will continue to lead, to retail store ownership—direct or indirect, full or partial—and operation of retail stores by manufacturers.

Certain environmental conditions favor circumvention of traditional wholesalers:

1. The greater the perishability of the product, the more necessary direct contact between manufacturers and retailers becomes. The

higher the unit value and the greater the installation and repair service, the more practical it becomes to sell direct to retailers or industrial users.

2. In general, the larger the scale and the greater the financial strength of the manufacturer, the more feasible it is to sell direct. If the production is fairly routinized, direct channels may be employed. Also, if a manufacturer has a long line of products, large orders can be obtained from each customer, thereby justifying direct contact.

3. Direct contact may result when the market is composed of large-scale retailers or users, large-scale purchases by small retailers, small numbers of customers, or geographically concentrated customers.

4. Manufacturers may establish their own sales branches when independent wholesalers are inefficient, incompetent, or not available.

QUESTIONS FOR DISCUSSION

1. What is the difference between the macro and micro levels of wholesaling?

2. What have been the basic structural shifts in the wholesaling industry?

3. (a) What are the ancillary functions of a wholesaler?
   (b) Are they becoming more or less important? Why?

4. McKeon states, "A wholesaling operation can be eliminated as an entity, but someone must perform the wholesaling tasks and absorb the costs formerly done by the agency, assuming the wholesaling tasks are necessary." Do you agree?

Chapter 4

Conflict and Cooperation in Marketing Channels

CONFLICT HAS BEEN DEFINED as tension and disagreement that results from incompatible desires and needs of each party. It is an extremely relevant concept in channel analysis since independent business firms frequently have divergent business objectives. An illustrative situation is the STP Corporation introduction of the STP oil filter. *The Wall Street Journal* noted that "... STP has alienated some auto-supply middlemen by bypassing parts of the industry's elaborate distribution setup in selling STP additives and these wholesalers might retaliate by not stocking the filters."[1] The president of STP, Andy Granatelli, scoffed at the possible wholesaler boycott. He stated that he was using a "pulling" strategy and that customers for his oil filters would demand them, forcing both retailers and wholesalers to carry his products.[2]

Another eample of a conflict situation takes place in petroleum marketing. *Business Week* has observed, "Dealers and jobbers are in revolt against the pricing policies of the majors, and are pressing damage suits in half-a-dozen states."[3] Briefly, there are two basic problems. One involves the majors selling gasoline to independent dealers at lower prices than are available to the affiliates of the major. Secondly, the dealers claim that they are being threatened by the majors to follow their marketing and operating procedures or risk the cancellation of their lease or operating agreement.[4]

Cooperation is often defined as the association of persons for their mutual benefit. Again, this is a very meaningful concept in channel analysis. For example, there has been a significant increase in the use of point-of-purchase (P.O.P.) displays designed by the manufacturer for use in retail establishments. A leader in this field is the Pillsbury Company through its Creative Marketing Services International Di-

1. Frederick C. Klein, "Andy Granatelli, His STP Additive Labeled Superfluous, Tries to Get Firm Rolling Again," *The Wall Street Journal* (June 13, 1972), p. 32.
2. *Ibid.*
3. "The Oil Giants Fight the Independents," *Business Week* (May 13, 1972), p. 135.
4. *Ibid.*

vision. This group tailor-makes P.O.P.s for each retail chain, so that the stores obtain displays that are fully compatible with the image the retailer is trying to project. Dean F. Thomas, a Pillsbury vice president, stated, "Each retailer stacks up a certain amount of credit with his purchases and he gets a comparable amount of P.O.P. service. Before we did it this way, the waste was unbelievable."[5]

Another example of channel cooperation is Eastman Kodak's emphasis on helping retailers effectively merchandise Kodak cameras. Kodak's president, Gerald Zornow, has noted, "At the retail level in cameras, . . . we have to get into such matters as store design, sales strategies, management, and human relations. Over the long haul, you sell more by helping people get the results they want than you do by simply loading them up with products."[6]

Channel cooperation is becoming a recognized means by which all participants increase their sales and earnings. David R. Foster, president of Colgate-Palmolive Company, states, "We've adopted the practice of using someone else's technology and our own worldwide reach."[7] Colgate distributes many non-competing products through its extremely comprehensive marketing channel network. These include such products as Stretch 'n Seal, Handiwipes, Wilkinson razor blades and Alpen cereal.[8]

A final situation illustrating the importance of channel cooperation is the Ball Corporation's recent introduction of food containers that will compete directly with The Tupperware Corporation. The latter firm distributes its products primarily by consumer parties in which the product is shown and explained. Ball will use a more traditional marketing channel institution—the supermarket. *Business Week* commented, "Ball's marketing campaign relies heavily on its solid contacts with the nation's supermarket chains."[9]

The first selection by Bruce Mallen is a channel classic that clearly sets forth the fundamentals of conflict and cooperation in a marketing channel. It is followed by a stimulating discussion of the effect of conflict on channel efficiency. All too often in the past, the literature has assumed that channel conflict always creates a negative effect on overall channel efficiency. Rosenbloom points out that in certain situations, conflict can be the catalyst that creates a positive environment conducive to increasing the total efficiency of the channel.

The next article by William L. Shanklin presents a lucid analysis of

5. "A.P.O.P. Art Form that Turns Shoppers On," *Business Week* (January 8, 1972), p. 38.

6. "How Kodak Will Exploit Its New Instamatic," *Business Week* (March 18, 1972), p. 46.

7. "Why Colgate Sells Other People's Products," *Business Week* (April 20, 1974), p. 109.

8. *Ibid.*

9. "A Jar Maker Takes on Tupperware," *Business Week* (April 26, 1976), p. 108.

the conflicts involved in *dual distribution.* This refers to the practice of manufacturers selling their products through two or more competing channels of distribution. The article concludes by suggesting a number of techniques designed to reduce the inherent conflict found in dual distribution.

The final selection in this chapter presents a little-known but growing method for the resolution of channel conflict. Professors Weigand and Wasson examine the usage of arbitration to reduce channel conflict before it expands to the point of causing serious channel disruption.

4.1 CONFLICT AND COOPERATION IN MARKETING CHANNELS

Bruce Mallen

"But despite some of the conflict dynamics and forced cooperation, channel members usually have more harmonious and common interests than conflicting ones . . . They have a singular goal to reach, and here they are allies.

The purpose of this article is to advance the hypotheses that between member firms of a marketing channel there exists a dynamic field of conflicting and cooperating objectives; that if the conflicting objectives outweigh the cooperating ones, the effectiveness of the channel will be reduced and efficient distribution impeded; and that implementation of certain methods of cooperation will lead to increased channel efficiency.

DEFINITION OF CHANNEL

The concept of a marketing channel is slightly more involved than expected on initial study. One author in a recent paper[1] has identified "trading" channels, "non-trading" channels, "type" channels, "enterprise" channels, and "business-unit" channels. Another source[2] refers to channels as all the flows extending from the producer to the user. These include the flows of physical possession, ownership, promotion, negotiation, financing, risking, ordering, and payment.

The concept of channels to be used here involves only two of the

---

Reprinted by permission of the author and publisher. Bruce Mallen, "Conflict and Cooperation in Marketing Channels," *Progress in Marketing*, edited by L. George Smith (Chicago: American Marketing Association, 1964), pp. 65–85.

1. Ralph F. Breyer, "Some Observations on Structural Formation And The Growth of Marketing Channels," in *Theory In Marketing*, Reavis Cox, Wroe Alderson, Stanley J. Shapiro, Eds. (Homewood, Illinois: Richard D. Irwin, Inc., 1964), pp. 163–175.

2. Roland S. Vaile, E. T. Grether, and Reavis Cox, *Marketing In the American Economy* (New York: Ronald Press, 1952), pp. 121 and 124.

above-mentioned flows: ownership and negotiation. The first draws merchants, both wholesalers and retailers, into the channel definition, and the second draws in agent middlemen. Both, of course, include producers and consumers. This definition roughly corresponds to Professor Breyer's "trading channel," though the latter does not restrict (nor will this paper) the definition to actual flows, but to "flow-capacity." "A trading channel is formed when trading relations, making possible the passage of title and/or possession (usually both) of goods from the producer to the ultimate consumer, is consummated by the component trading concerns of the system."[3] In addition, this paper will deal with trading channels in the broadest manner and so will be concentrating on "type-trading" channels rather than "enterprise" or "business-unit" channels. This means that there will be little discussion of problems peculiar to integrated or semi-integrated channels, or peculiar to specific channels and firms.

CONFLICT

Palamountain isolated three forms of distributive conflict.[4]

1. Horizontal competition—this is competition between middlemen of the same type; for example, discount store *versus* discount store.
2. Intertype competition—this is competition between middlemen of different types in the same channel sector; for example, discount store *versus* department store.
3. Vertical conflict—this is conflict between channel members of different levels; for example, discount store *versus* manufacturer.

The first form, horizontal competition, is well covered in traditional economic analysis and is usually referred to simply as "competition." However, both intertype competition and vertical conflict, particularly the latter, are neglected in the usual micro-economic discussion.

The concepts of "intertype competition" and "distributive innovation" are closely related and require some discussion. Intertype competition will be divided into two categories; (a) "traditional intertype competition" and (b) "innovative intertype competition." The first category includes the usual price and promotional competition between two or more different types of channel members at the same channel level. The second category involves the action on the part of traditional channel members to prevent channel innovators from establishing themselves.

3. Breyer, *op. cit.*, p. 165.
4. Joseph C. Palamountain, *The Politics of Distribution* (Cambridge: Harvard University Press, 1955).

For example, in Canada there is a strong campaign, on the part of traditional department stores, to prevent the discount operation from taking a firm hold on the Canadian market.[5]

Distributive innovation will also be divided into two categories: a) "intrafirm innovative conflict" and b) "innovative intertype competition." The first category involves the action of channel member firms to prevent sweeping changes within their own companies. The second category "innovative intertype competition" is identical to the second category of intertype competition.

Thus the concepts of intertype competition and distributive innovation give rise to three forms of conflict, the second of which is a combination of both: (1) traditional intertype competition, (2) innovative intertype competition, and (3) intrafirm innovative conflict.

It is to this second form that this paper now turns before going on to vertical conflict.

INNOVATIVE INTERTYPE COMPETITION

Professor McCammon has identified several sources, both intrafirm and intertype, of innovative conflict in distribution, i.e., where there are barriers to change within the marketing structure.[6]

Traditional members of a channel have several motives for maintaining the channel status quo against outside innovators. The traditional members are particularly strong in this conflict where they can band together in some formal or informal manner—when there is strong reseller solidarity.

Both entrepreneurs and professional managers may resist outside innovators, not only for economic reasons, but because change "violates group norms, creates uncertainty, and results in a loss of status." The traditional channel members (the insiders) and their affiliated members (the strivers and complementors) are emotionally and financially committed to the dominant channel and are interested in perpetuating it against the minor irritations of the "transient" channel members and the major attacks of the "outside innovators."

Thus, against a background of horizontal and intertype channel conflict, this paper now moves to its area of major concern; vertical conflict and cooperation.

5. Isaiah A. Litvak and Bruce E. Mallen, *Marketing: Canada* (Toronto: McGraw-Hill of Canada, Limited, 1964), pp. 196–197.

6. This section is based on Bert C. McCammon, Jr., "Alternative Explanations of Institutional Change and Channel Evolution," in *Toward Scientific Marketing*, Stephen A. Greyser, ed. (Chicago: American Marketing Association, 1963), pp. 477–490.

VERTICAL CONFLICT—PRICE

The Exchange Act.   The act of exchange is composed of two elements: a sale and a purchase. It is to the advantage of the seller to obtain the highest return possible from such an exchange and the exact opposite is the desire of the buyer. This exchange act takes place between any kind of buyer and seller. If the consumer is the buyer, then that side of the act is termed shopping; if the manufacturer, purchasing; if the government, procurement; and if a retailer, buying. Thus, between each level in the channel an exchange will take place (except if a channel member is an agent rather than a merchant).

One must look to the process of the exchange act for the basic source of conflict between channel members. This is not to say the exchange act itself is a conflict. Indeed, the act or transaction is a sign that the element of price conflict has been resolved to the mutual satisfaction of both principals. Only along the road to this mutual satisfaction point or exchange price do the principals have opposing interests. This is no less true even if they work out the exchange price together, as in mass retailers' specification-buying programs.

It is quite natural for the selling member in an exchange to want a higher price than the buying member. The conflict is subdued through persuasion or force by one member over the other, or it is subdued by the fact that the exchange act or transaction does not take place, or finally, as mentioned above, it is eliminated if the act does take place.

Suppliers may emphasize the customer aspect of a reseller rather than the channel member aspect. As a customer the reseller is somebody to persuade, manipulate, or even fool. Conversely, under the marketing concept, the view of the reseller as a customer or channel member is identical. Under this philosophy he is somebody to aid, help, and serve. However, it is by no means certain that even a large minority of suppliers have accepted the marketing concept.

To view the reseller as simply the opposing principal in the act of exchange may be channel myopia, but this view exists. On the other hand, failure to recognize this basic opposing interest is also a conceptual fault.

When the opposite principals in an exchange act are of unequal strength, the stronger is very likely to force or persuade the weaker to adhere to the former's desires. However, when they are of equal strength, the basic conflict cannot so easily be resolved. Hence, the growth of big retailers who can match the power of big producers has possibly led to greater open conflict between channel members, not only with regard to exchange, but also to other conflict sources.

There are other sources of conflict within the pricing area outside of the basic one discussed above.

A supplier may force a product onto its resellers, who dare not oppose, but who retaliate in other ways, such as using it as a loss leader. Large manufacturers may try to dictate the resale price of their merchandise; this may be less or more than the price at which resellers wish to sell it. Occasionally, a local market may be more competitive for a reseller than is true nationally. The manufacturer may not recognize the difference in competition and refuse to help this channel member.

Resellers complain of manufacturers' special price concessions to competitors and rebel at the attempt of manufacturers to control resale prices. Manufacturers complain of resellers' deceptive and misleading price advertising, nonadherence to resale price suggestions, bootlegging to unauthorized outlets, seeking special price concessions by unfair methods, and misrepresenting offers by competitive suppliers.

Other points of price conflict are the paper-work aspects of pricing. Resellers complain of delays in price change notices and complicated price sheets.

Price Theory.   If one looks upon a channel as a series of markets or as the vertical exchange mechanism between buyers and sellers, one can adapt several theories and concepts to the channel situation which can aid marketing theory in this important area of channel conflict.[7] For example, the exchange mechanism between a manufacturer as a seller and a wholesaler as a buyer is one market. A second market is the exchange mechanism between the wholesaler as a seller and the retailer as a buyer. Finally, the exchange mechanism between the retailer as a seller and the consumer as a buyer is a third market. Thus, a manufacturer-wholesaler-retailer-consumer channel can be looked upon as a series of three markets.

The type of market can be defined according to its degree of competitiveness, which depends to a great extent on the number of buyers and sellers in a market. Some possible combinations are shown in Table 1.

A discussion of monopoly in a channel context may show the value of integrating economic theory with channel concepts.

If one channel member is a monopolist and the others pure competitors, the consumer pays a price equivalent to that of an integrated monopolist; and the monopolist member reaps all the channel's pure profits; that is, the sum of the pure profits of all channel members. Pure profits are, of course, the economist's concept of those profits over and above the minimum return on investment required to keep a firm in business.

7. Bruce Mallen, "Introducing The Marketing Channel to Price Theory," *Journal of Marketing*, July, 1964, pp. 29–33.

TABLE 1   Classification of Economic Markets

Suppliers (sellers)	Middlemen (buyers)	Market situation
Pure competitor	Pure competitor	Pure competition
Oligopolist	Pure competitor	Oligopoly
Monopolist	Pure competitor	Monopoly
Pure competitor	Oligopsonist	Oligoposony
Pure competitor	Monopsonist	Monopsony
Oligopoly	Oligoposonist	Bilateral oligopoly
Monopolist	Monopsonist	Bilateral monopoly
Monopolist	Monopolist	Successive monopoly

Assume that the retailer is the monopolist and the others (wholesalers and manufacturers) are pure competitors, as for example, a single department store in an isolated town. Total costs to the retailer are composed of the total cost of the other levels plus his own costs. No pure profits of the other levels are included in his costs, as they make none by definition (they are pure competitors).

The retailer would be in the same buying price position, so far as the lack of suppliers' profits are concerned, as would the vertically integrated firm. Thus, he charges the same price as the integrated monopolist and makes the same profits.

If the manufacturer were the monopolist and the other channel members pure competitors, he would calculate the maximizing profits for the channel and then charge the wholesaler his cost plus the total channel's pure profits—all of which would go to him since the others are pure competitors. The wholesaler would take this price, add it on to his own costs, and the result would be the price to retailers. Then the retailers would do likewise for the consumer price.

Thus, the prices to the wholesaler and to the retailer are higher than in the first case (retailer monopoly), since the channel's pure profits are added on before the retail level. The price to the consumer is the same as in the first case. It is of no concern to the consumer if the pure profit elements in his price are added on by the manufacturer, wholesaler, or retailer.

Thus, under integrated monopoly, manufacturer monopoly, wholesaler monopoly, or retailer monopoly, the consumer price is the same; but the prices within the channel are the lowest with the retailer monopoly and the highest with the manufacturer monopoly. Of course, the non-monopolistic channel members' pure profits are not affected by this intrachannel price variation, as they have no such profits in any case.

VERTICAL CONFLICT—NON PRICE

Channel conflict not only finds its source in the exchange act and pricing, but it permeates all areas of marketing. Thus, a manufacturer may wish to promote a product in one manner or to a certain degree while his resellers oppose this. Another manufacturer may wish to get information from his resellers on a certain aspect relating to his product, but his resellers may refuse to provide this information. A producer may want to distribute his product extensively, but his resellers may demand exclusives.

There is also conflict because of the tendency for both manufacturers and retailers to want the elimination of the wholesaler.

One very basic source of channel conflict is the possible difference in the primary business philosophy of channel members. Writing in the *Harvard Business Review*, Wittreich says:

> In essence, then, the key to understanding management's problem of crossed purpose is the recognition that the fundamental (philosophy) in life of the high-level corporate manager and the typical (small) retail dealer in the distribution system are quite different. The former's (philosophy) can be characterized as being essentially dynamic in nature, continuously evolving and emerging; the latter, which are in sharp contrast, can be characterized as being essentially static in nature, reaching a point and leveling off into a continuously satisfying plateau.[8]

While the big members of the channel may want growth, the small retail members may be satisfied with stability and a "good living."

ANARCHY[9]

The channel can adjust to its conflicting-cooperating environment in three distinct ways. *First*, it can have a leader (one of the channel members) who "forces" members to cooperate; this in an autocratic relationship. *Second*, it can have a leader who "helps" members to cooperate, creating a democratic relationship. *Finally*, it can do nothing, and so have an anarchistic relationship. Lewis B. Sappington and C. G. Browne, writing on the problem of internal company organizations, state:

> The first classification may be called "autocracy." In this approach to the group the leader determines the policy and dictates or assigns the work tasks. There are no group deliberations, no group decisions . . .

8. Warren J. Wittreich, "Misunderstanding the Retailer," *Harvard Business Review*, May–June, 1962, p. 149.

9. The term "anarchy" as used in this paper connotes "no leadership" and nothing more.

The second classification may be called "democracy." In this approach the leader allows all policies to be decided by the group with his participation. The group members work with each other as they wish. The group determines the division and assignment of tasks . . .

The third classification may be called "anarchy." In anarchy there is complete freedom of the group or the individual regarding policies or task assignments, without leader participation.[10]

Advanced in this paper is the hypothesis that if anarchy exists, there is a great chance of the conflicting dynamics destroying the channel. If autocracy exists, there is less chance of this happening. However, the latter method creates a state of cooperation based on power and control. This controlled cooperation is really subdued conflict and makes for a more unstable equilibrium than does voluntary democratic cooperation.

CONTROLLED COOPERATION

The usual pattern in the establishment of channel relationships is that there is a leader, an initiator who puts structure into this relationship and who holds it together. This leader controls, whether through command or cooperation, i.e., through an autocratic or a democratic system.

Too often it is automatically assumed that the manufacturer or producer will be the channel leader and that the middlemen will be the channel followers. This has not always been so, nor will it necessarily be so in the future. The growth of mass retailers is increasingly challenging the manufacturer for channel leadership, as the manufacturer challenged the wholesaler in the early part of this century.

The following historical discussion will concentrate on the three-ring struggle between manufacturer, wholesaler, and retailer rather than on the changing patterns of distribution within a channel sector, i.e., between service wholesaler and agent middleman or discount and department store. This will lay the necessary background for a discussion of the present-day manufacturer-dominated *versus* retailer-dominated struggle.

EARLY HISTORY

The simple distribution system of Colonial days gave way to a more complex one. Among the forces of change were the growth of population, the long distances involved, the increasing complexity of new products, the increase of wealth, and the increase of consumption.

10. Lewis B. Sappington and C. G. Browne, "The Skills of Creative Leadership," in *Managerial Marketing*, rev. ed., William Lazer and Eugene J. Kelley, eds. (Homewood, Ill.: Richard D. Irwin, Inc., 1962), p. 350.

The United States was ready for specialists to provide a growing and widely dispersed populace with the many new goods and services required. The more primitive methods of public markets and barter could not efficiently handle the situation. This type of system required short distances, few products, and a small population, to operate properly.

19TH CENTURY HISTORY

In the same period that this older system was dissolving the retailer was still a very small merchant who, especially in the West, lived in relative isolation from his supply sources. Aside from being small, he further diminished his power position by spreading himself thin over many merchandise lines. The retailer certainly was no specialist but was as general as a general store can be. His opposite channel member, the manufacturer, was also a small businessman, too concerned with production and financial problems to fuss with marketing.

Obviously, both these channel members were in no position to assume leadership. However, somebody had to perform all the various marketing functions between production and retailing if the economy was to function. The wholesaler filled this vacuum and became the channel leader of the 19th century.

The wholesaler became the selling force of the manufacturer and the latter's link to the widely scattered retailers over the nation. He became the retailer's life line to these distant domestic and even more important foreign sources of supply.

These wholesalers carried any type of product from any manufacturer and sold any type of product to the general retailers. They can be described as general merchandise wholesalers. They were concentrated at those transportation points in the country which gave them access to both the interior and its retailers, and the exterior and its foreign suppliers.

EARLY 20TH CENTURY

The end of the century saw the wholesaler's power on the decline. The manufacturer had grown larger and more financially secure with the shift from a foreign-oriented economy to a domestic-oriented one. He could now finance his marketing in a manner impossible to him in early times. His thoughts shifted to some extent from production problems to marketing problems.

Prodding the manufacturer on was the increased rivalry of his other domestic competitors. The increased investment in captal and inventory made it necessary that he maintain volume. He tended to locate himself in the larger market areas, and thus, did not have great distances to travel to see his retail customers. In addition, he started to produce various products; and because of his new multi-product production, he could reach—even more efficiently—these already more accessible markets.

The advent of the automobile and highways almost clinched the manufacturer's bid for power. For now he could reach a much vaster market (and they could reach him) and reap the benefits of economics of scale.

The branding of his products projected him to the channel leadership. No longer did he have as great a need for a specialist in reaching widely dispersed customers, nor did he need them to the same extent for their contacts. The market knew where the product came from. The age of wholesaler dominance declined. That of manufacturer dominance emerged.

Is it still here? What is its future? How strong is the challenge by retailers? Is one "better" than the other? These are the questions of the next section.

DISAGREEMENT AMONG SCHOLARS

No topic seems to generate so much heat and bias in marketing as the question of who should be the channel leader, and more strangely, who is the channel leader. Depending on where the author sits, he can give numerous reasons why his particular choice should take the channel initiative.

Authors of sales management and general marketing books say the manufacturer is and should be the chief institution in the channel. Retailing authors feel the same way about retailers, and wholesaling authors (as few as there are), though not blinded to the fact that wholesaling is not "captain," still imply that they should be, and talk about the coming resurrection of wholesalers. Yet a final and compromising view is put forth by those who believe that a balance of power, rather than a general and prolonged dominance of any channel member, is best.

> The truth is that an immediate reaction would set in against any temporary dominance by a channel member. In that sense, there is a constant tendency toward the equilibrium of market forces. The present view is that public interest is served by a balance of power rather than by a general and prolonged predominance of any one level in marketing channels.[11]

John Kenneth Galbraith's concept of countervailing also holds to this last view.

11. Wroe Alderson, "Factors Governing the Development of Marketing Channels," in *Marketing Channels for Manufactured Products*, Richard M. Clewett, ed. (Homewood, Richard D. Irwin, Inc., 1954), p. 30.

For the retailer:

In the opinion of the writer, "retailer-dominated marketing" has yielded, and will continue to yield in the future greater net benefits to consumers than "manufacturer-dominated marketing," as the central-buying mass distributor continues to play a role of ever-increasing importance in the marketing of goods in our economy. . . .

. . . In the years to come, as more and more large-scale multiple-unit retailers follow the central buying patterns set by Sears and Penneys, as leaders in their respective fields (hard lines and soft goods), ever-greater benefits should flow to consumers in the way of more goods better adjusted to their demands, at lower prices.[12]

. . . In a long run buyer's market, such as we probably face in this country, the retailers have the inherent advantage of economy in distribution and will, therefore, become increasingly important.[13]

The retailer cannot be the selling agent of the manufacturer because he holds a higher commission; he is the purchasing agent for the public.[14]

For the wholesaler:

The wholesaling sector is, first of all, the most significant part of the entire marketing organization.[15]

. . . The orthodox wholesaler and affiliated types have had a resurgence to previous 1929 levels of sales importance.[16]

. . . Wholesalers have since made a comeback.[17] This revival of wholesaling has resulted from infusion of new management blood and the adoption of new techniques.[18]

For the manufacturer:

. . . The final decision in channel selection rests with the seller, manufacturer and will continue to rest with him as long as he has the legal right to choose to sell to some potential customers and refuse to sell to others.[19]

These channel decisions are primarily problems for the manufacturer. They rarely arise for general wholesalers. . . .[20]

12. Arnold Corbin, *Central Buying in Relation to the Merchandising of Multiple Retail Units* (New York, unpublished doctoral dissertation at New York University, 1954), pp. 708–709.

13. David Craig and Werner Gabler, "The Competitive Struggle for Market Control," in *Readings in Marketing*, Howard J. Westing, ed. (New York, Prentice-Hall, 1953), p. 46.

14. Lew Hahn, *Stores, Merchants and Customers* (New York, Fairchild Publications, 1952), p. 12.

15. David A. Revzan, *Wholesaling in Marketing Organization* (New York: John Wiley & Sons, Inc., 1961), p. 606.

16. *Ibid.*, p. 202.

17. E. Jerome McCarthy, *Basic Marketing* (Homewood, Illinois: Richard D. Irwin, Inc., 1960), p. 419.

18. *Ibid.*, p. 420.

19. Eli P. Cox, *Federal Quantity Discount Limitations and Its Possible Effects on Distribution Channel Dynamics* (unpublished doctoral dissertation, University of Texas, 1956), p. 12.

20. Milton Brown, Wilbur B. England, John B. Matthews Jr., *Problems in Marketing*, 3rd ed. (New York: McGraw-Hill Book Co., Inc., 1961), p. 239.

Of all the historical tendencies in the field of marketing, no other is so distinctly apparent as the tendency for the manufacturer to assume greater control over the distribution of his product. . . .[21]

. . . Marketing policies at other levels can be viewed as extensions of policies established by marketing managers in manufacturing firms; and, furthermore, . . . the nature and function can adequately be surveyed by looking at the relationship to manufacturers.[22]

PRO-MANUFACTURE

The argument for manufacturer leadership is production oriented. It claims that they must assure themselves of increasing volume. This is needed to derive the benefits of production scale economies, to spread their overhead over many units, to meet increasingly stiff competition, and to justify the investment risk they, not the retailers, are taking. Since retailers will not do this job for them properly, the manufacturer must control the channel.

Another major argumentative point for manufacturer dominance is that neither the public nor retailers can create new products even under a market-oriented system. The most the public can do is to select and choose among those that manufacturers have developed. They cannot select products that they cannot conceive. This argument would say that it is of no use to ask consumers and retailers what they want because they cannot articulate abstract needs into tangible goods; indeed, the need can be created by the goods rather than vice-versa.

This argument may hold well when applied to consumers, but a study of the specification-buying programs of the mass retailers will show that the latter can indeed create new products and need not be relegated to simply selecting among alternatives.

PRO-RETAILER

This writer sees the mass retailer as the natural leader of the channel for consumer goods under the marketing concept. The retailer stands closest to the consumer; he feels the pulse of consumer wants and needs day in and day out. The retailer can easily undertake consumer research right on his own premises and can best interpret what is wanted, how much is wanted, and when it is wanted.

An equilibrium in the channel conflict may come about when small retailers join forces with big manufacturers in a manufacturer leader-

21. Maynard D. Phelps and Howard J. Westing, *Marketing Management*, rev. ed. (Homewood, Ill.: Richard D. Irwin, Inc., 1960), p. 11.
22. Kenneth Davis, *Marketing Management* (New York: The Ronald Press Co., 1961), p. 131.

ship channel to compete with a small manufacturer-big retailer leadership channel.

PRO-WHOLESALER

It would seem that the wholesaler has a choice in this domination problem as well. Unlike the manufacturer and retailer though, his method is not mainly through a power struggle. This problem is almost settled for him once he chooses the type of wholesaling business he wishes to enter. A manufacturers' agent and purchasing agent are manufacturer-dominated, a sales agent dominates the manufacturer. A resident buyer and voluntary group wholesaler are retail-dominated.

METHODS OF MANUFACTURER DOMINATION

How does a channel leader dominate his fellow members? What are his tools in this channel power struggle? A manufacturer has many domination weapons at his disposal. His arsenal can be divided into promotional, legal, negative, suggestive, and ironically, voluntary cooperative compartments.

Promotional. Probably the major method that the manufacturer has used is the building of a consumer franchise through advertising, sales promotion, and packaging of his branded products. When he has developed some degree of consumer loyalty, the other channel members must bow to his leadership. The more successful this identification through the promotion process, the more assured is the manufacturer of his leadership.

Legal. The legal weapon has also been a poignant force for the manufacturer. It can take many forms, such as, where permissible, resale price maintenance. Other contractual methods are franchises, where the channel members may become mere shells of legal entities. Through this weapon the automobile manufacturers have achieved an almost absolute dominance over their dealers.

Even more absolute is resort to legal ownership of channel members, called forward vertical integration. Vertical integration is the ultimate in manufacturer dominance of the channel. Another legal weapon is the use of consignment sales. Under this method the channel members must by law sell the goods as designated by the owner (manufacturer). Consignment selling is in a sense vertical integration; it is keeping legal ownership of the goods until they reach the consumer, rather than keeping legal ownership of the institutions which are involved in the process.

Negative Methods.   Among the "negative" methods of dominance are refusal to sell to possibly uncooperative retailers or refusal to concentrate a large percentage of one's volume with any one customer.

A spreading of sales makes for a concentrating of manufacturer power, while a concentrating of sales may make for a thinning of manufacturer power. Of course, if a manufacturer is one of the few resources available and if there are many available retailers, then a concentrating of sales will also make for a concentrating of power.

The avoidance and refusal tactics, of course, eliminate the possibility of opposing dominating institutions.

Suggestives.   A rather weak group of dominating weapons are the "suggestives." Thus, a manufacturer can issue price sheets and discounts, preticket and premark resale prices on goods, recommend, suggest, and advertise resale prices.

These methods are not powerful unless supplemented by promotional, legal, and/or negative weapons. It is common for these methods to boomerang. Thus a manufacturer pretickets or advertises resale prices, and a retailer cuts this price, pointing with pride to the manufacturer's suggested retail price.

Voluntary Cooperative Devices.   There is one more group of dominating weapons, and these are really all the voluntary cooperating weapons to be mentioned later. The promise to provide these, or to withdraw them, can have a "whip and carrot" effect on the channel members.

RETAILERS' DOMINATING WEAPONS

Retailers also have numerous domination weapons at their disposal. As with manufacturers, their strongest weapon is the building of a consumer franchise through advertising, sales promotion, and branding. The growth of private brands is the growth of retail dominance.

Attempts at concentrating a retailer's purchasing power are a further group of weapons and are analogous to a manufacturer's attempts to disperse his volume. The more a retailer can concentrate his purchasing, the more dominating he can become; the more he spreads his purchasing, the more dominated he becomes. Again, if the resource is one of only a few, this generalization reverses itself.

Such legal contracts as specification buying, vertical integration (of the threat of it), and entry into manufacturing can also be effective. Even semiproduction, such as the packaging of goods received in bulk by the supermarket can be a weapon of dominance.

Retailers can dilute the dominance of manufacturers by patronizing those with excess capacity and those who are "hungry" for the extra volume. There is also the subtlety, which retailers may recognize, that a strong manufacturer may concede to their wishes just to avoid an open conflict with a customer.

VOLUNTARY COOPERATION

But despite some of the conflict dynamics and forced cooperation, channel members usually have more harmonious and common interests than conflicting ones. A team effort to market a producer's product will probably help all involved. All members have a common interest in selling the product; only in the division of total channel profits are they in conflict. They have a singular goal to reach, and here they are allies. If any one of them fails in the team effort, this weak link in the chain can destroy them all. As such, all members are concerned with one another's welfare (unless a member can be easily replaced).

ORGANIZATIONAL EXTENSION CONCEPT

This emphasis on the cooperating, rather than the conflicting objectives of channel members, has led to the concept of the channel as simply an extension of one's own internal organization. Conflict in such a system is to be expected even as it is to be expected within an organization. However, it is the common or "macro-objective" that is the center of concentration. Members are to sacrifice their selfish "micro-objectives" to this cause. By increasing the profit pie they will all be better off than squabbling over pieces of a smaller one. The goal is to minimize conflict and maximize cooperation. This view has been expounded in various articles by Peter Drucker, Ralph Alexander, and Valentine Ridgeway.

> Together, the manufacturer with his suppliers and/or dealers comprise a system in which the manufacturer may be designated the primary organization and the dealers and suppliers designated as secondary organizations. This system is in competition with similar systems in the economy; and in order for the system to operate effectively as an integrated whole, there must be some administration of the system as a whole, not merely administration of the separate organizations within that system.[23]

Peter Drucker[24] has pleaded against the conceptual blindness that the idea of the legal entity generates. A legal entity is not a marketing entity. Since often half of the cost to the consumer is added on after the

23. Valentine F. Ridgeway, "Administration of Manufacturer-Dealer Systems," in *Managerial Marketing*, rev. ed., William Lazer and Eugene J. Kelley, eds. (Homewood, Ill.: Richard D. Irwin, Inc., 1962), p. 480.

24. Peter Drucker, "The Economy's Dark Continent," *Fortune*, April 1962, pp. 103 ff.

product leaves the producer, the latter should think of his channel members as part of his firm. General Motors is an example of an organization which does this.

> Both businessmen and students of marketing often define too narrowly the problem of marketing channels. Many of them tend to define the term channels of distribution as a complex of relationships between the firm on the one hand, and marketing establishments exterior to the firm by which the products of the firm are moved to market, on the other . . . . . A much broader more constructive concept embraces the relationships with external agents or units as part of the marketing organization of the company. From this viewpoint, the complex of external relationships may be regarded as merely an extension of the marketing organization of the firm. When we look at the problem in this way, we are much less likely to lose sight of the interdependence of the two structures and more likely to be constantly aware that they are closely related parts of the marketing machine. The fact that the internal organization structure is linked together by a system of employment contracts, while the external one is set up and maintained by a series of transactions, contracts of purchase and sale, tends to obscure their common purpose and close relationship.[25]

COOPERATION METHODS

But how does a supplier project its organization into the channel? How does it make organization and channel into one? It accomplishes this by doing many things for its resellers that it does for its own organization. It sells, advertises, trains, plans, and promotes for these firms. A brief elaboration of these methods follows.

Missionary salesmen aid the sales of channel members, as well as bolster the whole system's level of activity and selling effort. Training of resellers' salesmen and executives is an effective weapon of cooperation. The channels operate more efficiently when all are educated in the promotional techniques and uses of the products involved.

Involvement in the planning functions of its channel members could be another poignant weapon of the supplier. Helping resellers to set quotas for their customers, studying the market potential for them, forecasting a member's sales volume, inventory planning and protection, etc., are all aspects of this latter method.

Aid in promotion through the provision of advertising materials (mats, displays, commercials, literature, direct-mail pieces), ideas, funds (cooperative advertising), sales contests, store layout designs, push money (PM's or spiffs), is another form of cooperation.

The big supplier can act as management consultant to the members, dispensing advice in all areas of their business, including accounting,

25. Ralph S. Alexander, James S. Cross, Ross M. Cunningham, *Industrial Marketing*, rev. ed. (Homewood, Ill.: Richard D. Irwin, Inc., 1961), p. 266.

personnel, planning, control, finance, buying, paper systems or office procedure, and site selection. Aid in financing may include extended credit terms, consignment selling, and loans.

By no means do these methods of coordination take a one-way route. All members of the channel, including supplier and reseller, see their own organizations meshing with the others, and so provide coordinating weapons in accordance with their ability. Thus, the manufacturer would undertake a marketing research project for his channel, and also expect his resellers to keep records and vital information for the manufacturer's use. A supplier may also expect his channel members to service the product after the sale.

A useful device for fostering cooperation is a channel advisory council composed of the supplier and his resellers.

Finally, a manufacturer or reseller can avoid associations with potentially uncooperative channel members. Thus, a price-conservative manufacturer may avoid linking to a price-cutting retailer.

E. B. Weiss has developed an impressive, though admittedly incomplete list of cooperation methods (Table 2). Paradoxically, many of these instruments of cooperation are also weapons of control (forced cooperation) to be used by both middlemen and manufacturers. However, this is not so strange if one keeps in mind that control is subdued conflict and a form of cooperation—even though perhaps involuntary cooperation.

EXTENSION CONCEPT IS THE MARKETING CONCEPT

The philosophy of cooperation is described in the following quote:

> The essence of the marketing concept is of course customer orientation at all levels of distribution. It is particularly important that customer orientation motivate all relations between a manufacturer and his customer— both immediate and ultimate. It must permeate his entire channels-of-distribution policy.[26]

This quote synthesizes the extension-of-the-organization system concept of channels with the marketing concept. Indeed, it shows that the former is, in essence, "the" marketing concept applied to the channel area in marketing. To continue:

> The characteristics of the highly competitive markets of today naturally put a distinct premium on harmonious manufacturer-distributor relationships. Their very mutuality of interest demands that the manufacturer base his distribution program not only on what he would like from distributors, but perhaps more importantly, on what they would like from him. In order to get the cooperation of the best distributors, and thus maximum

26. Hector Lazo and Arnold Corbin, *Management in Marketing* (New York: McGraw Hill Book Company, Inc., 1961), p. 379.

TABLE 2   Methods of Cooperation as Listed[27]

1. Cooperative advertising allowances
2. Payments for interior displays including shelf-extenders, dump displays, "A" locations, aisle displays, etc.
3. P.M.'s for salespeople
4. Contests for buyers, salespeople, etc.
5. Allowances for a variety of warehousing functions
6. Payments for window display space, plus installation costs
7. Detail men who check inventory, put up stock, set up complete promotions, etc.
8. Demonstrators
9. On certain canned food, a "swell" allowance
10. Label allowance
11. Coupon handling allowance
12. Free goods
13. Guaranteed sales
14. In-store and window display material
15. Local research work
16. Mail-in premium offers to consumer
17. Preticketing
18. Automatic reorder systems
19. Delivery costs to individual stores of large retailers
20. Studies of innumerable types, such as studies of merchandise management accounting
21. Payments for mailings to store lists
22. Liberal return privileges
23. Contributions to favorite charities of store personnel
24. Contributions to special store anniversaries
25. Prizes, etc., to store buyers when visiting showrooms—plus entertainment, of course
26. Training retail salespeople
27. Payments for store fixtures
28. Payments for new store costs, for more improvements, including painting
29. An infinite variety of promotion allowances
30. Special payments for exclusive franchises
31. Pavements of part of salary of retail salespeople
32. Deals of innumerable types
33. Time spent on actual selling floor by manufacturer, salesmen
34. Inventory price adjustments
35. Store name mention in manufacturer's advertising

exposure for his line among the various market segments, he must adjust his policies to serve their best interest and, thereby, his own. In other words, he must put the principles of the marketing concept to work for him. By so doing, he will inspire in his customers a feeling of mutual interest and trust and will help convince them that they are essential members of his marketing team.[28]

SUMMARY

Figure 1 summarizes this whole paper. Each person within each department will cooperate, control, and conflict with each other (notice

27. Edward B. Weiss, "How Much of a Retailer Is the Manufacturer," in *Advertising Age*, July 21, 1958, p. 68.
28. Lazo and Corbin, *loc. cit.*

arrows). Together they form a department (notice department box contains person boxes) which will be best off when cooperating (or cooperation through control) forces weigh heavier than conflicting forces. Now each department cooperates, controls, and conflicts with each other. Departments together also form a higher level organization—the firm (manufacturer, wholesaler, and retailer). Again, the firm will be better off if department cooperation is maximized and conflict minimized. Finally, firms standing vertically to each other cooperate, control, and conflict. Together they form a distribution channel that will be best off under conditions of optimum cooperation leading to consumer and profit satisfaction.

CONCLUSIONS AND HYPOTHESES

1. Channel relationships are set against a background of cooperation and conflict; horizontal, intertype, and vertical.

2. An autocratic relationship exists when one channel member controls conflict and forces the others to cooperate. A democratic relationship exists when all members agree to cooperate without a power play. An anarchistic relationship exists when there is open conflict, with no member able to impose his will on the others. This last form could destroy or seriously reduce the effectiveness of the channel.

3. The process of the exchange act where one member is a seller and the other is a buyer is the basic source of channel conflict. Economic theory can aid in comprehending this phenomenon. There are, however, many other areas of conflict, such as differences in business philosophy or primary objectives.

4. Reasons for cooperation, however, usually outweigh reasons for conflict. This had led to the concept of the channel as an extension of a firm's organization.

5. This concept drops the facade of "legal entity" and treats channel members as one great organization with the leader providing each with various forms of assistance. These are called cooperating weapons.

6. It is argued that this concept is actually the marketing concept adapted to a channel situation.

7. In an autocratic or democratic channel relationship, there must be a leader. This leadership has shifted and is shifting between the various channel levels.

8. The wholesaler was the leader in the last century, the manufacturer now, and it appears that the mass retailer is next in line.

9. There is much disagreement on the above point, however,

FIG. 1 Organization

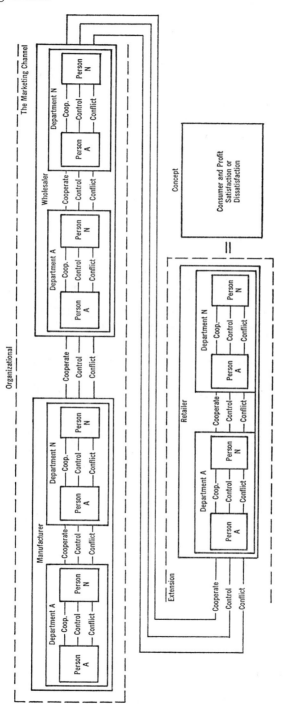

especially on who should be the leader. Various authors have differing arguments to advance for their choice.

10. In the opinion of this writer, the mass retailer appears to be best adapted for leadership under the marketing concept.

11. As there are weapons of cooperation, so are there weapons of domination. Indeed the former paradoxically are one group of the latter. The other groups are promotional, legal, negative, and suggestive methods. Both manufacturers and retailers have at their disposal these dominating weapons.

12. *For maximization of channel profits and consumer satisfaction, the channel must act as a unit.*

QUESTIONS FOR DISCUSSION

1. (a) What precisely does the author mean when he refers to channel conflict?
   (b) What is vertical conflict?
   (c) Why does it take place?
   (d) What can be done to lessen the intensity of vertical conflict?
2. (a) What does "controlled cooperation" signify?
   (b) In what ways can channel members effectively cooperate with each other?

3. Present an argument for the channel member that you believe should be the channel leader or "captain."

4. Why does the author believe that retailers should be the channel leaders?

5. Discuss at least five specific areas of potential conflict between the manufacturer and the channel members. Which of these five problems do you believe is the most serious? Defend your answer.

4.2 CONFLICT AND CHANNEL EFFICIENCY: SOME CONCEPTUAL MODELS FOR THE DECISION MAKER

Bert Rosenbloom

". . . The 'diseases' of the marketing channel are very real and, if anything, have been neglected too long."

Walter Wentz recently wrote that the marketing literature seems to be characterized by too many cures looking around for diseases.[1] The marketing manager charged with making decisions has little time for what appears to him to be esoteric theory in which he can find little or no relevance to his problems. Most of the literature on the marketing channel, however, cannot be accused of this syndrome. Rather it seems that the "diseases" of the marketing channel are very real, and, if anything, have been neglected too long.[2]

One particular aspect of the marketing channel which has come under increasing scrutiny in the last several years is conflict.[3] Recent examinations of conflict in the marketing channel take a broad perspective in viewing the marketing channel as a social system subject to the same behavioral processes characteristic of all social systems, with conflict as one such process.[4] Hence, the door has been opened to examine mar-

Reprinted by permission from the author and publisher. Bert Rosenbloom, "Conflict and Channel Efficiency: Some Conceptual Models for the Decision Maker," *Journal of Marketing* (July 1973), pp. 26–30.

1. Walter B. Wentz, *Marketing Research: Management and Methods* (New York: Harper and Row Publishers, 1972), p. xi.

2. Bert C. McCammon, Jr. and Robert W. Little, "Marketing Channels: Analytical Systems and Approaches," in *Science in Marketing*, George Swartz, ed. (New York: John Wiley & Sons, Inc., 1965), p. 322.

3. See, for example, Louis W. Stern and Ronald H. Gorman, "Conflict in Distribution Channels: An Exploration," *Distribution Channels: Behavioral Dimensions*, Louis W. Stern, ed. (Boston: Houghton-Mifflin Company 1969), pp. 156–175; Larry J. Rosenberg and Louis W. Stern, "Toward the Analysis of Conflict in Distribution Channels: A Descriptive Model," *Journal of Marketing Research*, Vol. 8 (November 1971), pp. 437–442.

4. For a discussion of the social systems perspective, see Louis W. Stern and Jay W. Brown, "Distribution Channels: A Social Systems Approach," in *Distribution Channels: Behavioral Dimensions*, Louis W. Stern, ed., (Boston: Houghton-Mifflin

keting channel conflict using many of the concepts and tools developed in the behavioral sciences. To the marketing manager this social systems perspective is both a blessing and a curse. On the one hand, the "tool kit" which is potentially available to aid decision making has been significantly augmented and enriched. On the other hand, the numerous concepts, terminologies, and approaches of the various treatments can create confusion leading to avoidance. A partial solution to this dilemma suggests the need for more straightforward conceptual structures or models which the manager can use as a skeleton or framework. Such models might help him gain the benefits of an enriched bag of behavioral tools and at the same time provide direction and insight for the possible use of some of these tools in dealing with a process such as conflict as it occurs in the marketing channel.

The purpose of this article is to develop several such conceptual models which can help the marketing manager gain further insight into how he might use behavioral concepts of conflict as input for channel decision making. More specifically, the following discussion will prevent several simple models which illustrate the possible effects of conflict on the efficiency with which a firm's channel decisions are executed.

CONFLICT AND CHANNEL EFFICIENCY

Various relationships and effects of conflict in the marketing channel have been discussed recently in the marketing literature. For example, Dixon and Layton argue that conflict can result in a threat to the survival of the channel.[5] Stern avers that conflict can be detrimental to the effective performance of the marketing channel.[6] Assael discusses possible positive results of conflict on the channel.[7]

What is lacking, however, *from the standpoint of the decision maker* in any given *unit of the channel*, is a convenient and uniform criterion against which to appraise the possible effects of conflict on channel de-

Company, 1969), pp. 6–19. For some earlier examples of channel literature which take a social systems viewpoint, see Wroe Alderson, *Dynamic Marketing Behavior* (Homewood, Ill.: Richard D. Irwin, Inc., 1965), pp. 239–258; and Joseph C. Palamountain, *The Politics of Distribution* (Cambridge, Mass.: Harvard University Press, 1955).

5. Donald F. Dixon and Rodger A. Layton, "Initiating Change in Channel Systems," *New Essays in Marketing Theory*, George Fisk, ed., (Boston: Allyn and Bacon, Inc., 1971), p. 315.

6. Louis W. Stern, "The Interorganization Management of Distribution Channels: Prerequisites and Prescriptions," in *New Essays in Marketing Theory*, George Fisk, ed. (Boston: Allyn and Bacon, Inc. 1971), p. 314.

7. Henry Assael, "Construction Role of Interorganization Conflict," *Administrative Science Quarterly*, Vol. 14 (December 1969), pp. 573–575.

cisions he makes. Without such a criterion, many of the ideas concerning the various effects of conflict on the marketing channel may have little meaning for him in that he may not see the relevance of such effects for his particular unit in the channel.[8] In other words, what is especially significant to the decision maker in any firm operating as a member of the channel is a criterion that relates possible effects of channel conflict as they affect *his* decisions in *his* particular firm in the channel.

It is suggested here that such a criterion might be called *channel efficiency*. For the purposes of this discussion, the firm means simply the degree to which the total investment in the various inputs necessary to effect a given channel decision can be optimized in terms of outputs. The greater the degree of optimization of inputs in carrying out a particular marketing channel decision, the higher the efficiency and vice versa. The inputs can include anything necessary to achieve the goal explicit or implicit in the firm's channel decision. Thus, for example, a particular wholesaler might make a decision to attempt to get, say, 60% of his retailers to carry a new line of his merchandise. Suppose that, in attempting to achieve this goal, the wholesaler runs into heavy resistance from his retailers, most of whom feel that they are already carrying too much inventory from this wholesaler. The resulting conflict could cause the wholesaler to direct his salesmen to spend an extraordinary amount of time and effort to convince the reluctant retailers to carry the new line. In this example, the extra input used to execute the decision would be salesmen time and effort, which could also be translated into dollars and cents. Had this wholesaler been able to gain the acceptance of his new line with less salesmen effort (and without substantially increasing other inputs) he could have achieved his decision goal with less total input; and a greater degree of channel efficiency, as defined here, would have been achieved.

This concept of channel efficiency should have significance for *any* manager making channel decisions in *any* particular unit of the channel in that conflict is a factor which can influence how efficiently his channel-related decisions are consummated. Some simple models are developed below which conveniently illustrate possible effects of conflict on this concept of channel efficiency.

NEGATIVE EFFECT—REDUCED EFFICIENCY

Figure 1 illustrates what is probably the most commonly held but often implicit belief concerning the effect of conflict on channel efficiency.

8. Phillip McVey, "Are Channels of Distribution What the Textbooks Say?" *Journal of Marketing*, Vol. 24 (January 1960), p. 62.

Figure 1 illustrates a negative relationship: as the level of conflict increases, channel efficiency is reduced.

FIG. 1   Conflict and Channel Efficiency—Negative Effect.

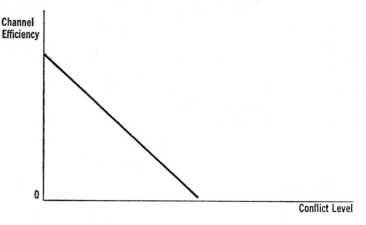

Following is an example of a conflict situation which is consistent with and illustrative of the relationship expressed in Figure 1. Assume a large retailer X carries similar products from manufacturers A, B, and C. At some point, manufacturer A notices that retailer X has substantially reduced his purchases from A. Manufacturer A becomes concerned over the reduction and makes a decision to attempt to regain the previous volume level from retailer X. This decision has set up a goal (regain previous volume from X) which manufacturer A will attempt to achieve. The level of input which manufacturer A utilizes to reach this goal is the measure of efficiency. Suppose manufacturer A tries gentle persuasion in the form of a friendly visit by his marketing manager to retailer X, but it turns out that X is doing very well with the products from manufacturers B and C and feels he cannot carry more products from A. Manufacturer A then moves to coercion, perhaps in the form of a threat to cut off several of his product lines which X still buys and finds very profitable. Yet suppose as a reaction to the threats from A, retailer X further reduces purchases from A and begins to disparage A's products in the eyes of his customers. The conflict continues to build with each subsequent action by the two parties. Manufacturer A not only finds it necessary to devote more and more of his sales effort to get retailer X to give in, but he may also feel the need to increase the advertising component of his promotional mix in an effort to create more consumer pull for added leverage on retailer X to carry A's products. It now becomes increasingly difficult for A to move his products through the channel of which retailer X is a member. That is, A has to use greater amounts of input (personal selling and advertising) to do so. Thus, the level of channel efficiency from manufacturer A's standpoint declines; and, as the conflict becomes more intense (movement along the horizontal axis in Figure 1), the level of efficiency for A continues to decline.

NO EFFECT—EFFICIENCY REMAINS CONSTANT

Another possible relationship between conflict and channel efficiency is illustrated in Figure 2. In this relationship, the existence of conflict has caused no change in channel efficiency. Hence, the effect of the conflict on input levels necessary to execute channel decisions is inconsequential.

FIG. 2   Conflict and Channel Efficiency—No Effect.

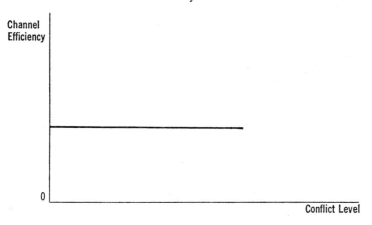

An explanation for the lack of effect of conflict on channel efficiency may be found in the conscious or unconscious awareness of the parties operating in the channel of the necessary nature of their relationship to one another. That is, the parties may feel that their need for each other to achieve their respective goals is so great that the conflict can have no more than a superficial effect on their efficiency in executing decisions to achieve these goals. In other words, the channel members learn to live with the conflict; even though there may exist a certain amount of hostility and acrimony, the parties become inured to the conflict to the extent that efficient performance may not be affected.[9]

9. Same reference as footnote 2, p. 329.

One of the earliest discussions of channel conflict, by Ivey, alludes to this view. In this early work, Ivey noted that in channel structures where integration was virtually impossible, firms were forced to live with each other so that, in spite of hostilities or conflict, the performance efficiency of the channel members apparently was not affected.[10]

POSITIVE EFFECT—CHANNEL
EFFICIENCY INCREASED

Figure 3 illustrates yet another possible effect of conflict on channel efficiency in that it suggests the possibility of conflict causing an increase in channel efficiency as the level of conflict increases.

FIG. 3   Conflict and Channel Efficiency—Positive Effect.

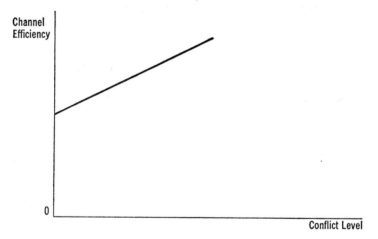

The following brief example serves to illustrate how conflict may have such a positive effect. Assume a particular wholesaler finds that a manufacturer with whom he had enjoyed a profitable relationship has decided to bypass him with respect to certain products and instead is attempting to sell directly to retailers, because the manufacturer feels that this wholesaler has not been selling these products with sufficient alacrity. The initial reaction of the wholesaler might be one of indignation and hostility toward what he could at first consider to be an ungrateful manufacturer. The seeds of conflict might develop further and ultimately result in a conflict situation which could negatively affect the

10. Paul W. Ivey, "The Manufacturer's Marketing Problem," *Administration*, Vol. 1 (March 1921), pp. 346–347.

efficiency in carrying out channel goals for one or both of the parties to the conflict. (See "Negative Effect" above and Figure 1.) However, the conflict might serve as an impetus for either or both of these channel members to reappraise their respective policies.[11] For example, the wholesaler might rise above his hostility to examine his own performance and find it lacking. He might determine that his previous level of selling effort for this manufacturer's products was not as high as it could have been within the context of his role prescriptions as an independent wholesaler.[12] Thus, he might view the manufacturer's actions as justified under the circumstances and attempt to make changes to do a more effective selling job.

The manufacturer also might reexamine his policies and find his efforts on behalf of this wholesaler to be lacking. He may decide that more special effort and inducements are necessary to maintain the support of the wholesaler.[13]

The effect of this two-party reappraisal could be a reallocation of inputs based on the comparative advantages enjoyed by each channel member in performing the tasks necessary to achieve his respective channel goals. The combination of inputs after reallocation between the two parties might be better and result in higher efficiency for one or possibly both parties in the channel. In this example, the conflict provided an impetus which led to a more efficient allocation of inputs.

CONFLICT AND CHANNEL EFFICIENCY— GENERAL CURVE

When the above models are combined, it is possible to visualize a general curve depicting the possible effects of conflict on channel efficiency. Figure 4 suggests a kind of tolerance range OC_1 over which the conflict has no effect on channel efficiency. Over the range C_1C_2, the effect of conflict is positive; while beyond C_2, the effect is negative. The level C_2 in Figure 4 suggests a threshold effect of conflict first discussed in a nonmarketing context by Boulding[14] and later applied to the marketing channel by Rosenberg and Stern.[15] Figure 4 is essentially a graphical

11. Same reference as footnote 7, pp. 576–577.

12. Lynn E. Gill and Louis W. Stern, "Roles and Role Theory in Distribution Channel Systems," *Distribution Channels: Behavioral Dimensions*, Louis W. Stern, ed. (Boston: Houghton-Mifflin Company, 1969), pp. 22–25.

13. For some examples of special inducements in support of wholesalers see: Martin R. Warshaw, "Pricing to Gain Wholesalers' Selling Support," *Journal of Marketing*, Vol. 26 (July 1962), pp. 50–54.

14. Kenneth E. Boulding, "The Economics of Human Conflict," *The Nature of Human Conflict*, Elton B. McNeil, ed. (Englewood Cliffs, N.J.: Prentice-Hall, Inc., 1965), pp. 172–191.

15. Rosenberg and Stern, same reference as footnote 3, pp. 45–46.

FIG. 4   Conflict and Channel Efficiency—General Curve.

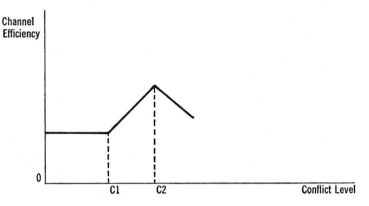

interpretation of this threshold concept of conflict which is related to a particular definition of channel efficiency (but which also includes a no effect or tolerance range OC_1). Thus, once the tolerance range is passed, the higher the level of conflict between C_1C_2, the greater the level of channel efficiency. Beyond C_2 (the threshold level) the greater the conflict level, the lower will be the level of channel efficiency.

CONCLUSION

Unfortunately, there is little empirical evidence currently available to determine when conflict would have no effect, a negative effect, or a positive effect. As Rosenberg and Stern point out, "whether the impact of conflict upon a channel member's performance is functional or dysfunctional remains to be settled."[16]

At this point, then, the marketing manager might justifiably ask how he is supposed to deal with conflict in his channel decisions when so little "hard evidence" of the effects of conflict exists. It has been suggested here that the decision maker has something to gain simply by thinking about conflict in terms of channel efficiency as defined above. Conflict, which is an inherent aspect of the system within which the manager involved with channel decisions operates, *can* be incorporated into his decisions. At first, of course, these incorporations will be crude. As times goes by, however, empirical information on the effects of conflict in the marketing channel will be increasingly accessible as more and more empirical studies are conducted. If the manager has developed a facility for using conceptual models on possible conflict re-

16. Same reference as footnote 15, p. 46.

lationships in the marketing channel, such as those presented here, the findings coming out of future empirical studies are more likely to "find a home" as part of his relevant input for making channel decisions. Therefore, the probability that the marketing manager will be able to *use* such findings as potentially beneficial information for channel decision making should go up, and behavioral examinations of conflict already discussed in the marketing literature as well as those studies which are sure to be forthcoming should hold greater meaning for him.

QUESTIONS FOR DISCUSSION

1. Historically, most channel literature has assumed that conflict had what effect on channel efficiency? Explain.

2. Rosenbloom argues that a number of potential outcomes are possible when a conflict situation arises in a marketing channel. Discuss carefully each possible result on channel efficiency.

3. Of the various outcomes discussed by Professor Rosenbloom when channel conflict occurs, which outcome do you feel is the most likely? Why?

4. The author states, "When the above models are combined, it is possible to visualize a general curve depicting the possible effects of conflict on channel efficiency." Discuss the shape and logic of the generalized curve.

4.3 DUAL DISTRIBUTION AS A SOURCE OF CHANNEL CONFLICT

William L. Shanklin

"Duality, no brand differentiation, has injured numerous independent business people and menaces countless more at every level of distribution."

Dual distribution encompasses situations in which "the manufacturer of a branded good sells that brand through two or more competing distribution channels" and/or "the manufacturer sells two brands of basically the same product through two competing kinds of distribution networks."[1] For clarity, when specifically making reference to the first type of dual distribution, it is denoted as dual distribution, no brand differentiation. The second kind of duality is called dual distribution, brand differentiation.

One rationale for dual distribution is that duality offers manufacturers opportunities to augment sales in existing target markets and to concomitantly develop new frontiers. As sales volume increases, the marginal costs of production and marketing may actually decrease because of economies of scale. Sales increments accompanied by cost decrements naturally make duality even more attractive from the standpoint of profitability. Another rationale for duality is that when dual distribution, brand differentiation is utilized, the manufacturer frequently gains the benefit of attaining intensive market coverage without sacrificing or endangering the favorable imagery connoted by a selectively or exclusively distributed name brand product or product line.

Dual distribution is not without costs. A firm opting to implement the strategy is vulnerable to risks. Channel relationships are almost certain to deteriorate. Alienation of channel members creates conflict ranging from minimal to warfare. In addition, the manufacturing enterprise employing dual distribution is exposing itself to the possibilities of legis-

---

Reprinted by permission from William L. Shanklin, "Dual Distribution As a Source of Channel Conflict," *Proceedings of the Southern Marketing Association* (Blacksburg, Va.: Virginia Polytechnic Institute and State University, 1974), pp. 357–361.

1. U.S. Congress, House, Subcommittee No. 4, Select Committee on Small Business, *Hearings, The Impact Upon Small Business of Dual Distribution and Related Vertical Integration*, 88th Congress (1st Session, 1963), p. 4.

lative, regulatory, and legal maneuvers. Institutions allegedly harmed by duality, in particular the independent retailer, have tended to receive sympathetic treatment from governmental authorities.

Executives are often induced to use the strategy of duality by competitive pressures emanating from the marketplace. Some executives form the attitude—and understandably so—"if we don't sell to these customers, someone else will." On the other hand, a number of marketing managers have resisted the enticements of duality. They believe that the practice is counterproductive. Their contention is that the goodwill of the independent retailing forces that sell their products is at stake. A Maytag executive has condemned duality as being incongruent with good channel relations. In his words:

> I'm enough of a businessman to know that my future is wrapped up in the sale of my products through normal distributive channels—by sales through dealers to the ultimate consumer. I know that I can't serve two causes at the same time. I can't forever work both sides of the street.[2]

In the discussion which follows, the focus is on the problems that can and do arise from duality. Primary emphasis is on dual distribution as it affects the independent retailer. Actual corporate experiences are used. Possible antidotes to conflict originating from the strategy are examined within the context of governmental, and other significant constraints upon their implementation.

CONFLICTS AND DUAL DISTRIBUTION— CAUSES AND EFFECTS

Duality, no brand differentiation has injured numerous independent businessmen and menaces countless more at every level of distribution. For instance, an independent fabricator of structural steel was subjected to a severe price squeeze by his own major raw material suppliers who were selling identical products to the fabricator's customers at bargain prices. A paint retailer in Louisiana was forced to sell his business when three well-known paint manufacturers began to compete with him through company-owned outlets and direct factory sales to consumers.[3] A more detailed illustration of the problems sometimes caused by this kind of duality is given below. A pseudonym has been used for the manufacturer involved.

The Western Wood Corporation is a large vertically integrated manufacturer of plywood and wood-related products. Western Wood has no

2. Thomas J. Murray, "Dual Distribution vs. the Small Retailer," *Dun's Review* (August 1964), p. 57.
3. *Ibid.*, pp. 29, 55c–56.

company-owned retail outlets; it sells to independent lumber yards, to lumber chains, and to general merchandise retailers through over 120 company-owned distribution centers located in metropolitan areas of the U.S.

On occasion, Western Wood has tried to institute duality by drop-shipping carloads of materials to building contractors. As a result, bitter altercations have often ensued between Western Wood distribution center managers and irate independent lumber dealers. Lumber yards consider the lucrative, high volume contractor market to be their domain. Some independents also strenuously object to Western Wood's practice of selling to outlets such as Sears. Their reasoning is that this type of institution is not a bona fide lumber dealer. The independents have thus far been largely successful in circumventing Western Wood's moves to distribute through multiple channels.

Turning to dual distribution, brand differentiation, it is evident that private brands—many of which are supplied by name brand manufacturers—have been notably successful, in a variety of product lines, in competing with national brands. One significant factor accounting for the rapid growth of private brands since World War II, when their importance was negligible, is increased awareness among consumers of which manufacturers supply specific retailers with what products for store branding. The print medium has contributed to educating consumers in this respect. For instance a consumer-advice magazine[4] recently compiled and published a rather lengthy list describing which producers supply prominent retailers with items for store branding.

Albeit knowledge of who manufactures store-branded products is often valuable information to consumers, retailers of name brands of the same products may be damaged by the knowledge. A major appliance manufacturer-dealer system is a case in point.

The manufacturer involved sells a major brand to independent retailers, to chains, and to contractors for installation in new dwellings. Another major brand is distributed in a similar manner. The company also sells products to a few large chains carrying store brands. Extensive distribution is achieved through this arrangement but channel relationships are also adversely affected. One dealer aligned with the manufacturer resents the fact that a number of his prospective customers have subsequently purchased private-branded appliances from department stores at prices far below those he could offer. He attributes lost sales to a growing awareness, among the public, that when they buy certain appliances from store-branders, they are, in fact, buying products produced by leading, and often identifiable manufacturers. Another independent retailer of the supplier's products terms the use of two major

4. "Name Brands vs. House Brands," *Changing Times* (August 1973), p. 27.

brands a "marketing trick." This mode of thinking is hardly conducive to the maintenance of harmonious manufacturer-dealer relations.

Conflict over duality, brand differentiation has sometimes led to legal battles. Perhaps the most publicized case is the Federal Trade Commission vs. the Borden Company.[5] Since the case is well-documented in the marketing literature it is not elaborated upon.

CONFLICT RESOLUTION

Manufacturers experiencing conflict with channel members agitated over duality have at least four major alternatives available to them which may have the effect of ameliorating channel harmony. These alternatives, and constraints upon their implementation are briefly considered.

Vertical integration into retailing is an alternative that has been pursued by a sizeable number of producers. Intensifying competition in many industries has prompted manufacturers to open their own outlets in market areas where suitable coverage did not previously exist. The Justice Department's stricter attitude toward external expansion through merger has left many large companies with vertical integration as the only major expansion route. As retailing has shifted to the suburbs, the small retailer has often been unable to raise the capital needed to relocate in shopping centers. Manufacturers have had to fill this void by opening their own stores. The lure of extra profits generated by eliminating the independent retailer and selling directly to the ultimate consumer through company-owned retail outlets has also contributed to the growth of vertical integration.[6]

If successfully implemented, total vertical integration may have the long-run effect of eliminating conflict entirely since there are ultimately no retailers independent of the manufacturer's control left to contend with. In the short-run, there is likely to be resistance arising from the process of phasing-out the independent retail firms which sell the manufacturer's goods.

Vertical integration seems to be an attractive alternative; yet, it is not always achievable. For small manufacturers, opening and maintaining a network of retail outlets is usually not viable because of the resources needed to accomplish the task. It would not be possible for even a giant corporation to establish the number of retail outlets required to achieve the extensive distribution needed for convenience items. Massive ver-

5. Federal Trade Commission vs. Borden Company, 86 S. Ct. 1092 (March 1966).
6. Murray, pp. 54–55c.

tical integration into retailing is, for the most part, open only to large manufacturers of some consumer durables, prestige products, and industrial goods.

Beyond the question of monetary costs, an additional impediment to vertical integration is governmental intervention. Any move that threatens to restrict competition or to eliminate the small businessman is indeed risky. For instance, Connecticut, Florida, and the Federal Trade Commission have all filed antitrust suits against the major oil companies attacking them for vertical integration. The Attorney General of Connecticut states that: "Crude oil prices and profits would be measurably lower if the major oil companies were not integrated all the way from crude production down through branded stations."[7] Other cases where companies have been assailed for vertical integration are a matter of record.

Franchising is a second alternative. This practice does not eliminate duality unless other measures are taken. As two authors[8] have observed, "if a single supplier of products markets some of them, or some brands, through franchisees and others through independent (or formally integrated) outlets, then dual distribution occurs." The producer must eliminate distribution of both manufacturers' and private-branded products to nonfranchised independents and through corporate-owned outlets if franchising is to be effective in minimizing conflict. Otherwise, duality remains and all parties concerned are left with the source of conflict that franchising was intended to alleviate in the first place.

Franchising may have the potential to remedy the conflicts arising from dual distribution, if properly implemented, but the strategy is not always feasible. The Federal government is likely to object to the phasing-out of independents, as shown recently when the U.S. Senate passed legislation[9] intended, in part, to protect independent oil distributors and retailers.

A third approach for manufacturers is to do nothing but continue the status quo. It may be possible for producers to practice duality and simultaneously placate channel members through various administrative strategies. This is what might be termed an enclave strategy since the problem is not solved, but rather, is contained at best. The option can be advantageous in the short-run but the benefits derived may be temporal. The growing riskiness of a "do nothing" approach on the part of manufacturers engaged in dual distribution is manifest. The U.S. government is becoming more and more concerned with the competitive

7. "Who Benefits?," *The Wall Street Journal* (August 20, 1973), p. 4.

8. Lee E. Preston and Arthur E. Schramm, Jr., "Dual Distribution and Its Impact on Marketing Organization," *California Management Review* (Winter, 1965), p. 61.

9. S. Res. 1570, 93rd Congress, (1st Session, 1973).

denouements of the practice—e.g., duality has prompted numerous inquiries by the Congress and the Chief of Evaluation for the Antitrust Division of the Justice Department has recently addressed himself to the issue.[10]

A fourth approach is to cease the practice of duality altogether. As previously mentioned, vertical integration into retailing and franchising are two means that can sometimes be used to accomplish this goal. Three further possibilities that are available to a manufacturer wishing to cease duality are delineated.

A manufacturer practicing dual distribution, brand differentiation might elect to abolish private labeling entirely. This strategy would not be wise where a substantial portion of a producer's sales is accounted for by private label purchases. A manufacturer using duality, brand differentiation might choose to abolish all of its name brand products and instead sell exclusively to private labelers. This option is especially suited to small manufacturers whose name brands hold negligible market shares. A manufacturer employing dual distribution, no brand differentiation could divest itself of all company-owned retail outlets and curtail direct from factory sales to consumers. In so doing, it would circumvent charges that it competes with, and therefore harms its own customers.

This paper is not meant to thoroughly evaluate the merits and limitations of all of the options open to manufacturers concerned with conflict and potential or actual legal problems resulting from duality. Moreover, generalizations are inappropriate because the solution which is best for a specific company depends upon endogenous constraints, the degree of existing cooperation among channel members, profitability derived from duality, environmental factors, and a number of other considerations. The intention has been to illustrate that decisions pertaining to dual distribution are difficult ones. Management must weigh the advantages of the additional market penetrating and market development that duality usually brings against the undesirable consequences of creating conflict within marketing channels and/or eliciting governmental response.

QUESTIONS FOR DISCUSSION

1. What is dual distribution? What are its benefits to a manufacturer? Discuss fully.

2. Why do channel members believe that dual distribution is responsible for an abnormal amount of channel conflict?

10. Michael Duggan, "Dual Distribution Poses Antitrust Problems," *Marketing News*, August 1, 1973, p. 8.

3. Discuss the difference between brand differentiation and no brand differentiation in dual distribution. Which tends to reduce the overall level of channel conflict? Defend your answer.

4. Explain several techniques of conflict resolution in the area of dual distribution.

4.4 ARBITRATION IN THE MARKETING CHANNEL

Robert E. Weigand and Hilda C. Wasson

"In an era when the alternatives to a peaceful solution are so costly and permanent, arbitration is an approach that holds great managerial promise."

Businessmen who find that some aspect of an arrangement with their suppliers or customers is intolerable usually "vote with their feet"; the arrangement is terminated and business is taken elsewhere. The offended buyer or seller believes he "will know better the next time," and uses his freedom and ability to locate someone else with whom to do business. Unfortunately, such a solution does not assure either a fair outcome to the other party or the short-run efficiency of the marketing system.

A less common solution is to resolve conflicts through litigation. If a courtroom solution is sought, each party is represented by counsel, arguments are heard before a judge, the merits of each side are carefully weighed, and a decision is rendered publicly. Antagonists are often reluctant to seek justice in the courts since it virtually amounts to a declaration of war between the parties in a marketing channel. Most cases do not go to trial because each side is anxious to avoid a long, costly, and perhaps embarrassing fight. The disputes are settled by negotiation between the parties before the case goes to trial, often because of a willingness to compromise rather than any particular effort to adhere to the strict letter of the law. In either case—whether by adjudication in the court or through an out-of-court settlement brought by the attorneys for the parties involved—it is unlikely that normal business relations can ever again be restored.

A still different, highly pragmatic approach, apparently growing in importance, is to provide for a third party to enter and resolve a dispute before it becomes too difficult to settle in a reasonably friendly fashion. The following are examples of disputes that might be settled in this way:

Reprinted by permission from Robert E. Weigand and Hilda C. Wasson, "Arbitration in the Marketing Channel," *Business Horizons* (October, 1974), pp. 39–47.

A manufacturer promises an exclusive territory to a retailer in return for the retailer's "majority effort" to generate business in the area. Sales increase nicely, but the manufacturer believes it is due more to population growth in the area than to the effort of the store owner, who is spending too much time on the golf course.

A fast food franchisor promises "expert promotional assistance" to his retailers as partial explanation for the franchise fee. One of the retailers believes that the help he is getting is anything but expert and that the benefits do not correspond with what he was promised.

Another franchisor agrees to furnish accounting services and financial analysis as a regular part of his services. The franchisee believes that the accountant is nothing more than a "glorified bookkeeper" and that the financial analysis consists of several pages of ratios that are incomprehensible.

A third franchisor insists that his franchisees should maintain a minimum stock of certain items that are regularly promoted throughout the area. Arguments arise as to whether the franchisor's recommendations constitute a threat, while the franchisee is particularly concerned about protecting his trade name.

Each of these examples is an important conflict to the participants. However, the disputes may not be so important that they should be allowed to disrupt the relationship.

Arbitration offers a number of advantages to the pragmatic businessman:

Arbitration is fast. The parties to a dispute can be quickly informed that a quarrel exists and told the time of a hearing, the evidence heard by the panel, and the decision rendered—all within a few weeks.

Arbitration preserves secrecy. Outside parties can be barred from the hearings. Decisions which are not matters of public record can be kept secret.

Arbitration is less expensive than litigating. There is an element of "corner-cutting" that takes place which reduces the cost of a tolerable decision.

Arbitration confronts problems in their incipient stage when they are easier to solve. The attitude can become: "We have a potential problem here; let us solve it before positions and opinions get too fixed."

Arbitration often takes place before industry experts. In many instances, the arbitrator or the arbitration panel is composed of those who know an industry and its practices. Some argue that this produces a fairer decision.

Arbitration of commercial disputes is an old practice that can be traced back for centuries, but it is not as well-known among business-men as labor arbitration. In an era when the alternatives to a peaceful solution are so costly and permanent, arbitration is an approach that holds great managerial promise. This article deals with the process of commercial arbitration as it applies to businesses that make up a marketing channel, with particular emphasis on franchise operations.

ARBITRATION PRECEDENTS

In an early study of commercial arbitration, Soia Mentschikoff argued that submission of business disputes to a third party is particularly likely under certain circumstances. First, associations made up of those who engage extensively in foreign trade are more likely to provide a mechanism for arbitration than are associations oriented toward domestic trade. International laws dealing with business disputes are sometimes vague; legal jurisdiction often is inadequately defined. Hence, international traders were among the first to find an expedient nonlitigant device for resolving disputes.

Second, arbitration is more likely to occur when the quality of the traded product is an important and frequently disputed issue and where a third-party expert is capable of discerning quality differences. For example, the quality of grain or livestock is a crucial matter between seller and buyer. Fortunately, widely accepted standards or grades exist for each. It is rather easy for an arbitrator to distinguish among the qualities and to determine relief to the damaged party, usually in the form of a modified exchange price. At the other extreme would be hard goods such as refrigerators or automobiles where a defect seldom can be remedied by a modest price concession. Here the solution is more likely to take the form of repair or replacement. Mentschikoff discovered that arbitration is extremely rare in adjudicating disputes between manufacturers of hard goods and their customers.

Finally, Mentschikoff argued that arbitration is more likely to occur in commercial disputes between suppliers and merchants who purchase goods for resale. Trade associations in which merchant membership is high are better equipped to deal with intrachannel conflicts than are other types of associations. The explanation seems to be that merchants are particularly interested in the speed and low cost features inherent in arbitration.[1]

For example, arbitration is a common practice in the textile industry, where a poor season can make or break a manufacturer or retailer. One

1. Soia Mentschikoff, "Commercial Arbitration," *Columbia Law Review*, LXI (May 1961), pp. 850–52.

important problem often subjected to arbitration is whether the goods shipped by a manufacturer match the quality originally promised. If a retailer's selling season is not going well, he might elect to return an order of dresses to his supplier with the allegation that the finished product does not meet the standards initially shown. Indeed, it is not unknown for manufacturers to substitute cloth of poorer quality or tolerate poorer workmanship when producing the final product than was shown in the samples.

Another type of dispute that arises in the industry develops when merchandise is shipped too late in the season to be sold at full mark-up, at least in the opinion of the retailer. His complaint may be valid, because manufacturers sometimes accept more orders than they can fill during the short time ahead, calculating that there surely will be cancellations. Such disagreements are common and are regularly handled by third-party arbitrators.

THE ADMINISTRATIVE MECHANISM

The Dealer Relations Board established at General Motors in 1938 by Alfred P. Sloan is an interesting forerunner of present-day arbitration practices. The board was created to adjudicate quarrels between the various General Motors' divisions and individual dealers. Each party to the dispute was expected to prepare its case as thoroughly as possible and defend its position. Sloan argued that "the chief benefit of the board was a preventive one. Divisions made very sure they had a sound case and were observing all the equities in taking action against any dealer, for it was the division itself, as well as the dealer, that came up for executive review."

Sloan was chairman of the first board, which was in fact composed exclusively of General Motors' executives. The major flaw of such an inhouse board is obvious; Sloan and the others were responsible for the survival and profit of General Motors and could not be expected to show objectivity with respect to manufacturer-dealer relations. Indeed, Sloan describes his firm's "liberal" policy when a dealer was terminated: the company would buy back unsold new automobiles, certain signs, special tools, and parts for newer model cars, and would help the dealer with any loss he might incur from any nonterminable lease he might have had on his facilities.[2]

In more recent arbitration agreements, the nature of the disputes and the techniques for solving them increasingly have been spelled out in the seller-buyer contracts. Contrary to what some might expect, provisions for negotiations are often initiated by the stronger party in the

2. Alfred P. Sloan, *My Years with General Motors* (Garden City, N.Y.: Doubleday, 1964), pp. 293–94.

relationship, generally meaning the franchisor. A recent arbitration plan that is often cited as a model for other firms and industries is the agreement initiated in 1965 by Carling Brewing Company to guide its relationships with its distributors. If a dispute arises between Carling and one of its distributors, the latter may submit the facts of the disagreement to the president. If the argument is not settled satisfactorily within ten days, it may be submitted to an arbitration tribunal for a solution.

An interesting feature of the arrangement is that arbitration is optional with the distributor; he may elect some other choice such as relief through the courts. But if the distributor chooses arbitration, the company is allowed no such choice; it is obliged to arbitrate. The commercial arbitration rules of the American Arbitration Association (AAA) generally are used, and the association helps administer the exchange of documents dealing with the case. In addition, the association may be asked to appoint a third person to the arbitration tribunal if the first two appointees (one appointed by the company and one by the distributor) cannot agree on the third member. The three arbitrators submit their decision to the association, which promptly notifies both the company and the distributor. Each is bound to abide by the conclusions of the tribunal.

When arbitration seems appropriate, the AAA is commonly used to adjudicate disputes; it is often named in contracts as the "official" body responsible for administrating a case in the event a dispute should arise. The association, established in 1926, administered 103,841 cases during its first forty years. Although the majority were labor cases, 23,633 commercial cases were handled during those forty years. It is the only national arbitration association that is willing to deal with such a variety of issues. The association maintains a list of about 20,000 professional arbitrators throughout the country who have expressed a willingness to sit in on disputes; the list is made available to each party just as soon as a disagreement is presented—an arrangement that is likely to accelerate the resolution of the case.

Under U.S. law either party can oblige the other to arbitrate differences if such a provision is contained in whatever contract exists between the two. However, it is easy for either party to engage in delaying tactics if such behavior seems useful. An agreement in the franchisor-franchisee contract to abide by the rules of the association lessens such possibilities. In short, the association provides a mechanism for routinizing what could otherwise be an administrative quagmire.

LEGAL LIMITS AND IMPLICATIONS

One of the reasons why the stronger party in the seller-buyer relationship may agree to arbitration is that it allows for the agreement to be tailored to the needs of the stronger party. Under these circumstances, seeking a fair or just relationship between the two parties is more apparent than real. One particular area where power is often badly balanced is in franchisor-franchisee relationships. Franchisees have not yet found a nonlitigant way to countervail the often very powerful franchisor, many of whom have added arbitration agreements to their contracts.

An example of a lukewarm approach to arbitration is provided by a franchising subsidiary of one of America's largest companies, which requires arbitration of all disputes except for money, eviction, or injunctive relief, and presentation of all claims within a year. In another instance, a franchisor insisted that a dispute be arbitrated in Los Angeles, even though the franchisee's restaurant was in Missouri. Such limits on the role of arbitration lead one to suspect that the franchisor is dragging himself rather reluctantly to any out-of-court resolution of disputes with his franchisees. By writing such limitations into the contract, it is virtually assured that arbitration will be infrequently used.

In addition to whatever limitations may be written into the contract, there is widespread doubt whether antitrust activities such as price fixing, tying arrangements, and price discrimination are legally arbitrable. The public's right to be represented in channel disputes where antitrust issues are at stake is probably the single most important reason for arguments that such questions are non-arbitrable. In the absence of advisors from either the Federal Trade Commission or the Antitrust Division of the Department of Justice, parties to an agreement to arbitrate must presumably agree whether or not an issue has antitrust implications, and, thus, either is or is not arbitrable.

Among the specific matters commonly arbitrated that affect a franchisor-franchisee relationship are restrictions on the source of supply of raw materials and on products and equipment used in the franchise; the minimum standards of design, quality, and appearance of the product being sold; the geographic limitations imposed on the franchisee; and restrictions that might be placed on products or services sold by the franchisee that compete with the franchisor. However, it takes only a little imagination to realize that two persons viewing the same problem may interpret the facts entirely differently. Indeed, the following questions serve to illustrate the delicate issues involved:

> If a food franchisor offers a menu to his franchisees that contains prices, is he merely providing another service to his franchisees or is he subtly attempting to fix the retail price of the product?
>
> If a franchisor provides a carefully drawn list of specifications that the products of the franchisee's suppliers must meet, at what

point does the list become so complex that the franchisee gives up in despair and buys his requirements from the franchisor?

If a franchisor collaborates with his franchisees in establishing an advisory council, what activities can the franchisees engage in that will not be considered conspiratorial?[3]

There are other objections to arbitration. First, arbitration proceedings are conducted under a cloak of secrecy, and decisions generally are rendered orally. Such practices do not further the businessman's understanding of the dimensions of acceptable business behavior, nor do they inform the public concerning what it can expect of its businessmen-servants.

A second objection to arbitration is that the law is less precisely followed in extra-court proceedings. Since these proceedings are often directed by those untrained in the law, only the roughest sort of justice may win out. A complete understanding of the long history of antitrust law and the legal rights of each party may be lacking.

Third, a binding obligation to engage in arbitration may be legally unenforceable, since a party that is obliged to submit disputes to arbitration may be relinquishing its right to demand its case be litigated in court. This becomes particularly important since the courts usually have been reluctant to upset arbitration decisions rendered by third-party negotiators. For example, the U.S. Supreme Court recently held that Merrill Lynch could not require that a former account executive settle his dispute with the firm through arbitration, even though he had signed an employment contract that required it. The former executive elected to sue the firm for his accrued profit-sharing benefits rather than submit to rules promulgated by the New York Stock Exchange. The court held that the former employee had the right to sue and the case should be initiated in the California state courts. While it cannot be inferred that the courts would hand down a similar ruling in a case between commercial enterprises, the case allows for interesting speculation.

Finally, arbitrators generally do not have the legal power to insist that vital documents be produced, although witnesses can be compelled to appear before the tribunal. If certain documents are essential for justice to be assured, and if the party holding the documents elects to withhold them, there is no assurance that the case will be resolved fairly. Some of these arguments would seem to be applicable to arbitration dealing with any issue, whether in the antitrust area or not. Furthermore, some would also apply to other nonlitigant practices such as consent orders.

3. Harold L. Rudnick, "Use of Arbitration Clauses," speech to the American Bar Association annual meeting, San Francisco, August 16, 1972.

The nonarbitrable nature of antitrust issues combined with the fuzzy picture of what constitutes an antitrust question present an interesting possibility for avoiding arbitration when it suits either party. If either party wants to throw the disputed issue into litigation, that party can rather easily argue that antitrust questions are involved. Such an argument can be used by either franchisor or franchisee as a matter of legal strategy designed to make the other party conciliatory rather than as an expression of an honest belief that antitrust issues are involved. An essential ingredient for successful arbitration—at least for most channel disputes—is the good faith of both parties. Without it, the arbitration amounts to little more than a public relations stunt.

BUSINESS-GOVERNMENT INTEREST

FRANCHISOR-FRANCHISEE AGREEMENT

Astute franchisors usually manage their businesses in such a way that disputes calling for arbitration are infrequent and litigation is rare. A sophisticated management information system is able to detect areas where franchisors and their franchisees have quite different expectations. Such disputes are completely normal where businesses interact not only frequently but over a long period of time. One need not call on a third party to resolve conflicts that often are attributable to misunderstanding or lack of coordination.

Arbitration takes place when two parties find that they cannot settle a dispute without help from a neutral third party, and when the two parties prefer that the third party not be the courts. There is evidence that businessmen, the judicial system, and legislatures prefer to see such quarrels settled quickly, inexpensively, and with as little recrimination as possible. It is not at all clear just how widespread arbitration of channel disputes is in American businesses, largely because businessmen often do not know that they have a policy that favors arbitration until they are faced with a need for it. Such informal arbitration takes place when a dispute has arisen between two or more parties that have never entered into a covenant to arbitrate disputes but, after realizing the serious nature of the disagreement, decide that arbitration is a handy mechanism that may solve their problem.[4] In one survey jointly conducted by the American Arbitration Association and the International

4. Harold L. Rudnick, General Counsel for the International Franchise Association, points out the difference between formal and informal arbitration: formal arbitration takes place when the channel members agree in advance to submit disputes to a third party while informal arbitration occurs when the agreement takes place after a disagreement has arisen. See his "Arbitration of Disputes Between Franchisors and Franchisees," *Illinois Bar Journal* (September 1966), p. 59.

Franchise Association (IFA), only a minority of the franchisors (ten out of fifty-one) indicated that arbitration clauses were contained in their contracts. Twenty-three respondents indicated that they would consider using arbitration if certain unspecified circumstances arose. In another study limited to fast food, convenience grocery, and laundry and dry cleaning franchising, 23 percent of the franchisors indicated that the contracts with their franchisees contained arbitration clauses.[5]

The IFA tends to be overrepresented by large franchising operations, so it is doubtful that the limited data can be projected to all types and sizes of franchise operations. It may well be that members of the IFA are more likely to engage in arbitration than non-members not only because of their size—if, indeed, this is a factor—but also because they are almost certain to be aware of the mechanism and are encouraged to use it. Smaller franchisors may be less inclined to anticipate channel disputes and only vaguely aware of how third-party intermediaries can be used.

The IFA argues that virtually all of the country's major franchisors are members and must surely be aware of the association's "code of ethics." The eleventh provision states, "A franchisor shall make every effort to resolve complaints, grievances, and disputes with its franchisees with good faith and good will through fair and reasonable direct communication and negotiation. Failing this, recourse should be made, if possible, to arbitration, with litigation pursued only as a last resort."

PROPOSED LEGISLATION

During the last several years, legislators have increasingly incorporated a variety of provisions into federal or state legislative proposals that in some manner explicitly allude to arbitration of channel disputes. Most of the proposals have not been enacted into law, but enthusiasm for the idea is not dead.

1. Senate Bill 2321 was introduced in 1967 to the 90th Congress by Senator Philip A. Hart. The bill would have provided for compensation for the franchisee in the event that the franchisor either terminated the franchise without his consent or entered into competition with him.

The franchisor would have been obliged to purchase the terminated franchisee's buildings, operating equipment, and material, and pay an amount for the goodwill built up in the territory; the franchisor would

5. The full study is presented in "The Economic Effects of Franchising" by Urban B. Ozanne and Shelby D. Hunt, for the Select Committee on Small Business. The same study appears in "Franchising: Vertical Relationship Issues and Public Policy Recommendations," an unpublished paper by Urban B. Ozanne presented at Northwestern University, June 1972.

also have been required to pay a "sum equal to the reasonable value of the customers' accounts, including goodwill," where the franchisor elected to expropriate the market for himself. However, the legislation also would have exempted those franchisors whose contracts contained a provision for "fair and equitable arbitration" of disputes involving termination or direct dealing.

2. Senate Bill 1967, sponsored by Philip A. Hart, George D. Aiken, Birch Bayh, and Thomas J. Dodd, provided that terminations could only be effected after at least ninety days notice and then only if the franchisee had not complied with the terms of the franchise or had acted in bad faith. Channel contracts that provided for binding arbitration of the disputes just described would be exempt. Bill 1967 stated that the rules of the AAA would be defined as acceptable arbitration procedures.

3. The Gasoline Dealers' Day-in-Court Act, introduced by Senator Sam J. Ervin, Jr. in May 1972 and passed by the Senate in June 1973, is the most recently proposed legislation that alludes to arbitration. It provides that petroleum distributors would be liable for damages or other relief incurred by a franchised retailer in the event he should be terminated without cause. Distributors would be allowed to defend themselves against such allegations by demonstrating that the terminated dealer had not complied with "essential and reasonable requirements of the franchise agreement" or had not acted "in good faith in carrying out the terms of the franchise."

However, the proposed legislation further provides that no legal action could be brought cancelling termination if the franchise agreement provides for the binding arbitration of disputes related to the termination, cancellation, or nonrenewal of such franchise, in accordance with the rules of the AAA.

4. A number of states—Washington, California, Arkansas, Florida, Nebraska, Massachusetts, and Connecticut—have passed legislation that has been distressing to franchisors. Many other states have threatened similar laws. The purposes of the state legislation are varied but generally they are designed to give the prospective franchisee more information about his relationship with the franchisor before entering into a contract; assure that he does not pay a higher royalty than others for use of the franchisor's trademark, trade name, or service mark; limit the franchisor's power to terminate the relationship; and secure certain rights for the franchisee in the event the franchise should be terminated.

For example, in Massachusetts, the Franchise Fair Dealing Act provides for the licensing of automobile salesmen and full disclosure of information about the franchisor-franchisee relationship. It also provides for final and binding arbitration and specifies that the procedures of the arbitration be fair and reasonable, containing the now familiar clause, "it being acknowledged that the rules and procedures of the AAA satisfy such standards." This legislation passed through hearings, but eventually was melded into a more limited act that applies only to automobile franchises.

5. The Federal Trade Commission (FTC) recently charged both Standard Oil Company (Ohio) and Phillips Petroleum Company with violation of the Federal Trade Commission Act. The practices were much the same, consisting primarily of restricting the dealers' freedom to purchase their tires, batteries, and accessories from any available supplier, and maintaining the freedom to cancel a dealer's contract without cause on either thirty-day (Standard Oil) or ten-day (Phillips) notice.

Although neither case has been settled at this writing, an identical provision for compulsory arbitration is being considered by the commission on matters dealing with franchise termination by either firm. It would include "prohibition against refusal by respondent, upon request by a cancelled leasee dealer, to submit to arbitration the question of whether the dealer's lease cancellation was for good cause."

6. In June 1974, the FTC lost an attempt to require Adolph Coors, the country's fourth largest brewer, to provide an arbitration mechanism for distributors who had been terminated. The system would have provided for settlement of the dispute in the distributor's own city of operation, and most expenses would have been borne by Coors. The FTC won most of its points in the Appeals Court decision, but lost its fight for a provision for arbitration. Coors has indicated that it will take the case to the Supreme Court.

REASONS FOR GROWTH

Arbitration is an ancient solution for certain kinds of disputes and a relatively unknown one for others. There is evidence that it is growing in importance, particularly in resolving disputes between franchisors and franchisees. There are several possible explanations for its popularity, all of them speculative.

One explanation for the growth of arbitration is that more businessmen are discovering the importance of system continuity and the inevitability of conflicts. In the past both businessmen and academicians have been slow to recognize that the marketing channel is often a system of complementary businesses meant to function together over an extended period of time.

Where system continuity is essential—and franchising is one such area—the parties to the system seem to be recognizing that arbitration is a useful device for conflict resolution and systems maintenance. A decision to sever the business relationship when a dispute arises is a poor solution for either party, each of which entered the arrangement with the expectation that it would prove profitable in the long run.

As has already been suggested, litigation is not only slow and costly, but makes resumption of normal business activities extremely difficult. It is not conducive to the development of a strong bond between a franchisor and his franchisee, each of whom should have respect and trust for the other. And to permit disagreements to go unresolved is an unhappy solution.

Another possible explanation for the increased use of arbitration is that larger firms may be hoping to lessen some of the sting that they foresee in impending legislation. Many franchisors have simply observed the increasingly tough stance taken by both the courts and the legislatures, and have modified their operating and legal relationship with their franchisees so that they are more closely attuned to the direction of the shift. Most businesses would prefer to police themselves rather than take their marching orders from Washington or one of the state capitols.

Much of the agitation for legislation is the consequence of massive abuses and the heavy-handed use of power; it is not generated by the occasional dishonest, misguided, or unthinking executive who acts in bad faith. Consequently, if the country's largest franchise agreements contained arbitration clauses, some of the presently proposed legislation would be unnecessary or at least would undergo substantial modification.

Reactions to this explanation for increased arbitration depend on whether one is a defender or critic of business. The defenders will see arbitration as nothing more than another step in big business's orderly and inevitable movement toward fairer treatment of their customers. Critics will interpret arbitration as an attempt either to manipulate legislation dealing with buyer-seller relations or an effort to thwart it altogether.

A final possible explanation, more Machiavellian in character, is that franchisors may perceive an increasingly litigant business environment, and arbitration may suit the needs of the franchisor better than a courtroom solution. It can be argued that arbitration, a seemingly conscientious attempt to arrive at a fair solution to all parties, can be prostituted to favor the franchisor. A contract can be written that permits arbitration, but it may also describe the issues to be negotiated, the method of selection of the arbitrators, the manner in which they are paid, the location of arbitration, and other factors.

Any one of these factors can affect the decision of the arbitration panel and can be used to manipulate the decision. The decision of an arbitration panel can generally be appealed to the courts, but the courts historically have been reluctant to upset such decisions unless they have been patently unfair. Where decision manipulation is the intent of an arbitration clause, the franchisor presents only an illusion of fairness.

QUESTIONS FOR DISCUSSION

1. What is arbitration? Discuss how it can be utilized to resolve channel conflict situations.

2. Explain the arbitration plan initiated at General Motors by Alfred P. Sloan.

3. What potential problems are involved in using litigation to resolve channel conflict?

4. Discuss the role of the American Arbitration Association in arbitration proceedings.

5. Explain how arbitration can be used in the franchising industry. Identify several specific issues in franchising likely to be resolved by arbitration.

Chapter 5

Channel Control

IT IS PROBABLY a safe statement to assert that most channel members would prefer to have as much channel control over the other channel members as possible. As will become clear after reading the selections in this section, it cannot be said *a priori* which channel member will be the controlling or dominant link in any given marketing channel.

One major retailer appears to be the channel controller in the appliance industry in Philadelphia. The firm is Silo, Inc. and it has 10 percent of the appliance business in Philadelphia. Silo has no allegiance to any manufacturer and supplier, and this, its managers claim, is their major strength. *Business Week* noted that, "When a supplier's prices and products are not producing satisfactory margins, he hears about it quickly. One observer, sitting outside an executive's office, saw two salespersons figuratively tossed out by the seat of their pants with the imprecation to 'come back when you've got the right price' ringing in their ears."[1]

In other industries the channel controller is the manufacturer. Thus, when Ethan Allen Industries decided to control the marketing channels for their Early American line of furniture, they established a network of 200 dealer outlets. To date, Ethan Allen's exclusive dealer system has proven very successful. Sales have nearly doubled between 1965 and 1971. Nathan S. Ancell, President of Ethan Allen, points out, "For years people in the furniture industry have been telling me I'll lose money if I keep selling my own products. They keep insisting that a manufacturer can't make it in the retail end."[2] Apparently Mr. Ancell is disproving his critics.

In an attempt to maximize its channel control, Litton Industries' Power Transmission Division is currently using salespersons who also represent other customers. *Sales Management* noted that Stephen Brand, divisional sales manager, ". . . admits that, like most sales managers, he'd perfer his own direct sales force. He'd have greater control of

1. "An Appliance Dealer With a Real Clout," *Business Week* (November 6, 1971), p. 76.
2. "Ethan Allen Breaks With Tradition," *Business Week* (June 10, 1972), p. 22.

direct salesmen, he says, and would know they were spending eight hours a day selling Litton products. 'But I don't have a money machine. I couldn't afford to maintain a 2,000-man force that could see and service customers all over the country on a day-to-day basis.'"[3]

In many consumer goods industries, the retailer is clearly assuming the role of channel captain. A 1976 article in *Business Week* noted that the major consumer food companies were having their salespeople call on supermarkets two to four times more often than they did five years before. A General Mills executive remarked, "With fewer products coming to the marketplace, the fight for shelf space is changing. We are no longer just fighting to get products on display. We also have to make it attractive for the grocer to display them longer."[4] To achieve this objective, General Mills stresses packaging with eye appeal, forceful advertising, and more lucrative trade deals for the grocers. Another GM executive stated, "There is no such thing as the 'safe' account any more. Couponing and incentives are becoming much more important."[5]

A final illustration is provided by the Sherwin-Williams Company, a large manufacturer of paint and related products. Frustrated by the lack of aggressiveness shown by retailers selling their products, the firm established its own chain of 1,600 retail outlets. In 1975, Sherwin-Williams experienced an 18 percent increase in sales to $459 million.[6]

The first selection provides an excellent introduction to the subject of channel control by attempting to answer the perplexing question of who should ideally be the channel captain. It is followed by Stern's article which examines interorganizational cooperation and control. Stern concludes that unless each channel member coordinates his activities with the other participants in the channel, the total channel effort will be less than optimum.

The third selection by Professor Moyer delves into the ramifications of the retailer serving as channel captain. In the conclusion to this well-researched article Moyer states, "In the marketplace, mass retailers are important channel captains, and in academia they are usually the favored ones. Yet they are often less understanding of their environments than has been commonly thought."

The next selection has become a channel classic. Professor McCammon presents a thorough discussion of one of the most significant ongoing trends in marketing channels—vertical contractually integrated marketing channels. As the author states, one of the prime motivating forces

3. "Don't Just Stand There—Talk to Them," *Sales Management* (September 15, 1970), p. 25.
4. "The Hard Road of the Food Processors," *Business Week* (March 8, 1976), p. 53.
5. *Ibid.*
6. "A Paintmaker Puts a Fresh Coat on its Marketing," *Business Week* (February 23, 1976), p. 95.

for this trend is to prohibit "static" or "noise" in the channel and to achieve a greater degree of control over the other channel members.

The next selection by Professors Foran and McGann examines marketing channels as social systems. It is noted that viewing the channel as a system of activities, interactions, and sentiments can lead to fresh insights into channel strategy.

The next selection is a fast moving roundtable discussion dealing with distributor incentive programs. As this article indicates, if maximum efficiency and control are to be achieved, both sides must clearly appreciate the benefits of participating in the program. The final selection is from *Sales and Marketing Management*. J. D. Kimball, vice-president-marketing of the Sola Electric Company, presents a number of pragmatic techniques for a manufacturer to use in order to maintain the cooperation and sales efforts of the manufacturers' representative.

5.1 THE MARKETING CHANNEL: WHO SHOULD LEAD THIS EXTRACORPORATE ORGANIZATION?

Robert W. Little

"An attempt is made to answer the implicit question: Who should be the 'Channel Captain'?"

This inquiry is directed toward the potential for leadership and control of marketing channels. Various types of firms, in the narrow sense, comprise a marketing channel and any one theoretically could serve as its leader. An attempt is made to answer the implicit question: Who should be the "Channel Captain"? First, the relevance of the question and then the case for central direction will be briefly discussed. The bases for control of an interorganizational network follow. The analysis is primarily devoted to the identification of the principals who might direct the channel, and to the answer of the following questions: Who is in the best position to lead the channel? Who has the power to do so? Who should lead?

THE QUESTION OF LEADERSHIP

"Leadership" and "control" are abstract terms and are often used interchangeably. Here, control is interpreted as the ability to predict events or to achieve a desired outcome. This can be realized by the capacity to direct or command the activity or behavior of others. Leadership is a somewhat broader term which suggests the *exercise* of control. This can come about in channel terms, primarily through the use of economic sanctions or incentives. It can also be realized by persuasiveness—the capacity to communicate and negotiate with different parties to achieve a better understanding of common goals and therefore more effective cooperation. A change in the behavior or perception of any channel member toward a position or goal desired by the leader is evidence of effective control through leadership.

Reprinted by permission from Robert W. Little, "The Marketing Channel: Who Should Lead this Extracorporate Organization?" *Journal of Marketing*, Vol. 34 (January 1970), pp. 31–38.

The questions raised in this article provide an approach to understanding the need for leadership in marketing channels. Knowledge of the bases for control, initial judgments regarding what institution(s) can lead the channel, and some limited suggestions about who should lead can evolve. These judgments and understandings are necessary for firms that want to control *their* marketing channels. Important strategy considerations for potential channel leaders may also be suggested. Other channel members will also benefit because they should understand more fully their role in channel operations as well as their relationships with others in the system. They can capitalize on this knowledge to enhance their own positions when bargaining with the channel leader and others in the system. Scholars with public policy interests will find this inquiry relevant, too. If channel direction is likely to be pursued at any rate, and achieved in many cases, those concerned with the role of channel activities in the economy can begin to judge who should be the channel leader, and under what conditions. They can proceed to decisions regarding what limitations, if any, are necessary outside the channel itself.

THE CASE FOR CHANNEL LEADERSHIP

In an advanced, high mass consumption economy, marketing channels should be directed by some member firm. At least two logical bases support this assertion. The first rests on simple observation and deduction. Many firms have sought and achieved control of significant portions of their channel(s). In the absence of strong goals superordinate to a profit motive, they seek control because profits are perceived to be enhanced. The widespread existence of integrated firms constitutes presumptive evidence that economies are realized by formal organization of all or part of the channel. Examples are voluntary and cooperative chains, corporate chains, franchise alignments, manufacturers' dealer organizations, and sales branches and offices. To argue that partial integration is accomplished merely to secure greater profits through market control in an oligopolistic or monopolistic sense is simply too easy a response: Heflebower supports this view at least partially in his conjectures on mass distribution.[1]

A second and more persuasive logical base rests on the simple recognition of the marketing channel as an interorganizational system. It has the disadvantages of large-scale organizations. Because firms are

---

1. Richard B. Heflebower, "Mass Distribution: A Phase of Bilateral Oligopoly or of Competition?" *American Economic Review*, Vol. XLVII (May, 1957), pp. 274–285; published concurrently in *Adaptive Behavior in Marketing*, Robert D. Buzzell, ed. (Chicago, Ill.: American Marketing Association, 1957), pp. 139–152.

loosely arranged, the advantages of central direction are in large measure missing. The absence of single ownership, or close contractual agreements, means that the benefits of a formal power (superior, subordinate) base are not realized. The reward and penalty system is not as precise and is less easily effected. Similarly, overall planning for the entire system is uncoordinated and the perspective necessary to maximize total system effort is diffused. Less recognition of common goals by various member firms in the channel, as compared to a formally structured organization, is also probable.

ARGUMENT AGAINST CENTRAL
DIRECTION OF THE CHANNEL

Some would argue that the best ordering of firms and their relationships one with another is determined by the free play of market forces, the assignment of functions, and activities being the result of continuing "make or buy" decisions by different firms. Middlemen and other specialized agencies offer external economies to manufacturers or to others by absorbing one or more activities for several firms and, by aggregating these, achieve an optimum scale operation not available to individual client firms. These arguments, however, are based on the constraints of the traditional competitive models. Entrepreneurs *do* seek to gain control over the activities of others, and they realize it in varying degrees. They do so because their operations are affected, often quite significantly, by the activities of others in the channel.

BASES FOR CHANNELS CONTROL AND LEADERSHIP

The bases for control in channels arise most logically from the sources of inefficiency inherent in any organization. These are summed up in the three broad classes of conflict—structure, communications, and joint decision making.[2] In order to reduce these, some form of power must be exercised. A restrictive and simplified perspective is proposed which is especially relevant for economic institutions. Only two forms of power are generalized—economic and position power. Although innumerable sources of economic power exist, it is ultimately manifest in concentration of capital resources. Position power evolves from the placement of

2. Russell L. Ackoff, "Structural Conflict Within Organizations," pp. 427–438, and Richard E. Walton, "Theory of Conflict in Lateral Organizational Relationships," pp. 409–426, both in *Operational Research and the Social Sciences* (London, England: Tavistock Publications, 1966). The close parallel between these conflicts and Alderson's characteristics of the organized behavior system will not be lost on marketing scholars.

a firm, function, or activity in a given structure. The locus of a particular establishment in a channel (geographically or in terms of a functional or activity flow, for example, negotiation or ownership transfer) may confer power—a capacity to direct or to change—on the person or firm who holds that place or position. Juxtaposition between two firms or activities may also prove to be a significant nodal point to which a power element accrues. At a more specific level of analysis, differences between physical distribution flows and others might lead to shifts or simply different arrangements of power.

POTENTIAL CHANNEL LEADERS

In a complex, high mass consumption economy, small retailers and wholesalers have neither the position to lead nor the necessary economic power to do so. The key consideration in terms of position power is access to markets. Small retailers and wholesalers offer only a few customers to the channel system, and thus their bargaining position vis-à-vis large firms at any level in the channel is insignificant. However, they are in a position to provide market information. They should be intimately familiar with customers' preferences and habits. But often they neither acquire these data nor, if they do, share them with others. There are several reasons to explain such reticence. For example, their goals are different from large firms. Often they do not recognize the importance of formal collection and analysis of these data, and lack sufficient funds and time to do so. Small retailers and wholesalers have little economic power either; by definition they are *small* and therefore have few capital resources.

If not small middlemen, who can lead? Large manufacturers can lead, and sometimes small ones, too. But first large wholesalers and retailers must be considered. A new context is suggested for their study.

THE MULTI-LEVEL MERCHANDISER

An analysis of "pure" wholesalers and retailers excludes too much channel activity when the greater part of consumer and industrial-commercial exchanges are considered. Most trade flows through integrated marketing institutions. In the United States, and probably in any high mass consumption economy, there is no such thing as just a "large retailer." There are only large, or huge, retail-wholesale integrated organizations. Whether corporate chain, voluntary chain, or retailer-cooperative, the distinctions between them are less significant than their points of commonality. In any of these categories, many retail outlets are tied directly to some form of wholesale organization. Small "inde-

pendent," retailer members attached to a voluntary or cooperative organization have, in reality, quite limited sources of supply outside their
own retail-wholesale channel. In practice they are nearly as limited in
their choices as are retail unit managers in many corporate chains.
Outside the system, additional contractual and transactional costs are
most often exorbitant. McVey suggests that some wholesalers command
access to their local markets,[3] but almost no small retailer has such
power. He chooses from the key wholesale establishment with which he
is aligned, and perhaps from two or three others. In customary terms,
then, to consider retailers or wholesalers as potential channel captains
is misleading. The relevant institution is the combined wholesale-retail
organization. The term W-R or R-W, the lead symbol denoting the force
of leadership, indicates this marketing agency.

In addition, many conventionally identified manufacturers are ex-
cluded since ownership of their own sales branches and offices removes
them from any reasonable concept of a "pure" unaligned entity. Also,
many vertical relationships between manufacturers and distributors are
of a rigid contractual nature. When these involve relatively permanent
commitments over a wide range of functional requirements by both
parties, they resemble more closely an ownership arrangement than the
concept of independent operations. These organizations are identified
as M-W and W-M.

Finally, there are the fully integrated organizations. The huge, general
merchandise retail organizations include not only Sears and Penney
types of operation, but also national department store chains such as
Allied Stores and Marshall Field (R-W-M). These are not simply combined retail-wholesale organizations, but represent direct ownership
(sometimes extensive) or control (often extensive) of manufacturing
and service facilities. In addition, major automobile, appliance, and petroleum refiners, and perhaps a few others, own retail outlets or have
tight, contractual, semi-permanent relationships with retailers (M-W-R).

There is, finally, the W $_{\cdot M}^{\cdot R}$ integrated organization—McKesson, for
example—where the wholesaler makes central decisions for some manufacturer and retailer components of the channel. For the moment, this is
treated as an aberration which will drift ultimately to M-W-R or R-W-M.

There are seven potential channel leaders to consider, and each
should be classified into two types. One encompasses all organizations
integrated by direct ownership; the other includes those maintained by
long-standing, contractual relationships. They cover a wide range of

3. Philip McVey, "Are Channels of Distribution What the Textbooks Say?"
Journal of Marketing, Vol. 25 (January, 1960), pp. 61–65.

required activities and go well beyond the simple buy-sell relationships established by independent firms.

In order to keep the number of institutional types manageable, a new institution, the multi-level merchandiser (MLM), is introduced. The MLM includes all retail- and wholesale-directed organizations: the R-W, the W-R, the W_{M}^{R}, the R-W-M, and the W-M. This is not an unreasonable grouping; the distinction between corporate chains, retailer-cooperatives, and wholesale voluntaries is much less than their similarity. The R-W-M also has many points in common with the previous two although more differences exist; approximately the same analysis can be used for all of these. Although rare, the W-M and the W_{M}^{R} are by definition, merchandising oriented and, to the extent they exist, are considered MLM. The analysis of manufacturer-integrated organizations, M-W-R and M-W, parallels the discussion of the manufacturer, and is considered later. In spite of the problems involved, this generalization eliminates much of the confusion and obscurity inherent in the present definitional literature. The introduction of these new terms does not solve the existing taxonomy problems; indeed, it is compounded by adding new terms. However, the different perspective is believed to provide a useful point of departure for channel study.[4]

Craig and Gabler provided the landmark study of partial integration. They observed that integration organized backward from the retailer (R-W) went with the market situation and integration organized forward from the wholesaler (W-R) went against the market situation. Their ultimate conclusion was that from "... the strictly business interest of the consumer . . . the retailer-guided system of distribution is to be preferred."[5] But operational differences today between wholesaler-sponsored voluntary chains and retailer-cooperative chains (and even retail-corporate chains) are insubstantial. In fact, it is difficult to distinguish one from another. To the extent that they apply today, Craig and Gabler's conclusions can be safely extended to all MLM organiza-

4. See Louis P. Bucklin, "The Economic Structure of Channels of Distribution," in *Marketing: A Maturing Discipline*, Martin T. Bell, ed. (Chicago, Ill.: American Marketing Association, 1960), pp. 379–385, for an excellent basis for diagramming internal channel functions to supplement this MLM genus. See also Louis P. Bucklin and Stanley F. Stasch, "Basic Problems in the Study of Channels," Working Paper No. 35 (Berkeley, Calif.: University of California, Institute of Business and Economic Research, November, 1967). The authors offer a persuasive argument for adoption of polythetic marketing taxonomies.

5. David R. Craig and Werner K. Gabler, "The Competitive Struggle for Market Control," *The Annals of the American Academy of Political and Social Science*, Vol. 209 (May, 1940), pp. 84–107, at p. 99.

tions. Most MLM organizations are large enough to have considerable economic power and, in addition, their position affords them access to large markets. They are also in a position to provide market information. Certainly, they can be considered as potential channel leaders.

THE MANUFACTURER

Large manufacturers are potential leaders of channels, by definition, since they have economic power. But small manufacturers may also serve as potential sources of control and direction of a vertical, interorganizational structure. As Borden has emphasized, limited economic power hampers their opportunity, but a good product offers control possibilities.[6] This is a manifestation of position strength. Those in the position of controlling a new product—desired by many consumers—can elect to offer or withhold their product from various middlemen and therefore exercise control. Craig and Gabler observed this long ago.

> As long as the existing demand or newly awakened demands exceed the supply, selling was easy and its costs were low. Whoever could make the wanted merchandise was in a strategic position to guide and direct its distribution.[7]

Clearly, large manufacturers enjoy similar position strength.

Although they observed a shift to sellers' markets later on, and followed this with the judgment that retailer-guided channel systems were best, Craig and Gabler failed to consider the enormous diversity and dynamism in an advanced, technologically diverse, economy. Many different products are in different states of development at the same time. There is no such thing as a *general* buyers' or sellers' market. Consequently, manufacturers—large and small—and MLM organizations are potential leaders of marketing channels.

THE LEADER—MLM OR MANUFACTURER?

ECONOMIC POWER

Either an MLM organization or a large manufacturer can lead because ability rests on economic power. They can control resources, "buy" time by utilizing staff specialists, and employ their resources in a manner to help the channel reduce conflict arising from any of the basic sources

6. Neil H. Borden, *Acceptance of New Products by Supermarkets* (Boston, Mass.: Division of Research, Graduate School of Business Administration, Harvard University, 1968), p. 13.

7. Same reference as footnote 5, p. 85.

of organizational conflict. For example, either organization can employ research personnel to learn more about customers and markets and therefore reduce uncertainty and improve communications throughout the channel. They have the economic power to communicate and enforce a greater recognition of the system's common goals which are congruent with some goals in each member firm. They have the ability to enforce, through economic sanction, a reward and penalty system within the interorganizational structure. They are thus able to design and administer joint-decision efforts and responsibilities in a manner that can lead to less conflict than would likely be the case without their intervention.

POSITION POWER

The MLM.   Position in the channel offers unique advantages to each party. The MLM has access to large markets manufacturers seek to reach. The larger the MLM and the greater the market its establishments serve, the more important is its adoption decision to most manufacturers; therefore, the MLM holds a strong potential for leadership. The strength of the MLM is much more than just a simple bargaining coalition which, Kuhn observes, ". . . differs from an organization in that it does not jointly produce anything, but only raises bargaining power by limiting the opponent's alternatives—i.e. by reducing competition."[8]

The MLM creates additional values for the system. In terms of decision making, its assembled resources, technology, skill, and experience place it in a unique position to reduce system inefficiencies. And it can realize substantial economies from the routinization of transactions. When considering structural changes, the MLM's power is often enormous. Because of its size and position in the market, the MLM can absorb directly a large measure of uncertainty for manufacturers regarding the acceptance of products by assuring them access to widespread markets. Indirectly, uncertainty may also be reduced for other manufacturers when the MLM markets its own brand.

These organizations are estimated to make merchandising decisions for two-thirds or more of all retail markets, since even many "convenience store" merchandising decisions, as well as decisions by corporate and contractual chains, are determined by the MLMs. The MLM chooses from many manufacturers' offerings which it may add, exclude, or drop almost at will. It has extraordinary influence over the degree of success realized by even the largest manufacturers. For example, in six markets studied by Borden, five corporate chains and two voluntary organizations controlled 65% of the grocery market in the least concentrated

8. Alfred Kuhn, *The Study of Society: A Multidisciplinary Approach* (London, England: Tavistock Publications, 1960), p. 385.

market. In the most concentrated market, six corporate chains and two voluntary organizations controlled 93% of the market.[9] Market concentration in most non-grocery fields is undoubtedly lower but still strong enough to support similar conclusions.

Limitations on the MLM.   Leadership and direction appear heavily weighted toward the MLM, but there are important offsetting factors to consider. When product development and demand-creation functions are considered, the MLM's position strength is substantially diminished. Only rarely are product modifications different enough to suggest that the MLM has provided any real sense of direction when offering its own reseller brands. Strength is minimal because the MLM's principal function is selecting and maintaining wanted stocks. The MLM is in no position to pursue demand creation or product-development functions. Many have the financial strength to accomplish this, but it is not their role. In theory, retail units are closest to the consumer and therefore the MLM is in a good position to lead by identifying user preferences. In reality, its specialists are much too concerned with selecting and maintaining stocks, and providing and merchandising the services that accompany them, to be able to meet this role. Retailers' brands are economically feasible only after widespread market acceptance has been established. Only with fully accepted generic products can the MLM assume the risk of introducing its own brands. This is summarized in the following generalization.

> The greater the acceptance by final users of a generic class of goods, the more likely control over channels through which these products flow will be held by the MLM.

The Manufacturer.   Manufacturers have significant position strength although it varies with changing market conditions. With a new product and substantial financial resources, the manufacturer can establish strong consumer demand, and control of channels is relatively easily established. Middlemen tend to accept complete, multifaceted, well-planned programs of new product introductions.[10] However, only large manufacturers are able to develop total programs for new product introduction and promotion and can, therefore, be clearly identified as channel leaders for new products.

With a good product but little financial strength, the manufacturer must offer high gross margins and other incentives to encourage middleman support. (The *Colgate Doctrine*, supporting refusal to deal, is still the small manufacturer's most fundamental protection.[11]) Position

---

9. Same reference as footnote 6, p. 10.
10. Same reference as footnote 6, pp. 180–184.
11. *United States vs. Colgate*, 250 U. S. 300 (1919).

strength and control is exercised by the small manufacturer, but it is less easily realized and maintained.

Once a strong consumer franchise is established, however, even the small manufacturer enjoys fairly easy control which is often maintained into market maturity.

Limitations on Manufacturers. But there are also offsetting influences regarding manufacturers' position strength. The MLM controls all the products branded for its organization. Also, MLMs, where territories overlap, are in competition with one another. Some handle the same manufacturer's products and others handle close substitutes. This complicates the analysis in a sense and adds some confusion because the MLM prefers exclusive territorial rights. Greater position strength for the manufacturer is, therefore, suggested. In general, however, the desire for full market coverage by manufacturers tends to weaken their position, and as a result probably more than offsets the apparent strength noted above.

In addition, even a strong manufacturer brand is weakened by the nature of the MLM's operation. As Sevin has aptly remarked:

> All merchandising decision making . . . is necessarily done at the level of the individual item—e.g., what to buy, display, promote; how to price, etc.[12]

Beyond the initial choice of a generalized assortment, any middleman must base his product selection on the basis of gross-margin dollars. Loyalty to selected channel members and/or antagonism to others should not interfere with his individual item decisions; he operates within a fixed space and returns per cubic foot concern him most.

Furthermore, even the largest manufacturer seldom can afford the luxury of his own distribution system. While a few may be able to achieve broad enough coverage through their own sales branches and offices, most manufacturers will be forced to use independent wholesalers and MLMs to reach a variety of customer types in addition to those who can be reached through their own system. Those controlling their own retail outlets almost always will be forced to secure additional representation in other retail stores. Most items stocked by the MLM have close substitutes. Usually, the reverse is not the case—the supplier needs many different MLMs.

Finally, market maturity is usually reached when there are substantial increases in industry capacity, through the entry of close substitutes from other manufacturers' and resellers' brands. This more or less defines market acceptance of the generic product class; economic power is then the ultimate determinant of channel control. At this final stage, effective

12. Charles H. Sevin, *Marketing Productivity Analysis* (New York, N.Y.: McGraw-Hill Book Company, Inc., 1965), p. 34.

control tends to lean toward the MLM, especially for the small manufacturer.

SUMMARY

Strength of position and economic power is indeterminate. Throughout a product's life cycle, the manufacturer's income and consumer franchise will increase while his exclusiveness, unless he has a very uncopiable product, will tend to depreciate. As this takes place, the manufacturer's *position* strength will tend to decline because less uncertainty surrounds the product and more substitutes are available, but his *ability* to direct will increase because his economic power is enhanced. Similarly, movement through the cycle alters the MLM's strength. With products of long standing acceptance where demand creation is less necessary, the MLM can enter the market with its own generic product, and thus create and direct a new channel. At the same time, however, the increasing strength of the manufacturer's brand makes the MLM less able to reject the product than before. Too many of its customers demand it.

In general, the MLM and the manufacturer must share leadership of the channel. In a period of generic product acceptance, however, the MLM tends to hold the greater measure of power. The MLM not only can decide to enter the market with its own brand, but it can decide *which* of the leading brands it will stock. The producer's power is substantially weakened under these conditions. The wider distribution requirements of most manufacturers, then, suggest a distinct imbalance in favor of MLM organization.

Three generalizations help to summarize the channel leadership role.

MLM organizations are in the best position to lead channels because the value to the manufacturer of market access provided by each MLM far exceeds the value of one more product to the MLM merchandising mix.

The more product sources are available to the MLM within a channel system, the more the locus of power will tend to shift toward the MLM.

Reciprocally, the wider the manufacturer's product line, the greater his economic significance to MLM organizations and the greater his potential power.

RELEVANCE FOR MARKETING MANAGEMENT

The value and uses of economic power to seek leadership of the channel should be clear to the manufacturer and the MLM. The manufacturer can use economic power to establish a stronger consumer franchise for his product(s) and to gain its acceptance by desired middlemen. The MLM can enjoy its resources to provide more and better market access for its suppliers. Both can utilize their capital resources to "encourage" greater recognition of common goals that, by definition, all channel members share in part. Their economic and position strength can also be used to coordinate more effectively the joint decision responsibilities of various member firms, and to facilitate communication and understanding between and among all members. Both can also use economic resources to support more careful studies of market structures and functions which should lead to the searching out of new alignment alternatives . . . the discovery of "better" channels.

For the MLM, knowledge of its role in the channel network can support a more effective bargaining stance with suppliers and buyers, and can lead to a fuller realization of its own goals. How many consumers' foods manufacturers do not want space in A&P or Super-Valu stores? The manufacturer, on the other hand, can use the knowledge of his unique position with greater force. He should know more about his final users than other channel members. In addition, he knows more about his own product(s) than does anyone else. He can and should exploit this knowledge in convincing the desired middleman to accept and/ or continue his products. In addition, a manufacturer's strong product franchise, accompanied by a realistic gross margin, severely limits the MLM's ability to bargain. Are there many appropriate retail outlets that do not carry Crest or Gillette?

Small wholesalers, retailers, and manufacturers who are not leaders can also benefit from the knowledge of who holds a strategic position and economic power. The recognition of the source of leadership gives them the opportunity to seek out channels guided by those who appear to be best able to contribute to their own individual goals. Understanding the relationships between all members in the channel should also lead to acceptance of one's role within the channel(s) involved. Also, non-leader members should recognize the *reality* of competing channel systems. This is simply an extension of the valuable concept of Smith and Kelley's competing retail systems.[13] A retailer, for example, must realize that much of his competition comes not only from similar establishments close by but also from retail outlets linked with other vertical market structures.

Knowledge of the economic and position strength of various channel members is also valuable to those outside the channel. It is important to those who wish to study the overall institutional structure of the

13. Paul E. Smith and Eugene J. Kelley, "Competing Retail Systems: The Shopping Central Business District," *Journal of Retailing*, Vol. XXXVI (Spring, 1960), pp. 11–18.

economy and specifically the role of marketing channels in contributing to growth and welfare. This is part of the final question considered in this article.

WHO SHOULD LEAD?

The preceding questions about position and ability are at least conducive to empirical measures. Although the discussion is theoretical, limited historical data lend some support to the conclusions. Now a move further away from the empirical measures is necessary. Who should lead? The question is important, although there are no definitive answers and subjective standards must be employed.

CHOICE AND EFFICIENCY

Two measures, choice and efficiency, guide the following analysis. They are necessarily conflicting goals in a narrow sense, but compatible in the broader perspective. The United States has supported the ideal, and in large measure, the reality of widespread individual choice which is most succinctly expressed in Lord Acton's paraphrased words: "The degree of civilization is directly proportional to the degree of choice." This requires an important qualification. Choice means "real" choice, choice from knowledge. When a buyer selects "A" rather than "B" on the basis of presumed differences that are in fact mere distortions, the choice process is perverted. A second difference is manifest in product complexity. Given reasonable knowledge and effort, if a buyer is unable to learn the relevant factors involved in an exchange, he chooses from ignorance rather than from knowledge. Channel agencies, and more specifically their employees in dealing with others, can help to confound or to clarify "real" choice.

The second criterion is efficiency—matching goods and consumption at the least cost consistent with widespread choice. The efficiency criterion implies that nonmaterial goals are enhanced or made more attainable, by material progress.

GENERALIZATIONS ON WHO SHOULD LEAD

Who should lead? Not nearly enough is known; however, some logical bases exist, relative to analyzing this question and several hypotheses can be developed.

That part of the marketing mix which is most difficult to match is the essence of competition. Wasson identifies product as the most important competitive tool because "... what one man can do another can find a way to copy, sooner or later. Thus, all differential advantages are temporary, and the successful can remain so only through continual innovation." [14] His view is a good one, but needs qualification. The most important competitive tool is the one most difficult to copy. For a local producer of liquid detergent, the competitive issue is the advertising budget. The factor most difficult for him to match, in his struggle with Procter and Gamble, Lever Brothers, and others, is the size of the advertising budget. In competition with Magnavox or Bell and Howell, another manufacturer might find the discovery and control of the channel as the competitive issue. For many the research capacity of DuPont is most difficult to match. From any perspective, size is most difficult to match if the small firm is compared vis-à-vis the large.

Competitive advantage must be identified for each prospective channel leader in order to determine which will encourage the greatest choice at the highest efficiency. The manufacturer's best opportunity for differential advantage is the development of new products and services. The resulting consumer franchise is his principal means to economic power and other goals. If new products and services are matched, the manufacturer's advantage is lost.

Merchandising organizations, MLM, seek differential advantage primarily through location. While customer and merchandising services are important, location of retail outlets is *the* competitive variable because it is the most difficult to match. The merchandiser's own brands also provide differential advantage but are more easily duplicated. In terms of choice, the MLM offers little to the consumer that is especially different when it selects various generic products for its own brand. These comprise a small part of its stock anyway, and it cannot accept the risk of new product introduction.

Both the manufacturer's and the MLM's ploys extend consumer choice. But in a high mass consumption society, wedded to the automobile and characterized by excess transport capacity, consumer choice is advanced more by new product introductions than it is by new brand introductions and additional retail locations. This is true unless brand proliferation, to which both the manufacturer and MLM contribute, leads to such an array of substitute products that the consumer cannot learn important differences.

If new products provide more choice than new locations, then the manufacturer should lead marketing channels. But the efficiency question must be answered too. Manufacturers' new product costs must be compared with MLMs' costs absorbed in selecting and developing additional locations. They must also be compared with MLMs' costs in diverse locations, many of which operate at less than optimum scale. To

14. Chester R. Wasson, *The Economics of Managerial Decision* (New York: Appleton-Century-Crofts, 1965), p. 3.

measure which of these is greater is difficult if not impossible. But the efficiency criterion is stated as requiring system performance at the least cost consistent with widespread choice, and choice is always costly. Narrowly observed, distribution of one electric razor through one channel is more efficient than distribution of ten razors through 15 channels. Choice is expanded in the latter case, however, and society has decided that choice is safer and worth the additional cost. Thus, unless the cost of developing new products rises beyond socially acceptable limits, manufacturer-directed channel systems are best suited to achieve consumer goals; therefore, manufacturers should lead.

REPRISE

Speculation, theory, and model building have far outstripped the quest for empirical verification. We must have more reports in the classic mold of Cox and Goodman, and Craig and Gabler.[15] In marketing, we use a few scientific tools, but the facts are mostly literary.[16] This is not really surprising in view of the enormously complicated relationships involved. The questions, answers, and perspectives set out in this paper have been shaped by some of the things we know and by some of the things we should know. But they are unfulfilled. More empiricism is needed. For example, data indicating the relative strength of MLM organizations in various industries would establish more clearly a need for further study. Determining the nature and extent of diseconomies in large corporate and highly contractually integrated channels, as opposed to less formally organized ones, could add important insights. Analysis of the relative efficiency of formal and informal channels for each basic marketing flow or function—physical distribution, promotion, information, and communication, for example—is needed. Finally, the conclusion suggested here regarding who should lead is highly subjective. Attempts to establish appropriate empirical measures should be pursued.

QUESTIONS FOR DISCUSSION

1. What are the basic characteristics of a "channel captain?"

2. What is a "multi-level merchandiser?"

15. Reavis Cox and C. S. Goodman, "Marketing of Housebuilding Materials," *Journal of Marketing*, Vol. 21 (July, 1956), pp. 36–61. Also see same reference as footnote 5.
16. Kenneth E. Boulding, *The Impact of the Social Sciences* (New Brunswick, New Jersey: The Rutgers University Press, 1966), pp. 3–23.

3. a. Who does Little believe should be the channel captain in a period of generic product acceptance? Why?

   b. Do you agree with Little's conclusion?

4. What generalizations can you develop regarding how a channel member can be more efficient when he or she has an understanding of the channel captain concept?

5. Present an argument in favor of the manufacturer assuming the role of channel captain.

5.2 CHANNEL CONTROL AND INTERORGANIZATION MANAGEMENT

Louis W. Stern

"It has become apparent to the author that an individual firm's objective of maximizing its own performance without regard to the performance of those other firms in the channel with which it does business is invalid in the long run."

DEFINITION OF CHANNEL CONTROL

Channel control is used here to signify the ability of one member of a marketing channel for a given product (or brand) to stipulate marketing policies to other channel members. For example, in a simple channel where a buyer interacts directly with a seller, the party gaining control in the bargaining process either through the use of sheer economic power, political or legal means, superior knowledge, more subtle promotional aids, or other methods, obtains a major advantage in all aspects of their relationship. When marketing policies may be stipulated by any one party, this may have a marked influence on the efficiencies of both. Their goals may not be totally compatible; therefore, by complying with the dictates of buyers, for example, sellers may frequently be forced to alter their methods of operation in a manner that is not often profitable for them.

The exercise of channel control can, of course, vary widely. At one extreme are situations of channel tyranny in which one channel member insists on compliance to policies and practices from other members that he believes are in his best interests but which may not be in theirs. At the other extreme are situations of benevolent channel leadership in which the most powerful member is able to manage the channel so that overall channel performance can be increased.[1] In the former case the

---

Reprinted by permission from Louis W. Stern, "Channel Control and Inter-Organization Management," *Marketing and Economic Development*, edited by Peter D. Bennett (Chicago: American Marketing Association, 1965), pp. 655–665.

1. Bruce Mallen describes various channel relationships as approaching either

application of current management theories and tools to intrafirm problems often fosters narrow, self-oriented goal definitions and may result in decisions which impair the performance of other firms within the channel, thereby diminishing the performance of the entire system.[2] In the latter case benevolence may be identified with enlightened long-run considerations on the part of the most powerful channel member.

TWO EXAMPLES OF CHANNEL CONTROL

Buyers or sellers rarely achieve complete control over the marketing activities of their channel opposites. One group or member may, however, exercise the balance of channel power. This latter factor provides the means by which the "victors" in the vertical conflict are able to stipulate marketing policies to the vanquished. It is also likely that the extent of control achieved by a channel member may vary with the type of vertical conflict involved. For example, the seller may establish the price discount schedule for various quantities, but the buyer still determines (within the constraints of the seller's policy) the quantity actually purchased, which may or may not be the most profitable from the standpoint of the seller. In addition, there may also be an ephemeral quality to channel control. The following two examples serve to illustrate the emergence and/or existence of control at opposite ends of the channel of distribution.

EXAMPLE 1: THE AUTOMOBILE INDUSTRY

Concerning the distribution of automobiles, Ridgeway has made the following observations: (1) An automobile manufacturer is in a strategic position to try to bring order and uniformity to the marketing channel for his products, because he occupies a centralized position with it. (2) "Manufacturers seek to control the activities and operation of the dealers individually and collectively." The term "control" refers to "the ability of the manufacturer to have the dealer operate for the benefit of the system." (3) The manufacturer with his supplies and/or dealers comprise a system, and "this system is in competition with similar systems

autocracy, democracy, or anarchy in "Conflict and Cooperation in Marketing Channels," *Reflections on Progress in Marketing*, L. George Smith, ed. (Chicago: American Marketing Association, 1965), pp. 65–85.

2. For a further discussion of similar reasoning, see Thomas L. Berg, "Designing the Distribution System," *The Social Responsibilities of Marketing*, William D. Stevens, ed. (Chicago: American Marketing Association, 1962), pp. 481–490.

in the economy. In order for the system to operate effectively as an integrated whole, there must be some administration of the system as a whole, not merely administration of the separate organizations within that system."[3]

If, as Ridgeway appears to suggest, the marketing channels for automobiles can be controlled by manufacturers so that the final result of their interorganizational management is desirable from the standpoint of all parties involved, then such a situation would approximate that of benevolent channel leadership. There is, unfortunately, no tangible evidence that this optimum situation has been reached. In fact, there is some historical evidence that indicates that automobile manufacturers have exercised despotic control within the channel to achieve their short-run objectives.

In the years immediately following World War II, dealers were able to increase sales yearly. During this period, manufacturers became intensely interested in achieving even higher rates of growth than the dealers were supplying. As a result, dealers were placed under tight franchise agreements and were assigned sales quotas that were designed to permit the manufacturers to realize maximum operating economies as well as to increase their overall growth rates. Dealers were forced to pay for shipments on delivery and then were expected to sell all the cars shipped by the plants. Dealers were also held to pricing and servicing standards set by the factory and were assessed part of the national advertising costs. If a dealer disagreed with these policy stipulations, he was disenfranchised. The manufacturers maintained this form of control until the middle 1950s, when the market for new automobiles slumped drastically. At that time the dealers found it impossible to sell all of the automobiles being shipped and began to revolt against the inequities imposed by the manufacturers.[4]

It is not certain whether or not the remedial measures taken by the manufacturers as a result of the revolt have eradicated the form of control existing during the decade after World War II. Ridgeway's conclusions cited previously apparently refer to an idealized situation that would no doubt be satisfactory to all channel members. It is unlikely, however, that the form of control has changed so radically in the past ten years to bring the industry full circle from channel tyranny to benevolent channel leadership.

3. Valentine P. Ridgeway, "Administration of Manufacturer-Dealer Systems," *Explorations in Retailing*, Stanley C. Hollander, ed. (Bureau of Business and Economic Research, Michigan State University, 1959), p. 250 and 256.

4. The dealer revolt was well publicized. A description of it can be found in the following issues of *Business Week:* February 4, 1956 (p. 29); March 3, 1956 (p. 104); March 23, 1957 (p. 65); February 2, 1957 (p. 25); and April 6, 1957 (p. 173).

EXAMPLE 2: THE WOOD HOUSEHOLD FURNITURE INDUSTRY[5]

The wood household furniture industry (including both manufacturers and retailers in the term "industry") is bilaterally competitive. In other words, the industry is characterized by low degrees of market concentration on both the manufacturing and retailing levels in the channel of distribution. Channel control in the hands of either retailers or manufacturers should be nonexistent or, at best, weak, because according to economic theory, the operation of open market forces should dictate the basic modes of doing business and thus should militate against the establishment of control in any one level of the channel. But control does, in actuality, exist in the wood household furniture industry; it resides at the retail level because furniture retailers have gained the greatest influence over the final sale of the products of the industry.

The fact of this control is illustrated in retailers' buying methods. Many of the manufacturers' marketing practices have been stipulated by, administered by, and/or enacted to placate furniture retailers, even though some of these policies and practices work to the detriment of manufacturers. For example, the furniture market system, under which manufacturers' exhibits are held periodically in major manufacturing and retailing centers, provides buyers with the opportunity to play off one manufacturer against another in the space of a few minutes within the same building. Manufacturers do complete a considerable volume of sales during the markets, but they have continually deplored their adverse bargaining positions and have sought ways to eliminate the markets for this and other reasons. Buyer insistence, however, has been a causal factor in influencing the manufacturers' policies with regard to market attendance and continuation.

Other examples of retail buying methods that often work to the disadvantage of manufacturers are: (1) the emphasis on sold-order buying whereby retailers carry minimum inventories, thereby forcing manufacturers to maintain large inventories and to ship in uneconomical lot sizes, (2) demands for exclusive, and (3) the desire for cumulative (as opposed to noncumulative) quantity discounts. In addition, furniture retailers look askance at, and have effectively forestalled, manufacturers' attempts to establish strong brand identity, especially where manufacturers may have wide distribution in the retailers' particular locales. The reason for this is that retailers know that consumers will shop for furniture and, if brand identity is established, will compare price from store to store on the same advertised pieces. The retailers also fear that if consumers become highly confident in their choices prior to entering

5. A more detailed description of channel control in this industry is found in an unpublished manuscript by the author entitled, "Bilateral Competition and Channel Control."

a store, a furniture salesman's selling latitude will be limited. "Switching" by sales personnel from low margin to high margin items within the store is a jealously guarded and accepted retail practice.

In sum, the retailers' buying methods mentioned above indicate that in the wood household furniture industry, retailers appear to have gained control over the channel in the sense that they have been able to stipulate many of the important marketing policies within the channel.[6]

CONTRIBUTIONS OF ECONOMIC THEORY

In cases of vertical conflict, the locus of channel control is frequently related to the types of markets in which both sellers and buyers compete. In an excellent discussion, Heflebower has described the bargaining relationships between supplying and distributing industries when these industries compete in markets characterized as oligopolistic and competitive.[7] Despite some of Heflebower's negative conclusions regarding the appropriateness of bilateral oligopoly theory for explaining the emergence of channel power among mass distributors, it is possible to attempt to make some modifications of his findings in order to show their applicability to the concept of channel control.[8]

Buyers or sellers operating in oligopolistic markets can frequently gain channel control when dealing with sellers or buyers operating in more competitive markets. One theoretical reason to explain the emergence of channel control in these situations is that oligopolists have to some extent stabilized competition among themselves. They interact under the constrainst of a rather well-defined oligopolistic rationale, while actors in a theoretically more competitive environment cannot rely on such a rationale to maintain some semblance of market stability. The latter have, almost by definition, less information about competitors' current and possible market activities and less available expertise. There is, therefore, little uniformity of action among competitors, and even if there were an opportunity for more competitive commonality, deviates would always be willing and ready to spoil the tranquility

6. Preliminary investigations indicate that situations of channel control may be found within specific segments of the food industry. For documented examples of channel control in a variety of industries, see Valentine P. Ridgeway, *op. cit.*; *The policies of Distribution* (Cambridge, Mass.: Harvard University Press, 1955); Ralph Cassady, Jr. and Wylie L. Jones, *The Changing Competitive Structure in the Wholesale Grocery Trade* (Berkeley and Los Angeles: University of California Press, 1949); and Bruce Mallen, *op. cit.*

7. See Richard B. Heflebower, "Mass Distribution: A Phase of Bilateral Oligopoly or of Competition?" *Explorations in Retailing, op. cit.*, pp. 193–204. The situation whereby "competitive-like suppliers" sell to "competitive-like distributive trades" is mentioned but not discussed by Heflebower.

8. *Ibid.*, pp. 201–203.

of the market. Another theoretical reason, among others, that might explain the emergence of channel control is the ability of oligopolists to utilize relatively large profits, gained through joint maximization, in developing strong consumer loyalties to their products or brands.

In addition, the theory of countervailing power can be extended to a theory of reaction to control. When a group of sellers, for example, "enjoys a measure of monopoly power and is reaping a measure of monopoly return as a result," and when that power can be exploited by large buyers,[9] the process of such exploitation is a factor signifying a shift in control. For example, through an increased emphasis on private labels, retailers have found an opportunity to share the gains of manufacturers' market and channel power, especially with regard to physically undifferentiated (or highly similar) items within a given product category. Retailers have used private labels as impressive bargaining levers in their negotiations with manufacturers. The implied threat by retailers to push their private labels at the expense of manufacturers' brands through the manipulation of shelf space, prices, and promotion has created the need for new and more retailer-oriented (oftentimes stipulated) marketing policies on the part of manufacturers in order to forestall possible disastrous consequences for their own brands. In many cases manufacturers have been too slow in developing these policies, and retailers have, therefore, placed even more emphasis on private labels.[10] As retail markets have become more concentrated, the locus of control has begun to shift away from manufacturers, and the private label phenomenon has been an important vehicle influencing the shift.[11]

In sum, if, in a number of industries, control and concomitantly the balance of bargaining power are centralized in one organization within a system of interrelated organizations, e.g., a marketing channel, the application of existing economic theory should provide a means by which the location of control can be determined. On the other hand, a weakness in economic theory is that it too often concentrates on price manipulation as the main determinant in bargaining situations. A lasting contribution of marketing studies to economic theory has been the discovery that in most situations price manipulation is only one element in the mix of competitive methods available to firms and that even if price is stabilized, control can be established and maintained through the manipulation of other elements. Further, implicit in economic literature is the sometimes unstated bias against central channel control, born out of a distrust for the powerful business firm.

9. See John K. Galbraith, *American Capitalism* (Boston: Houghton Mifflin Company, 1956), pp. 111–112.

10. Additional thoughts relating to the effects of increased private label activity may be found in a manuscript by the author entitled "The New World of Private Brands" to be published by the *California Management Review*.

11. See Richard B. Heflebower, *op. cit.*

INTERORGANIZATION MANAGEMENT: THE
NEEDS AND THE OBSTACLES

It was suggested earlier that, in situations approximating channel tyranny as opposed to benevolent channel leadership, the results may work to the benefit of the controlling party and possibly to the detriment of other members of the channel of distribution. For example, Balderston has delineated problems that may arise because of intraorganizational conflict, and his remarks can be easily related to marketing channels viewed as organizations or systems. He has written that:

> Conflicts often arise between groups of functionally specialized executives, e.g., between physical distribution executives and merchandising men. For display and other promotional reasons, the merchants may favor large retail units and the holding of correspondingly large inventories at the retail level, whereas physical distribution men will point to the economies of holding stocks in intermediate warehouses and of restocking retail units according to notions of efficient physical commodity flow. Similar conflicts may arise over the broadening of "captive" manufacturing facilities, and many other issues. Fundamentally, these difficulties arise in power struggles over priorities, criteria of performance, and assignments of responsibility.[12]

In this regard, various members of the channel react in like manner to the executives Balderston describes. They have vested interests and attempt to enhance these interests through the adoption of narrow, self-oriented goal definitions. In a system in which members are inflexible or where there is no leader to direct channel activities, the outcome may be chaotic or, at best, inefficient.

From a management theory point of view, there is altogether too much effort wasted in vertical conflict within any given channel of distribution. According to March and Simon:

> Many of the phenomena of intergroup conflict are almost indistinguishable from the phenomena that we might consider under (conflict within organizations) . . .[13]
>
> The distinction between units in a production-distribution process that are "in" the organization and those that are "out" of the organization typically follows the legal definition of a particular firm. We find it fruitful to use a more functional criterion that includes both the suppliers and the distributors of the manufacturing core of the organization (or its analogue where the core of the organization is not manufacturing) . . .[14]

12. F. E. Balderston, "Discussion," *Explorations in Retailing, op. cit.*, p. 206.
13. James G. March and Herbert A. Simon, *Organizations* (New York: John Wiley and Sons, Inc., 1958), p. 131 (Parenthesis supplied).
14. *Ibid.*, p. 89.

The need to view the channel as an organization of an interrelated group of firms rather than as a loose and oftentimes temporary amalgamation of competing parties has been urged by Balderston, Ridgeway, Berg, Alderson, March, Simon, Mallen, and others.

For example, Berg has emphasized that:

> Connections with suppliers, networks of financial intermediaries, and trade channels are examples of external organizations. Although they may not appear on company charts or in manuals, these should be regarded as logical extensions to the internal organization of the firm. Internal and external organizations are similar in that both deal with economic functions performed by interdependent human agents requiring motivation and coordination through communication. Both involve continuous personal relationships, routinized tasks, and stable expectations of reciprocal performance.[15]

In practice, the beginning point in organizing a channel or in forming a coalition among channel members would be to locate a potential channel leader through an economic and sociological analysis of the existing power structure within the channel. The next step would be to convince this channel member to adopt a managerial philosophy that would permit the channel, through his leadership, to achieve effective overall performance. A recent study by McKinsey and Company is certainly an example of an effort to bring this important message to the food industry.[16]

There is, however, the necessity of obtaining a leader who would be capable of formulating and directing the adoption of a set of interorganization policies and practices. If the channel is to be managed as an organization, it must be characterized by explicit goals, an elaborate system of explicit rules and regulations, and a formal status structure with clearly marked lines of communication and authority.[17] The task of manipulating such an organization will no doubt be complex. As Talcott Parsons has written:

> . . . the integrative problem within an organization most directly concerns the human agents. This point can be generalized to interorganizational integration. The central problem concerns the institutionalized norms which can effectively bind the actions of individuals in their commitments to organizations. An important feature of all complex societies is that the normal individual is involved in a multiplicity of roles. From one point of

15. Thomas L. Berg, *op. cit.*, p. 482.
16. McKinsey & Company, Inc., *Opportunities to Improve Relations Between Chains and Manufacturers* (Washington, D. C.: National Association of Food Chains, October, 1962), and *The Economics of Food Distributors* (New York: General Foods Corporation, October, 1963).
17. Peter W. Blau and W. Richard Scott, *Formal Organizations* (San Francisco: Chandler Publishing Company, 1962), p. 14.

view these roles constitute membership in or commitments to collectivities, of which in turn organizations are one principal type. The focus of the integrative problem on a transorganizational level, then, is the problem of the determination of the loyalties of participant persons . . . Clearly this allocation of loyalties, not within the organization but within the society between collectivities, is intimately connected with values.[18]

Parsons also suggests that:

. . . the management of the organization must, to some degree, take or be ready to take measures to counteract the centrifugal pull, to keep employment turnover at least down to tolerable levels, and . . . to bring the performances of subunits . . . more closely into line with the requirements of the organization than would otherwise be the case. These measures can take any one or a combination of three fundamental forms: (1) coercion—in that penalties for noncooperation are set, (2) inducement—in that rewards for valued performance are instituted, and (3) "therapy"—in that by a complex and judicious combination of measures the motivational obstacles to satisfactory cooperation are dealt with on a level which "goes behind" the overt ostensible reasons for the difficulty by the persons involved.[19]

THE NEED FOR REDIRECTION THROUGH RESEARCH

Although there may be some agreement among certain writers that coordination of the activities in marketing channels through interorganizational management is desirable, especially after they have noted the negative effects of vertical conflict,[20] such coordination demands a major redirection of individual organization efforts and objectives. To date, little research has been completed that tests the applicability of intraorganization management principles to the "management" of interorganization coalitions, that indicates the means by which coordination might be achieved, or that estimates the probable results of such coordination, once accomplished. To this end, J. L. Heskett and the author have formulated a set of tentative hypotheses to be used as a basis for research. These hypotheses are presented below. In large part they represent a summary and conclusion to this article. It is hoped, however, that they will evoke constructive criticism from others who have an interest in the subject matter.

1. Power (in the form of interorganizational control) gravitates to one organization within a system of interrelated organizations. The

18. Talcott Parsons, *Structure and Process in Modern Societies* (Glencoe, Illinois: The Free Press, 1960), pp. 36–37.
19. *Ibid.*, pp. 33–35.
20. For example, see John A. Jamison, *The California Fresh Deciduous Fruit Industry: Structure, Organization and Practices* (Giannini Foundation of Agricultural Economics Report No. 275, April, 1964), pp. 95–96.

emergence of a leader within such a system is not likely, but inevitable.

2. Power structures within interfirm organizations more commonly than not permit the formulation and pursuit of a set of interorganization policies and practices.

3. The performance of an interorganization coalition depends, to a significant extent, on the acceptance of broad long-run considerations by the coalition member with which the greatest power rests.

4. The use of current management theories and modern decision tools which contribute to rational[21] intrafirm management decisions: (*a*) fosters narrow, self-oriented goal definitions, and (*b*) often results in decisions which impair the performance of individual firms within a group of interrelated firms, thereby diminishing the performance of the entire system.

5. In a system characterized by vertically linked activities (such as a channel of distribution), a set of positive or negative incentives can be established on a systematic basis by the interorganization leader to encourage the development of coordinated behavior among its members.

6. The means now exist to expand management theory and restate decision tools, where necessary, to allow a conscious pursuit of long-run, effective, overall performance for a group of interrelated firms.

Channel control is, in a great sense, a central concept underlying the above hypotheses. But the most significant premise is that interorganizational management, once accomplished, can achieve effective channel performance and a more efficient allocation of resources among channel members.

It has become apparent to the author that an individual firm's objective of maximizing its own performance without regard to the performance of those other firms in the channel with which it does business is invalid in the long run. The overall success of a channel, in terms of the profit and/or stability it can return to its members, may very well depend on a process of coordinated action.

QUESTIONS FOR DISCUSSION

1. Based on your personal experiences, can you recall any examples of channel captains who are either tyrants or benevolent leaders?

2. Is the theory of countervailing power relevant to channel analysis? Why?

21. "Rational" is used here to denote that which seeks to maximize, optimize, or satisfice.

3. Why is each firm in better financial health in the long run if it actively cooperates with the other channel members?

4. Refer to the tenative hypotheses at the end of the article.
   a. Do you agree with them? Why?
   b. Can you think of any additional ones that should appear on this list? If so, enumerate them and their basic underlying rationales.

5. Many firms tend to downgrade channel analysis in relation to the other aspects of the marketing mix. Explain why this often occurs.

5.3 TOWARD MORE RESPONSIVE MARKETING CHANNELS

M. S. Moyer

*". . . As leading merchants move explicitly to
defining and designing systems of satisfactions,
their existing contact with the consumer becomes
relatively crude and increasingly inadequate."*

THE PROBLEM OF RESPONSIVENESS

One of the most significant changes in the shape of North America's
distributive network is the advance of vertical marketing alliances. In
fact, it has been argued that "Conventional marketing systems are being
rapidly replaced by vertically organized marketing systems as the dominant distribution mechanism in the American economy."[1]

Typically, these systems are captained by a major channel participant.
Some have concluded that "the emergence of a leader within such a system is not likely, but inevitable."[2]

One candidate for this role is the leading retailer in the channel. Indeed, it would appear that the rise of retailing organizations sufficiently
strong to challenge the earlier dominance of wholesalers and manufacturers is one of the marks of an advanced marketing system.

These two developments—the emergence of vertical marketing systems and the rise of retailers as channel captains—raise important policy
questions. One central issue is whether these new channel forms, with
their highly systematized operations, can be sufficiently responsive to
changing market requirements.

The question of adaptability is important for scholars, marketers, and
consumers alike. Especially in recent years, it has been emphasized that
"The market system is so central to the functioning of American society

Reprinted by permission from M. S. Moyer, "Toward More Responsive Marketing
Channels," *Journal of Retailing* (Spring, 1975), pp. 7–19ff.

1. William R. Davidson, "Changes in Distributive Institutions," *Journal of Marketing*, 34, No. 1 (January 1970), p. 7.

2. Louis W. Stern, "Channel Control and Interorganization Management," Peter
D. Bennett, ed., *Marketing and Economic Development* (Chicago: American Marketing Association, 1965), p. 665.

that the students of that system . . . cannot afford to pass over questions concerning the performance of that system"[3] and that one aspect of performance must be "the adjustment of the system to the consumer needs."[4]

The purpose of this article is to highlight a problem of responsiveness in retailer-led marketing channels and to suggest how scholars and marketers might begin to deal with it.

THE CAUSES OF UNRESPONSIVENESS

FROM COTTAGE INDUSTRY TO MATURE INDUSTRY

Briefly, the problem is that channels led by retailers, and therefore sizable parts of our marketing system, are suffering a loss of responsiveness.

To redeem this loss, one must examine its causes. In general, they lie in the advancing maturity of the retailing industry. In considerable part, retailing continues to be a cottage industry: run from the home, using unpaid family workers, operating on a small scale, dependent on the capital of its suppliers, and led by untrained and unprofessional managers. Its prototype is the marginal mom and pop store. In recent decades, however, growing sectors of the retailing industry have adopted the attitudes, aims, forms, and methods of "big business." Their prototype is the "free-form corporation . . . with a newfound willingness to go anywhere and do anything in distribution."[5]

In many respects, this trend must be welcomed. It has produced increases in real output per retail worker, gains in real income for the marketing labor force, and, in many ways, more efficient operations at the point where marketing channels touch their customers.

But these gains have not been costless. In the retailing industry, the cost of maturity has been the loss of some sensitivity to the consumer. As a consequence, the price of progress in marketing has been the loss of some adaptability in retailer-led vertical marketing systems. The following sections analyse that process in greater detail.

CAPITAL INTENSIVENESS

First, a maturing industry tends to become less labor-intensive and more capital-intensive. In this, the marketing process has lagged the produc-

---

3. Frederick D. Sturdivant, "Distribution in American Society: Some Questions of Efficiency and Relevance," Louis P. Bucklin, ed., *Vertical Marketing Systems* (Glenview, Ill.: Scott, Foresman and Company, 1970), p. 99.

4. Louis P. Bucklin and Stanley F. Stasch, "Problems in the Study of Vertical Marketing Systems," Louis P. Bucklin, ed., *Vertical Marketing Systems* (Glenview, Ill.: Scott, Foreman and Company, 1970), pp. 5–6.

5. Davidson, "Changes in Distributive Institutions," p. 9.

tion process. However, with the passage of time, retailing's production function is almost surely giving less weight to labor and more weight to capital. Off the sales floor the modern retail organization is equipped with increasingly expensive capital equipment, notably for materials handling and data processing. On the sales floor, it is becoming a self-service operation staffed by fewer manual workers. Moreover, the industry is converting to "automated front ends"—systems made up of electronic cash registers, optical scanners, and in-store mini-computers —which save labor costs but raise equipment costs. In a very real way, then, the modern store is becoming a factory of distribution.

This development has its price. How high a price was illustrated by a recent cartoon set in a supermarket. It appeared at about the same time that some food chains were advertising that one should "Get to know the friendly man behind the meat counter." It pictured that friendly man seated at his meat counter, holding a snuffling matron on his knee, his face shining with compassion as he murmured, "Now Mrs. Swartz, tell me about last Thursday's pot roast."

The cartoonist was picturing the other side of capital intensiveness: the widespread disappearance of the salesperson for whom retailing is a chosen career and a serious calling. His departure tends to remove from the point of purchase one agent that retail managers once had in their efforts to know their clientele and to understand their markets. Thus industrial maturity in the form of capital intensiveness has probably reduced the openness of retailing enterprises.

MASS PRODUCTION

Second, as Knauth[6] and Galbraith[7] have emphasized, a maturing industry moves from sporadic activities to continuous operations. "Businessmen, in meeting the exigencies of the modern world, have fashioned a new . . . system of production and distribution . . . whose main idea is to administer the business . . . in the interest of continuity."[8] In other industries, the quest for continuity takes the form of mass production methods and round-the-clock operations.

Here, too, retailing seems to be adopting the animus of other, more mature sectors of the economy. Being increasingly capital intensive, merchandising facilities, like manufacturing plants, must avoid down time. In retailing, this imperative is manifested in the extension of evening hours and the advance of open Sundays. Significantly, it has gen-

6. Oswald Knauth, *Managerial Enterprise: Its Growth and Methods of Operation,* (New York: W. W. Norton and Company, Inc., 1948).
7. John Kenneth Galbraith, *The New Industrial State,* 2d ed., rev. (Boston: Houghton-Mifflin, 1971).
8. Knauth, *Managerial Enterprise,* p. 11.

erally been the independent merchant, whose operations are not large-scale and capital-intensive, who has not supported the stretching of store hours.

Again, industry leaders have incurred some concomitant costs. To mass produce retail transactions the merchant must follow another formula of the factory, which is shift work. To staff those extra shifts, he must use more part-time people. Now these workers have in common that for them retailing is an occasional and incidental activity. Large retailing organizations rely on such personnel for a large portion of their total revenues. This means that as dominant retailing organizations move toward continuous high-level operations, a growing proportion of their personnel are amateurs.

Such people can have some difficulty in knowing the merchandise and substantial difficulty in knowing the market. One evidence of this is that the "want book"—a device whereby knowledgeable salespeople signalled unmet needs to their superiors—has all but disappeared from the point of purchase. To that extent, management loses another link with its constituency.

Alderson showed how the routinization of transactions can lead directly to efficiency in a marketing system.[9] It must be added that mass production methods at the point of purchase can lead indirectly to insensitivity in a distributive system.

THE SELLING OF SYSTEMS

Third, a maturing industry seems to shift to the selling of systems rather than isolated products. That trend is evident elsewhere in marketing.[10] Again, so it is with retailing. There was a day when the merchant sold merchandise and little else. Now it is recognized that just as the package can sell, so can the outlet. Consequently, as one retail president has put it, "Retailing is . . . changing from the selling of products to the marketing of stores."[11] Moreover, merchants and scholars are recognizing that, in a market with more discretionary time and money, a widening range of human needs can be met in the shopping experience.[12] Hence the retailer, like other marketers, is becoming a seller of systems: systems of satisfactions.

9. Wroe Alderson, *Marketing Behavior and Executive Action* (Homewood, Ill.: Richard D. Irwin, Inc., 1957), pp. 296–304.

10. Elmer P. Lotshaw, "Industrial Marketing: Trends and Challenges," *Journal of Marketing*, 34, No. 1 (January 1970), 23–24.

11. Dean Muncaster, "The Marketing Function in Retail Merchandising," (address to the 14th Annual Management Seminar of the Toronto Chapter of the American Marketing Association, Toronto, Jan. 11, 1964).

12. Philip Kotler, "Atmospherics as a Marketing Tool," *Journal of Retailing*, 49, No. 4 (Winter 1973–1974).

As a result, along with other marketers, the merchant is finding that his conventional sensing devices are insufficient for understanding the environment. When pennies counted, comparison shoppers checking competing prices could report fairly accurately the relative appeal of rival stores. When merchandise had primarily to be serviceable to be salable, a department manager with little more than an innate feel of the cloth could reckon reasonably well his relative drawing power. When shopper's needs were unsubtle, a merchandising manager by merely patrolling the sales floor could come close to divining consumer needs. "We've got the greatest market testing place in the world right here in our store. You can stand on the floor of our store and get more ideas. It's fantastic." At an earlier stage of market maturity, then, retail decision-makers could sensibly rely on information systems that were personal, informal, and unsophisticated.

But the selling of systems is a more demanding undertaking. As proponents of the marketing concept have so clearly established, the vending of "bundles of value satisfactions" requires not only an imaginative definition of corporate mission, but an insightful reading of market needs. Large retailing organizations share this problem. Systems of satisfaction cannot be accurately priced by comparison shoppers, cannot be readily felt by central buyers, and cannot be easily calibrated by department managers standing on the sales floor waiting for insight to strike.

In short, as leading merchants move more explicitly to defining and designing systems of satisfactions, their existing contact with the consumer becomes relatively crude and increasingly inadequate. In this way, too, as large retailing organizations progress as marketers they may well be losing some of their empathy with their markets.

LARGER ENTERPRISES

Fourth, a maturing industry seems to cluster into larger units. In retailing, this trend takes the form of larger outlets, larger companies, and more economic concentration.

The enlargement of the typical store is well-documented. During the last three decades, the average output per retail establishment, in real terms, has increased more than three times.[13] Measures of company growth are more fragmentary, but a similar trend is indicated. "Those data available indicate that the retailing sector has participated fully in the merger movements that swept all of American industry."[14] The most comprehensive study on the subject concludes that "Through the

13. Louis P. Bucklin, *Competition and Evolution in the Distributive Trades* (Englewood Cliffs, N.J.: Prentice-Hall, Inc., 1972), p. 74.
14. *Ibid.*, p. 134.

most recent period we have seen a continuing consolidation of the retail sector in the hands of fewer and fewer large-scale firms."[15]

In developing these aggregations, retailers have paid another penalty: executive isolation. As one critic has said, ". . . many . . . mass retailers have retreated to . . . penthouse offices . . . overlooking artificial gardens—far from the madding shopper. . . ."[16] One of the dangers of executive isolation is a poverty of intelligence on the environment. This problem is inherent in evolving organizations; it threatens the leadership ability of large enterprises in industry, in government, in religion, and elsewhere.[17] It is therefore an inescapable issue for "leading" retailing firms.

CENTRAL STAFF SPECIALISTS

Fifth, a maturing industry appears to use more central staff specialists. While measures are unavailable, retailing is almost surely doing so. "Centrally coordinated systems are gradually displacing conventional marketing channels as the dominant distribution mechanism. . . ."[18] As part of this situation, key decisions are moving from the sales floor to the upstairs office, from the hustings to head office, and from the jack-of-all-trades to the master of one.

In this case it could be argued that one encounters an exception to the rule; that the effect of maturity is not to reduce contact with consumers, but to increase it. For one of these specialists is the central buyer, whose mandate is to keep the company in tune with the market.

On the face of it, that seems a reasonable conclusion. The central buyer does seem well connected to the environment of the enterprise. His reports are voluminous, his travels are wide, and his knowledge is impressive. But one must observe his activities. In a large distributive organization, he visits retail stores, but briefly and infrequently, and then it is usually to meet retailers, not to consult customers. He skims trade journals, but they tend to tell him how other merchants are merchandising, not how his own markets are moving. He scans sales and inventory reports, but because the computer can convey no more than it can capture, his reports deal with the past rather than the future;

15. *Ibid.*, p. 167.
16. Steven Masters, in an address to a seminar of the National Retail Merchants Association, in New York, 1962.
17. Harold L. Wilensky, *Organizational Intelligence: Knowledge and Policy in Government and Industry* (New York: Basic Books, Inc., 1967).
18. Bert C. McCammon, Jr., and Albert D. Bates, "The Emergence and Growth of Contractually Integrated Channels in the American Economy," P. D. Bennett, ed., *Economic Growth, Competitive* and *World Markets* (Chicago: American Marketing Association, 1965), p. 496.

they tell him about his merchandise rather than his customers, and they tell him how he is doing rather than why. In short, they tell him about the market needs that he is meeting rather than about the market needs that he is neglecting.

Also, he spends much time with his suppliers. Here the information he gets is enormous; it should not be underestimated. But neither should it be overestimated. Most of the intelligence available from suppliers concerns their own offerings. Needless to say, it is detailed and direct. Intelligence about end users is much scarcer. And when it is offered it is of much lower quality, for it comes from company executives, many of whom have conducted no direct investigations among consumers, none of whom share the full results of such studies as have been made, and all of whom have an ax to grind. Therefore, suppliers' insights on the market must be deduced from recent sales, inferred from other retailers' takings, and spun together from the talk of the trade. Altogether, a second look reveals a somewhat different picture. When it is said that the central buyer knows the market, what is meant is that he knows what his sales figures (a reflection rather than a picture of the market) *imply* about the market, and what his suppliers (themselves twice removed from the market) *say* about the market.

These differences have not been widely remarked. Indeed, it is a measure of the unconsciously inverted orientation of a maturing retailing industry that when a central buyer states that he is going "into the market" he means that he is going to visit, not his customers, but his suppliers.

Thus, on closer inspection, central buying emerges as a mixed blessing. About the supply of merchandise it makes information more direct, detailed, and authoritative; about the wants of consumers, it makes information more indirect, crude, and speculative. About products, then, the organization knows much; about markets, it knows much less. The difference is profound. Again, maturity has imposed its penalty.

THE FULL PRICE

In many ways, therefore, as retailing progresses it pays a price. In particular, as the industry matures, the firms in it undergo five key changes which increase internal efficiency but decrease external empathy.

This unspoken exchange can alter the strengths and weaknesses of leading retailing organizations. It can make them more powerful, but less permeable. It can make them more informed about operations, but less insightful about shoppers. It can make them more dominant in the marketplace, but less directed by market demand. It is a tradeoff which deserves to be weighed.

EMERGING EVIDENCE

These conclusions find some support in empirical studies. In recent years several researchers have tested a retailer's understanding of his market and found it often misinformed. For example, a probe of a sizable group of major electrical appliance dealers concluded that "Many . . . demonstrated little knowledge about their customers' characteristics. . . . Such results were quite unexpected, since it has generally been hypothesized that the retailer is particularly knowledgeable about his customers and the manufacturer often depends on the dealer as a primary source of consumer information."[19] In the same way, in an examination of seventeen retail businesses, again in a variety of product fields, other researchers found that none of the firms had at hand a summary profile of its credit customers by income, occupation, sex, or age.[20] On examining the market information available in eight leading retailing organizations in fields as diverse as food, auto accessories, apparel, hardware, and variety merchandise, the author also frequently found that key decision-makers lacked basic, actionable facts about their markets.

The process does not end with the absence of information. When a decision-maker continually lacks facts, he can be moved to invent them. When merchants lack data on their markets, they fall back on plausible hypotheses. This leads to unsupported generalizations about shoppers, their characteristics, motivations, and behavior. The result can be misguided marketing effort.

Again, scholarly investigations attest to this phenomenon. One was a study of both the customers and executives of department stores and specialty stores. In their beliefs that delivery was a less wanted service on small packages than on large items, that lower-income women bought more often by phone than others, and that telephone sales tended to replace floor sales, management was largely contradicted by examination of shoppers themselves. The study concluded that "those findings . . . which revealed a situation somewhat different from what many store executives had assumed, suggest that these two services might play a large role in building sales"[21] for the stores involved.

Another was a study of householders and retailers of refrigerators, stoves, and automatic washers. It found that the retailers concerned

19. John K. Ryans, Jr. "An Analysis of Appliance Retailer Perceptions of Retail Strategy and Decision Processes," Peter D. Bennett (ed.), *Marketing and Economic Development* (Chicago: American Marketing Association, 1965), p. 669.

20. Thomas V. Greer and Charles G. Walters, "Credit Records: Information Tool for Planning," *Journal of Retailing*, 42, No. 1 (Spring 1966), pp. 11–18ff.

21. Stuart U. Rich, *Shopping Behavior of Department Store Customers* (Boston: Division of Research, Graduate School of Business Administration, Harvard University, 1963), p. 227.

often overestimated the price differences that consumers perceived between competing brands, and consistently underestimated the weight that consumers gave to service and warranty, ease of use, and style in the purchase decision. It concluded that many of the stores examined could be pursuing ill-considered marketing strategies.[22]

Another was a study of the buyers and retailers of bathing suits. It found that on the importance of brand names, on the relative frequency of visits to rival stores, and on the best and least liked features of each store, the merchants' beliefs were badly mistaken when tested against the actual behavior and attitudes of the customers themselves. It closed with the conclusion that "Most retailers do not even know the key strengths and weaknesses of their own stores," with the result that each type of outlet studied was missing major opportunities to develop a uniquely effective marketing strategy.[23]

Another was a study of the patrons, reputed and real, of a particular department store. It found that in visualizing a separate "basement store customer" and "upstairs customer," store executives had invented largely fictional characters and that the biggest customer for either a basement or upstairs department was, unexpectedly, the customer who bought from both. It concluded that, having developed a marketing mix to insulate the basement customer from the upstairs customer, management was discouraging its best patrons.[24]

This evidence cannot show how often retailers hobble themselves for lack of facts or bemuse themselves with believable misinformation. However, it does demonstrate that it is not difficult for modern mass retailers to make basic marketing decisions, on behalf of consumers and suppliers, using facts about the market which are implicit, plausible, and wrong. To the extent that such mistakes occur, they reduce the responsiveness of marketing channels and invite a search for corrective action.

POSSIBLE RESPONSES

ACTIONS BY ACADEMICS

For scholars, the major consequence should be a re-examination of accepted views on channel leadership.

22. Peter J. McClure and John K. Ryans, Jr. "Differences Between Retailers' and Consumers' Perceptions," *Journal of Marketing Research*, 5, No. 1 (February 1968), pp. 35–40.

23. H. Lawrence Isaacson, *Store Choice: A Case Study of Consumer Decision Making* (New York: Retail Research Institute, National Retail Merchants Association, 1966), p. 78.

24. Donald F. Blankertz, "The Basement-Store Customer," *Journal of Marketing*, 15, No. 1 (January 1951), pp. 336–40.

The emergence of vertical marketing systems has raised the question, "Who should lead this extracorporate organization?"[25] Most academics have leaned toward the retailer as leader. On this there has not been unanimity, of course; the wholesaler and the manufacturer have had their champions. Nevertheless, it seems fair to say that most would concur with the conclusion that "the mass retailer appears to be best adapted for leadership under the marketing concept."[26]

The endorsement of retailer-captained channels has had various origins. Those who have sought a more rationalized marketing process have reasoned that the retailer-led channel is the most streamlined one attainable.[27] Those who have sought to preserve traditional price competition have valued the retailer's private label as a beneficent threat to entrenched national brands and ossified channel margins.

But there is one line of reasoning that has had broad appeal. It has seemed unarguable that, relative to other marketing institutions, the retailing firm is close to the consumer. "The retailer . . . feels the pulse of consumer wants and needs day in and day out."[28] From there it has been easy to reason that, of all marketers, it is the retailer who is best able to consult the consumer, to comprehend his wishes, and to reflect his wants. Moreover, retailers are seen to be relatively uncommitted to any particular, partisan brand. In keeping with this preferred position, retailers cast themselves in a heroic role; as one has said, "The retailer cannot be the selling agent of the manufacturer because he holds a higher commission; he is the purchasing agent for the public."[29] It has therefore seemed a reasonable conclusion that, relative to other possible channel leaders, the retailing organization is the most likely to captain a vertical marketing system which is truly responsive to consumer needs. Thus one close student of retailing concludes that "As the . . . mass distributor continues to play a role of ever-increasing importance in the marketing of goods in our economy . . . ever-greater benefits should flow to consumers in the way of more goods better adjusted to their demands, at lower prices."[30]

25. Robert W. Little, "The Marketing Channel: Who Should Lead This Extracorporate Organization," *Journal of Marketing*, 34, No. 1 (January 1970), pp. 31–38; David R. Craig and Werner K. Gabler, "The Competitive Struggle for Market Control," *The Annals of the American Academy of Political and Social Science*, 209 (May, 1940), pp. 84–107; and Valentine F. Ridgeway, "Administration of Manufacturer–Dealer Systems," *Administrative Science Quarterly* (March 1957), pp. 464–67.

26. Bruce Mallen, "A Theory of Retailer–Supplier Conflict, Control and Co-Operation," *Journal of Retailing*, 39, No. 2 (Summer 1963), p. 32.

27. Craig and Gabler, "The Competitive Struggle."

28. Mallen, "A Theory of Retailer–Supplier Conflict," p. 31.

29. Lew Hahn, *Stores, Merchants, and Customers* (New York: Fairchild Publications, 1952), p. 12.

30. Arnold Corbin, "Central Buying in Relation to the Merchandising of Multiple

That chain of logic now seems to underestimate the price of progress. In particular, it tends to disregard the several ways in which, in becoming large enough to lead marketing channels, mass retailers have lost their ready communion with the consumer. This unacknowledged cost could revise the case for retailers as channel leaders. It could be that as major merchandising firms become more able to control marketing channels, they become less qualified to guide them. For proximity does not equal empathy. The prior analysis underlines that "Just as an organism may literally starve to death in the presence of available food, so can a management gradually succumb to factual malnutrition while . . . necessary information abounds on all sides."[31] Scholars should consider the possibility that as retailers capture channels, it could lead to vertical marketing systems which are more effective in terms of transaction efficiency but less effective in terms of responsiveness.

ACTIONS BY PRACTITIONERS

Among retailers, several actions would be opportune. To compensate for their loss of automatic communion with the consumer, merchants should aggressively adopt the new point-of-sale devices which are now becoming available. These include electronic cash registers, in-store minicomputers, and optical scanners. Together, they make it possible for the retailer to capture, in machine language and at the moment of purchase, every detail of every transaction, including the identity of the item and of the buyer. Thus "electronic checkouts" or "automated front ends" allow a breakthrough in the marketer's quest for full and timely information on the sources of his sales.[32] This opportunity should be grasped.

Even "automated front ends" have their limitations, however. Thus, to further enrich their understanding of their marketers, major retailers should adopt another practice uncommon in retailing today: formal market research. Contrary to many merchant's fears, this research need not be elaborate, expensive, inconclusive, or slow. Properly managed, it can produce large payoffs.[33]

Armed with the kind of commercial intelligence that is available from emerging informational technology and established market research techniques, large retailing organizations would then be better able to

---

Retail Units" (New York: Unpublished doctoral dissertation, New York University, 1954), pp. 708–9.

31. Charles K. Ramond, "How to Starve in the Midst of Plenty," *Journal of Advertising Research*, 3, No. 4 (December 1963), p. 59.

32. M. S. Moyer, "The Marketing Implications of Point-of-Sale Systems," *The Business Quarterly*, Spring 1975.

33. M. S. Moyer, "Market Intelligence for Modern Merchants," *California Management Review*, 14, No. 4 (Summer 1972), pp. 63–69.

respond to marketing opportunities. Two examples will illustrate the new capabilities that could follow.

RETAILERS AS PRODUCT INNOVATORS

Captained channels have "high vertical programming potential."[34] In retailer-led marketing channels, an attractive use of that potential is to absorb some of the manufacturer's product planning function through specification buying. But here the merchant's paucity of market information becomes an increasing penalty. In unambitious forms of private branding, retailers can get by on simple "knockoffs" of supplier's makes. Most do. To date then, private branding has required the ability to imitate rather than innovate. But if retailers are to grasp their full potential as channel captains, they will need to develop forms of specification buying that can generate something more than "me too" products. Then there will be a new need to discover unique, wanted, product features. As has been shown, the price of progress is that they lack that capability. However, if through market research and automated front ends retailers could steep themselves more deeply in consumer's unmet wants and needs, then retailer-managed marketing systems could more fully exploit their vertical programming potential.

RETAILERS AS CONSUMER ADVOCATES

Similarly, there might be another role the leading retailer could play: that of consumer advocate. The complexity and impersonality of the modern marketplace have created, in the public mind, a need for new allies who will champion the consumer's cause.

Filling that need has activated several institutions outside of conventional marketing channels. Newspaper actionlines, radio hotlines, and government complaint bureaus attract a considerable chorus of consumer questions, complaints, and suggestions, many of them concerning retailers and their channel partners. By contrast, large retailers have often been so insulated from consumers as to be largely untouched by this traffic in feelings and ideas. As a salesclerk reminded a matron in a recent cartoon, "Madam, in this store you are a voice crying in the wilderness." Again one sees the enervating effects of inadequate consumer contact.

Aggressive consumer advocacy is not a role suited to all large retailers. On the other hand, it has been employed by some leading merchants, especially grocery chains.[35] It is a strategic opportunity that should be

34. Davidson, "Changes in Distributive Institutions," p. 8.
35. Esther Peterson, "Consumerism as a Retailer's Asset," *Harvard Business Review*, 52, No. 3 (May–June 1974), pp. 91–101.

accepted or rejected on its merits, not lost by default. In this way, too, by moving to improved instruments for understanding their markets, retail management would open up for themselves new marketing options.

CONCLUSION

In an era of advancing vertical marketing systems, it is increasingly realistic to see the channel of distribution as a unit of competition. If these units are to be truly responsive to public needs and expectations, they must be led by channel captains who are well tuned to their constituencies.

In the marketplace, mass retailers are important channel captains, and in academia they are usually favored ones. Yet they are often less understanding of their environments than has been commonly thought. Their unresponsiveness stems less from lack of will than from fundamental changes in the retailing industry. However, the retailer's capacity and credentials for channel captaincy are correspondingly diminished.

This situation has consequences for scholar and marketer alike. For academics, it should mean less reliance on deductive derivations of plausible abstractions about how distribution works, more empiricism in addressing the question of where channel leadership should lie, and a scrapping of the maxim that large retailers are automatically well endowed for channel captaincy. For retailers it should mean abandonment of the comfortable untruth that they are by definition "close" to the market, an early conversion to automated front ends, a discriminating use of formal market research, an imaginative exploitation of the information generated by "automated front ends," and an opportunistic exploration of those roles—such as product innovator and consumer advocate—which capitalize on a combination of market knowledge and marketing power.

Out of these actions should come more responsive marketing channels.

QUESTIONS FOR DISCUSSION

1. Professor Moyer argues that retailers are suffering from a loss of responsiveness. Discuss the reasons suggested for this situation.

2. Is retailing a "maturing" industry? Discuss fully.

3. Explain the relationship between central staff specialists and a "mature" industry.

4. What is the relationship between retailers, channel captains, and vertical marketing systems?

5. What courses of action does the author state or imply that retailers should be taking in the late 1970s and 1980s?

5.4 THE EMERGENCE AND GROWTH OF CONTRACTUALLY INTEGRATED CHANNELS IN THE AMERICAN ECONOMY

Bert C. McCammon, Jr.

"Recent changes in the structure of distribution suggest that centrally coordinated systems are gradually displacing conventional marketing channels as the dominant distribution mechanism in the American economy."

INTRODUCTION

Marketing channels have been traditionally viewed as fragmented, potentially unstable, networks, in which vertically aligned firms bargain with each other at arm's length, terminate relationships with impunity, and otherwise behave autonomously. McVey, for example, argues that channels are a series of vertical markets,[1] rather than operating systems *per se*, and several economists, including Stigler and Coase, regard channel behavior as an extension of the theory of the firm.[2] These, and similar, constructs can be used effectively to explain the rationale of conventional marketing channels, which consist of relatively small and autonomous units. Unfortunately, they do not provide an adequate basis for analyzing the economies that can be achieved through vertical coordination of marketing activities.

Recent changes in the structure of distribution suggest that centrally coordinated systems are gradually displacing conventional marketing channels as the dominant distribution mechanism in the American

Reprinted by permission from the author and publisher. Bert C. McCammon, Jr., "The Emergence and Growth of Contractually Integrated Channels in the American Economy," *Marketing and Economic Development*, edited by Peter D. Bennett (Chicago: American Marketing Association, 1965), pp. 496–515.

1. Philip McVey, "Are Channels of Distribution What the Textbooks Say?" *Journal of Marketing* (January, 1960), pp. 61–65.

2. See George J. Stigler, "The Division of Labor is Limited by the Extent of the Market," *Journal of Political Economy*, June, 1951, 11.185–193; and R. H. Coase, "The Nature of the Firm" *Economica*, New Series, November, 1937, pp. 386–405.

economy. Furthermore, competition, to an increasing extent, involves rivalry between systems, as well as between the individual units that comprise them. Thus, centrally coordinated systems have emerged as a basic component of the competitive process.

There are at least three types of centrally coordinated systems—corporate, administered, and contractual—that compete for differential advantage in the marketplace. This paper is concerned, to some extent, with all three types of systems, but it focuses on the emergence and growth of contractual networks, with particular emphasis on the recent expansion of franchise programs and voluntary and cooperative groups. Consequently, the paragraphs that follow are selective rather than comprehensive in their coverage, and descriptive, rather than theoretical, in their content.

CORPORATE, CONTRACTUAL AND ADMINISTERED SYSTEMS

Corporate marketing systems, which combine successive stages of production and distribution under a single ownership, have existed for an extended period of time, but their importance has risen in recent years as a result of mergers and internal expansion. The Federal Trade Commission, for example, recently concluded that 22.5 per cent of the mergers and acquisitions consummated between 1949 and 1954 involved forward or backward integration.[3] Futhermore, many of the corporations emerging from these consolidations, now operate manufacturing facilities, warehousing points, and retail outlets. Thus, they have combined the principal stages of production and distribution under a single ownership, which results in coordinated and concerted marketing activity. Sherwin-Williams, for example, operates over 2,000 paint stores; Hart Schaffner and Marx, a long established manufacturer in the men's wear field, owns over 100 clothing outlets; Sears has an ownership equity in production facilities that supply over 30 per cent of the company's inventory requirements; and, large food chains obtain almost 10 per cent of their requirements from captive manufacturing facilities, many of which were acquired in the 1950's.[4]

Large corporations have also created relatively self-sufficient marketing systems through internal expansion, and this trend is particularly noticeable at the wholesale level. The authors analyzed the relative importance of primary channels in 72 industries for the 1939–1958 period.

3. *Report on Corporate Mergers and Acquisitions*, Federal Trade Commission, Washington, D. C., 1955, p. 7.
4. For a brief, but useful discussion of vertical integration in marketing, "Vertical Integration," *Business Management* (January, 1965), pp. 47–49 and 78.

In 56 of these industries, a higher proportion of total output was distributed through manufacturer's sales branches and offices in 1958 than in 1939.[5] These facilities are frequently a partial or complete substitute for independent middlemen; thus the growing importance of manufacturer's sales branches and offices suggests that considerable vertical integration has taken place at the wholesale level since World War II. In summary, corporate vertical integration can be used as a device to coordinate marketing activities, and available data, though fragmentary, suggest that *corporate systems*, arising through merger or internal expansion, have become more important in the American economy during recent years.

Administrative strategies, as opposed to ownership, can also be used to coordinate the flow of goods and services and thereby achieve systemic economies.[6] Individual enterprises, by exerting leadership, can often influence or otherwise control the behavior of adjacent firms within the channel; as a result, vertically aligned companies work closely with each other to achieve transportation, warehousing, data processing, and advertising economies, which reduce "total" costs within the system. Numerous manufacturing firms have historically relied on administrative expertise to coordinate reseller marketing efforts. Suppliers with dominant brands usually experience the least difficulty in securing strong trade support, but many manufacturers with "fringe" items have been able to elicit reseller cooperation through the use of liberal distribution policies, which take the form of attractive discounts (or discount substitutes), financial assistance, and various types of concessions that protect resellers from one or more of the risks of doing business.[7] Consequently, administrative strategies, of both a formal and informal nature, can be, and have been, used to reduce friction within channels and produce coordinated marketing effort. When these conditions prevail, the resulting channel may be designated as an *administered system*.

Finally, and most significantly, channel coordination can be effected through the use of contractual agreements. That is, independent firms at different levels can coordinate their activities on a contractual basis to obtain systemic economies and market impact that could not be achieved through individual action. *Contractual systems* have grown more rapidly

5. Authors' calculations based on *Distribution of Manufacturers' Sales By Class of Customer*, 1939 and 1958, Census of Manufacturers, U. S. Department of Commerce, Washington, D. C.

6. For an excellent discussion of administered marketing systems, see Valentine F. Ridgeway, "Administration of Manufacturer-Dealer Systems," *Administrative Science Quarterly*, March, 1957, pp. 464–467.

7. For a more extended treatment of this subject, see Bert C. McCammon, Jr., "The Role of Distribution Policies in the Manufacturer's Promotional Mix," *Proceedings of the First Sales Promotion Management Seminar*, Association of National Advertisers, Inc., New York, 1965.

in recent years than their corporate or administered counterparts, and this development, in retrospect, may be one of the most significant trends to emerge during the 1950–1965 period.

Contractual integration is an unusually flexible economic device, and thus there are a variety of possible affiliations from which individual firms may choose. Despite this diversity, the principal types of contractual systems can be clasified as follows:

CONTRACTUAL SYSTEMS INVOLVING BACKWARD INTEGRATION

Retail cooperative groups
Retail and wholesale buying groups
Retail promotional groups
Non-profit shipping associations (sponsored by consignees)
Retail resident buying office (particularly those operated on a programmed basis or owned cooperatively)
Industrial, wholesale, and retail procurement contracts
Producer buying cooperatives

CONTRACTUAL SYSTEMS INVOLVING FORWARD INTEGRATION

Retail voluntary groups
Retail programmed groups
Retail franchise programs for individual brands and specific departments
Retail franchise programs covering all phases of licensee operations
Non-profit shipping associations (operated by shippers)
Leased department arrangements (particularly those involving subsidiaries of manufacturing and wholesaling enterprises)
Producer marketing cooperatives

These systems, as suggested above, differ in a variety of respects, but all represent attempts on the part of affiliated firms to achieve the efficiencies required in competitive markets, without totally sacrificing enterprise identity and autonomy.

REASONS UNDERLYING THE GROWTH OF CENTRALLY COORDINATED MARKETING SYSTEMS

Corporate, administered, and contractual marketing systems have grown in relative importance during recent years, and their development has been particularly rapid since World War II. In fact, these systems are becoming a principal element in the competitive process, and they are gradually displacing conventional marketing channels as the dominant distribution mechanism in the American economy. The growth of centrally coordinated systems can be attributed to several factors, although cause and effect relationships are predictably difficult to identify and measure.

INCREASED CAPITAL REQUIREMENTS AND HIGHER FIXED COSTS

The capital required to implement competitive manufacturing and marketing programs rose continuously between 1948 and 1965. Fixed costs, particularly those connected with the use of capital, increased, too. As a result, a growing number of firms were confronted by constantly rising break-even points, which forced them to maintain sales at unusually high levels in order to obtain adequate rates of return on investment. The need for assured volume encouraged the growth of centrally coordinated systems in which individual units can predict and/or control the behavior of others.[8]

The increases that occurred in capital requirements between 1948 and 1965 were impressive, indeed. Average investment per manufacturing employee, for example, rose from $8,089 in 1949 to $18,227 in 1960,[9] and comparable gains occurred in wholesaling and retailing, e.g., construction outlays for new supermarkets rose from $285,200 per unit in 1959 to $388,200 in 1964—a gain of 36.1 per cent—and average construction costs for new variety stores climbed from $238,800 to $341,300—an increase of 43.3 per cent—during the same period.[10] These illustrations tend to support Schultze's contention that capital related costs rose more rapidly than any other expense category following World War II. More specifically, he estimates that capital consumption allowances per unit of output increased by 112 per cent between 1947 and 1957.[11] Furthermore, he notes that other fixed costs, particularly those incurred to compensate "overhead" personnel, increased rapidly, too.[12] In short, the trend towards more capital-intensive operations has raised break-even points and created a need to maintain volume at unprecedented

8. For an extended and early treatment of this subject, see Oswald Knauth, *Business Practices, Trade Position, and Competition,* Columbia University Press, New York, 1956.

9. *The Economic Almanac 1964,* National Industrial Conference Board, New York, p. 244.

10. Authors' calculations and "Annual Survey of Construction and Modernization Expenditures," *Chain Store Age,* (1959–1964 editions).

11. Charles L. Schultze, *Prices, Costs and Output for the Post War Decade: 1947–1951,* Committee for Economic Development, New York, 1960, p. 53.

12. *Ibid.,* p. 57.

levels, which has encouraged the formation of centrally coordinated marketing systems.

DECLINING PROFIT MARGINS AND RATES OF RETURN ON INVESTMENT

Internal Revenue Service data indicate that manufacturing, wholesaling, and retailing corporations experienced significant declines in operating profit margins and rates of return on investment between 1950 and 1962. For manufacturing corporations, net profits (after taxes) on net sales declined from 6.16 per cent in 1950 to 3.09 per cent in 1962, and net profits (after taxes) on tangible net worth decreased from 13.54 to 6.49 per cent during the same period. Operating profit margins (after taxes) for wholesaling corporations sagged from 2.17 to 1.05 per cent between 1950 and 1962, and their composite rate of return on tangible net worth declined from 13.06 to 6.67 per cent over the same interval. Finally, net profits (after taxes) as a percent of sales for retailing corporations decreased from 2.84 to 1.11 per cent during the 1950–1962 period, and net profits (after taxes) on tangible net worth fell precipitously, too—declining from 11.82 to 5.83 per cent during the thirteen years in question.[13] These declines in relative profitability were the result of growing competition—of both a conventional and innovative nature—and rising costs. New approaches were clearly required to ameliorate these pressures, and thus a growing number of firms attempted to achieve economies and market impact through vertical affiliations and mergers.

GROWING COMPLEXITY OF MARKETING PROCESSES

Coordinating the flow of goods and services became increasingly more complicated between 1948 and 1965 due to the expansion in number of items, the increased emphasis placed on fashion merchandising, and the advances in management technology which occurred during this period. The number of items carried in a typical supermarket, for example, rose from 3,705 in 1950 to over 6,800 in 1963,[14] and variety stores, between 1956 and 1961, increased the number of housewares items stocked by 75 per cent; notions by 50 per cent; apparel by 40 per cent; drugs, toiletries, and stationery by 25 per cent; and confectionaries, cosmetics, and yardgoods, by 20 per cent.[15] Furthermore, a substantial number of merchandise categories, traditionally dominanted by staple items, were

13. *Statistics of Income: Corporation Income Tax Returns*, (1950–1962 editions), Internal Revenue Service, Washington, D. C.

14. Robert W. Mueller, *Grocery Business Annual Report*, Progressive Grocer, New York, 1964, p. 3.

15. "Profit Engineering Demands Revaluation and Close Control of Assortments," *Variety Store Merchandiser*, August, 1961, p. 11.

revitalized through the use of fashion programs, with children's ready-to-wear, domestics, and housewares being conspicuous examples of this development. Finally, significant advances were made in management technology and accompanying data processing systems. A variety of distribution cost accounting methods—including SOSCA, Merchandise Management Accounting, Production Unit Accounting, and others—were introduced between 1950 and 1965; mathematical models for inventory control and supporting computer programs, such as IBM's IMPACT System, were developed, too; and several relatively sophisticated decision criteria enjoyed widespread use. As a result of these factors, marketing in general, and retailing in particular, became increasingly more complex, and many enterprises were literally forced to merge or affiliate with large systems to obtain the specialized assistance and other services needed to compete in complex markets.

POTENTIAL ECONOMIES IN CENTRALLY COORDINATED MARKETING SYSTEMS

Centrally coordinated marketing systems also grew in importance, because they are the source of three types of economies, which are relatively difficult to obtain in conventional channels. First, centrally coordinated systems are often able to achieve scheduling efficiencies, because the requirements and intentions of member units can be predicted and/or controlled. There is also more data available for planning purposes in a centrally coordinated system than in a conventional channel. Consequently, manufacturing, warehousing, and promotional activities can be scheduled to minimize "total" costs. Second, centrally coordinated marketing systems also achieve economies by eliminating, simplifying, and repositioning marketing activities. Field selling costs, as an illustration, are often eliminated, or at least minimized, in centrally coordinated systems, and various activities such as ordering, financing, and billing are drastically simplified or reduced to programmed routines, which lowers expense ratios and "creates" more time for planning activities. Furthermore, certain functions can be shifted forward or backward within the system to achieve scalar economies. The marking of merchandise, for example, is often moved backward in centrally coordinated systems, because the originating supplier can perform this function at a lower cost per unit than resellers. In similar fashion, warehousing, data processing, and other facilities are often relocated to obtain systemic efficiencies. Quite obviously, this repositioning can be accomplished more expeditiously in a centrally coordinated system than in a conventional channel. Third, centrally coordinated systems, in practice, often have substantial horizontal outreach which permits individual units to obtain economies of scale, or failing this, to achieve the savings that accrue to enterprises using existing facilities intensively.[16]

OTHER FACTORS AND SUMMARY

Other factors, such as the expansion and relocation of markets which occurred in the 1950's, also favored the growth of centrally coordinated systems. Furthermore, as new products were introduced or as new markets developed, various types of systems, particularly franchise networks, emerged to capitalize on these newly created opportunities.

In short, the 1948–1965 period was one that encouraged large scale undertakings and the formation of centrally coordinated marketing systems. Predictably, a response, counter-response pattern soon developed. That is, as one system achieved market power in a line of trade, others were quickly formed to counteract this competitive thrust. Consequently, all three types of systems experienced substantial growth between 1948 and 1965, with contractually integrated networks—particularly voluntary groups, cooperative groups, and franchise programs—expanding at the most rapid rate.

VOLUNTARY AND COOPERATIVE GROUPS

CURRENT STATUS

Voluntary and cooperative groups have been in existence for an extended period of time. Several retail cooperatives were established in the food field before the turn of the century; the first drug cooperative was founded in 1902;[17] and a substantial number of voluntaries—including IGA, Red & White, Western Auto, Ben Franklin and others—operated on an extensive scale as early as the 1930's. Despite these historical precedents, voluntary and cooperative groups were largely confined to the food field prior to the middle 1950's. Since that time, however, voluntaries and cooperatives have expanded rapidly, particularly in drug, hardware, automotive, and variety retailing, and continued growth is predicted for the future.

16. For a more extended discussion of channel theory, see Bert C. McCammon, Jr. and Robert W. Little, "Marketing Channels: Analytical Systems and Approaches," *Science in Marketing*, (George Schwartz, ed.), John Wiley and Sons, Inc., New York, 1965.

17. For an excellent discussion of the history of contractual systems in the drug field, see William T. Kelley, "The Franchise System in Co-operative Drugstores," *Journal of Retailing*, Winter, 1957–1958, p. 485.

Retailers affiliated with voluntary and cooperative groups normally operate their stores under the same name, contribute to a common advertising and sales promotion fund, adhere to comparable operating procedures, and purchase most of their inventory requirements from a sponsoring wholesaler (in the case of voluntaries) or from a retail-owned warehouse (in the case of cooperatives). Conversely, the sponsoring wholesaler or warehouse offers a variety of supporting services to affiliated stores so that they can compete against chain outlets on a roughly equal basis.

Retailers belonging to voluntary and cooperative groups have been particularly successful in the food field since World War II. Their share of total food store sales rose from 32 per cent in 1950 to 49 per cent in 1963, while the share held by corporate chains climbed from 37 to only 41 per cent during the same period. Significantly, the proportion of total volume obtained by unaffiliated independents shrank from 33 to 10 per cent between 1950 and 1963.[18] Thus, independent retailers, purchasing from voluntary or cooperative warehouses, have become the dominant form of distribution in this important sector of the economy. On a dollar basis, voluntary group wholesalers increased their sales from approximately $3.2 billion in 1956 to over $6.5 billion in 1963, and cooperative warehouses boosted their volume from $2.0 billion to $4.2 billion during the same period.[19] Furthermore, several of these organizations now rank among the nation's largest merchandising enterprises. Super Valu's volume amounted to $412.2 million in 1964, and Fleming and Wetterau, two IGA affiliates, had sales of $261.7 and $120.0 million respectively, during the same year.[20] Leading cooperatives such as Allied, Thrifty, Affiliated, Certified, and others, also obtain annual sales well in excess of $100 million.

Voluntaries and cooperatives have been active in the drug field since the turn of the century, but their growth has been relatively sluggish until recent years. Rexall and Walgreen, through their wholesale divisions, currently sponsor the most extensive voluntary programs. These organizations supply affiliated druggists with private brand merchandise and numerous supporting services, including financial, merchandising, advertising, and promotional assistance. In 1963, over 14,000 independent druggists were either Walgreen or Rexall "agency" outlets, and these stores, because of their number alone, are a significant competitive factor in the market.[21]

Conventional drug wholesalers began to sponsor voluntary groups

18. Mueller, *op. cit.* (1950 and 1962 editions).
19. *Ibid.*, p. 20.
20. "The Best of Both Possible Worlds," *Forbes*, November 15, 1964, p. 48.
21. *Fairchild's Financial Manual of Retail Stores*, Fairchild Publications, Inc., New York, 1964.

in the early 1960's, and by 1963, aproximately 8.4 per cent of these firms serviced affiliated outlets on a contractual basis.[22] Admittedly, many of the voluntary programs in the drug field are administrative devices for redistributing cooperative advertising allowances, but a growing number of wholesalers offer a substantial number of services to affiliated stores, and most trade authorities believe that existing programs will become increasingly more comprehensive. McKesson & Robbins, as an illustration, already provides numerous services to retailers affiliated with its Independent Druggist's League plan. Over 1,200 outlets, located in 26 major markets, participated in this program in 1963, and continued growth is planned for the future.[23] In total, an estimated 9,914 independent druggists participated in wholesaler-sponsored voluntary programs during 1963, and these outlets, in addition to those participating in the Rexall and Walgreen plans, represented approximately 47.5 per cent of all drugstores in operation during the year.[24]

The growth of cooperative groups in the drug field has also been impressive in recent years. Leader Drug Stores, Inc., which serves affiliated outlets in Cleveland, Buffalo, Toledo, and Pittsburgh, is the largest of the cooperative groups currently in operation. This organization was formed by 34 independent druggists in 1949, and it has grown steadily since that time. Member stores currently account for 60 per cent of total drug sales in the Buffalo market, and the warehouse in Cleveland increased its volume from $7.5 million in 1962 to over $10 million in 1964—a gain of more than 33 per cent.[25] Significantly, the leading cooperatives in the drug field formed a national association on July 1, 1964. At the present time, the organizations belonging to the National Drug Cooperative Association service 850 affiliated outlets, which is over twice the number of stores operated by Walgreen, the largest chain in the field.[26]

The rapid growth of voluntaries and cooperatives in drug retailing is symptomatic of growing competition in the industry. Several major food chains, including Safeway, Kroger and Jewel, acquired drug subsidiaries during the 1950's, and each of these organizations operates over 100 outlets at the present time. Discounting has become a more important factor, too. Over 51 per cent of the discount department stores in operation contain drug departments, which generated annual sales of

22. Findings of a survey undertaken by the editors of *American Druggist* as reported in Bob Vereen, "Where is the Hardware Industry Headed?" *Hardware Retailer*, October, 1964, p. 69.

23. Stanley Siegelman, "Corporate Portrait: McKesson & Robbins," *Drug News Weekly*, July 8, 1964, p. 8.

24. Vereen, *op. cit.*, p. 69.

25. "Independents Counterattack," *Drug News Weekly*, April 19, 1965, p. 4.

26. Warren Moulds, "National Co-op Group Becomes Reality," *Drug News Weekly*, July 19, 1965, p. 1.

$380 million in 1964.[27] As a result of these and other competitive developments, a growing number of drug retailers joined voluntary or cooperative groups.

The voluntary and cooperative movement has also gained momentum in the hardware field. Trade authorities estimate that 10,575 hardware stores—or 35.9 per cent of the total—participated in wholesaler-sponsored programs in 1964.[28] Furthermore, a recent survey of 189 wholesalers indicates that 71 of these firms—or 37.6 per cent—sponsored voluntary groups in 1964, and 28—or 14.8 per cent—plan to develop such programs in the future.[29] Finally, large wholesalers in the hardware field, such as Ace and Cotter, offer a wide variety of services to affiliated stores, as is indicated in Table 1.

The voluntary group concept has been used extensively in the automotive field, too. There are several major programs that involve wholesaling enterprises exclusively, and a substantial number that extend to the retail level. The National Automotive Parts Association, founded in 1924, is the largest voluntary group in the industry. The program is sponsored by 45 warehouse distributors that service approximately 4,000 affiliated wholesalers. NAPA warehouses buy private label and nationally branded merchandise on a contractual basis from a limited number of resources for subsequent redistribution through affiliated jobber outlets. These warehouses also provide a variety of supporting services to automotive wholesalers, which enables the latter to compete more effectively in the marketplace. Gulf and Western's American Parts System, which supplies 450 affiliated jobbers, is quite similar to the NAPA program, as is the recently formed AllCar group, which consists of 12 warehouse distributors and an unannounced number of affiliated jobbers. These data suggest that approximately 20 per cent of the wholesalers engaged in the distribution of automotive parts, accessories, and chemicals belong to voluntary programs sponsored by warehouse distributors.[30]

Voluntary groups are also active in the so-called "home and auto" field, which is an important part of the automotive aftermarket. This segment of retailing, which has grown rapidly in recent years, is dominated by a mixture of franchise and voluntary stores. Of the 33,000 home and auto stores in operation during 1963, approximately 16,300 held Firestone, Goodyear or Goodrich franchises. Over 4,900 of the remaining stores participated in voluntary programs sponsored by West-

27. *The True Look of the Discount Industry*, Super Market Publishing Company, Inc., New York, 1964.

28. Bob Vereen, *op. cit.*, p. 65.

29. *Ibid.*, p. 67.

30. For an excellent discussion of the structure of distribution in the automotive field, see Charles N. Davison, *The Marketing of Automotive Parts*, University of Michigan, Ann Arbor, 1954.

Table 1 Services Provided by Voluntary Group Wholesalers in the Hardware Field United States 1964

Service Provided to Retailer	Percentage of Voluntary Group Wholesalers Providing Designated Service
Consumer circulars and/or catalogs	91.5%
Private brand merchandise	90.3
Monthly promotional specials	73.6
Store-wide promotional kits	73.6
Extended dating programs	69.4
Management and merchandising counseling services	68.1
Cooperative newspaper advertising programs	67.0
Member store identification programs	63.9
Store planning and modernization assistance	62.5
Inventory control systems	58.3
Drop-shipping program	58.3
Bin-tickets for inventory control	55.6
Sales training programs	51.4
Supply and installation of store fixtures	50.0
Catalog order service for consumers	48.6
Preprinted order forms	48.6
Sponsorship of retail advisory committee	44.4
Programmed merchandise deliveries	41.7
Preretailed invoices	31.9
Store location or relocation assistance	29.2
Consumer credit program	27.8
Window display service	22.2
Pool-car buying program	20.8
Centralized accounting service	6.9

Source: "Where is The Hardware Industry Headed?" *Hardware Retailer*, October, 1964, p. 91.

ern Auto, Gamble-Skogmo, and Coast-to-Coast Stores. In summary, roughly 21,200 home and auto stores—or 64.2 per cent of the total—participated in franchise or voluntary group programs during the most recent year for which comprehensive data are available.[31]

Finally, voluntary group retailers are an important factor in the variety field, which has been traditionally dominated by large national chains and their regional counterparts. These organizations accounted for 71.5 per cent of total variety sales in 1964, and their market share has increased steadily since the early 1950's.[32] Retailers affiliated with the Ben Franklin program are the only other significant factor in the mar-

31. "The Anatomy of a Market," *Home & Auto Retailer*, July, 1965, p. 14.
32. "Annual Report on the Variety Store Field," *Variety Store Merchandiser*, March, 1965, p. 23.

ket at the present time. Over 2,400 variety stores participated in this program during 1964, and their aggregate volume amounted to approximately $300 million, which represented 6.0 per cent of total variety sales.[33]

EMERGING TRENDS

There are several recent developments in the voluntary and cooperative field that have particular significance. First, a substantial number of voluntary and cooperative groups have expanded their private brand programs. Ben Franklin retailers, for example, obtained 15 per cent of their sales from private label merchandise in 1963.[34] Stores affiliated with the Super Valu program relied on private brands for 10 per cent of their volume in 1964, and IGA outlets exceeded even this percentage.[35]

TABLE 2   Private Brand Programs Sponsored by Voluntary Group Wholesalers in the Hardware Field United States 1964

Merchandise Category	Percentage of Voluntary Group Wholesalers Stocking Private Brands in Designated Category
Traffic appliances	87.5%
Power tools	86.1
Power mowers and equipment	86.1
Hand tools	84.7
Lawn and garden supplies	76.4
Paint sundries	76.4
Hardware	75.0
Fishing tackle	65.3
Paint	61.1
Sporting goods	58.3
Lawn and garden chemicals	37.5

Source: "Where is The Hardware Industry Headed?" *Hardware Retailer*, October, 1964, p. 87.

Furthermore, a substantial percentage of voluntary wholesalers in the hardware field inventoried private brands in 1964, as is indicated in Table 2. Consequently, this approach to merchandising has apparently

33. A. J. Vogl, "Franchising: The New American Dream," *Modern Franchising*, September–October, 1964, p. 10.
34. *Annual Report*, City Products Corporation, Des Plaines, Illinois, 1964, p. 8.
35. "A Supermarket Chain that Isn't a Chain," *Business Week*, August 22, 1964, p. 82.

become an established part of the voluntary and cooperative movement, and it could become increasingly more important in the future. Second, voluntary and cooperative wholesalers have diversified their inventories in recent years to better serve affiliated retailers, and this trend is particularly apparent in the food field. In 1963, for example, 93 per cent of all voluntary food wholesalers stocked health and beauty aids; 49 per cent handled housewares, and a substantial proportion also carried garden supplies, small appliances, glassware and greeting cards.[36] Cooperative food wholesalers were equally as aggressive in their inventory diversification programs as were their counterparts in the drug, hardware and home and auto fields. Available data suggest that this trend will accelerate, rather than diminish, during the decade ahead, which indicates that intertype competition at the retail level may become more intense. Third, both voluntary and cooperative wholesalers are expanding the range of services offered to affiliated stores, and this development is particularly pronounced in the drug and hardware fields. Many drug wholesalers, sponsoring voluntary programs, routinely sign shopping center leases to secure prime locations for their accounts and others provide a centralized accounting service. Voluntary hardware wholesalers are expanding their retail assistance programs at a comparable rate, which suggests that voluntary programs in these fields, at least, will become as comprehensive as those used in food retailing.

FRANCHISE PROGRAMS

Franchising involves a contractual arrangement between originating suppliers (manufacturers or service organizations) and affiliated outlets.[37] These agreements vary in scope and content, but all contain provisions in which the franchisee is given the right to sell a designated product or service, in a generally defined geographical area, in exchange for his promise to market the product or service in a specified manner.[38] Furthermore, the franchise agreement may cover the entire outlet, a department within the outlet, or a brand within the department. As is the case with other forms of contractual integration, franchising is a long established method of distribution. The Singer Sewing Machine Company, for example, developed an extensive and successful franchise network shortly after the Civil War; automobile manufacturers converted

36. Robert W. Mueller, *op. cit.*, p. 21.
37. For an excellent discussion of the legal aspects of franchising, see Charles M. Hewitt, "The Furor Over Dealer Franchises," *Business Horizons*, Winter, 1958, pp. 80–87.
38. For an interesting analysis of the differences in franchise agreements, see Edwin A. Lewis and Robert S. Hancock, *The Franchise System of Distribution*, University of Minnesota, 1963.

to a franchise system of distribution in 1911 which is still being used today; and the integrated oil companies, which obtain approximately 90 per cent of their volume from franchised outlets, adopted this method of distribution during the 1920's and 1930's.[39] As a result of these and similar programs, franchising systems have been an integral and important part of the marketing structure for almost 100 years. Franchising did not become a pervasive phenomenon until the early 1950's, however, when a growing number of companies entered the field for the first time.

Franchise programs, covering consumer goods and services, experienced particularly rapid growth between 1950 and 1965. Many of these programs, such as those sponsored by Fanny Farmer, Loft's, Russell Stover, Barton's, Barricini, and other candy companies, involve departmental franchises which are granted on a selective basis. There were approximately 15,000 franchised candy departments in operation during 1964,[40] and comparable expansion has occurred in other merchandise categories, including cosmetics, ready-to-wear, and vacuum cleaners. Franchise agreements covering specific brands which are normally merchandised with competing brands, may have grown in importance too, but data regarding these programs are fragmentary. Certainly, individual manufacturers—including Maytag, Zenith, Magnavox, and Karastan—have strengthened their position in recent years through the use of intelligently conceived franchise programs. These developments, though significant in terms of marketing strategy, have had little impact on the structure of retailing. In sharp contrast, franchise programs covering all phases of an outlet's operations have dramatically affected competitive relationships, and these programs are the ones usually described by chroniclers of the "franchise movement."

Comprehensive franchise programs grew rapidly between 1950 and 1965, and they have become a particularly significant factor in the marketing of the following goods and services: laundry and dry cleaning services, soft ice cream, hearing aids, carpet and upholstery cleaning services, water conditioning systems, and swimming pools. Furthermore, a growing number of restaurants, motels, and part-time employment agencies are operated on a franchise basis (the relative importance of franchising in these and other industries as of the end of 1963 is shown in Table 3). On a national basis trade authorities estimate that there were approximately 100,000 franchised outlets (excluding service sta-

39. For an analysis of the growth of franchise systems in the petroleum industry, see John Godfrey MacLean and Robert William Haigh, *The Growth of Integrated Oil Companies*, Harvard University, Boston, 1954.

40. "Store-Within-Store Franchise A Big Step," *Drug News Weekly*, March 29, 1965, p. 7.

tions and automobile dealers) in operation by the end of 1963. These enterprises generated aggregate sales of over $5 billion and competed in at least 80 lines of trade under franchises granted by over 400 organizations, including Dairy Queen, Tastee Freez, A & W Root Beer, the Mary Carter Paint Company, Howard Johnson's, McDonald's System, Inc., and others.[41] Furthermore, most of the firms sponsoring, or affiliated with, franchise programs were either founded after 1950 or have experienced their most rapid rate of growth since that time.

TABLE 3 Number of Franchised Outlets by Line of Retail Trade of Service Category United States 1963

Line of Retail Trade or Service Category	Number of Franchised Outlets	Estimated Sales (Millions of Dollars)
Laundry and Dry Cleaning	35,700	$ 509
Restaurants and Refreshment Stands	24,590	1,410
Household Goods Moving Companies	5,000	1,000
Carpet and Upholstery Cleaning	4,000	100
Hearing Aids	3,500	70
Water Conditioning Systems	2,300	207
Swimming Pools	1,000	40
Part-time Employment Agencies	500	100
Total	76,590	$3,436

Source: David B. Slater, "Some Socio-Economic Footnotes on Franchising," *Boston University Business Review*, Summer, 1964, p. 19.

Franchising has expanded most rapidly in the food service field. At the present time, 10 of the 20 largest franchising organizations supply restaurants and soft ice cream outlets. The rapid growth of these programs can be effectively illustrated by examining the history of the soft ice cream industry. Only 100 outlets served this product after World War II, but by 1964 there were over 18,000 franchised dairy stands in operation.[42] Franchised restaurants have grown almost as rapidly, as indicated by the following corporate illustrations:

Chicken Delight, Inc. expanded from one franchise outlet in 1952 to over 511 in 1964. Furthermore, the company's total revenue, including sales, commissions, and fees, was over $40 million during the latter year.

McDonald's System, Inc. generated total sales of $100 million in 1964, after expanding from a small regional base 10 years earlier.

Howard Johnson's, a long established restaurant chain, accelerated its

41. Steven S. Andreder, "License for Growth," *Barron's*, November 27, 1961, p. 3.
42. "Franchise Selling Catches On," *Business Week*, February 6, 1960, p. 90.

expansion through the use of a franchise program. The company serviced 675 restaurants in 1964, and half of these outlets were operated by franchisees.[43]

In summary, the franchise movement is well established in the food service field. There were over 24,590 franchised restaurants or roadside stands in operation by the end of 1963, and these outlets accounted for approximately 12.8 per cent of total food service sales.[44]

Franchised motels have become a significant competitive factor, too. There are three major types of contractual arrangements in this field: conventional franchise programs, co-owner franchise programs, and referral groups. Conventional franchise programs—such as those sponsored by Quality Courts Motels, Holiday Inns, and Congress Inns—involve contractual agreemnts between the sponsoring organization and affiliated motels in which the latter adhere to specified architectural standards, contribute to a common advertising and sales promotion fund, follow recommended operating procedures, and purchase most of their equipment and supplies from the franchisor. Co-owner franchise programs are virtually identical to their conventional counterparts, except that the sponsoring organization has an equity interest in affiliated units. TraveLodge, which developed the concept, Imperial 400, MoteLodge, and Hyatt Chalets, are the principal proponents of co-owner franchise programs. Motels belonging to referral groups, the third type of contractual system in the field, constitute a loose economic coalition. These outlets often differ markedly in terms of their size, pricing practices, and operating methods. As a result, they do not project the unified image or maintain the consistency of service that is usually found in conventional or co-owner programs. However, referral group motels contribute to a common advertising and sales promotion fund, consolidate their orders to lower purchasing costs, and refer customers to affiliated outlets; thus, they achieve systemic economies and substantial market impact. Best Western Motels, Superior Motels, and Emmons Walker are the largest of the referral groups currently in operation, and their growth has been unusually rapid in recent years. By the end of 1964, 1,723 motels were affiliated with conventional franchise programs, 544 participated in co-owner programs, and 2,324 were members of referral groups. These franchised motels contained over 279,500 rooms, which represented approximately 30 per cent of the industry's capacity at the end of the year.[45]

Franchising programs, as indicated above, tend to be offensive align-

43. A. J. Vogl, *op. cit.*, p. 11.

44. David B. Slater, "Some Socio-Economic Footnotes on Franchising," *Boston University Business Review*, Summer, 1964, pp. 19–28.

45. Ralph Dellevie, "Chain and Referral Groups," *Tourist Court Journal*, June, 1964, pp. 8–12.

ments. Sponsoring firms, by using this technique, can obtain extensive market coverage with a minimum capital investment. Similarly, franchisees tend to be entrepreneurs entering the market for the first time. As a result, franchising programs can significantly disrupt the competitive *status quo* in a relatively short period of time, and this innovative potential has been dramatically realized in the motel, restaurant, and dry cleaning fields, as well as others.

With respect to emerging trends, there are two significant developments that deserve particular emphasis. First, franchising will probably be used in a growing number of industries during the decade ahead, including home furnishings and ready-to-wear. Several pilot programs are already underway and early results are encouraging. Second, multiple operations will probably emerge. TraveLodge and the Pure Oil Company, for example, are now developing TOURest units, which include a motel, service station and restaurant, all of which are franchised operations.[46] This type of arrangement has considerable appeal for affiliated operators because it broadens their market base, and thus continued growth can be expected.

SOME UNRESOLVED PROBLEMS CONFRONTING MEMBERS OF FRANCHISE, VOLUNTARY AND COOPERATIVE GROUPS

The future growth of franchise networks and voluntary and cooperative groups may be somewhat inhibited, because these contractual systems have not solved several significant problems. First, there is the problem of management succession. The firms participating in franchise, voluntary, and cooperative programs are usually small scale enterprises operated by first generation enterpreneurs. Such organizations have historically experienced difficulty in ensuring continuity of capable management, and affiliation has not significantly eased this problem. As a result, the economic performance of franchise networks and voluntary and cooperative groups may deteriorate in the future due to a decline in the managerial capability of affiliated units. Second, the administrators of franchise, voluntary, and cooperative programs will probably continue to encounter difficulty in maintaining uniformity of operations throughout the system. Affiliated outlets, particularly in voluntary and cooperative groups, often differ markedly in terms of their store layouts, inventory assortments, pricing practices, and other characteristics. These variations are frequently difficult to eradicate, because member firms possess considerable autonomy; consequently, executives in contractual

---

46. Reuben Polen, "TOURest—New Concept Combines Three Basics," *Tourist Court Journal*, October, 1963, p. 16.

networks have much less control over marketing activities than their counterparts in corporate systems, which suggests that the former may have fewer opportunities than the latter to effect systemic economies. Admittedly, this lack of centralized control *may* result in prompter adjustments to demand and stronger management incentives at the *local* level, but such arguments lose much of their validity in the context of recent advances in data processing and executive development techniques. Third, financial limitations may dampen growth rates in the franchise, voluntary and cooperative fields. The firms affiliated with these systems tend to be undercapitalized, and virtually all of them depend on local sources of funds to finance their operations. As a result, they often experience difficulty in raising capital for expansion and modernization. Comparable units in corporate systems, on the other hand, have relatively easy access to the capital market, since their line of credit is based on the performance of the total system, rather than that of individual outlets. In addition, corporate systems offer lendors and investors the advantage of diversification of risk which the individual entrepreneur, operating at a single location, cannot. Fourth, voluntary and cooperative groups, in particular, have not been conspicuously successful in their attempts to compete in large urban markets. Affiliated outlets are typically located in small and medium size communities, which will decline in relative importance as the American economy becomes more urbanized. Consequently, the future growth of voluntary and cooperative programs is partially conditional on their ability to penetrate highly competitive urban areas. Fifth, and finally, franchisees and members of voluntary and cooperative groups have not solved their estate tax problems through affiliation. That is, entrepreneurs, interested in fragmenting and diversifying their holdings for estate tax purposes, cannot achieve this goal through contractual integration. Consequently, owner-managers, desirous of diversifying their holdings, must still merge their operations with publicly owned corporations or negotiate an outright sale. If a growing number of affiliated entrepreneurs become concerned about estate tax problems, many may decide to liquidate their investments, and thus contractual integration may be a prelude to corporate integration.

The problems cited above are rather formidable, and each of them deserves careful study and additional research. Despite these reservations, however, franchise, voluntary, and cooperative groups will probably continue to expand in the future, since they have clearly demonstrated their ability to compete against corporate and administered systems. Furthermore, franchising has proved to be an effective device for obtaining consumer acceptance of new products, new services, and new methods of operation; thus, this distribution technique should continue to be of interest to prospective market entrants.

QUESTIONS FOR DISCUSSION

1. What are the basic characteristics of:
   a. a corporate system?
   b. a contractual system?
   c. an administered system?

2. What reasons do you believe best explain the significant growth in contractual, corporate, and administered systems?

3. What emerging trends:
   a. does McCammon see in this area?
   b. do you predict in this area? Why?

4. Where does franchising fit into this area? Why?

5. Do you believe that planned integrated vertical channels will become more or less important in the 1980s? Defend your answer.

5.5 A SCHEME FOR EXAMINING MARKETING CHANNELS AS SOCIAL SYSTEMS

Michael F. Foran and Anthony F. McGann

"The real leader, however, may not be the official leader. This is why an analysis of the activities, interactions and sentiments between members of the marketing channels is a necessity."

The marketing literature has reflected the fact that marketing channels are something more than mere paths in which goods or services flow from one organization to another. It is now being recognized that channels are, in reality, systems with social significance. This paper sets forth a scheme for examining the channel as a social system. This analysis assumes a system composed of intermediate and ultimate customers.

CHANNEL IDENTIFICATION

A critical problem in channel analysis is the identification of the entire channel. McCammon and Little state "most manufacturers, on the basis of their internal records, know very little about the composition of the market below the first stage of distribution."[1] Similarly, Clewett points out that:

> channels are not 'flagged' (identified by name) on your operating records. No item on the profit and loss statement makes you focus attention on distribution channels, as is the case of advertising, personal selling, and other expenses.[2]

Reprinted by permission from the authors and publisher. Michael F. Foran and Anthony F. McGann, "A Scheme for Examining Marketing Channels as Social Systems," *Business Ideas and Facts* (Fall, 1974), pp. 51–54.

1. B. C. McCammon, Jr., and R. W. Little, "Marketing Channels: Analytical Systems and Approaches," *Science in Marketing*, ed. G. Schwartz (New York: John Wiley & Sons, Inc., 1965), p. 325.

2. R. M. Clewett, "Checking Your Marketing Channels," *Readings in Marketing*,

Channel identification, however, need not take place only on the basis of financial or accounting records. These records can be most helpful in identifying the first stage of distribution (e.g., through customer analysis). But these data should be supplemented with data from sales, product service, advertising and sales promotion, product planning and marketing research. An analysis of the nature of the product itself could also indicate the type of channel needed. This, in turn, provides a basis for the implementation of the analysis set forth in this paper.

ACTIVITIES, INTERACTION, SENTIMENTS

The primary concern of this paper will be with a focal organization and the other organizations which deal with it as members of the marketing channel.

> Channel members pursue a hierarchy of individual goals and they pursue channel goals that are perceived to contribute to fuller realization of their own goals. System goals are strong enough in some sense to hold members within the channel; otherwise it would not exist.[3]

Thus, the system's goals are something more than the sum of the goals of the individual organizations. Also, the system's performance in distributing goods and services is an output which depends on the behavior of the members.

> The designation of the distribution channel as a system has a number of important implications, some of which are: (1) each member of a distribution channel is dependent upon the behavior of other channel members; (2) a behavior change at any point in the channel causes change throughout the channel; and (3) the whole channel must operate effectively if the desires of any one member are to be realized. These three implications derive from the central characteristic of all systems—mutual dependency among components.[4]

Given the interdependence of channel member organizations, a certain pattern of activities is required of each member. These activities, in turn, require a specific set of interactions among the firms. The interactions then bring about sentiments concerning the working relationships in-

ed. C. J. Dirksen, A. Kroeger, and L. C. Lockley (2d ed. rev.: Homewood, Illinois: Richard D. Irwin, Inc., 1968), p. 263.

3. R. W. Little, "Power and Leadership in Marketing Channels," (An unpublished paper presented at the AMA Proceedings of the 1968 Fall Conference, Denver, Colo.), p. 3.

4. L. W. Stern (ed.), *Distribution Channels: Behavioral Dimensions* (Boston: Houghton-Mifflin Company, 1969), p. 2.

volved. These sentiments, thus determined, feed back to and affect the organization's behavior in the required activities and the cycle repeats itself. "The activities, interactions and sentiments of the group members, together with the mutual relations of these elements with one another during the time the group is active, constitute what we shall call the social system.[5]

Activities, interactions and sentiments of group members bring about the emergence of group norms. On this point, McCammon and Little hold that:

> the behavior of channel members, particularly in a well established channel is 'regulated' by a code that specifies types of acceptable competitive behavior. The occupational code consists of informally established group norms, and a subtle but clear array of sanctions is used in most channels to control the behavior of participants.[6]

This idea of group norm emergence must be acknowledged as both a critical and useful one. It can be used not only to classify various members of the channel from other participating and influential groups performing a similar function (i.e., insiders, strivers, complementors, transients),[7] but can also be used to determine the channel leader. This is so because "the leader gets his power only by conforming more closely than anyone else to the norms of the group."[8] In other words, the leader will have the highest social rank, his sentiments will carry the greatest weight, and he will be at the center of interaction.[9] The real leader, however, may not be the official leader. This is why an analysis of the activities, interactions and sentiments between members of the marketing channels is a necessity.

Once the leader has been identified, the social structure of the channel can be charted. This can be done because "the interfirm linkages that prevail in the marketplace reflect status as well as economic operations."[10] Thus, the channel leader will usually originate interaction and will ordinarily do so through those members who are immediately below him in social rank. These, in turn, will pass information to the next social rank and so on. Therefore, both origination and direction of the interactions within the social system are important aspects of the analysis.

5. G. C. Homans, *The Human Group* (New York: Harcourt, Brace and Company, 1950), p. 87.

6. McCammon and Little, p. 330.

7. L. Kriesberg, "Occupational Controls Among Steel Distributors," *American Journal of Sociology*, November, 1955, pp. 203–212.

8. Homans, p. 149.

9. *Ibid.*, p. 141, 181, 418.

10. McCammon and Little, p. 347.

APPLICATION

For consumer goods the initial analysis is to classify the product as being a convenience, shopping or specialty good. Then the product can be analyzed from the viewpoint of the activity, interaction and sentiment associated with it. Evident in this analysis is the fact that the consumer is and should be considered a channel member. This is nothing more than the marketing concept.

The leader of the traditional channel depends on the consumer's perception of the product. For instance, if the customer wants to buy (activity) a specialty good (positive sentiments) then he is actually interacting with the manufacturer even though he makes the purchase through a retail store. He is looking to the manufacturer to meet his needs and, in this instance, sees the retail store as merely an outlet for the manufacturer's product. Thus, if the purchase of this specialty good does not meet the expectation of the customer, then his purchases from the manufacturer will decrease, his sentiments for the manufacturer will become negative, and the interaction between producer and consumer will fall off. The retailer may suffer little, if any, damage through this series of events and may even benefit. This can be the case because if the customer returns the good to the retailer (activity and interaction with the retailer increases) and is pleased with the service of the retail establishment (increasing positive sentiments for the retailer) he may do additional business there—thus, increasing the retailer's position in other channels.

In the specialty good example, it must be remembered that manufacturers have circumvented distributors, and appealed directly to the consumers. By developing directly a consumer demand for specialty goods, the manufacturer has influenced wholesalers and retailers to stock his goods.[11] In this example, the manufacturer has become the de facto leader of the [distributor] channel. As such he "has many domination weapons at his disposal. His arsenal can be divided into promotional, legal, negative, suggestive, and ironically, voluntary cooperative compartments."[12] Whether he uses any of his arsenal or not, however, he must always keep in mind the consumer's sentiments for his products. These sentiments govern the activities and interactions of the consumer and are the principal determinants of leadership within the channel.

11. D. R. Craig and W. K. Gabler, "The Competitive Struggle for Market Control," *The Annals of the American Academy of Political and Social Science*, (May, 1940), pp. 85–86.

12. B. Mallen, "Conflict and Cooperation in Marketing Channels," *The Marketing Channel*, ed. B. Mallen (New York: John Wiley and Sons, Inc., 1967), p. 130.

This analysis can also be used for convenience good and shopping good categories. As a general rule, specialty goods would have a manufacturer leading the traditional channel, a convenience good would have a retail leader, and a shopping good would have a wholesale leader. Of course, there will be exceptions to all of the categories (i.e., private branded specialty good), but the analysis of activities, interactions, and sentiments of the consumer will indicate these variations in the general rule.

OTHER IMPORTANT SOCIAL SYSTEM ELEMENTS

Although detailed discussion is beyond the scope of this paper, other elements must be considered when viewing the marketing channel from a social system viewpoint. Stern and Brown emphasize this by reminding us that:

> a social systems approach, once adopted, requires an investigation of the factors influencing the structural and functional variables of such systems. For distribution channels, pertinent factors (among others) are role expectations, the exercise of power, the existence of conflict, and the presence and use of viable communication networks.[13]

All of these factors will have a vital effect on the ability of the channels to become an effective and efficient system which will accomplish both the goals of the individual organizations and those of the channel. A valuable insight into all of these areas will be provided by adopting the scheme set forth in this paper. A thorough analysis of the marketing channel through the concepts of activities, interactions and sentiments can set forth and emphasize the problems associated with power, conflict and communication within the channel. In addition, the parties involved in channel problems as well as probable causes of the problem will be obtained from the analysis.

SUMMARY

This paper set forth a scheme of analysis for the examination of the marketing channel as a social system. It emphasized studying the system from the viewpoint of activities, interactions and sentiments.[14] In addition to indicating the channel leader, the division of labor established for the channel, the social status attached to each level, and the

13. L. W. Stern and J. W. Brown, "Distribution Channels: A Social Systems Approach," *Distribution Channels: Behavioral Dimensions*, ed. L. W. Stern (New York: Houghton Mifflin Company, 1969), p. 17.
14. Homans, p. 87.

working relationships within the channel, this scheme can also be a basis for analyzing the uses and problems associated with power, conflict and communication. All of this information must be known if the channel is to be analyzed as a social system.

QUESTIONS FOR DISCUSSION

1. Explain the value of viewing marketing channels as social systems.

2. Discuss the interface between social systems and the channel captain.

3. The authors state, ". . . if the customer wants to buy a specialty good then he is actually interacting with the manufacturer even though he makes the purchase through a retail store." Discuss the implications of this statement on channel strategy.

5.6 DISTRIBUTOR INCENTIVE PROGRAMS —YOU BOTH SHOULD WIN: AN EXECUTIVE ROUNDTABLE

"When an independent distributor sells your product, your 'real' competition may be not your competitors' products but the other lines competing for the distribution salesperson's attention."

WHYS AND WHEREFORES

SM: Why use incentive programs for distributors and their salesmen? What specific sales goals can they help you reach?

WATERS: In today's economy, we feel that we're competing against many other manufacturers for the distributor's time. For example, at the CSG Group of Certain-teed, we have about 500 distributors handling our insulating products nationwide. We recently had an incentive program on a duct system we were introducing because our distributors were already handling competitive products. The idea was to show the distributors how they could profit with our line, and to help them move their inventories.

NAGEL: At Lily, we're dealing with over 1,000 distributors, and they are definitely nonexclusive. We use incentives to create loyalty for our company, and to encourage distributors to spend a greater proportion of their discretionary sales time on our line.

GARVIN: At ESB, our programs are heavily oriented to getting new customers.

SM: What types of incentive programs work best?

GROSSMANN: Probably the best programs for salesmen are those in which everyone can be a winner. American Hospital Supply Div. sells products made by 1,200 manufacturers. We have 300 salesmen. So if we had a year-long promotion in which only 10 salespersons could win, by midyear the effectiveness of the incentive would be greatly reduced because the majority would realize, by then, that they could not win.

Reprinted by permission from the publisher. "Distributor Incentive Programs—You Both Should Win: An Executive Roundtable," *Sales Management* (September 8, 1975), pp. 44–48.

TOBIN: I work with distributors primarily in the electronic tube area. Sylvania's Electronic Components Group has about 650 distributors nationwide, and I deal with them in terms of the TV repair market, picture tubes, receiving tubes, and so on. We use a lot of incentive programs with these people. For example, we have a dealer program with a nine-month promotion that's aimed at the TV serviceman who buys from the distributor, and there is a lot of competition for his business. We also have a year-long travel incentive program for the distributor himself. We encourage him to use our trips as an incentive within his own organization.

SM: Do you also give incentives directly to distributor salesmen?

TOBIN: We've tried distributor salesmen programs in the past with the approval of the distributors. But many times, it is to the distributor's disadvantage to implement a manufacturer's program because his salesmen will promote a particular model of a particular line, and that will quickly unbalance the inventory situation in the distributorship. Thus many distributors would rather run their own incentive programs. In those cases, I help them organize programs for their own people.

SHORT-TERM VS. LONG-TERM PROGRAMS

NAGEL: There is a fair amount of controversy in the incentive field as to whether it's better to offer short-term programs that capture immediate interest and move a particular product or a longer program that builds loyalty and interest over a period of time. I'm somewhat opposed to short-term programs because they tend to balloon the distributor's inventory.

GROSSMANN: I think there are two aspects to that issue, Bob. If you're promoting a full line, as you apparently are at Lily, then I think a longer program is better. If you're promoting a narrow product line or a specific product, then perhaps you should use the shorter term. The way we handle the inventory problem when participating in a manufacturer's program is to make a payout only for sales to the customer, not on what we buy. That way, our managers are not loading their inventory.

PROBLEMS OF PRICE-CUTTING

JONAS: As a distributor, I guess most manufacturers would think I would be in favor of incentives and other promotions. Really, I'm not. Some are based strictly on price, and, quite honestly, a lot of them seem absurd. One of our suppliers has 10 price promotions a year involving five groups of products. Each one is promoted twice a year. Now our business is selling parts, and we can only sell a part when it is needed. A customer is not going to buy a washing machine pump and hang it on his wall. Nonetheless, when the manufacturer's price cut comes, many distributors go out and start cutting their prices to customers. Which is one reason why I'm against price incentives: when there is regular price-cutting, market prices start getting muddied up. And I don't think it's good for a distributor or good for a manufacturer.

WATERS: We as manufacturers have one motive for incentives: to move product in a down economy. We feel that to do this at the expense of our distributors isn't going to help us at all because that's when they hang us over the cliff after the program is over. Extending credit terms temporarily is an incentive, and we prefer to use something like that rather than a price cut. In a volatile market, if we cut prices and our competitors pick up on it, the whole market is down the tube.

SPIFFING SALESMEN

SM: What do you think of using spiffs for salesmen?

McELVEEN: I don't want to sound like a hypocrite, but that's one area I'm not really for. If a slow mover is spiffed, which is customary in many trades, then the salesman is prone to sell that model even though it may not be the model with the most profit to the dealer. However, this year, for the first time in the history of the Friedrich company, we gave a retail incentive because it's a tough market and other people are spiffing. We gave retail salesmen prime steaks shipped from the Midwest. The incentive amounted to about $4 per unit, and I have to admit I don't know what I'd have done without it.

WATERS: We offered a spiff as part of the total incentive program when we introduced our duct system. It was aimed at the distributor salesman who, we feel, is the guy who creates the first sale for us, the guy who puts the pressure on the buying agent to carry our line.

GARVIN: One way to make spiffs effective is to get the head of the distributorship to pay part of the cost, even if it is only 10%. If his money is there, he's going to push the program.

GROSSMANN: If the spiff or any other incentive is going to succeed, it has to fit the product. The wholesaler can't have his men mismanaging their time on commodity products. It would be a poor management decision if a company allowed its salesmen to be spiffed on a low-profit item.

SETTING GOALS

SM: How do you go about setting goals for distributor incentive programs?

NAGEL: The best advice is to get some outside consulting help to determine exactly what your distributors are after. You may think you know them. We did. But when we had a couple of surveys done, the results were surprising. Even within what we thought was a homogeneous distributor family, there were wide variations in the way distributors looked at incentives and promotions. You could almost categorize them. Multibranch and professionally managed organizations had a totally different view about incentives than did the more entrepreneurial ones.

SM: In what way, Bob?

NAGEL: The smaller distributor is usually most concerned about increasing local sales and enhancing his image in the community. So if we offer a trip or merchandise award, he is interested in going himself or in sending one or two of his top salesmen.

If you go to large companies, it is very difficult to interest them in a promotional program because they have their own internal setup and the computer generates orders based on analysis of inventory and sales. So it is difficult to come in and say, We have a program; wouldn't you like to plug it in? It's sort of like coming in with a 110 plug and finding a 220 socket.

SM: Then how do you set your goals?

TOBIN: Our quotas for all our distributors are pretty much based on their purchases the previous year in our industry. In many cases, the distributor is buying the same item from two or three different manufacturers and he can decide which he is going to buy from.

GARVIN: At ESB, we try to group like-volume distributors and have various levels of prizes so that everybody can win something. The quota is what they did last year in the same period plus an increase of 5% or whatever. Each salesman has a list of his accounts and which level of program we think he can sell the guy. The distributor might get a trip to Rome for buying 5,000 batteries, to Bermuda for 2,500, and so on down to where he gets a weekend in his local Holiday Inn. The distributor commits to the level he thinks he can achieve; then he either makes it or he doesn't.

SM: Do you do anything special to get new distributors to participate?

GARVIN: Actually, as I've said, all our programs are heavily oriented to getting new customers. Our salesman walks in to a prospect and says, Here is our program; if you sign within the next 30 days, we're going to count every battery you buy double. The distributor decides what level he wants to try for. And that's another good thing as far as we're concerned. The distributor knows he either makes it or he doesn't.

A lot of times, salesmen are the biggest liars in the world. If we ever paid any attention to what the salesmen said the new accounts were going to sell, I could have retired a long time ago. I cut everything in half and I'm still 50% too high. But the distributor knows he isn't going to get the trip if he doesn't make it, so he starts being honest with us.

SM: What advantage is there to setting levels of commitment rather than just assigning individual quotas?

NAGEL: Say Joe has a guy working for him who Joe figures could sell about 2,500 batteries this year. If the commitment levels are set at 2,000, 3,000, 4,000, and so on, and you let the distributor choose his own level, most of the time he'll try to stretch a little rather than take the easiest route out. So he's going to sell more than he would have if you'd given him that 2,500 quota. Also, because he picked his own objective, he's probably going to work harder to reach it than if you just assigned him a quota.

AWARDS AND REWARDS

SM: What awards seem to be most effective?

WATERS: A lot of surveys show that the No. 1 incentive for a salesman is dollars, No. 2 is trips, and No. 3 is merchandise or point catalogues.

GARVIN: We've found that travel is the best type if you can afford it.

GROSSMANN: Our salesmen are on straight commission, so cash incentives are important—or something that has emotional value. I'm wearing an anniversary watch that we offered in a program three years ago. You could get one only by achieving your goal, and it drove our guys just crazy. They had to have that watch.

McELVEEN: I don't think that the prize is as important as the amount of pride that is involved in getting it.

TOBIN: We refer to that as "trophy value." We use a lot of that now.

NAGEL: You can't underestimate it. A plaque that costs $5 can have more value to the winner than something of greater material worth.

JONAS: A few years ago, one of the manufacturers we represent had a program based on record keeping and volume sales. The prize was one watch for every X% the company achieved over its quota. The watch had value to our people, and it was impossible to win enough for everyone. But we felt that all our salesmen and managers had helped make the promotion successful, and we wanted to reward all of them. So I asked the manufacturer if I could buy some extra watches. That way, I was able to give them to our entire sales team. And it was a very meaningful thing. Whenever the people from this company come around, our men show them the watch.

NAGEL: You can get a lot of people to work hard for what comes out to be 2% or 3% of sales because you are generally purchasing things that they couldn't get on their own for that. I'm thinking mostly of travel, which combines the aspects of recognition and image along with having a nice vacation. If you wanted to promote with a price cut, you'd have to cut by 5% or more to get anyone's interest.

TOBIN: Also, from a promotion viewpoint, I think price-cutting is the worst type of incentive because it is the most easily matched by your competition.

SM: Where does the supplier's sales force come into the picture?

WATERS: Incentive programs are a tool for our men. We purposely key our incentives to such things as the profitability of the distributor's product mix, or his salesmen's presentations. That gives our salesman an opportunity to go in and talk with the distributor about how he runs his business and how we can help him increase his profit, cash flow, or whatever.

TOBIN: We have found that incentive programs also help us as a sales training tool. When we introduce an incentive plan, we kick it off at a meeting with our salesmen. After talking about the program, we say, O.K., let's get back to basics. Then we review some of the basic selling techniques that they may have forgotten over the last several months.

MCELVEEN: We always talk with our field salespeople before we introduce a program. We've found we'd better heed them if they tell us it will never sell.

WHY DISTRIBUTORS SAY NO

SM: What percentage of the programs that you are offered do you actually accept?

GROSSMANN: About 10%—and we tailor those.

JONAS: Somewhere around 25%.

SM: What determines which ones you accept?

GROSSMANN: We have a basic marketing plan and profitability goals. We'll consider the incentives that are offered to us on the more profitable lines. Then, if the plan doesn't fit our marketing program or if mechanically it is just too difficult to implement, we decline it.

JONAS: We are running our business to make money, and we won't bring in inventory just to make a trip or whatever. But the relationship we have with the supplier's salesman does have an effect on whether or not we accept an incentive program. If our relationship is generally good and the program won't hurt us, we'll run it. In fact, there are times we'll run one just because the manufacturer would like to run one or because we feel that the competition will accept it and it could hurt us if we don't match it.

SM: Do you ever feel pushed into overbuying because of the competitive pressures of incentive contests?

JONAS: No. We don't make any superhuman efforts, and occasionally we haven't made a promotion. But the pressure really does get to some people. In one travel program we were involved in, for instance, the manufacturer grouped distributors on four or five levels based on volume. Every month, we got a mimeographed sheet listing the different groups and who was at what percentage of quota. People started thinking, Gee, I want to be on top, and they started buying like crazy. That's great for the manufacturer but not for the distributor.

GARVIN: But you're saying it works.

JONAS: Yes, for the manufacturer—but I'm not a manufacturer.

GARVIN: But I am. The ones that overbought used poor judgment. Anyone who is running a business isn't going to last very long if he loads in a lot of inventory in order to go to Hanoi or whatever. But the program does work as far as the manufacturer's objective is concerned.

I think we've got to be careful that we don't generalize and say that all loading programs are bad. If the objective is to load, why downgrade it? Every incentive should have a goal. If you reach that goal, the program is successful.

SM: *What if the distributor, feeling he is going to be loaded, refuses the program?*

GROSSMANN: A manufacturer can go around the distributor. Say that we're not interested in your program because it doesn't fit into our marketing plan. You can always go direct to the buyer with a promotion and thereby force the distributor to get on your bandwagon.

MEASURING SUCCESS

SM: *How can manufacturers measure a program's success?*

McELVEEN: The product has to move through the pipeline. If it stops anywhere along the line, the program isn't any good.

GARVIN: It depends on your goal. You may want to take the product through the warehouse distributor, to the jobber, to the dealer, and out to the consumer. If the program breaks down anyplace, it's unsuccessful. But if your incentive was designed to load and that's what it did, it was successful.

TOBIN: We try to do both by offering an incentive to purchase and a program to pull the product out of the distributor's inventory—in other words, to help him unload.

WATERS: That's how we sell our programs to the distributor. He's smart enough to tell when someone is loading him, so then our salesman shows him the unloader program.

TOBIN: If you want a guy to buy more than he bought the previous year, you can't just say, I want 10% more than you did last year, and walk away. You also have to say, Here's a program that's going to help you sell more, and our sales representative is here to help you implement it. Our distributors look to us for that type of leadership. Let's face it, most of them are not experts at promotion.

NAGEL: Do you use any rules of thumb for judging the success of the program?

TOBIN: We measure it against incremental profits plus business.

McELVEEN: That's how we do it—except this year. I look at it this way: how much less business would we have gotten this year had we not used an incentive?

Supplier Representatives:

Joseph P. Garvin, marketing manager, ESB Brands, Cleveland
L. P. McElveen, Jr., sales vice president, Room Air Conditioner Division, Friedrich Refrigerators, San Antonio
Robert B. Nagel, distributor marketing manager, Lily Division, Owens-Illinois, Toledo
James E. Tobin, sales promotion manager, GTE Sylvania Electronic Components Group, Waltham, Mass.
Gerald M. Waters, national sales manager, CSG Group, Certain-teed Products, Valley Forge, Pa.

Distributor Representatives:

Frederic Grossmann, marketing vice president, American Hospital Supply, McGaw Park, Ill.
Elliott Jonas, vice president, All Appliance Parts of New York, Huntington Station, N. Y.

QUESTIONS FOR DISCUSSION

1. Discuss the general problems involved in distributor incentive programs.

2. What types of dealer incentive programs tend to work best? Why?

3. Are long-term or short-term dealer incentive programs better? Why?

4. Identify the chief problems associated with price-decrease incentive programs.

5. What is a "spiff"? What are their advantages and disadvantages?

6. What determines which dealer incentive programs are actually used by the manufacturer representative firms?

5.7 GET THE REP'S ATTENTION BY GIVING HIM ATTENTION

J. D. Kimball

"Being afraid of all those other lines your reps handle is, in my opinion, nothing more than marketing paranoia."

Independent sales representatives offer a highly effective and clearly economical way to take products to market. They are particularly good at selling technical products, which often call for shirt-sleeve sessions with designers to help iron out the details of specifying. That's why many suppliers in industrial businesses rely so completely on independent representatives as their primary link with both OEM (original equipment manufacturer) customers and distributors.

But among those suppliers who don't like selling through independent reps, one of the major objections is that reps "never seem to give our line the attention it deserves."

When Sola Electric ended some 20 years of direct selling and shifted to almost complete reliance on reps in 1970, we quickly learned that that kind of complaint is more an indictment of the supplier than of the rep system. Any company that isn't getting the representation that it deserves has probably brought that situation upon itself by failing to give reps that handle its products the attention and support *they* deserve.

The complainers' central point is usually that reps handle multiple lines. From that, they draw the conclusion that "all those other lines must be taking too much time away from selling our line." I refuse to accept that point of view. I believe that the supplier is likely to get more selling, rather than less, from reps than from direct factory salesmen. And our experience at Sola Electric during the last few years has supported my belief.

Reps selling multiple lines are actually doing their principals a marketing favor. Multiple-line selling practically assures multiple-market exposure. Because of the other products they sell, reps go to many customers you've never sold, many of them in markets you've never ap-

Reprinted by permission from the publisher. J. D. Kimball, "Get the Rep's Attention By Giving Him Attention," *Sales and Marketing Management* (February 23, 1976), pp. 52–56.

proached. Every time reps do that, your products go in there with them. And because the reps' income, reputation, and future depend directly on their performance, you can bet that they are constantly eyeing other customers for any sign that your product might be sold to them, too.

Those other lines, then, are drawing you and your products into new customers and new markets a lot faster than you could possibly drive into them with a direct selling force. Thus you benefit by reducing your sales costs and by shaving your own work load.

Moreover, reps usually sell more easily and more quickly than direct salespeople. Hour for hour, the time they spend with your product will be more productive than the same amount of time spent by direct salesmen. Why do they sell more easily? Primarily because most reps have invested their lives in cultivating their territories. Because of their other lines, reps know the buyers intimately. And, more importantly, the buyers know them intimately. Mutual trust is long established. In the hands of a good rep, your product has a lot less resistance to overcome, and this is particularly important when you're trying to crack new markets.

Being afraid of all those other lines your reps handle is, in my opinion, nothing more than marketing paranoia. Those other lines are helping you more than you realize. It is true that the more aggressive principals will put out extra effort to win even a little extra share of the reps' time, just as they put out extra effort to field a stronger advertising and promotion program, or build broader distribution, or generate a better R&D effort to keep their products ahead of their competitors. But this is entirely within the rules of good business, no matter how you choose to take your products to market.

If you want to get ahead, you simply have to put out a little extra effort of your own. And this brings me back to the original premise that getting more of the reps' attention is basically a matter of giving the reps more of your attention.

Reps are independent businessmen. They are profit oriented, just as their principals are, so the most important form of attention you can give is to make sure your line is profitable for them. An equally important form of attention is to make sure they understand how and why your line is profitable for them. The former does not automatically beget the latter. You have to work at it. Some suggestions:

If profit depends on volume, make it easy for reps to get volume. If profit results from a high unit cost, make it easy for the rep to justify that cost to his customers in terms of benefits and advantages. Check to see that you are supporting him from the plant with good shipping, sensitive engineering assistance, and fast troubleshooting. Provide good selling tools—easy-to-use catalogues, uncomplicated ordering procedures, and well-done application or technical literature. Command a powerful position in the marketplace with solid advertising, direct mail, and public relations programs. Set up a system for qualifying inquiries promptly, getting those qualified leads into the rep's hands quickly, and then following up to let him know you care.

Make sure you communicate with your reps regularly, but do it sparingly. Make them aware of all the things you're doing to develop more attractive products, to presell their customers, to enhance your company and brand-name reputation, and to open the doors to new accounts.

If you use distributors, the rep's success depends in large part upon how well those distributors perform. Make sure you have a clear-cut and attractive distributor program, with competitive pricing policies. Develop periodic promotions to rekindle distributor enthusiasm.

Try to let your reps grow with their accounts. Don't snatch accounts away as they ripen into high-volume customers unless it's clear that the rep either cannot or would rather not handle them. Reps are usually in an excellent position to expand the business of current accounts as well as find new accounts, and letting them enjoy the fruits of their labor is a terrific incentive for them to continue building your business.

Remember, too, that education and motivation are essential to getting a new rep off to a fast, profitable start or getting an existing rep reoriented to supporting your line more aggressively. Make sure you have effective ways to give the rep a quick but thorough understanding of your product line, your support programs, and your company's position in the marketplace. Conduct presentations for rep firm personnel whenever possible, or at least make good materials available for them to conduct their own training sessions.

Finally, consider establishing a rep advisory council and letting it play a significant role in your market planning and new product development. This shows the reps that you are sensitive to their needs, and it gives them a sense of involvement in your marketing program and a stronger commitment to make that program work. It also rewards you with very candid and objective feedback about how the market looks at your company and what the market might respond to in terms of new products.

'REP SUGGESTIONS ARE VITAL...'

In Sola Electric Advisory Council meetings, we generally focus on three main areas of discussion: success stories, rep suggestions, and management proposals.

By success stories, we mean a sharing of any experience in which something unusually effective was accomplished. This serves as a warm-up for our meeting, and it's meaningful because any technique or approach that worked well for one rep can probably work equally well for others. So everyone gains from hearing about it.

In another sense, the success story can provide marketing insights that lead to new product development. As an example, one Council member told of noticing that an unusually high amount of a standard Sola item had been sold for application with electronic 24-hour banking equipment. The Sola units were being shipped to individual bank branches to solve a common on-location problem that was occurring after the equipment was already installed and operating. This problem and its solution were reviewed with the equipment OEM, and as a result, the rep closed a $100,000 OEM order. As a longer-term result, we developed a modified version of this product to meet the needs of similar manufacturers, and the modified product is now being sold as a standard item in our line.

Rep suggestions are vital to all Council meetings because they reveal objective thinking that invariably leads to better ways for the rep and manufacturer to work together.

The third area of discussion, management proposals, is where we put our ideas on the table—procedures we'd like to see changed, problems we'd like to see solved, products we'd like to introduce, etc.—and see what reactions the reps have.

In order to make the Council more meaningful for all our reps, we distribute a recap memo after each meeting so everybody knows what was discussed, what conclusions were reached, and what action is to be taken. Also, in preparation for the next meeting, the Council appoints a rep spokesman who serves in the interim as an ombudsman, an individual to whom the entire rep network can direct questions.

Approximately one month prior to the coming meeting, we send a rough agenda to all our reps asking them to convey their comments to the rep spokesman. In this way we give all reps an easy way to guide their Advisory Council members and exert individual influence more effectively in Council activities.

Much of what I've been proposing here may sound like simple common sense—and it is. It's so simple, in fact, that it very often gets overlooked. There are still a surprising number of companies that will appoint a rep, send him some samples and a ream of data sheets, and then sit back and wait for the orders to swarm in. Months go by, nothing happens, and management starts grousing because the rep isn't giving the line enough attention.

But the simple truth is that appointing reps does not signal the end of your company's responsibility to cultivate markets for its products. Quite the opposite. Setting up a rep force is only the beginning. Whether it will turn out to be the beginning of something successful and mutually profitable depends largely on what you do for your reps after you appoint them.

QUESTIONS FOR DISCUSSION

1. Discuss the basic advantages and disadvantages of using manufacturers' representatives.

2. J. D. Kimball states, "I believe that the supplier is likely to get more selling, rather than less, from reps than from direct factory salesmen." Explain why the author takes this position.

3. Discuss the value of suggestions from manufacturers' representatives.

4. Identify several techniques designed to insure that the representative devotes sufficient time and efforts to a firm's products.

5. What is a "rep advisory council"? Should one be implemented? Why?

Chapter 6

Marketing Channels for Industrial Goods

INDUSTRIAL CHANNELS of distribution are frequently assumed to have exactly the same procedures and problems as are found in consumer products. While this statement is more correct than false, differences do exist. Industrial outlets tend to be fewer in number, carry larger inventories, and tend to stress service and repair-parts inventories. International Harvester recently reorganized its heavy truck distribution network of 2,067 franchised dealers. Prior to the reorganization the firm's marketing was divided into 15 sales regions, each responsible for sales policies, pricing and marketing research. To correct the resultant problems caused by operating without a unified direction, the regions were eliminated and the entire United States is served by four centralized divisions—heavy and medium trucks, small trucks, parts and service, and company dealerships. Each is operated as a profit center. The new distribution organization has significantly increased the level of customer service available to franchise dealers.[1]

The first selection in this chapter presents the parameters that differentiate industrial and consumer channels. Professor William E. Matthews carefully explains the *nature* of industrial channels, their *composition*, the *role* of an industrial channel and the *relationship* between the channel members and the manufacturer. The article concludes with a thought-provoking analysis of why change takes place in industrial channels. A model is developed that is characterized by four phases—establishment, takeoff, growth and maturity.

The second selection is entitled "The Chain Reaction That's Rocking Industrial Distribution." The author, John G. Main, indicates that industrial distribution, with $25 *billion* in sales, is one of America's largest and least well-known industries. The major change in this field is the steadily increasing power of the distributor chains. The advance of the chains is bringing with it a shift in market power similar to that which accompanied the rapid growth of food and drug chains during the early postwar years. Thus thousands of suppliers, distributors, and

1. "International Tries to Cut Its Truck Losses," *Business Week* (February 16, 1976), p. 99.

end users face major, if not life-and-death business decisions.

The last two articles in this chapter address the issue of availability of repair-parts inventory. Both articles discuss distributor chains that are offering superior service to their customers and, in so doing, are achieving increasing market shares.

6.1 CHALLENGE FOR INDUSTRIAL MARKETERS: CHANGING CHANNELS OF DISTRIBUTION

William E. Matthews

"As a broad generalization, newly formed companies tend to rely initially on an external marketing organization, often utilizing manufacturers' representatives which provide sales effort plus some technical expertise."

A manufacturer of industrial goods is not operating in a static system, but in a changing environment. From time to time, top management receives signals that "all is not well" with its channels of distribution and that it ought to evaluate possible changes. The role of any marketing or product manager, who is concerned with the distribution of one or more products or product lines, should be able (*a*) to recognize the pressures for channel changes as quickly as possible, (*b*) to implement policies that lead to an effective evaluation of alternative responses to such pressures, and (*c*) to take appropriate action by following through with the necessary channel change.

TYPES OF CHANNEL CHANGE

Given that a channel of distribution consists of a number of channel members performing certain functions in the movement of the product from the manufacturer to the customer, a manufacturer can then implement four types of channel change—namely, in the *nature* of the channel, *composition* of the channel, *role* of the channel, and in the *relationship* between the channel and the manufacturer.

NATURE OF THE CHANNEL

Theoretically, a manufacturing company selecting the channel of distribution through which to market its products has a number of alter-

Reprinted by permission from William E. Matthews, "Challenge for Industrial Marketers: Changing Channels of Distribution," Marketing Science Institute Working Paper (August, 1972).

natives. For example, it can utilize an "internal" channel (its own sales force), or one of a wide variety of "external" channels (distributors, representatives, agents, brokers). In reality, however, not all channel alternatives are available to the manufacturer at the time the channel decision has to be made. Thus, the manufacturer chooses among *available* channels. This decision may later prove to be nonoptimal and lead to growing pressure for a change in the channel of distribution.

More important, the industrial goods' manufacturer operates in a changing environment. Not only does the nature of the manufacturing operation itself change through the addition or deletion of products, but actions by competitors affect the manufacturer's position in the marketplace. These and other changes in the marketing environment create pressures for change in the channel of distribution so that the manufacturer can remain competitive.

At the extreme, the manufacturer may completely discontinue the use of one channel of distribution and replace it by another distinctly separate channel. For example, a manufacturer with a nationwide network of distributors might decide to sell only through the company's own sales force. In most situations, however, the manufacturer can neither justify the complete discontinuance of a channel, nor is such a channel change appropriate. In this case, a manufacturer selling through distributors may develop so many large customers in one geographic area that they could justifiably be handled on a direct basis. In other areas, however, the number of large customers might be insufficient to justify direct sales. Under these circumstances, the manufacturer might replace only a part of the channel of distribution for the product. Such a change can be classified as a *channel shift*.

A second distinct type of channel shift involves the establishment of a new channel of distribution to handle an existing product. Let us say that a manufacturer decides to sell a product in a new market segment not previously covered by the existing channel of distribution. The existing channel continues to handle the product so there is no shift in terms of the channel itself. However, a shift does occur in terms of the product since it is now handled by a second channel.

COMPOSITION OF THE CHANNEL

While a channel shift affects distribution as a whole, a more common and numerous form of change affects individual members of the channel, as in the case where members are replaced without reference to other channel members. This type of channel change can be characterized as a *channel alteration*.

A manufacturer using an internal channel normally expects a turnover in personnel as a result of either promotion, transfer, or dismissal.

On the one hand, a manufacturer utilizing an external channel may force a turnover in individual members either due to dissatisfaction with the marketing performance (insufficient sales effort, ineffective technical assistance to customers, and so on), or because management has an opportunity to upgrade its representation by adding a competitive channel member. On the other hand, a channel alteration may also be forced on the manufacturer should the channel member become dissatisfied with its relationship with the manufacturer and choose to carry the products of another manufacturer.

ROLE OF THE CHANNEL

In the channel of distribution, each member performs specific marketing tasks for the manufacturer. The role of the channel can be changed, however, in two major respects by the nature of the market served, and by the services provided.

Market served. The channel of distribution represents the manufacturer's sales effort within a geographic area and, over a period of time, develops a specific set of customers. In the event that a new market segment develops within that geographic area, the manufacturer has the options of (*a*) utilizing a separate channel of distribution for the new market segment, (*b*) making a channel alteration, or (*c*) modifying the role of the existing channel member.

In view of the fact that I have already discussed the first two alternatives, let us look at the manufacturer's third option: a *channel role modification.* This is more easily implemented when an internal channel is being used since an external member may be unable or unwilling to make such a change. An example of this type of channel role modification might be sales by a manufacturer through distributors to maintenance and repair customers but not to original equipment manufacturers. If the company wishes to expand into the latter market, it is faced with either a modification in terms of its existing members, a channel alteration, or a channel shift.

Similarly, the manufacturer can limit the number of customers to which the channel members sell, thus effectively changing the role of the channel member. Though it is illegal to reserve customers,[1] it is legal to follow pricing policies which de facto limit the customers to whom the external channel sells.

For example, a volume discount for an extremely large volume pur-

---

1. In the past, a company could legally reserve certain customers for the internal channel, and external members were not allowed to sell to these reserved customers. In 1965, the Supreme Court, in United States v. Arnold Schwinn Co., interpreted such practices as illegal under Section 1 of the Sherman Act.

chase may be attractive only to large user-customers. If the volume is above the level which a channel member could justifiably purchase and warehouse, the channel member's role may be limited to smaller customers. This limitation of customers also can be obtained by formal contracts between the manufacturer and user-customer. Such a contract may be for the user-customer's total requirements of a product or product line, or for a guaranteed purchase volume.

Services provided.   While the channel performs a specific set of functions, there is always the possibility that the manufacturer will respond to the changing market environment by a channel role modification. Such a modification can represent either the addition of new functions to the channel's role or the removal of existing functions. Thus, a manufacturer may decide that a product requires extensive technical assistance, and may provide a technical sales force to support the channel members. As the product matures, technical assistance may become less important and the manufacturer may delegate this function to the independent channel members.

RELATIONSHIP BETWEEN THE MANUFACTURER AND THE CHANNEL

While the manufacturer and the channel are both concerned with profitability, each is concerned with its own profitability, not that of the overall system. Therefore, the goals and strategies of the two parties do not necessarily coincide. The manufacturing company can alter its relationship with the channel either by modifying its rewards to the channel or by exerting pressure on the channel.

The modification of the rewards to the channel normally involves a change in the commission or discount allowed the external member, or in the salary and/or commission paid to the internal channel member. The value of the commission or discount can be varied depending upon the manufacturer's objectives. For example, the manufacturer may introduce a reward system designed to encourage the channel to handle a specific product, to encourage pioneering effort of a highly technical nature, and so forth. Variations in the rewards are of major concern to the channel and are often a source of conflict between the channel member and the manufacturer. Intense dissatisfaction on the part of the member may force a channel alteration.

In addition to changes in the financial rewards, a manufacturer can affect the relationship with channel members in ways which have indirect financial implications. Thus, the manufacturer may assist the channel member in financing its inventory, in developing and financing an advertising program, and so on.

At the other end of the spectrum is the pressure that the manufacturer can exert on the channel. However, such pressure is relatively limited in scope. While, in the case of the internal channel, the manufacturer can tie remuneration to performance by the establishment of goals and quotas, similar pressure is considerably more difficult to apply to the independent external channel.

PRESSURES LEADING TO CHANNEL CHANGES

Possibly the best way to consider any pressure for channel change is to view it as a metamorphosis model. William H. Starbuck describes metamorphosis models as those which "take the view that growth is not a smooth, continuous process, but is marked by abrupt and discrete changes in the conditions for organizational persistence and in the structures appropriate to these conditions."[2] Among the most useful of the numerous metamorphosis models are the two of D. G. Moore[3] and Alan C. Filley and R. T. House,[4] both of whom envisage three stages of growth.

These two models form the basis for the model that I propose. However, unlike Moore's model, which implies that an organization passes through stages from disorganized creativity to organized professionalism, my model suggests that there are a series of channel changes (associated with a specific stage in the organization's growth) which are appropriate to a well run company.

My proposed model can be characterized in terms of the four phases —establishment, takeoff, growth, and maturity.

PHASE 1: ESTABLISHMENT

The newly formed company normally has a single product or product line and, characteristically, severely limited financial and personal resources. The company's concern is often focused on the manufacturing processes and, more generally, on the solution of day-to-day operating problems. The major task facing the company is that of communicating with its potential customers. This process of communication, education, and persuasion can be a lengthy one often complicated not only by the number of persons involved in the purchasing decision but also by the need to test new products under operating conditions.

2. James G. Marsh, ed., "Organizational Growth and Development," *Handbook of Organizations* (Chicago: Rand McNally, 1968), chap. II.

3. W. L. Warner and N. H. Martini, eds., "Managerial Strategies," *Industrial Man* (New York: Harper, 1959), pp. 220–22.

4. *Managerial Process and Organizational Behavior* (Glenview, Ill.: Scott, Foresman and Company, 1969), pp. 443–51.

The first channel of distribution decision faced by the company, therefore, is whether (*a*) to attempt this communication process internally by utilizing management's own time and efforts, or (*b*) to rely on an external sales organization. The critical factors in this decision appear to be the company's financial status, its personnel resources, the number of potential customers, the nature of the selling task, the skills of different types of channel members, and the availability of suitable members.

If the *financial status* is relatively weak, then it is likely that the company will be unable to afford a direct sales effort and will have to rely on an external sales effort. Similarly, a company with limited *personnel resources* is likely to rely initially on an external channel. The number of *potential customers* affects the channel decision since the larger the number of potential customers—the wider their geographic distribution —the more expensive a direct sales effort becomes. Management, however, may be able to identify a number of companies with high sales potential, and may wish to concentrate its own sales effort on those prospects while utilizing an external channel for the remainder of the effort.

The *nature of the selling task* also has a major impact on the channel decision. If it is highly technical, requiring extensive interaction between the seller and the customer, then the manufacturer may choose to perform the task on a direct basis; a less technical selling task, however, may be adequately handled by the external channel. If the task is expected to be a lengthy one, it is likely that management will rely on the external channel to reduce costs, especially if it is largely that of maintaining continuing contact until the sale is consummated.

Finally, the *skills of different types of channel members* in the newly formed organization's industry and the *availability of suitable members* are critical. The manufacturer does not choose a specific channel because it has the correct name but because it provides certain critical skills at an acceptable cost. However, as mentioned earlier, not all channels of distribution are open to the manufacturer at the time the decision is made, and thus the company is forced to select its channel members from among those that are available.

As a broad generalization, newly formed companies tend to rely initially on an external marketing organization, often utilizing manufacturer's representatives who provide sales effort plus some technical expertise. There is, however, no automatic selection rule. It depends very much on the various influencing factors mentioned above. Thus, an electronics component manufacturer with a highly sophisticated product might first utilize distributors who possess engineering and sales staffs with the specialized training, knowledge, and contacts to do the necessary "door opening" work and to gain acceptance of the product.

However, unless the product requires a highly sophisticated sales force, the initial decision is normally to utilize manufacturer's representatives. The manufacturing company usually supports its sales representatives with technical assistance provided by its own skilled personnel. The company's advantage in utilizing representatives is that they have at least some technical skill and they are motivated by the commissions on actual sales. The sales coverage may, however, be fairly limited, and the length and extent of the sales effort may be less than the manufacturer might desire.

Therefore, the first pressure for channel change may result from the performance of one or more of the representatives. If a representative does not perform up to the manufacturer's standard, then there is an inevitable pressure for a channel alteration—that is, the replacement of the representative by another in the same geographic area.

PHASE 2: TAKEOFF

Whereas the problem facing the manufacturer in Phase 1 is deciding which channel alternative to select given a number of important constraints, Phase 2 sees the development of pressures for channel change. These pressures stem from the very success of the manufacturer in the education of potential customers, the acceptance of the product, and the growth of sales.

Let us return to the previous example of the manufacturer selling through representatives. Once the representative's primary function of sales generation has been achieved, the focus shifts to satisfying the need of the customer which the manufacturer's representative cannot normally satisfy. Namely, it is rapid service through the existence of a local stock. In addition, in many cases, the manufacturer's representative is not interested in providing long-term technical assistance with less certain rewards than the generation of new sales.

The pressure developing in this situation is for the replacement of the existing channel by a local channel better able to satisfy the customer's need. This pressure is further supported by the fact that as potential customers become more aware of the product they begin to contact both the manufacturer *and* the local distributor with whom they normally do business. The local distributor then becomes interested in carrying the product since there is now a demand for it.

The replacement of manufacturers' representatives by distributors presupposes the existence of suitable distributors. If the product is new and has demonstrable advantages, the manufacturer may have little difficulty in obtaining new distributors. In many instances, however, the manufacturer will find that the leading local distributors already represent other industrial companies and are thus unwilling to carry the potentially competitive line. As a result, the manufacturer will be forced to utilize smaller and possibly less effective distributors. Sometimes the manufacturer may find that adequate distributors are obtainable in certain geographic areas and not in others. In the case of the latter, the company is forced to continue to sell through manufacturers' representatives.

The replacement of manufacturers' representatives by distributors also presupposes that the manufacturer's personnel are capable of administering a distributor network. The absence of such in-house capability may force the manufacturer to continue to use representatives to assist in administrating and controlling the distributor network.

Obviously, the control of the distributor network by manufacturers' representatives contains the seeds of a further channel change. First, there is the danger of discord between the two organizations. The manufacturer's representatives and distributors may have conflicting motivations and objectives. Second, pressure may result from the economics of the two-step control of the channel. External pricing systems (by manufacturers who sell either through their own sales organization or directly through distributors) may force the company to change its channel of distribution in order to be competitive.

Phase 2, therefore, is primarily concerned with channel shift. The pressures for channel alteration are relatively limited during this phase since the manufacturer may still have only a minor position in the industry and thus may not be in a position to attract new members to replace the existing channel. Channel role modification and relationship modifications are possible during this phase, but they are not likely to be implemented.

Since the company's position vis-à-vis the channel members is still extremely weak, it is in no position to implement changes either in the role of the channel member or in the interrelationship. In fact, it is conceivable that the channel members will be in a sufficiently strong position to force changes on the manufacturer.

In Phase 2, the manufacturer tends to be primarily concerned with the general functioning of the channel rather than with specific problems associated with the performance of the members.

PHASE 3: GROWTH

The growth phase sees a broadening of the pressures for channel change. Not only does further growth result in additional pressures for change, but there are also pressures generated by changes in the product itself and by changes in the nature of the user-customer.

Expanded product sales.   As a result of the distributor's sales effort, certain large user-customers begin to emerge and a small number of them begin to account for a high percentage of the manufacturer's sales. As a result, the manufacturer begins to focus increasing attention on these customers and to spend more time in direct contact with them.

Pressure develops, therefore, to bypass the distributor in favor of direct sales to these customers. The subsequent channel shift reflects not so much the company's dissatisfaction with the former channel's performance but, rather, a change in the economic balance of the relationship between the manufacturer and the customer. The volume of business generated now makes direct sales more economical and enables the company to offer the new channel volume discounts which would not have been a feasible arrangement with the old channel.

Product maturation.   If a product at the time of its introduction involves (a) new technology or new applications, (b) extensive education of the user-customer, or (c) a long testing period (and hence a long-term relationship between the manufacturer and the user-customer), then the manufacturer may utilize a specific channel of distribution. Once the educational task is complete, however, that channel may no longer be attractive or desirable. Other channels may now be in a better position to provide the manufacturer's needed services. Thus, as the product matures from its initial introductory state to that of a commodity (when a number of competitors offer a product basically indistinguishable from that of the original manufacturer), there is increasing pressure for either a channel shift or a channel relationship modification.

A channel shift is relatively unlikely to occur unless the product is the only one sold through the specific channel. More likely, the product will be one unit in a product line sold through the channel. Under these circumstances, the manufacturer might choose to modify the channel's relationship through, say, a reduction in the channel's margins, thus attempting to put the emphasis on other products. If the manufacturer originally sold the product through a primary channel with back-up support from a secondary channel, then as the product matures the manufacturer might implement a channel change involving the reduction of the role of the secondary channel (a) by limiting the back-up sales effort to major customers, or (b) by eliminating company-owned inventory points and requiring that adequate inventory be carried by the primary channel.

Product line expansion.   The introduction of a new product may have little direct impact on the existing channel if it is either the addition of a product only slightly different from existing products, or a new product so dissimilar that it requires a separate channel of distribution. An example of the latter would be the addition of a high-priced product to an otherwise low-priced line selling to a different market. (From a managerial viewpoint, modification of the existing channel is conceptually simpler than the establishment of a new channel. For this reason, the manufacturer will tend to incorporate the new product into the existing channel. This in itself contains the seeds of pressure for channel change. The situation is basically unstable if the channel selected does not satisfy the needs and requirements of the product for which it was established.)

In certain circumstances, however, the broadening of the product line may have a major impact on the channel of distribution. For example, a company may have been restricted to a specific channel because of its limited line. The addition of new products may give the manufacturer a full line, and thus enable him to shift to a new channel. Similarly, as a result of broadening the product line, total sales of *all* products in a specific area may become sufficiently large to justify a direct sales effort. Thus, there may be pressure for a channel shift to take advantage of the changed economics associated with sales to that geographic area.

The addition of a new product to an existing product line may also result in pressure for a channel relationship modification. For example, a manufacturer may introduce a new product which provides a certain level of profitability and has a certain long-range sales potential. The channel, however, may neither perceive the potential for this product nor be impressed by the anticipated rewards, and thus may make little effort to sell the new product. The manufacturer may therefore be forced to alter the margins on existing products to generate the desired sales effort.

Customer changes.   Even when the product remains unchanged, both the nature of the customer and his purchasing behavior can and do change. A channel of distribution, established to satisfy the requirements of one set of customers, may be unable to satisfy a second set. If either the customer's nature or his requirements change, then there is likely to be pressure for a channel change.

Consider first the *nature of the customer*. Over a period of time, the number of customers may change through an increase or decrease in the *total* number. If the expansion in the number of customers occurs in the same industry, then the manufacturer is faced with the need to expand the coverage of the existing channel or to implement a channel shift to cover certain segments of the market. For example, a company marketing through an internal channel to a small number of customers might be faced with the emergence of a large number of extremely small customers. Under these circumstances, expansion of the internal channel might be uneconomical, and thus a channel shift would be necessary to serve this growing segment of the market.

The nature of the customer can change in ways other than an increase or decrease in number. For example, the growth or decline of *one* segment of the market can result in pressure for either a channel shift or alteration. As we have seen, the initial channel decision is implemented because the chosen channel is best suited to meet the objectives of the manufacturer and the needs of a specific set of customers. Yet the market for the product may shift to one not served by the original channel. The exact nature of the change would depend upon the magnitude of the differences between the customer characteristics in each industry.

In some cases, a channel alteration in which individual members in the channel are replaced by new units with a different orientation might be sufficient. In many instances, however, it may be extremely difficult to find channel members capable of serving effectively both the old *and* new segments of the marketplace. Under these circumstances, management must decide among three alternative courses of action:

1. To ignore the emerging market segment completely.
2. To focus on the older market segment, and market to the new segment only where convenient.
3. To implement a channel shift designed to enable the company to add an additional channel to handle the emerging new markets.

Another way in which the nature of the customer can change is on a geographic basis. This normally represents a broadening of the area in which potential customers are located. For example, in the early stages of an industry's development, potential customers cluster in those geographic areas with optimal economics. As the industry develops, however, technological innovations and improvements in transportation, power supply, and so on enable industry members to expand into new areas. The channel of distribution, established to satisfy the initial geographic distribution of the customer, is unlikely to be able to satisfy the expanded market, and thus there will be a growing pressure either for an expansion of the existing channel or the addition of a second channel.

The second major change is in terms of the customer's *purchasing behavior*. In recent years, many larger companies have turned their attention to the economies associated with optimal purchasing such as annual buy contracts. These changes in purchasing behavior have resulted in growing pressures for channel change. For example, an external channel which has regularly serviced a specific account may find itself unable to compete should the customer, who previously purchased on a plant basis, decide to purchase his nationwide requirements on a bid basis.

Under these circumstances, the channel may no longer be able to compete effectively since regular pricing schedules may offer inadequate margins to obtain the business.

Management is then faced with three alternative courses of action:

1. To maintain the existing channel structure and face the loss of this particular type of business.

2. To implement a channel shift by establishing a new channel capable of competing for the business.

3. To implement a channel relationship modification to enable the existing channel to compete by offering additional volume price discounts, reduced selling prices, and similar measures.

PHASE 4: MATURITY

This phase reflects the situation in which (a) the organization is firmly established, (b) the product no longer involves high technological inputs, and (c) the nature of the customers has reached a position of relative stability.

The organization, however, still experiences a wide variety of pressures for channel change during the maturity phase. In fact, certain pressures become extremely important for the first time.

Maturity is often characterized by increased competition leading to reduced selling prices and margins. With limited flexibility in pricing, management normally experiences a profit squeeze as labor and material costs increase. There is, therefore, pressure for any type of channel change which will lower selling costs. Thus, there is growing pressure for a channel shift in order to utilize a less expensive channel.

Management action, however, may be difficult because (a) the existing channel underwent changes during the earlier phases and is now best adapted to fit the marketplace, (b) there is a high level of involvement with and commitment to the existing channel, (c) the existing channel accounts for a large volume of sales, and management is reluctant to disturb the status quo, and (d) the existing channel has considerable power vis-à-vis the manufacturer and will resist any change.

During the maturity phase, a normal channel shift is relatively rare. However, management may consider a special type of channel shift— namely, the acquisition of channel members so that in effect they become a direct sales effort. By taking over the profitability of the distribution function, management attempts to restore the overall profitability of the operation.

An alternative means of improving the profitability is to increase the volume of sales (assuming that there are production economies of scale). One way of doing this is to replace weaker channel members by others who are more aggressive and effective. In those situations where the manufacturer utilizes an internal channel, the continual upgrading of the channel is feasible (through both normal attrition and transfer of weak members). In the case of the external channel, however, the upgrading process has generally continued throughout the first three phases and thus, to a very large extent, the weaker members have already been weeded out. Those channel members that remain represent the best available to the manufacturer, and to some extent the company is locked into the existing channel. For this reason, channel alterations are much less common during this fourth phase.

The two most important and common types of channel change during the maturity phase are channel role and channel relationship modification. Channel role modification becomes important because the manufacturer is primarily concerned with obtaining a competitive edge relative to the competition. If a price advantage cannot be achieved, the manufacturer is forced to fall back on other means of satisfying the customer's needs and requirements.

For this reason, the manufacturing company looks more closely at the roles played by its own organization and by the channel of distribution. For example, the manufacturer may be able to gain a competitive edge by providing extensive warehouse stocks, direct credit, drop shipments, and other inducements to the user-customers.

Equally important during the maturity phase is the channel relationship modification through changes in the margins and discounts offered to the members. In theory, this is a relatively simple type of channel change to implement. However, in reality it can prove to be extremely difficult. The manufacturer treads a narrow path between gaining increased profitability and losing the support of the channel of distribution. By the maturity phase, the channel is not only aware of its power position in the system but it also tends to represent an important position in the manufacturer's sales effort.

Therefore, the manufacturer may face extensive resistance to any relationship modification; in fact, the company may find that it has very limited flexibility. This is particularly true in those situations where the manufacturer has encouraged the channel to take on additional responsibility for part of the "manufacturing" process (finishing, cutting to size, and so forth).

During this fourth phase, pressures for both channel role and channel relationship modification may result from the channel itself as it exerts the power of its position. The channel may feel that it is not competitive with the members representing other manufacturers and may thus request further assistance which requires a channel change by the manufacturer.

As stated earlier, certain types of channel change appear to be both more common and more appropriate at different phases of an organization's growth. The accompanying table suggests a ranking of the importance of different types of channel change.

	Ranking		
	Phase 2 takeoff	*Phase 3 growth*	*Phase 4 maturity*
Channel shift	1	1	3
Channel alteration	2	3	4
Channel role modification	—	4	1
Channel relationship modification	—	2	2

QUESTIONS FOR DISCUSSION

1. Discuss fully *each* of the four types of channel change discussed in this article.

2. What is "channel role modification"? Why is it an important concept in channel selection?

3. Professor Matthews notes that, "The manufacturing company can alter its relationship with the channel either by modifying its rewards to the channel or by exerting pressure on the channel." Discuss this statement fully.

4. Matthews develops a thought-provoking four phase *metamorphosis* model. Explain each of the four phases in this model.

5. Identify and evaluate the strengths and weaknesses of the four phase model suggested by Professor Matthews.

6.2 THE CHAIN REACTION THAT'S ROCKING INDUSTRIAL DISTRIBUTION

John G. Main

"Although some suppliers have gone over to chain-oriented policies entirely, most must strike a delicate balance between chains, which are here to stay, and independents, through which the bulk of product volume still flows."

With nearly $25 billion in sales, industrial distribution is one of America's largest industries. In addition, because it supplies industry with such ubiquitous products as nuts and bolts, bearings, belts, power-transmission equipment, and component parts for large pieces of equipment, it is one of the least-known industries.

This anonymity may be dispelled, however, when people recognize the implications of an important industry trend: the rise of distributor chains. Our research shows that 20 or so leading chains now account for a total of $2.5 billion in sales, or about 10% of the industry. Among the largest are W. W. Grainger, Chicago (annual distribution revenues: $283.9 million); Noland Co., Newport News, Va. ($226.3 million); Ducommun, Los Angeles ($210.3 million); and Bearings, Inc. ($156.2 million), Premier Industrial ($137.1 million), and Curtis Noll ($104.3 million), all of Cleveland.

The advance of the chains is bringing with it a shift in market power similar to that which accompanied the rapid growth of food and drug chains during the early postwar years. Thus thousands of suppliers, distributors, and end users face major, if not life-and-death, business decisions.

Like food and drug retailing, industrial distribution is tremendously fragmented: products, uses, and users are bewilderingly varied. There are about 6,500 distribution firms and 11,000 outlets. The small, privately owned, single-warehouse firm did and still does form the core of the industry.

Reprinted by permission from the publisher. John G. Main, "The Chain Reaction That's Rocking Industrial Distribution," *Sales and Marketing Management* (February 23, 1976), pp. 41–45.

This enormous scattering and diversity make the industry ripe for some clever entrepreneurs to come in and clean up. The method: Buy or start up multiple outlets, and achieve significant economies of scale by establishing one highly sophisticated central inventory, purchasing, and distribution system. Here is what's happening:

The merger trend is strengthening, particularly among bearing and power-transmission distributors. Some chains have opened new outlets, but because personal service is a strong marketing factor, they prefer to buy out established distributors. Helping that trend along is the constant cash squeeze on small firms: Almost 70% of all distributorships were established after World War II; this, plus the intensifying competition of much stronger outfits, means that many of those owners are ready to sell out and retire.

Inventory power is concentrating, so chain inventories are not only deeper and cheaper but broader and more diversified.

Central warehouses to serve many outlets are being built by chains to (1) cut warehousing costs per outlet, (2) justify highly sophisticated computerized systems, and (3) permit purchasing in quantity and stocking in depth. So strong is this trend that many suppliers are closing out their own warehouses and passing along their savings to the chains.

A quantity discount pricing structure is thereby being created in direct violation of the traditional class-of-trade discount structure. This permits chains to sell much more cheaply than independents.

Multiple brand coverage is cutting into supplier exclusives. Overlaps between chains' coverage and local exclusives have forced suppliers to retract demands that distributors carry their line and no others. This enables chains to offer a tremendous selection of branded products.

Private labelling is also gaining momentum, particularly in product lines such as bearings; electrical motors and equipment; and expendable maintenance, repair, and replacement supplies. For some distributors, private labels constitute far and away the bulk of total sales (for example, Associated Spring, almost 100%; W. W. Grainger, 75%; and Lawson Products, 90%).

Thus as in food and drug, the three main factors powering the industrial chaining trend are (1) price discounts, (2) one-stop shopping for all needs, and (3) a wide choice of products for even the most brand-conscious buyer.

'MOM AND POP' FOUGHT BACK IN FOOD

Today, food and drug chains, both corporates and cooperatives, are an accepted part of the consumer landscape, with independent stores filling only special or strictly local needs. We can see now that the shift was inevitable. In the early days it wasn't so clear because small stores dominated the market. Precedents for chaining existed, but few observers could then envision a concentration of power so extreme.

So the independents fought back, tooth and nail. They formed protective associations, lobbied in state and federal legislatures, and invoked fair trade laws. They loudly proclaimed the higher quality of the lines they carried and the personalized service they provided. Most effective—as long as it *was* effective—was their boycott of any supplier they discovered selling to chains at a discount.

In industrial distribution, matters are nowhere near as advanced, but the parallels are clear. Suppliers are denying publicly that they give quantity discounts to chains, but privately they ask to be considered for contract sales.

Independents have instituted lobbies and formed a number of cooperatives. The Midwest Sixty have mounted a lobby against quantity pricing. They also have plans for central warehouses in Columbus to help them compete against power-transmission chains in the event that their lobby fails.

Another approach is the so-called moral consortium. One such organization in Wisconsin consists of 52 firms, five of them distributors. They provide one another with services and supplies and are committed to maintaining members' independence, but through mutual cooperation and appeals for solidarity—not by playing the chains' price-war game.

Other measures are also being tried. To counter the chains' enormous inventory power, independents are setting up inventory exchange agreements to cut warehousing costs yet still carry a wide selection.

TIME FOR SUPPLIERS TO START PLACING BETS

For most suppliers, the situation is still a bit of a bog, and they look forward to reaching solid ground. In the interim, they must recognize the threats, review their operations, and resolve some critically important questions. Although some suppliers have gone over to chain-oriented policies entirely, most must strike a delicate balance between chains, which are here to stay, and independents, through which the bulk of product volume still flows.

To strike that balance, the marketing director must ask and resolve the following questions—not once, but probably every three to six months:

1. *Can we afford to offer exclusives* to independents? to chains? If we offer them to independents, is there any way to protect existing exclusives and still sell to chains?

2. *How do we sell to chains?* At what level do we approach them?

Do we coordinate salesmen selling to independents with salesmen selling to chains that overlap the independents' territories? Can both salesmen present a consistent policy?

3. *Is our volume to chains* with centralized warehousing large enough to permit us to withdraw our branch warehousing support to independents? Is there any way we can offset the reduction in service to independents that would result? What about helping independents to pool? How large a reduction in price are we willing to grant chains for assuming the entire warehousing burden (say, for assembly-to-truck contracts)?

4. *Do we want to cultivate private label sales?* Do we now have excess capacity we need to fill? Will the incremental profit offset the chunk it could take out of our branded volume?

5. *What kind of discounting structure do we want?* If we didn't offer quantity discounts to chains, how much volume—and profit—would we forfeit? If we do give quantity discounts, can we offer our loyal smaller independents some compensating help?

Where will it all come out? The chances are that the trend to chaining will intensify for the distribution of commodity items—those without much quality differentiation among brands. Thus industrial chains with high-quality technical service as well as warehousing power will do very well.

But the concentration of chains will probably never be as great as in food and drugs, simply because the uses to which the thousands of industrial products are put are so diverse. This won't block the chains but will surely slow them down, ensuring that the feisty independents will survive.

QUESTIONS FOR DISCUSSION

1. Discuss the rationale for the significant increase in chain distributors for industrial products.

2. In what ways can "mom and pop" stores compete with the chain distributors?

3. Explain the concept of the moral consortium. Do you believe it will be effective? Defend your answer.

4. What are some of the key issues that manufacturers must consider in choosing an independent and/or chain distributor?

5. Do you believe chain distributors will become more or less important in the 1980s? Explain.

6.3 THE McDONALD'S OF AUTO PARTS

*"Genuine has a rather unusual set-up. In one sense,
it operates an auto-parts franchising system, its
jobbers being independently owned and operated.
In actual practice, they are tightly controlled, rather
like a McDonald's of the auto-parts business."*

Recessions weren't supposed to hurt the automobile replacement parts business. They were supposed to help it, since car owners would try to make their old buggies last longer by repairing them. But the current recession, the worst in 42 years, has exposed the limits of that wisdom. Monroe Auto Equipment, Maremont Corp. and even venerable Champion Spark Plug, all with upwards of 90% of their businesses from repair parts, suffered earnings declines last year. Champion may improve a bit this year, but the others are expected to be down again.

All of which makes the record of Atlanta's Genuine Parts Co. even more impressive. Over the last five years, through two recessions, Genuine's profits have more than doubled, to $24 million, on sales of $573 million. This year it figures to lift its volume some 15% and profits by at least 8%, to around $1.65 per share, as against the $1.53 that it earned last year.

While it serves the general market as other replacement-parts companies do, Genuine is a very different kind of outfit. Monroe, Maremont, Champion are essentially manufacturers who do some distributing. Genuine is purely and simply a distributor. This enables it to have by far the broadest product line. It distributes 100,000 different parts, which it sells to 3,400 independent jobbers. The jobbers, in turn, sell them to your local service station or auto repair garage. Genuine manufactures not a single item; it buys from literally hundreds of different sources, including Champion, Maremont and Monroe. Because of the powerful image of Champion, Genuine sells spark plugs under that name; in most other cases it sells under house names.

This broad spread gives Genuine a great deal of stability. Car owners

Reprinted by permission of *Forbes* Magazine from the August 15, 1975 issue, pp. 54–55.

can clean and regap spark plugs if their budgets are tight. They can put off buying new shock absorbers. But eventually they will be forced into buying some parts. As Genuine's Chairman Wilton Looney puts it: "When a fellow needs a water pump, he needs a water pump."

EVERYWHERE

More important than the breadth of its product line, however, is the nationwide reach of Genuine's distribution setup. Other than the Big Three automakers, who get roughly 40% of the replacement-parts business, Genuine is the only truly nationwide distributor. Over the past decade or so Gulf & Western's American Parts System has put together a similar though somewhat smaller parts distribution system. The rest of the business is divided up among a number of small, regional and mostly privately owned enterprises.

Genuine has a rather unusual setup. In one sense, it operates an auto-parts franchising system, its jobbers being independently owned and operated. In actual practice, they are tightly controlled, rather like a McDonald's of the auto-parts business.

Here's how it works. Around 90% of the parts sold by Genuine's jobbers carry the company's own private label. Its best known brand is NAPA. (NAPA is an acronym for National Auto Parts Association, which was put together in 1925 by a group of parts distributors so they could buy parts in bulk and thus at lower prices. Over the years, Genuine has acquired most of the businesses of the old NAPA members.) A Genuine-NAPA jobber must sell only NAPA parts and must pay at list —or what is known in the trade as "blue sheet" prices.

This strategy does two things for Genuine. It protects its operating profit margin, which has increased over the past ten years from 7.8% to 9.5%, by insuring that its jobbers won't go bargain hunting. In the parts business it is common practice for local parts distributors to drum up business by selling some lines, such as spark plugs, at, say, 10% off list price. Should an NAPA jobber, however, try to take advantage of an outside cut-price deal, Genuine quickly jumps him. Says one small east coast distributor who refuses to be identified: "They tell him to stay in line or they'll open a jobber right across the street from him." In return for the support Genuine gives them, its jobbers have to give up some of their independence.

Does this mean that car owners end up paying higher prices for NAPA parts? That all depends on whether the non-NAPA jobber pockets the extra profit or passes it on to his customers. Either way, Looney, 56, who has been running the company since 1955, isn't worried. He claims the business isn't price-sensitive, "So we're not going to become price-cutters. We're just going to offer better service."

KEEPING TABS

By "service" Looney means NAPA jobbers carry a better inventory of most-often-sold auto parts. What Genuine does is keep tabs on the sales trends of all parts needed to keep cars running (both U.S. and foreign makes 15 years old or younger). For instance, Genuine knows that a brake master cylinder on a five-year-old Ford wears out faster than that on a Chevrolet of the same age. Genuine also shows its jobbers how to set up an inventory-control system, and for a nominal fee the company will even keep books. By eliminating such business headaches, which other jobbers must deal with, Looney claims his jobbers have more time to sell parts.

Looney has also set up 37 parts distribution warehouses around the country, and Genuine even operates its own fleet of delivery trucks. Thus, he says, Genuine can give quicker delivery service than the competition. As a result, he claims many former non-NAPA jobbers have signed for a Genuine franchise.

Looney's plans include adding about 200 new jobbers a year and expanding the company's automotive parts distribution networks in Europe and Canada. In addition, he is branching out into other lines of business. So far, he has gone into distributing household hardware goods, such as lawn and garden tools, and office supplies. He never forgets that he is in distribution rather than, strictly speaking, in auto parts. The stock market is so impressed with Genuine's setup that the stock currently sells at 24 times last year's earnings and nearly four times book value—a rare tribute in the 1975 environment.

QUESTIONS FOR DISCUSSION

1. Discuss the general business operations of Genuine Parts Company.

2. What power does Genuine have over its independent wholesalers?

3. What are "blue sheet" prices? Are they legal? Comment.

4. What services does Genuine provide for its independent wholesalers?

6.4 PARTS FOR ALL SEASONS

"Large chain distributors, although they now control only about 5 percent of the independents' market, are by far the fastest growing segment."

Your Perfection Tooling widget-part-maker has just broken down, and your PT salesman says the parts you need are out of stock. Each hour the machine is down is costing you $100 in lost production. Soon you'll have to turn off another machine, which needs the components the first one makes. But all is not lost. Though it's 8 P.M., you call your local industrial distributor at the home number he has given you. He promises to call back in ten minutes. The parts you need are out of stock in the regional warehouse, but the central computer has located them in another warehouse halfway across the country. They will be airshipped tomorrow and you'll have them by noon. The next day, at 11:45, the salesman arrives with your parts. He helps set up the machine again, and readjusts some gears so next time the parts won't wear out so fast.

For that, you'd gladly pay the $150 he charges instead of the manufacturer's price of $100, wouldn't you?

Of course. And so would the managers of thousands of plants, fleets, cafeterias, schools, hospitals, dams and other facilities that need parts, maintenance and repairs. The vast majority of them are too small to call, say, Timken Co.: "Please send me four No. 3982 bearings, fast." They buy from industrial distributors. But most industrial distributors are single-warehouse operations and like as not would carry in stock only the faster-moving No. 3980 bearings. That is, until recently.

Although the individual orders are usually quite small, this is no peanut of an industry. It handles ball bearings, hose clamps, small engines, lubricants, tennis court coatings, fan belts, key blanks and even roach killers. American industry spends $40 billion a year buying maintenance and replacement parts for its increasingly complex machines and equipment. A substantial portion of this, $26 billion perhaps, is channeled not through the manufacturers but through independent dis-

Reprinted by permission of *Forbes* Magazine from the February 15, 1976 issue, p. 44.

tributors. As the business grows bigger and more complex, however, the number of such distributors is shrinking. A decade ago there were—according to *Industrial Distribution* magazine—7,600 such distributors; now there are only 6,500. What is happening is that although sales are growing at 8% a year, the smaller firms are disappearing, often through acquisition by the bigger ones. Large chain distributors, although they now control only about 5% of the independents' market, are by far the fastest growing segment.

Every one of the chains listed below uses an elaborate computer system to keep track of its inventories in precise detail. Shipping articles cross-country from warehouse to warehouse and then to the customer in a matter of hours is a regular business procedure. But service means more than that. Many salesmen function almost like country doctors. "These guys are trained to call on the maintenance foreman," says one follower of the industry. "In some lines, much of what they sell is small enough not to need authorization from up top, so they don't waste time with the purchasing department."

BUYING YOUR WAY IN

This intimate relationship between buyer and seller is one reason many of the chains started out by acquiring established businesses. Motion Industries, for example, made five acquisitions in 1973, helping to raise its sales from $29 million in 1972 to close to $80 million for 1975. In most cases, the chains started as specialists and then began branching out. Premier Industrial, for example, began as a seller of automotive parts. But now Premier has 14 completely separate divisions, each with its own sales force, serving distinct markets, from J.I. Holcomb Manufacturing, which sells cleaning agents, brushes, insecticides and the like, to Certanium Alloys & Research Co., which sells welding electrodes, brazing alloys, solders and other welding aids.

Some such acquisitions—though not Premier's—have attracted questions from the FTC or the Department of Justice, although they ultimately registered no objections. But even the largest companies in this field are still so small in relation to the market that they can find new geographic territory without encroaching on government ideas of fairness. Moreover, as the companies grow bigger and better known, acquisitions—except for ventures into new markets—become unnecessary.

As the figures below show, this is a profitable enough business to finance expansion without resort to mergers or debt: Return on equity ranges from 17% to 30% among the companies listed here. They seem to have found an ideal market: In a recession, people tend to repair machines rather than replace them, and they also make repairs that might be postponed in more prosperous times. On the other hand, during a boom the base of capital equipment requiring parts and maintenance is expanding and businesses are more willing to spend.

So far Wall Street has paid scant attention to most of these companies. Although getting bigger fast, they are still small, and much of their stock is closely held. By and large, they are headquartered outside New York City in the Midwest or the Southeast, and their products are things most white-collar people never think about. Which perhaps explains why Wall Street doesn't consider them growth stocks in spite of their impressive growth.

Leading Publicly Held Industrial Distributors

Company	Recent Price	Latest 12 Mos. Earns. Per Share	Price/Earnings Ratio	Est. 1975 Sales (millions)	Return on Equity	5-Yr. Sales Growth (ann. avg.)	Shares Outstanding (millions)	Shares Closely Held
Bearings, Inc.	22	$2.16	10	$180*	16.9%	14%	4.0	20%
Curtis Noll	15	2.37	6	120	18.8	14	2.3	16
W. W. Grainger	28	1.27	22	325	16.5	17	14.0	28
Kar Products	15	1.53	9	30†	29.1	20	1.7	67
Lawson Products	19	1.10	17	40	29.7	28	3.3	45
Motion Industries	18	1.47	12	80	19.0	33	1.9	35
Premier Industrial	11	1.43	8	165††	18.0	10	6.9	64

* Actual, year ended June 30. † Actual, year ended Nov. 30. †† Actual, year ended May 31.

QUESTIONS FOR DISCUSSION

1. Why are the chain distributors experiencing such rapid growth?

2. Explain *how* chains are able to provide their customers a higher level of customer service.

3. Why have the chains been able to generate such a large return on invested capital?

Chapter 7

Franchising

THE GROWTH OF franchise operations has been nothing short of phenomenal over the last decade. In 1972, there were 406,000 franchising units in the United States—from hamburger stands to art galleries—generating $131 billion a year in sales.[1] By 1976 the Commerce Department estimated that 460,000 franchised outlets with combined annual sales of approximately $177 billion were operating in the United States. This included 189,000 gasoline stations, 52,000 auto product and service centers, and 47,000 fast-food restaurants.[2]

The first selection in this chapter explores the extent to which franchisors engage in deceptive practices in selling franchises and in negotiating franchise agreements. It then examines whether franchisees need protection from deceptive selling practices of franchisors and evaluates some of the legislative proposals designed to protect franchisees. In March, 1976, the FTC completed their rules which govern all new franchise agreements in interstate commerce. These regulations, which are similar to those discussed in the first article, went into effect in September, 1976.[3]

The following selection discusses the recent trend in franchising in which the franchisor actually owns and operates a larger percentage of the total number of units. The reasons for this trend are clearly enumerated and its ramifications are examined.

The final selection on franchising discusses a very common cause of franchising conflict—the tying contract. Such a contract forces the franchisee to purchase certain products exclusively from the parent franchisor. This situation has resulted in a number of lawsuits.[4] Professors Hunt and Nevin examine the legal issues involved in tying agreements and then present arguments both for and against this franchising practice.

1. James D. Snyder, "Selling the Hustings Instead of Headquarters," *Sales Management* (January 24, 1972), p. 19.
2. Burt Schorr, "FTC Staff Completes Its Draft of Rules to Curb Abuses in Franchise Operations," *The Wall Street Journal* (March 31, 1976), p. 2.
3. *Ibid.*
4. See: "Cramping the Business Style of Franchisers," *Business Week* (June 16, 1975), p. 82.

7.1 FULL DISCLOSURE AND THE FRANCHISE SYSTEM OF DISTRIBUTION

Shelby D. Hunt

"Franchising literally abounds with deceptive selling practices."

No student of marketing would contest that the franchise system of distribution plays a prominent role in distributing goods and services in our national economy. Some have estimated that up to 25% of total retail sales are accounted for by franchised outlets.[1]

Recently, franchising has come under attack from the courts as being an anti-competitive system of distribution.[2] Franchising critics have also charged that franchisors do not treat their existing franchisees fairly[3] and that franchisors provide potential franchisees with misleading information when negotiating the franchise agreement.[4]

The purpose of this article is to explore whether franchisors engage in deceptive practices in the selling of franchises and in negotiating

Reprinted by permission from Shelby D. Hunt, "Full Disclosure and the Franchise System of Distribution," *Proceedings of the 1972 Fall Conference of the American Marketing Association* (Chicago: American Marketing Association, 1973), pp. 3–12.

1. Hart, Senator Philip A., *Congressional Record* Proceedings and Debates of the 92nd Congress, First Session, Vol 117, No. 124.

2. Brown Shoe Co. v. United States, 370 U.S. 294 (1962); Atlantic Refining Co. v. Federal Trade Commission, 381 U.S. 357 (1965); Harvey Siegel and Elaine Siegel, *et al.*, v. Chicken Delight, Inc., CCH73, 146 (D.C.V. Col., April, 1970); BNA ATRR No. 458 (April 21, 1970) A-1, X-1; United States v. Arnold Schwinn & Co., 388 U.S. 365 (1967); United States v. General Motors, 234 F. Supp. 85 (S.D. Col. 1964) reversed 384 U.S. 127 (1966); Lester J. Albrecht v. The Herald Co., 389 U.S. (decided March 4, 1968); United States v. Sealy Inc., 35 U.S. Law Week 4571 (decided June 12, 1967).

3. Shuman, Jerome, "Franchising—*Quo Vadis?* The Future of Franchising and Trade Regulation" *Franchise Legislation* Hearings before the Subcommittee on Antitrust and Monopoly of the Committee on the Judiciary, United States Senate (U.S. Gov. Printing Office, 1967) p. 514. Corliss, Robert F. "Franchising: Time for a New Beginning?," *Boston Bar Journal* Vol. 15 No. 8 (Sept. 1971) p. 10. Brown, Harold, *Franchising: Trap for the Trusting* (Toronto: Little Brown and Co., 1969) p. 27.

4. Brown, Harold, "Franchising: Legislating Full Disclosure, Good Faith and Fair Dealing," *Boston Bar Journal* Vol. 15 No. 8 (Sept. 1971).

franchise agreements. The article will also examine whether franchisees need protection from the deceptive selling practices of franchisors and will evaluate some of the legislative proposals to protect franchisees.

METHOD

The data result from a two-year investigation of "fast food", convenience grocery, and laundry/dry cleaning franchising which was founded by a grant from the Small Business Administration.[5] The study employed a probability sample of nearly 1000 completed questionnaires from franchisees, 151 franchise contracts provided by franchisors, and 146 completed questionnaires from franchisors.

DO FRANCHISORS ENGAGE IN DECEPTIVE PRACTICES IN SELLING FRANCHISES?

Franchising literally abounds with deceptive selling practices. First, and most importantly, many franchisors systematically mislead prospective franchisees about the potential profitability of their franchises. The study obtained the pro-forma income statements which 67 fast food franchisors show to prospective franchisees as profit projections. The study also had detailed profit data from 282 franchisees associated with the chains who used the pro-forma income statements. The results were dramatic: 73% of the franchisees had incomes *below* the minimum projected by the pro-forma statements; 92% had incomes below the average projected figures; and 99% had incomes below the maximum projected incomes. The results demonstrate conclusively that the pro-forma income statements of many fast food franchisors are not based on the average performance of their franchisees and would, therefore, mislead potential franchisees as to the profitability of the franchises.

Further evidence of misrepresentation comes from the probability sample of 878 fast food franchisees. Thirty-seven percent said that their franchisors had either *overestimated or greatly overestimated* their potential profits; whereas, only 7% said that their franchisors had *underestimated* their protential profits.

A second deceptive practice concerns franchisors relying completely on pro-forma statements and refusing to show actual profit and loss statements to potential franchisees. Of the 890 fast food franchisees responding, 41% stated that their franchisors did *not* show them actual

5. Ozanne, Urban B. and Hunt, Shelby D., *The Economic Effects of Franchising* (Washington D.C.: The United States Senate—U. S. Government Printing Office, 1971).

profit and loss statements. As might be expected, those franchisees who did *not* see actual profit and loss statements had markedly *lower* profits than those who *did* see actual operating statements. The results were statistically significant at the 0.05 level with a Kruskal-Wallis "H" test.[6]

A third deceptive practice concerns the prices franchisees are charged for services and supplies. Sometimes there is a "hidden charge" for a service like bookkeeping where the franchisee is led to believe the service will be free. Most franchisees (70% of our sample) are required to purchase some of their operating supplies from their franchisors. Table 1 shows that a substantial number (46%) believe that they could purchase equivalent items at lower prices elsewhere.

TABLE 1   Prices Franchisees Pay for Supplies From Franchisor

Response Category [1]	N	Percent
Franchisor's prices are over 25% higher	76	12.3
Franchisor's prices are 5% to 25% higher	208	33.7
Franchisor's prices are about the same	181	29.3
Franchisor's prices are 5% to 25% lower	147	23.8
Franchisor's prices are over 25% lower	5	0.8
Total	617	99.9 [2]

[1] Question (EQ34b): Which statement best describes the prices you are charged as compared with prices of equivalent items you could purchase elsewhere?
[2] Rounding error.

Potential franchisees are frequently misled into believing that because the franchisor "buys in bulk" the franchisee will get a *lower* price on his supplies. Our research also showed that (significant at the 0.05 level) franchisees who were required to purchase a high percentage of their supplies from the franchisor were less profitable than franchisees who purchased a low percentage of their supplies from their franchisor.

Another facet of the "supplies" issue involves "kickbacks." A "kickback" is a rebate which is illegally demanded or received. Most franchisors retain the right to approve their franchisees' major suppliers. In response to the question, "To the best of your knowledge, does your franchisor receive a commission from any of your suppliers when they sell supplies to you," 41% of the franchisees responded affirmatively; 20% responded negatively; and 39% said they didn't know. Now, believing something to be the case does not make it so, but the fact that 41% of the franchisees believed that their franchisors are taking "kickbacks" cannot be entirely dismissed as misperception.

6. Siegel, Sidney, *Nonparametric Statistics*, (New York: McGraw-Hill Book Co., Inc., 1956).

A fourth deceptive practice concerns using a celebrity's name to promote the sale of a franchise. Potential franchisees are led to believe that a celebrity would not lend his name to a franchise system if it were not a sound business investment for the franchisee. The performance of many of these systems has shown this to be an unwarranted assumption. Many of these systems have fallen on hard times, if not bankruptcy.[7] In recent months few new celebrity franchise systems have been established.

A fifth deceptive practice concerns the organizational ability of the franchisor to deliver on his promises of service and support to the franchisee. Franchisors have been known to attempt to set up a nationwide franchise system without first operating a "pilot" unit to ensure that the franchise concept was sound and before developing an organization to service their franchisees. Thirty-five percent of our sample of franchisees were dissatisfied with the quality of day-to-day business advice being provided by their franchisors and 30% of the franchisees felt that thier field supervisors were of below average or poor quality. Franchisors should provide in their promotional material a bibliography of the background and business experience of their principal officers. Potential franchisees could then evaluate whether the franchisor has the business experience to provide the services he promises. Unfortunately, the study indicated that many franchisors do not provide this information in their promotional material.

A sixth deceptive practice concerns the high pressure tactics involved in closing the sale of a franchise. Franchisees are urged to make up their minds quickly in order to "get in on the ground floor." As a franchisee with one of the largest and best known franchise systems in the country put it in the "comments" section on the back of his questionnaire:

> We paid $1500 (to talk). Agreed to forfeit this for expenses if, after mailing check to home office and receiving agreement, we failed to go ahead once the site was selected by company and pay approximately $22,500. We paid by check and were told that the builder would be over . . . to make arrangements in a week. We were given unsigned copies of pages and pages of legal documents and contracts late at night and allowed 20 minutes to read, absorb, digest, and make a decision (to jump or lose $1500 deposit).

The preceding six deceptive practices cover most of the major kinds of misrepresentation in franchising. Although not all franchisors engage in these practices, they are sufficiently widespread to be a cause for alarm. The substantial misrepresentation in franchising raises the issue of whether potential franchisees should be protected.

7. "Fullback Brown Gets Thrown for a Loss," *Business Week* Jan. 10, 1970, p. 58. Also "Athletes Fail to Carry Success on the Field into Business Ventures", *Wall Street Journal* Jan. 4, 1971, p. 1. "Franchises Often Just use Names," *Wisconsin State Journal* Jan. 22, 1971, p. 3.

DO FRANCHISEES NEED PROTECTION FROM THE
DECEPTIVE SELLING PRACTICES OF FRANCHISORS?

The doctrine of *caveat emptor* is dead. Both the federal government and the various state and local governments have long taken the position that protecting the consumer is a legitimate governmental concern. As will be demonstrated, the *consumer of franchises* needs protection.

At the present time, many potential franchisees simply do not have enough information to make an informed investment decision. Since the franchisor alone knows which of his claims are fact and which are fiction, the potential franchisee is at an extreme negotiating disadvantage.

In addition to the imbalance of information between the franchisor and the potential franchisee, both the popular press and the low level of business sophistication of potential franchisees contribute to the problem. The numerous "rags to riches" stories in the popular press about franchising in many cases have *presold* potential franchisees that owning a franchise is the key to success.[8]

The lack of business sophistication is exemplified by the fact that 68% of our sample of franchisees did not own a business prior to their franchised business and half the franchisees had incomes below $10,000 prior to buying their franchise. The unsophisticated nature of potential franchisees is further illustrated by the fact that 39% of our sample did not consult a lawyer prior to signing the franchise agreement. This is amazing, considering that these agreements are extremely complex documents with much fine print and will govern the basic relationship between franchisee and franchisor for a period of years.

The fact that many potential franchisees are unsophisticated in business, combined with the fact that they are often presold on franchising through the popular press, and that franchisors hold unique access to the information that franchisees need to make an informed investment decision, creates a situation where the opportunity for deception is ripe and the need for protection is clear. The demonstrated need for protection raises the issue of who should provide this protection.

LEGISLATION TO PROTECT POTENTIAL FRANCHISEES

Four agencies are candidates for insisting on full disclosure in franchising: (1) self-regulation by the franchising industry, (2) the state legislatures, (3) the Congress, and (4) the Federal Trade Commission.

8. Kursh, Harry, *The Franchise Boom* (New York: Prentice Hall, 1969); "Franchising—No end to its Growth?", *Printers Ink* (August 13, 1965).

SELF-REGULATION

Effective self-regulation by either of the two trade associations (the International Franchise Association and the National Association of Franchise Companies) seems unlikely. Although both have codes of ethics, since there remain hundreds of franchisors that belong to neither association and since both lack effective sanctions, they could not enforce full disclosure.

STATE LEGISLATION

The states have already begun to act on full disclosure. The legislatures of California, Washington, and Wisconsin have passed full disclosure bills.[9] Other states are considering similar legislation.

Most of the state legislation on full disclosure follows the California model. The general provisions are:

1. Regulation of full disclosure for franchising is carried out by the state commissioner of securities.
2. All franchisors (except certain large franchisors which are exempted) must register a prospectus with the Office of Securities.
3. A *sample* of the items which must be included in the prospectus are:
   a. The disclosure of the background of the principals involved with the franchisor (especially any felonies committed by the principals).
   b. Recent financial statement.
   c. Sample franchise contract.
   d. The policy of the franchisor concerning franchise fees, royalties, and supplies.
   e. Contract termination provisions.
   f. Substantiation for any profit projections in pro-forma statements.
   g. Disclosures relating to using the name of a public figure.
   h. Territorial protection given to the franchisee.
4. All franchisors must show the preceding prospectus to all potential franchisees at least 48 hours before signing the agreement (or receiving any consideration).
5. All advertisements for franchisees must be registered with the commissioner at least 3 business days prior to publication of the advertisement.

CONGRESSIONAL LEGISLATION

The United States Senate has under consideration Senate Bill 3844, the Franchise Full Disclosure Act. All franchisors would be required to register a disclosure prospectus with the Securities and Exchange Com-

9. "Franchise Investment Law," Division 5, Added to Title 4 of the Corporation Code of the State of California, operative on Jan. 1, 1971. Also Senate Bill No. 755 regulating franchising in the State of Washington, and Senate Bill No. 784 regulating franchising in Wisconsin, effective April 18, 1972.

mission. The kinds of disclosures required parallel to a large degree those of the state bills. Likewise, the Senate bill requires franchisors to supply potential franchisees with a copy of the prospectus. The major difference between the Senate bill and the various state bills is that the Senate bill does not require franchisors to submit advance copies of their advertisements to the SEC. This bill has not yet reached the floor of the Senate for a vote.

FEDERAL TRADE COMMISSION

During February of 1972 Federal Trade Commission held hearings on a proposed trade regulation rule concerning full disclosure in franchising. Once again, the actual disclosure provisions would parallel the Senate bill and the state legislation. The major differences between the proposed rule and the state legislation are three: (1) Instead of requiring a pre-registration procedure, the FTC would simply require franchisors to furnish at the end of each year copies of all disclosures made during the year, (2) prior clearance of advertisements is not required, and (3) a "cooling off" period is provided. During the "cooling-off" period of 10 days after the contract is signed, the franchisee could cancel the contract for any reason and get his money back. The "cooling-off" period is designed to prevent franchisors from using high pressure tactics in selling franchises. The F.T.C. has not yet given a final judgment on the proposed ruling.

CONCLUSIONS

Many franchisors do engage in deceptive and misleading practices when selling franchises. Franchisors exaggerate the potential profitability of their franchises and refuse to show actual profit and loss statements to prospective franchisees. Other deceptive practices include overcharging franchisees for supplies, taking "kickbacks" from the franchisee's suppliers, failing to have the organizational ability to deliver on promises of service and support, misusing a celebrity's name in selling franchises, and using high pressure tactics in closing the sale.

Many franchisors do not provide prospective franchisees with sufficient unbiased information to enable the franchisee to make a sound investment decision. Just as the purchaser of stocks and bonds must rely on the issuer to make a full and accurate disclosure, the purchaser of franchises must rely on the franchisor to make full disclosure.

Although the intent of the previously described state full disclosure legislation is good, a plethora of legislation at the state level may endanger the viability of the franchise system of distribution. Different registration and full disclosure procedures in each of the states may prove so costly that many franchisors may simply avoid franchising altogether in favor of expansion via company-operated units. This would be extremely undesirable, given the many positive advantages of franchising.

Federal action seems much more desirable since franchisors would have to make only one disclosure to one agency, thus providing the uniformity so necessary to keep franchising a viable part of the economy. Either Congress or the Federal Trade Commission should take decisive action on this problem of national concern.

QUESTIONS FOR DISCUSSION

1. What conclusion does Hunt make concerning the issue of deceptive practices in selling franchises?

2. Specifically, what deceptive practices were found most frequently?

3. Does Hunt think that franchisees need additional legislative protection? Do you agree? Explain.

4. Assuming some sort of additional regulation is needed, what type and in what problem areas do you believe it to be most relevant?

7.2 THE TREND TOWARD COMPANY-OPERATED UNITS IN FRANCHISE CHAINS

Shelby D. Hunt

". . . The 'franchising ethic' says that franchised units combine the best of both worlds, access to the sophisticated business procedures of a large company (the franchisor), while retaining the drive and initiative of the independent owner-manager."

An article in the JOURNAL OF RETAILING by Alfred R. Oxenfeldt and Anthony O. Kelly raised the issue of whether successful franchise systems would ultimately become wholly-owned chains.[1] The authors concluded:

> Hopefully, we have demonstrated that powerful forces at play on both franchisor and franchisee tend to bring about that result: namely, changes in objectives sought; diminishing alternative investment opportunities; the frustrations involved in operating through independent businessmen; and fundamental shifts in the capabilities and resources of each. Clearly, to arrive at definitive conclusions on this important issue, much empirical evidence would be needed.[2]

This article will provide empirical evidence to support the hypothesis of Oxenfeldt and Kelly. The data come from the recently completed study on the economic effects of franchising funded by a grant from the Small Business Administration.[3] The study focused on franchising in the three areas of fast food, convenience grocery, and laundry/dry cleaning.

Reprinted by permission from the author and publisher. Shelby D. Hunt, "The Trend Toward Company-Operated Units in Franchise Chains," *Journal of Retailing* (Summer, 1973), pp. 3–12.

1. Alfred R. Oxenfeldt and Anthony O. Kelly, "Will Successful Franchise Systems Ultimately Become Wholly Owned Chains?" *Journals of Retailing*, 44, No. 4 (Winter 1968–1969).

2. *Ibid.*, p. 38.

3. U. B. Ozanne and Shelby D. Hunt, *The Economic Effects of Franchising* (Washington, D.C.: The United States Senate, United States Government Printing Office, 1971).

The data result from a probability sample of nearly one thousand completed questionnaires from franchisees, 151 franchise contracts provided by franchisors, and 146 completed questionnaires from franchisors.

FACTORS FAVORING FRANCHISED UNITS

Why do firms seek franchised units? The primary motivations appear to be six:

LACK OF AVAILABLE CAPITAL

Firms often choose the route of franchised units because they simply do not have access to the capital required to expand via company-operated units. Many franchisors candidly admit that they would have preferred all company-operated units but that capital requirements dictated franchising:

> Hardee's would have preferred not to have franchised a single location. We prefer company-owned locations. Here again profits. But due to the heavy capital investment required we could only expand company-owned locations to a certain degree—from there we had to stop. Each operation represents an investment in excess of $100,000; therefore, we entered the franchise business.[4]

THE "FRANCHISING ETHIC"

A second reason some firms enter franchising is a belief in the "franchising ethic." Simply put, the "franchising ethic" says that franchised units combine the best of both worlds, access to the sophisticated business procedures of a large company (the franchisor), while retaining the drive and initiative of the independent owner-manager. Some franchisors do believe that there is no substitute for the owner-manager, and at least one small empirical study lends support to the proposition that franchisors can make more money out of a unit run by a franchisee than the same unit with a company manager because of the superior performance of the owner-manager.[5] However, as will be shown later, there is significant evidence contrary to the "franchising ethic," at least regarding the proposed benefits to the franchisor.

4. Robert E. Bennett, "To Franchise or Not—How to Decide: Pro-Why, How, Advantages," C. L. Vaughn and D. B. Slater (eds.), *Franchising Today: 1966–1967* (New York: Matthew Bender and Company, Inc., 1967), p. 20.

5. John P. Shelton, "Allocative Efficiency vs. 'X Efficiency': A Comment," *American Economic Review*, LVII, No. 5 (December 1967), pp. 1252–258.

RAPID EXPANSION

Speed of expansion constitutes a third factor contributing to the development of franchise chain. Even if a firm has ample capital, it may not have the human resources necessary for rapid expansion via company-operated units. Some franchise chains (e.g., "Minnie Pearl Fried Chicken") have sprung up almost overnight.

THE ISOLATED UNIT

Managing several company-operated units in close physical proximity can provide significant economies of scale. Consequently, a firm may prefer to franchise a unit that is physically isolated. Careful observation of the "buy-backs" of several chains (e.g., McDonalds) shows a tendency to repurchase units in metropolitan areas where managerial economies of scale ought to occur.

LOW-PROFIT UNITS

The overall profitability of the units of some franchise chains is so low that if the parent company installed company managers, the salaries of the company managers would absorb all of the "profit" of the units. Clearly, franchisees with these chains are merely "buying" a manager's job, since real "profit" for a franchisee begins only *after* he pays himself a salary for managing the unit.

A second aspect of the low-profit-unit motive is the simple fact that good, high-volume locations are scarce. Consequently, franchise chains may reserve their best locations for company-operated units and franchise the less desirable locations.

FRANCHISE FEES

Almost all fast food franchisors charge a franchise fee, the mean of which this study found to be almost $9,000. These fees are normally nonrefundable according to most contracts.

The potential revenues to be collected solely in the form of franchise fees constitute a final (albeit unsavory) reason for franchising. A few "fast buck artists" enter franchising with little or no intention of actually *operating* a franchise chain, but simply to collect franchise fees from unsuspecting franchisees. The present study was not designed to empirically assess the extent of this practice.

Another unsavory practice occasionally associated with franchise fees might be called "churning." The franchisor sells an unprofitable unit to a franchisee for a healthy franchise fee. After a few months, the franchisee realizes that the unit will never be profitable and decides to "cut his losses" by selling it back to the franchisor at a fraction of his original investment. The franchisor is then free to sell the unit again to another unsuspecting franchisee and collect another franchise fee.

FACTORS FAVORING COMPANY-OPERATED UNITS

The factors favoring company-operated units appear to be five:

HIGHER PROFITS PER UNIT

In certain instances, a franchisor can reap much greater profits from a company-operated unit than from a franchised one. For example, John Y. Brown, head of Kentucky Fried Chicken, has said, "We'll make more profit from 300 company-owned stores than we will from 2,100 franchise outlets."[6] Similarly, McDonald's received two-thirds of its revenues from company-operated units.[7] In addressing the Fifth International Management Conference on Franchising, John Jay Hooker commented:

> As all of you know, the name of the game is not really franchising. The name of the game is company stores. I was looking at some figures not too long ago and saw where a big company in America had 1,600–1,700 units, and only two hundred of those were company owned, but the two hundred company-owned units were producing 60 percent of the net after taxes. It becomes obvious to you, if two hundred company-owned units out of 1,600–1,700 overall units produce 60 percent of the net after tax profits, the real name of the game is owning the stores yourself.[8]

Similarly, Lawrence E. Singer, president of Royal Castle System, Inc., has noted "we make more profit, per company-operated unit, than we could possibly make in franchising. This fact has been acknowledged by many of the franchise operators. For this reason, we operate company-owned stores."[9] Finally, William Ware of PKI Foods, Inc. (Aunt Jemima's Kitchens) makes the same point:

> More profits can be gained from company-owned stores. A break-even analysis of operations in the $225,000 to $300,000 range shows this fact to be very true. Since our stores average $270,000 per unit per year and some

6. "Franchising's Troubled Dream World," *Fortune* (March 1970), p. 121.
7. "The Chains Profit by Buying the Links," *Business Week* (June 27, 1970), p. 55.
8. John J. Hooker, "The Story of Minnie Pearl," *Franchising Today* (Lynbrook, N.Y.: Farnsworth Publishing Company Inc., 1970), p. 171.
9. Lawrence E. Singer, "To Franchise or Not—How to Decide, Con: Why, Company-Owned Units," C. L. Vaughn and D. B. Slater (eds.), *Franchising Today: 1966–1967* (New York: Matthew Bender and Company, Inc., 1967), p. 24.

clear between $50,000 and $100,000, it becomes evident that our stores are more profitable than if franchised.[10]

Although the present research design did not yield comparative profit figures on franchised units vs. company-operated units, it did generate accurate information on a closely associated figure—sales per unit. In 1970 the mean fast food franchised unit had sales of $150,000, whereas the mean company-operated unit was 81 percent greater at $271,000.

GREATER CONTROL

A second factor favoring company-operated units is the need for control. Company ownership provides sanctions that simply are not available under franchising. As Robert E. Bennett, vice president of Hardee's Food Systems, Inc., puts it:

> Better management control is another reason that we have company-owned stores. I saw a recent situation where a franchise competitor wanted to change his prices and he went through considerable turmoil in order to convince his franchise operators to go along with the price increase. He ended up changing some of the prices, not all of them, and he is still working on the problem of raising prices. Policies, graphics, advertising, merchandising, quality control, remodeling repairs—how do you convince a franchise dealer that even if a store is only ten years old, he must invest more of his money for remodeling?

> There is more flexibility in company-owned stores. Our capacity to react more swiftly to the need for change, we find to be to our advantage in the company-owned store.[11]

LEGAL PROBLEMS

Legal difficulties alone may be sufficient to push many potential franchisors toward company-operated units. Not only are there the substantial legal costs of devising and negotiating franchise agreements, but also, franchisees are increasingly taking their franchisors to court to redress grievances, both real and imagined. Since the "Chicken Delight" class action suit,[12] rumblings abound of new suits against franchisors. The franchisees of over two dozen fast food franchise chains

10. William Ware, "To Franchise or Not—How to Decide, Con: Why Company-Owned Units," C. L. Vaughn and D. B. Slater (eds.), *Franchising Today: 1966–1967* (New York: Matthew Bender and Company, Inc., 1967), p. 29.

11. Bennett, "To Franchise or Not," p. 25.

12. Harvery Siegel and Elaine Siegel, et al., Chicken Delight, Inc., et al., and Vance E. Shephard and Ben Zachary, et al., Intervening Plaintiffs, CCH 73, 146 (D.C. V. Cal., April 1970); BNA ATRR No. 458 (April 21, 1970) A-1, x-1.

have formed individual franchise associations and a fledgling national association has been formed, The National Association of Franchised Businessmen, headquartered in Washington, D.C.

NEW RESTRICTIVE LEGISLATION

The possibility of new restrictive legislation may push some franchisors toward company-operated units. Such legislation may severely curtail franchisors' rights to terminate a franchise and may substantially increase the amount and kinds of information that franchisors must show potential franchisees. Similar "full disclosure" type legislation has already passed the legislature in California.

RESULTS

The study yielded three kinds of evidence concerning company-operated units: the aggregate trend of the fast food franchising industry toward company-operated units, the relationship between the size of the franchise system and the percentage of company-operated units and the relationship between the age of the franchise system and the percentage of company-operated units. The aggregate data in Table I illustrate the rapid growth in fast food franchised units during the past decade. The number of fast food franchised units grew from 16,200 in 1960 to over 38,000 in 1970. The number of company-operated units rose from 200 in 1960 to 4,000 in 1970. Consequently, the percentage of total units that was company-operated increased steadily from a low of only 1.2 percent in 1960 to 9.5 percent in 1970, and the figure is expected to be 11.3 percent at the end of 1971.

Aggregate data, as in Table II, do not necessarily imply that individual franchise systems are increasing their percentage of company-operated units. The trend in Table I might possibly result from the entry into franchising of fast food chains which already had large numbers of company-operated units. Disaggregated data, such as Tables II and III provide additional evidence.

Table II shows the relationship between the size (franchised units plus company-owned units) of the franchise system and the percentage change in company-operated units between 1968 and 1971. Since the primary hypothesis is that lack of capital is the major factor influencing firms to franchise, and since access to capital should increase with size of the system, larger systems should show a greater tendency toward increasing the percentage of company-operated units than smaller systems. The numbers in parentheses in Table II show the expected number in each cell under the null hypothesis that the two variables are not related. With a significant chi square of 7.4, Table II indicates that among the 95 fast food franchise systems for which we had complete data, the larger franchise systems were disproportionately increasing their percentage of company-operated units.

In addition to size, the age of the franchise system should be positively associated with access to capital for expansion. Therefore, if lack of capital is the primary motivator for franchising, then older, successful systems should be concentrating on developing company-operated units. Table III indicates that, as predicted, the older franchise systems show a disproportionate tendency to increase the percentage of units which are company-operated.

SOURCE OF COMPANY-OPERATED UNIT EXPANSION

Franchise chains can expand their company-operated units either via new construction or by buying back units from their franchisees. Although considerable attention has been focused on "buy-backs,"[13]

TABLE 1   Fast Food Franchised and Company-Operated Units

Type	1960 *	1968	1969	1970	1971 †
Franchised	16,200	31,100	35,000	38,100	41,000
Company-operated	200	2,200	2,900	4,000	5,200
Total	16,400	33,300	37,900	42,100	46,200
Company-operated as percent of total	1.2%	6.6%	7.7%	9.5%	11.3%

* All figures are as of December 31 of that year.
† Projected estimate provided by franchisors.

most of the actual expansion has been by new construction. The data indicated that in 1969 there were 360 franchised units converted to company operation by fast food franchisors and 150 company-operated units converted to franchise operation, leaving a net change from franchised to company-operated of 210 units. Therefore, about 30 percent of the increase in company-operated units in 1969 resulted from "buy-backs," whereas 70 percent came from new construction.

13. "Food Franchiser's Merry Go Round," p. 122, "Franchising's Troubled Dream World," *Fortune*, p. 121, and "The Chains' Profit by Buying the Links," *Business Week*, p. 55.

FUTURE TREND FOR COMPANY-OPERATED UNITS

Will successful franchise chains ultimately become wholly-owned chains? If "wholly-owned" implies literally "100 percent," then the answer is probably no. Three factors mitigate against a franchise chain buying back *all* its franchised units:

1. Once a large franchise system is set up, extrication by the franchisor can be difficult. Franchise contracts typically cover long periods of time (we found the median length to be 15 years) and frequently the franchisee has an option to renew. If franchisees do not wish to sell

TABLE 2 Size of Fast Food Franchise System vs. Trend in Company-Owned Units

	Trend for Company-Owned Units			
Size [*]	Increasing [†]	Same [‡]	Decreasing [¶]	Total
1–24	18(20)	9(13)	33(27)	60
25 and greater	13(11)	12(8)	10(16)	35
Total	31	21	43	95
Chi square=7.4	p<.05 (2d.f.)			

[*] Includes both franchised and company-owned units as of the end of 1968.
[†] Shows the number of franchise systems whose percent change was greater than or equal to 1 percent where: percent change=(percent company-owned in 1971) −(percent company-owned in 1968).
[‡] Number of systems whose percent change was < 1 percent but > −1 percent.
[¶] Number of systems whose percent change was ≤ −1 percent.

their units, there is little a franchisor can do short of unethical, and perhaps illegal, coercion. Legislation may make coercive termination techniques specifically illegal.

2. A second factor mitigating against 100 percent company-operated units would be the existence of physically isolated franchised units for which supervision from the home office might be uneconomical.

3. Finally, all franchise chains have at least some units that have low profitability. There would be no reason for a franchisor to buy back these units except a strong desire to get out of franchising altogether.

Although most franchise chains will probably not become 100 percent company-operated, the percentage of units that are company-operated will undoubtedly continue to rise. When we asked franchisors what would be the "ideal" percentage of units that should be company-

TABLE 3   Age of Fast Food Franchise System vs. Trend in Company-Owned
Units

| Age of System | Trend in Company-Owned Units | | | Total |
	Increasing *	Same †	Decreasing ‡	
Five years or less	9(15)	5(10)	31(20)	45
Five years and older	22(16)	16(11)	12(23)	50
Total	31	21	43	95
Chi square=16.0	p<.005.			

* Shows the number of franchise systems whose percent change was greater than
or equal to 1 per cent where: percent change=(percent company-owned in 1971)
−(percent company-owned in 1968).
† Number of systems whose percent change was < 1 percent but > −1 percent.
‡ Number of systems whose percent change was ≤ −1 percent.

operated, the mean response was 42 percent. Since the "ideal" percentage is almost four times higher than the actual percentage, if franchisors have access to the necessary capital, they will probably continue
to concentrate their efforts on company-operated units.

Other evidence that the trend will continue comes from the franchisees themselves. Thirteen percent of our sample of franchisees indicated that their franchisors had expressed interest in buying back their
franchises. A Kruskal-Wallis "H" test, which was significant at the 0.005
level, showed that the franchisors were primarily seeking to buy back
the more profitable units.[14]

THE SOCIOECONOMIC CONSEQUENCES OF THE
TREND TOWARD COMPANY-OPERATED UNITS

The fact that many firms are apparently "using" franchising as a vehicle
to obtain the necessary capital to expand via company-operated units
is not of itself undesirable. The procedure is actually conceptually similar to a corporation selling common stock to raise capital for expansion. In the first case the buyer gets a franchised unit and the right to
a part of the profits from the unit and in the second case the buyer gets
a share of stock and the right to a part of the profits from the total corporation. Since selling equity is frequently not a viable alternative for
the small firm, franchising often becomes the best way for small firms
to capitalize on a unique concept and grow. Increasing the alternative

14. Sidney Siegel, *Nonparametric Statistics* (New York: McGraw-Hill Book
Company, Inc., 1956), pp. 184–94.

ways to finance growth would seem to be desirable from society's perspective.

Franchising as a means to raise capital for expansion has socially undesirable consequences when franchisors treat their franchisees unfairly. Two such unfair practices would be coercing franchisees to sell their franchises and misleading potential franchisees as to the expected profits and risks from franchised units. From the potential franchisee's point of view, the complete absence of company-operated units in a large franchise chain could well mean that the units are so low in profitability that the franchise chain cannot *afford* to have company-operated units.

QUESTIONS FOR DISCUSSION

1. Discuss fully the advantages to the franchisor of using independent franchisees.

2. Explain why many firms are beginning to operate more of their outlets as company-run units rather than as franchisee outlets.

3. The article discusses the "isolated" unit. Discuss this idea from a franchising efficiency viewpoint.

4. Hunt states, "In certain instances, a franchisor can reap much greater profits from a company-operated unit than from a franchised one." Explain the rationale of this statement.

5. Do you believe that company-owned units will become more or less important in franchising during the 1980s? Why?

7.3 TYING AGREEMENTS IN FRANCHISING

Shelby D. Hunt and John R. Nevin

"*A gallon of maraschino cherries costing $1.50 was just relabeled by Howard Johnson and priced at $4.50. Shakey's charges $21.50 for the spice blend which costs them $3.00.*"

The franchise system of distribution continues to grow in importance. Retail sales of the approximately 380,000 franchising firms—both independent and company owned—approached $151 billion in 1973, nearly one-third of the $497 billion estimate for total retail sales. Independent, franchisee-owned units dominated the franchise system's retail sales, accounting for approximately 85% of the total. For 1974, franchising firms expected sales to exceed $159 billion, which would at least maintain their 30% share of total retail sales volume.[1] Concomitant with this rapid growth, however, has been the rise of substantial legal problems in franchising.

This article examines the legal problems confronting franchising and the efforts currently being made to help solve these problems. The controversy surrounding one of the most serious legal problems in franchising, the tying agreement problem, is reviewed. Finally, the results of an empirical study are presented to provide a better understanding of the impact of tying agreements on the franchise system of distribution.

LEGAL PROBLEMS IN FRANCHISING

In recent years, the franchise system of distribution has been deluged with legislation and litigation. Franchisee versus franchisor litigation has proliferated to the extent that some legal experts consider the legal problems facing the franchise industry to be of crisis proportions. Many

Reprinted by permission of the authors and publisher. Shelby D. Hunt and John R. Nevin, "Tying Agreements in Franchising," *Journal of Marketing* (July 1975), pp. 20–26.

1. U.S. Department of Commerce, *Franchising in the Economy, 1972–1974* (Washington, D.C.: U.S. Government Printing Office, 1974).

prominent franchising companies have found themselves in court as a result of disenchanted franchisees. These companies include Shakey's, Mister Donut of America, Midas Muffler, Chicken Delight, Schwinn, H&R Block, Chick N'Joy, Chock Full O'Nuts, Mr. Steak, Electric Computer Programming Institute, The Southland Corporation (7-Eleven Stores), Network Cinema Corporation (Jerry Lewis), and A&W.

Sidney Diamond suggests that the current legal problems confronting franchising fall into three main areas: (1) misrepresentations by franchisors to potential franchisees about the operation of the franchise (the "disclosure" problem), (2) restrictions by franchisors on the source of supplies or services purchased by their franchisees (the "tying agreement" problem), and (3) onerous termination provisions in the franchise agreement (the "capricious termination" problem).[2] These problems are receiving the attention of trade associations in the franchising industry, state legislatures, the Congress, and the Federal Trade Commission (FTC),[3] as discussed below.

The two major franchising trade associations, The International Franchise Association and the National Association of Franchise Companies, are concerned about the legal problems facing their members and have tried to establish self-regulation through codes of ethics. However, since there are hundreds of franchisors that do not belong to either association, and since both associations lack effective sanctions to enforce their ethical codes, trade association efforts alone are unlikely to eliminate the problems confronting franchising.

The individual states have begun to pass laws regulating the franchise industry. Although these state laws are chiefly of the "full disclosure" variety, a few states have also passed so-called fair practice laws. Full disclosure laws are designed to protect prospective franchisees from franchisor misrepresentations by requiring franchisors to provide each prospective franchisee with sufficient unbiased information to enable him to make a sound investment decision.[4] As part of the full disclosure provisions, franchisors usually must disclose any requirements that the franchisee purchase supplies from the franchisor or his designated suppliers. Full disclosure laws have been passed (as of this writing) in the legislatures of California, Hawaii, Illinois, Michigan, Minnesota, Oregon, Rhode Island, South Dakota, Washington, Wisconsin, and the Province of Alberta, Canada.

Fair practice laws have been passed in the legislatures of California,

2. Sidney A. Diamond, "Federal Trade Commissioners Warn of Abuses in Franchising," *Marketing Insights*, October 27, 1969, p. 17.

3. Shelby D. Hunt, "Full Disclosure and the Franchise System of Distribution," *Dynamic Marketing in a Changing World*, Boris W. Becker and Helmut Becker, eds., (Chicago: American Marketing Assn., 1975), pp. 301–304.

4. See same reference as footnote 3, for a detailed discussion of the provisions of full disclosure laws.

Connecticut, Delaware, New Jersey, Virginia, Washington, and Wisconsin. These laws are designed to protect the franchisee by prohibiting the franchisor from using unfair or deceptive acts or practices. Although fair practice laws differ substantially from state to state, franchisors are usually prohibited from such practices as: (1) requiring a franchisee to purchase goods or services from the franchisor or his designated suppliers unless it is reasonably necessary to maintain control over the nature and quality of the goods or services; (2) discriminating between franchisees in the charges of royalties, goods, services, advertising services, and the like, unless reasonably justifiable; (3) selling a product or service to a franchisee for more than a fair or reasonable price; (4) competing with, or granting franchises to compete with, a franchisee in the relevant market area specifically listed in the franchisee agreement; and (5) from terminating, canceling, or failing to renew a franchise without good cause. The burden of proving good cause or reasonability of a restrictive purchasing agreement is the responsibility of the franchisor.

On the federal level, the U.S. Senate has been considering a franchise full disclosure act, which would require disclosures similar to those of the state bills. Likewise, during February of 1972 the Federal Trade Commission held hearings on a proposed trade regulation rule concerning full disclosure in franchising.[5] Again, the actual provisions would parallel the Senate bill and the state legislation. The FTC has not yet given final judgment on the proposed ruling.

TYING AGREEMENTS IN FRANCHISING

As the state legislatures, Congress, and the FTC both pass and ponder legislative solutions, the flood of franchisee versus franchisor litigation continues. Much of the litigation concerns restrictions by the franchisor on the source of supplies. The Select Committee on Small Business feels that

> one of the more serious problems facing franchisors is the matter of "tie-ins," the policy whereby a seller, by conditioning the sale of a desirable product over which he has sufficient control, upon the purchase of other less desirable products, requires the purchaser to buy both the "tying" and the "tied" products from him.[6]

5. FTC Proposed Rule Involving Disclosure Requirements and Prohibitions Concerning Franchising, 4 T. R. Rules 38,029 (February 1972).

6. *The Impact of Franchising on Small Business*, Hearings Before the Subcommittee on Urban and Rural Economic Development (Washington, D.C.: U.S. Government Printing Office, 1970), p. 23.

In the case of franchising, the tying product is the franchise itself and the tied products are the supplies the franchisee must purchase to operate his business. Benjamin Glosband, a legal expert, believes the problem of restrictions on the source of supplies or services is at the heart of almost every complaint pending against franchisors:

> The Federal Trade Commission has received numerous complaints alleging that the franchisor is requiring the franchisee to purchase supplies at outrageous prices from the franchisor or designated supplier. This type of complaint has been the basis of a number of antitrust suits—governmental and private—charging the franchisor with involvement in an exclusive dealing arrangement or a tie-in arrangement.[7]

The present article will first examine the pros and cons of tying agreements in franchising, will briefly review the legal status of tying agreements, and then will present the results of an empirical investigation of three basic questions concerning the impact of tying agreements in franchising: (1) How widespread is the practice of franchisees being required to purchase supplies from their franchisors? (2) Do franchisees who are required to purchase supplies from their franchisors pay competitive prices for these supplies? (3) What are the effects, if any, on franchisees of this requirement?

TYING AGREEMENTS: PRO

Franchisors give two primary justifications for requiring their franchisees to purchase supplies from them: (1) the franchisor can buy the supplies cheaper because of volume purchases, and (2) the purchase requirements are necessary to insure uniform quality control throughout the franchise system. Many franchisors indicate in their brochures that their mass purchasing power is one of the advantages of being a franchise member. For example, one brochure states that the franchisor

> negotiates volume contracts with all purveyors and suppliers. These contracts are based on high quality and low prices. [The franchisor] makes all items available to the individual operator at the exact price of the contract. The overall advantage of this centralized buying power reflects a saving to the operator of approximately 4 percent of his gross, for which he is paying only 2.5 percent. . . .[8]

Many franchisors also maintain that purchase requirements are the only effective means of insuring quality control. According to William Sandberg, contributing editor of the *Franchise Journal*, there are num-

7. Benjamin A. Glosband, "The Franchising Dilemma," *Trial*, Vol. 8 (July–August 1972), p. 34.
8. *Weekly Digest*, October 5, 1968, p. 8.

erous cases where franchisees have completely ignored quality standards when the franchisor relinquished strict control over the franchisees' purchasing procedures.[9] A. L. Lapin, Jr., past president of the International Franchise Association, contends that franchisors, franchisees, and American consumers are all harmed when quality control cannot be assured. He maintains that:

> The franchisor, who cannot be assured of his ability to direct the uniformity and preserve the quality of his product, will simply elect to cease franchising. The franchisee, who cannot be assured that the consumer acceptance of his franchised goods or services can be protected by the franchisor, will have lost much of the value of his investment. The American consumer cannot but be harmed by the deterioration in quality and the decreased confidence in the individual outlet which will inevitably flow from the atrophy of the franchising system.[10]

TYING AGREEMENTS: CON

In addition to royalty payments, franchise fees, and rent payments, a major way for franchisors to secure revenue is through the sale of supplies and raw materials to their franchisees.[11] Equity suggests that franchisors should be permitted to make a return on this service as long as franchisees reap the benefits claimed for centralized or mass purchasing. However, critics claim that franchisors are requiring franchisees to purchase supplies and raw materials at prices far above those of the competitive market. Numerous cases have been cited in support of this contention. As examples of this practice, the Select Committee on Small Business reported that: "A gallon of maraschino cherries costing $1.50 was just relabeled by Howard Johnson and priced at $4.50. Shakey's charges $21.50 for the spice blend which costs them $3.00."[12] In the committee's eyes, these were but two examples where franchisors were requiring their franchisees to purchase supplies at exorbitant prices.

According to Harold Brown, a strong critic of franchising, one hardly need speculate on the consequences of overcharges. As an illustration, Brown cites the case of a prominent restaurant chain with more than 500 outlets:

> In 1945, about 20 percent were owned by the franchisor and 80 percent by the franchisees. By 1960, the situation had reversed, and the franchisor

9. William Sandberg, "Are Franchise Controls Necessary?" *Franchise Journal*, March 1971, p. 21.

10. Same reference as footnote 6, p. 267.

11. Milton Woll, "Sources of Revenue to the Franchisor and Their Strategic Implications," *Journal of Retailing*, Vol. 44 (Winter 1968–69), p. 14.

12. Same reference as footnote 6, p. 5.

owned more than 80 percent of the outlets. The financially pressed franchisees had cut down on servings and service, borrowed to the limit, and ultimately surrendered their franchises to the franchisor—expressing gratitude for being released from personal guaranty.[13]

Brown argues that preventing the franchisee from buying on the open market harms the franchisee, the third-party supplier, and the consumer.[14] Franchisees are prevented from making purchases at the lowest prices and on the best available terms. Third-party suppliers, therefore, lose the opportunity to compete for the trade of the franchisees. And, in turn, the consumer suffers because of the secondary interference with the normal operation of the marketplace.

TYING AGREEMENTS: LEGAL ISSUES

Is it legal for franchisors to have purchase requirements or tying agreements? As previously discussed, tying agreements may arise out of a franchisor's effort to control both the quality and the uniformity of his trademarked products or services. Such control can be both legally and commercially necessary. Federal law, according to the Lanham Act, provides that a trademark owner *must* insure that the products or services identified by the mark meet all owner quality standards or risk cancellation or abandonment of his trademark rights.[15] The Lanham Act, however, specifically provides that an antitrust violation is not condoned by trademark law.

Tying provisions in franchise agreements have to date presented both a trade regulation problem under Section 5 of the Federal Trade Commission Act and an antitrust problem under Section 1 of the Sherman Act and Section 3 of the Clayton Act. Franchisors should be aware of the conditions under which tying agreements are considered illegal. FTC Commissioner Wilbur Dixon suggests that four criteria should be applied in determining whether tying arrangements are illegal: (1) Does the arrangement in question involve two or more distinct items, one of which (the tying product—the franchise) may be obtained only if the other(s) is also purchased? (2) Is the tying item invested with sufficient economic power to restrain competition in the tied product(s)? (3) Is a "not insubstantial" amount of commerce affected by the arrangement? And, if these first three questions can be answered affirmatively, (4) Is the respondent able to demonstrate by way of affirmative defense that the tie-in is necessary to ensure the quality of

13. Harold Brown, *Franchising-Realities* and *Remedies* (New York: Law Journal Press, 1973), p. 28.
14. Same reference as footnote 13.
15. The Lanham Act, 15 U.S.C. 1055, 1064 (e) (1) 1127 (1964).

its products, or that no less restrictive means than the tie-in may be used to ensure such quality?[16]

In the Carvel case, the FTC dismissed a proceeding under Section 5 of the FTC Act against Carvel (a soft-service ice cream franchise), despite Carvel's requirements that its ice cream mix was to be purchased only from Carvel-designated sources.[17] The commission chose not to define the restriction as an illegal tie-in; rather, it decided to examine whether the supply restrictions were reasonably ancillary to the protection of the trademark and vindicated Carvel on this basis. In *Susser v. Carvel*, the court found that a tie-in did exist, but concluded that ingredient-supply restrictions were justified by the need for quality control connected with the problem of ingredient secrecy.[18]

In the Chicken Delight case, several franchisees challenged Chicken Delight's franchising contracts under Section 1 of the Sherman Act, seeking treble damages.[19] Chicken Delight required that its franchisees purchase specified cookers, packaging items, and food preparation mixes. Apparently, the prices they were required to pay for these products were higher than those of similar products generally available from alternate sources. The franchisees challenged the agreements as unlawful tying arrangements. The court rejected the "quality control" defense of the franchisor as applied to the packaging products. The court reasoned that any competent packaging manufacturer could have supplied satisfactory packaging upon proper specification of printing type and color. However, as to the tied dips, spices, and cookers, which allegedly impart a secret unique flavor to the Chicken Delight product, the district court recognized that, under *Carvel*, "the quality control defense is relevant." The court then sent this issue to the jury with the instructions that it accept the "quality control" defense only if "specifications for a substitute would be so detailed that they could not practically be supplied."[20] The jury determined that quality control could have been effected by means other than a tie-in.

A recent timely decision concerning Chock Full O'Nuts Corporation provides further clarification as to how the FTC will interpret the "quality control" defense.[21] Chock Full O'Nuts required its 38 franchisees to purchase from it a large number of: (a) food products manufactured by the franchisor (e.g., coffee, bakery goods, and hamburger), (b) food

---

16. In re Chock Full O'Nuts Corp., Inc., 3 Trade Reg. Rep. π 20,441 (October 1973).

17. In re Carvel Corp., [Transfer Binder] Trade Reg. Rep. π 17,298 (August, 1965).

18. *Susser v. Carvel*, 332 F. 2d 505 (1964).

19. *Siegel v. Chicken Delight*, 448 F. 2d 43 (1971).

20. In re Siegel v. Chicken Delight, BNA ATRR No. 467 (June 23, 1970), B-1, B-4.

21. Same reference as footnote 16.

products *not* manufactured by the franchisor (e.g., milk, french fries, and soft drink syrups), and (c) nonfood products *not* manufactured by the franchisor (e.g., napkins, straws, and glasses). Chock Full O'Nuts defended its practice of tying the sale of these products to the sale of the franchise by asserting that it was necessary to maintain uniform quality throughout all its restaurants. The FTC held that the "quality control" defense was applicable *only* where it was not practicable to specify the ingredients in such a way as to render the item duplicable by competing manufacturers. Upon examining the difficulty of adequately specifying the ingredients for the various tied products, the FTC ruled:

> [Chock Full O'Nuts Corp.] successfully proved its affirmative defense [to tying charges] of maintaining quality control with regard to its coffee and baked goods, but not as to its other distinctive products that franchisees were obligated to purchase.[22]

This decision seems consistent with *Carvel* and *Chicken Delight*.

The franchisor faces the conflict between his duty under the Lanham Act to protect the trademark through quality control and his duty to avoid violations in the various antitrust laws. This dilemma has been referred to as the "revolving door" since, by satisfying the requirements of one statute, the franchisor may find that he has violated another.[23] Several experts have suggested that in the vast majority of cases quality control can be accomplished by less restrictive means than tying agreements.[24] In those cases where quality control considerations dictate tying agreements, prudence suggests that franchisors charge prices that are reasonably competitive with other suppliers.

IMPACT OF TYING AGREEMENTS IN FRANCHISING

The data used to explore the three basic questions concerning the impact of tying agreements in franchising came from a study on the economic effects of franchising conducted at the University of Wisconsin-Madison.[25] The data base is a national probability sample of 664 completed questionnaires from franchisees in the fast-food restaurant area. The sample of franchisees was drawn from lists of franchisee names and addresses supplied by franchisors and from the yellow pages of telephone directories. Empirical results from this survey are presented for each of the three questions.

22. Same reference as footnote 16.
23. Same reference as footnote 13, p. 150.
24. Donald F. Turner, "The Validity of Tying Arrangements Under the Antitrust Laws," *Harvard Law Review*, Vol. 72 (November 1958), p. 64.
25. Urban B. Ozanne and Shelby D. Hunt, *The Economic Effects of Franchising* (Washington, D.C.: U.S. Government Printing Office, 1971).

EXTENT OF PRACTICE

The first question examined was: *How widespread is the practice of franchisees being required to purchase supplies from their franchisors?* The results of the survey indicated that about 70% of the responding franchisees were required to purchase at least some of their operating supplies from their franchisors. Of those franchisees who had to purchase from their franchisors, the median percentage of total operating supplies that they purchased from this source was 50%. It appears that tying agreements, far from being just an isolated practice that involves only a few franchisors, affect the overwhelming majority of franchisees, who must purchase at least some of their supplies from their franchisors.

PRICES CHARGED FOR SUPPLIES

The second research question asked: *Do franchisees who are required to purchase supplies from their franchisors pay competitive prices for these supplies?* The results, reported in Table 1, show that only 24.8% of

TABLE 1   Franchisees' Perceptions of the Competitiveness of Franchisor Prices for Supplies

Response Category [a]	N	Percent
1. Franchisor's prices are over 25% lower	3	.7
2. Franchisor's prices are 5% to 25% lower	107	24.1
3. Franchisor's prices are about the same	125	28.2
4. Franchisor's prices are 5% to 25% higher	150	33.9
5. Franchisor's prices are over 25% higher	58	13.1
Total	443 [b]	100.0

[a] Response categories to the following question: Which statement best describes the prices you are charged as compared with prices of equivalent items you could purchase elsewhere?

[b] Only the 464 franchisees who purchased supplies from their franchisors answered this question. Twenty-one of these 464 either did not answer the question or said they did not know.

the franchisees believed they paid lower prices to the franchisor than they would in the open market, while 47.0% believed they paid higher prices to the franchisor. The remaining 28.2% perceived their franchisors' prices to be about the same as the prices of equivalent items they could purchase elsewhere. Therefore, although a substantial number of franchisees apparently felt they got a price advantage by purchasing from their franchisors, many more believed they were being overcharged.

EFFECTS OF PURCHASE REQUIREMENTS

The third basic question concerned: *What are the effects, if any, on franchisees of being required to purchase supplies from their franchisors?* In order to investigate or draw any conclusions with respect to this extremely broad question, three specific questions on the effects of purchase requirements should be explored: (1) Do franchisees who are required to purchase supplies from their franchisors have lower incomes than other franchisees? (2) Are franchisees who are required to purchase a large proportion of their supplies from the franchisor less satisfied with the franchise relationship than franchisees who must purchase only a small proportion of their supplies from their franchisors? (3) Are franchisees who are charged high prices by their franchisors less satisfied with the franchise relationship than franchisees who are charged low prices? These issues were approached in the questionnaire by asking the franchisee: (1) what his family income was from his franchised business before taxes, (2) whether he planned to renew his franchise agreement when it expired, and (3) how satisfied he was with the profitability of his franchised business up to this time.

Using an F test, it was determined that franchisees required to purchase supplies from their franchisors had significantly lower incomes than franchisees not required to purchase supplies from their franchisors. As used in this study, franchisee income included profit plus owner's salary and any salaries paid to spouse and unmarried children.

The results, as reported in Table 2, also indicate that the proportion of supplies franchisees were required to purchase from their franchisors was negatively related to both measures of franchisee satisfaction. Franchisees who did not plan to renew their franchises were required to purchase a significantly higher percentage of their supplies from their franchisors than franchisees who planned to renew their franchises. Likewise, franchisees who were very dissatisfied with the profitability of their franchised business were required to purchase a high percentage of their supplies from the franchisor, while franchisees who were very satisfied with the profitability of their franchises purchased a smaller proportion from their franchisors.

The results in Table 2 also indicate that the prices franchisees paid for supplies were negatively related to both measures of franchisee satisfaction. Franchisees who did not plan to renew their franchises reported paying higher prices to their franchisors for supplies than fran-

TABLE 2   Franchisee Satisfaction as a Function of Two Franchisor Supply Practices

Measures of Satisfaction	Proportion of Supplies Required [a]	Prices Paid for Supplies [b]
Plans to Renew Franchise		
1. If no	43.2%	3.8
2. If yes	29.8	3.3
Satisfaction with Franchise Profitability		
1. Very dissatisfied	48.9	3.9
2. Dissatisfied	42.4	3.6
3. Neither satisfied nor dissatisfied	42.1	3.3
4. Satisfied	31.6	3.3
5. Very satisfied	12.1	3.2

[a] Mean responses are reported in percents.

[b] Mean responses are reported. "Prices paid for supplies" was measured using the five-point scale shown in Table 1, where higher scale values indicate higher prices.

Note: All the relationships depicted in this table were found statistically significant at the .001 level by Kruskal-Wallis H tests.

chisees who did plan to renew their franchises. Franchisees who indicated dissatisfaction with the profitability of the franchise also reported paying higher prices to their franchisors for supplies than franchisees who indicated satisfaction with the profitability of their franchises.

SUMMARY, CONCLUSIONS, AND RECOMMENDATIONS

The numerous complaints charging franchisors with involvement in tying arrangements suggest that the practice is quite widespread. In the study of fast-food franchises reported here, approximately 70% of the respondents indicated that they were required to purchase at least some of their supplies from the franchisor. Of those franchisees who were required to purchase from the franchisor, the median percentage of total operating supplies involved was 50%.

Proponents of franchising justify tying agreements on the basis of mass purchasing and quality control. Critics of franchising, in contrast, allege that franchisors are charging franchisees exorbitant prices for supplies. The results of this study show that, as perceived by franchisees, some franchisors do, in fact, pass along bargain prices on supplies due to volume purchasing discounts. However, many more franchises perceived their franchisors to be charging prices that were higher than competitive market prices.

When franchisors use tying agreements as a means to extract higher than competitive market prices, tying agreements may have deleterious effects on the franchisee's income and his satisfaction with the franchise relationship. The results reported here showed that franchisees who were required to purchase supplies from their franchisors had lower incomes than franchisees who were not required to purchase supplies from their franchisors. The results also showed that franchisees who were required to purchase a greater proportion of supplies from their franchisors and were charged higher prices by franchisors for supplies were less satisfied with the franchise relationship.

The preceding discussion strongly suggests that the widespread practice of tying agreements has deleterious effects on the franchise system of distribution. Franchisors obviously have a vested interest in the health of the franchise system and, therefore, should reconsider their policies of using tying agreements to surreptitiously generate revenue from their franchisees. Franchisors who are currently using tying agreements to generate the revenue needed to maintain their franchise programs should consider offering their franchisees new agreements with provisions that reflect an adequate royalty and a less restrictive supply program. With respect to franchisees who reject the new contract, franchisors legally may be able to continue to impose the purchase requirements. Several franchisors have successfully converted the majority of their franchisees to royalty contracts, and these companies do continue to collect income from nonroyalty franchisees in the form of surcharges on certain supplies.[26] Efforts by franchisors to correct the problems associated with tying arrangements in franchising may forestall onerous, restrictive legislation and regulation, slow down the flood of litigation, and strengthen the franchising system of distribution.

QUESTIONS FOR DISCUSSION

1. Explain the use of tying contracts in the franchising industry.

2. Discuss the basic legal aspects of tying contracts.

3. How prevalent are tying contracts in the franchising industry?

4. Present an argument in *favor* of tying contracts in franchising.

5. Present an argument *against* tying contracts in franchising.

26. *Franchising and Antitrust*, Sixth Annual Legal and Government Affairs Symposium (Washington, D.C.: International Franchise Association, 1973), p. 14.

Chapter 8

International Channels

AMERICAN BUSINESS EXECUTIVES are becoming increasingly aware of the tremendous markets available to them in foreign countries. Half of Caterpillar Tractors' 1975 sales of $4.6 billion involved foreign sales; IBM had revenues of $13.7 billion in 1975, with 47 percent from foreign customers; and Minnesota Mining and Manufacturing secured 40.5 percent of its $3.2 billion in sales from foreign accounts.

The purpose of this chapter is to acquaint the reader with some of the channel differences that are found in foreign markets. No attempt is made to present a comprehensive discussion of foreign channels. Instead, the articles selected indicate sufficient differences in foreign channel systems so that the reader will appreciate the need to give special emphasis and study to this aspect of international marketing.

An example of the channel differences is illustrated by J. C. Penney's expansion into Italy. Penney secured the assistance of the Brustio family, a noted Italian retailing family. Thus, *Business Week* noted, ". . . Penney needs the help of experiencd Italian merchandisers such as the Brustios to thread its way past the obstacles to a major new retailing venture in Italy."[1]

Other firms, such as Colgate-Palmolive, are actively attempting to initiate new strategies designed to increase their product acceptance in foreign countries. Bill Dorn of CP states, "In Denmark, for instance, we have one-third of the pet food market through a joint venture with a company there; and another joint venture in Germany has us marketing Gard hair products to growing acceptance. The thinking no longer is U.S. market vs. international market; now we consider the U.S. just one of all our markets."[2]

The lead article in this chapter by Professor Hollander outlines the activities of American retailers in foreign countries. It is followed by a selection discussing public policies toward retailing around the world.

1. "J. C. Penney Italian-Style," *Business Week* (January 10, 1970), p. 50.
2. "Why Colgate Sells Other People's Products," *Business Week* (April 20, 1974), p. 111.

Professors Boddewyn and Hollander note that few countries even approximate a stated public policy toward the retailing sector.

The next three selections present a comprehensive channel analysis of an important U.S. trading partner—Japan. "Cumbersome" is the first word in the title of the lead article analyzing the Japanese distribution system. The next article from *Fortune* builds on the first by examining the complexity of Japanese channel activity. The article demonstrates the reasons why many observers agree that the Japanese system is an excellent example of "how *not* to do it." The selection by Professor Weigand presents a discussion of the techniques used by Japanese manufacturers to maintain control over the long marketing channels that are typical in their country.

The final article in this chapter examines the successes and failures experienced by the McDonalds Corporation when expanding into the European market. An interesting aspect of this article is the impact of cultural differences in Europe on fast-food resturants.

8.1 THE INTERNATIONAL RETAILERS

Stanley C. Hollander

"The major problem, aside from difficulties in executive recruitment and development, is the danger of competitive and nationalistic resentment and reprisal."

It is difficult to decide which is more interesting: the international retailing that doesn't exist or the international retailing that is in actual operation.

On the one hand, the functions of retailing—the job of assembling merchandise and putting it on display for customer selection—would seem to be highly similar from country to country. Consequently one might expect that the strongest and most able merchants would have easily spread across national boundaries and garnered enormous shares of the world's retail market. Yet even today, in spite of all modern improvements in transportation and communication, foreign-owned or foreign-affiliated retailers normally handle only a small percentage of the total sales in most monetized nations. The resistances to internationalization, including some skilled firms' lack of interest in foreign growth, have sharply curtailed cosmopolitanism in retail trade. (Resident members of certain ethnic groups do handle much of the retail trade in some developing countries—the roles of Chinese and East Indian groups in much of Africa, the South Pacific and Southeast Asia are well known— but regardless of what some ardent nationalists might say, that is not international retailing as you and I understand the term).

On the other hand, truly international retail organizations are more numerous, more varied, more significant and enjoy a longer history than is generally assumed. In spring 1969, I completed a descriptive study of some of the firms and organizations engaged in "transferring retail techniques, management skills, buying power, and/or investment across national boundaries."[1] My inventory, incomplete as it probably was, included the following types of international retailing efforts.[2]

Reprinted by permission from Stanley C. Hollander, "The International Retailers," *Relevance in Marketing: Problems, Research, Action* edited by Fred C. Allvine (Chicago: American Marketing Association, 1972), pp. 271–274.

1. Published as *Multinational Retailing*. East Lansing: Institute of International Business and Economic Development Studies, Michigan State University, 1970.
2. These categories are neither completely parallel, discrete nor exhaustive, but

I

FOREIGN-OWNED RETAILING

A

Retail businesses conducted as auxiliaries to non-retailing business endeavors.

1.   Commissaries intended for fellow-resident expatriates, including military post exchanges and canteens for civilian executives at remote foreign establishments. Although foreign in location, these outlets are essentially extensions of the sponsor's nationality in spirit, purpose and clientele.

2.   Foreign manufacturers' "showcase" or demonstration stores, designed primarily to impress local retailers and to teach them how the lines should be displayed.

3.   Trading company establishments in the less developed countries where the firm may have to sell at retail to provide incentives for its commodity suppliers. Over time such retail businesses tend to become separated from commodity procurement and may take on new importance in their own right. United Africa Company's Nigerian retail ventures, including the Kingsway department store group, provide a good illustration of this tendency.

B

Retail businesses conducted in hopes of retail profit-making. This category seems to include representatives of almost every type of retailing, whether classified on the basis of operation method, merchandise lines, price level, or degree of vertical backward integration.

1.   Operating method. The international retail firms include:
    a. Mail order firms, such as Quelle and Neckermann (German), La Redoute (French) and Littlewoods (British), with foreign subsidiaries.
    b. In-home selling plans, exemplified on world-wide scales by Singer, Avon and Tupperware.
    c. Store operation, naturally the most common type of international as well as domestic retailing.

---

they do suggest some of the prime motives for internationalization in retailing, some of the organizations that experience those motivations, and some of the ways in which they respond.

d. Automatic vending. Although some of the major U.S. vending companies have experienced difficulties in expanding their own operations beyond the U.S. and Canada, at least one international firm, Eurovend, has been established in Europe.

2. Various merchandise lines, including
a. Firms with very general merchandise assortments, such as department stores (Sears Roebuck, Great Universal Stores), discount department stores and hypermarkets (K-Mart, Woolco, Jewel, Carrefour), junior department and variety stores (Penney, Prisunic, EPA), and supermarkets (Safeway, Weston).
b. More specialized firms in such varied fields as clothing (C. & A. Brenninkmeyer, Montague Burton, Etam), infantswear and supplies (Prenatal-Mothercare), pharmacy (Walgreen), wines and liquors (International Distillers & Vintners, Ltd), garden supplies (Wickes), newspapers and magazines (W. H. Smith & Sons), and, to a very surprising degrees, shoes (Salamander, Bally, Bata, Andre).
c. Nonmerchandise, or service, firms closely resembling the retail trade, such as beauty parlors (Glemby, Seligman & Latz), shoes repair (Industrial and Merchandising Services), and TV rentals (Granada).

3. Various price levels. Some of the types cited above, especially the discount and variety outlets, use mass merchandising pricing policies. But internationalization can be, and often, is a positive marketing asset in such luxury trades as jewelry, high-style clothing, and art dealerships.

4. Varying degrees of vertical integration. Some firms use their foreign retail branches to sell goods that they themselves manufacture in their homeland; some establish indigenous factories to supply the foreign stores; some devote themselves to reselling imported or domestically purchased goods; and some pursue combinations of these three possibilities.

II

Quasi-integrated, Contractual and Agency Relationships.

A

Franchising: Automobile manufacturers, petroleum refiners, soft drink syrup firms, and some appliance manufacturers have used world-wide franchising techniques for quite some time. International franchising also plays a part in marketing high-style clothing and accessories through the emergence of designer-licensed boutiques, such as Cardin's and St. Laurent's Rive Gauche. The newer fast food and service trade franchisors have not made as much international progress, although several are now represented abroad and many plan substantial expansion during the next five years.[3]

B

International voluntary chains, such as Spar and VeGe, have become major factors in European food retailing. Although the voluntary system is most pronounced in food marketing, Catena and Jarnia are significant hardware voluntary chains, Euro-Seldis is a major international textile organization, and some of the new hypermarket discount firms are licensing affiliates under a type of franchising-voluntary chain arrangement.

C

International cooperative chains, buying pools and groups, including the highly successful Nordisk Andelsforbund combined purchasing agency for the Scandinavian consumer cooperative societies and some of their other European and British counterparts, as well as a number of joint buying agreements in the private sector.

D

Resident buying offices serving foreign merchants.

III

A wide variety of governmental, nonprofit, and private consultancy and advisory services, international trade associations and information exchanges, and development assistance efforts. At least two foreign retail ventures, the International Basic Economy Corp. supermarkets in Latin America and the Migros-Turk markets in Istanbul were established primarily to demonstrate "what can be done."

Even a cursory examination of the trade press suggests that North American, British and European retailers have become even more internationalized since that inventory was completed two years ago. But in-

3. "Franchising," *Marketing in Europe*, Annual Supplement 1970, pp. 27–38 at pp. 34–36.

ternational retailing remains diverse and varied, and not susceptible to easy generalization. Nevertheless, a few observations can be made concerning problems and policies—the subject of this afternoon's meeting.

A firm establishing foreign retail outlets may strive for competitive advantage through differentiated merchandise, differentiated retail services, or a combination of the two. The firms that introduce new retailing techniques may be more interesting and may have more profound effects upon domestic marketing systems. But historically, and even currently, a very substantial part of international retailing has a product-oriented base. Manufacturing-retailers, commissaries, trading company outlets, luxury goods importers, and some buying combines and franchise arrangements often depend upon the ability to supply goods that are at least somewhat different from competitive offerings. Many of the firms that introduce new retailing techniques, for example the direct selling firms, also tend to have private merchandise lines that are not exactly reproducible. The retail outlets that are tied to particular producers or products may reproduce their supplier's life cycle; they will at least usually share the supplier's misfortunes even if they do not participate in all his good fortunes.

A life cycle pattern, somewhat analogous to the product life-cycle, may also be characteristic of attempts to introduce distinctive retailing services. Much more intensive research is needed to define the pattern and all of its variations, but at least some characteristic phases and problems can be isolated.

THE INTRODUCTORY PHASE

A few high-style or novelty ventures seem to win acceptance almost immediately upon being introduced into a new national market. Such acceptance often rests upon an extremely fickle base, and thus can involve the danger of an equally rapid decline. But the introductory phase is usually long and arduous. Firms that have had little experience in entering new countries generally underestimate the time, effort and managerial attention required to place a foreign retail division on the road to success.

Determination of the appropriate merchandise and service mixes almost always requires a certain amount of trial and error—usually many errors and many trials. Personnel recruitment can be a problem, yet excessive reliance upon home-country expatriates is both prohibitively expensive and politically unwise.

Appraisal of competitive and market conditions is often difficult. Foreign retailers seem especially prone to errors in site selection, even in neighboring and supposedly familiar countries. The joint venture approach will ease some of these difficulties, but it presents problems of its own.

Attempts to introduce mass-marketing or so-called "modern" retailing into the LDC.'s involves another peculiar problem. These institutions usually cannot draw, at least initially, upon the same socioeconomic segments that they appeal to at home. Instead they must try to attract upper income customers and then perhaps trickle down the income pyramid. The upper income customers, on the other hand, often delegate shopping to servants who characteristically prefer the sociability and financial rewards of patronizing indigenous full-service establishments. The new retailer may have to offer a wide range of labor intensive services to attract his best potential clientele in the face of their normal reliance upon servants, or he may have to hunt for rare groups of progressive middle-class consumers.

ACCEPTANCE AND GROWTH

It seems tautological to say that growth is necessary for successful foreign retailing, but it does point up a basic economy of scale. A single foreign branch in a given country may be satisfactory if the establishment is intended as an instrument of some more basic policy; e.g. a manufacturer's "showcase" store designed to demonstrate ways of displaying the product, or a London or Paris branch intended to add a little international glamor to the domestic operation. A single foreign unit may also be satisfactory for a small, family-owned specialty business when most of the family members want to remain at home while one or two migrate, permanently or temporarily, to another country. Most large-scale international firms, however, require a number of branches per country to support the management overhead and to provide satisfactory economies of scale.

Organizational controls usually run directly from international headquarters to each national subsidiary. Each national subsidiary is likely to be a discrete career and promotional ladder, and often experts and general manager sent out from the homeland constitute the only international personnel transfers. Tariff barriers, time and cost considerations, and market differences inhibit inter-country merchandise transfers. Consequently each national subsidiary often becomes an entity, and the economies of scale relate more to the number of stores within a country than to the total number of countries entered.

Nevertheless, the growth period can be an exhilarating one. The economies of scale do emerge, and customer acceptance can exhibit bandwagon effects as the new retailing organization wins increasing favor.

The major problem, aside from difficulties in executive recruitment and development, is the danger of competitive and nationalistic resentment and reprisal. Sometimes the mere announcement of planned entry is enough to trigger protest and political action; if the firm successfully overcomes or avoids that crisis, the growth period constitutes the next danger point.

The international retailer often must rely upon his uniqueness to draw customers. Yet a low profile may be necessary to avert nationalistic attacks. The high-style store and the luxury boutique may profitably proclaim their foreign origin, not so the large-scale retailer. Even though he conducts his business with foreign techniques, he may wisely refrain from any public emphasis upon his foreign connections.

MATURATION

International retailing is subject to all of the dangers of maturation in any other business plus one additional hazard. Many international retailing firms are suprisingly centralized in control and administration. This high degree of internal integration helps in exporting the firm's unique techniques, facilitates home office procurement for the foreign branches, permits easy transfer of home-trained personnel to the overseas branches, and maintains consistency throughout the operation. But it also hinders local adjustment and adaptation. This may not be a serious problem during the growth state, when the firm's methods are unusual and desired in the host country. Sooner or later, however, indigenous merchants who understand the local market better than the foreigner are likely to copy its techniques. In such instances, the local firms, wise in the ways of the market, are likely to beat the foreign organization at its own game.

In spite of this danger and all of the other problems, an increasing number of international retailers are currently successfully crossing national boundaries, are earning profits in the process, and are enhancing the competitive structures of the countries they enter. On balance, international retailing seems to be both a salutary and a growing phenomenon.

QUESTIONS FOR DISCUSSION

1. a. In what types of retailing have international operations been most successful in recent years?
   b. Why have these areas been more rewarding than others?

2. The author mentioned a life-cycle pattern for international retailing. What is this concept? Do you believe it will be a valid thesis in the next decade? Defend your answer.

3. Identify the major problems that a successful retailer is likely to experience in expanding into foreign countries.

4. Professor Hollander has stated, "international retailing is subject to all the dangers of maturation in any other business plus one additional hazard." Discuss this statement fully.

8.2 PUBLIC POLICIES TOWARD RETAILING AROUND THE WORLD

J. Boddewyn and S. C. Hollander

*"Politically, small retailers frequently represent
a sizeable pressure group which various parties
like to placate if not favor. Besides, kicking
out the foreigners is popular in many underdeveloped
countries."*

Few countries even approximate a public policy toward retailing, but many more have a set of policies which deal with critical components of this socio-economic function, and/or which affect it significantly in the context of other public objectives, such as the protection of small businessmen and consumers and the improvement of competitive conditions.

FACTORS

Considering the importance of retailing in terms of employment and value added and of its impact on sundry economic and social goals, this lack of an explicit, complete, and coherent public policy toward retailing may seem strange, particularly considering the existence of agricultural and industrial policies in many nations. The explanation of this situation boils down to: (1) the long association of economic growth with industry rather than trade; (2) the assumption that distribution will automatically adjust to greater industrial outputs and consumer demands; and (3) an essentially parasitic view of commerce associated with consumer exploitation and the wasteful use of economic resources.[1]

This neglect is being slowly corrected, however, on account of a va-

Reprinted by permission from the authors and publisher. J. Boddewyn and S. C. Hollander, "Public Policies Toward Retailing Around the World," in Thomas V. Greer, ed., *Increasing Marketing Productivity*, American Marketing Association 1973 Proceedings (Chicago: 1974), pp. 83–86.

1. Fuller analysis of these arguments can be found in the literature on "marketing and economic development" and in J. Boddewyn, "Marketing in Economy and Society: Theory and Public Policy," in George Fisk, ed., *New Essays in Marketing Theory* (Boston, Mass: Allyn & Bacon, 1971), pp. 409–421.

riety of factors. *Economically*, retailing partakes of the tertiary sector which is absolutely and relatively growing in most countries, and thus receives more attention from the authorities on account of the calls it makes on various resources, and of its implications for employment, price stability, and productivity. More generally, affluence and high levels of economic development have been associated with greater tolerance of retailing innovations, and with the allocation of public resources to compensate for the socio-economic dislocations these innovations create.

Socially, consumers are receiving more attention as they demand more, better, and cheaper goods; and as they need more protection against distributors and manufacturers but also against their own unbridled appetites (the regulation of credit sales typically exhibits both motives). This situation leads to greater regulation of retailing. Outside of socialist countries, there is also concern about protecting small businessmen against the large modern forms of distribution; while the new nations of Africa and Asia want to make room for a native class of traders in lieu of the expatriates that have dominated the field.

On the *physical side*, spreading urbanization demands new retail facilities; while suburbanization threatens older shopping areas and makes demand on the land, thus leading to greater physical planning of land-use—a growing phenomenon in any case. Pollution problems also generate the regulation of containers and their return.

Politically, small retailers frequently represent a sizeable and significant pressure group which various parties like to placate if not favor (for example, voting Communist is not at all exceptional in France and Italy). Besides, kicking out the foreigners is popular in many underdeveloped countries. The growing role and spread of governments also bring them increasingly into the retail scene, either as regulators, owners (e.g., in Italy), or as sponsors of various cooperative schemes (Latin America). Foreign influences are important here as they disclose new problems and solutions; as they create precedents (e.g., for nationalization); as they serve as reference points (e.g., Great Britain for Australia); and as supranational institutions (e.g., EEC, OECD, FOA, WHO) and agreements (e.g., on trademarks) contribute to the harmonization of some regulations.

Internal factors also affect the development of public policy toward retailing as the emergence of new retailing types, kinds, and practices create tensions within the system as well as demands (often successful) for regulatory restrictions and/or compensating public assistance. The competition for trade and favors thus remains active between small and large stores, between full-time and part-time (marginal) retailers, between sedentary and itinerant traders (including the newer mail-order

houses, vending machines, and house-parties), between large-scale retailers and large-scale manufacturers, and between traditional and innovative merchants of all stripes. All of these factors contribute to the
new interest in developing public policies toward the retail trade.

OBJECTIVES

PROTECTING SMALL RETAILERS

In developed countries, the drive for protection has been strongest during periods of depression, such as the 1930's in Europe and North America, when the retailing middle class felt threatened and saw no avenues
of escape into other employment. On the other hand, the pressure for
such protection diminishes during periods of business expansion and
manpower shortages, as exemplified by the post-World War II relaxation
of trade-restrictive legislation in these two geographical areas. To some
extent, the desire for "nativization" of retail trade in many of the developing countries is another illustration of efforts to protect small
traders, but it also flows from ethnic and nationalistic motivations.

To protect small tradesmen, governments have: (1) restricted the
expansion of large and marginal stores (e.g., through discriminatory
taxes, limited opening hours, and anti-price-discrimination legislation);
and (2) helped smaller stores survive and/or expand (e.g., through
subsidized educational programs, low-cost credit, and the encouragement of voluntary chains). In the new countries of Africa and Asia, this
protection has often taken the form of expelling foreign retail minorities
that have traditionally dominated the field.

IMPROVING RETAILING'S EFFICIENCY

This goal often reflects the need to remove obstacles to the growth of
other sectors such as agriculture and manufacturing by releasing manpower and/or by providing low-cost and effective channels of distribution to these sectors. Still, retailing is also increasingly being considered
as a sector whose own efficiency is worthy of special attention on account
of the fast-rising cost of distribution. Communist countries have been
particularly anxious to increase the efficiency of retailing through input
minimization rather than output maximization even though not always
willing to make the necessary investments.

Governments here have encouraged new, more efficient and competitive retail forms, often of a larger size; and/or they have tried to raise the

productivity of existing organizations through better people, methods, and structures (e.g., more qualified employees and owner-managers; self-service; voluntary chains). The authorities are increasingly willing to bear the expenses involved in the second approach since the latter can be fairly readily reconciled with the goal of protecting small retailers. Hence, follows the growth of subsidized credit and educational programs, licensure, and the encouragement of associational endeavors.

STABILIZING RETAIL PRICES

Price stabilization objectives vary in importance in direct relationship to the severity of economic changes. This objective normally becomes paramount when prices are unusually depressed or unusually inflated.

Inflation has long been rampant in underdeveloped countries, but it is a recurrent problem in more advanced economies although Communist countries have been much better able to prevent it through their comprehensive management of the economy. Price controls are thus becoming more prevalent, although competition is also being encouraged to achieve price stability (witness the decreasing public support of resale price maintenance and of various forms of collusion).

CONSUMER PROTECTION

Commercial codes generally include provisions against fraud and deception, but an increasing demand is being voiced for expanded consumer protection. In some instances, public policy has singled out certain types of retailers as being particularly prone to untoward practices—at least this is often the avowed rationale for measures aimed at auctions, itinerant vendors, house-to-house canvassers, and other marginal dealers. More often, however, consumeristic measures are directed against practices considered inimical to consumer welfare. Hence the development of regulations concerned with labeling, weights and measures, consumer credit, price posting, "truth in advertising," liquidations, special sales, etc. In the light of current experience, it is tempting to associate consumer protection with prosperity since consumeristic issues tend to come to the fore when prosperity-induced expectations outrun the benefits that the system actually delivers.

PROTECTING THE ENVIRONMENT

The ecological-environmental considerations which are just beginning to influence retailing regulation (land-use planning, waste disposal rules, product limitation, etc.) in the more prosperous countries are, at least so far, clearly correlated with affluence. On the other hand, the less developed countries have generally felt that ecological problems are primarily artifacts of overabundance and should rank low on the scale of national priorities.

INSTRUMENTS AND MEASURES

FROM CONTRACT TO REGULATION AND STATUS

The nineteenth century emphasis on protecting the freedom of individual wills as expressed in contracts and as interpreted in the light of customs has been progressively superseded by imperative rules which limit the wills of individuals and do even upset business customs. First, various measures *forbade* fraudulent and unhealthy practices, and obliged the guilty party to repair or compensate for the harm done. Now, the tendency is toward *preventing* such harm by requiring the advance testing of products and validation of advertising claims; and toward *extending control beyond the transaction* (e.g., by allowing the consumer to change his mind) and *over the life of a product* in such matters as warranties.

One observes also a certain historical tendency to restrict the practice of retailing to certain people and groups, and to recognize certain rights to particular categories, instead of letting individuals or parties decide freely. Of course, minors, criminals, bankrupts, mental incompetents, and even women, have usually been restricted; while natives, invalids, and veterans have often received preferential access to certain occupations. Licensure, where it exists, stresses the right "inputs" (such as minimum education, experience, credit and equipment, but also one's parents' occupation) rather than "output." While licensure is not spreading very fast, special credit assistance (e.g., low-interest loans) is often limited to certain types of retailers considered worthy of protection or promotion.

Such measures affect particularly entry and growth, but also process and structure as the law now tends to favor buyers (particularly the ultimate customers) over sellers, tenants over landlords, licensees over licensors, and debtors over creditors. The trends are both toward protecting vested rights, and those of the party considered weaker. There is also a tendency toward defining certain practices as "unfair" to the interest of *particular* categories of suppliers, competitors and customers, rather than focusing on a broader concern for the general *interest*.

GREATER VARIETY AND PERVASIVENESS OF REGULATIONS

Governments no longer limit themselves to setting the *general rules* of the game, but have developed many measures of control over most marketing activities—from relations with suppliers, landlords and licensors to pricing, product and promotion practices; and land-use planning promises to increase their number. While control is associated with prohibitions and restrictions, governments are also increasingly in a position to promote a certain sector (or part of it) and to encourage certain practices through various *monetary* measures where the granting of cheaper (or more abundant) credit figures prominently, although its refusal or withdrawal has also been used to affect retailing (e.g., in the matter of consumer credit). Besides, *fiscal* measures have been used against itinerant traders and chain stores; while the tax-on-value-added system is beginning to have some *structural* effect on retailing. Furthermore, *public expenditures* on commercial education, research, and statistics, and on the administration of these programs, are also more evident. Finally, there are now more *public and semi-public institutions* to group and represent retailers.

Such instruments have been translated into numerous measures of regulation, promotion, intervention, suasion, consultation, self-regulation, and contractual agreements with private parties. However, lack of action, threats of regulation, and delays in making or applying policy have also been used to further government objectives.

This growing pervasiveness of regulation and institutionalization is almost a perfect illustration of the principle that all the facets of marketing (price, product, promotion, and place-time) are interrelated and can be substituted for one another. Hence, public policy has to progressively blanket all retailing operations because otherwise ways can be found around the regulation found bothersome. Installment-sales legislation illustrates this point because to be effective, it has to deal with interest rates (price), goods and services covered (product), truth-in-lending (promotion), and—in some countries—the registration and/or limitation of lenders (place).

Yet, it would be erroneous to visualize the trend as being only away from laissez-faire and toward complete state interventionism—all the way to the Russian type. As a matter of fact, governments are often delegating some regulatory powers to professional associations, chambers of commerce, and businessmen's tribunals considered better equipped to determine what is "fair" and "unfair." This trend reveals the growing complexity of economic life which sets limits to what the state can achieve. It also demonstrates the increasing demand for participation in the making and application of policies. Corporativist tendencies are thus more evident nowadays—particularly outside of the United States and the socialist countries.

Besides, programs of consumer education and small-business credit reveal that state intervention is not exclusively couched in restrictive terms. Moreover, regulation helps retailing when it clarifies the status of certain types and practices in statutory-law countries where these types and practices (e.g., supermarkets in Brazil and franchising in Belgium) would otherwise remain unused for lack of clear legal standing.

GREATER REGULATORY FLEXIBILITY AND DISCRETION

The growth of regulation can easily be interpreted as meaning greater rigidity in public policy. However, this trend is not as obvious as it may appear. For one thing, measures get changed and adapted as when "Weekly closing" replaces "Sunday closing." Besides, the authorities are aware of the growing need for flexibility on account of frequent changes in retailing. Moreover, policy now extends its reach to more complex problems (e.g., land-use planning) that do not present any easy or permanent solution. Such a situation demands more flexible legislation than can be applied through decrees according to the current situation and without resorting to the lengthier legislative process. This development leads to more discretionary powers for the executive and judiciary bodies who apply laws through decrees and court decisions but also through administrative rulings and "bargained solutions" with private firms or trade associations. The outcome is, of course, much more indeterminate as it depends on the judgment and respective powers of the parties—not to mention venality—but change and complexity seem to dictate this course which can and should be guarded with more appeal procedures.

RESULTS AND PROSPECTS

1. In the short or medium run, the policy of *protecting small retailers* has usually succeeded in slowing down retail innovations. However, in the long run, economic and other factors have usually nullified or greatly reduced its effectiveness. Public policy can thus only retard or postpone the evolution of retailing.

2. Improving the *efficiency of retailing* has been a more recent and sporadic goal; and it has proved rather complex and slow to achieve even under central-planning conditions. In general, the furthering of such economic goals must be constantly reconciled with that of

maintaining social equilibrium; and this slows down the process
of economic development while raising its cost.

3. *Stable retail prices* are easier to achieve in socialist economies
than in more liberal ones since price controls (against undue rises)
are fairly effective in the short run but cannot fundamentally alter
demand and supply conditions in the long run. On the other hand,
the ultimate aim of price stabilization in periods of stagnation and/or
of rapid innovations (e.g., discount houses) has usually been one
of protecting small and traditional retailers under the guise of
"fair trade."

4. *Protecting consumers* is the oldest goal of public policy toward
retailing, and it finds applications both in periods of stagnation and
of rapid change. However, the enforcement and effectiveness of
measures in this area have waxed and waned because this objective
has not benefited from the pressures of a strong consumer movement until recently. On the other hand, consumers have benefited
from the pursuit of other goals such as price stability and increased
efficiency.

5. It is too early to appraise *protection of the environment* but
the latter is bound to reduce consumer convenience and/or to
increase the cost of retailing.

6. Finally, *one should not overemphasize the role of public policy*
because many changes in retailing actors, processes, structures, and
functions have succeeded or failed in the absence of any policy
addressed to them, or even irrespective to it (e.g., discount houses in
Brazil, or trading stamps in the United States). Similarly, general
policies designed to insure a reasonably prosperous and orderly
economy have probably achieved more for retailing than any specific
public policy addressed to it, since many problems take care of
themselves when business is good.

PROSPECTS AND IDEALS

Partial and indirect approaches to the problems and opportunities associated with retailing are likely to remain the norm around the world
until some critical mass is reached, and a full-fledged policy is felt
needed and considered possible. For that matter, it is not yet proven
that a separate policy toward retailing is completely desirable, although
it would obviously give greater attention and visibility to this sector and
insure better harmonization with other policies and sectors. The dangers
of such a separate policy lie in: (1) considering retailing as an end
rather than as a means toward the achievement of more primary economic and social goals; and (2) getting more than one bargained for

as the history of retail regulations has often been a recital of stubborn and hard-to-remove barriers against progress. On the other hand, there is agreement that governments should support the development of information so that their policies may be better framed and implemented.

Ultimately, any resulting public policy toward retailing should be guided by the following principles:

1. It should not only be negative in its emphasis on combatting abuses, but also recognize and encourage the *positive* aspects and contributions of retailing—a much needed emphasis in many countries.

2. Policy should be *non-discriminatory*, and support all forms of retailing that contribute to current economic and social goals: small as well as large firms; old and new; foreign and domestic; existing and potential. Special assistance here should be largely limited to help the laggard firms catch up with their times.

3. Policy should be *flexible* in order to accommodate changing situations, and this may well require supple grants of power to the executive government in lieu of rigid and hard-to-amend laws.

4. Finally, policy should be *limited* according to the principle of "As little as possible, as much as necessary." Essentially, this means: (1) banning or restricting practices that are clearly harmful and/or fraudulent; (2) leaving the main regulatory role to competition and self-regulation (watched by the State, of course); and (3) providing social measures to alleviate the human costs of economic evolution so as to take care of those "condemned to progress."

QUESTIONS FOR DISCUSSION

1. Discuss in general terms some of the major aspects of public policy toward retailing in foreign countries.

2. Discuss *why* many countries believe that the retailing sector is sufficiently important to encourage it to become more efficient.

3. When government policy does exist for the retailing sector of the economy, what *objectives* are typically sought?

4. Do you believe more or less governmental control will assist the retailing sector of foreign countries in becoming more efficient? Defend your answer.

5. The authors suggest that a country's public policy toward retailing should be guided by four general policies. Identify and explain each of these policies.

8.3 CUMBERSOME JAPANESE DISTRIBUTION SYSTEM STUMPS U.S. CONCERNS

William D. Hartley

> *"Those who have encountered the Japanese system say it may well rank as the most inefficient, most complex, and most costly of any in the industrialized world, a lesson in how not to do it."*

Consider a can of Del Monte peach halves and its Japanese odyssey.

The peaches land in Yokohama at 26 cents a can. Immediately, customs and handling charges add nine cents to the price. Then the importer sticks on a bit more than a penny. He sells it to a wholesaler, who adds another three cents. The wholesaler sells it to another wholesaler, who adds a further two cents. He sells it to a grocery store, which adds an additional 11 cents.

The retail price: 52 cents a can—a far cry from the 30 cents or so the 15-ounce can might command in a suburban U.S. supermarket. So it's no surprise that in a typical Japanese city, some 90% of the imported canned peaches are sold wrapped as expensive gifts.

The peaches are victims of a phenomenon that is stumping many American businessmen there these days: the Japanese distribution system. Those who have encountered the Japanese system say it may well rank as the most inefficient, most complex and most costly of any in the industrialized world, a lesson in how not to do it. So many eager middlemen handle each item that wholesale volume runs about five times retail volume, one expert calculates. In the U.S., the comparable wholesale figure is only twice the retail volume.

STUBBORN ANACHRONISM

Thus, while Japan's well-publicized industrial efficiency grows and grows, its distribution system remains a strange and stubborn anachronism.

The system here affects a growing number of American companies trying to sell to the Japanese market. These companies figure that the

Reprinted by permission from the publisher. William D. Hartley, "Cumbersome Japanese Distribution System Stumps U.S. Concerns," *Wall Street Journal* (March 2, 1972), pp. 1, 12.

U.S. dollar devaluation and the upward revaluation of the Japanese yen will make American goods more competitive here. Moreover, Japan is gradually liberalizing its regulations to allow more imports. But companies are finding that many obstacles remain before imported goods can wend their way through the complex distribution system at a price Japanese consumers can afford.

The distribution system socks consumers heavily. While the wholesale price index in Japan remains remarkably steady, the consumer price level climbs sharply. "It reflects the cost of distribution," shrugs an official of the Ministry of International Trade and Industry. This problem particularly affects imported goods, which must naturally pass through even more distribution channels than competing domestic products.

The workings of the system sometimes stagger foreigners. One who imports art reproductions tried to sell directly to a department store. He was soon told he had to deal through a wholesaler who had an account with the store. So today, the wholesaler simply lends his name and gets a cut—which, of course, adds to the cost.

"It's an unwritten rule you don't sell to department stores; our distributor would take offense if we did," says Saul David Levy, senior executive president of Barclay & Co., a liquor and wine importer.

Playing by the rules, Levi Strauss & Co. of San Francisco, first sold blue jeans through 20 Japanese wholesalers. But these companies also carried competitive brands and Levis sometimes didn't get much display effort, says Edwin C. Gibson, the company's general manager here. With admitted trepidations, Levi Strauss finally recided to service retailers directly. Most agreed, but some still refuse to handle the goods because they haven't gone through channels, says Mr. Gibson.

"The stores aren't going to risk getting a bad relationship with a major supplier just to carry a relatively small brand," he says.

The rebate system can also mean trouble. In the United States, it is normal for the manufacturer to give a wholesaler a discount of about 2% for cash, says Gordon L. Wogsland, senior general manager of Morinaga General Mills Ltd., a joint venture of General Mills Inc. and a Japanese concern. But here, there are rebates for cash, rebates for volume, rebates for promotion and rebates for all kinds of other services, he says. In the case of a Morinaga General Mills corn snack called "Spins," rebates total between 13% and 15% of the manufacturer's price, Mr. Wogsland says.

A CHECKLESS SOCIETY

Besides all this, there's the legwork. "So many transactions are for cash in this nearly checkless society that you've got to go around and collect by hand, which is also expensive," says one management consultant.

Because very few retail outlets keep a back-shop inventory, resupply must be frequent—and therefore costly. Most of the shops must buy on credit, too. Says Mr. Levy, the liquor importer: "We get 60-days to 90-days promissory notes. The whole distribution economy is based on P-notes." Naturally, all this financing involves interest, which further boosts costs.

But costs aren't the only worry. Says Mr. Wogsland of Morinaga General Mills: "The problem is you are far away from your consumer when you have to go through so many levels." He says promotion is difficult because manufacturers often can't learn the results of a campaign for many months. Goods get lost in the cycle, too. "We're still getting back cake mix that we discontinued two years ago," sighs Mr. Wogsland.

A few companies try to buck the system. Coca-Cola Co.'s 16 bottlers in Japan created their own distribution network years ago; it sells directly to more than a million retail outlets. If successful, such moves can slash costs. Barclay & Co. "cut out some small people" in the distribution of Mogen David wine and could thus cut the retail price about $1 a bottle to $4.85, says the company's Mr. Levy.

But most foreign and Japanese companies alike figure they can't win and don't try to fight the system. "Most companies that come in here and buck the system come around to join it," says John Wiggins, executive vice president of Yamazaki Nabisco Co., a venture of National Biscuit Co. "If you come in here with an item and deliver it the way we do in the States, each stop would take in maybe $2 in goods, the truck would make 17 or 18 stops a day—and you'd be out of business," he adds.

The structure of Japanese retailing creates this problem. Japan has 1.5 million stores—about the same as the United States, which has twice the population and 25 times the land area. Outlets here are midget stores tucked away in tiny neighborhoods on narrow back streets. As no big wholesaler could hope to know them all, he sells to regional wholesalers who sell to neighborhood wholesalers. These, in turn, form tight, personal relationships with a few retail outlets.

Despite its immense size and appearance as a modern city, Tokyo is a collection of thousands of small villages. At least in shopping, these have little contact with each other.

"The average Japanese housewife shops every day within 500 yards of her home," says Fred Perry, an official of Audience Studies Inc., a market research firm owned by Columbia Pictures Industries Inc. She typically spends 1,000 yen ($3.25) each time, he adds. "You must have a great number of points of supply for this; it is the logistics of bits and pieces," says the official.

Historically, the complex system grew from the early development of Japanese villages, which commonly distrusted each other. "Neutral" middlemen were needed to sell goods from one village to the next. Then, as trading companies began to appear in the late 19th Century, they became so prominent in buying and selling that many manufacturing companies never bothered to develop sales arms. Moreover, Japan has very little vertical integration of industry to eliminate middlemen.

But there are glimmerings of change. Japan built its first "super-market" in 1958. Today the country has 9,000 of these outlets, and they handle nearly 9% of retail sales—twice the percentage in 1964.

Many of these markets deal directly with suppliers, and executives believe that supermarkets offer a major hope to beat the present system. But even the biggest markets here are far smaller than any American version. Change is slow.

QUESTIONS FOR DISCUSSION

1. Why is the Japanese distribution system so inefficient?

2. What is the typical outcome if someone tries to eliminate traditional middlemen from a marketing channel?

3. Why do you think the Coca-Cola Company is successful in selling directly to their retail customers?

4. What factors are at work that will probably make the Japanese system more efficient in coming years?

8.4 JAPAN IS OPENING UP FOR GAIJIN WHO KNOW HOW

Louis Kraar

"Aggressive, hard-selling techniques clash with the overwhelming Japanese concern for harmony. Though competition is fierce, there is a tacit understanding that no company will abruptly take away too much of a rival's share of a market."

From the flood of gloomy reports in American papers recently, U.S. businessmen might easily conclude that Japan's economy is tumbling into a crisis that will cripple opportunities for their companies in that promising market. But the impact of Arab oil cutbacks has been much exaggerated. The resilient economy has never been threatened with collapse. In fact, Japan has been receiving adequate energy supplies. Over the past few years a surprisingly wide range of U.S. companies have broken into the long-closed Japanese market, and nearly all of them are pushing ahead with expansion plans made before the Mideast erupted last fall.

U.S. executives on the scene plainly see rich prospects in Japan, though there are economic problems. The greatest is raging inflation. But one problem that used to be the most formidable—stubborn Japanese resistance to letting foreigners conduct business in their country —is rapidly receding.

The lopsided trade relationship that frustrated Americans for many years is no longer so lopsided. Not long ago, the Japanese were grabbing rich segments of the U.S. market (such as cameras, television sets, and compact cars), but American corporations couldn't gain equal access to Japan's consumers. Now that the country has opened its doors, many U.S. companies are making the most of it. A quarter of Coca-Cola's worldwide earnings flow from its subsidiary in Tokyo. And Brunswick Corp. receives 24 percent of its total net profits from a joint venture that sells bowling equipment in Japan.

"The Japanese market must be viewed as the largest overseas opportunity for U.S. business," says James Abegglen, president of the Boston Consulting Group, which advises corporate clients about how to sell in Japan. "Most of the old protectionist barriers are down, and the rest are fast disappearing."

TOWARD A WESTERN LIFE STYLE

Only in the last year and a half has the Japanese government, under relentless international pressure, eased the major restrictions against foreign enterprises. A voluntary 20 percent across-the-board tariff cut on manufactured items put Japan's import duties roughly on par with those in the U.S. and Europe. Import quotas on non-agricultural products were largely removed. And the government adopted a sweeping liberalization policy that allows foreign investment in nearly all industries. The few notable exceptions, such as computers and pharmaceuticals, will be opened before the end of 1976, according to a precise timetable.

Consumers in Japan, who have attained buying power comparable to those in Western Europe, are especially ready for U.S. goods. After long years of self-denial to speed economic growth, they want to improve the quality of their lives. The Japanese, in fact, are moving toward a life style somewhat closer to the Western pattern. They eat an increasingly varied diet, pursue leisure activities with frantic zest, and are spending huge sums to improve and replace their generally shabby, cramped housing.

A SPIDER WEB THAT RESISTS OUTSIDERS

But the key to Japan's locked market was the ability of some U.S. corporations to perceive that doing business there requires considerably different techniques than in any other country. Companies that have accepted the unique environment and adjusted to it are doing well. They point the way for others to follow if they have the wit and patience to learn. The main business obstacle, often underestimated in the past, is the clannishness of the Japanese. In this homogeneous, tight-knit society, foreigners are not only called *gaijin*—outsiders—but are instinctively treated as such. The Japanese business system resembles an intricate spider web of personal and financial relationships. It is inherently difficult, though not impossible, for an outsider to enter.

U.S. businessmen face a costly, multilayered distribution system, bound together by credit arrangements and friendships, which is very difficult to crack. Salesmen since feudal days have enjoyed little status;

even now they mainly take orders from wholesalers. Aggressive, hard-selling techniques clash with the overwhelming Japanese concern for harmony. Though competition is fierce, there is a tacit understanding that no company will abruptly take away too much of a rival's share of a market.

Ingrained corporate practices pose formidable difficulties. Japanese corporations recruit the best students right out of school, nurture them with paternalism and fat annual pay increases (20 percent last year), and keep them for life. As a result, foreign companies find it is so difficult to attract talented Japanese employees that few of them can operate independently. Though wholly foreign-owned ventures are now permitted in most fields, most companies find it necessary to take a Japanese partner.

SEARS MAKES A QUICK START

A new Sears, Roebuck venture illustrates the possibilities open to companies that adopt a deft approach. Without making any capital investment, the world's largest retailer offers virtually its entire U.S. line to Japanese consumers. The Seibu Group of Retail Enterprises, a family-controlled company with over $2 billion annual sales, serves as a sales agent on a commission basis. Already seventeen Seibu outlets have opened Sears mail-order centers. The Japanese have responded enthusiastically to the Sears way of merchandising and to Sears's prices. Though sales started only eight months ago, customers have snapped up 200,000 catalogues, and monthly volume in merchandise is about $1 million.

Sears owes its quick start mainly to the selection of an able local associate, which shares its aims. Seibu eagerly accepts the Sears policy of money-back guarantees on catalogue sales—far from the usual retailing practice in Japan. Robert Ingersoll, a Chicagoan and former business executive who helped arrange the Sears venture while he was Ambassador to Japan, points out: "They're really taking a market survey, and it will lead to much more later—even though Sears top management doesn't fully realize it yet."

COKE'S GIFT TO THE COMPETITION

Few foreign businesses have had more success in Japan than Coca-Cola —or had more troubles because of it. From the start in late 1957, the company avoided the cumbersome local distribution system. Instead, Coke followed its normal practice of franchising bottlers. They are controlled by powerful Japanese corporations, such as Mitsubishi and Mitsui, which have sufficient influence to defy the system and sell directly to dealers for cash.

But as sales skyrocketed toward their present 40 percent of the country's soft-drink market, disgruntled Japanese competitors counterattacked. Small local soft-drink bottlers charged that a "foreign invasion" was driving them into bankruptcy. The press widely publicized claims that large Coke bottles mysteriously exploded. Although the company says it has had no such complaints in any other country, it brought out new bottles reinforced with a double coat of epoxy resin. Even the Coke slogan—"It's the real thing"—was forbidden by Japan's Fair Trade Commission on grounds that it implied other drinks were somehow not genuine.

Finally Coca-Cola turned to what was widely regarded as the major source of its trouble. The company appointed a Japanese as president; he arranged payment of $550,000 to the protesting local bottlers as a conciliation gift, a traditional gesture. The moves have calmed criticism and protected the company's dominant market position.

A "SOFT TOUCH" THAT SELLS COPIERS

Xerox found an extraordinary way to bridge the gap between American business methods and Japanese culture. Its joint-venture partner, Fuji Photo Film, completely manages daily operations without a single Western senior executive or board member in residence. The solid local image has helped to attract bright, young employees who readily adopt —and adapt—Xerox sales techniques. The company has held the lion's share of an expanding market for copying machines, despite intense competition recently. In the past seven years, sales have grown an average of about 40 percent annually to $200 million last year, and net profits have generally approached 10 percent of sales.

Fuji Xerox thrives by blending aggressive Western marketing with subtle Oriental touches. Signing up rental customers poses special problems in a land that has habitually looked down upon salesmen. So senior management not only advises new recruits that selling is the path to rapid promotion, but also rewards the best performers with prestige titles. "It means something socially, so we call them managers—even if there aren't many people reporting to them," says Yotaro Kobayashi, managing director and general manager for marketing.

At Xerox's urging, the company bucked custom by providing personal monetary incentives to salesmen. The difficulty is that Japanese regard group effort as more important than individual accomplishment. Moreover, most employees feel insecure working on a commission basis. "Our feeling at the beginning was that this was really against the Japanese grain," say Kobayashi, "but we really wanted better results." So Fuji Xerox set sales goals as team objectives. Salesmen collect regular salaries and benefits, but teams that exceed targets receive extra payments in the bonuses given all personnel twice annually. The system works.

One innovative Japanese approach to customers succeeded so well that Xerox is trying it in other countries. Fuji Xerox created a completely new job category, the customer-service officer (C.S.O.), and filled it mainly with attractive women college graduates. They regularly visit offices that already have the rented machines and offer advice about their use. The "soft touch from an intelligent woman," as Kobayashi puts it, helps to retain contacts and persuade customers to convert to more profitable newer models. The C.S.O.'s proved especially resourceful in countering a wave of cancellations two years ago, when rival machines were offered at lower prices. Nowadays many of its customers call Fuji Xerox with requests to arrange marriages with C.S.O. women, for matchmaking is an enduring Japanese custom.

The U.S. company initially considered the C.S.O. system unnecessary. But as an American executive of Xerox explains: "We're smart enough to realize that there are lots of things about doing business in Japan that we really don't comprehend."

LEARNING TO LIVE WITH GROUP DECISION MAKING

The joint venture started in 1962 as a compromise, for Fuji wanted a straight licensing agreement and Xerox sought majority ownership. Each settled for 50 percent of the joint company. Fuji insisted on managing the venture, but its executives rely heavily on Xerox for advice and technology. Almost all the machines rented in Japan are manufactured locally. Major decisions, including introduction of new products and annual budgets, must be approved by a board on which both partners are equally represented; neither can act alone.

A major advantage of the setup is that Japanese employees and customers regard the corporation as one of their own. Fuji preserves such venerable practices as group decision making; a proposed policy or action plan is circulated among all connected with the problem and discussed until a consensus is reached. By Western standards, it is a lengthy process and often appears to dilute the authority of top executives. But Kobayashi maintains, "Any plan has to be backed up by those who carry it out. People tend to stay with a company here, so you don't want to make enemies of those you'll be working with for many years."

Fierce competition is putting the Xerox arrangement to a severe test. Ten rivals are wooing its customers with lower-priced copying machines.

This is a common tactic in Japan, where companies invest heavily to increase market share even at the sacrifice of immediate profits. Even though it is the industry leader, Fuji Xerox is vulnerable because rising operating costs and profit-consciousness rule out price cuts. So the company is responding in other ways that draw on resources of both joint-venture partners. For the first time, Japanese engineers are participating in the design of new products in the U.S. so that Fuji Xerox can introduce them simultaneously. Previously, there was a year or more of delay because American machines had to be adapted for the larger standard paper sizes used in Japan.

A LOSS OF FACE

By contrast, Caterpillar Tractor oversees its joint venture with a large team of Americans. The resulting clash of cultures has caused plenty of management problems. For the past ten years, Caterpillar has politely but firmly "advised" Japanese managers to do things its way—and often succeeded. Says a Caterpillar senior executive, "It's like working with independent U.S. dealers, who must be persuaded to do things but never forced." Half the company is owned by Mitsubishi Heavy Industries, which belongs to Japan's largest zaibatsu; it is known for strong-minded executives, too. Says one insider: "Mitsubishi people are very proud. When Caterpillar told them what to do, they felt a loss of face."

Initially, U.S. executives sharply questioned the relatively high salaries and fringe benefits of employees that Mitsubishi assigned to the joint venture from its other companies. But Caterpillar had to accept them. As startup costs mounted, it was Mitsubishi's turn to worry. Japanese companies plan ahead, but they don't make the highly detailed financial projections common in the U.S. Having carefully calculated the costs of building a huge plant outside Tokyo and establishing dealerships, Caterpillar expected a large cumulative deficit. Much to the consternation of Mitsubishi Group officials, the losses eventually reached some $38 million. It was early 1972—right on the Caterpillar timetable—before profits erased the red ink.

IT'S HARD TO SAY "NO"

Caterpillar guides the company by means of a tandem management set-up that has become the talk of Tokyo. Twenty-two Americans sit close by Japanese executives who have precisely the same responsibilities; the Caterpillar men advise their counterparts, who give orders down the line. At every level, each official is supposedly coequal. But Caterpillar managers reinforce their influence by reporting to the chairman of the joint venture, an American. He takes the case to the president, a Japanese. "Above all, we avoid confrontations and adjust details to get results," insists E. J. Schlegel, who was chairman of Caterpillar Mitsubishi from 1970 through 1973 and is now a Caterpillar vice president in Peoria. "There are times that we say, 'Okay, we'll do it your way.'"

Getting the joint venture to adopt Caterpillar's manufacturing and sales methods demands long rounds of meetings that are often beset by snarled communication. Neither partner is completely fluent in the other's language. "Sometimes we come out with completely different impressions of what's been decided," says Schlegel. One reason is that in Japan both the ambiguities of the language and customary politeness make it difficult to express a blunt "no."

The most difficult task was persuading Mitsubishi to adopt the Caterpillar marketing system, which relies on sizable dealerships to provide customers with parts and servicing. Normally in Japan, there's a much greater division of labor: manufacturers sell to trading companies, which in turn finance dealers, who have little capital of their own. Maintenance and repairs are left to small independent shops. The Caterpillar-type dealerships have enabled the joint venture to snare about 30 percent of the country's annual sales of earthmoving equipment.

Though the business relationship seems to be working, it has to be conceded that personal relations at Caterpillar Mitsubishi are somewhat tense. In the managers' dining room, one sees Caterpillar people choose tables on one side, while all the Mitsubishi men sit on the opposite side of the room. Few of the Americans have close personal relations with their Japanese associates, and turnover among the Mitsubishi executives has been high, because they prefer to go back to other divisions of the zaibatsu where they feel the atmosphere is more congenial. Profits hold the joint venture together.

HOW HEINZ GOT OUT OF THE SOUP

One of the most inviting opportunities for U.S. companies is the processed-food industry, which is increasingly receptive to Western products. But, again, the convoluted distribution system poses an implacable barrier to most outsiders who tackle it alone. Selling any brand involves pushing it through a maze of intermediaries into thousands of tiny retail outlets. When H. J. Heinz tried to buck the system, the result was a fiasco. To enter Japan, Heinz hastily took a minority interest in a joint venture with Nichiro Fisheries, which lacked both capital and broad distribution channels. Heinz ketchup, canned goods, and baby foods reached the Japanese market in 1963—and flopped. One problem: Nichiro's name on the label gave many housewives the false impression that the contents were fish-flavored.

As losses mounted, the partners argued bitterly over what to do about them; Heinz finally bought 80 percent of the joint venture in 1967 and began using American-style marketing. It bypassed primary wholesalers and sold directly to smaller ones; then it began dealing directly with large retailers. The whole Japanese food network banded together in a boycott of Heinz products.

To repair the damage, Heinz turned in December, 1970, to a gentle Japanese executive, Kazuo Asai. He had marketing experience in both countries (having worked for a Japanese trading firm), a degree from the Wharton School of Finance, and a willingness to leave his last employer, Dow Corning. Asai also has what counts most in Japan—an acute sensitivity for human relationships and good personal connections through his wealthy family. In a year as president of Nichiro Heinz, he turned the chaos into profit.

"My predecessors didn't understand the delicate situation here," says Asai. He put Heinz back into normal distribution channels through the sort of personal effort that most impresses his countrymen: he visited every major wholesaler and profusely apologized for bypassing them. "At first, most of them wouldn't even listen and several said, 'Go to hell.' I kept going back until they were convinced we were sincere," he recalls. Asai purposely offered no additional monetary incentives to distributors. "No matter how much money you offer or how many big geisha parties you give, it makes no difference if people don't trust you. That was our problem." Within the company, Asai conducted a similar campaign of persuasion to restore morale, which had been shattered by high turnover of personnel.

Once harmony was restored between Heinz and Japan, the company's products gained increasing acceptance. Its market share of canned soups, for instance, has doubled, to 60 percent. In addition to regular retail outlets, Asai has developed substantial business with hotels and restaurants by carefully cultivating a relatively small group of specialized wholesalers. Heinz has also broadened its appeal by making products in Japan (among them curry-flavored ketchup) that cater to long-standing local tastes.

Since the Japanese president took over, sales have risen by an average of 30 percent annually, to nearly $4 million last year. Asai expects they will climb 50 percent this year and next because of a shift to an even more traditional distribution channel. Mitsubishi Corp., Japan's largest trading firm, now handles all Heinz products. The trader's extensive contacts and credit facilities will greatly increase outlets for Heinz.

DOING "THINGS WE NEVER DREAMED OF"

Unlike Heinz, Brunswick Corp. bet on the right strategy immediately when it came into Japan in 1961. It formed a joint venture to sell bowling equipment—and then shrewdly used its presence to develop ever widening business in other lines, ranging from boat motors to medical supplies. Each activity has enhanced Brunswick's ability to move into another.

Taking a long-range view of the potential returns, Brunswick asked for no royalties when it teamed up with Mitsui & Co., a major trading house. Instead, the company waited for profits from the fifty-fifty joint venture, called Nippon Brunswick. It overcame a sluggish start when the new Japanese bent for leisure brought on a bowling boom. The company has provided a third of the country's 130,000 lanes—and profited immensely. Among corporations with substantial foreign capital, its pretax earnings of $58.6 million were second only to I.B.M.'s, according to Japanese tax returns published last year.

From the start, Brunswick itself has also been expanding its activities through an independent Tokyo branch. One big reason the company has been able to do so successfully is that, unlike most American corporations, Brunswick keeps U.S. executives in Japan for long periods and expects them to learn the language. Garrett M. Flint, managing director of the Tokyo branch for nine years, speaks Japanese fluently. "Just because you're here leads to all sorts of other things—things we never dreamed of at first," says Flint. The Japanese mania for golf opened the way for MacGregor clubs and bags, which bring Brunswick $10 million in annual sales. In status-conscious Japan, golf is now the prestige game and name-brand clubs bestow extra cachet. By being on the scene, Brunswick spotted the trend early and built up volume gradually. The clubs are exported from America; the bags are manufactured in Japan by a licensee. Initially, the U.S. company sold through normal wholesale channels. But Flint saw that he could cut prices and raise margins by selling directly to retailers. That's a risky step in Japan, but the company made the switch in 1970 without stumbling.

"You can do things differently here if you know what you're doing and proceed in the right way," says Flint. He bypassed distributors by working through Brunswick's Japanese staff. The staff concluded that the shift was feasible, recruited a larger sales force, and—most delicately—broke the news to wholesalers. Brunswick now provides credit to 300 mostly small retailers who were previously financed by wholesalers.

Brunswick uses its association with large corporations to good advantage too. In 1968 its own sales force started promoting products for Sherwood Medical Industries, a U.S. subsidiary that makes disposable hypodermic needles and syringes. But Flint found that he needed better contacts with Japanese hospitals. So Brunswick turned to Mitsui, which is in touch with every major industry through its own teams of specialists. Last year Brunswick and Mitsui formed a new company, Nippon Sherwood, to manufacture and sell the medical items.

"There's certainly a synergistic effect," observes Flint. "The more contacts you have, the more power you have to get things done. I don't mean dictating, but skill in finding your way through the labyrinth of negotiations and achieving results."

THE SALESLADY HAS TO BE
FORMALLY INTRODUCED

Business contacts normally begin with formal introductions through mutual friends and rarely occur in Japanese homes. In the face of these strong traditions, Avon has launched door-to-door sales of cosmetics. But the system it uses in seventeen other countries had to be modified to suit the sensitivities of Japan—as did many of its products.

Under its well-tested system, the company has found 20,000 housewives willing to become sales representatives on a commission basis. As elsewhere, each is called an "Avon lady." But the similarity ends there. In Western countries, Avon sales representatives routinely call on people they don't know and often obtain an order on the first visit. Japanese, on the other hand, regard their homes as sacrosanct, and any sales relationship is fraught with fear that one of the parties—buyer or seller—may lose face. Not surprisingly, as George E. Gustin, Avon general manager in Japan reports, "the Avon lady here is not as aggressive and outgoing as her counterpart in the West."

After much hand wringing and experimentation, Avon started adapting its approach to meet these special challenges. Through friends and relatives, area managers around the country arrange formal introductions of Avon ladies to prospective customers. To help overcome the innate shyness of its sales force, the company appeals to Japanese group-consciousness; as it does nowhere else, Avon holds large "beauty class" meetings, where it dispenses product data and pep talks.

Even though Avon offers up to a 33 percent commission on sales in Japan, the company has discovered it can't be too blunt about monetary rewards alone; working only for money seems crass to most Japanese. Thus Avon inspires its Oriental ladies by discussing things of value they can buy with earnings, such as a TV set or refrigerator, and stressing what Gustin calls "pleasant objectives," such as helping make customers look better.

Average sales of a Japanese Avon lady still lag behind those in most other countries where the company operates. But each Japanese customer buys more. So far, Avon has garnered about 2 percent of Japan's cosmetics market, which has reached a wholesale volume of $1.2 billion a year (the world's second largest after the U.S.). If the company continues to overcome the social barriers, it expects to earn profits in Japan starting next year. It is showing its confidence by investing $5 million to build a plant near Tokyo to meet anticipated demand for the next decade.

Both the successes and the failures of American companies in Japan demonstrate that the only way to operate there is to accept the country's ways and adapt to them. Once the Japanese are met on their own terms, there is a lot of latitude for introducing fresh techniques in sales and management.

Above all, things get done through personal contacts, not just formal business transactions. Cultivating the essential friendships requires more time than the usual two- or three-year executive assignment. Most corporations would be better served by keeping men in Japan for five or even ten years. Top executives need not speak Japanese fluently, but some knowledge of the language not only smooths social relations but also affords valuable insights into the Japanese way of thinking.

Patience, grace, and the ability to communicate are especially important in Japan. Even a seemingly relaxed evening of entertainment, for instance, may be a crucial test to a Japanese of an American's compatibility. Smart U.S. executives never talk business at such gatherings.

When they do get down to business, always in the office, Japanese executives are just as interested in harmonious relations as in profits. Brisk Americans eager to sign contracts are likely to run into delays; the Japanese move deliberately and prefer to rely on overall understanding rather than legal contracts. There are few business secrets in Japan. As many U.S. companies have learned, anyone who discusses investment plans with a government ministry can expect the whole local industry to know about it, too. Thus it is usually best to meet Japanese competitors and tell them directly, for their acceptance is also vital. Avon, among others, did this before entering Japan.

NEW HELP FOR U.S. EXPORTERS

The Japanese themselves have belatedly recognized that their cohesive business system and insular customs remain formidable barriers. To prove that the old protectionism has ended, several of the nation's leading exporters have assumed a new role—helping U.S. companies sell in Japan. Sony is distributing through its own facilities about fifty products, including Shick electric razors, Heathkit amplifiers, and Whirlpool refrigerators.

Still, the best starting point for many U.S. export items is a Japanese trading company. Some of the giant traders are already so busy handling rival products that they may give newcomers insufficient attention, but hundreds of smaller, specialized firms are eager to exploit Japanese enthusiasm for international name brands and unusual products. Some fifty companies expressed interest in teaming up with Sears for catalogue sales. "There are still a lot more opportunities here than American companies are aware of," says former U.S. Ambassador Ingersoll, "but first they must know more about Japan."

QUESTIONS FOR DISCUSSION

1. Discuss the differences between channel structure in the United States and in Japan.

2. Kraar states, "The main business obstacle, often underestimated in the past, is the clannishness of the Japanese." Discuss this statement and relate it to appropriate marketing strategies in Japan.

3. Discuss the techniques used by Sears, Coca-Cola, and Xerox in Japan to successfully market their products.

4. Explain the usage of C.S.O.'s by Xerox in Japan.

5. Discuss how the Caterpillar Corporation markets its products in Japan.

6. Summarize the Avon marketing program in Japan.

7. The author states, "Still, the best starting point for many U.S. export items is a Japanese trading company." Discuss the rationale of this statement.

8.5 ASPECTS OF RETAIL PRICING IN JAPAN

Robert E. Weigand

"Although members of a marketing channel often have a close working relationship in Japan, long channels are not usually conducive to unified action. Where a product must pass through several stages, the manufacturer finds it much more difficult to enforce throughout the length of the channel what he perceives as desirable policies."

Those who are involved in international business invariably face the problem of separating the familiar from the unknown. There are a few institutions, beliefs, attitudes, and practices that are similar in countries that geographically are quite remote from each other. Businessmen are quick to borrow ideas from wherever in the world they may find them and use them—either intact, or by adapting them to the domestic culture. Other aspects of culture seem to be highly localized and bear little resemblance to what occurs in the rest of the world. They seem uniquely applicable to the domestic situation and have not been borrowed for use in other countries.

The American businessman in Japan faces this problem. He must decide what aspects of business operations are about the same in Tokyo as in New York, and what ones are different. This is not an easy task since his answer will be modified as he observes the two cultures under a vast array of different circumstances. Indeed it has been said that no country offers a greater opportunity for a discussant to be agreeably disagreeable than Japan. Almost any general comment can be followed by "Yes, but . . . ," and a recitation of contrary evidence. Presumably such supplemental and opposite remarks can, in turn, be contested. Several vignettes suggest how business behavior can be roughly the same between the United States and Japan but sufficiently different that we dare not overlook the details:

A Japanese employer commonly pays a bonus of significant proportion

Robert E. Weigand, "Aspects of Retail Pricing in Japan," *MSU Business Topics*, Vol. 18 (Winter 1970), pp. 23–30. Reprinted by permission of the publisher, Division of Research, Graduate School of Business Administration, Michigan State University.

to his employees twice a year. This not only affects consumer purchase patterns but represents an unavoidable expense to employers whose pricing system must be sufficiently flexible to generate income to pay for the bonus and other employee benefits.

A sidewalk merchant in the Tsukiji section of Tokyo sells nothing but cricket cages and does so at a fixed price; he is largely influenced in his pricing by the implicit cost of his family's time in constructing the boxes, and he is largely free of government interference.

A full-service department store a mile away sells television sets on an installment plan controlled by the manufacturer, but the customer can save over 40 percent if he pays cash; the government is a very close observer of the pricing behavior of the department store.

In the Akihabara section of Tokyo, only a few miles away, a "discount house" sells the same model at a higher price; but the discount house will accept any one of several credit cards.

And in Akasaka, a group of retailers are entertained at the Mikado, probably the world's largest night club, as guests of a supplier who regularly strengthens his relationship with his dealers in this manner; it may be an unevenly balanced relationship that has lasted for many years.

This article deals with some of the major factors that affect the pricing practices of Japanese retailers, with particular emphasis on the relatively recent tendency to discounting from "standard" price.[1] There are many similarities between the United States and Japan with respect to the types of goods discounted, the historic origin of low margin retailers, the difficult problem of defining a discount sale, and the response of traditional retail outlets. But there are also differences between the countries, some of which are quite basic.

PATERNALISM AND FIXED COSTS

One conspicuous feature of Japan that has often attracted the attention of the Western world is the long-term paternalistic attitude of management toward its employees. Managerial concern for the employee can be viewed as an extension of the traditional Japanese view of the family or the *ie*. Included in the responsibilities of the head of an *ie* were supervising the family enterprise, arranging marriages, assigning work to be done, providing for retirement of the elderly, assuring that proper homage was paid to the deceased, and taking precautions to assure the health of the living.[2] Only when a member voluntarily left the *ie*,

1. The Japanese prefer to say "standard price" since the word "list" has little meaning to them in conjunction with price.
2. The role of the *ie* in Japanese life has been dealt with rather thoroughly in the literature. For a recent explanation of the decline of its importance among middle

died, or was adopted by another *ie,* was the head absolved of his
responsibilities.

The view held by the modern Japanese businessman of his responsibilities toward his employees has been somewhat diluted by the increased number of employment opportunities open to workers, the
growth of labor unions and social legislation, and the decline of support
accorded paternalism by the educational system.[3] None the less, he continues to see himself as more responsible for the welfare of his workers
than does the American businessman. The consequence of this view
is that labor must be defined as a type of cost that is not susceptible to
significant reduction by termination of an employee during times of
economic stress; such termination is not generally an acceptable business practice.[4] Labor costs are not only unavoidable in Japan but include perquisites that are considered personal expenses in most other
countries. Low cost, company-subsidized housing for both married and
single employees; meals; vacation areas; concerts, dances, movies, lec-
tures, and other after-hour activities; high school courses, and expense
accounts for a large number of managerial personnel who do not engage
in public contact work are employee benefits furnished by Japanese
businesses that usually are individually borne by employees in the
Western world.

As a consequence of the Japanese commitment toward their employees, Japanese sellers must view prices as a highly flexible marketing instrument. The notion of marginal pricing and the importance of selling
at prices that contribute to unavoidable costs is well understood both
by businessmen and by academicians. The significant distinction of
Japanese managerial practice, however, is that labor costs are more
likely to be treated as unavoidable and thus irrelevant to short-term
strategy. Prices may be cut at any level in the marketing channel by
firms that must have sufficient immediate income to meet their unavoidable costs, but the move ultimately will affect the retailers' cost of goods.

THE ANTI-MONOPOLY ACT

An early step of the post-World War II occupation forces was to insist
that the Japanese Diet pass antitrust legislation that would reduce the
degree of economic concentration and the prevalence of "unfair" busi-

income families, see Ezra F. Vogel, *Japan's New Middle Class* (Berkeley and Los
Angeles: University of California Press, 1965), ch. 8. For its significance in Japan's
large business, see Yasuzo Horie, "The Role of the *ie* in the Economic Modernization of Japan," *The Kyoto University Economic Review*, April 1966, pp. 1–16. For
its relationship to labor relations, Masu-ichi Honda, "Managing Personnel in Japanese Industry," *Personnel Journal*, March 1968, p. 191.

3. M. Y. Yoshino, *Japan's Managerial System: Tradition and Innovation* (Cambridge, Mass.: The M.I.T. Press, 1968), pp. 113–17.

4. Warren S. Hunsberger, *Japan and the United States in World Trade* (New
York and Evanston: Harper and Row, 1964), p. 167.

ness practices that had typified Japan. The Anti-Monopoly Act, specifically designed to prevent monopoly, restraint of trade, and unfair business practices, was passed in 1947 and contains many terms which suggest American guidance.[5]

The act was amended in 1953 in several ways, one of which was to allow certain manufacturers to enter into resale price maintenance agreements with those to whom they sell. The price maintenance part of the act is different in several ways from American legislation. Perhaps the most conspicuous difference is that a manufacturer who elects to maintain the price of his re-seller must petition the Fair Trade Commission (Kosei Torihiki Iinkai) for permission to do so and approval must be specifically granted. The responsibilities of the commission may be confusing to Americans if they equate it with administering resale price maintenance agreements. It is responsible for, among other things, judicial interpretation of the Anti-Monopoly Act. The resale price maintenance provision is but a small part of that act.

To guide the commission in its decisions, the law specifies that the products for which price maintenance contracts may be approved must be in daily use by the consumer, must be easily identifiable, and must be in free and open competition with similar products. The commission has been slow to allow vertical pricing contracts that are viewed as dissonant with its role of preventing restrictive business practices.[6] By March 1967, it had approved 120 price maintenance agreements, primarily for cosmetics, medicine, soap, hair dye, and toothpaste.[7]

A second major difference between American and Japanese practice is that American manufacturers may rely upon court injunctions to prevent price cutting if their case is strong enough and if they are willing to finance some very costly court appearances. In Japan, the manufacturer who receives the commission's approval to maintain standard price throughout the length of the channel enforces his effort by refusing to deal with the price cutter. The Anti-Monopoly Act specifically declares that a sale that restricts the activities of other parties to a transaction is an "unfair business practice." Only those products specifically designated by the commission are exempt from the act's application. Many brands of cosmetics, medicines, and the other products that have received commission approval are regularly and conspicuously sold at less than standard price. One American company—Smith, Kline and French—is said to have been relatively successful at maintaining standard price for Contac cold remedy by selective distribution and use of the price maintenance provision of the Anti-Monopoly Act.[8] The firm

5. More formally known as an "Act Concerning Prohibition of Private Monopoly and Maintenance of Fair Trade."

6. *1966 Annual Report of the Fair Trade Commission*, pp. 120–23.

7. Anti-Monopoly Law, Part I, Section 2, Paragraph 7-IV.

8. Masafusa Miyashita, "Distribution Channels of Daily Consumer Goods," *Industrial Japan*, July 1968, pp. 36–39.

uses only nine wholesalers to distribute throughout Japan and has signed price maintenance contracts with each of them. The wholesalers, in turn, have contracts with about 7,000 retailers who re-sell the product. There is no nonsigner clause in the Japanese law although Yoshio Kanazawa states that the wording of the law is unclear.

LONG MARKETING CHANNELS

The ability of retailers to deviate from standard price if they choose to do so is partially attributed to the long distribution channels through which many Japanese products are said to pass. Although members of a marketing channel often have a close working relationship in Japan, long channels are not usually conducive to unified action. Where a product must pass through several stages the manufacturer finds it much more difficult to enforce throughout the length of the channel what he perceives as desirable policies.

The Akihabara area of Tokyo, for example, has several dozen small shops that specialize in electrical goods at prices substantially below standard price. These small stores sell television sets, air conditioners, rice cookers, blenders, water coolers, refrigerators, and all the other types of merchandise one would see in an American discount house; they feature brand names such as National, Columbia, Hitachi, and Sony; they are conveniently located and accept one or more credit cards such as Japan Credit Bureau, Million Card, Nippon Shinpan, Partners Diamond, or Bank Americard. Retailers such as these in Akihabara seldom acknowledge a close relationship with their supplying manufacturer and may, in fact, be obtaining their merchandise from nearby wholesalers or even other neighboring retailers. Proximity to supply facilitates minimum inventory positions, a practice in which Japanese retailers have long engaged; this also results in long marketing channels.

The length of marketing channels in Japan is suggested by comparing "class of customer" sales for Japanese wholesalers with similar census data from the United States. Both the Ministry of International Trade and Industry in Japan and the Bureau of the Census in the United States ask wholesalers about the type of customers to whom they sell and the proportion of sales that flows to each type. Table 1 indicates the portion of wholesaler sales that go to other wholesalers, industrial buyers, retailers, household consumers, and export markets. Of particular importance is the fact that there are a great many more wholesaler-to-wholesaler transactions in Japan than in the United States. Such sales take place both in the United States and Japan because wholesalers cannot stock all the commodities for which they have orders, yet find it im-

TABLE 1 Wholesalers' Sales by Class of Customer in Japan and the United States

Country	To Other Wholesalers (percent)	To Industrial Buyers (percent)	To Retailers (percent)	To Household Consumers (percent)	To Export Market (percent)	Total (percent)
Japan	42.2	30.0	19.4	3.1	5.2	100
United States	19.2	41.3	33.5	1.1	4.8	100

Source: The Japanese data were obtained and translated for this article by Professor Yusaku Furuhasi of the University of Notre Dame, and are derived from the Inter-Sectoral Circular Flow part of the Census of Distribution (1962) conducted by the Ministry of International Trade and Industry. The American data are from U.S. Bureau of the Census, *U.S. Census of Business: 1963*, vol. 4, *Wholesale Trade—Summary Statistics, Part I* (Washington, D.C.: Government Printing Office, 1966), p. 4–11.

portant to give the appearance of selling a full line. The limited line wholesaler can achieve this appearance if he can easily and quickly purchase supplementary goods from others. Another seeming explanation for wholesaler-to-wholesaler transactions, particularly in the United States, is the geographic vastness of the market. In assuring market coverage of an area so large, it is almost inevitable that large wholesalers (or re-sellers by some other name) will sell to smaller wholesalers in more remote areas. If size of territory is a partial explanation of the length of a marketing channel, it would seem that American channels should be characterized by more wholesaler-to-wholesaler transactions than would be true in Japan. However, this is not the case.

Long marketing channels generate serious policing problems for those manufacturers who hope to enforce sales at standard prices. A short channel of carefully selected dealers is more conducive to maintenance of standard price than longer channels where tracing the product becomes more difficult. Long channels make price maintenance particularly difficult in Japan since the commission only allows manufacturers to refuse to deal with price cutters, a remedy quite different from the American approach. When merchandise passes through several re-sellers and ultimately is discounted by a retailer who refuses to reveal his source, price maintenance becomes almost impossible.

THE FAIR TRADE COMMISSION AND UNFAIR BUSINESS PRACTICES

One view of the role of both the Fair Trade Commission and the Ministry of International Trade and Industry is that they must "umpire" the changes that are taking place in Japan as those who are employed in low productivity activities are gradually absorbed by high productivity industries. The shift of workers away from what can be viewed as an inefficient activity, retailing, toward higher productivity occupations is slow for a host of reasons. Among them are the unwillingness of industry to accept older workers, worker preference for a particular geographic area, a lack of awareness that greater opportunities exist, and the inability or unwillingness of some workers to learn new skills. As more low margin retailers such as Summit Stores, Super Daiei, Seidensha, or Meidiya become more popular, fewer people should be attracted to the traditional type of retailing operation. If the transition of the work force to higher productivity activities occurs too rapidly, however, it could result in serious social, economic, and political complications. Both MITI and the FTC are kept aware of this problem by trade associations of smaller stores as the All Japan Federation Retailers Association and the Federation of Specialty Stores Association.

The changes that were made in the Anti-Monopoly Act in 1953 are usually considered to have made the Japanese economy less competitive. One part of the legislation, however, is sufficiently general to allow the Fair Trade Commission to decide just how rigorous competition should be. Article 19 of the act states that, "No entrepreneur shall employ unfair business practices," and it designates six activities that are unfair. One such unfair practice is selling at "undue prices," a term that requires commission interpretation. The commission often has warned various sellers that their prices or terms of trade have been unreasonable and has taken action against them. In September 1968, for example, it warned the National Federation of Electrical Appliances Retailers Association of Japan that the premiums given to buyers of color television sets were excessive. The premiums consisted of weekend excursions to vacation areas—popular bonuses to good customers as well as to loyal employees in Japan. In February 1968, the FTC warned many Tokyo retailers that premiums accorded buyers of air-conditioners were unduly large.[9]

THE JAPANESE VIEW:
COMPETITION AND GROUP RELATIONSHIPS

One of the more basic differences that exists between American and Japanese businessmen is their view toward competition. Although there are many instances in which Japanese firms compete fiercely with each other, using all the marketing weapons at their disposal, there are many other cases in which competition is less intense. Those who have com-

9. "FTC Warns Retailers on Color TV Premiums," *The Japan Times*, September 5, 1968, p. 9.

mented on this issue generally state that the American version is more spirited. Although attitudes have changed since Ruth Benedict wrote her classic book, her description of the ways in which the Japanese avoid direct competition or potentially embarrassing situations provides an interesting insight into their business behavior.[10] Subjecting a professor to questions which he cannot answer, entering into a romance or marriage without the benefit of an intermediary, asking favors that cannot be carried out, making work demands that are unrealistically high, and developing reward systems that are based on individual rather than group accomplishment are less likely to occur in Japan than in the United States. American businessmen who do business in Japan often have favorite stories to tell about letters that go unanswered, contracts that are violated in some manner, and schedules that are not met. Those who are familiar with Japan usually explain that such problems are derived from the difficult position in which hard driving Americans have put their Japanese partners; the Americans have neglected to allow the Japanese an "out" for an embarrassing situation.

Soon after the Japan-United States peace treaty was signed, the antitrust legislation that reflected an American view of competition began to undergo both legislative as well as interpretive changes. The direction generally was toward a form of competition in which most existing retailers could survive. Depression cartels, although infrequently used, became a legal possibility. Associations where public sanitation would be affected, such as restaurants, bath houses, beauty shops, and theaters, were allowed to impose regulations that were alleged to be in the public interest. Export associations that would portion out "voluntary" quotas were formed for such products as textiles and flatware (and, it appears at this writing, for steel). Operating decisions such as the number of days a retailer may open each month, closing hours, and services that can be extended to the consumer are controlled by MITI under the Department Store Act of 1956. All in all, a host of ways have been devised by the Japanese to control competition; they are ways that are known and used in the United States, but with less frequency.[11]

Japanese competition tends toward emphasizing the accomplishments of the group rather than the individual. Hence, the prospect of individual shame is lessened or at least shared by all the members. There are times, of course, when the reward system must center on the individual. Yet even under these circumstances the basis for the reward is more likely to be one's own previous accomplishments rather than those of the group norm.

10. Ruth Benedict, *The Chrysanthemum and the Sword* (Cambridge, Mass.: The Riverside Press, 1946), especially ch. 8.
11. See especially William W. Lockwood, "Japan's 'New Capitalism,' " *The State and Economic Enterprise in Japan*, William W. Lockwood, ed. (Princeton, N.J.: Princeton University Press, 1965), p. 498 †.

Japanese manufacturers appear to be more likely to look upon their re-sellers as members of their group than are American executives, although power in the group and rewards to each member may be badly balanced. Those executives who were interviewed sometimes alluded to a closeness to their wholesalers and retailers that is difficult to document but none the less very real. This is a psychological feeling of closeness brought about perhaps by both the time span of business commitments which tends to be very long and by the deep-felt need to commit one's effort to a group cause.

DEALER INCENTIVE PLANS

In spite of the long marketing channels that typify Japan, manufacturers often find ways of creating group feeling with their retailers.[12] Dealer incentive plans are well known in the United States, but they appear to be much more common in Japan. A night at Kabuki or a large cabaret, a weekend in Hong Kong, or even a week in Hawaii are rather common incentives for retailers. Another practice that draws the retailer and manufacturer close together is the use of manufacturer-paid demonstrators in the retail outlets. The practice is not much different in Japan than in the United States except for its legality. Japan's proscription against the use of paid demonstrators appears to be less restrictive than the American interpretation of the law. The most specific statement concerns unfair business practices in department stores, a statement made in December 1954.[13] The FTC warned against the "unfair use" of a supplier's own employees in retail outlets. However, it has been suggested by Japanese business observers that the practice continues to be a common one, perhaps largely due to the limited applicability of the law and the problem of knowing what "unfair use" of the practice means.

The long-term commitment of the retailer to the manufacturer is not entirely explained by the significance of group competition. A great deal of control can be levied by the manufacturer or the trading company because he has greater access to capital than does the retailer. The Japanese banking system traditionally has engaged in long-term financing toward large businesses and has used less of its funds for making loans for working capital needs.[14] Small businesses look to their supplier as their "banker," often taking several months to pay for merchandise

12. For an American view that the marketing channel is an operating system of businesses that sometimes collaborate over an extended time period, see Wroe Alderson, *Marketing Behavior and Executive Action* (Homewood, Ill.: Richard D. Irwin, Inc., 1957), p. 156 †.

13. *Department Stores in Japan: 1968* (Tokyo: Japan Department Stores Association, n.d.), pp. 8–9.

14. For a description of the attitude of Japanese banks toward short-term loans, particularly to smaller businesses, see Hubert F. Schiffer, S.J., *The Modern Japanese Banking System* (New York: University Publishers, Inc., 1962), ch. 13.

that would be sold on thirty-day terms in the United States. Manufacturers have been known to attempt to use this power to influence retail pricing practices. In particular, appliance manufacturers have established finance subsidiaries to factor the installment-plan paper of some of their retailers who are incapable of carrying their customers for an extended time. The merchandise is pre-ticketed by the manufacturer, who states the terms of the sale. For example, Tokyo Shibaura (Toshiba) recently pre-ticketed a twelve-inch black and white television set for Yen 39,800 ($111.17). The ticket also indicated that the customer could pay for the set in seven equal monthly installments totaling Yen 41,800 ($116.70), eleven installments totaling Yen 42,600 ($119.00), or thirteen installments totaling Yen 43,000 ($120.10).

Such pre-ticketing is common and can be used to encourage a price system desired by the manufacturer. One manufacturer, for example, will factor only the accounts where the retail sale has occurred at standard price; the retailer who discounts must carry his own installment customers or make other financing arrangements. Although the success of this system is largely a secret, it is susceptible to several serious weaknesses which prevent it from being an effective deterrent to price cutting. First, the disparity between the cash and installment price is so great that it would seem to encourage cash sales. The television set that was pre-ticketed to sell for as much as Yen 43,000 ($120.10) was being widely discounted at stores readily accessible to a large proportion of prospective buyers. One large Tokyo department store was discounting the product to sell for Yen 29,800 ($83.25). This cash price was observed in one of Tokyo's largest full-service department stores, raising the oft-asked rhetorical question about defining a discount house. Another manufacturer had pre-ticketed a similar television set to sell for Yen 45,800 ($127.90) in fifteen equal monthly installments but the cash price was Yen 26,800 ($74.90). Although we know too little about how the consumer views installment terms, it appears that the charge for installment purchases can be very high.

Another factor that limits the capacity of the manufacturer to control the retailer's pricing policy by his more ready access to the banking system is the increasing number of sources of funds available to the Japanese consumer. Credit cards have become popular in recent years, some of the unions make funds available to assist their members with small purchases, companies sometimes will lend money to their employees from the retirement fund that is being accumulated, a substantial semiannual bonus is a common practice, and many purchases come from personal or family savings. Consequently, those buyers who want immediate possession of a product are not at the mercy of those who sell at standard price but can finance the purchase through any of a variety of institutions.

Finally, the method is not particularly useful for maintaining retail prices in a nation where consumer credit is not yet accepted by a large segment of the population. The Japanese are not unlike many other people who hold the attitude that most purchases should be delayed until there are funds to buy for cash.

CONCLUSIONS

The perceptive international observer is likely to notice about as many similarities as differences in the practices of retailers in the developed countries. He probably will be about as comfortable in a department store in Paris, London, Tel Aviv, or Tokyo as in a large American city. The services that he is accorded such as credit, delivery, exchange privileges, or guarantees will be roughly the same, although the details may differ.

Anyone who studies the Japanese retailing system would surely see numerous ways in which American and Japanese practices are outwardly the same. In particular, he would notice that each country had experienced an increasing amount of discounting by certain retailers from the price recommended by the manufacturer. The discounting is most widespread when it is applied to well-known products where traditional retail margins are disconsonant with services performed by the retailer. He would also notice that both countries have attempted to mitigate the harshest forms of competition that might change the distributive system too quickly. Critics are quite aware that "soft" competition is brought by those who believe that there is great advantage in gradually allowing the smallest and perhaps least efficient businesses to become extinct by nonreplacement rather than by big business power. An observer would also notice that, as in the United States, the government's role of umpire between large and small business is not an easy one. Manufacturers, usually larger than those middlemen who make up the marketing channel, hold significant power that some believe must be controlled by government. At the first level of observation, there are many similarities between the United States and Japan.

There are some significant differences behind such similarities as the growth of discounting, laws to moderate the fiercest competitive practices, the problem of enforcing resale price maintenance laws, and efforts by the manufacturers to control the marketing channel.

First, this article centered on the different ways in which Japanese and American businessmen perceive labor costs. The Japanese historically have tended to view them as unavoidable expenses. Americans increasingly are accepting this idea, but for different reasons than the Japanese. Although the underlying reasons differ, the effect is the same; since a major cost item is an inflexible expenditure, price must be a flexible selling weapon.

Second, the manner in which retail prices are maintained by use of the law is quite different in Japan than in the United States. In Japan, price maintenance is attained by gaining the permission of the Fair Trade Commission to refuse to sell to price cutters. Refusal to deal with recalcitrant middlemen generally would be illegal without commission approval; but even when approval is given, policing adherence to a price policy becomes difficult because of Japan's long distributive channels.

Third, the feeling of group membership, so widely observed but difficult to document, probably plays a part in minimizing price cutting. Japanese retailers are said to feel a closeness to their suppliers that is not as strong in American channels. This group feeling permeates many aspects of Japanese political, social, and economic life, and channel relations are simply one of its manifestations. Such feeling lends itself to price stability.

Finally, power in Japan's marketing channel has the appearance of being more weighted in favor of the manufacturer than in the United States. In addition, access to capital is easier for the Japanese manufacturer than it is for the retailer. The retailer with limited capital may be obliged to request lenient credit terms from his supplier, a request that is more likely to be met if the retailer is compliant with the manufacturer's pricing policies.

QUESTIONS FOR DISCUSSION

1. How does the Anti-Monopoly Act affect a manufacturer's pricing its products with other channel members?

2. Why does Japan have such long marketing channels?

3. What techniques does the Japanese manufacturer use to control the price charged by the other channel members who are distributing the firm's products?

4. Should American manufacturers use the techniques of Japanese manufacturers in controlling the other channel members? Defend your answer.

8.6 NOT FOR EXPORT?

> *"Barnes concedes that McDonald's made mistakes.
> It thought it should put its first European store—
> Amsterdam—in the suburbs, just as it had started
> up in suburban Chicago. But, as Barnes soon learned,
> the suburbs are not where it's at in Europe."*

With all the fervor of the Pilgrims returned, McDonald's set out to introduce Europe to the joys of the *real* American hamburger. Most people assumed that golden arches, like blue jeans and Coke, would sprout up overnight across the Continent. A few years back McDonald's set a goal of 300 European stores by 1977. So far, there are 38. After four years, the company has lost none of its zeal. But it has learned the hard way about doing business with the natives.

"It's corny," says smiling, silver-haired Steve Barnes, head of McDonald's international operations, "but I feel like a missionary over here." Barnes, based at McDonald's Oak Brook, Ill. headquarters, and his 37-year-old European manager, Tony Klaus, talk enthusiastically about providing a place where the French are not embarrassed to bring their children and where the Germans can taste "a better bun." Says Dutch-born Klaus: "We're bringing one of the purest American things to good old Europe." Reflecting this, McDonald's starred-and-striped sales campaign in Britain features "The United Tastes of America."

But Barnes and Klaus would rather talk mission than money. Understandably. European sales are probably no more than $18 million out of $2 billion worldwide. Financial chief Richard Boylan says for the first time non-North American operations are making enough to cover operating and expansion costs this year. But that includes Japan and Australia; he won't say whether this is true of Europe.

Carl DeBiase of Fourteen Research Corp., who is very bullish on the company domestically, thinks it may take a decade before McDonald's makes real money in Europe. Analyst Al Simon of Sanford C. Bernstein estimates that, with a few notable exceptions like the record-breaking Stockholm store, European stores average $480,000 in yearly sales

Reprinted by permission of *Forbes* Magazine from the October 15, 1975 issue, pp. 23–24.

against $740,000 worldwide. For company stores, Simon puts average unit profit margins in European and Australian stores at 11%, though this is up from 6% last year, compared with 19% for American and Canadian stores.

Some of the qualities that made McDonald's so successful in North America may be nibbling at its margins abroad. Fast service for one thing, which gives McDonald's much higher labor costs than Kentucky Fried Chicken or Britain's Wimpy International. It takes four people per shift to sell take-out chicken; McDonald's averages up to 30 in its London stores. McDonald's is fanatical about quality. A Big Mac tastes the same in Des Moines as in London or in Amsterdam. The company adheres to strict specifications for meat, buns, apple pies and most everything else, specifications that may differ from those of European suppliers. So it must either import long distance (french fries from Canada, pies from Tulsa) or place special and more costly orders locally. When McDonald's has blanketed an area with stores, it can promise big orders and get discounts. Until that day arrives, the company will have to pay for being finicky.

Wimpy hamburger bars, by contrast, don't worry so much about consistency, and most franchisees solve their supply problems by buying from Wimpy's giant parent food company, J. Lyons ($1.4-billion sales). Wimpy's quality may suffer, but profits don't.

It takes under $25,000 to open a Wimpy or KFC store in Britain. A McDonald's costs over $200,000. This big capital requirement—and the fact that there are fewer entrepreneurs in Europe than in the U.S.—will make it hard for the company to find franchisees abroad, especially in capital-scarce Britain. Ten of the European stores are franchised, compared with 73% of the U.S. stores. Klaus concedes European development would come much faster if franchising could be pushed.

In Europe, the competitors who ostensibly thought small—either with low per-store capital costs like Wimpy and KFC or with limited expansion plans like Switzerland's Mövenpick—have already made big strides in European fast foods, where McDonald's is just getting going. KFC, in the U.K. since 1965, has 254 stores there and 4 on the Continent, while Wimpy has 950 outlets all over Europe. Both have mostly franchise stores. Mövenpick has 16 Swiss quick-service restaurants with varied menus that have the advantage of being identified with the company's 49 dining-room-type restaurants throughout Switzerland and Germany.

Barnes concedes that McDonald's made mistakes. It thought it should put its first European store—Amsterdam—in the suburbs, just as it had started up in suburban Chicago. But as Barnes soon learned, the suburbs are not where it's at in Europe. Most people still live in cities, and they are less mobile than Americans. The out-of-town shopping centers that sprang up all over the U.S. and provided good sites for fast-fooders have not caught on in much of Europe. The original Amsterdam store was moved into town. "We learned our lesson," Barnes recalls. "Now we are choosing shop-front sites in the cities." But rents in those areas are often astronomical, and all four of the new London stores are more or less suburban.

McDonald's says that, as in the States, it is aiming to get the whole family in. McDonald's contrasts its relaxed approach to the more refined European restaurant, where the waiter may look askance at messy, noisy children. But Vice President Mario Wang of Mövenpick has his doubts, at least about Germany where McDonald's has made its biggest European commitment with 22 stores. "The Germans and Swiss are still quite traditional, and we are more gastronomically minded. Even if the wife works, dinner means a home-cooked meal. And once the family is home at the end of the day, it is not likely to go out again." So the real promise seems to lie with the lunchtime and Saturday shopping crowds.

FROM HAMBURGERS TO BEER

McDonald's has made a few changes in its menu to accommodate European tastes: tea in Britain, beer and—to head off Kentucky Fried—chicken on the Continent. As for expansion in Europe, "We don't really make projections," said Barnes when *Forbes* first talked with him. "We work on a one-by-one basis with our stores." Financial Chief Richard Boylan ventured that there are 13 European stores under construction, but wouldn't say how many more are planned. Surprisingly, Barnes talked more recently of 40 new stores by the end of 1976. Time will tell.

New York Times columnist Tom Wicker recently lamented that McDonald's was luring Swedes away from their good old smoked herring. His worry may prove to have been a bit premature. Even missionaries have to adapt.

QUESTIONS FOR DISCUSSION

1. Discuss the major problems experienced by McDonald's in Europe.

2. What *cultural* differences in Europe have affected the McDonald's marketing program?

3. Do you feel McDonald's should substantially alter their stores, menus, and operating procedures in Europe rather than continuing to export those utilized in the U.S.? Defend your answer.

Chapter 9

Legal Issues in Marketing Channels

EVEN THE MOST CASUAL observer of the business press is aware of the significant involvement of governmental regulation in the business sphere of the 1970s. Furthermore, upon more careful reading, one is struck by the fact that a disproportionately large portion of the regulation involves marketing activities. This situation probably is a result of the fact that marketing is the most "observable" business practice. That is, it is the business activity that is most frequently seen by the consumer. Because the public is most aware of marketing abuses, it is easier to legislate regulation in this area.

The following are some examples of business publications discussing legal issues involving marketing channels. One issue of *The Wall Street Journal* discussed an antitrust investigation involving the wholesaling activities of a newspaper and magazine distributor. This Justice Department investigation was initiated because more than 600 local wholesalers in this area have no competition. Some wholesalers claimed that competition in their industry would be detrimental to the public good. One such advocate claimed, "It (competition) would create a war that would put a lot of wholesalers and publishers out of business."[1] Other distributors believe competition would be good for the industry. One observed, "The way it is now, if a news dealer wants to do business with another wholesaler there's no place to go. As a result, the retailer gets poor service and selection, and the wholesaler gets high profits."[2]

Another *Wall Street Journal* article examined the Supreme Court's current interpretation of the antitrust laws as they affect closed sales territories. This case involved Topco, a cooperative association of approximately 24 regional supermarket chains. The supermarket chains, in turn, own all of the Topco stock. Topco distributes both food and non-food items to its member chains. At issue was an agreement among the members that each firm had a territorial license granting the exclusive rights to sell Topco products in that area. A provision did allow

1. Ronald Kessler, "Crime Strike Force Begins Investigation Into Garfinkle News-Distributing Firms," *The Wall Street Journal* (August 6, 1969), p. 30.
2. *Ibid.*

a member to expand into another's area if the first seller in the area approved of the second's expansion. The Justice Department charged that the territorial restriction violated the Sherman Act because it prevented retail competition in Topco products. The high court upheld the Department of Justice's suit and Justice Thurgood Marshall declared, "We think it is clear that the restraint in this case is a horizontal one. . ."[3] He further stated that the companies involved would normally be competitors and therefore their agreement was illegal.[4]

In May 1976, the FTC charged the Levi Strauss Company with violating the antitrust laws. The government alleged that Levi Strauss told its 15,000 dealers what to charge for the jeans and other clothing they sold, and also forced them via tying contracts to purchase products they did not desire in order to receive Levi's most popular items. Levi responded by stating, "Levi's marketing system as it is functioning today is wholly lawful, and the company is prepared to defend itself."[5] The FTC complaint states that Levi uses various forms of coercion, discipline, and surveillance. Specifically, it was alleged that the firm terminates retailers who do not comply or are suspected of not complying; refuses to deal with dealers who it believes will not comply; and does not reimburse firms for cooperative advertising unless the retailers follow Levi's suggested prices.[6]

The first selection in this chapter is a fast-moving *Business Week* feature article entitled, "Is John Sherman's Antitrust Obsolete?" It presents an excellent survey of the various interfaces between the antitrust laws and marketing channel strategy. The second selection by Professor Burley examines the current legal status of distribution system territorial restrictions. The recent Schwinn and Coors cases are examined and implications for channel strategy are discussed.

The third selection is entitled "Farewell to Fair Trade" and it examines a controversial forty-five year experiment in U.S. retailing. It is followed by an analysis of several recent legal actions involving shopping center development.

The fifth selection presents the very interesting case history of the Magnavox company and the legal and other problems involved in its channels of distribution. The final selection again illustrates the vigor of the Federal Trade Commission, in this instance as it attacks the problems of reciprocity. The article describes how the FTC attempts to protect smaller competitors in a marketing channel by the use of the "pernicious" test.

3. Louis M. Kohlmeier, "Supreme Court Rules Ford Can't Make Spark Plugs for 10 Years, Must Sell Line," *The Wall Street Journal* (March 30, 1972), p. 3.
4. *Ibid.*
5. "Levi Strauss Accused In Price Fix Count," *Tulsa Daily World* (May 8, 1976), p. B-3.
6. *Ibid.*

9.1 IS JOHN SHERMAN'S ANTITRUST OBSOLETE?

"Many businesspersons wonder whether their companies are often targets of antitrust prosecution simply because they are big and successful."

The head of the major U.S. corporation spoke feelingly: "I would be very glad if we knew exactly where we stand, if we could be free from danger, trouble, and criticism." His plea could have been made yesterday, by executives at IBM, Xerox, GTE, General Motors, AT&T, Exxon, Standard Brands, Chrysler, or dozens of other large companies that have recently stood in the dock, accused of violating the nation's antitrust laws.

It was, in fact, said back in 1912 by Elbert H. Gary, chairman of U.S. Steel Corp. He was giving a Congressional committee his views on the need for updating the country's first antitrust law, the Sherman Act, to which Ohio Senator John Sherman gave his name in 1890. Echoing the sentiments of many executives, Gary complained bitterly of the restraints imposed by the antitrust law on his company's ability to compete in world markets. Business had grown too big and complex, Gary maintained, to be shoehorned into laws drawn from Adam Smith's economic model of many small companies competing in local markets.

Two years later Congress gave Gary an unwelcome answer to his plea. It passed an even more restrictive antitrust measure, the Clayton Act, and set up the Federal Trade Commission to police business practices and methods of competition even more closely.

Today business faces much the same danger, trouble, and criticism that disturbed Gary, and is raising much the same complaints against antitrust. The International Telephone & Telegraph Corp. scandal and corporate participation in Watergate has stirred up deep public distrust of national institutions, including business. In response, as in Gary's day, the antitrust wind is rising, blown up currently by the oil crisis and fanned by consumerists, such as Ralph Nader, who argue that antitrust

Reprinted by permission from the publisher. "Is John Sherman's Antitrust Obsolete," *Business Week* (March 23, 1974), pp. 47–51ff.

weapons have been used like peashooters against dinosaurs. Business almost certainly faces even tougher antitrust enforcement and possibly even a new antitrust law aimed at breaking up the corporate giants in the country's basic industries.

This prospect points up the underlying question businessmen ask about antitrust: Are laws framed more than three-quarters of a century ago appropriate legal weapons in a market system grown increasingly large, complex, and multinational? In raising this basic issue, business-men can point to a far-reaching, intricate web of laws and rules that has made the government the regulator, watchdog, and even partner of business. Wage and price controls, health and safety regulations, and disclosure laws, are all a far cry from the economy of Sherman's or Gary's day.

Businessmen complain of the unsettling vagueness of the antitrust laws, which permits antitrusters to attack many long-standing business practices in their effort to root out restraints of trade and monopoly. The FTC, for example, is now suing Kellogg, General Foods, General Mills, and Quaker Oats, alleging that such procedures as having route men arrange their breakfast cereals on supermarket shelves are anticompeti-tive. The Justice Dept. has a similar suit against tire makers Goodyear and Firestone.

Executives of International Business Machines Corp., caught by both government and private antitrust suits attacking pricing and promotion policies, privately declare that they are baffled over what they can legally do. Bertram C. Dedman, vice-president and general counsel for INA Corp., echoes a widely held view: "We never really know precisely what antitrust means. It's frequently strictly a matter of opinion."

Enormous economic stakes are involved in antitrust enforcement. Such current cases as those against IBM, Xerox Corp., and other giants involve billions of dollars' worth of capital investment and stockholder interests. Executives fear that such suits give broad power to courts not schooled in business, economics, or industrial technology. This power was dramatically illustrated last fall when U.S. District Judge A. Sher-man Christensen announced a $352-million judgment against IBM and then confessed error, sending IBM's stock into wild gyrations.

Many businessmen wonder whether their companies are often targets of antitrust prosecution simply because they are big and successful. Philadelphia lawyer Edward D. Slevin sums up this attitude: "If the free market is pushed to its fullest extent, somebody wins. But the Jus-tice Dept. seems to say: 'Now that you've won, you've cornered the market. We're going to break you up and start over.'"

All this, say many executives, makes it increasingly difficult for Ameri-can business to compete internationally. Douglas Grymes, president of Koppers Co., argues that "big corporations are the only ones that can compete with big corporations in world markets." He says that the antitrust laws seem to equate bigness itself with monopoly and thus hinder American corporations from reaching the size necessary for world competition.

HOW JUSTICE AND THE FTC COMPETE

The antitrust laws exist to preserve the values of competition, so it may be entirely logical that two agencies compete to administer them. On paper, the Antitrust Div. of the Justice Dept. and the Federal Trade Commission are different kinds of agencies. Justice is the law enforcement branch of the Executive Branch, the FTC is an independent regulatory commission. But in their antitrust responsibilities they are quite similar.

The Antitrust Div. headed by Thomas E. Kauper, is responsible for enforcing the Sherman and Clayton Acts. It has the exclusive power to bring criminal prosecutions. It also tries to enjoin anticompetitive mergers and a variety of collusive practices. The FTC's power springs from the Federal Trade Commission Act of 1914. Over the years, the courts have interpreted Section 5 of that Act to include all offenses proscribed by the other antitrust laws, giving the FTC equal civil jurisdiction with Justice. In fact, it has a broader civil authority, since it is required to proceed against "unfair methods of competition" and, as added by the Wheeler-Lea Act of 1938, against "unfair or deceptive acts or practices in commerce." These phrases permit the FTC to go after business conduct that is not necessarily collusive. The FTC for example, has premised the cases against four big cereal makers on a variety of practices that it charges are unfair methods of competition, allegations that are not open to the Justice Dept. to make.

RESOURCES

The Antitrust Div. has an annual budget of some $14-million, the FTC $15-million for antitrust purposes. Both together represent tiny sums contrasted with the resources private business is able to draw on. International Business Machines Corp., for example, reimbursed Control Data Corp. $15 million in legal fees and expenses in settling the private suit CDC filed against IBM.

Occasionally the agencies take potshots at each other. The FTC last year finally got the power, formerly reserved to the Justice Dept., to go into court on its own to enforce its own decrees. The FTC complained that Justice sat on requests for action. Justice countered that the requests were poorly framed.

But the agencies usually work reasonably well together. Now, when good politics dictates making headlines as tough antitrusters, the brass at each shop says the rivalry between the two to bring and win significant cases serves as a spur to both. The rivalry, says Justice's Kauper, is a "friendly" one. "Each has kept the other at it," he says. The FTC's Halverson concurs, citing "good practical results" from the existence of two agencies.

Neither agency launches an investigation without first clearing it with the other. The first agency to propose a particular investigation gets it, provided there is no conflict with the other's on-going work. Disagreements are settled at weekly liaison meetings. When a conflict cannot be settled at meetings, the assistant attorney general and the chairman of the FTC, Lewis A. Engman, deal with it.

The home for a particular kind of case is partly a matter of historical accident and partly the predilection of staff lawyers. Price discrimination cases under the Robinson-Patman Act are traditionally prosecuted by the FTC, which also generally probes problems in food and textile industries. Justice almost always gets steel cases. While Justice must proceed on a case-by-case basis, the FTC has the power also to issue rules with the force of law, in effect to promulgate codes of commercial conduct. Until recently, Justice alone had specific authority to try to block an unconsummated merger. But the FTC just gained similar powers in the law authorizing the Alaska pipeline.

TOUGHER ENFORCEMENT LIKELY

Despite all these deeply felt concerns, the antitrust laws are likely to become even tougher and more restrictive. Starting with the Sherman Act, antitrust has been a product more of politics than of economics. Today's rising populist sentiment has led to demands for tighter antitrust enforcement. Only a decade ago historian Richard Hofstadter wrote, "The antitrust movement is one of the faded passions of American reform." Today it is the darling of reform. As James T. Halverson, director of the FTC's Bureau of Competition, sums up: "The political atmosphere is very favorable to antitrust right now."

The many signs of stepped-up antitrust activity in the last one or two years make an impressively lengthy list. They include:

NEW INVESTIGATIONS

Last week three federal agencies—Justice, the FTC, and the SEC—as well as some congressmen, revealed that they are turning to a little-used section of the Clayton Act to investigate the complex of interlocking directorships among major oil companies.

NEW LEGISLATION

The industrial reorganization bill that Senator Philip A. Hart (D-Mich.) introduced in Congress last year would provide a new legal basis for breaking up leading companies in the nation's most basic industries: autos, iron and steel, nonferrous metals, chemicals and drugs, electrical machinery and equipment, electronic computing and communications equipment, and energy. It is given no immediate chance to pass, but its ideas could find their way into future legislation. Another bill introduced by Senator John V. Tunney (D-Calif.), already approved by the Senate and taking a back seat to impeachment considerations in the House, would increase the current maximum criminal antitrust fine from $50,000 to $500,000 for corporations and $100,000 for executives. It would also require the Justice Dept. to explain publicly its reasons for accepting a consent decree instead of preparing a case and actually going to trial.

BIGGER ENFORCEMENT BUDGETS

The Administration is seeking large increases, by usually puny antitrust standards, in the fiscal 1975 budgets of both the Justice Dept. and the FTC for their antitrust departments. If Congress approves, Justice's Antitrust Div. will pick up 83 additional staff slots, more than half lawyers and economists. At the last big increase, fiscal 1970, the division got only 20. The FTC is due for an additional $3-million, or a 20% increase in its present antitrust budget.

GROWING MUSCLE AT FTC

After a long hibernation, the FTC is stepping out as a feisty agency with a new esprit, a highly professional staff, and a taste for going after bigness. It filed the monopoly suits against Xerox Corp. and the four biggest cereal makers. It has a special unit with an extra $1-million appropriation to litigate its case to break up the eight leading oil companies. And it got important new powers from Congress last year, including the right to demand otherwise unavailable product-line sales and profit figures from companies without first clearing with the Office of Management & Budget.

REORGANIZING JUSTICE

If the Justice Dept's monopoly case against IBM, filed more than five years ago, is successful, it would give new spirit to the Antitrust Div., which at least until recently has been demoralized by the successive shocks of ITT and Watergate. Even so, the division reorganized and beefed up its economics staff last fall to enable it to undertake investigations and prosecutions with a sharper eye to the economic impact of its actions.

More and tougher antitrust enforcement is foreshadowed by more subtle changes in mood and belief as well as by these specific developments. One such change is a growing recognition that the government itself creates monopoly power. Several weeks ago Columbia Law School called together many of the nation's leading industrial economists and antitrust lawyers for a conference on industrial concentration. The participants examined what business concentration means both for the economy and for antitrust policy. About the only thing generally agreed on was that governmental attempts to regulate an industry often result in preserving the monopoly power of those being regulated. In line with this belief, insiders say that the Antitrust Div. will step up its policy of intervening in other government proceedings to shape regulatory policy consistent with antitrust principles. Last January, for example, the division formally intervened in FCC proceedings in an attempt to deny renewal of the broadcasting license of Cowles Communications, Inc., in Des Moines, and those of Pulitzer Publishing Co. and Newhouse Broadcasting Corp. in St. Louis. All these companies also own newspapers.

Another change has been the dramatic multiplication of private antitrust suits—those brought by one company against another. These include the 40-odd private business suits against IBM, ITT's suit to split up General Telephone & Electronics Corp., and the large class actions against plumbing and wallboard manufacturers. In fiscal 1973 the government filed 45 antitrust suits. By comparison, businesssmen and other private parties filed 1,152, making the business community itself a significant factor in antitrust enforcement.

All this is leading to an antitrust Congress. Victor H. Kramer, director of Washington's Institute for Public Interest Representation and a leading antitrust lawyer, expects that "more supporters of an effective antimonopoly program are going to be elected to the 94th Congress than to any previous Congress in many years."

THE ALTERNATIVES

But as antitrust action steps up, so do the conflicts over the direction antitrust policy should take. The populists contend that antitrust enforcement in the past has been spineless. Businessmen complain that current policy paralyzes corporations because they are uncertain what practices are lawful and that they are being punished for being successfully competitive. Who is right?

The conflicts lead many businessmen to push for an up-dating of the antitrust laws. Richard L. Kattel, president of Atlanta's Citizens & Southern National Bank, which has been sparring with the Justice Dept. over the bank's expansion plans, feels that the antitrust laws "need complete revamping."

Major revamping, though, will not come because there is no general agreement on what form it should take. Most of the Columbia conference participants believe that the economic evidence for a change in policy is scanty and inconclusive. Suggestions ranged from doing nothing to pushing the tough Hart bill through Congress.

In approaching antitrust policy, there are alternatives:

1. ABOLISH THE LAWS ALTOGETHER

A very few economists, such as Yale Brozen of the University of Chicago, talk as though antitrust laws are largely unnecessary. But as Robert L. Werner, executive vice-president and general counsel of RCA Corp., told a Conference Board antitrust seminar earlier this month: "There should be little disagreement by industry over the basic validity of the doctrine of antitrust. Certainly no businessman would seriously suggest that we scuttle that doctrine and return to a pre-Shermanite jungle." The courts have ruled that such practices as fixing prices, dividing markets, boycotting, some mergers, and predatory pricing designed to destroy competitors unlawfully impose restraints on the market.

2. CLARIFY THE LAWS BY SPECIFYING PRECISELY WHAT BUSINESS PRACTICES ARE UNLAWFUL

If various practices can be identified and prohibited through case-by-case litigation, why not draft a detailed code of conduct?

But the very difficulty of identifying such practices when business conditions are constantly changing led to the broad wording of the Sherman Act originally. No one has ever produced an all-inclusive list of anticompetitive conduct. No one can possibly delineate all the circumstances that amount to price fixing and other illegal practices. If publication of future prices by members of a trade association is unlawful, as the Supreme Court held in 1921, is dissemination of past inventory figures and prices equally unlawful? (No, said the Court in 1925.) Moreover, as Thomas M. Scanlon, chairman of the American Bar Assn.'s 8,500-member antitrust section points out: "There's uncertainty in any kind of litigation. Laws intended to bring more certainty often bring less."

3. REPLACE ANTITRUST LAWS WITH DIRECT REGULATION

U.S. Steel's Gary favored and Koppers' Grymes favors a business-government partnership with this approval. Its advocates agree with John Kenneth Galbraith that antitrust is a "charade," that it has not and cannot produce a competitive economy in the face of the technological imperatives of large corporations. University of Chicago's George J. Stigler concludes that antitrust has not been "a major force" on the economy to date. "The government has won most of its 1,800 cases," he points out, "and there has been no important secular decline in concentration." On the other hand, many economists and lawyers would argue that Stigler has drawn the wrong conclusion. As Almarin Phillips, professor of economics and law at the Wharton School of Finance & Commerce, puts it: "The success of antitrust can only be measured by the hundreds of mergers and price-fixing situations that never happened."

Moreover, in the view of an increasing number of observers, regulation that is designed to mitigate the effects of "natural" monopolies, such as telephone service, often winds up fostering them instead. Civil Aeronautics Board regulations for example, have compelled higher airline rates than have prevailed on shorter, nonregulated interstate flights. Wesley James Liebler, recently named director of policy planning at the FTC, says: "What the airline industry needs is a little competition. In the long run we should get rid of the CAB and let in some free competition." Liebler also wants to abolish fixed commission rates for stockbrokers.

Much of the energy of regulatory commissions seems to be devoted to anticompetitive ends. The Federal Communications Commission promulgated rules several years ago designed to stifle the growth of pay-cable television. Sports events, for example, may not be broadcast on pay-cable TV if similar events have been shown on commercial television any time during the previous five years.

Walter Adams, a Michigan State University economist, notes that regulatory commissions can exclude competitors through licensing power, maintain price supports by regulating rates, create concentration through merger surveillance, and harass the weak by supervising practices that the strong do not like. To combat this kind of government behavior, the Antitrust Div. itself has, for the past several years, been intervening or attempting to intervene in such agencies as the ICC, CAB, and SEC to force decisions that spur competition in industry.

In support of their position, reformers make a further point: Large corporations have the political muscle to force the government to support their anticompetitive goals. Adams charges that the government has established an industrywide cartel for the oil companies through publishing monthly estimates of demand; through establishing quotas for each state pursuant to the Interstate Oil Compact, which Congress approved at behest of the oil companies; and through "prorationing devices" that dictate how much each well can produce. It is illegal to ship excess production in interstate commerce. Tariffs and import quotas protect only the producers, Adams says.

What this all amounts to is maintenance of shared monopoly power with the active cooperation of government. Only when the power of large companies is reduced, argue the populists, will the government be able to guide a competitive economy rather than serve as a prop for large interests. This was one of the original arguments for the Sherman Act in the 1880s.

4. MOVE TOWARD TOUGHER ENFORCEMENT

Populist critics of antitrust, such as Nader and Senator Hart, agree with Galbraith that antitrust has been all too ineffectual, but they move in the opposite policy direction. Since they believe that government regulation usually entrenches the power of big firms and concentrated industries, they favor a get-tough antitrust approach. They argue for two related tactics: extending existing law through the courts to curtail many practices of large firms in concentrated industries and getting Congressional legislation such as the Hart bill to attack the structure of these industries.

The Hart bill would permit the prosecution of companies because of their size alone. The history of antitrust has largely been to define and prosecute practices that courts would rule were restraints of trade, such as price fixing by agreement among competitors. But with increasing fervor, "structuralists" argue that size itself can be harmful.

HISTORICAL DEFICIENCIES

Before the Civil War, Americans felt uncomfortable with corporate bigness. The image of the yeoman farmer and the small, fiercely competitive businessman largely reflected economic reality. But the growth of railroads, with their "pools" carving up markets, changed all that. By 1871, Charles Francis Adams, grandson and great-grandson of presidents, was writing that corporations "have declared war, negotiated peace, reduced courts, legislatures, and sovereign states to an unqualified obedience to their will."

Populist politics, such as the formation of the Grange movement, picked up steam, but at the same time, in 1882, the first big trust, Standard Oil of Ohio, was born, followed by the Whiskey Trust, the Sugar Trust, the Lead Trust, and the Cotton Oil Trust. Senator Sherman warned that without federal action the country would confront "a trust for every production and a master to fix the price for every necessity of life." The upshot was his Sherman Act.

But federal prosecutions were limited, aimed mostly at fledgling labor unions, and the Sherman Act failed to curb bigness. Corporate mergers speeded up. U. S. Steel, Standard Oil (New Jersey), American Tobacco, American Can, International Harvester, and United Shoe Machinery were all put together at this time. As a result, antitrusters increased pressure for even tougher laws and an independent agency, which could develop industrial expertise, to enforce them.

These efforts came to fruition in 1914, with the passage of the Clayton and Federal Trade Commission Acts. The Clayton Act specifically banned anticompetitive mergers, while the FTC Act set up an agency to police "unfair competition" in the marketplace but not to regulate prices and output.

Like the Sherman Act, the Clayton Act proved ineffectual for many years, largely because of the way courts interpreted the law. As recently as 1948 the Court permitted U.S. Steel to acquire one of its own customers.

Partly in response to this decision, Congress passed the Celler-Kefauver Act in 1950, amending the Clayton Act to prohibit mergers through acquisition of assets or stock as well as those that would tend to foreclose competition in any market in the country. This effectively closed the door on many mergers. But the merger wave of the late 1960s comprised so-called conglomerate get-togethers of companies in different, often unrelated, industries. The case intended to settle this issue—ITT—never got to the Supreme Court because it was settled by a consent decree.

Mergers became the target of antitrusters because they mean the disappearance of independent competitors and lead to concentrations of industrial power. And, argue antitrusters, a few large companies may "share" monopoly power simply by dominating a given market. But unless collusion among competitors can be proved, there is no way under conventional enforcement to prosecute them.

CONFLICTING VIEWS

To remedy this supposed defect Senator Hart's new law would create a presumption of monopoly power whenever:

A company's average rate of return is greater than 15% of its net worth for each of five consecutive years.

There has been no substantial price competition for three consecutive years among two or more corporations within an industry.

Four or fewer companies account for half or more of an industry's sales in a single year.

Clearly, these criteria create a net that would sweep up hundreds of large corporations. Hart's staff estimates, for example, that a quarter to a third of all U.S. manufacturing concerns meet the third condition.

A company that met any of these criteria would not automatically have to divest. Its defense before the special agency and court the bill would create could be either that its position rests on legally acquired patents or that divesting would deprive it of "substantial economies." (At present economics are not a defense.)

Howard O'Leary, chief counsel to Hart's antitrust subcommittee, argues that without "some mandate" from Congress, the Justice Dept. would be unlikely to embark "on an antitrust crusade." The bill would provide that mandate.

Senator Hart asserts that statistics can be misleading. He cites concentration ratios which according to economists show competition in the oil industry. But, says Hart, "Look at the evidence of joint ventures, banking interlocks, vertical integration, joint ownership of facilities, joint production, absence of real price competition, and lockstep decision-making, and one must wonder."

Economist Walter Adams agrees. He points out that between 1956 and 1968, 20 major oil companies were involved in 226 mergers and thereby gained control over a variety of substitute fuels, such as coal and atomic energy. The oil companies also moved into allied businesses, such as fertilizers, plastics, and chemicals, through vertical integration. Adams believes that a new law is necessary to fragment the power of the companies in the oil and other industries.

The only businessmen to come forward so far in support of at least the thrust of what Senator Hart is trying to do, says O'Leary, are some in communications and data processing. Through a series of hearings the subcommittee hopes, says O'Leary, "to persuade politicians and to some extent the public that it is feasible to come up with more firms than now exist, that the market won't crash, and that jobs won't be lost."

Most other businessmen see little good in the Hart bill. Carl H. Madden, chief economist for the U. S. Chamber of Commerce, brands its basic thrust as "faulty." He told Senate hearings last spring that the bill would thwart competition, not aid it, "by changing the legally permitted goal and cutting back the prizes."

Legal experts have many other objections. Richard Posner, of the University of Chicago Law School, feels that the Hart bill is symptomatic of "antitrust off on a tangent." Antitrust chief Thomas E. Kauper is not "satisfied with the economic evidence favoring broad deconcentration statutes." Kellogg Co. vice-president and corporate counsel J. Robert O'Brien says: "There is no reason whatever to assume that a 'concentrated' industry will necessarily be any less competitive than a fractionated industry. A course of antitrust enforcement that seeks to break up companies and restructure industries by looking at little more than concentration levels is misguided, to say the least."

Many have pointed out that among the defects in Hart's approach is the difficulty of measuring and the ease of manipulating rates of return. Further, even Ralph Nader, a supporter of the bill, says that deconcentrating an industry "is a 15-year job, at least."

THE SUPREME COURT'S TOUGHER STANCE

Although there have been hundreds of antitrust decisions, the following Supreme Court cases would be on any list as landmarks on the road to tougher antitrust:

Standard Oil Co. of N. J. v. U. S. (1911).   Only "unreasonable" restraints of trade are prohibited. To be guilty of monopolization, a company must have "purpose or intent" to exercise monopoly power.

American Column & Lumber Co v. U. S. (1921).   Control of competition through a trade association that distributes current price and inventory information and company-by-company forecasts, is unlawful.

Maple Flooring Manufacturers Assn. v. U. S. (1925).   Mere dissemination of cost and past price and inventory statistics through a trade association is not unlawful.

U. S. v. Trenton Potteries Co. (1927).   Price-fixing is inherently unreasonable and any such agreement is a per se violation of the Sherman Act.

Interstate Circuit, Inc., v. U. S. (1939).   Consciously parallel behavior, where each competitor knew, even without direct communication with the others, how to act in order to control the market, is unlawful.

U. S. v. Socony Vacuum Oil Co. (1940).   Program by a group of oil companies to purchase surplus gasoline on spot market from independent refiners in order to stabilize price violates the Sherman Act.

Fashion Originators Guild v. FTC (1941).   Group boycotts are per se unlawful.

U. S. v. Aluminum Co. (1945).   It is not a defense to a charge of monopolization that the company was not morally derelict or predatory in its abuse of monopoly power. Even though monopoly may have been "thrust upon" the company because of its superior foresight, actions designed to prevent competition from arising constitute unlawful monopolization.

International Salt Co. v. U. S. (1947).   Tying agreements are unlawful per se.

Theatre Enterprises v. Paramount Film Distributing Corp. (1954). Parallel behavior in the absence of any collusive activity is not unlawful per se.

U. S. v. United Shoe Machinery Corp. (1954).   Business practices that "further the dominance of a particular firm" are unlawful where the company has monopoly power.

Du Pont-GM Case (1956).   The government may move to undo a merger not only immediately after stock is acquired but whenever the requisite lessening of competition is likely to occur, even if that is decades after the merger.

Brown Shoe Co. v. U. S. (1962).   For purposes of determining a merger's effects on competition, there may be broad markets "determined by the reasonable interchangeability" of products and also "well-defined submarkets," whose boundaries may be determined by examining industrial customs and practices.

U. S. v. Philadelphia National Bank (1963).   "A merger which produces a firm controlling an undue percentage share of the relevant market and results in a significant increase in the concentration of firms in that market, is so inherently likely to lessen competition substantially that it must be enjoined in the absence of evidence clearly showing that the merger is not likely to have such anticompetitive effects."

El Paso Natural Gas Co. v. U. S. (1964).   A merger that eliminates substantial potential competition violates the Clayton Act.

U. S. v. Penn-Olin Chemical Co. (1964).   A joint venture by two competitors may violate the Clayton Act.

U. S. v. Pabst Brewing Co. (1966).   A merger with "substantial anti-competitive effect somewhere in the U. S." is unlawful.

U. S. v. Arnold, Schwinn & Co. (1967).   It is unlawful per se for a manufacturer to limit its wholesalers' rights to sell goods purchased from the manufacturer.

U. S. v. Topco Associates (1972).   All territorial allocations among distributors are unlawful, even if they might foster competition against others.

WHEN COMPANIES SUE EACH OTHER

Professor George J. Stigler of the University of Chicago, chairman of President Nixon's Task Force on Antitrust, finds the whole subject of antitrust "a dull field with few sensations." He makes an exception of the rise of the private antitrust case, which he calls "fascinating."

In recent years private companies have been suing each other furiously under the antitrust laws, far outpacing the government. In the past two fiscal years the government filed 108 antitrust suits against private business. But in the same period companies filed 2,451 suits against other companies. In fiscal 1960 there were only a paltry 228 private suits.

Dr. Irwin M. Stelzer, president of National Economic Research Associates, Inc., a large antitrust-oriented consulting firm, explains that private suits began to increase markedly following the electrical equipment price-fixing conspiracy cases in the early 1960s. State public utility commissions said, in effect, that if utilities had a remedy for overcharges as a result of antitrust violations but failed to bring suit to recover, the commission would not approve rate increases to cover the losses. The same principle applied to all corporations: Failure to pursue antitrust remedies could subject them to stockholder derivative suits. So, according to Stelzer, what had seemed to the big names in the antitrust bar as seamy litigation far beneath their notice, like chasing ambulances, suddenly became necessary and glamorous.

Maxwell Blecher, antitrust attorney in Los Angeles, sees the rise of private antitrust suits in the past 10 years as a transfer of power. "The government has failed to act and the private sector has filled the vacuum," he says. He attributes the change in part to different business attitudes. "Management is now result-oriented rather than concerned about being accepted at the club." He expects the number of private suits to to continue to increase.

Anyone can sue. Stigler strongly supports the private use of the antitrust laws, a concept introduced into the Clayton Act in 1914. Anyone injured by a violation of the laws can sue as a "private attorney general." To sweeten the burden, courtroom success is rewarded with triple money damages plus attorneys' fees. "Anybody should be able to enforce the antitrust laws," says Stigler. "There is no way for bureaucrats to know what is happening. The only way the government finds out is through letters of complaint."

In 1966 the Supreme Court approved changes in the procedural rules governing class actions, making it easier for large classes of people or groups to pool common claims and seek relief through coordinated efforts of their attorneys. The number of private antitrust suits soared.

Businessmen began to see the specter of numerous nuisance suits. Victor H. Kramer of the Institute for Public Interest Representation agrees that there may be some but believes that "this is a fair price" for the meritorious suits. Thomas E. Kauper, Justice Dept. antitrust chief, says there is some basis for the businessman's concern, but he thinks that the courts will become increasingly experienced in using the class action rules to strike a fair balance. George R. Kucik, an antitrust attorney with Arent, Fox, Kintner, Plotkin & Kahn in Washington, suggests that consideration be given to changing the law with respect to the large class action sponsored by municipal or state governments in order to permit ordinary, not treble, damages. "If the pool is big enough to begin with," he says, "there is no need for the trebling." This idea is embodied in the Uniform State Antitrust Act, a new law being pushed by the National Conference of Commissioners on Uniform State Laws. It permits individuals and businesses to seek treble damages but holds governmental units to actual damages plus attorneys' fees.

OTHER TACTICS

Antitrusters are not holding their breath waiting for legislation. In a series of cases initiated during the past five years, they are using existing laws prohibiting monopolization and unfair methods of competition to check alleged anticompetitive conditions in concentrated industries.

The FTC's suit against Xerox and the Justice Dept's against IBM represent marked change from the past. The government has brought very few cases against single companies for alleged monopoly, partly because of limited prosecution budgets, partly because of political pressure from business, and partly because officials thought them unnecessary. These two recent suits single out a variety of practices—pricing policies, for example, and such things as announcing products embodying new technology far in advance of actual availability—that are alleged ways the two companies exercise monopoly power. The antitrust subcommittee's O'Leary says, "The IBM case is potentially very significant, if it is won and a remedy can be found. It is the first such case in 25 years."

The Justice Dept. also brought suit last August against Goodyear and Firestone, charging them with monopolizing the replacement tire market through a combination of practices, including acquisitions, periods of uneconomically low prices designed to drive out competitive products, service station tie-ins, and reciprocity deals. The two companies are charged with acting independently to maintain their dominant positions; they are not charged with collusion.

Perhaps the most innovative case is the FTC's suit against the four leading breakfast food makers, charging them with a variety of unfair methods of competition. The Commission is not claiming any conspiracy among the companies. It is trying to prove, instead, that a lengthy list of long-standing industry practices are anticompetitive and permit the companies, whose market shares have gone from 68% in 1940 to 90% today, to "share" monopoly power in their respective industries. If successful, this suit would strengthen the commission's ability to use its statute to go after many heavily concentrated industries.

The FTC's current prosecution against the eight major oil companies also attempts to break new ground. The key allegation is that the majors have been "pursuing a common course" in using control of crude oil and shipping facilities to stall the development of independent refineries. This includes eliminating retail competition by keeping prices low at the refinery and marketing end and high at the production end of the business. The FTC also charges the companies with such practices as using barter and exchange agreements to keep crude oil in their own hands and reluctance to sell to independent marketers. Unlike the cereal suits, the FTC charges that some of the oil practices are collusive.

CAN WE COMPETE?

In the face of government attack, some businessmen wonder whether such antitrust action aimed at cutting down corporate size might not handicap U. S. companies in keeping pace with the growing number of multinational corporations around the world. Koppers Co.'s Grymes, who argues for permitting mergers, would prefer to see the government "adopt a whole new philosophy of life." He would like to see 26 steel companies, for example, merged into five or six. "Let them get together, produce together, sell together," he says. He concedes that to make up for the absence of competition, the government would have to levy an excess-profits tax or put limitations on investments. He vigorously opposes the Hart bill.

So does J. Fred Weston, a professor at the University of California at Los Angeles' Graduate School of Management, and for similar reasons. "The world market requires increasingly large firms," he argues. "If we hold on to the 18th century idea of a nation of small shopkeepers and small farms, we will become a small nation." Unlike Grymes, Weston would not encourage mergers. Rather, he is against "fighting a rearguard battle to prevent deconcentration based on invalid premises." Corporate size, he insists, should be judged in relation to the world market. "If there are firms of increasing size abroad and there are economies of scale, U. S. firms have to be able to compete."

Supporters of deconcentration policy do not quarrel with the premise that U. S. companies must be able to compete, but they do argue that existing levels of concentration in many industries are more than adequate. They believe that size alone is not a guarantee of economies of scale or of efficiencies. And they point to industrial studies indicating that economies of scale relate primarily to plant size but not necessarily to the numbers of plants that any one manufacturer controls.

Frederic M. Scherer, the FTC's incoming economics bureau chief, believes that economic studies show that many industries are more concentrated than efficiency requires. Nader argues that the best evidence is "clinical, not statistical." He says that studies of industries that have become less concentrated would show consumer gains without loss of efficiency. The arrival of a new supermarket chain in the Washington metropolitan area several years ago, he says, forced prices down, and he cites the aluminum industry after Aluminum Co. of America had to face competition. It was still able to compete.

Moreover, the fact that a company can be efficient does not mean that it will be. On the contrary, absence of competition may make the company fat and lazy—capable of efficiency but acting inefficiently because it is not spurred by the need to compete.

In the 1950 Congressional hearings on monopoly power, Benjamin Fairless, president of U. S. Steel, admitted that his company had less efficient production processes than its competitors, including much smaller foreign companies. Studies have demonstrated that American steel producers lagged woefully in innovation. Between 1940 and 1955, 13 major inventions came from abroad, yet American steel boasted the largest companies in the world.

The basic oxygen process, which Avery C. Adams, chairman and president of Jones & Laughlin Steel Corp., described in 1959 as "the only major technological breakthrough at the ingot level in the steel industry since before the turn of the century," was perfected by a tiny

Austrian steel company in 1950. It was introduced into the U. S. in 1954 by McLouth Steel Corp., which then had less than 1% of American ingot capacity. Jones & Laughlin waited until 1957, and U. S. Steel and Bethlehem Steel Corp. waited until 1964 to adopt the process, resulting in lost profits to the steel industry, according to one study, of some $216-million after taxes by 1960 alone.

As for ability to compete abroad, there is practically no evidence that the Justice Dept. has impaired the competitive posture of U. S. companies in world markets. In the past few years the Justice, Commerce, and Treasury Depts., as well as Congressional committees, have practically pleaded for businessmen to come forward with examples of how Americans have been hurt, with minimal results. The Antitrust Div.'s recent release of business review letters from 1968 through 1972 indicates not a single turndown of joint export ventures.

David H. Baker, director of the Commerce Dept.'s Office of Export Development, made an intense search for examples of antitrust harm. A large food company wanted to enter a joint venture with another big U. S. outfit to bid on a plant an Eastern European government planned to build. The Justice Dept. indicated it might refuse to approve the deal, and the food company pulled out. A small U. S. company then bid for the contract on its own and won.

A NEW APPROACH

Some experts believe that the government cannot deal with business complaints adequately unless it develops a comprehensive approach to competition generally. Victor Kramer suggests the creation of an "office of antimonopoly affairs" within the Executive Office of the President. The function of this office, Kramer says, would be to implement a new executive order he would like to see promulgated, directing all federal agencies to act to promote a "free competitive enterprise system." It would require the federal departments and bureaus to prepare antitrust impact statements whenever they suggest action that would "significantly affect competition in the private sector."

Professor Neil H. Jacoby, of UCLA's Graduate School of Management, agrees with the general thrust of Kramer's suggestion. Jacoby, who believes that oligopoly is here to stay, proposes the creation of a Federal Competition Agency, either as an independent commission or within the White House. He would have it submit a "competition impact report" for "all proposed federal legislation."

Kramer concludes that his policy would have compelled the State Dept. to evaluate publicly the competitive impact of the voluntary steel import agreements with Japan and European nations. The Pentagon would have been called on to explain how the public benefits from the awarding of nonbid contracts. The Internal Revenue Service and the White House, he believes, would have to consider the competitive effects of proposed changes in tax laws.

This broadened approach to competition could come closer to resolving the conflicts between the tendency of companies to exert control over their markets and the public requirement that monopoly be held in check. Short of this, the evidence suggests that antitrust is the best we have.

QUESTIONS FOR DISCUSSION

1. The antitrust laws are known to be relatively vague and ambiguous. Discuss a number of specific examples that illustrate the complexity of the antitrust laws.

2. The FTC and the Justice Department are increasing the vigor with which the antitrust laws are enforced. Why has this taken place?

3. The article mentions that the FTC and the Justice Department "compete." Explain.

4. Discuss fully each of the four basic alternatives to the present antitrust laws.

5. Explain Senator Hart's proposed changes in the antitrust laws.

6. Under what circumstances can companies sue each other under the antitrust laws?

7. The article states, "Some experts believe that the government cannot deal with business complaints adequately unless it develops a comprehensive approach to competition generally." Assume you are a consultant to the U. S. Government. Develop the comprehensive approach to competition which is desired.

9.2 TERRITORIAL RESTRICTIONS IN DISTRIBUTION SYSTEMS: CURRENT LEGAL DEVELOPMENTS

James R. Burley

". . . Those firms that rely on restrictive distribution arrangements must assess their present situation to determine if their distribution systems are in violation of any of these recent holdings."

Any business in the United States that produces a product that is in any way unique may, at some point, want to develop a method to control the distribution of that product. Familiar control techniques include resale price maintenance as well as resale restrictions on the types of customers or territories serviced by the company's distributors and dealers. Recently the Supreme Court upheld a 1974 decision that may have tremendous impact on every business that uses resale restrictions. This article will examine the present legal situation with respect to resale restrictions on territories or customers and will show why the Supreme Court decision in the Coors case may have an impact on the marketing strategy of many firms in this country.

IMPORTANCE TO MARKETING STRATEGISTS

Territorial restrictions have become an accepted practice in the distribution of many products. Some wholesale and retail firms will not consider distributing a product unless a reasonable protection of the investment made to promote and service it is guaranteed by the manufacturer. Likewise, many manufacturers have elected to restrict the distribution of their products for strategic reasons such as limited productive capability or image protection. Many firms at both the manufacturing and distributing levels of the channel rely on territorial restrictions to facilitate

Reprinted by permission from James R. Burley, "Territorial Restrictions in Distribution Systems: Current Legal Developments," *Journal of Marketing* (October 1975), pp. 52–56.

the orderly distribution of a product. However, recent antitrust decisions have held many territorial or customer restrictions to be in violation of the law. Clearly, those firms that rely on restrictive distribution arrangements must assess their present situation to determine if their distribution systems are in violation of any of these recent holdings. In addition, marketing managers must be aware of regulatory changes that are taking place in distribution in order to plan future marketing strategies.

LEGAL DEVELOPMENT OF TERRITORIAL RESTRICTION SITUATIONS

Territorial and customer restrictions were allowed under antitrust interpretations until 1963. At that time, in the White Motor case, the Supreme Court enunciated the "rule of reason" doctrine for evaluating territorial or customer restrictions.[1] The Court indicated that the reasonableness of the particular restriction would be used to determine if a restraint of trade had occurred. The "rule of reason" prevailed as the method used to determine the legality of territorial or customer restrictions until the Schwinn decision in 1967.[2] In the Schwinn decision, the Supreme Court declared all control techniques associated with territorial allocation or restriction to be per se violations of the Sherman Antitrust Act if title to the product had passed to the dealer. The only exception mentioned in the decision was for those reasonable restrictions used by failing companies or newcomers to a market. This decision negated the White Motor doctrine, which had established the requirement of testing the restriction for its reasonableness. The "per se" rule established in the Schwinn case meant that the reasonableness of the restraints would no longer be evaluated. *Any* restraint of territory or customer used by an established prospering company was illegal if title had passed from manufacturer to dealer.

Because the Schwinn decision declared vertical territorial restraints imposed on distribution channel members to be illegal per se, many manufacturers altered their distribution structures to either eliminate territorial restraints or to establish consignment sales systems by which they maintained ownership of the product until transfer to the final consumer.

Many subsequent lower court decisions, however, have not followed the Schwinn per se rule but have distinguished their arguments on some particular point. (See Figure 1.) The majority of these decisions deal with the statement in the per se ruling that describes the reasonable

1. *White Motor Co. v. United States*, 372 U.S. 253 (1963).
2. *United States v. Arnold, Schwinn and Co.*, 388 U.S. 365 (1967).

defenses available to failing companies or newcomers. Those defenses have been expanded to include other reasonable exceptions to the Schwinn rules, and the Supreme Court has not acted to close the gap in interpretation. The following discussion examines the primary exceptions to the Schwinn doctrine and those cases where the doctrine has been upheld.

EXCEPTIONS TO THE SCHWINN DOCTRINE

The narrowed view of the Schwinn decision has received some attention in the legal literature. In two of these articles, the commentators point out the types of lower court decisions that have expanded the exceptions to the per se doctrine as well as the test of what constitutes a reasonable restraint.[3] These types of exceptions are discussed below.

NOT FIRM AND RESOLUTE IN REFUSING TO DEAL

The first group of exceptions to the per se rule can be classified as those involving companies that are not "firm and resolute" in their policy of refusing to deal with dealers that do not adhere to territorial restrictions. In a case where no proof was offered that the firm had ever enforced its territorial sales restrictions, the court found that the practice needed to be tested under the rule of reason and was not per se illegal, even though the situation involved the sale of a product.[4] In a similar situation in which sales territories were assigned but not enforced, the court said: "assignment of territories or customers, even in a contract, is insufficient to establish a per se violation; some element of enforcement of the restriction on the part of the manufacturer is required."[5] Finally, this approach was repeated in a case where the distribution territories were assigned but not enforced.[6] Thus, the imposition of territorial restraints, even in the presence of sale, may not constitute a per se violation of the Sherman Act if the company has not been firm

3. Comment, "Territorial and Customer Restrictions: A Trend Toward a Broader Rule of Reason?" *George Washington Law Review*, Vol. 30 (1971), p. 123; and Comment, "Vertical Territorial and Customer Restrictions Under the Sherman Act: Decisions Since United States v. Arnold Schwinn & Co.," *Journal of Public Law*, Vol. 22 (1973), p. 483.

4. *Janel Sales Corp. v. Lanvin Parfums, Inc.*, 396 F. 2d, 398 (2d Cir. 1968), 303 U. W. 938 (1968).

5. *United States v. Eaton, Yale & Towne, Inc.*, Trade Cases ¶ 73, 889 (D. Conn. 1972).

6. *Colorado Pump & Supply Co. v. Febco, Inc.*, 472 F. 2d 637 (10th Cir. 1973), 411 U.S. 987 (1973).

FIG. 9.1   Legal Development of Territorial and Customer Restrictions.

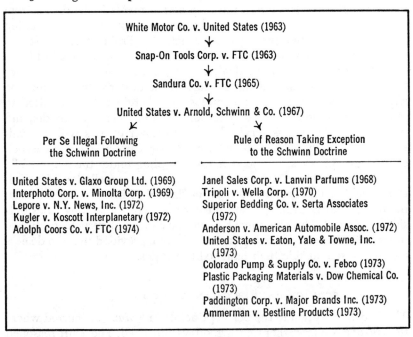

White Motor Co. v. United States (1963)

Snap-On Tools Corp. v. FTC (1963)

Sandura Co. v. FTC (1965)

United States v. Arnold, Schwinn & Co. (1967)

Per Se Illegal Following the Schwinn Doctrine	Rule of Reason Taking Exception to the Schwinn Doctrine
United States v. Glaxo Group Ltd. (1969)	Janel Sales Corp. v. Lanvin Parfums (1968)
Interphoto Corp. v. Minolta Corp. (1969)	Tripoli v. Wella Corp. (1970)
Lepore v. N.Y. News, Inc. (1972)	Superior Bedding Co. v. Serta Associates (1972)
Kugler v. Koscott Interplanetary (1972)	Anderson v. American Automobile Assoc. (1972)
Adolph Coors Co. v. FTC (1974)	United States v. Eaton, Yale & Towne, Inc. (1973)
	Colorado Pump & Supply Co. v. Febco (1973)
	Plastic Packaging Materials v. Dow Chemical Co. (1973)
	Paddington Corp. v. Major Brands Inc. (1973)
	Ammerman v. Bestline Products (1973)

and resolute in forcing compliance with the assignment by canceling franchises or other techniques.

DANGEROUS PRODUCTS

A second exception to the Schwinn rule deals with dangerous products. In a case where special haircolor application procedures were necessary to prevent blindness and other equally undesirable effects resulting from improper application, the court held that the restraints that allowed sales only to qualified applicators were reasonable.[7] Another case suggested that safety factors may be justification for territorial restrictions as well as customer restrictions.[8] Exception to the per se rule has occurred where the products are dangerous or have inherent safety characteristics that require qualified dealers or distributors.

AREAS OF PRIMARY RESPONSIBILITY

A third exception to the Schwinn rule has occurred in the definition in franchise agreements of "areas of primary responsibility." Such agree-

7. *Tripoli v. Wella Corp.*, 425 F. 2d 932 (3d Cir. 1970), 400 U.S. 831 (1970).
8. *United States v. Safety First Products Corp.*, Trade Cases π 74, 223 (S. D. N. Y. 1972).

ments designate the geographic region within which the dealer is to make his primary sales effort, but they do not preclude the dealer from selling outside that territory.[9] Another case involving primary trading areas deal with the profit-passover activity. Profit-passover clauses are used to compensate a dealer for sales that are made within his assigned territory by another dealer. The justification for such clauses rests on the argument that the demand in the dealer's territory may be affected by his advertising and promotion; therefore, he is entitled to some compensation as the party responsible for generating the demand that another dealer has serviced. Profit-passover clauses will be evaluated on an individual basis to determine their reasonableness since such clauses are not per se illegal.[10] A similar ruling under the Automobile Dealers' Day in Court Act was used to allow the cancellation of a dealer's franchise. The dealer had been neglectful of his responsibilities to the manufacturer in his primary area while actively seeking sales outside his area.[11] The assignment of primary areas of responsibility appears to be a reasonable exception to *Schwinn*, provided that the dealers are free to sell outside their assigned territories.

SALE OF A SERVICE RATHER THAN A GOOD

The fourth exception to the per se principle in *Schwinn* occurred where the sale of a service rather than a good was involved. The court reasoned that since the per se rule applied to the sale of a good in the Schwinn language, the sale of services, with territorial restraints, needed to be tested under the rule of reason.[12] This decision points out one of the confusing aspects of *Schwinn*: the sale of services does not receive the same treatment as the sale of goods.

OTHER EXCEPTIONS

Other cases have departed from the basic Schwinn rule for a number of reasons. One exception occurred where a firm was allowed to sell goods to foreign distributors at a lower price than he sold to U.S. distributors, provided that the goods not be resold in the United States, thereby escaping the duty on the goods.[13] In another action, involving the sale of

9. *Plastic Packaging Materials, Inc. v. Dow Chemical Co.*, 327 F. Supp. 213 (E. D. Pa. 1971).

10. *Superior Bedding Co. v. Serta Associates, Inc.* 353 F. Supp. 1143 (N.D. Ill. 1972).

11. *Frank Chevrolet Co. v. General Motors Corp.*, 419 F. 2d. 1054 (6th Cir. 1969).

12. *Anderson v. American Automobile Assoc.*, 454 F. 2d 1240 (9th Cir. 1972).

13. *Paddington Corp. v. Major Brands, Inc.*, 359 F. Supp. 1244 (W. D. Okla. 1973). This decision is consistent with the immunity granted to exporters under the Webb-Pomerene Act, 15 U.S.C. 61065 (1918).

home cleaning products combined with territorial restrictions, the court, rather than follow *Schwinn* and declare a per se violation, requested a test of the reasonableness of the territorial restrictions. This ruling constitutes an effective recognition of exceptions to the Schwinn doctrine.[14] Thus, expansion of the exceptions available as defenses under the Schwinn doctrine has occurred outside the previously identified major areas.

CASES UPHOLDING THE SCHWINN DOCTRINE

During this same period, a number of cases have upheld the Schwinn doctrine by declaring sales situations coupled with territorial restriction to be per se violations of the Sherman Act.[15] Such a ruling was applied to a newspaper that assigned carriers specific territories. The court said:

> I find that by inference from the exclusive territory provisions of the carrier agreements, the plaintiffs have not been permitted to sell the *News* outside their own territories. This is a per se violation of Section 1 of the Sherman Act.[16]

Likewise, in a pyramid distribution structure that specified that each dealer could buy only from his supplier and could sell only to his own organization, the court found the territorial and customer restraints to be per se illegal.[17] Another case that followed the Schwinn doctrine involved a moving company agent who was not allowed to solicit business inside another agent's territory. The territorial restrictions were allowed when applied in this agency situation, because the agency relationship meant that title had not passed and, therefore, the restrictions had to be tested under the rule of reason.[18]

The Minolta case, which also followed *Schwinn*, overturned an argument of reasonableness because of the need for orderly marketing. Minolta had contracted with independent distributors for coverage of certain regions where Minolta did not have a factory-owned distributor. In fringe areas (bordering a company distributor and factory distributor) many retail dealers tried to convince the nearby independent distributors to sell at lower than factory prices. This arrangement could increase the distributor's total volume and not affect sales within his assigned area. Minolta argued that cancellations of franchises of dis-

14. *Ammerman v. Bestline Products, Inc.*, 352 F. Supp. 1077 (E. D. Wis. 1973).
15. *United States v. Glaxo Group Ltd.*, 302 F. Supp. 1 (D. D. C. 1969).
16. *Lepore v. New York News, Inc.*, 347 F. Supp. 755, 761 (S.D.N.Y. 1972).
17. *Kugler v. Koscott Interplanetary, Inc.*, 293 F. 2d. 682 (N.J. 1972).
18. *Clemmer v. North American Van Lines*, Trade Cases ¶ 72, 936 (E. D. Pa. 1969).

tributors who sold in the factory distributor's territory were allowed because of the need for orderly marketing. Minolta's dealers were not sure which distributor to purchase from, and Minolta encountered problems in the distribution of its products because of this confusion. However, the court rejected this argument on the basis of the Schwinn doctrine of the per se illegality of such restrictions.[19]

A 1974 decision in the Coors Brewery case found a vertical territorial restraint system to be in violation of the Sherman Act.[20] The decision was rendered by the circuit court of appeals and an appeal to the Supreme Court has been denied, thereby upholding the lower court's ruling. The Coors decision was also decided in a manner consistent with the Schwinn decision, but it raises new issues of major significance to distribution.

Adolph Coors Company, a beer manufacturer located in Golden, Colorado, used a distribution system that included territories allocated to the firm's 166 independent distributors. The court said that the territorial restrictions were a per se violation of the Sherman Act, following the Schwinn doctrine. Coors argued that because its beer was produced using a much costlier process, because it needed special refrigeration at the distributor level, and because it had a very limited shelf life, the restrictions were reasonable. The firm pointed out that since it was necessary for a Coors distributor to make a larger investment in physical facilities to insure the freshness of the beer, the protective provisions were justified. The need to insure freshness was the reason the manufacturer had dropped central warehouse accounts in 1966. The large retailers' central warehouses could not insure freshness of the product and maintain the tight turnover requirements that were imposed upon distributors. Restricted distribution also provided the high market penetration rates necessary to make a single-brewery production system profitable.

The court of appeals could not accept the argument that the reasonableness of the territorial restrictions should be tested because the beer required specialized distribution techniques. Rather, the court followed the Schwinn doctrine and declared the restrictions per se violations of the Sherman Act.

IMPLICATIONS AND FUTURE DEVELOPMENTS

Present business practices recognize the importance of the exclusive distribution process that has been established in the United States. When the Supreme Court denied the appeal in the Coors case, it was in fact

19. *Interphoto Corp. v. Minolta Corp.*, 295 F. Supp. 711 (S.D.N.Y. 1969).
20. *Adolph Coors Co. v. FTC*, 497 F. 2d 1178 (10th Cir. 1974).

approving the lower court's ruling. This indicates that the Schwinn doctrine—that control techniques associated with territorial allocation or restriction are per se violations of the Sherman Act if title to the product has passed to the dealer—is still considered the guiding rule in territorial restriction. The Coors decision, along with previous vertical territorial restriction cases, has created a dilemma for the marketing manager. Since a number of exceptions have been allowed under the Schwinn doctrine, the firm contemplating the use of a vertical territorial restriction should determine if the product falls into one of the categories of exceptions. If one of the exceptions is not available to the firm, alternative control strategies will be necessary.

The only allowable control technique available to the manufacturer under a strict interpretation of the Schwinn doctrine is an agency distribution structure wherein the manufacturer maintains title, dominion, and risk over the product until it is transferred to the ultimate consumer. Under such a system, resale and customer or territorial restrictions can be maintained. The cost of such a system will place exceptional demands for capital on the manufacturers, who will need to maintain ownership until the sale is consummated. Many manufacturers who have established substantial preferences for their product by quality control or strict dealer selection may be forced to relinquish control over the resale of their products and hence lose some of the differential advantage they have established. It must be concluded that a strict interpretation of the doctrine places severe limitations on manufacturers who wish to control some aspect of the distribution of their product.

If the manufacturers elect not to maintain control over their distribution channels, then hardships for intermediaries could result. In the Coors distribution system, each of the distributors was required to make a substantial investment in refrigerated storage facilities. If the Coors distributors were not assured some reasonable protected market, there would be no justification for the additional investment (when compared to other beer distributors) necessary to be a Coors distributor. A similar situation can be expected for every distribution channel member who is required to make substantial investments in equipment, training, or promotional activities in support of a manufacturer's product. Without some assurance that a competitor will not open a business next door, the additional investment necessary to carry some products may not be justifiable.

CONCLUSION

The conclusion must be reached that the Supreme Court's refusal to hear the appeal in the Coors case means the question of restrictive distribution must remain undecided for a time. Whether a further expansion of exceptions will occur is also questionable. The Court's acceptance of the Coors decision has meant that:

1. Confusion over the manufacturer's ability to control the distribution of his output is increased.

2. Since the per se rule has been applied in some situations, continuation of selective or exclusive distribution systems will be possible where individual state statutes permit, but national exclusive distribution is a questionable business practice given the treble damage private antitrust implications under the Sherman Act.

The Supreme Court has an important role to play in the final determination of the future form of distribution in the United States. As a result of the Court's role, the distribution structure will undoubtedly undergo change. These changes may cost manufacturers much of the goodwill and/or brand preference that may have built up over the years. Because of the importance of this issue to the general economy, it is imperative that the Court clarify its present position with respect to territorial restrictions on resale. Until the Court speaks in a more definitive way, however, business executives will need to monitor the various legal developments to insure that their distribution structures are consistent with one of the possible positions that can be defended under the present legal structure.

QUESTIONS FOR DISCUSSION

1. Discuss the Schwinn case and indicate why it is considered a landmark case in marketing channel legal analysis.

2. What are the exceptions to the Schwinn Doctrine?

3. Discuss the Coors case and its ramifications.

4. Do you believe that the antitrust laws increase or decrease the overall level of competition in the marketplace? Defend your answer.

9.3 FAREWELL TO FAIR TRADE

James C. Johnson and Louis E. Boone

"An editorial in Consumers Electronics Monthly, *referring to manufacturers who support fair trade, stated that 'they are certainly to be applauded for their principled and determined, if ofttimes lonely efforts to maintain their good names and to keep retailers from drowning in a swamp of profitless selling'."*

On 12 December 1975, President Gerald R. Ford signed Public Law 94–145, entitled the *Consumer Goods Pricing Act of 1975*. This law terminated all interstate utilization of fair trade or resale price maintenance. The death of fair trade officially took place on 11 March 1976, ninety days after Ford's signature. This ended a highly controversial and emotional issue that has either plagued or blessed marketing practitioners since 1931. When signing the above legislation, Ford noted that "the best way we can protect the consumer is to identify and eliminate costly, inefficient, and obsolete laws and regulations. Thus, I take particular pleasure in signing this bill for the benefit of the American consumer."[1]

Ford's position regarding the viability of fair trade is far from unanimous. Defenders of fair trade have made numerous charges.

An editorial in *Consumers Electronics Monthly*, referring to manufacturers who support fair trade, stated that "they are certainly to be applauded for their principled and determined, if ofttimes lonely efforts to maintain their good names and to keep retailers from drowning in a swamp of profitless selling."[2]

In a court brief, Sony discussed the situation when a retailer disregarded fair-trade regulations: "Never in the history of fair trade has

James C. Johnson and Louis E. Boone, "Farewell to Fair Trade," pp. 22–30, *MSU Business Topics*, Spring 1976. Reprinted by permission of the publisher, Division of Research, Graduate School of Business Administration, Michigan State University.

1. "Statement by the President Upon Signing H.R. 6971," *Weekly Compilations of Presidential Documents* 11, no. 50 (15 December 1975): 1368.
2. Leonard Wiener, "Congress May Retire Depression Era's Fair-Trade Laws," *Marketing News*, 28 Feb. 1975, p. 5.

the goodwill of a manufacturer been so sorely abused and appropriated to the unfair advantage of another."[3]

A Washington, D.C., lawyer, Arthur Berndtson, hired by fair-trade proponents, observed: "Price maintenance has a tremendous backing in this country. Without it, consumers will have fewer alternatives, and discounters will squeeze the quality out of our products."[4]

William Day, director of consumer relations and product safety at Westinghouse Electric Corporation, stated that "it is beneficial to the consumer and the dealer in the New York area. If you eliminate fair trade there, then the dealers would lose control of their pricing and eventually would stop carrying the item. This would reduce the number of places where the item is available, and price would go up."[5]

Opponents of fair trade have been equally vociferous.

In 1974, then Attorney General William Saxbe declared: "Whatever feeble justification may have once existed for fair trade, there is today no reason to place such heavy burdens on the consuming public."[6]

Then Governor Nelson Rockefeller, asking for repeal of New York's fair-trade law, stated in 1973 that it was "an affront to the American system of competitive free enterprise."[7]

New York State Judge Joseph Kunzeman after reluctantly fining a violator of the state's fair-trade law referred to it as "an anachronistic leftover from the 1930s [which] at the present time serves primarily as an anti-consumer device."[8]

This article will succinctly examine the legislative history of the fair-trade laws, their usage and enforcement, and the primary arguments pro and con regarding this highly disputed issue. Effects of fair trade will be discussed and the probable consequences of the recent death of fair trade in interstate commerce will be analyzed by the authors.

LEGISLATIVE HISTORY OF FAIR TRADE

Manufacturers have historically desired the ability to control the retail price of their products.[9] One procedure involved refusal to sell to distributors who sell the manufacturer's product at less than the suggested retail price. Refusal-to-deal is specifically authorized by Section 2 of

3. "Will Congress End Fair Trade?" *Business Week*, 17 February 1975, p. 84.
4. "Fair Trade: How Fair," *Forbes*, 1 December 1974, p. 15.
5. "Will Congress End Fair Trade?" *Business Week*, 17 February 1975, p. 82.
6. "Fair Trade: How Fair," p. 15.
7. Johnathan Kwitny, "Discounters Campaign Against Laws That Let Retail Prices Be Fixed," *The Wall Street Journal*, 10 May 1975, p. 1.
8. *Ibid.*, p. 19.
9. The reasons for this situation are examined in the section under the subheading "Fair-Trade: Favorable Arguments" in this article.

the Clayton Act which declares that "persons engaged in selling goods, wares, or merchandise in commerce [have] the right to select their own customers in bona fide transactions and not in restraint of trade." However, in the landmark case which established the *Colgate Doctrine*, the Supreme Court restricted the ability of manufacturers to utilize the refusal-to-deal concept.[10] Specifically, manufacturers were not allowed to warn, discipline, spy on, or threaten distributors who did not follow their suggested retail prices.[11] The manufacturer could only announce a suggested retail price, and if there was noncompliance, the only recourse for the manufacturer was to unilaterally refuse to deal with the offending party.[12]

Frustrated manufacturers were then joined by a powerful ally—trade associations representing independent retail proprietors. Spearheading the latter group was the National Association of Retail Druggists (NARD). It originally sought a national fair-trade or resale price maintenance law. In every congressional session from 1914 to 1936, bills to effect that outcome were introduced—but all were defeated.[13] Undaunted by these failures, the NARD decided to seek fair-trade laws at the state level and drafted a model statue which was originally enacted into law in California in 1931. It specifically exempted manufacturer price fixing from the state's antitrust law. However, individual retailers in California were able to circumvent the law because they had not signed a contract agreeing to be bound by the manufacturer's suggested minimum retail price. To correct this situation, a 1933 amendment established the notorious "non-signers" clause. It stated that when any California retailer agreed to abide by the manufacturer's suggested minimum price, all other retailers in the state were also bound by the same agreement as soon as they were properly notified of the agreement between the manufacturer and a retailer.

The NARD and other manufacturer and retailer organizations worked diligently to have similar laws passed in the other states. Within the first year after California enacted its fair-trade law, twenty-eight additional states followed suit. By 1941, fair-trade laws had been enacted by forty-five states. Many states passed verbatim the NARD drafted model statue which was first enacted in California. Clair Wilcox has noted:

> The statutes legalizing resale price maintenance were whipped through the legislatures at breakneck speed. There is no record of hearings having

10. *U.S. v. Colgate & Co.*, 150 U.S. 300 (1919).

11. *See Beechnut Packing Co. v. F.T.C.*, 247 U.S. 441 (1972).

12. Robert E. Weigand and Hilda C. Wasson, "Refusal to Deal—A Case History," in Louis E. Boone and James C. Johnson, eds., *Marketing Channels* (Morristown, N.J.: General Learning Press, 1973), pp. 354–63.

13. Stanley C. Hollander. "[Fair-Trade in the] United States of America," in B. S. Yancy, ed., *Resale Price Maintenance* (Chicago: Aldine Publishing Co., 1966), p. 68.

been held in forty states. There is no transcript of hearings available in any state. The California law was supposed to contain a provision authorizing a producer to require "any dealer" to maintain a stipulated price. The text enacted, however, was garbled. Instead of "any dealer," it read "in delivery," so that the authorization made no sense. The care with which the laws were considered is indicated by the fact that this version was passed by the House and Senate and signed by the governor, not only in California, but also in Arizona, Iowa, Louisiana, New Jersey, New York, Pennsylvania, and Tennessee. The NARD held the hoop and cracked the whip. The legislators and the executives obediently jumped.[14]

Because of the obvious support for fair trade at the state level, Congress reconsidered its position regarding resale price maintenance. The Miller-Tydings Act of 1937 allowed a manufacturer in one state to enforce the fair-trade law in another state in which the product was sold, assuming the latter state had enacted a fair-trade law. Although enacted into law, the *Miller-Tydings Act* had only lukewam support in Congress. It did *not* mandate fair trade in those states which had not individually passed resale price maintenance laws. Ironically the District of Columbia which was legislatively controlled by Congress, did not, nor has it ever enacted a fair-trade law.

The *Miller-Tydings Act* thus amended the *Sherman Act* to allow vertical price control in interstate commerce. President Roosevelt opposed any weakening of the antitrust laws and had indicated he would veto the *Miller-Tydings Act*. In a shrewd political maneuver just before adjournment in 1937, Congress attached the *Miller-Tydings Act* to the *District of Columbia Appropriations Act*. Although Franklin D. Roosevelt publicly stated that he opposed the rider, he signed the legislative "package" in order to assure the District of Columbia of operating funds for the next term.

In 1951, the *Miller-Tydings Act* was significantly weakened by a Supreme Court decision.[15] A supermarket in Louisiana refused to follow Calvert's suggested retail price for liquor, arguing that the manager of the store had not signed a fair-trade contract, and since the *Miller-Tydings Act* did not mention the legality of the non-signers clause, it was not valid in interstate commerce. This position was upheld by the Supreme Court. The Schwegmann decision significantly crippled fair trade in interstate commerce. Selected cities did experience substantial price wars following this decision.[16] However, the price wars were short-lived and in most cases lasted less than six weeks.

Powerful pressure groups exerted tremendous influence on Congress to correct the problem which resulted in Schwegmann's victory. The

14. Clair Wilcox, *Public Policies Toward Business*, 3d ed. (Homewood, Ill.: Richard D. Irwin, Inc., 1966), p. 709.
15. *Schwegmann Bros. v. Calvert Corp.*, 341 U.S. 384 (1951).
16. Wilcox, *Public Policies*, p. 711.

American Fair Trade Council (representing manufacturers of branded products), the Bureau of Education on Fair Trade (organized by retail druggists), and similar organizations launched a united effort to return fair trade to the pre-Schwegmann situation. Congress was bombarded by letters, telephone calls, telegrams, and delegations. At the congressional hearings, the American Bar Association, the Justice Department, and many other groups opposed changing the current situation regarding fair trade. Notwithstanding this opposition, the *McGuire-Keogh Fair-Trade Enabling Act* (1952) was enacted into law and passed by the House of Representatives 196 to 10 and the Senate by 64 to 16.

The Report of the House Committee on Interstate and Foreign Commerce summarized the purpose and intent of the *McGuire Act.*

> The primary purpose of the [McGuire] bill is to reaffirm the very same proposition which, in the committee's opinion, the Congress intended to enact into law when it passed the Miller-Tydings Act . . . , to the effect that the application and enforcement of State fair-trade laws—including the nonsigner provisions of such laws—with regard to interstate transactions shall not constitute a violation of the Federal Trade Commission Act or the Sherman Antitrust Act. This reaffirmation is made necessary because of the decision of a divided Supreme Court in Schwegmann Bros. v. Calvert Distillers Corp.[17]

FAIR TRADE UTILIZATION AND ENFORCEMENT

A substantial variety of products has been subjected to fair-trade laws. The most important product categories include power tools, major appliances, glassware, wearing apparel, jewelry, bedding, television sets, watches, and cosmetics. Recently the high-fidelity components field was one of the most strongly committed to enforcing fair trade. U.S. Pioneer Electronics Corporation, the largest manufacturer of high-fidelity components, budgeted $1 million in 1975 to enforce fair trade among its distributors.[18]

It is generally conceded that the golden age for fair trade was 1950–1952, when the American Fair-Trade Council stated that 1,600 manufacturers enforced fair trade. Estimates indicate that during this period approximately 10 percent of total retail sales was subjected to fair-trade enforcement. By 1954, E. S. Herman estimated the percentage dropped to 7 percent[19] and in 1975 it was approximately 4 percent.[20]

17. As quoted in Robert N. Corley and Robert L. Black, *The Legal Environment of Business*, 3d ed. (New York: McGraw-Hill Book Co., 1973), p. 320.

18. Wiener, *Congress May Retire*, p. 5.

19. E. S. Herman, "A Statistical Note on Fair-Trade," *Antitrust Bulletin* 4 (1959): 583–92.

20. Louis J. Haugh, "Effect of Fair Trade Drop on Co-op Ads Uncertain," *Advertising Age*, 18 August 1975, p. 216.

Fair trade is enforced by the use of two basic techniques. The first technique involves cooperation of manufacturers and retailers to ensure that dissident retailers and manufacturers follow fair trade. Retailers' associations in the late 1930s acted to force wayward retailers to follow fair-trade prices and also to ensure that manufacturers sold and enforced their products under fair trade. Blacklists of uncooperating manufacturers were maintained and the retailers' association boycotted their products. In 1937, the manufacturers of Pepsodent toothpaste refused to fair trade this product. Starting in California and spreading rapidly towards the East Coast, druggists put the product "under-the-counter." Because of the product's unavailability, other toothpaste brands rapidly experienced significant increases in market share. Within a few months, Pepsodent was again being fair traded nationally.[21]

The strength of retailer associations has waned during recent years. Therefore, the second method of enforcement has become the dominant method. This technique involves the manufacturer's use of private detective agencies (referred to as *shopper's services*) to purchase products and report the names of retailers selling at less than the fair-trade price. Typically, the offending retailer receives a letter warning him that the fair-trade price must be maintained. If the retailer refuses, the manufacturer will file a suit in the appropriate state court. The court often issues an injunction prohibiting sale of the product in question at less than the fair-trade price. In some cases small fines are assessed against frequent violators. A *Wall Street Journal* reporter sampled a dozen fair-trade suits in the New York Supreme Court in 1973 and found the largest fine was $250. State judges appeared to be sympathetic with the retailers and consistently awarded the minimum penalties prescribed by law.[22]

FAIR TRADE: FAVORABLE ARGUMENTS

Although there are many variations, four basic arguments form the bulwark for the defenders of fair trade. The first involves the manufacturer's loss of goodwill. The thrust of this argument is that consumers use price as a surrogate indicator of quality. They believe in the slogan: "You get what you pay for." Thus, if the retailer cuts the price of the manufacturer's product, the consumer is led to believe that the manufacturer has compromised quality in order for the product to sell at the

21. It should be noted that retail association boycotts, blacklists, and so forth, were generally found by the courts to be illegal. See *Business Week*, 28 August 1937.
22. Kwitny, *Discounters Campaign*, p. 19.

lower price. Sony and Westinghouse recently have used this argument against a retailer violating fair trade.[23]

The second argument deals with "loss leaders." This is the practice of retailers selling an item at an unusually low price, and in some cases at an actual loss. The rationale is to entice into the store customers who would then purchase other products besides the loss leader. Selected manufacturers have argued that the usage of their products as loss leaders is detrimental to their marketing efforts. Why? Because once the product is used by one retailer as a loss leader, other retailers will put the product "under-the-counter" because they do not want to face the unpleasantness of a direct price comparison. The classic example is the Ingersoll Watch Company, which capitulated prior to World War I.

> Some retailers throughout the country decided to use the Ingersoll watch as a loss leader. They began to sell it for less than one dollar. The price went down and down as competition increased, until finally it was selling for fifty-seven cents, far below the wholesale price. The retailers who were selling it at that price were making up their losses on sales of other merchandise in their large stores. Small business retailers were forced to drop the Ingersoll dollar watch. They could not sell it if they charged more than fifty-seven cents, and they could not afford to sell the watch at that price and take the loss involved in each sale. The result was that the manufacturer lost his market and was forced out of business.[24]

The third and most fervent rationale deals with protecting the viability of small retailers. Without minimum prices established by retailers, highly efficient giant discounters and other retail gargantuans would spell the demise of the small retailer. Also predatory price cutting would become common, driving the small retailer out of business. John E. Lewis, vice president of the National Small Business Association, sent a letter in 1975 to President Ford chiding him for his position in favor of abolishing fair trade. Lewis called Ford's position "an attack on small business." Similarly, Thomas Rockwell, an antitrust lawyer for a brand-name manufacturers' trade association—The Marketing Policy Institute—declared, "If Congress adopts this repeal legislation, it will be killing thousands of small businesses across the nation."[25] Finally, a retail jewelry lobbyist observed that Congress would not repeal fair trade because "Fair Trade laws were enacted in the 1930s to slow down the number of retail store bankruptcies. Why are today's conditions any less valid?"[26]

23. "Will Congress End Fair Trade?", p. 84.
24. *Congressional Record*, 1 July 1952, pp. 8935–6.
25. "Fair Trade Pricing Draws New Foes," *Tulsa Daily World*, 2 July 1975, p. 2.
26. "Fair Trade: Looking for a Direction," *Sales Management*, 3 March 1975, p. 15.

Consumer protection is the final basic argument. Fair trade protects small retail outlets and, therefore, a greater number of outlets sell any particular product. Also, the higher margins give all retailers an incentive to "push" the product and, therefore, the manufacturer's sales volume increases. The increased volume allows the manufacturer to achieve economies-of-scale in production which eventually results in lower retail prices to the consumer. Henry Michel, Black and Decker's director of public affairs, noted that repeal of fair trade would be detrimental to the public: "Because of lower margins, the number of retailers handling our products would go down and the others wouldn't carry as broad a line."[27] The likely result is lower sales and higher production costs. Michel stated that in 1972 his company sold a battery-powered grass shear for $19.99. Because of fair trade, retailers aggressively sold the product, production cost decreased, and its retail price in late 1974 was $14.99.

Another aspect of consumer protection is that fair trade assures the customer of selecting the correct product because of knowledgeable, well-paid sales personnel. Walter Bennett, a spokesman for General Electric noted that ". . . years ago, it was very difficult to go into a nice, well-lighted store and get a salesman's attention. Stores that were selling appliances were running on a shoestring."[28]

FAIR TRADE: NEGATIVE ARGUMENTS

After distillation, there are four basic arguments against fair trade. The first states that fair trade is unfair to the consuming public. Louis A. Engman, Chairman of the Federal Trade Commission, strongly supported the repeal of fair trade. In 1975 he noted:

> Though most government regulation was enacted under the guise of protecting the consumer from abuse, much of today's regulatory machinery does little more than shelter producers from the normal competitive consequences of lassitiude and inefficiency. . . . In any case, the consumer, for whatever presumed abuse he is being spared, is paying plenty in the form of government-sanctioned price fixing.[29]

Thirty years before, the FTC argued forcefully against fair trade, stating: "The Commission believes that the consumer is not only entitled to competition between rival products but to competition between dealers handling the same branded product."[30] It cannot be argued

27. "Fair Trade: How Fair?", p. 15.
28. *Discounters Campaign*, p. 19.
29. Lewis A. Engman, "Inflation and Regulation," *Antitrust Law and Economics*, 7, no. 3 (1975): 38–39.
30. Federal Trade Commission, *Report on Resale Price Maintenance* (Washington, D.C.: U.S. Government Printing Office, 1945): lxiv.

that fair trade has kept retail prices higher than they would have been in the absence of this law. A nineteen-inch Sony color television set recently sold for $459.95 in Massachusetts (no fair trade) and at the same time the same retail chain sold this product for $569.95 in New York because of their fair-trade law.[31] One successful discounter and open violator of the fair-trade laws, Jerry Rosenberg, stated that the traditional profit margin on most fair-traded items he sold is 27 to 35 percent, but that his firm does very well with a 13 percent margin.[32] Senator Edward Brooke, the Senate's most outspoken advocate for fair-trade repeal, stated that consumers in 1974 paid $2.1 billion more than if the law had not existed. He said: "To remove that unnecessary burden from our economy would be one of the most immediate anti-inflationary steps we could take."[33]

The second argument deals with fair trade and its effect on retailers. Fair-trade laws tend to penalize efficient retailers, because they are not permitted to lower their prices based on their efficient operations. A Canadian study group reported:

> The crux of the problem of resale price maintenance is whether the consumer should reap the benefits of the most efficient form of retailing or . . . should be forced to pay more in order to make retailing . . . a more comfortable occupation.[34]

It is often pointed out that the fair-trade laws have not been successful, in any case, in protecting small retailers against the larger, more efficient retailer. An FTC attorney, Ronald Bloch, stated, "The little guys thought fair trade would keep them alive. They got it and they still died."[35] A drug store study indicated that from 1958 to 1967 there was a 5 percent increase in drug store outlets in non fair-trade states and a 2 percent decline in fair-trade states.[36] Professor Stanley C. Hollander extensively reviewed the literature and concluded, "There seems to be little evidence that resale price maintenance reduces retail failure rates."[37]

The third argument states that laws which are difficult or impossible to enforce should be repealed. Fair-trade laws have historically been ignored by many segments of the retailing community. Enforcement of fair trade is difficult because there are so many ways "to beat the system." Generous trade-in allowance can be granted, such as $150 for a

31. "Fair Trade Pricing Draws New Foes," p. 2.
32. *Discounters Campaign*, p. 1.
33. "Looking for a Direction," p. 15.
34. *Resale Price Maintenance, An Interim Report of the Committee to Study Combines Legislation* (Ottawa, 1951), p. 16, as found in Wilcox, *Public Policies*, p. 716.
35. "Fair Trade: How Fair?", p. 15.
36. "Will Congress End Fair Trade?", p. 82.
37. Hollander, in *Resale Price Maintenance*, p. 94.

hand-push lawnmower on a fair-traded $700 riding lawnmower. Manufacturer's refusal-to-deal with fair-trade violators can be circumvented by using untraditional channels-of-distribution, which often involves using wholesalers in other states. In addition, enforcement is complicated because a manufacturer must enforce its fair-trade policies uniformly in all areas where fair trade is legal. The manufacturer cannot choose to ignore violators in certain areas and then prosecute others.[38]

Because of the manufacturers' difficulties of enforcing fair trade, retailers are notorious for violating it. Simon Hindelly, manager of a radio store in Manhattan, observed: "Fair trade is important and we honor it. But I won't let a customer walk out if a competitor is breaking it. You have a lot of consumers today who just won't pay fair trade."[39]

The final argument asks: Why should manufacturers be concerned about retailers cutting price on their products and hence selling more of it? Hollander, a leading expert on marketing channel strategy, questions why "a manufacturer wants to cut himself off from what may be some of the most vigorous and important outlets in the market."[40]

FAIR TRADE: ITS EFFECT BEFORE REPEAL

Fair trade has been partially responsible for two fundamental changes in post-World War II marketing practices. The first involves the significant growth of discount stores. Managers of the discount stores openly and flagrantly violated the fair-trade laws. Why? Donald V. Harper has noted, "When they sold merchandise at less than the established fair-trade prices, they could easily prove to customers that they were receiving genuine price reductions; customers could easily recognize and appreciate these reductions."[41] Thus fair-trade violations helped to establish the credibility of discount stores.

Second, since many retailers refused to openly violate the fair-trade laws, they circumvented this situation by starting to stock private brands or retail-label products. These products, of course, were not subject to the fair-trade laws and, therefore, the retailer could be as price competitive as desired.

THE REPEAL OF FAIR TRADE: WHAT TO EXPECT

Fair trade died on 11 March 1976. Prognosticators have stated that the repeal of fair trade will precipitate changes in marketing practices; some

38. Corley and Black, *The Legal Environment*, p. 320.
39. *Discounters Campaign*, p. 19.
40. Hollander, p. 82.
41. Donald V. Harper, *Price Policy and Procedure* (New York: Harcourt, Brace & World, Inc., 1966), p. 263.

predict very significant structural shifts while others believe the differences to be imperceptible. Four basic areas of change will be examined. First, will price wars become rampant? History indicates that prices will drop immediately after the end of fair trade, and then slowly increase and stabilize at a level somewhat below the former fair-trade price. After the Supreme Court's 1951 decision in favor of the Schwegmann Brothers, there were price wars in many cities, including New York, Detroit, Denver, New Orleans, and forty others. However, no price wars developed in eighty other major cities, including Boston, Philadelphia, Cleveland, Chicago, and Los Angeles. The price wars lasted about six weeks and then prices moved up and stabilized.[42]

A recent study of the effect of fair-trade repeal in Rhode Island indicated that prices did not "universally collapse." Professors Hourihan and Markham concluded:

> It would appear to us that both opponents and defenders of fair trade have frequently exaggerated both the disadvantages and advantages of fair trade—indeed, the very importance of fair-trade laws. Prices of previously fair-traded products did not universally collapse following the repeal of Rhode Island's fair trade law, nor did the law's repeal materially affect the sales volume of product availability of most of the product lines surveyed.[43]

The prevailing opinion is best summed up by Ray Steiner, senior vice-president of Sony's American subsidiary. He said, "There probably will be lower prices generally to start with. Perhaps on a $569 set, a dealer will knock off a $20 bill. Then, after a time, I think prices will stabilize close to what they had been."[44]

A second issue is the overall effect on small retailers. Although some observers believe that the demise of fair trade will significantly weaken small retailers, this viewpoint is in the minority. The majority position is stated by Oliver O. Ward, president of the Smaller Business Association of New England, who observed that small retailers "can be competitive and thrive through flexibility and extra service."[45] In the District of Columbia (which never has had fair trade) small drug stores, liquor stores, and appliance dealers exist side-by-side with giant discount stores. The small retailers, instead of competing on price, stress personalizing service, such as home delivery, and neighborhood convenience.[46]

There has been speculation that the end of trade will significantly affect the advertising practices of manufacturers. Ed Libov, an expert in

---

42. *Public Policies*, p. 711.

43. "Prices 'Did Not Universally Collapse' After Rhode Island Fair-Trade Repeal," *Marketing News*, 28 February 1975, p. 5.

44. N. R. Kleinfield, "Fair-Trade Laws Fall In State After State, but Impact Is Small," *The Wall Street Journal*, 11 June 1975, p. 1.

45. "Looking for a Direction," p. 15.

46. "Fair Trade Draws New Foes," p. 2.

co-operative advertising, believes that up to $1 billion will be added to co-op advertising. His rationale is the following:

> Manufacturers and retailers emerging from the protective cocoon of fair trade will find immediate need to chart a whole new marketing game plan. More of the pricing, advertising and promotional planning and activities will need to be originated at the local grass roots level instead of the other way around. To put it another way: "Uptown" fair trade manufacturers will have to make it on "Main Street," where the retailers and customers are. And "Main Street" always has meant coop advertising with both parties sharing media, and in many cases, production costs.[47]

This position is far from unanimous and most observers believe that coop advertising will not significantly be affected by the repeal of fair trade. Spokesmen for Sony and General Electric, strict adherers to fair trade where legal, have stated that they did not anticipate any change in coop advertising if fair trade were to be repealed.[48] Most manufacturers appear to be taking a conservative "wait and see" attitude regarding their advertising and promotional budgets.

A fourth trend is fairly certain to materialize. Manufacturers who are strongly committed to controlling retail prices can do so by consignment selling, in which the manufacturer retains title to the products in the retail outlet. Since the retailer is acting strictly as an agent for the manufacturer, the latter has complete freedom to establish any retail price desired. Although consignment selling is likely to become more common, it is not expected to achieve substantial growth. Why? Because it is very expensive in that it ties-up a significant amount of the manufacturer's capital in inventory awaiting sale in the retailer's store. Also, courts generally have used rigorous tests to differentiate between consignment and outright sales. The manufacturer must absorb *all* the costs and risks normally associated with the retailer. These include insurance costs, personal property taxes, and the risk that manufacturers cannot be paid for the merchandise until the merchandise has been sold.

CONCLUSION

The death of fair trade in the United States appears to have been long overdue. In the authors' opinion, the arguments against fair trade are substantially more powerful than the counter position. Many foreign countries came to the same conclusion regarding fair trade and they

47. Ed Libov, "Good-Bye, Fair-Trade; Hello, $1 Billion in New Co-op Advertising," *Broadcasting*, 7 July 1975, p. 10. See also, John Soloway, "Adman Sees Boom In Co-op with Repeal of Fair Trade," *Editor and Publisher*, 28 June 1975, p. 20.

48. Louis J. Haugh, "Effect of Fair Trade Drop on Co-op Ads Uncertain," *Advertising Age*, 18 August 1975, p. 216.

also repealed it; these include: Canada, Sweden, Denmark, Holland, Germany, Italy, the United Kingdom, and France.[49]

QUESTIONS FOR DISCUSSION

1. Outline the legislative history of the fair trade laws.

2. Explain the utilization and enforcement procedures for the fair trade laws.

3. Discuss the basic arguments in *favor* of the continuation of the fair trade laws.

4. What are the basic arguments *against* the continuation of the fair trade laws?

5. What effect did the fair trade laws have before their repeal in 1976?

6. What are the likely outcomes as a result of the repeal of fair trade?

49. For an excellent discussion of fair trade in other countries, see Yancy, *Resale Price Maintenance*.

9.4 POWER AND CHANNEL CONFLICTS IN SHOPPING CENTER DEVELOPMENT

Joseph Barry Mason

". . . It is questionable whether many of the small outlets that seem to support the current FTC stance can survive in a shopping center without the pulling power of a major anchor tenant to generate a large volume of traffic which the small outlets cannot attract on their own."

Recent legal actions relative to the shopping center development process provide a meaningful focus for channel power and conflict relationships in this process as well as for the changes that are likely to affect all parties involved with it. Some recent actions are: (1) Federal Trade Commission (FTC) restraint of trade complaints, one against a Virginia regional shopping center and three of its major tenants, and another against Gimbel Brothers; (2) a Justice Department investigation of shopping center leasing practices; and (3) a number of miscellaneous items, including private class action suits by a gift shop franchisor against several of the nation's largest shopping center developers.

Power and conflict issues often have an important effect on the efficiency of marketing operations. Conflict in this context is usually defined as a process of change that causes realignments in relationships between channel system members. Channel decisions tend to be long-term decisions, and the development of channel relationships involves much economic and psychological investment. Because of this investment, it is in the interest of all parties to maintain cooperative relationships if at all possible.

Conflict that occurs between tenants and developers of shopping centers arises, at least partially, as a result of the process of shopping center development. The shopping center developer seeks to choose and obtain, at satisfactory rental rates, those tenants who will provide the

Reprinted by permission of the author and publisher. Joseph Barry Mason, "Power and Channel Conflicts in Shopping Center Development," *Journal of Marketing* (April 1975), pp. 28–35.

greatest amount of customer satisfaction. He also wants to lease to those tenants who will create an image for his center that will maximize center traffic and thus sales for the total project. This factor typically is also the basis on which financial institutions judge the merits of a shopping center developer's mortgage. As has been stated:

> Traditionally, such developers seek as anchor tenants full-line department stores, which they feel will not only draw traffic but will fit the center's image. Most developers need long-term commitments from large retailers before they can get permanent financing. To lure the big stores, developers offer leases and operating agreements that permit the stores to protect their investments by protecting themselves against too much competition, particularly from discount operations.[1]

The power base of anchor tenants in shopping centers results largely from the restrictive clauses that are currently under attack. From their positions of power, major tenants can force the developer to grant concessions which, they argue, are for self-protection. To a large extent, these firms dictate the operations of the entire center. The major tenants typically are granted concessions in operating policy, location, and rental rates; while the independents are, in turn, restricted in their operations by these concessions. In their negotiations with the developer, major tenants often determine such items as prohibition of discounting, a requirement that all of the center's stores join a merchants association, and control over other stores' operations. Traditionally, the developer has had little alternative but concession if he wanted to obtain the triple-A tenants necessary to satisfy the mortgage terms for obtaining a loan.

The purpose of this article is to focus attention on recent investigations and litigation affecting shopping center development. Through careful analysis of the complaints and rulings issued by the FTC and others, the author hopes to provide greater insights into the dynamics of channel conflict and power shifts, as well as into the possible strategy alternatives that now face the major parties in this process—namely, the developer, the anchor tenants, the satellite tenants, and the financing institutions.

FTC RESTRAINT OF TRADE COMPLAINTS

The FTC has concerned itself with undue channel power in shopping centers in two recent cases. In July 1971, the FTC issued a proposed

1. "The FTC Zeroes in on Shopping Center," *Business Week*, February 19, 1972, p. 22.

complaint against Tysons Corner Regional Shopping Center under Section 5 of the FTC Act. In October 1971, a similar complaint was issued against Gimbel Brothers. The first FTC complaint was aimed at Tysons Corner and its three major department store tenants—City Stores, operating as Lansburghs: May Department Stores, operating as Hecht Co.; and Woodward and Lothrop, Inc. The Gimbels action covered 24 allegedly restrictive shopping center leases in several metropolitan areas. The FTC proposed complaints against both Tysons and Gimbels contended their lease provisions were anticompetitive.[2]

Tysons Corner is one of the nation's largest regional shopping centers and has over 100 retail stores and 1.2 million square feet of floor space, of which Lansburghs, Hecht, and Woodward and Lothrop occupy approximately 450,000 square feet. The proposed complaint contended that restrictive lease provisions enabled the three major tenants to exclude competitors, fix retail prices, eliminate discount selling, and otherwise restrain trade.

The proposed complaint against Gimbels stated that the challenged lease provisions tended to eliminate, discourage, and hinder discount store operations in shopping centers; and to unlawfully restrain trade by fixing retail prices and by allowing Gimbels to select its competitors and coerce shopping center developers in their choice of potential tenants. The formal complaints against Tysons Corner and Gimbels were issued on May 8, 1972. Consent orders to cease and desist were issued in late 1973 for Tysons Corner[3] and in January 1974 for Gimbels.[4] In each case the result of federal action was a reduction of the power major tenants could hold in the channel.

2. Tysons Corner Regional Shopping Center et al., Proposed Complaint, [Transfer Binder] Trade Reg. Rep. ¶ 19,720 (July 1971); Gimbel Brothers, Inc., Proposed Complaint, [Transfer Binder] Trade Reg. Rep. ¶ 19,834 (October 1971).

3. An administrative law judge's order certifying a joint application for withdrawal from adjudication by May Department Stores Co. and Woodward and Lothrop, Inc., was issued on September 27, 1973: see Tysons Corner Regional Shopping Center et al., [Transfer Binder] Trade Reg. Rep. ¶ 20,455 (September 1973); and on October 9, 1973 for Tysons Corner, [Transfer Binder] Trade Reg. Rep. ¶ 20,446 (October 1973). For details of the cease and desist order issued on June 26, 1974, see Tyson's Corner Regional Shopping Center et al., [Transfer Binder] Trade Reg. Rep. ¶ 30,532 (June 1974). In the case of City Stores, the commission held that City Stores' proposed consent order would not be an appropriate disposition of the matter and that City Stores' alternative request for dismissal of the complaint should be denied. See Tysons Corner Regional Shopping Center et al., Order Returning Matter to Adjudication as to Respondent City Stores Company, [Transfer Binder] Trade Reg. Rep. ¶ 20,533 (March 1974); see also, "Tysons Corner and FTC Reach Consent Accord," ICSC Newsletter, February–March 1974, p. 1.

4. Gimbel Brothers, Inc. Consent Order to Cease and Desist [Transfer Binder] Trade Reg. Rep. ¶ 30,478 (January 1974); see also, "Gimbels Agrees to Limited Center Rule in FTC Accord," ICSC Newsletter, December 1973, p. 1.

PROHIBITED RESTRAINT OF TRADE
LEASE PROVISIONS

The lease provisions that control tenant composition and marketing policies are the key in shopping center development, and these provisions have been severely restricted by the FTC. The lease provisions challenged by the FTC were, for the most part, the same in both cases. The key points for Tysons Corner were that the respondents were prohibited from entering into leases or carrying out agreements that granted them the right to approve tenants, to approve the amount of floor space of other tenants, to exclude particular tenants or classes of tenants, to approve the types or brands of merchandise to be sold by other tenants, to specify particular prices or price ranges of other tenants, to approve the center location of other tenants, to control the advertising of other tenants, and to prohibit price advertising.[5]

The consent decree for Gimbel Brothers went further and also prohibited any agreement that would prevent expansion of a center. However, the language in the Gimbels decree was limited specifically to "retailers" and did not make reference to "all tenants," as did the Tysons Corner decree. The action against Tysons Corner was more restrictive than the action taken against Gimbels.

PERMISSIBLE TENANT LEASE PROVISIONS

Realistically, developers must be allowed to exert some control over the development process to insure a balanced tenant mix and a proper return on their investment. Thus, in its consent decree, Tysons Corner was permitted to enter into agreements with tenants that allowed the tenants to insist that Tysons: (1) maintain a balanced grouping of retail stores; (2) prohibit occupancy of space by objectionable types of tenants such as those selling pornographic materials; (3) not force them to occupy space immediately proximate to tenants who create undue noise, litter, or odor; (4) require reasonable standards of appearance; and (5) establish a layout of the shopping center that designates the tenants' stores and sets forth the location, size, and height of all buildings.[6]

Gimbels was also allowed to have certain very general radius restrictions in its leases that would be applicable to stores located not more than 150 feet of mall frontage from Gimbels' outlets and 200 feet from

5. [Transfer Binder] Trade Reg. Rep ¶ 20,532, same reference as footnote 3.
6. [Transfer Binder] Trade Reg. Rep. ¶ 20,532, same reference as footnote 3.

the Saks Fifth Avenue outlets of Gimbels. Specifically, Gimbels was allowed to establish reasonable categories of retailers from which a developer could select tenants. However, the categories chosen could not specify price ranges, price lines, trade names, store names, trademarks, brands or lines of merchandise of retailers, or the identity of particular retailers, including even the listing of particular retailers as examples of a category.[7]

Finally, Tysons was required to cease and desist from entering into any agreement with a tenant that allowed the tenant to specify or control prices of merchandise or services sold by any other retailers, to control discounting by any other retailer, or to exclude any retailer from Tysons shopping center because the retailer engaged in discount selling or discount advertising.[8] The FTC rulings in these two cases prohibited virtually all previously accepted practices in the shopping center development process.

DISCUSSION

Until the issuance of the complaints against Tysons Corner and Gimbels, virtually no shopping center antitrust litigation had appeared and there was little overt evidence of channel conflict in such centers. This was probably due to a tendency on the part of regulatory agencies to treat shopping center developments as real estate phenomena and to treat problems when they arose as contractual in nature. The antitrust actions in these two situations represent the application of basic antitrust principles, but these principles are new to the shopping center industry and may do much to shift the power bases in that industry.

The prime concern of the FTC in these two precedent-setting cases is the so-called right of tenant approval and tenant exclusion clauses.[9] Specifically, this is the right given to some merchants to approve other tenants of a center. The FTC contends that all of the traditional arguments, such as image preservation, elimination of cut-throat competition, preservation of investment, and the like, are simply efforts to eliminate competition unfairly. The commission contends that all space in the center should be free and open, and sees no difference between the shopping center of today and central business district locations. Tenant approvals are not allowed in downtown areas.[10]

7. [Transfer Binder] Trade Reg. Rep. ¶ 20,478, same reference as footnote 3.
8. [Transfer Binder] Trade Reg. Rep. ¶ 20,532, same reference as footnote 3.
9. Ernest G. Barnes, *The Federal Trade Commission and Shopping Centers* (New York: International Council of Shopping Centers, 1972), p. 4.
10. E. J. Caldecott, "The Developer and Anti-Trust Problems Concerning Construction, Operation and Reciprocal Easement Agreements," in *The Shopping Center Industry and Anti-Trust Laws*, Proceedings of a Law Conference Held on Safety

Second, concern is also evident over approval-of-location clauses where the effect is anticompetitive. Clearly, some limited approval appears to be in order. For example, the location of an ice cream parlor next to a shop featuring exclusive women's dresses probably is undesirable if one is concerned with preventing undue merchandise damage. However, blanket approval over the location of all other tenants cannot be justified.

A third major concern evident in these cases is market divisions by a developer. The FTC contends that "an overly rigid notion of tenant mix is market division."[11] Developers typically specify that one retailer will sell high-priced goods, a second medium-priced goods, and a third low-priced goods. Under antitrust terms, this is market allocation. Closely aligned is the practice of price fixing, which prohibits discounting, warehouse sales, and similar practices. The FTC contends that price-fixing agreements and market division agreements are per se illegal.

Clearly, the traditional power base of the anchor tenants, formed by their ability to require developers to engage in anticompetitive practices on their behalf, has been badly damaged. However, the conflict issues are likely to become even more pronounced as a result of the FTC actions. The financial institutions will continue to insist on triple-A long-term leases from major tenants before providing the financing for a given center. Also, the anchor tenants will continue to seek various types of safeguards designed to insure a satisfactory return on their investment. Lastly, the satellite tenants are now in a position to require more flexible leases from the developer by utilizing the implicit threat of FTC action. Thus, the developer is without any power base from which to operate. As a result of these fast-changing channel dynamics, the key question becomes: What form is the shopping center development process likely to take as a result of these changing relationships? The developer remains the key in the development process, but the options available to him in insuring a financially successful venture are no longer clear.

CONTRASTING COURT DECISIONS

Part of the uncertainty as to the changes imposed on the development process are conflicts between FTC decrees, court rulings, and decisions rendered in private action cases. The FTC decree in the Tysons Corner matter was somewhat different from an earlier 1970 U.S. district court

---

Spa Harbor, Florida (New York: International Council of Shopping Centers, 1973), p. 50.

11. Same reference as footnote 9, p. 6.

ruling.[12] Dalmo Sales charged that Tysons Corner and the Hecht and Woodward and Lothrop department stores had conspired to prevent the renting of space to Dalmo because of its discounting activities and that this was a group boycott per se violative of the Sherman Act. In denying a preliminary injunction that would have prohibited the lease of the space by Tysons until the outcome of the dispute, the district court stated that

> it is clear that the successful development of Tysons Corner or any similar regional shopping center is dependent on obtaining the prior long term commitments of large department stores. . . . The heavy financial stake of Tysons Corner and the department stores which are parties to long-term leases in the future success of such an enterprise may very well give them the right to select and approve tenants who in their judgement will contribute to the success of the enterprise without being subject to the *per se* rule of illegality. . . . Any restraint involved in the sharing by Tysons Corner of such rights with the department stores whose prior commitments are necessary to the success of the enterprise may very well be deemed to be a reasonable one under the anti-trust laws.[13]

The case was appealed to the U.S. Court of Appeals, which refused to overturn the ruling of the district court.[14] The appeals court recognized that discount prices and sales below list price were offered by Woodward and Lothrop and some of the satellite stores, and thus held that discount pricing alone was not a controlling consideration in the action of Tysons Corner.

Differences in the philosophy of the courts and of the FTC are evident in these two cases. In the 1970 decisions, the courts recognized that Tysons had the right to enter into restrictive leases with anchor tenants but they did not directly address the question of arbitrary exclusion of discounters. However, the 1973 FTC consent decree prohibited restrictive leases with virtually no exceptions. Apparently, in both the FTC consent decree and the appeals court decision, some general guidelines emerged as to permissible lease arrangements with anchor tenants. It seems anchor tenants can insist on elimination or control relative to tenants who would create excessive noise, odor, or litter. It also appears that developers can exclude stores that do not meet specified standards of appearance and, therefore, are not in harmony with the overall image of the center.

In other matters, the stance taken by the U.S. Justice Department seems to be similar to that of the FTC, at least based on its ruling in a recent antitrust case involving shopping center restrictive leases. In

12. *Dalmo Sales, Inc., et al. v. Tysons Corner Regional Shopping Center et al.,* Trade Cases ¶ 73,024 (1970).

13. Same reference as footnote 12.

14. *Dalmo Sales, Inc., et al. v. Tysons Corner Regional Shopping Center et al.,* Trade Cases ¶ 73,206 (1970).

1972, Wachovia Bank and Trust Company was barred by the U.S. Justice Department from entering into any arrangement that would limit or restrict the number, location, or use of night depository branch banking offices or other banking facilities in a shopping center by a third person.[15]

In addition to these federal actions, several private cases have also been brought by Plum Tree, Inc., a franchisor of a nationwide chain of retail shops, against a number of shopping center developers. In these cases, Plum Tree alleged various restraint violations, including fixing retail prices, prohibiting discounting, setting store hours, and the like. In 1973, out-of-court settlements were reached in all four Plum Tree cases. Terms of settlement were not announced.[16]

Actions in the various shopping center cases have been brought as actions by the FTC as in the Gimbels and Tysons Corner cases, as actions by the Justice Department as in the Wachovia case, and as private suits as in the Plum Tree cases. This raises a series of questions as to who makes or changes policy in these matters, whether the FTC decisions will be overturned, and the like.

When the Anti-Trust Division of the U.S. Department of Justice or a private individual seeks civil redress against alleged violations of the federal antitrust laws, suits are brought in a U.S. federal district court. From that point forward, they are handled as any other suit before the courts.

The FTC case procedure is different in that that FTC is not a court of law but an administrative agency and its charges are brought before its administrative law judges. All formal FTC complaints stem from commission investigations or from complaints by businesspeople or consumers. When the commission issues a complaint, it can be settled by a consent order to correct or discontinue a challenged practice. If the proposed order is not agreed to, the case is heard by an FTC hearing examiner. The examiner hears the case and either affirms the consent order or dismisses the case. Either side may ultimately appeal to the U.S. Supreme Court.

In antitrust matters, the Justice Department and the FTC have overlapping jurisdiction. However, the jurisdictional power of the Justice Department is somewhat broader in that it requires only that an alleged action "affect" interstate commerce, while the FTC Act requires that the "act" or practice be "in" interstate commerce. There is liaison be-

15. *United States v. Wachovia Bank and Trust Co.*, NA, Trade Cases ¶ 74,109 (1972).
16. See *Plum Tree, Inc. v. Rouse Company* et al., Trade Cases ¶ 74,243 (1972). See also, "Billion Dollar Anti-Trust Suit Against Rouse May Be First of Many in Industry," *Chain Store Age*, January 1972, "Plum Tree Sues Forbes-Cohen, Others," *Chain Store Age*, June 1972, p. E-6; and "Plum Tree Sues Another Developer Group," *Chain Store Age*, June 1972, p. E-16.

tween the two agencies so that they are not moving against the same practice simultaneously. The Wachovia Bank case was handled by the Justice Department because banks are outside the jurisdiction of the FTC.[17]

As to the powers of the FTC in these matters, it has been stated that "the ultimate validity or invalidity of these shopping center covenants, and the remedy therefore if they are found to be unlawful," will have to be determined through litigation.[18] As long as the FTC and the defendants agree on consent orders, no clear body of guidelines is likely to emerge. The same is true with the out-of-court settlements of private suits, as in the Plum Tree cases.[19] Also, the authority of the FTC to issue industrywide regulations is now in doubt.

Chain Store Age editors recently published a statement by Irving Scher, a lawyer involved in the Tysons Corner case, to the effect that "Federal Trade Commission consent orders are not legal precedents, so the worst thing for the shopping center industry to do would be to take the terms of the Gimbels and Tysons Corner consent orders and turn them into 'de facto trade regulation rules.'"[20]

Carrying this idea a little further, it may well be that the anchor tenants will seek legal redress through the courts to restore the damaged sources of their power in the shopping center development process. At this point, however, the consent orders seem to be generally preferred to binding legal precedents that could be established by the courts and that would have far more damaging industry effects. The FTC is insisting, however, on a court determination of the legality of the restrictive clauses in the leases before the commission issues trade regulation rules of any type.[21]

It is possible that at least one court test of the various challenged provisions of the FTC may occur in the near future. The International Council of Shopping Centers (ICSC) reported at its Spring 1974 Conference that even though May Department Stores, Woodward and Lothrop, and the developers of Tysons Corner have agreed to consent decrees, City Stores "has decided to continue fighting [the] FTC."[22] However, supporters of the traditional practices in shopping center development are

17. Same reference as footnote 15.
18. Same reference as footnote 9, p. 7.
19. Same reference as footnote 16.
20. "Lawyer Says That FTC Rulings Aren't Precedents," *Chain Store Age*, July 1974, p. E-5.
21. Same reference as footnote 9, p. 12.
22. "Discuss Impact of Federal Trade Commission Rulings on Shopping Center Leasing Practices," *ICSC Convention Bulletin*, June 1974, p. 6. The case was heard in court in early August; see "FTC v. City Stores," *ICSC Newsletter*, September 1974, p. 3.

heartened by the court's ruling in the Dalmo case. In its refusal to grant a preliminary injunction in this case, the court stated that: "The presence of novel legal issues, which require resolution at trial, preclude the grant of a preliminary injunction."[23] The defendants argued that, ultimately, "the best defense is the application of the so-called 'rule of reason'" as implied in the ruling of the U.S. district court.[24] If court tests of the various restrictions are undertaken, it may be years before meaningful tenant restriction guidelines emerge.

ADDITIONAL EXAMPLES OF CHANNEL CONFLICT

Several other relevant, but less publicized, court rulings have emerged in recent years. These also have important strategy implications for shopping center developers and provide different insights into channel dynamics.

THE INTERSTATE COMMERCE TEST

For restraint of trade cases to be successfully prosecuted under the Sherman Act, the violation must be part of interstate commerce. In 1970, a shopping center restrictive covenant contention was refused a hearing under the Sherman Act because the action was not proved to restrain interstate commerce. The plaintiff challenged a restrictive covenant in a lease to a food supermarket that prohibited the lessor from leasing or selling property within the shopping center to another food supermarket.[25] The district court held that for an offense to be unlawful under federal laws, the practice must restrain trade in interstate commerce.

The issue of interstate commerce is murky at best. For example, when Ernest G. Barnes, assistant director of the FTC Bureau of Competition, was questioned on this point, he stated that

> you have different forces at play in a shopping center and jurisdictional requirements of each may be different. Now, for example, a major chain such as Gimbels, located in a local shopping center, might be more subject to our jurisdiction than the developer himself. I would say that there might

23. Same reference as footnote 12.

24. Walter A. Bossert, Jr., "The Department Stores and Shopping Center Controls," in *The Shopping Center Industry and Anti-Trust Laws*, Proceedings of a Law Conference Held at Safety Spa Harbor, Florida (New York: International Council of Shopping Centers, 1973), p. 48.

25. *St. Anthony/Minneapolis, Inc. v. Red Owl Stores, Inc.*, Trade Cases ¶ 73,408 (1971); see also, *Mandeville Island Farms v. American Crystal Sugar Co.*, Trade Cases ¶ 62,251 (1948).

be some problems as to whether or not we had jurisdiction over every merchant in a shopping center or over the developer. Situations will vary.[26]

However, even if the interstate commerce test is not met, violations of state antitrust statutes are possible in this context, as several recent cases have revealed.[27]

HOURS RESTRICTIONS

A requirement for common hours of operation by all center stores has traditionally been a part of many shopping center lease agreements. A U.S. district court held in 1972 that shopping center lease provisions that require tenant stores to remain open for business for a minimum number of hours are not per se illegal and must be tested under the rule of reason.[28] Thus, the district court exhibited a benefit-cost philosophy and indicated that good reasons may exist for the hours provisions. However, the burden was placed upon the plaintiff to demonstrate the benefits of the provisions.

DISCRIMINATION IN LEASE TERMS

Center developers also traditionally have charged different rents for equal square footage depending on the type of merchandise sold. In a suit against N. K. Winston Corporation, Plum Tree charged these shopping center developers not only with restrictive lease arrangements and a variety of other antitrust claims, but also with price discrimination under the Robinson-Patman Act in their lease arrangements.[29] The discrimination prohibited under the act is "between different purchasers of commodities of like grade and quantity." Plum Tree contended that commodities under the act are equivalent to lease holds in shopping centers and that a landlord must charge equal rent for equal space. The court held that a lease for real property is not "selling goods, wares or merchandise." Thus, the court apparently left the way open for continuing discrimination in the price of equal space between different tenants. The court did not address the economic justification for different rents for equal space, however.

26. Same reference as footnote 9, pp. 9–10.

27. *Neiman-Marcus Company et al. v. Lewis J. Hexter et al.*, Trade Cases ¶ 72,144 (1967). *Meyer Braun, d/b/a/ Rex the Tailor, Plaintiff-Appelant v. Theordore W. Berenson, d/b/a/ Gulfgate Shopping Center et. al., Defendants-Appellees*, Trade Cases ¶ 73,338 (1970); see also, "Ohio Store Faces Law Suit," *ICSC Newsletter*, July 1974, p. 2.

28. *Amajac, Ltd. of Georgia v. Northlake Mall et al.*, Trade Cases ¶ 74,510 (1973).

29. *Plum Tree, Inc. v. N. K. Winston Corp. et al.*, Trade Cases ¶ 74,245 (1972).

DISCUSSION AND IMPLICATIONS

The FTC consent decrees may mean the end of many tenant restrictions that are frequently but tacitly imposed by major center department stores in cooperation with shopping center developers. These restrictions typically include limitations on what the smaller store can sell, the merchandise price lines they can offer, advertising policy, the hours and days the outlets open, expansion of existing stores, and merchant association membership. These consent decrees may spark a revolt throughout the industry, which would see similar restrictions in hundreds of centers become null and void as the power bases of the parties involved were changed.

Some headway in loosening the restrictions has already occurred, as certain trade associations and similar groups endeavor to respond to the increasing restlessness and conflict among all parties in the development process. For example, the International Council of Shopping Centers (ICSC) recently approved full retail membership in the organization, including giving retailers the right to vote and hold office. Further, the group approved membership rights for insurance companies, banks, savings and loan associations, real estate firms, and other sources of mortgage and construction financing.[30] Clearly, a sharing of the power bases in a more equal frame is emerging.

It appears that merchants association participation clauses will also increasingly come under attack. The previously unquestioned fact that tenants will sign clauses agreeing to participate in, and pay dues to, a shopping center merchants association will become a question mark for some chain retailers as they seek greater independence in their actions. This seems particularly true for certain national chains, who feel the dollars allocated to a merchants association could be more effectively spent on national brand advertising. Whatever the final outcome, it is likely to be a major area of discussion. Various concessions possibly will be granted by the shopping centers to lessen emerging conflict, including perhaps allowing more involvement and participative management on behalf of national franchisors who may have a franchisee located within a given shopping center.[31]

The future of the exclusion clause, long a major feature of most shopping center leases, also is open to question. As Allan Ransom, of the FTC's Bureau of Competition, recently stated: "Privileged classes of retailers and the elimination of competition will not stand up in the face of antitrust laws." Mr. Ransom was responding to what he said were

30. "ICSC Approves Full Retailer Membership," *Chain Store Age*, November 1972, p. E-12.
31. "Participation Clauses," *Chain Store Age*, September 1972, p. 20.

complaints from a number of druggists that they were frozen out of shopping centers and that they did not have access to shopping center locations on equal terms with other retailers. Mr. Ransom indicated that "a desirable method of attacking such injustices" would be class action suits.[32]

One of the biggest concerns to both developers and tenants, however, seems to be the question of discounters in shopping centers. The issue of discounters is a difficult one for all parties. On the one hand, many discounters would generally like to have the right to move into shopping centers. On the other hand, some are not particularly anxious to do so because of the high rent rates they would have to pay and because they are better suited to drawing traffic to a free-standing location.

Developers have their own problems. They would like to lease to anyone who is capable of paying the lease. Yet they are totally dependent on major department store anchors for the long-term leases necessary to secure financing for the centers.

Gimbels, in its retort to the FTC charges against it, stated that because of the FTC ruling large department store companies would be forced, more and more, to channel their expansion activities into free-standing stores rather than into shopping centers. Prior to the FTC ruling, Gimbels said that if the FTC won the case, the result would be to "deprive local independent retailers and national chain store organizations of the opportunity to compete [with Gimbels]—and other large department stores for retail sales dollars heretofore generated by retail shopping centers."[33] Clearly, Gimbels and probably other large retailers will develop more free-standing outlets to preserve and perhaps enhance their power bases, which are in danger of being eroded as a result of the current conflict. This is the action taken by Penney's in its Treasure Island outlets and by other major retailers. These types of retailers are able to succeed without adjacent competition. However, it is questionable whether many of the small outlets that seem to support the current FTC stance can survive in a shopping center without the pulling power of a major anchor tenant to generate a large volume of traffic which the small outlets cannot attract on their own. Their success often depends on sharing in the customer volume generated by the major anchor tenants.

The ultimate effect of this conflict in channel relationships in unclear. However, these regulatory actions may cause Gimbels and other major tenants to avoid making the long-term financial commitments that are

32. "FTC Is Probing Shopping Center 'Exclusives': Class Action Filed," *American Druggist*, April 17, 1972, p. 30.

33. Gimbel Says FTC Wants Big Stores Out of Centers," *American Druggist*, August 21, 1972, p. 23.

necessary to the development of retail shopping centers if they cannot be assured of meaningful ways to protect their investments.

One must also question whether a proper and balanced tenant mix will continue to exist, particularly if the actions taken in the cease and desist orders become industrywide. Because of the difficulties that the shopping center developer may face as a result of these rulings, he may begin to accept virtually any type of tenant in order to remain financially solvent. If this becomes the case, the shopping center's image may change and the investments of both the large and the small tenants could be damaged.

Regardless, the result is likely to be fewer shopping center developers. Developers with large amounts of capital and excellent tie-ins with major anchor tenants probably will become the rule, while the small, independent shopping center developer will be virtually eliminated from the channel. It is also possible that consortia will begin to put together centers that will feature the ownership of many types of establishments by a few major companies. This will eliminate the need for negotiating leases with increasingly large numbers of small tenants and will greatly lessen the number of parties involved in the inevitable power and conflict relationships. Clearly, this is an area in which empirical investigations of power and conflict relationships are badly needed.

QUESTIONS FOR DISCUSSION

1. Discuss fully the various issues involved in the Tysons Corner case.

2. Explain the legal issues involved in lease provisions that allegedly result in restraint of trade.

3. What are the *permissible* tenant lease provisions?

4. Summarize the contrasting court decisions involving shopping center development.

5. Discuss the importance of anchor tenants to shopping center developments. What legal issues are raised in the article regarding "special" treatment given to anchor tenants?

6. Do you believe the FTC is overly involved in shopping center development? Defend your answer.

9.5 REFUSAL TO DEAL—A CASE HISTORY

Robert E. Weigand and Hilda C. Wasson

*"The threat of termination is the ultimate
weapon in the hands of a strong manufacturer."*

Businessmen and academicians share the view that much of marketing consists of seeking ways to increase sales while keeping costs within tolerable bounds. Very little attention is devoted to the seller who discriminates among prospective buyers to the point of refusing to deal with those whose practices do not conform to supplier policies. "Refusal to deal" is a well known concept in the law, and has a rich history that is generally conceded to have started with the U.S. vs. Colgate and Company case[1] in 1919. In earlier years marketing professors generally taught that retail prices could be maintained by careful selection and quick termination of recalcitrant dealers who refused to abide by the manufacturer's wishes. Consignment selling, use of "Fair Trade" laws, and moral suasion of one sort or another completed the list of tools available to manufacturers who cared enough to try to enforce prices. With the rampant discounting that took place in the 1950's, price maintenance became less important—at least in the classroom. It appears to have become more important again as we seek to learn about quasivertical integration taking place through franchising.

The article focuses attention on the history of Magnavox Consumer Electronics Company's[2] efforts to build a small and carefully controlled marketing channel and an attempt to explain how a recent Federal Trade Commission consent order might affect that company. The origin of the marketing channel for the consumer electronics portion of Magnavox's business—meaning such products as television, radios, phonographs, stereo sets, and tape equipment—should be traced to 1938 when Frank M. Freimann took over the consumer product operations.[3]

Reprinted by permission of the authors and publisher from Robert E. Weigand and Hilda C. Wasson, "Refusal to Deal—A Case History," of which an abstract is contained in *The Journal of Business Research* (May 1972).

1. 250 U.S. 300, 1919.
2. A subsidiary of the Magnavox Company.
3. For an interesting but now somewhat dated description of the Magnavox history, see "Magnavox Goes Its Own Golden Way," *Fortune* (February, 1964), p. 114.†

The first important product developed under Freimann's guidance was a high quality—at least by the standards of the day—home phonograph that would retail for $69.00. Although this price was higher than that of rival products, the quality was also thought to be superior. To elicit extra effort out of the retailers who agreed to sell the product, distribution was limited to department stores and music stores, and outlets were carefully spaced so that Magnavox dealers would not normally compete with each other. The manufacturer by-passed distributors and argued that much of the 16 percent margin that other manufacturers were paying their distributors at the time was being passed on to the retailers. Such care with a marketing system is unusual in the appliance industry and almost inevitably means fewer outlets than other manufacturers will use who sell indiscriminately. By 1970, Magnavox is believed to have had about 2,600 franchised outlets.[4] Zenith claims to be the present sales leader in consumer electronics,[5] but Admiral, Motorola, and private-brand sellers are also important forces in the industry. Since the larger manufacturers sell through distributors and their products are sold through virtually any kind of outlet, there is no particularly reliable way of estimating how many "big name" outlets blanket the country. Probably few would argue with the statement that Zenith has ten times as many outlets as does Magnavox.

In February, 1970, the Federal Trade Commission proposed a complaint against the Company's marketing system,[6] one directed at its efforts to enforce its pricing, exclusive dealing, full-line forcing, and other policies on its dealers. The company responded that, "Management believes present practices do not violate the Federal Trade Commission Act and is satisfied it will demonstrate this to the Commission or in the courts if necessary."[7] The Company later stated it had "... reorganized personnel and practices to insure an effective solution ... (to the complaint), and that the final outcome might take many years to settle."[8] However, in April, 1971, Magnavox accepted an initial order barring it from a number of practices that signalled a dramatic change in its marketing system,[9] and a final order became effective a month later.

The final decision and order[10] suggests the nature of Magnavox's mar-

---

4. "Magnavox Company," *Standard and Poors Corporation Records,* Standard and Poors Corporation Pub., Vol. 32, No. 25, p. 2416.

5. "Zenith Radio," *Value Line Survey* (May 28, 1971).

6. Magnavox Illegally Fixes, Controls Prices of TV Sets and Other Items, FTC Alleges," *The Wall Street Journal* (February 17, 1970), p. 6.

7. *The Magnavox Company: Annual Report: 1969,* p. 4.

8. *The Magnavox Company, Annual Report: 1970,* p. 4.

9. "Magnavox Company Agrees To FTC Order Barring Alleged Price Fixing," *The Wall Street Journal,* (April 21, 1971), p. 9.

10. "In the Matter of The Magnavox Company, a Corporation," Docket Number C-869, Decision and Order, The Federal Trade Commission, December 23, 1964.

keting channel in recent years, and it clearly indicates that significant changes might now take place. The order contains thirty-four different obligations to perform involving such matters as Magnavox's influence over the dealers' pricing and inventory functions, exemption of the pricing section of the order in fair trade states, re-instatement of terminated dealers, and notification of present and terminated dealers of the changes brought by the decree.

The order bars Magnavox from attempting in any way to influence the price at which its dealers sell the company's products. Enforcement of a price maintenance system is enjoined for the duration of the decree, although the manufacturer may revert to suggesting a price after a two-year period. The order prohibits Magnavox from stipulating the price at which its dealers may advertise its products, from offering any co-operative advertising plans in which adherence to a specific price is a condition of participation, attempting to affect trade-in prices, learning the names of uncooperative retailers through others, or terminating or in just about any other way making it difficult for price-cutting retailers to do business. However, Magnavox may continue to use its efforts in those states with valid legislation which permits manufacturer price-fixing. Yet even here, the Commission takes a tough stance; Magnavox may not stipulate the retail price in any Standard Metropolitan Statistical Area that encompasses both a fair trade and a non-fair trade state.

Magnavox's efforts to control its channel for consumer electronics is further impaired by the limits placed on its attempts to control the retailers' inventories. It may no longer require the dealer to sell only Magnavox products, promote the entire line of Magnavox products, or agree to tied purchases. However, the Commission has permitted the Company to insist that dealers maintain a "representative" inventory of products.

The Company is further obliged to notify all dealers in twelve listed states and the District of Columbia who were terminated during the previous five years that they might qualify for re-instatement. No dealer has a right to automatic re-instatement, but Magnavox must show that the retailer lacks proper credit or that its facilities are inadequate; otherwise the retailer may elect to be re-instated. Although not specifically stated, the twelve states and District of Columbia where Magnavox must act appear to be those areas without fair trade laws and no overlapping Standard Metropolitan Statistical Areas. The rest of the order deals with notification that the company is obliged to give its dealers about their presumably greater operating freedom and reports of compliance that must be made to the Commission.

Magnavox was involved in an earlier consent decree dealing with its marketing practices, but the major thrust dealt with deceptive advertising.

THE REASONS WHY—CONJECTURES

It appears that Magnavox has elected to change its marketing system, or at least allow the system to change, by submitting to a rather severe consent order preventing most of the forms of control that it historically has exercised over its dealers. It is interesting to attempt to discern its reason for doing so. One explanation may be that the company underwent an important managerial change in 1968 and the new chief executive may not be willing to spend the substantial legal fees necessary to police the firm's channels. The threat of termination is the ultimate weapon in the hands of a strong manufacturer. Refusal to deal under certain conditions is still acknowledged by the Commission in its Advisory Opinions. The Commission recently wrote that

> . . . its view of the present state of the law in this area was that a seller not acting to create or maintain a monopoly may make a unilateral announcement of his policy as to those with whom he will deal, including policies affecting price, and he may refuse to deal with those who do not observe that policy. However, when the seller's actions . . . go beyond a mere announcement of his policy and the simple refusal to deal, and he employs other means which effect adherence to his policy, he is in serious danger of having put together a combination in violation of the antitrust laws.[11]

Furthermore, the courts have not declared refusal to deal to be a *per se* violation of the antitrust laws. One legal scholar states,

> Since, in the absence of an attempt to achieve or maintain a monopoly, Colgate guarantees the right of customer selection, a manufacturer must be free, in so far as the antitrust laws are concerned, to replace an existing distributor with a new one regardless of the hardship for the former and even in the absence of any plausible justification. The courts have consistently so held.[12]

However, management at Magnavox may have agreed to the order because it believes that present FTC and Court interpretation of the Colgate doctrine permits dealer termination under such confined circumstances that it is not a viable threat to price-cutting or otherwise uncooperating retailers. Indeed, the General Counsel for the Company writes,

> Our decision to settle the FTC proceeding by the acceptance of a consent order was not the abandonment of the 'Colgate Doctrine' or any other doctrine. Rather, it was a recognition that taking into consideration the present composition of the Federal Trade Commission and the appellate

11. "Publication of Dealer Sales Standards . . . ," *Advisory Opinion Digest Number 163,* published in News Summary: F.T.C., (January 31, 1968), unpaged.
12. Carl H. Fulda, "Individual Refusals to Deal . . ." *Law and Contemporary Problems,* (Summer, 1965), p. 597.

courts, Magnavox would be unable to prevail on the factual issue of whether, in the non-fair trade areas, we had gone beyond what Colgate allows.[13]

One scholar argues that suppliers who are strong enough to announce in advance that they will refuse to deal with price cutters or otherwise deviant customers can do so only through coercion.[14] The coercion results in a combination that restrains trade, and any subsequent refusal to deal with outlets will be illegal. What this means is that the seller must actually terminate a number of dealers and their termination must be widely publicized among the remaining dealers so that the message is clear. Those suppliers who prefer a price maintenance policy quite understandably would prefer some sort of warning system in which price-cutters would be given three strikes before being counted out. However, the courts have often held that it is fatal to warn re-sellers that they will be terminated if they continue to sell at cut prices or to terminate and then reinstate them with a warning not to do it again. Isaac's conclusion is that, ". . . Colgate will be limited to those cases where it is unnecessary."[15]

A second and highly plausible explanation is that Magnavox's management may have perceived elements of the consumer electronics industry as being in a mature state where older practices are no longer germane. The literature dealing with the mature or declining industry is limited, but the concept generally suggests that unit marketing costs are lower, distribution is often more widespread, and that transactions are more routine than in the introductory or growth states. Trade association evidence indicates that monochrome (black and white) television sets appear to have reached their sales peak of $910,000,000 in 1965 and then to have fallen to $518,000,000 in 1970. Although the evidence is less clear for color television equipment, it appears that maturity will be reached quickly. More specifically, sales of color television sets have declined to $1,684,000,000 in 1970 from a high point of $2,086,000,000.[16] About 95 percent of wired homes in the United States have at least one television set,[17] but since slightly less than one-third of the country's sets presently in use are color,[18] the sales decline may be temporary. Indeed, preliminary figures from the Electronic Industries Association indicate that 1971 sales should be about 25 percent higher

13. Letter to the authors from Mr. Samuel J. Rozel, General Counsel for the Magnavox Company, August 31, 1971.

14. William M. Issac, "Unilateral Refusal To Deal: King Colgate to Deal!" *The Ohio State Law Journal*, (1969), p. 537.

15. *Ibid.*, p. 547.

16. *Electronic Market Data Book*; 1971, (Washington, D.C.: Electronic Industries Association, 1971), p. 3.

17. *Ibid.*, Table 11.

18. *Ibid.*, Table 3.

than in 1970. Little can be learned about management's perception of where color television is in its life cycle from recent pricing changes. Magnavox raised its price on color television to dealers about seven percent in early May, only about two weeks after the preliminary consent decree, attributing some of the increase to higher costs and some to product improvements.[19] However, three months later RCA, Sylvania, Sears, and Philco-Ford announced temporary cuts,[20] and Magnavox followed a week later.[21] Unit manufacturing and marketing costs should decline during the drive to maturity, and this may well be what is happening with respect to color television sets. Home radios and phonographs are less important items to the industry and are not growing rapidly, and may even be declining; tape equipment, on the other hand, seems to be one of the industry's most rapidly growing products.[22]

Data furnished by retailers also show that elements of the consumer electronics industry are in the mature state of their life cycle. Reported gross margins in percent terms for one recent month were lower for television sets than for any of fourteen other categories except small appliances. The margins for portable color television sets averaged 22.4 percent while color consoles averaged 24 percent. On the other hand, margins for stereo sets, garbage disposals, and tape recorders all averaged slightly over 30 percent.[23] The average price in 1969 for color television sets was $440, and the average price of monochrome sets was $120.[24] Product improvements make historic price comparisons difficult, but it appears that even during the short history of color television, retail prices have declined about one-third. Still another piece of evidence that can be used to indicate product maturity is the proportion of sales where a trade-in is involved. During the early years, there should be few trade-ins since most sales are derived from new buyers. The evidence does not support this view, at least with respect to appliances. During the most recent year for which figures are available, only 25 percent of the television sets sold involved a trade-in. This figure is less than half what it was during the early 1960's. The explanation seems to be that few retailers want to be bothered with trade-ins and retail prices are as low as they can go with or without a trade-in.[25] In addition, many

19. "Magnavox Raises Color TV Prices About 7% Average," *The Wall Street Journal*, (May 7, 1971), p. 2.

20. "Color TV Prices On Portables Cut by Some Makers," *The Wall Street Journal* (August 12, 1971) p. 2.

21. "Magnavox Cuts Prices Up to $76 on Color TV's to Meet Competition, *The Wall Street Journal*, (August 18, 1971), p. 16.

22. *Ibid.*, Table 2.

23. "A-R-TV Dealers' Gross Margin," National Appliance and Radio-TV Dealers Association, (Volume IV, Number 6, July 1, 1971), p. 2.

24. *24th Annual Costs of Doing Business Survey*, National Appliance and Radio-TV Dealers Association, (1970), p. 7.

25. *Ibid.*, p. 9.

householders have found places in or outside the home to put the old set even though it may work imperfectly.

That the consumer electronics industry has a number of important products that are well past the introductory stage is well established. That Magnavox's management is loosening its control over its channel for this reason is a much more tenuous proposition. Life cycle theory generally suggests that mature products will be more widely distributed and subjected to much price cutting. However, the various products of multi-product firms often go through the same channel, and sellers cannot easily pursue one strategy for older products and a different one for products just being introduced. It is largely conjecture as to how Magnavox views the relationship of its well established products to its new ones, but it may have had an important influence on its thinking.

A third possible explanation for the company's acquiescence is that much channel control can still be exercised, the consent decree not withstanding. Unlike most appliance manufacturers, Magnavox does not use distributors or wholesalers. Rather, it deals directly with its retailers, a factor which has made dealer control and termination so easy in the past. There is little doubt that Magnavox dealers are watching carefully for changes either in Magnavox's attitudes or for changes in retailer strategy. One rather obvious hint would be the willingness of Magnavox to maintain retail prices in those states where fair trade pricing is still legal. If Magnavox relentlessly pursues price-cutters and brings them to court, managerial intent is known. On the other hand, if policing is rather superficial, it may be the spark that leads to price-cutting throughout the country. That elusive trait that can be called "channel discipline" is not always brought by legal means. This explanation infers that if Magnavox is to exercise non-legal control over its dealers it must select its new dealers with great care. The company has always been careful in its choice of retailers, but mistakes cannot now be corrected by abrupt termination.

Wroe Alderson succinctly states, "The nonintegrated marketing channel is often in direct competition with the fully integrated channel. In order that the nonintegrated channel may survive, which is a condition for the survival of the independent units which make it up, it must achieve balance and coordination in its operations."[26] If Magnavox polices retail prices in fair-trade states, does not impose unreal sales quotas, and does not add new dealers who will be perceived by entrenched retailers as encroaching on their economic turf, there may be few immediate changes in the way Magnavox's products reach the public.

A final factor that should be mentioned, perhaps more a consquence of the consent decree than a reason for it, is the prospect of Magnavox's entry into retailing. The literature on vertical integration generally in-

26. Wroe Alderson, *Marketing Behavior and Executive Action*, (Homewood, Illinois: Richard D. Irwin, Inc., 1957), pp. 157–8.

dicates that manufacturers enter retailing reluctantly, but they seem to do so with considerable regularity. City areas seem to offer the greatest dollar volume potential so it is not unusual to find manufacturer-owned outlets in metropolitan areas. Vertical integration is not easy to achieve but offers the greatest assurance that management's policies will be followed. If Magnavox's management is intent on continuing to control its marketing channels and is unable to do so through moral suasion, vertical integration remains a possibility, albeit a remote one.

Vertical integration often results in dual marketing channels, since the manufacturer's outlets compete with independent retailers unless there are powerful barriers that prevent cross-territorial customer movement. However, dual distribution has also grown to be a problem of giant proportions in the appliance industry as large manufacturers sell to large non-retailer customers. It is generally acknowledged that manufacturers sell large quantities of certain types of appliances direct to home and apartment builders, mobile home builders, and contractors for commercial and office buildings.[27] The legality of what retailers perceive to be encroachment on their market recently was challenged in 1970 by an Austin, Texas, retailer who argued that General Electric violated the Robinson-Patman Act by selling appliances to builders at lower prices than those charged retailers.[28] The suit indicated that as much as 30 percent of appliances sales now by-pass the retailer. The case was settled out of court, so we know little more about the law than we did before. Historically, newly constructed homes and apartments have been offered for sale with refrigerators, laundry/dryer units, and, increasingly include home entertainment units as a part of the total package. If this should occur, Magnavox and other manufacturers will increasingly deal directly with building contractors. To the extent that this occurs, traditional retailers will play a less important role in the firm's marketing operations.

George Stigler and others argue that vertical re-integration of production and marketing functions is probably the expected course for mature industries and certainly for declining ones.[29] This does not mean that manufacturers will fully assume the risk function in a single step, but generally is interpreted to mean a gradually increased manufacturer interest in selected activities normally associated with retailing. There probably are fewer examples of manufacturers who integrate forward than there are of retailers who integrate backward. However, the recent

27. "Appliance Dealers Industry," *The Impact Upon Small Business of Dual Distribution and Related Vertical Integration*, Select Committee on Small Business of the House of Representatives, 88th Congress, 2nd session, (Washington, D.C.: 1964), p. 26. See also, *ibid.*, Volume 5, pp. 1126–9.

28. "GE's Appliance Pricing Is Challenged in Court by a Dealer In Texas," *The Wall Street Journal*, (December 7, 1970), p. 17.

29. George J. Stigler, "The Division of Labor is Limited by the Extent of the Market," *The Journal of Political Economy*, (June, 1951), p. 185.

movement of mens' clothing manufacturers into retailing in order to assure themselves of outlets in important markets offers an interesting example of how the "routinization" of retailing in a mature industry permits manufacturer-owned outlets to survive. We are unwilling to state that this is occurring in the consumer electronics industry, but it represents an interesting long-term possibility. No doubt much of the manufacturers' reluctance to enter retailing is fear of political and legal pressure brought by about-to-be expropriated retailers. There is ample evidence that the courts stand ready to prevent manufacturers from unjust enrichment when they enter into retailing at the expense of those retailers who initially developed the market.[30]

A FINAL IRONY

It has not been long since many observers hailed franchising as a happy marriage between a strong supplier who has managerial know-how and retailers who were willing to work hard but lacked a basic understanding of how business operates. Franchisor assistance could, and in many instances certainly has, turned small businessmen with modest abilities into moderately wealthy entrepreneurs. A certain amount of submission was necessary as a condition of entry into the system and power used by the suppliers almost certainly was heavy-handed in many instances. The Magnavox Company was able to build up a powerful marketing organization that probably has been irrevocably changed by the recent consent order. It would be ironic if the strong system of participating dealers through which Magnavox was able to compete with larger rivals would be weakened by the decree.

QUESTIONS FOR DISCUSSION

1. Why did Magnavox wish to exercise a high degree of control over its marketing channels?

2. a. What can Magnavox do to control the retail prices of its products?

   b. What legal issues are involved in this situation?

   c. Do you believe there should be more or less regulation regarding Magnavox's control of retail prices? Why?

3. Why do you believe the Magnavox Company elected to change its existing program of channel control? Discuss fully.

30. This is a particularly important issue in the automobile industry. The "Big Three" face numerous court challenges around the country for opening dealer-owned agencies that are geographically proximate to independent outlets.

9.6 RECIPROCITY IS "DEAD"

". . . (The) FTC has spent time and money warning
marketers that trade relations is naughty. From now
on, anyone caught at the game had better be ready
for a formal complaint and—if necessary— a
court fight."

"Effective immediately," said the official announcement, "the Federal Trade Commission will not . . . accept Assurances of Voluntary Compliance from corporations engaging in reciprocal dealings . . . where they use their purchasing and selling power to secure business from other firms."

Translation: FTC has spent enough time and money warning marketers that trade relations is naughty. From now on, anyone caught at the game had better be ready for a formal complaint and—if necessary—a court fight.

Indeed, marketers can't say they haven't been warned. In recent months, the FTC has wrung promises to halt the practice from American Standard, Inc., Chase Bag Co., Celanese Corp., GAF Corp. (formerly General Aniline & Film), Sun Chemical Corp., and Union Camp. During the same span, FTC's antitrust enforcement twin, the Justice Dept., signed consent orders (which carry no admission of guilt) with Armco Steel Corp., Evans Products Co., Inland Steel Corp., Republic Steel Corp., and General Tire & Rubber Co., along with three of its subsidiaries.

The latter pact is typical of most signed to date. The government contended that General Tire subsidiaries Aerojet General (El Monte, Cal.), RKP-General, Inc. (New York City), and A.M. Byers Co. (Pittsburgh) had since 1961 "conspired to utilize their purchasing power to coerce and persuade suppliers to buy products from them." In addition, said the complaint, "the firms entered into reciprocal purchasing arrangements in which they agreed to buy products from suppliers if the suppliers in turn bought from them."

In what was also a typical settlement, the companies agreed to abolish

Reproduced by permission from *Sales Management* (October 15, 1970), pp. 27–28.

their trade relations departments, cease all internal communications "relating to a potential supplier's status as a customer," and stop generating statistical data designed to "further any relationship between purchasing and sales."[1]

In their intensified crackdown on reciprocity, FTC and Justice have not only decided to swap information and conduct joint investigations but to explore ways computer technology might be enlisted to spot potentially abusive companies and industries. How? "Right now it's possible to classify companies according to a five-digit Census code," says Harry A. Garfield, Assistant Director of FTC's newly formed Bureau of Competition. "You can then show the categories of products made by the company, as well as the categories of products it's likely to buy. The computer can take all this and help match up companies that would be likely to buy and sell from each other. Once we have that data, we could begin to go to specific companies and ask questions related to reciprocal dealing."

Despite the government's red flag waving, corporate trade relations departments remain surprisingly entrenched. Their spokesman, the Trade Relations Association (TRA), admits membership is "off somewhat" (to about 70 companies) but not enough, apparently, to crimp plans for its annual convention at the Greenbrier, in White Sulphur Springs, W. Va., this month. Moreover, TRA's roster continues to glitter with such corporate luminaries as American Machine & Foundry, Johns-Manville, Kaiser Aluminum, Martin Marietta, Signal Oil & Gas, and St. Regis Paper Co.

But TRA may be living on borrowed time. If FTC lawyers had their way, corporate trade relations departments would be banned altogether; and joining an *association* of such evildoers would rate the same reaction as throwing a brick through a precinct station window. Instead, TRA owes its continued life to the fact that neither practice has ever been declared a *per se* antitrust violation. The courts, in fact, have given antitrusters very few guidelines on how to proceed against reciprocal dealings. "Oh, we've won a few cases against guys who openly had ordered customers to buy from them or else," says FTC's Harry Garfield, "but we've never had a clear ruling on how far we can go on some of reciprocity's more subtle forms."

THE "PERNICIOUS TEST"

Right now, FTC's rule of thumb is that reciprocal dealing must be "systemized and pernicious" to justify federal intervention. "Reciprocity in

1. Other common names for trade relations departments—equally verboten to federal antitrusters—are sales coordination, business development, and corporate relations.

its most innocent form may very well not violate the law," says Garfield. "Our economists would probably find that if the practice carried no 'substantial foreclosure' and no upward pressure on prices, it probably wouldn't result in economic injury."

The Justice Dept. is inclined to be less liberal. "While such activities by themselves may be perfectly legal," says the antitrust division's Lewis Bernstein, "when the person to whom they are assigned also assists in sales promotion, then antitrust violations may occur." The same thing can happen, he adds, "when a corporation lets it be known that it has a trade relations department when it furnishes to its purchasing agent information about the volume of sales made to the prospective dealer."

Ironically, the biggest problem confronting reciprocity-watchers at FTC and Justice is that they've been unable to find a company willing to let them test their policies in court. It's a prime reason that the FTC stopped allowing accused offenders to settle by voluntary agreement. Clearly the agency is looking for a court fight. As Harry Garfield told *Sales Management*: "I can't see why any company would want to form a trade relations department unless it's willing to test the law."

QUESTIONS FOR DISCUSSION

1. Why is reciprocity illegal?
2. What steps is the FTC taking to find probable cases of reciprocity?
3. a. What is the "pernicious" test?
   b. Do you believe it will be effective? Why?

Chapter 10

Societal Issues in Marketing Channels

OF ALL THE AREAS of marketing channels, the societal issues are the most fluid and challenging. Because of the constant change in this aspect of channels, the articles presented are designed to make the reader aware of some of the basic current issues. No attempt has been made to present an all-inclusive set of articles on the societal implications of marketing channel strategy. Indeed, it would be folly to do so, because the complexity and subtlety of this dynamic aspect would prevent a definitive analysis of the subject. The objective of this chapter, then, is to impart to the reader an appreciation of the type of issues and problems that are likely to be encountered in this area of channel management and to suggest some possible solutions.

Societal issues are a very important challenge and opportunity to marketing practitioners. Thus, Church and Dwight Co., best known for its Arm and Hammer brand of baking soda, recently introduced an ecology detergent. *Business Week* noted, "Davies' first new product was the detergent, an unlikely start when the competition is surveyed. But the company looked for an opening, spotted the ecology issue, and launched a product that was nonpolluting."[1]

The lead-off article by Professors Zikmund and Stanton is an extremely appropriate initial reading. This stimulating article looks at the recycling of solid wastes as a "backward" channels problem. The authors use channel strategy analysis to suggest a number of unique solutions to this most vexing current problem.

The second article deals with door-to-door selling. Many readers are not aware that this industry is very large and well established. Avon, the undisputed leader, in this channel, has 680,000 sales representatives selling 1,400 products to 85 million households around the world.[2] Professor Marvin A. Jolson presents a pragmatic view of the intricacies of door-to-door selling. Consumer complaints are discussed, along with the positive aspects of direct selling. Finally, the advantages and disadvantages of a door-to-door selling career are examined.

1. "The New Face of Arm & Hammer," *Business Week* (April 12, 1976), p. 60.
2. "Troubled Avon Tries a Face-Lifting," *Business Week* (May 11, 1974), p. 98.

The next article examines the benefits and problems involved in using open dating for perishable food products. The final article discusses the impact of unit pricing on the various channel members. This type of pricing, which has long been advocated by consumer interest groups, is now estimated to be used by about 40 percent of all supermarket food chains.

10.1 RECYCLING SOLID WASTES: A CHANNELS-OF-DISTRIBUTION PROBLEM

William G. Zikmund and William J. Stanton

". . . Specifically, recycling is primarily a channels-of-distribution problem, because the major cost of recycling waste products is their collection, sorting, and transportation."

In 1970 every American threw away approximately five and one-half pounds of solid waste (industrial construction, commercial, and household) each day which amounts to about a ton a year. This daily disposal rate is predicted to increase to eight pounds by 1980.[1] The escalation of public concern over environmental issues has, to an increasing extent, led government officials, business leaders, and conservationists to seek a solution to the problem of solid-waste pollution. One ecologically desirable technique for the disposal of trash is recycling. Simply stated, recycling consists of finding new ways of using previously discarded materials.

The recycling of solid wastes is being recognized as a tenable solution to cleaning up the cluttered environment. Scientists view recycling as a substitute for the declining supply of natural resources. Technology has responded to the recent interest in recycling with many new and sophisticated techniques capable of turning solid wastes into basic raw materials.

Although science and technological innovations are necessary aspects of recycling, the task of alleviating solid-waste pollution may be treated as a marketing activity; that is, the marketing of garbage and other waste materials. If it is a marketing function to distribute products and to add time and place utility to products, then, theoretically, it should make no difference whether the product is an empty, used beer can or a full one. More specifically, recycling is primarily a channels-of-distribution problem, because the major cost of recycling waste products

Reprinted by permission from the publisher and authors. William G. Zikmund and William J. Stanton, "Recycling Solid Wastes: A Channels-of-Distribution Problem," *Journal of Marketing,* Vol. 35 (July 1971), pp. 34–39.
    1. "Cash in Trash? Maybe," *Forbes,* Vol. 105 (January 15, 1970), p. 20.

is their collection, sorting, and transportation. The American Paper Institute estimates that over 90% of the cost of recycling paper is the cost of distribution.[2]

This article discusses the major alternative channels necessary to handle the waste materials created by the ultimate consumer, and identifies some of the major marketing problems involved in the recycling of these waste materials.

CONCEPT OF THE "BACKWARD" CHANNEL

If recycling is to be a feasible solution to the trash problem, there must be some means to channel the waste materials to the firm for future reuse. However, marketers have traditionally examined the channel of distribution starting with a producer; that is, a channel of distribution is the vehicle which facilitates the flow of goods from producer to consumer.

Recycling, on the other hand, is unusual from a marketing standpoint, because the ultimate consumer who recycles his waste materials must undergo a role change. The household consumer who returns his old newspapers and used bottles is the *de facto* producer of the waste materials which eventually will be reused. Thus, in this case the consumer becomes the first link in the channel of distribution rather than the last. The unique circumstances of recycling present an interesting marketing situation.

Recycling waste materials is essentially a "reverse-distribution" process. Reverse distribution is facilitated by a "backward" channel which returns the reusable packaging and other waste products from the consumer to the producer; it reverses the traditional physical flow of the product.

Conceptually, reverse distribution is identical to the traditional channel of distribution. The consumer has a product to sell and, in essence, he assumes the same position as a manufacturer selling a new product. The consumer's (seller's) role is to distribute his waste materials to the market that demands his product.

There is a practical difference, however, between the traditional channel and the "backward" channel. The consumer does not consider himself a producer of waste materials. Consequently, he is not concerned with planning a marketing strategy for his product—reusable wastes. Thus, for analytical purposes the recycling of waste materials will be considered as the reverse distribution of the original product, and the flow of the product from the consumer to the producer will be treated as the manufacturer's "backward" channel.

2. Walter P. Margulies, "Steel and Paper Industries Look to Recycling as an Answer to Pollution," *Advertising Age*, Vol. 41 (October 19, 1970), p. 63.

REVERSE DISTRIBUTION:
TYPES OF BACKWARD CHANNELS

One of the prime considerations in recycling household wastes is returning the waste product to a manufacturer for reuse. One of marketing's important roles is to determine the most efficient channel of distribution necessary to move the trash to the firm that will technically recycle the materials. The nature of the product and the nature of the market are as important in the determination of the backward channel as they are in the selection of the traditional channel of distribution. Thus, there is not an ideal channel that will typify all recycling efforts. The backward channel used to recycle an automobile is not likely to be the same channel used to recycle a glass bottle. However, some generalizations may be made about various backward channels, since a number of channel patterns is evident.

DIRECT BACKWARD CHANNEL—CONSUMER TO MANUFACTURER

Perhaps the simplest contemporary recycling attempt is exemplified by the plan of the Glass Container Manufacturing Institute (GCMI). Waste glass—known as a "cullet" in the industry—can supply 30% or more of the materials required to make new bottles. To obtain empty bottles and jars from the public, the manufacturer-members of GCMI have established approximately 100 bottle-redemption centers at glass container manufacturing plants in 25 states.[3]

It is doubtful that the modern consumer will make the effort to return his waste products directly to the manufacturer. The selection of any channel must consider the ultimate consumer's needs and it is unlikely that the modern consumer, accustomed to convenience, will exert any substantial effort to recycle his trash. The GCMI's recycling plan places the burden of recycling on the consumer. This innovative attempt to recycle glass is still in the "production-orientation" stage of development.

BACKWARD CHANNEL WITH AN ATYPICAL INTERMEDIARY

The absence of a middleman causes the consumer a number of inconveniences. Ecologically concerned civic and community groups which are sponsoring paper drives and community clean-up days are an im-

3. Walter P. Margulies, "Glass, Paper, Makers Tackle Our Packaging Pollution Woes," *Advertising Age*, Vol. 41 (September 21, 1970), p. 43.

portant link in the reverse-distribution process because they are performing the middleman's function in the backward channel.[4]

Considering the low prices paid for waste materials and the high cost of reverse distribution, it is not surprising that these organizations are the prime collectors of discarded newspapers, beer cans, and other waste materials. The collection and distribution of trash is a worthwhile venture for these associations because of the volume of their operations. It should be noted that the normal business costs are absent in paper drives and clean-up days, because expenses such as labor and collection vehicles are donated by the associations' membership. Since the main activity of these organizations is not the collection of waste materials, their performance of the middleman's reverse-distribution function tends to be sporadic. Even if community action recycling programs are conducted on a regular basis, it is not realistic to assume that they will be adequate to recycle the mountains of household wastes which will be generated in the coming years.

BACKWARD CHANNEL WITH TRADITIONAL MIDDLEMEN

Past recycling efforts used the traditional channel of distribution as the backward channel. Although recycling was not their major function, these intermediaries cooperated because the system was extremely convenient for the producer.

The recycling soft-drink bottles for a deposit provides a familiar example of one of the major attempts to recycle waste products and to reuse them in their existing forms.[5] This backward channel is literally the reverse of the normal channel for soft drinks.

During the 1930s and 1940s, packaging and wholesaling in the soft-drink industry was tied to the system of cycling the returnable bottle. The returnable bottle was desirable from the bottler's point of view, because every reuse reduced the "manufacturing" cost per bottle.

If this was the case, how can the steady growth of one-way bottles and cans be explained? Today, returnable bottles represent less than 50% of the soft-drink industry's business because both retailers and consumers resisted the returning and handling of empty bottles.[6] To maximize their profits, supermarkets emphasize the efficient utilization of space. Storing and handling empties was an additional task that retailers

4. See "Does Ecology Sell?" *Sales Management*, Vol. 105 (November 15, 1970), p. 20; and Walter P. Margulies, "Aluminum Industry is Already Hard at Work Against Pollution," *Advertising Age*, Vol. 41 (November 16, 1970), p. 64.

5. See "Will Returnables Make a Comeback?" *Business Week* (October 31, 1970), p. 25; and Sanford Rose, "The Economics of Environmental Quality," *Fortune*, Vol. LXXXI (February, 1970), p. 184.

6. "Packaging Advances Promise Much but Environment Dampens Outlook," *Soft Drink Industry*, Vol. 49 (May 27, 1970), p. 1.

were not willing to assume. Consequently, supermarkets influenced bottlers to introduce soft drinks in one-way bottles in 1948.[7]

One-way containers increased the bottler's manufacturing cost, and the consumer was required to bear the additional cost of throw-away bottles and cans. The response in the marketplace demonstrated the consumer's willingness to pay a few cents more for the convenience of one-way containers.

INDIRECT BACKWARD CHANNEL USING TRASH-COLLECTION SPECIALISTS

Various trash-collection specialists have developed to satisfy the consumer's need to dispose of his garbage and other solid wastes. In the past, the channel for recycling some household wastes included the "old rag and junk man" who served as a recycling-middleman specialist. By calling on homes and purchasing waste products such as rags, used papers, and discarded metal items, he provided both a service and a small-income source to consumers. However, he was part of a subsistence economy and a depression era. As people became more affluent, they preferred the convenience of throwing away their wastes. Moreover, his collection and processing costs were rising. Thus, the "old rag and junk man" disappeared largely because his role in the marketing of trash ceased to provide a sufficient service to household consumers or a profit to himself.

A contemporary waste-disposal specialist is the garbage or other trash-collection agency—either a private contractor or a unit in a municipal service system. At one time, these agencies made no attempt to recycle the wastes; they simply carried the rubbish to a city dump. Today many trash-collection agencies function as a link in a backward channel which recycles household wastes into landfill, power (via incineration), fertilizer, and other uses. The buyer of the trash (possibly after it has been sorted into basic materials) may be a power plant, a metals company, or a fertilizer company.[8]

Obviously this channel is convenient for the household consumer; he simply discards his rubbish into one or more trash cans. However, trash collection by an intermediary specialist is probably not the answer to the recycling channel problem. Unsorted trash used as landfill soon will exhaust available dumping sites. Trash sorted into various basic materials (e.g., glass, paper, and steel) for recycling increases the costs of these materials, although technology in this area is making significant

7. Robert K. Rogers, "Soft Drink Industry's Progress Paced by New Developments in Packaging," *Soft Drink Industry*, Vol. 49 (July 17, 1970), p. 17.

8. See "Turning Junk and Trash into a Resource," *Business Week* (October 10, 1970), p. 64; and "Aluminum Peddles its Own Recycle," *Business Week* (January 30, 1971), p. 21.

progress.[9] Sorted materials (e.g., glass bottles), frequently are too damaged to be reused in original form. Incinerated trash poses air pollution problems.

THE PROBLEMS OF RECYCLING

The development of effective backward channels should greatly facilitate recycling. However, in order to reach this goal, at least two major tasks must be accomplished. First, the ultimate consumer must be motivated to start the reverse flow of the product. Second, a greater degree of cooperation has to be achieved among channel members than is likely to occur under present conditions.

CONSUMER MOTIVATION

The greatest barrier to recycling household solid wastes is the consumer himself. The experience of the beer and soft-drink industries indicates that consumers have become accustomed to the luxury of convenience packaging and a throw-away economy. The purchase of 44 billion non-returnable beverage containers each year provides rather strong exemplary evidence that the consumer's cooperation will not be easy to obtain.[10]

The crux of any recycling plan must be to motivate the consumer to sort and return his waste products. Existing financial incentives such as a bottle deposit are not likely to elicit his cooperation. An appeal to a sense of civic duty or social responsibility so far has proven to be of momentary value, with little lasting effect.

In recognition of the fact that the present free-market system may not result in the recycling of consumer trash, various forms of government intervention are being tried to motivate consumers. Some legislators view packaging taxes and the banning of one-way containers as possible means of stimulating consumers to initiate the reverse distribution process. Some places (e.g., Bowie County, Maryland; South San Francisco, California; and British Columbia) have already passed laws restricting the sale of nonreturnables.[11] The President's Council on Environmental Quality has recommended promoting the idea of recycling bottles.[12]

9. "Gold in Garbage," *Time*, Vol. 97 (February 1, 1971), p. 61.
10. "Does Ecology Sell?" *Sales Management*, Vol. 105 (November 15, 1970), p. 20.
11. Same as footnote 10; and "Bottlers, Makers of Throw-away Cans Active in Ecological Programs," *Advertising Age*, Vol. 42 (March 1, 1971), p. 62.
12. "New Federal Programs May Strengthen Efforts to Guard Environment," *The Wall Street Journal*, Vol. CLXXVI (October 27, 1970), p. 1.

These attempts to force the consumer to recycle his trash are attacking only a symptom of the problem. The real problem is the consumers' throw-away life style. It probably will be a monumental task to change these attitudes, but it must be done before household solid wastes can be efficiently reused.

CHANNEL CONFLICT AND COOPERATION

Retailers and other middlemen must be willing to cooperate with the manufacturers if reverse distribution is to operate effectively. Generally, traditional middlemen in the backward channel have not been anxious to cooperate with recycling attempts, because it has not been profitable. The last 20 years in the soft-drink industry illustrate that retailers may resist recycling in order to utilize their space more efficiently. Consider the costs incurred by the outlet which collects waste materials from the consumer. The retailer must count or weigh the waste products, pay the consumer for his efforts, and store the materials for delivery to the manufacturer or another party in the backward channel.

No matter how delicately recycling is handled, conflict is inevitable in a backward channel. The middleman is an independent force, and he has the freedom to set his own objectives. Thus, he will need an additional incentive to participate in reverse distribution. A financial incentive may be adequate, but will the economics of recycling provide enough money to induce the middleman's support? Making products from new resources has been economically more feasible than recycling, because existing channels are not designed to recover and reuse old household products.

These middlemen will probably have to commit themselves to a higher order of social responsibility and a longer-range perspective than they customarily consider. They may have to become one of the cases Rosenberg and Stern envision as being malign for channel participants, but benign for the society at large.[13] It is questionable whether such a societal commitment can be reasonably expected from existing middlemen in traditional channels.

FUTURE OUTLOOK

The recycling of solid wastes is a major ecological goal. Although recycling is technologically feasible, reversing the flow of materials in channels of distribution presents a significant challenge. The existing

13. Larry J. Rosenberg and Louis W. Stern, "Toward the Analysis of Conflict in Distribution Channels: A Descriptive Model," *Journal of Marketing*, Vol. 34 (October, 1970), p. 45.

distribution system is designed to move products from the producer to the consumer. Existing backward channels are primitive, and financial incentives are inadequate. Most traditional middlemen recycle trash only as a sideline. Yet today, societal pressures and dwindling natural resources are forcing consumers to market their trash, even though the price paid for solid wastes is low, and the cost of collecting and processing these materials remains high.

NEW INSTITUTIONS

"A society, like any other open system, is an adaptive mechanism which responds to the demands of its environment. As it responds, a certain amount of internal adjustment, a large amount which is unpredictable, and the consequences, which are even less predictable, takes place."[14] Existing institutions must adapt to their environment or new institutions will arise to perform the job which is not being completed.

One new institution which may evolve in the reverse-distribution process is a *reclamation or recycling center*. In essence, this would be a modernized and streamlined "junkyard." These centers would be placed in locations convenient to the customer who would be paid an equitable amount for his goods. The recycling center, unlike the junkyard, would have a high turnover of wastes, because its prime goal would be the efficient collection and sorting of basic raw materials, rather than passively waiting for a buyer to purchase junk. If recycling centers perform some minor processing before shipping the basic raw materials to the various manufacturers, the centers might be very profitable operations.

If the recycling center is not convenient enough for the ultimate consumer, perhaps a modernized "rag and junk" man might work for the center, and periodically collect sanitized containers each containing the basic wastes (e.g., glass, paper, and aluminum). The consumers' use of garbage compactors and glass crushers could also enhance the economic feasibility of this operation.

Supermarket chains recycling their used cardboard packaging materials often employ *brokers* to negotiate sales to paper mills.[15] Brokers specializing in the recycling of trash could provide a useful service for small reclamation centers which may evolve into a significant institution in a backward channel.

To aid the recycling efforts of existing middlemen in traditional channels, *central processing warehousing* systems may develop to store trash and to perform limited processing operations on these waste materials.

---

14. Raymond A. Bauer, "Social Responsibility of Ego Enhancement," *The Journal of Social Issues*, Vol. XXI (April, 1965), p. 50.

15. "They're Finding Gold in Their Trash Bins," *Chain Store Age*, Vol. 45 (January, 1969), p. 18.

Existing middlemen typically have very limited space available for storing trash, and transportation is likely to represent a major portion of total recycling costs.

PACKAGING DESIGN AND MATERIALS

As part of their management of solid-waste disposal, marketers will have to reconsider the role of packaging in their marketing mix. The promotional benefits of superfluous packaging (such as shadow boxes) and the convenience factor in packaging (such as vegetables packaged in plastic cooking bags inside of cardboard boxes) will have to be re-evaluated in terms of the ecological problems they cause. Marketers could reduce the quantity of trash and facilitate the recycling of used packages through actions such as (1) building reuse value into the package (a jelly jar becomes a drinking glass); (2) avoiding unnecessary packaging (does an aspirin-bottle package have to be placed inside a cardboard box package?); (3) using materials which are degradable or which simplify recycling (the metal ring remaining on a glass bottle after a twist-off cap is removed causes a problem in the recycling of the bottle); and/or (4) placing a message on the package reminding the consumer to dispose of his trash properly (don't be a litterbug).

REVERSE DISTRIBUTION AS PART OF MARKETING STRATEGY

From the viewpoint of marketing management in a firm, reverse distribution should be treated as another ingredient in the market mix. As such, the success of any firm's recycling attempts will be contingent upon the marketing strategy employed. Educating the consumer via promotion, for example, will affect the consumer's willingness to use a firm's backward channel.

Management should recognize that waste products may be recycled in different ways:

1. The waste product may be reused in its existing form. For example, a Pepsi bottle is returned to the Pepsi bottler and reused as a Pepsi bottle.

2. The waste product may be reused as a raw material in the manufacture of additional units of the same product. For example, the aluminum from empty beer cans may be reused to make new beer cans.

3. The recycled waste product may become a different product, as when oil and tar are produced from old tires, or when organic wastes are converted to fertilizer.

The major factors in the selection of traditional channels of distribution are the nature of the product and the nature of the market. These factors are equally important in the selection of the backward channel, because the bulk and weight of the waste materials and the types of buyers and sellers will significantly influence the nature of the backward channel.

Each marketer contemplating the recycling of his product will have to choose one distribution strategy from a number of alternatives. The brewers of Coors beer, for instance, may wish to recycle their own beer cans exclusively. It is also possible that Coors's recycling strategy would have the backward channel return empty Budweiser beer cans which would then be reincarnated into Coors cans.

The type of reverse channel a company selects may influence the raw materials it purchases. A strategy of exclusively recycling waste products through traditional middlemen could provide the manufacturer with control over his sources of raw materials, thereby freeing him of dealing with some suppliers. In addition, the firm's environmental and ecological image may be enhanced if recycling is done by outlets identified with the manufacturer.

ROLE OF GOVERNMENT AND PUBLIC POLICY

In their role as citizens, people in the United States are demanding a cleaner environment, but when acting as consumers they have not been sufficiently motivated to help clean up that environment by recycling their trash. The result of this role conflict will undoubtedly mean an increase in the government's influence on a company's marketing policies with respect to recycling and reverse distribution. Previously, the article referred to a packaging tax and other local and state limitations on nonreturnable packaging. In addition, a bill was recently introduced at the federal level to ban the manufacture and sale of nonreturnable containers because they pose a threat to public welfare and the environment, and bcause they represent a high-cost form of litter and solid-waste management.[16] As Weiss observed, "When government moves in this radical new direction, can industry, can marketing, look in the other direction?"[17]

CONCLUSION

Predicting the future is difficult, but knowledge of society's needs helps us to know the general direction of the changing environment. One focus of the 1970s seems to center on the reduction of pollution in our environ-

16. U.S. Congress, House, 91st Congress, 2nd Session, H.R. 18773.
17. E. B. Weiss, "The Coming Change in Marketing: From Growthmanship to Shrinkmanship," *Advertising Age*, Vol. 42 (February 1, 1971), p. 63.

ment. The environmentalists who see recycling as the solution to the problem of solid-waste pollution must rely on marketing's help; technology alone is not enough. Lavidge has observed that "as it [marketing] matures, as it broadens in function and scope, marketing will become increasingly relevant during the 70's to the fulfillment of man. And as the impact of marketing on society increases, so does the social responsibility of marketing people."[18] Recycling waste materials is part of marketing's growing responsibility.

QUESTIONS FOR DISCUSSION

1. a. What is a "backward" channel?
   b. How is it different from a traditional channel?

2. a. What backward channels are suggested for solid wastes in this article?
   b. Which ones do you think will be most often used during the next decade?
   c. What backward channel concepts do you believe the authors failed to discuss?

3. What actions can a manufacturer take to facilitate reverse distribution channels of solid waste?

4. Should a manufacturer even be concerned about a product's waste return after it has been sold? Why?

5. a. Is the government involved in backward channels at this time?
   b. Should governmental agencies become involved in this area? Defend your answer.

18. Robert J. Lavidge, "The Growing Responsibilities of Marketing," *Journal of Marketing*, Vol. 34 (January, 1970), p. 28.

10.2 DIRECT SELLING: CONSUMER VS. SALESMAN

Marvin A. Jolson

". . . public condemnation of the direct selling method has done much to tag this distribution system with a label of rascality."

More than any other mode of retail distribution, door-to-door marketing is under attack by consumer advocates. The following article identifies the sources of conflict between the consumer and the sales person—what the advantages and what the disadvantages are to each in this approach to selling. From these evaluations, the author suggests ways management can help to reduce the level of stigma facing direct-to-home selling.

When Victor Buell investigated door-to-door selling from the firm's point of view seventeen years ago, he concluded that a well formulated and carefully implemented direct-selling program offered an opportunity for the individual manufacturer to secure a special competitive advantage.[1] During the ensuing years, direct selling has progressed considerably in some directions and suffered setbacks in others. It would probably be unfair to say that the "direct" system of product distribution has flopped. But there is nevertheless a lurking suspicion that the present level of consumer/sales force conflict is both disruptive to economic performance and a threat to the survival of this method of distribution.

The causes of conflict in the channel of distribution comprise the beginning phase of analysis.[2] Serious trouble indicators—such as a high sales force turnover rate and a rising rate of prohibitive or restrictive government legislation—are salient symptoms of conflict in direct-to-consumer channels.

Management seeks to discover, understand, and hopefully satisfy the

Reprinted by permission from Marvin A. Jolson, "Direct Selling: Consumer vs. Salesman," *Business Horizons* (October, 1972), pp. 87–95.

1. Victor P. Buell, "Door to Door Selling," *Harvard Business Review* (May–June 1954), pp. 113–123.

2. Larry J. Rosenberg and Louis W. Stern, "Toward the Analysis of Conflict in Distribution Channels: A Descriptive Model," *Journal of Marketing*, 34 (October, 1970), p. 44.

grievances of both consumers and sales force members without disturbing the advantages of the direct selling system. Therefore the design of this article is to summarize the pros and cons of direct selling as perceived by the key members of the channel system—the consumer and the direct salesman. Policy implications for the firm are discussed after a presentation and discussion of the basic findings.

The results and conclusions to follow are based largely upon a broader Baltimore study involving 200 households, 300 direct-to-home sales people, and 12 direct selling firms.[3]

CONSUMER COMPLAINTS

The findings indicate that direct selling has a disagreeable connotation to many consumers; salesmen are perceived as trying to trick or influence people into buying what they do not need. Consumers resent aggressive "foot in the door" tactics, unsolicited phone contacts, and high pressure sales presentations. Consumers complain of "one call closes," noncancellable binding contracts, invasion of privacy, and other conditions not normally encountered by customers who trade through conventional retail channels.

It is true that some direct salesmen who see a prospect only once will use high pressure tactics. Such a salesman is really interested only in the signed order and the resultant commission. Whether the customer actually needs the product or can afford it, and whether the product will perform as promised, is of little importance to this salesman. However, this offensive image fits only a small percentage of the nation's direct salesmen.

UPSETS RATIONAL PLANNING

It is probably more exact to say that the direct selling method upsets the consumer's rational planning and scheduling of his purchases. Many consumer purchases are essentially nonrationally determined. Needs exist of which the consumer may be conscious, but these are often reinforced by secondary needs of which he is only marginally aware or totally unconscious.

The sight of an article, the salesman's description of it, and especially a presentation of what it will do for the buyer cause the consumer to invest it with attributes and properties, real or fancied, which give it unusual value. At this point the product may be said to have "seduced"

3. Marvin A. Jolson, *Consumer Attitudes Toward Direct-to-Home Marketing System* (New York: Dunellen Publishing Co., 1970), pp. 65–82.

him. This is the point at which the consumer begins to discover that he likes the product and wants it. The procedure is analogous in many respects to the act of falling in love—and is equally irrational.[4]

INVASION OF PRIVACY

A prime difference between in-store and in-home buying is that the former method allows the consumer to buy at his own convenience at the seller's establishment. On the other hand, a large proportion of consumer contacts by direct selling firms involve uninvited phone calls and drop-ins. Often the consumer's written response to a magazine advertisement or direct mail circularization results in the surprise visit of the salesman who often arrives without having telephoned for an appointment.

The present study's analysis of consumer receptivity toward several frequently used methods of prospecting and customer contact revealed significant differences. Consumers are most receptive to sales contacts that they initiate themselves and least receptive to drop-in canvass calls.

PROFILE OF THE DIRECT SALESMAN

In the eyes of the consumer, the role of the salesman in consummating (closing) the sale may be summarized as follows:

1. The salesman is the "procurer" who uses the product presentation to seduce the prospect so that the latter falls in love with it and wants to buy it.

2. The salesman provides logical justifications to his prospect for performing what might appear to others as an irrational act, that is, the purchase of an article which the buyer neither needs nor can afford.

3. It is the salesman who, when necessary, applies the pressure to effect a "close."

In effect, the buyer is objecting to a purchase at the seller's convenience rather than at his own convenience.

The profile of the direct salesman as perceived by the consumer is shown in Figure 1.

CONSUMER ADVANTAGES

Despite consumer criticism, there are several reasons why consumers support the direct-to-home method of distribution.

4. Robert N. McMurry, "The Mystique of Super Salesmanship," *Harvard Business Review* (March–April 1961), pp. 113–115.

Fig. 1 Profile of the Direct Salesman As Perceived by the Consumer*

Educated...	Uneducated
High Income..	Low Income
Modern...	Old Fashioned
Neat...	Sloppy
Well Trained...	Poorly Trained
Polite...	Rude
Believable...	Generates Skepticism
Interesting..	Monotonous
Diplomatic...	Offensive
Sincere..	Phony
Wants to Satisfy My Needs..	Interested in Commission Only
No Pressure..	High Pressure
Energetic..	Lifeless
Accepts "No" Graciously..	Becomes Obnoxious when Rejected
Would Enjoy Him as a Friend..	Prefer Never to See Him Again
Prestige Job...	Necessary Job

* Reproduced from Marvin A. Jolson, *Consumer Attitudes Toward Direct-to-Home Marketing Systems* (New York: Dunellen Publishing Company, 1970), p. 106.

ENTIRE FAMILY CAN BE CONSULTED

Nearly 65 percent of the consumers sampled felt that a major advantage of direct selling is that all family members can inspect the product together so that a joint decision may be made. This is particularly important when higher priced items such as encyclopedias, storm windows, water softeners, vacuum cleaners, and so forth are being marketed. The average housewife is reluctant to take full responsibility for spending two or three hundred dollars or more. Most direct sellers of expensive products deliver a majority of their sales presentations during evening hours or on weekends. The net result is shared responsibility for the buying decision and a minimization of regret. The findings indicated that jointly signed contracts generate significantly less buyer's remorse than situations where a husband or wife enters into a contractual agreement in the absence of his or her spouse.

THE CONSUMER REQUIRES PERSUASION

Analysis of 490 purchase transactions indicated that 80 percent of the purchases would not have been made in the near future if a direct sales person had not made his unsolicited visit. Many consumers readily admitted that considerable persuasion took place but "they are now glad that the salesman talked them into making the purchase."

TRYING IN ADVANCE OF BUYING

Approximately 45 percent of the consumers interviewed confirmed the advantage of trying out the product under actual conditions of use. For example, the prospect housewife can operate the vacuum cleaner on her own carpeting, the prospect's children can verify the readability of the reference library, or the blending of the silverware pattern with the prospect's home environment can be examined. The prospect often desires special services, advice, and instructions about effective product use. Few people like the self-service principle for everything they buy.[5]

CONVENIENCE AND COMFORT OF IN-HOME BUYING

There is a growing demand by millions of consumers for shopping facilities that will save time, effort, and expense. Suburbanites seek to eliminate driving time, parking fees, and babysitting costs. Also there is substantial evidence that in-store shoppers are demanding but not receiving the required level of courteous, personal, and intimate treatment by salesmen.[6] This is partially due to the presence of queues in busy stores, the lack of familiarity of retail clerks with the profusion of available products, and the absence of financial incentives for the in-store sales person.

On the other hand, the direct seller usually carries only one product or a limited line of products; therefore, he is quite familiar with the features, benefits, and advantages of what he sells. There are no seller inflicted interruptions of the sales presentation and the typical result-

5. Albert Haring, "Can Door to Door Selling Perk Up Your Profit Picture," *Sales Management* (October 21, 1960), p. 101.

6. For example, see Gregory P. Stone, "City Shoppers and Urban Identification: Observations on the Social Psychology of City Life," *American Journal of Sociology,* 60 (1954), pp. 36–45; and Richard A. Smith, "The Ceiling on Selling," *Fortune* (August 1958), pp. 91–92.

oriented compensation plan motivates the seller to please the customer. As indicated by Figure 1, the consumer perceives the direct seller as being polite and well trained.

SALESMAN COMPLAINTS

More than 85 percent of the consumer respondents indicated that they would not consider employment as a direct sales person. People reluctant to try direct selling and those who have suffered disappointing experiences as direct sellers have a number of objections to the method of distribution.

IT "FORCES" PEOPLE TO BUY THINGS THEY DO NOT NEED

This observation is strongly related to direct distribution's objective of upsetting the consumer's rational planning and scheduling of purchases. The following transactions are pertinent examples:

1. the 21-year-old Washington, D.C. stewardess who purchased a double cemetery lot in suburban Maryland;
2. the 17-year-old San Antonio high school senior who purchased a $200 set of waterless cookware although she lived with her parents and had no immediate intentions of marriage or relocation of her residence;
3. the newly married Pennsylvania couple who purchased a $300 encyclopedia although their apartment was completely devoid of furniture due to their meager finances; and
4. the Hibbing, Minnesota couple who contracted for $389 worth of storm windows even though they lived in an apartment and had no specific plans to move into their own home.[7]

All of the above customers regretted their purchases and attempted to cancel their contractual agreements.

IT IS FRUSTRATING AND PROSTITUTING FOR THE SALESMAN

A certain amount of door-to-door canvassing (cold turkey) is required, depending upon the lead system of the company. Field sales positions have the disadvantage of being lonely. The representative must frequently work by himself, without the supportive presence of an associate or supervisor. Moreover, the salesman is often in an inferior status position vis-a-vis his prospect. He must be willing to accept rude-

7. Marvin A. Jolson, "Cooling Off the Direct-to-Home Seller," *Business and Economic Dimensions* (February 1971), pp. 8–9.

ness and rebuffs as a matter of course. In many instances, the salesman sees himself as the perpetual intruder, forcing himself on people and into homes where he is not only unwelcome, but often actively resented.[8]

THE FREQUENCY OF REJECTION IS HIGH

Consumers may resist the salesman on three separate levels—at the door, just preceding or during the sales presentation, and after the price is quoted. Put another way, the prospect may have as many as three decisions to make:

1. Will I admit this sales person to my home?
2. Will I listen to his story?
3. Will I buy this product or service?

An encyclopedia salesman, for example, may approach ten doors before being admitted. Once admitted, he may complete only one of three presentations. Only one of six presentations may be converted into a sale. Therefore, the salesman may suffer 179 turndowns in order to acquire one sale.

No one with a sensitive response to rejection could continue in this pattern on a prolonged basis.[9]

THERE IS NO SECURITY OF EARNINGS

The impact of 179 "no's" in exchange for each "yes" is especially tortuous when the salesman's earnings are totally dependent on sales. There are two undesirable effects of a straight commission plan: one is the actual low earnings when sales are scarce; the other is the anticipated non-uniformity of earnings. The first causes terminations; the second causes both terminations and a reluctance to seek a career in direct selling.

Many salesmen, both inexperienced and experienced, tend to exaggerate the drawbacks of a straight commission situation. Several examples were offered by respondent sales force members. Jim S. refused employment because he recalled a friend who failed on a straight commission basis. Bill T. decided to "try" a commissioned job; after three nonproductive days his fears were reinforced. George J. did well on straight commissions; however, he resigned because of fears that "some day" he would stop producing.

UNETHICAL CONDUCT IS REQUIRED

There is little doubt that the present level of consumer stigma and increasing legislation to protect the consumer from the door-to-door sales-

8. McMurry, "Mystique of Super Salesmanship," p. 116.
9. *Ibid.*

man has painted direct-to-home distribution in a shady color. Some of the charges are justified; others are not. Most direct sales people are trained by their firm to convey only reliable, correct statements to the consumer. Yet, there are some sales people who, in the interest of more sales and increased commissions, intentionally mislead the prospective customer. Unfortunately, the findings indicate that some direct selling firms train their salesmen to misrepresent their items.

As a result, public condemnation of the direct selling method has done much to tag this distribution system with a label of rascality. Potential career salesmen are concerned therefore with what they perceive to be a lack of status, dignity, ethics, and prestige.

SELLING MUST TAKE PLACE AT THE PROSPECT'S CONVENIENCE

Direct selling does not follow the job routine of five days a week, eight hours a day. The present findings have disclosed several advantages to the direct seller in delivering the sales presentation when both husband and wife are present. Husbands are significantly more at ease, more patient, and more willing to listen to a sales presentation than wives.

Consequently, companies are increasing the frequency of evening and weekend calls. The preference of the prospect for joint decision opportunities has already been discussed. In meeting the prospect's convenience, the firms also benefit in fewer call-backs and a reduced probability of cancellation under the cool-off option.[10]

Although there are advantages in adjusting the salesman's schedule to include the husband, the requirement for evening and weekend sales work imposes a burden of irregular working hours upon the sales person. Such a demand may adversely affect the living pattern that motivates his productivity.

SALESMAN ADVANTAGES

The person with little or no successful experience in direct selling often harbors unrealistic notions about "in-home" selling. He generally has heard about "getting in" and "closing" techniques. Probably, he thinks

10. The most common form of direct sales regulation requires a "cool-off" clause in the sales agreement which allows the customer to cancel his commitment within 24 to 96 hours following the signing of the contract. To date, cool-off statutes have been enacted in 22 states and others are following suit. For detailed descriptions of cool-off legislation see Orville C. Walker, Jr. and Neil M. Ford, "Can Cooling-off Laws Really Protect the Consumer," *Journal of Marketing*, 34 (April 1970), pp. 53–58; and Jolson, "Cooling-Off the Direct-to-Home Seller," pp. 7–17.

these processes are some kind of black art combination of hypnotism and jujitsu which allows a salesman, through guileful and violent methods, to make prospects buy something they do not want.

On the contrary, there is much evidence to establish that the image of today's direct salesman is far different from the sellers once considered men of "glittering eye and well-oiled tongue," each with a "large and heavy foot which he was ready to wedge into a doorway." Those old-time agents of an earlier era, bold and truculent, often carried samples slung from a harness under their coats. They were primarily wanderers who swept into a city or neighborhood, turned a quick profit, and moved away swiftly and silently. They preyed on ignorance and often charged prices three to four times the value of the product.

Even after the ranks of such agents had thinned, there still continued to be certain shady aspects of direct distribution. Justifiably, prospects were wary of anyone who announced that he had come to bring benefits to their households. But as time passed, people grew wiser and less susceptible to chicanery and sophistry. When consumers were not alert, various governmental agencies and Better Business Bureaus were.[11]

It was previously inferred that consumer/salesman conflict and buyer dissonance are greatly decreased when low ticket purchases are involved. Recent studies by Haring of over 15,000 direct-to-home sales people disclose that 80 percent of the respondents reported that three-fourths or more of those contacted received the sales person in a courteous and friendly manner and seemed to welcome his call. However, over 6,500 of these people sold Avon Products averaging under ten dollars per sale.[12] Thus the intensity of this problem area is not identical for all direct sellers.

Regardless of product price, today's successful direct salesman sees himself as an ethical businessman who fulfills an important need in America's marketing system. Moreover, he achieves a number of advantages over the salesman who operates in more conventional channels.

FEW QUALIFICATIONS FOR ENTRY

Direct selling requires only sound character and a self-motivated willingness to work. Age, sex, race, lack of education or experience, and time availability are not barriers.

11. Herman Kogan, *The Great E. B.* (Chicago: University of Press, 1958), pp. 300–302.

12. As reported by Professor Albert Haring during his testimony before the U.S. Congress, Senate, Consumer Subcommittee of the Committee on Commerce, *Hearings on Senate Bill Number 1599, Door-to-Door Sales Regulations*, 90th Congress, 2nd Session, March 4–5, 20–21, 1968, pp. 173–177.

FLEXIBLE HOURS

The direct salesman may work as much or as little as he wishes, with income related only to productivity.

REWARDS FOR PRODUCTIVITY

The average income of the direct salesman is similar to that of most other salesmen. However, the median income is low, which may be attributable to the high proportion of part-time direct sales people.

Often overlooked within the mass of data on direct selling are income phenomena which are seldom enjoyed by sales people who operate in other channels. A company in the home security field, which primarily recruits salesmen under 25 years of age, reported 28 salesmen earning in excess of $30,000 in 1970. Another firm, in the cookware industry, tells of three salesmen who entered the company in 1968 from non-selling positions; each in his first year of direct selling surpassed $40,000 in net earnings. A national cosmetics sales organization, which relies heavily on female representatives, reported that more than 300 of its sales women acquired more than $20,000 in personal earnings in 1969. An international publisher whose sales volume rises substantially during the summer season points with pride to more than 150 college students who netted incomes of more than $2,500 during a single summer.

ADVANCEMENT POTENTIAL

The successful salesman finds that advancement to a supervisory position is rapid and extremely rewarding. The field sales manager receives a commission or override on the sales of his six or eight assigned salesmen. The branch or district manager profits on all orders in a city or state. The regional manager typically receives compensation on all volume in a multistate territory. The product division sales manager may receive a substantial salary, an override on every sale in the nation, as well as sizeable bonuses and stock options. These combine to ensure a sizeable financial reward: six-figure incomes for direct-to-home sales executives (who are not corporate officers) frequently occur.

CONCLUSIONS AND POLICY IMPLICATIONS

The purpose of this article has been to examine the current state of in-home selling from both positive and negative viewpoints. The positive views may help to explain the magnetic lure of direct selling which is continuously attracting many new companies into the field. The negative views place consumer/salesman conflict problems in perspective for management and also identify certain consumer/company and sales force/company areas of conflict.

RECRUITMENT AND RETENTION

As a result of the negative perceptions of consumers and potential employees, "selling the job" is often more difficult than "selling the product."

While emphasizing the recruiting function, the firm's management often neglects the basic indoctrination and followup on sales training, planning, and control that are essential for manpower retention. Frequent consumer rejection, low earnings, and harassment by local municipalities and federal authorities contribute to a manpower turnover rate that often exceeds 500 percent annually. The interrelationships among these factors are shown in Figure 2.

IDEAS FOR PROGRESS

It is predicted that consumer and corporate interests will become more compatible. Adoption of some of the following suggestions may hasten the process.[13]

1. Direct selling executives should initiate an educational program directed at consumers, government officials, the Better Business Bureau, news media, and members of the university community. The emphasis of this program should be the benefits of direct marketing to consumers and the overall economy.

2. An accrediting organization, consisting of industry leaders working in conjunction with selected consumer agencies, should be established to develop, promote, and enforce a code of ethics and standards of operations acceptable to all parties concerned.

3. Companies marketing higher priced packages should initiate a post-sale system of verifying the sales transaction with the new customer for the purpose of uncovering misunderstanding, complaints, or buyer's remorse. The order should not be processed until any customer grievances have been settled.

4. Sales calls of new or questionable sales people should be monitored; unsatisfactory people should be corrected or terminated.

5. Companies should install a more rigorous, more objective per-

13. Several of the following suggestions were discussed at the National Roundtable Seminar on Direct Selling, October 8–10, 1970 at Vail, Colorado.

FIG. 2   Interrelationship of Problem Areas Facing Direct Selling Firms*

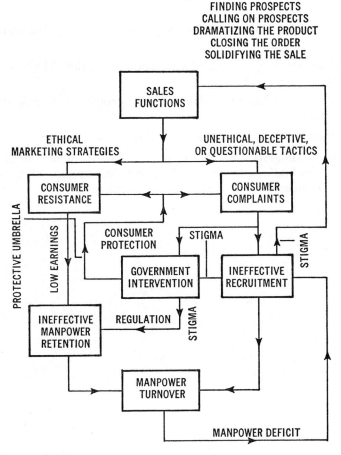

FINDING PROSPECTS
CALLING ON PROSPECTS
DRAMATIZING THE PRODUCT
CLOSING THE ORDER
SOLIDIFYING THE SALE

* Reproduced from Marvin A. Jolson, *Consumer Attitudes Toward Direct-to-Home Marketing Systems* (New York: Dunellen Publishing Company, 1970), p. 5.

sonnel selection system; a thorough check of the applicant's character and past employment record should be utilized.

6. Research must constantly be underway to keep abreast of attitudes of consumers and of present or former sales people. This information is crucial to combat ignorance and prejudice and to provide a sound base for policy decisions.

Effective management of direct selling requires a total integration and coordination of all the factors that can influence the final sale.

QUESTIONS FOR DISCUSSION

1. Discuss the chief consumer complaints that deal with door-to-door selling.

2. What are the *advantages* to the consumer of direct-to-home distribution?

3. Discuss the basic complaints of salespeople involved in door-to-door selling.

4. What are the *advantages* of direct selling as a career?

5. Jolson suggests a number of conclusions and policy implications based on his findings. Summarize these conclusions and policy implications. Do you agree with them? Defend your answer.

10.3 DOES OPEN DATING OF FOOD PRODUCTS BENEFIT THE CONSUMER?

Prabhaker Nayak and Larry J. Rosenberg

"According to the retailer, open dating seems to increase costs, directly and indirectly, and as such contributes to higher food prices."

On May 17, 1971, Congressman Benjamin Rosenthal and others introduced the Open Dating of Food Products Bill to amend the Fair Packaging and Labeling Act (1966).[1] Its main objective was to indicate clearly to the consumer, on packaged perishable or semiperishable foods, the "pull date" which is defined in the Bill as:

> The last date on which a perishable or semiperishable food can be sold for consumption without a high risk of spoilage or significant loss of nutritional value or palatability, if stored by the consumer after that date for the period which a consumer can reasonably be expected to store that food.[2]

Before the Bill was introduced in the House of Representatives, two limited surveys were made in the Washington, D.C., area. The results indicated that retailers did not rotate and remove stocks from the shelves and, therefore, sold a considerable amount of overage food.[3] At that time, no other significant research on open dating of food products had been undertaken.

Since the introduction of the Bill several studies have been conducted. This article (1) reviews the existing research studies on open dating, and (2) assesses the findings to determine the possible benefits to consumer and retailer.

BACKGROUND TO OPEN DATING PROPOSAL

The contemporary consumerism movement in the United States has been concerned with several issues, among them: consumer choice, in-

Reprinted by permission from Prabhaker Nayak and Larry J. Rosenberg, "Does Open Dating of Food Products Benefit the Consumer?" *Journal of Retailing* (Summer, 1975), pp. 10–20.

1. Bill to Amend the Fair Packaging and Labeling Act, 92nd Congress, 1st Session, H. R. 8438, House of Representatives, May 17, 1971.
2. *Ibid.*, p. 2.
3. Eileen Taylor, *Food Product Dating* (Washington, D.C.: Marketing and

formation, protection, and representation. The Fair Packaging and Labeling Act (1966) was designed to provide the consumer with more relevant information about products, thus enabling him to make price comparisons. The proposed Open Dating Bill is designed to provide the consumer with even more information and choice.

Open dating regulations are already in effect in Dade County, Florida. According to the provisions of the ordinance passed and adopted in Florida in October 1971, "perishable products," which include fresh packaged perishable meat, poultry, fish, and dairy products, must be conspicuously marked with a terminal shelf life date.[4] Massachusetts has passed a similar law which requires as of January 1, 1974, that perishable food, i.e., food having a shelf life of less than 60 days after manufacture, be labeled with the last date of sale.[5]

Open dating of food products is not generally practiced, the major exception being milk and yeast products. Open dating of milk is required by only one state and five municipalities (City of New York, Baltimore, St. Louis, Birmingham, and suburban Philadelphia). Some states do require dating, but these are not intended for use by consumers. Food processors have adopted open dating on most refrigerated dough products (which contain yeast).

STUDIES CONCERNING OPEN DATING

To assess the consumer benefits derived from open dating of food products, the results of six major research studies are examined. Since 1970, major studies have been sponsored by universities, government, and industry-supported organizations. They focus on a range of food products—perishable (dairy) to package (processed food)—and have sampled scientific experts, governments, stores, and consumers. They have sought to shed light on important aspects of open dating: technical validity, extent of usage, impact on marketing practices, consumer experience, and consumer attitudes.

THE MILK STUDY

The first and perhaps the most extensive study of open dating involved milk.[6] It was conducted in four phases:

Transportation Situation, United States Department of Agriculture, November 1970), p. 28.

4. "Proposed Rules and Regulations for Terminal Shelf Life Dates on Packaged Perishable Foods," Metropolitan Dade County, Florida, Consumer Protection Division, Ordinance No. 7180, October 19, 1971.

5. "Labeling Regulations," Massachusetts Department of Public Health Division of Food and Drugs, June 5, 1973, p. 72.

6. E. D. Glass, Jr., G. H. Watrous, Jr., W. T. Butz, W. F. Johnstone, and C. W.

1. *Influence of dating on quality of milk.* The objective of the first phase of the milk study was to review the recent literature on milk dating to determine the factors that can influence the quality of pasteurized milk and to evaluate the significance of these factors on quality.[7] The results showed that:

> Although the practice of dating may have had some value as a means of insuring quality of pasteurized milk in the past, significant technological innovations in milk production, processing, packaging, and distribution have improved the keeping quality of pasteurized milk to the point where dating as a public health measure may no longer be necessary.[8]

Thus, this study indicates that because of improvements in packaging and distribution of milk, there is no simple relationship between age and quality.

2. *Extent, nature, and trends in milk dating.* The second phase of the milk study assessed the number of states or other political subdivisions which currently require marking milk containers in a way that can be readily understood by consumers. The findings are as follows:

> Based on 1960 populations, markets requiring milk dating in 1957 included 14.9 percent of United States population. By 1969, however, only 9.3 percent of the 1960 population resided in dating markets. Marketing areas which have repealed dating legislation since 1957 contained 5.8 percent of United States population in 1960.[9]

As of September 1969, only the six areas mentioned above required dating of milk, compared with 21 in 1957.

The main reason for removal of dating ordinances by areas that formerly required dating was the adoption of the United States Public Health Grade "A" Pasteurized Milk Ordinance by many states.

> Many state and local public health officials have indicated that under modern methods of processing, refrigerating and retailing milk, dating of milk cannot be justified on grounds of protecting the health of consumers.[10]

3. *Delivery practices and costs.* The main objective of the third phase of the milk study was to ascertain any differences between dating and nondating markets with respect to processor practices and costs in

---

Pierce, *Quality and Economic Considerations in the Dating of Milk*, International Association of Milk, Food and Environmental Sanitarians, Inc., 1971; reprinted from *Journal of Milk and Food Technology*, 33 (December 1970), pp. 529–40 and 34 (January 1971), pp. 46–53.

7. *Ibid.*, p. 34.
8. *Ibid.*, p. 529.
9. *Ibid.*, p. 533.
10. *Ibid.*, p. 534.

delivering milk to stores. From the survey of delivery practices in 1969, it was found that stores located in dating markets generally received more deliveries per week than did stores in nondating markets. Since frequency of delivery directly influences the cost, unit costs of delivery were usually higher in dating than in nondating markets.[11] The study also suggested that these costs are eventually passed on to consumers.

4. *Milk handling practices in stores.* The fourth phase of the study sought to determine differences in store milk handling practices between dating and nondating markets with particular emphasis on differences in milk availability. Surveys were conducted in three paired sets of markets during the period August to December 1969: New York City (dating) and Chicago (nondating); Birmingham (dating) and Montgomery, Alabama (nondating); Camden, New Jersey (dating), and Philadelphia (nondating).[12] In each of the paired sets, milk was less available in the dating market. In the New York City/Chicago and Birmingham/Montgomery surveys, there were more special deliveries and lower inventories in the dating markets. The Camden/Philadelphia study, however, found that special deliveries were few, and there was no difference in inventory levels.[13]

In summary, the milk study indicates that technological innovations might help maintain quality in the product. To this extent, pull dates might discriminate against some products by implying a deterioration of quality which in fact did not yet occur. The importance of proper product handling in the distribution process has also been stressed. The need for temperature control seems to be more critical than dating.

In various dating markets the return of unsold milk was estimated to be higher than in the nondating markets. As a result, the costs of operating were estimated to be higher. Also, the lack of inventory in the dating markets could cause consumer inconvenience and higher costs of special delivery to replenish stocks. All these costs might be passed on to consumers.

Some of the areas of potential cost saving in dating markets would be in lower milk inventories which might tie up less capital; however, the study failed to consider this positive aspect of dating. This type of saving should be weighed against consumer inconvenience and possible loss of goodwill.

FOOD STABILITY SURVEY[14]

This 1971 study was conducted by Rutgers University for the New Jersey Department of Health. The first part concerns itself with the

11. *Ibid.*, p. 536.
12. *Ibid.*, p. 46.
13. *Ibid.*, p. 46–47.
14. Food Stability Survey, Vol. I (Washington, D.C.: Rutgers University De-

factors affecting the quality and shelf life of processed food in four areas: aesthetic, nutritional, microbial, and functional. A literature review in the study encompasses the available scientific and factual information on quality changes in food before, during, and after processing.

The study also indicates the problems involved in determining shelf life and it points out the difficulties of legislation on this particular issue:

> . . . the shelf-life prediction of one food company can differ from another's —even on the same product. Yet, both may be correct within the limitations of their own specific experimental methodology. Thus, shelf-life determination cannot be legislated and must remain as a variable in the hands of food producers. Other information on variety trials for specific types of processing, different methods of analyses, etc. is evident in the scientific literature.[15]

The second part of the study deals with the present practices of code dating/public dating of food products, primarily (1) voluntary food industry coding and monitoring, (2) legal or required coding/dating, and (3) influence of dating on quality maintenance. It concludes that coding has been used primarily by manufacturers to identify date of packaging, production plant, work shift, specific formulation, and raw-material mix. It is not meant for use by the consumer.

Some of the general findings of the study are:

1. With age, the loss of quality—particularly aesthetic quality (color, flavor, texture)—of packaged foods rarely produces health hazards.

2. Processed foods are less likely to deteriorate than are fresh foods. However, if food is "impaired," changes in its aesthetic qualities are obvious and the consumer will reject the food.

3. Food manufacturers use various codes on food products to help maintain quality and for inventory control.

4. Consumers may not find the actual date of processing useful in itself, as it does not indicate expected product durability.

5. In the absence of a guarantee of proper handling at the stages of distribution, an open date may be of doubtful validity.[16]

FOOD DATING IN SELECTED CHICAGO SUPERMARKETS[17]

This case study, conducted in early 1971, involved 18 supermarkets of a Chicago food chain—six each in low, middle, and higher income areas.

partment of Food Science and United States Department of Agriculture, Economic Research Service, February 1971).

15. *Ibid.*, p. 17.
16. *Ibid.*, pp. iv–v.
17. *A Case Study of Food Dating in Selected Chicago Supermarkets* (Wash-

It was launched with substantial publicity on the meaning of open dating, and dates were made highly legible on the products. The object was to examine: (1) shoppers' reactions to and in-store effects of freshness codes, (2) shoppers' awareness and use of the open dating program, and (3) their views on the program.

The study showed that more than 50 percent of 1,700 shoppers interviewed were aware, unaided, of readable dates on products. Also, in-depth interviews were conducted with 429 customers who had indicated awareness of the freshness code program. Only 20 percent of them could correctly interpret open date as "pull date"; 21 percent thought it was the expiration date (last day the product should be used); and 40 percent viewed the date as an assurance of freshness.

NATIONAL TELEPHONE SURVEY ON OPEN DATING[18]

This survey was conducted for the Consumer Research Institute by a private research organization during the period June 22–28, 1971. Telephone interviews were conducted on a random basis of 1,531 persons largely responsible for household grocery shopping. The important questions this survey addressed were: (1) consumers' experiences as to the frequency of buying food that was stale or spoiled; (2) satisfaction with the freshness of foods purchased; (3) observation of dated food products in stores; (4) practice of sorting through packages to look for the freshest item; and (5) opinion as to the meaning of the date.

Only 7 percent of consumers experiencing lack of freshness reported that it occurred often; the remaining 93 percent hardly ever or never received stale or bad products. Consumers with higher per family income indicated a 26 percent rate of some spoiled products, whereas those in the lower-income category reported a 17 percent rate. Those with less education exhibited a 14 percent rate, while those with more education had a 45 percent rate.

As to satisfaction with food purchases, 92 percent of the consumers were very satisfied or fairly satisfied with food freshness, with 8 percent registering dissatisfaction. Most cases of spoiled or stale foods were in the perishable and semiperishable categories (e.g., meat, dairy products, and fresh produce).

Consumers who noticed the date on food products totaled 41 percent 55 percent did not, and 4 percent were uncertain. Of the 628 respondents who noticed dates, 62 percent said they sorted through packages looking for the freshest item. However, 45 percent of the same 628 respon-

---

ington, D.C.: Economic Research Service, United States Department of Agriculture, Marketing Research Report No. 943, November 1971).

18. Consumer Research Institute, *Open Dating National Sample Survey* (Washington, D.C.: Unpublished Study, March 3, 1972).

dents identified the date as an expiration date; 30 percent thought it was a pull date (to be taken off the shelf); 15 percent said it was the date of packing; and 9 percent perceived it as the date the product was placed on display.

Among the 41 percent of respondents who did notice the date, it was found that women shoppers tended to exhibit a higher awareness index than did the men and that consumers who were younger, more affluent, and/or better educated seemed to be more aware than were their older, less affluent and/or less educated counterparts. Also, awareness of open dating information appeared to be higher in suburban areas (49 percent) than in urban (39 percent) and rural areas (38 percent).

The survey shows that the consumers' opinions on the freshness of purchased food and the frequency with which they encountered spoiled food was not influenced by the way dates were interpreted. Consumers who sorted through packages tended to express more dissatisfaction with the freshness of purchased food or to indicate more frequently that they received spoiled food.

IN-STORE OPEN DATING EXPERIMENT[19]

This 1973 study of 12 Kroger supermarkets in Ohio had as its principal objectives the determination of: (1) the influence that open dating will have on consumer reporting of receipt of spoiled or bad food; (2) the effectiveness of different open dating options—pull date (last date it should be sold), pack date (when packaged at the plant), or expiration date (last date it should be consumed). It was found that introduction of the open dating system with a large promotional campaign reduced the frequency of consumer complaints of spoiled food. Also evident was that both pull date and pack date systems were equally effective in reducing consumer complaints. The study concludes:

> The trend implies that the reduced frequency with which consumers report experiences with bad foods after introduction of open dating program is probably caused by psychological factors (i.e., a favorable change in the consumer's attitude toward store management) and not by any major improvement in the freshness of food purchased.[20]

AN EMPIRICAL STUDY OF CONSUMERS' ATTITUDES[21]

This 1973 study was concerned primarily with consumers' awareness and knowledge, priority, and willingness to pay for open dating service.

---

19. Consumer Research Institute, *Kroger In-Store Open Dating Experiment* (Washington, D.C.: Unpublished Study, March 3, 1973).
20. *Ibid.*, p. 34.
21. Prabhaker Nayak, "An Empirical Study of Consumers' Attitudes on Open Dating of Food Products," (New York: Unpublished Doctoral Dissertation, New York University, 1973).

The research was undertaken in five Pathmark stores in Passaic County, New Jersey, where 415 consumers were randomly interviewed. The findings indicated that 84 percent of consumers reported having received spoiled food products less than three or four times a year; 15 percent experienced no bad food. Also, nearly half of the sample expressed their awareness of open dating. These figures were much lower for consumers with less education and lower income. A majority of consumers gave low priority to open dating vis-à-vis other services—convenience, price, store reputation, and the like—and were unwilling to pay or to pay at most only "one cent on the dollar" for this service. This was especially true for consumers who had received spoiled food infrequently. Nonetheless, the majority of consumers "favored" open dating coding because it would give them greater confidence in the freshness of food products.

DISCUSSION OF FINDINGS

Research studies conducted within the last few years permit a preliminary assessment of the value to consumers of open dating of food products, although their findings fall short of conclusively determining the effectiveness and efficiency of this consumerism-inspired practice. Because the methodologies of these studies vary in quality, caution must be exercised regarding the findings. Also, because specific studies have dealt with different types of food products—milk to bread to catsup—all encompassed by the Bill's definition, generalizations regarding these products do not hold for every item on the spectrum.

From the accumulated data, it seems possible to make an initial attempt at evaluating the major issues involved in open dating: technical validity, impact on marketing, and consumer experience and attitudes.

Improvements in production, packaging, and distribution of processed food products and their high turnover in large volume stores have reduced the probability of spoilage. For refrigerated and frozen foods, the key to freshness is temperature control; therefore, food durability lengthened by technological progress can be shortened by problems in proper temperature maintenance. While quality still declines as a perishable product ages, reliability in the prediction of shelf life is elusive. Although this makes it difficult to legislate specific requirements, they can still be determined. Open dating *per se* is no guarantee of freshness; it has relevance to product durability only when there has been no lapse in temperature controls.

Different technical preparation of the thousands of food items in the modern supermarket makes it necessary to distinguish between product categories. Open dating on dairy, eggs, and dough products has been accepted, but produce, meat, bottled and canned foods may need attention.

A related issue to open dating involves the additives and artificial ingredients that extend the shelf life of numerous products. While their use may seem reasonable in a mass distribution and open-dating situation, concern has been expressed that they may eventually cause harm to consumers' health. Insufficient government and business research has been charged, but some instances of deleterious effects of "unnatural" additives have been reported.[22]

The impact of open dating on marketing activities and performance rests mainly on studies of milk. Stores that use open dating seem to have more frequent deliveries. This practice may be partially influenced by the smaller average size and higher transactions/sales per square foot of urban stores compared to those in the suburbs. Also, open dating tends to generate lower inventories, higher rates of dissatisfaction and/ or returns, and thus lower product availability for consumers. These conditions tend to increase operating costs, although it has not been reported how much; the costs are presumably passed on to the consumer. Again, in comparison to suburban stores, urban stores may experience more upward pressure on prices of open-dated foods because of higher rent and taxes per square foot and greater pilferage.

As with unit pricing[23] (another consumer-oriented practice), open dating may result in two benefits for the retailer: (1) it may enhance the firm's image as the consumer's friend; (2) it may increase the efficiency of stock rotation by providing a spur and double check on the performance of rotation duties by employees. Thus open dating, within a proconsumer orientation, may serve as a differential advantage over competing stores.

Consumer Reactions. Consumer experience with food freshness has been reported as basically favorable.[24] Although few consumers have complained about spoiled foods, the incidence of complaints increases with income and education levels. Upscale groups seem to be more perceptive and demanding. It may be reasonable to assume that persons with lower income and education (even if they find less-than-fresh food in the retail stores serving them) are basically unaccustomed to complaining about the situation. Or do they simply have less time to

22. "The Heat Is on Chemical Additives," *Business Week* (October 23, 1971), p. 83.

23. Kent B. Monroe and Peter J. LaPlaca, "What Are the Benefits of Unit Pricing," *Journal of Marketing*, 36 (July 1972), pp. 16–22.

24. For example, see "The Shoppers' Friend at Giant Supermarkets," *Business Week* (April 6, 1974), p. 38, and "How Pathmark Disarms the Crusaders," *Business Week* (May 8, 1971), p. 62–64.

make complaints because both heads of the household often work? In contrast to satisfied consumers, those who are dissatisfied tend to sort through food products more in making their selections, and they report finding more spoiled foods. Approximately half of consumers who shop in stores practicing open dating are aware of it, with the more aware generally being younger, more affluent, more educated, and suburban. A majority of consumers favor open dating. A major campaign promoting open dating did reduce complaints regarding bad foods, even when it was believed that no change in food freshness had occurred. Consumers often perceive open dating as an assurance of product freshness, although confusion exists as to what open date means. Among other marketing practices, consumers give a low priority to open dating, and few are willing to pay very much for it.

CONCLUSION

What ultimately determines the extent of the benefit that consumers derive from open dating depends upon the point of view from which it is considered. According to the retailer, open dating seems to increase costs, directly and indirectly, and as such contributes to higher food prices. The consumeristic viewpoint recognizes that consumers' rights must be protected. As Bell and Emory assert: "Although many consumers do not appreciate or use information, this is not adequate justification for denying such information or seeking to perpetuate buyer ignorance."[25]

A third and perhaps more realistic view is that open dating should be considered beneficial only if it improves the product freshness obtained by consumers. On the one hand, retailers who continue to sell stale and spoiled food products would not stay in business long because consumers overall are a perceptive group who would switch, when possible, from offending stores. On the other hand, rising expectations of consumers confront stores with the problem of moving inventories of many perishable foods. Moyer submits that "even if many ignore it, consumers should benefit from the pressure on retailers to be alert to the need for product freshness."[26] Assuming neither run-away cost increases nor highly adverse consumer reactions, the insistence on open dating notifies retailers and manufacturers that the consumer must be served with more product information and quality-assured foods.

25. Martin L. Bell and C. William Emory, "The Faltering Marketing Concept," *Journal of Marketing*, 35 (October 1971), p. 41.

26. Reed Moyer, *Macro Marketing: A Social Perspective* (New York: John Wiley and Sons, Inc., 1972), p. 116.

QUESTIONS FOR DISCUSSION

1. What is open dating? What benefits is it designed to produce for consumers?

2. Discuss the milk study and its major findings regarding the effect of open dating.

3. Summarize the findings of the national telephone survey on open dating.

4. The authors state, "Open dating *per se* is no guarantee of freshness; it has relevance to product durability only when there has been no lapse in temperature controls." Discuss this statement.

5. Professors Nayak and Rosenberg note, "Among other marketing practices, consumers give a low priority to open dating, and few are willing to pay very much for it." Discuss this statement.

10.4 THE IMPACT OF UNIT PRICING ON CHANNEL SYSTEMS

Lawrence M. Lamont and James T. Rothe

"A fundamental issue is channel control. Will unit pricing, like the private label programs, result in a further shift of channel control to the retailer?"

INTRODUCTION

Much of the impact of the consumer movement has been directed at the retail sector of the business community. Grocery retailers, in particular, have been the target of consumers dissatisfied with rising food prices and confused by the proliferation of products, brands, and packages. The consumers' difficulty in securing the necessary information to make more informed purchase decisions has resulted in frustration, boycotts, and pressure for protective legislation.

Recently some innovative responses to the consumer's need for information have come from the business community. The consumer's demand has been met by retail chain programs featuring "dual" or "unit" pricing, open dating, and nutrition labeling. Unit pricing is the subject of this paper.

THE RATIONALE OF UNIT PRICING

Unit pricing is intended to provide information which enables the consumer to rationally evaluate package sizes and brands. Pre-printed labels on grocery shelves show the package price and also the price per pound, ounce, quart, or other appropriate unit. Using this information the consumer can quickly tell what an item costs per standard measure, compare the unit price with other package sizes and brands, and hopefully make a more informed purchase decision.

THE CURRENT STATUS

In June of 1970 Benner Tea Company of Burlington, Iowa, became the first major grocery retailer to adopt unit pricing on a chain-wide basis.

Reprinted by permission from Lawrence M. Lamont and James T. Rothe, "The Impact of Unit Pricing on Channel Systems," *Relevance in Marketing: Problems, Research, Action*, edited by Fred C. Allvine (Chicago: American Marketing Association, 1972), pp. 653–658.

Other supermarket chains experimented with unit pricing to evaluate consumer appeal and the costs of implementation. During 1970 Safeway experimented at four stores in the Washington, D.C. area and Kroger conducted a study under the auspices of the Consumer Research Institute. Jewel's preliminary testing of unit pricing began in January, 1970, and concluded with a customer response survey in July. During this period Jewel introduced unit pricing on a limited basis in all of its 258 stores.

Many chains decided to forego experimentation and began chain-wide, store-wide programs. Among the first were King Soopers in Denver, Red Owl stores in Minnesota, Chatham Food Centers in Michigan, Kohls Food Stores in Wisconsin, and Ralph's Grocery Company of Los Angeles. The list of chains carrying such programs now numbers more than fifty.

THE CHANNEL IMPACT

While most of the literature on unit pricing has been focused at the retail end of the distribution channel, the grocery product manufacturers are concerned about the impact of unit pricing on their brands and marketing strategy. A fundamental issue is channel control. Will unit pricing, like the private label programs, result in a further shift of channel control to the retailer? The manufacturers' product strategies may also be affected. For many products satisfactory standards of measurement do exist. Some branded products, such as detergents and soups, are concentrated. Others are instant or freeze-dried and call for different amounts of water. The result is that while many products may offer superior values on a cost per serving or other performance measure, they show up at a disadvantage when priced on a unit basis. How will manufacturers respond? Some have changed packaging to make their products more attractive on a unit basis. Other changes in marketing strategy seem inevitable as the impact of unit pricing becomes more apparent.

THIS STUDY

The study reported in this paper was performed with the assistance of the King Soopers Division of the Dillon Corporation. The objectives were: (1) to evaluate unit pricing as a response to a consumerism problem, and (2) to determine the impact of unit pricing on the distribution channel—specifically the grocery retailer and grocery product manufacturer.

RESEARCH METHODOLOGY

On September 22, 1970. King Soopers introduced Chek-Mate unit pricing into their chain of 29 Colorado supermarkets. During November a University of Colorado research team conducted a telephone survey of 2,330 randomly selected households in the Denver metropolitan area to evaluate consumer awareness of Chek-Mate unit pricing and the extent of its use in the buying process.

Early in 1971 a main survey of 450 grocery product manufacturers was conducted to determine their attitudes toward unit pricing and probable marketing response. A return of 177 questionnaires enabled the identification of a variety of marketing responses.

A final portion of the study examined the costs and benefits of unit pricing at the retail level. Selling Areas—Marketing, Inc., (SAMI) warehouse withdrawal data for the Denver market was used to appraise the commercial impact of the program. Detailed cost data were also provided by King Soopers and contrasted with cost information reported by other chains.

TABLE 1   Hierarchy of Consumer Use of Chek-Mate Unit Pricing

	Based on 816 King Soopers Shoppers	Based on 668 King Soopers Shoppers Aware of Chek-Mate Pricing
Consumers Using Chek-Mate Information	53.3%	65.1%
Used Chek-Mate to Switch Sizes	38.2	46.7
Used Chek-Mate to Switch Brands	27.9	35.0
Switched Stores to Use Chek-Mate	7.8	9.5

THE CONSUMER RESPONSE

Consumer awareness was surprisingly high. Of the 2,330 respondents interviewed, 67.9 percent were aware of the Chek-Mate program. The awareness level was even higher for regular King Soopers shoppers. In this subsample of 816 respondents 82.0 percent were aware of the unit pricing program. Our survey found consumer awareness to be significantly related to income and occupation. The family head of the most knowledgeable group of consumers was usually a white collar professional or manager earning an annual income of $10,000 or more.

CONSUMER USE—BRAND AND SIZE SWITCHING

A more accurate measure of the program's acceptance is the actual use by consumers to make or change buying decisions. As shown in Table 1, 53.3 percent of all King Soopers shoppers (65.1 percent of those aware of the unit pricing program) reported actually using the unit pricing information during the shopping process. In addition, another 38.2 percent used the information to switch package sizes and 27.9 percent used it to change brands. The program also has significant competitive advantages. Of the chain's current customers surveyed, 7.8 percent reported changing stores to take advantage of unit pricing.

To focus more specifically on consumer use, brand and size switching were related to consumer demographics and shopping behavior. A number of relationships were significant.

1. Both size and brand switching were related to the respondent's age. The younger the respondent, the greater the reported frequency of size and brand switching.

2. A significant relationship was found between size and brand switching and the occupation of the household head. Both types of activity were most prevalent among respondents in which the head of the household was a manager or professional and least prevalent among respondents in which the head of the household was employed in a clerical position, unemployed or retired.

3. Purchase motivations were also related to brand and size switching. King Soopers shoppers mentioning store service and convenience as their most important patronage motives were not active size switchers. By comparison, the shoppers mentioning food quality or price as their major patronage motive were active size switchers. The brand switching data provided an interesting contrast. A similar trend was noted except that the shoppers mentioning food quality as their most important patronage motive were not as likely to be brand switchers. These shoppers use unit pricing to switch sizes of the same product, but their emphasis on purchasing quality inhibits them from using the information to change brands.

4. Both brand and size switching were related to store loyalty. The longer a respondent had been a regular King Soopers shopper, the less tendency there was to switch package sizes and brands. Continuous shopping at the same store tends to ingrain buying habits and increase resistance to using unit pricing information to change a buying decision.

Family size and occupation were significantly related to store switching activity. Patronage motives were only weakly related to store switching, but still provide an interesting dimension to this important consumer.

1. Of the respondents belonging to families having one or two members, 15 percent reported switching stores because of Chek-Mate pricing. Overall, almost 50 percent of the store switchers came from families of one or two members. By comparison only 7.5 percent of the respondents from families of three or more were store switchers.

2. Store switching occurred most frequently among families in which the head of the household was a white collar manager or professional. Almost 59.0 percent of the store switchers came from this occupation class.

3. There was no evidence that the store switcher was primarily a price buyer. Their interest in unit pricing seems to have been related to the fact that it helps to achieve a better price-quality relationship in their food purchases.

4. The store switchers proved to be active users of unit pricing information. Almost 55.0 percent of this consumer group reported changing brands (not surprising, since they were changing stores) and 61.0 percent changed package sizes.

CONCLUDING REMARKS

Brand and size switching data indicate that unit pricing is being used by shoppers. Use of unit pricing information during the shopping process, size switching, and brand switching are significantly related to age of respondent, occupation of the family head, patronage motives, and store loyalty. In general, unit pricing seems to have particular appeal to the younger shoppers in the middle class of society. Many of these individuals are educated well enough to understand unit pricing and have a need for information which enables them to shop more rationally.

The store switcher is somewhat different from the typical user of unit pricing. They are a mobile group of shoppers from small families— probably singles and households without children. They are also active users of unit pricing information and seem to be seeking a better price-quality relationship in their food purchases. The brand and size switching data also suggest that store switchers have lower brand loyalty and will not hesitate to take advantage of new shopping opportunities.

THE MANUFACTURER—IMPACT AND RESPONSE

Manufacturers expressed favorable attitudes toward unit pricing, but they were not optimistic about its impact on purchasing behavior. The majority felt (1) that unit pricing would result in only temporary changes in consumers' buying habits and (2) that very few consumers would actually use unit prices to make purchase decisions. Another 42.1 percent believed that unit pricing would result in higher food prices for the consumer.

Most manufacturers agreed that unit pricing poses a challenge to their marketing programs. However, this concern was not reflected in their actions. Only 41.0 percent indicated that they were actively studying unit pricing or planning to change existing market programs. Which firms were concerned about unit pricing?

1. Of the manufacturers having annual sales over $70.0 million, 61.0 percent either were studying unit pricing or planning to change their marketing programs. By comparison, only 26.2 percent of the firms with annual sales of $10.0 million or less were planning to take any action.

2. Among the manufacturers obtaining a majority of their sales from nationally distributed products, 61.2 percent were either studying unit pricing or planning to change their marketing programs. Of the firms deriving 50.0 percent or less of their sales from nationally distributed products, only 42.8 percent were actively involved with unit pricing.

Part of the reason for this response is that many regional manufacturers have not been confronted with unit pricing. Further, not all products will be affected by pricing. According to manufacturers, the products most likely to be influenced by the consumer's use of unit pricing would be (1) cereals and instant breakfasts, (2) cleaning and household supplies, (3) snacks and prepared foods, (4) specialty foods, (5) canned meat and fish, and (6) paper products. Many of the items in these categories have high unit prices, product substitutes, numerous competing private and national brands, as well as unit of measure problems. Consequently manufacturers are concerned about the impact of intensified price competition and the consumer's ability to use the information properly.

SELECTED EXAMPLES OF MARKETING RESPONSE

Manufacturers were asked to indicate the marketing strategies they would most likely use in response to unit pricing. Possible strategies included cents-off deals, coupons, special promotions, packaging changes, product reformulations, and advertising and adjustments in the product's price-quality relationship. Of the firms studying unit pricing or planning to change their marketing program, 44.6 percent indicated that they would emphasize the quality-price relationship in their advertising and sales promotion. Another 28.6 percent of the firms indicated that they were planning to change their packages to facilitate unit pricing. Some manufacturers are planning to change both the package and the product. A national manufacturer of frosting and cake mixes reformulated its products to increase the package size and contents by 10.0 percent. The larger package was then introduced at the previous price, thus giving the manufacturer a price reduction on a unit basis. This feature was promoted on the package label.

New product introductions of manufacturers are also being influenced by unit pricing. In one instance, a leading manufacturer introduced a dishwashing detergent with the product pre-priced at 89 cents for the 50-ounce size and 59-cents for the 35-ounce size. When converted to a unit price, the larger size was more expensive—thus forcing the consumer to purchase the smaller package. The chain forced the manufacturer to change the price structure to show a unit price advantage for the larger size.

The impact of unit pricing on sales promotion items such as cents-off deals, coupons, and premiums is not yet clearly defined. Survey respondents indicated that the use of cents-off deals would not increase as a result of unit pricing. Chains have discouraged their use by refusing to accept cents-off merchandise and instead passing the deal on to the consumer in the form of a manufacturer's special and a reduced unit price. Coupons and package premiums may well increase since they can be used to give the consumer a price reduction without requiring the retailer to change the unit price.

CONCLUDING REMARKS

The impact of unit pricing on the manufacturer is unclear at this time. However, early evidence indicates several areas of potential concern. For many grocery products the retail unit pricing program conflicts with the manufacturer's desire to build brand loyalty. Unit pricing encourages price comparison. Competition between brands will be intensified because a new dimension of rationality has been added to the buying process.

Other conflicts exist. Some of the product categories where pricing information might be used most often are also the categories in which the information is deceiving and ambiguous to the consumer. Manufacturers are concerned that even with unit pricing the consumer will not be able to properly evaluate the product. If this is correct, rivalry between frozen, dehydrated and canned foods, powders and liquids, and other product forms should increase. Unit pricing makes more apparent the opportunities that exist for substitution between similar products that have been processed or packaged by different methods.

How will manufacturers respond? The inability of most manufacturers to control the retail price suggests that the majority of marketing adjustments will take the form of product reformulations, package changes, and promotion programs designed to capitalize on a unit price advantage or offset a unit price disadvantage. During the research several strategies were observed in which manufacturers used non-price techniques to realign their products' price relationship with competing brands.

Examples of cooperation also exist. Manufacturers are providing more complete label information. The large sizes of many products have been priced to reflect an economic advantage to the consumer. The distributor is also playing a role in unit pricing. For retailers not having the financial means to unit price their products, the distributor will print the unit price labels and assist the retailer in the administration of a unit pricing program.

TABLE 2 Direct Installation and Maintenance Costs of King Soopers' Chek-Mate Program

		Total	Per-Store
Installation Costs [1]			
Unit Price Labels and Shelf Strips		$15,760	$ 544
Preparation	$4,050		
Materials	3,010		
Installation	8,700		
Promotion Costs		2,900	100
Executive—Program Planning			
and Introduction		10,700	369
Total Installation Costs		$29,360	$1,013
Maintenance Costs [2]		Total/Year	Store/Year
Labels and Protective Shelf Strips		$ 6,711	$ 231
Store Labor		$ 9,048	312
		$15,759	$ 543

[1] Based on 29 stores.
[2] Estimate based on four months data for 29 stores.

IMPACT ON THE RETAILER—COST AND BENEFITS

The direct costs of implementing and maintaining King Soopers' Chek-Mate program were examined in this study. As illustrated in Table 2, chain-wide installation costs amounted to $29,360 or approximately

$1,013 per store. The largest portion of this cost is attributed to the unit price labels. Preparation expenses include the cost of (1) computer programming to produce the labels and tie the program into the ordering and inventory control systems, and (2) the computer time to print labels for 29 stores and 12,000 grocery products. Materials costs covered the paper labels and protective plastic shelf strips. Installation costs represented the labor expense to fix the labels to the shelf facings. Promotion costs included displays and brochures to explain the program to the chain's customers. Executive expenses were incurred during the design, development and orientation phases.

Estimated yearly direct maintenance costs include label materials, key punching and printing, replacement of plastic shelf strips and distribution. The store labor needed to keep the system current is the most important maintenance item. It accounts for over 57 percent of the maintenance expense and amounts to two hours a week per store. The maintenance costs for the program compare favorably to those reported by other chains. Jewel, for example, reported yearly maintenance costs of $1000 per store, while the Kroger study indicated annual costs of $2,073 per store. Benner Tea reports a direct maintenance cost of $260 per store on a yearly basis.

SAMI warehouse withdrawal data covering 75 percent of the Denver metropolitan market was used to evaluate the change in King Soopers' competitive position. A comparative analysis of market share data covering the four month period before the introduction of Chek-Mate pricing and the four month period after the introduction indicated a new increase in market share of 15.0 percent.

An additional fact is available to assess the competitive impact. The consumer survey data indicated that about 2.8 percent of the households in the sample had switched stores to take advantage of unit pricing. Extending this estimate to all families in the Denver Metropolitan area and assuming an average weekly grocery purchase of $25 per family, the gain can be translated into an annual sales increase in the Denver market of between $8,500,000 and $14,000,000. Using a 1.5 percent margin of profit on sales it can be estimated (in a crude manner) that the program will cover the installation and maintenance costs and make a significant contribution to net profit.

The chain also believes that the unit pricing program has had a favorable impact on the private label business. Analysis of SAMI data for a number of grocery product categories suggests that the private label business increased in several areas including household supplies, household cleaners, condiments and paper products. The inability to control for many external market factors makes the findings of limited value.

The retail chains having unit pricing programs indicate that some of the costs are offset by internal operating efficiencies. They cite improved inventory control, reduced ordering costs, better control over pricing decisions and labor savings in shelf stocking. Many of these benefits are present in the King Soopers chain. They are difficult to attribute directly to unit pricing, however, because the Chek-Mate program was implemented simultaneously with the firms COSMOS merchandising program and automatic ordering system.

The unit pricing labels, for example, provide the consumer with information on the unit price, the retail price, the item description, the package size, and the item order number. Most of this label information is used not only for the unit pricing program but is an integral part of the other two programs that comprise the system. The overall impact has been improved inventory control at the store level, reduced ordering costs, and better control over direct vendor space allocation in the store.

CONCLUSIONS

Our study concludes that King Soopers unit pricing program has been well received by consumers. This acceptance is confirmed by the large percentage of shoppers that reported using the information during the shopping process to switch product sizes and brands.

The program has also had a favorable impact on retail performance. New customers have been attracted to the chain and several categories in the private label program appear to have been strengthened as a result. The profit impact indicates that the program will easily cover direct installation and maintenance costs and make a significant contribution to profit.

Manufacturers tend to support unit pricing as a response to consumerism, but they are concerned with its potential impact on their marketing strategies. Unit pricing conflicts with the manufacturers' desire to control the market because it encourages brand and size switching and more informed purchase behavior. Many would like to see the technology of unit pricing improved before it is actively promoted to consumers.

Preliminary evidence suggests that unit pricing will have an unfavorable impact on the manufacturer. Package and label changes will have to be made to accommodate unit pricing, and some products will have to be reformulated to be price competitive. Promotional strategy may also be modified as manufacturers discover new ways to capitalize on unit pricing. Cents-off deals will probably decline since they are inconsistent with unit pricing. Premiums and coupons may well increase because they provide a method of offsetting a unit price disadvantage.

QUESTIONS FOR DISCUSSION

1. What is unit pricing?

2. Do you think the average shopper would use unit pricing if it were available? Explain your answer.

3. What outcome do the authors predict on the impact of unit pricing on channel control?

4. What channel conflict areas, if any, does unit pricing precipitate?

Chapter 11

Emerging Trends in Marketing Channels

THE AREA OF MARKETING CHANNELS is one of the most dynamic aspects of marketing. The first article in this chapter discusses a retailing technique that may be the newest retailing institution in the United States —and one that conforms perfectly to the "wheel-of-retailing" theory. The discount-catalog showroom is experiencing explosive growth. *Business Week* stated, "Popularized by people who hate to spend hours shopping and who enjoy the rare combination of elegance and discount pricing, the discount-catalogue showroom business is quietly turning into one of today's hottest trends in retailing."[1]

The next two selections deal with the rapid growth of door-to-door selling. This sales technique, while not stressing low cost, offers very high levels of customer service. Many families, especially those with working wives, readily accept the ease and convenience of this form of shopping. As American families produce more discretionary income, it is generally predicted that direct selling will prosper.[2]

The fourth selection examines another emerging trend which also offers a high degree of convenience—mail order shopping. The mail-order industry is comprised of 3,000 active firms with $50 *billion* in sales for 1975.

Cooperative advertising is experiencing rapid growth as manufacturers and their channel members attempt to secure better working relationships. This interesting form of channel cooperation is examined in the selection entitled, "Co-op's Spirit of '76."

Another significant trend in channels is that of in-store servicing or detailing. These terms refer to persons who maintain the retailer's shelf, take inventory of the products, and in some cases automatically place the replacement order with the supplier. Traditionally, detailing has been done by salespersons for the wholesaler or the manufacturer. Recently, however, specialized firms have emerged that are performing

1. "Discount Catalogues: A New Way to Sell," *Business Week* (April 29, 1972), p. 72.
2. See: "How the Changing Age Mix Changes Markets," *Business Week* (January 12, 1976), pp. 74–75ff.

the detailing function for the wholesaler or manufacturer. Why would a company such as General Electric, prefer to hire detailers than have their sales force perform this function? Robert Ely, a salesperson for GE's Lamp Division indicates the rationale this way, "If you are paying a man to be a salesman, he can't devote his time to detailing."[3] This is based on the fact that Space Control, a detailing company, charges about $12.80 per hour of detailing, while a salesperson's time is worth about $28.75 per hour.[4] The article on in-store servicing provides a comprehensive treatment of this very important new channel member.

The final emerging trend to be discussed is the growth of the voluntary wholesaler in the grocery industry. The article notes that firms such as A&P are starting to use voluntary wholesalers instead of performing the wholesaling function themselves. Why? As the article points out, ". . . retailers have become increasingly reluctant to shell out the $3 million to $10 million nedeed to build or upgrade warehouses, capital for which might otherwise go to finance the new 'super' stores now in vogue."[5]

3. "Making Sure the Goods Get on the Shelves," *Business Week* (July 22, 1972), p. 46.
4. *Ibid.*
5. Carol Kurtis, "Bigger Slice of the Pie: Independent Grocers (and their Suppliers), Carve One," *Barron's* (March 29, 1976), p. 11.

11.1 THE CATALOG SHOWROOM BOOMS, REDUCES COSTS, MAKES SHOPPING EASIER

Stanley H. Slom

"Catalog warehousing is today at the same stage that discounting was 20 years ago."

A few years ago, Mrs. Patricia Porter might have bought her new toaster-oven at a department store or discount house. But a few weeks ago, the West Orange, N.J., housewife flipped through a catalog at home, selected a General Electric model and drove to the Summit Catalog Showroom in nearby Wayne. Within minutes, she paid her $21—$6 less than the price in a local department store—and drove off with the toaster-oven.

Attracted by the convenience and economy of such shopping, buyers like Mrs. Porter are creating a boom for catalog warehouses—and another challenge to traditional retailers. In such operations, customers simply pre-shop from a mailed catalog and buy at a warehouse—where all the goods are stored out of the shoplifters' reach. Operating costs are low, and profits can be high, owners say.

About 1,800 catalog showrooms now operate across the nation, at least double the number three years ago, says *Catalog & Showroom Merchandiser*, the industry's trade magazine. Volume of these outlets should soar to at least $2 billion this year from last year's $1 billion, predicts Ralph H. Sullivan, publisher of the magazine.

Some think catalog operations will succeed discount houses as retailing's big growth field. "Catalog warehousing is today at the same stage that discounting was 20 years ago," says Philip Wise, chairman and president of Volume Merchandise, Inc., New York, a discount chain that is entering the catalog field.

FOILING SHOPLIFTERS

Among other advantages, losses from shoplifting are slashed to about 0.5% of sales in a catalog warehouse from 6.5% in a traditional volume

Reprinted by permission from *Wall Street Journal* (July 5, 1972), pp. 1, 13.

discount store, Mr. Wise estimates. The catalog operations, which specialize in appliances, jewelry and other hard goods, keep most of their showroom merchandise in enclosed cases, the goods actually sold are kept in closed inventory rooms which may take up two-thirds of the outlet's space. At a time when shoplifting and pilferage costs business an estimated $3 billion a year, this security is one of the biggest attractions to a catalog operation, owners say.

In addition, the warehouse outlets cost less to operate than a discount store, partly because they require only about one-third as many sales people, owners say. As customers personally pick up about 95% of the merchandise sold, delivery costs and headaches are minimal. There are usually no accounts receivable problems; the only credit is handled through major credit-card companies and banks.

As a result, many companies active in discounting are turning to catalog operations. Vornado Inc. (operators of the Two Guys chain), Volume Merchandise, Giant Stores Corp., Dayton-Hudson Corp., Grand Union Co., Supermarkets General Corp., Zale Corp. and Gordon Jewelry Corp. have all either started catalog showrooms or are about to open them. E.F. MacDonald Co., which operates the Plaid Stamp merchandise program, has also said it will enter the field. And Designcraft Jewel Industries Inc., a jewelry supplier, has announced that it will open catalog showrooms in 38 states under a license from F. C. Dahnken Co., a catalog operation based in Salt Lake City.

As previously reported, May Department Stores Co., St. Louis, and Consumers Distributing Co., Toronto, last week said they reached agreement in principle to form a new joint venture that will operate a minimum of 150 catalog showroom outlets in the U.S. Officials at the May concern have "been studying this new form of retail distribution and are convinced it has tremendous potential," Stanley J. Goodman, chairman of the company said.

Some discount operations anxious to continue growing figure the catalog trend comes just at the right time. There are now over 6,000 discount houses in operation, up from 4,100 five years ago, estimates Kurt Barnard, director of the Mass Retailing Institute. Thus in many metropolitan areas, the market is glutted, industry sources complain.

"GREATEST GROWTH IN CATALOGS"

"Our greatest growth has to be with catalog showrooms," says Theodor Kaufman, chairman of Giant Stores Co., a new England discount chain. "We're not going to stop opening discount stores, but we will reduce the rate of openings," he adds.

"We net 2% on sales in our Giant Stores and 4% in our catalog showrooms," the official says. Catalog operations also produce a much higher return on invested capital, he adds. To open and stock a 50,000-square-foot discount store takes $500,000 to $600,000, but the cost for a catalog store capable of similar volume is only about $300,000, Mr. Kaufman says.

Like others in its field, the Giant Stores catalog operations avoid clothes and other soft goods. This eliminates worry about style changes and the complexities of sizes and makes it easier to replenish stocks, Mr. Kaufman says. Concentrating on appliances and jewelry, which are comparatively compact, boosts volume prospects. While a 20,000-square-foot discount house will generate $40 to $100 in sales per square foot each year, a similar catalog showroom will produce over $200 a square foot, Mr. Kaufman finds.

"We now have eight catalog showrooms and expect to have 15 by November, generating $20 million a year in sales," adds the official. "We expect to add 20 next year for a total of 35 doing about $80 million in the fiscal year ending Jan. 31, 1974," he says. The traditional discount stores should add another $80 million to sales, he predicts.

Besides other advantages, the catalog operation also helps retailers beat the rising cost of land. As buyers pre-shop in catalogs, locating showrooms in an expensive, high-traffic area isn't necessary, catalog men say. Leasing such expensive space in a good area for a discount store now costs about $1.85 a square foot per year, compared with only $1.35 five years ago, Giant Stores finds.

In contrast, Mr. Kaufman believes the most economic locations for catalog showrooms are old supermarkets or variety stores that have closed after their owners opened larger, more modern stores in nearby shopping centers. These older buildings are usually in low-rent areas, he says.

Other catalog men agree. "If we had our 'druthers,' we'd be two blocks away from shopping centers," says Andrew Lewis, vice president of Best Products Co., Richmond, Va., the largest publicly held catalog discount operation. "There's no use paying top dollar for the exposure because there's little impulse shopping," he explains.

Best Products' strategy seems to pay off. In its stores, which range from 60,000 square feet to 80,000 square feet, the company has annual sales averaging $117 a square foot. This compares with the $98 a square foot at K-Mart discount department stores, a division of S. S. Kresge Co. Many analysts consider K-Mart one of the best-managed discount chains in the U.S.

Best Products' has six showrooms in operation and expects to have 10 more units by Christmas, Mr. Lewis says. He declines to make any profit forecast, but says that security analysts are estimating the company earned 70 cents to 80 cents a share on sales of about $50 million in the fiscal year ending last Friday. This would compare with earnings of $1.02 million, or 50 cents a share (adjusted for two stock splits), on sales of $31.25 million last fiscal year.

Of course, catalog operations also have their own special problems—such as the need to produce the catalogs. Except for a few large chains, most catalog showrooms have their catalogs prepared by large merchandise distribution companies such as Creative Merchandising Inc., Jewelcor Inc. and American Merchandisers Inc. The catalogs generally cost the showroom 70 cents to $1.50 apiece. The catalog producers generally obtain the artwork free from the various manufacturers. The catalog showrooms then send the catalogs out in mass mailings in their areas.

In most cases, the catalog is the showroom's only advertising expense. But some large chains, such as Best Products, often blanket an area with newspaper and television advertising too.

Despite the growth of catalog showrooms, many retailers remain wary. The field mainly involves only a comparatively small range of goods, they note. If an operator doesn't have a strong knowledge of jewelry, small appliances and similar goods, catalog operations may be more troublesome than they look, warns one discounter who specializes in soft goods.

QUESTIONS FOR DISCUSSION

1. What are the basic operating advantages to this type of retailing?
2. Why do consumers like this method of retailing?
3. a. What type of products seem ideally suited to this form of retailing? Why?
   b. Which products are not well suited? Why?
4. Do you believe that catalog showrooms are a passing fad? Support your answer.

11.2 THE AWESOME POTENTIAL OF IN-HOME SELLING OR LOOK WHO'S AT THE DOOR

Sales Management

". . . The race to the front door is gathering such momentum that for some suburbanites hardly a day goes by without someone phoning to try to sell them something."

It hardly seems like the time for a revival of door-to-door selling. Congress once again is pondering "cooling off" legislation that would allow consumers to reconsider major purchases made in their living rooms, and the Federal Trade Commission is looking askance at some of the "pyramid" schemes that direct-selling companies use to multiply the ranks of their sales people. The 3,000 or so companies in the industry seem to be living up to their tradition of bringing the selling profession its worst publicity and some of its best management. You don't usually hear much about the latter.

Yet the race to the front door is gathering such momentum that for some suburbanites hardly a day goes by without someone phoning to try and sell them something. Phone, not lean on the doorbell. The hazards—and scant earnings—of the cold canvass have been largely left to such laggard areas of the business as magazine distributors and aluminum siding salesmen. The most successful of the modern direct sales companies work by appointment only and frequently back up their salespeople with all the sales forecasts and inventory control that a computer can provide.

Currently, the industry is attracting the attention of many diversified companies not generally associated with direct selling, such as General Foods, Bristol Myers, and Consolidated Foods. There are many reasons for the awakening interest, but a major one is a basic shift in American attitudes: After years of straining at the bonds of family life, people are spending more time at home.

Not only have shopping centers lost their allure because of increased traffic and indifferent sales clerks, but the average person in the next

Reprinted by permission from *Sales Management* (April 15, 1971), pp. 27–30.

decade is expected to spend a higher proportion of his income on his house and the things that go into it. Before he heads for a store, the consumer of the 1970s will at least consider ordering from a catalogue or welcoming a salesman into his living room.

To make sure they're invited, many companies now keep a variety of selling systems in gear. Stuart McGuire Co., Salem, Va., relies mainly on part-time salesmen to promote its apparel lines. Part of its $20 million annual volume, however, is generated by its own retail store and through its catalogue sales. Such sprawling concerns as Consolidated Foods, Dart Industries, and C.H. Stuart maintain two or more direct-selling companies, each with its designated market and separate sales force (see table).

TEN BIGGEST FEET IN THE DOOR

Company	Sales (Millions)
Avon Products, Inc.	$759.2
Consolidated Foods Corp.	
Electrolux	150.0
Fuller Brush Co.	90.0
Grolier, Inc.	228.0
Field Enterprises Educational Corp.	170.0
Encyclopaedia Britannica	165.0
Dart Industries, Inc.	
Tupperware	118.0
Vanda Beauty Counselor	23.0
West Bend Co. (Miracle Maid Div.)	1.5
Stanley Home Products, Inc.	126.5
Amway Corp.	120.0
Scott & Fetzer	116.4
C. H. Stuart & Co., Inc.	
Sarah Coventry, Inc.	57.0
Caroline Emmons	3.0
Nobility-Prestige Co.	2.0
C. W. Stuart & Co.	2.0

Some marketing analysts, looking forward to the day when much of the "mass market" will be broken into segments, predict that most major companies will resemble Stuart McGuire, with a hand in retailing, mail order, and in-home selling in addition to maintaining their usual sales forces for selling to chain stores and other retailers.

One company apparently heading in this direction is General Foods, which does its retailing through Burger Chef Systems fast food outlets and late last year acquired the mail-order seed business of W. Atlee Burpee Co. But the most intriguing move that GF has made toward establishing alternative distribution systems was its purchase late in 1969, of Viviane Woodard Corp., a highly profitable in-home cosmetics firm in Panorama City, Cal. What interests marketing people is not so much the acquisitions themselves, but trepidation about what a company with GF's resources might do with them. "As far as General Foods is concerned," one observer says, "Burpee and Viviane Woodard are laboratories first and profit-producers second."

It's not that the basic forms of in-home selling have changed radically. Tupperware and Wear-Ever Aluminum still bring in eye-popping profits by getting housewives to throw parties for them, and that vital ingredient of in-home selling, a referral "from your neighbor Mrs. Zilch," is still pure platinum to any salesman. But two things promise to affect the industry and much of consumer marketing over the next few years: (1) the interest of highly diversified manufacturers in direct selling opens up the possibility that a wider variety of products, including more consumer durables, will be sold in the home; (2) as members of the door-to-door establishment find their product lines maturing, they are looking for new lines to distribute.

Honeywell, Inc., which used to rely on wholesalers to reach most of its customers, is experimenting with a direct-to-home sales force for selling its new home security system, Concept 70. At a price of up to $700, Concept 70 is one of the more expensive items being peddled in the home. It could pale, however, alongside the ambitions of Charles L. Logan, who is piloting J. C. Penny Co. into an in-home selling operation for its home furnishings business.

A poor third to Sears, Roebuck and Montgomery Ward in the furniture trade, Penney's badly needed a way to expand its furnishings business beyond the limits of its store and catalogue customers. Logan's solution: an army of some 600 decorator-consultants, operating mainly from stores, trained to help a housewife set up a plan for decorating and furnishing her home right in her own living room. Drawing on a wide assortment of styles (80% of the line shown in the in-home catalogue is not available in Penney's stores) salespeople are in a position to program customers into a sizable commitment over a period of time. "They may start with slip covers and wind up with a brand new living room," Logan observes.

Though there's little talk about it in Detroit, the in-home movement may have gained momentum among car dealers during the current economic slowdown. "When people don't come in to buy cars, you've got to go out after them," says one man familiar with the dealer scene. The approach may be anything from a half-hour demonstration to the "use my car for the weekend" gambit.

Some predict that such techniques will increase in popularity even after the auto sales start to pick up. "Those guys in the auto showrooms have a pouncing image that really puts people off, especially women," one observer says. With car-buying now recognized as a family decision, many car salesmen may find they get better results in a low-pressure sales atmosphere where they can extol the virtues of the upholstery to wives and quote compression ratios to the family teen-ager.

Whether a similar approach is practical for other hard goods is anybody's guess. Sears, Roebuck uses in-home consultants to sell such things as washers and dryers. Other companies have even toyed with the idea of sending out mobile demonstration vans to drum up appliance business in neighborhoods.

Change is also having an impact on members of the direct-selling establishment. Although Avon Products, the undisputed leader with 400,000 representatives generating $760 million in sales, doesn't admit to having any serious competition in the in-home cosmetics trade, it is beginning to feel the effects of its more successful imitators, such as the Vanda Beauty Counselor division of Dart Industries, Inc. When Vanda began filling all its customers' orders in just two weeks last year, Avon promptly switched its entire force from a three-week delivery cycle to two weeks. Latest of the fraternity to challenge Avon is Field Enterprises Educational Corp. Having established its *World Book* as the nation's largest-selling encyclopedia, it is launching an in-home cosmetics operation called Field Creations in Atlanta.

But it's a small world. Sarah Coventry, most successful of the direct-selling ventures operated by C. H. Stuart & Co., Newark, N.Y., for the first time may get some serious competition in costume jewelry. The antagonist: Avon Products, which is testing the idea extensively.

Estimating the size of the in-home selling industry has always been a problem, even before the influx of companies into the field. Some say it is doing research on the subject, the Direct Selling Assn. can only say that the industry employs more than three million salespeople. Regardless of the numbers, direct selling offers specific marketing advantages for many consumer products.

"This is a business where you make only one cold call," a Manhattan marketing consultant says. "From then on, it's all referrals. The person you call on is not just a customer but an advertising medium and a research sample as well." The extent of feedback from the field varies widely from company to company, but most of the larger ones are able to monitor sales by computer, enabling them to assess within a week what styles and price categories are selling in every area of the country.

But it is the person-to-person aspect of the medium that makes it especially appropriate for the marketing environment of the 1970s, its proponents say. Not only does the neighborly sales approach pioneered by Avon and such household goods companies as Stanley Home Products and Amway Corp. fit the informal life-style of suburbia, but it helps recruiting. The knowledge that they aren't expected to deliver a hard sell makes the job acceptable to many people who might not otherwise become salespeople. And recruiting, along with training, is clearly the name of the game.

"It may sound corny, but this is a people business," says Frank Gagliardi, head of Field Creations. "You have to get managers excited about hiring good people, and from then on, it's a continuous job of motivating people in the field by finding out what they want out of life."

The economy also has played a role in the recruiting picture, especially during the current siege of unemployment and inflation that has sent many people scurrying to bolster family income. Al Winfrey, executive vice president of Sarah Coventry, credits the recession with helping to raise his "file count" to 22,000 representatives, compared to the 17,000 normally active at this time of year. Furthermore, memories of the recession may last, prompting many part-timers to stay with direct selling during better times to ensure their families a second source of income.

Money may talk, but the promise of personal fulfillment is easily as strong an inducement to try direct selling. For the woman whose day starts with a whimpering child and ends with a load of laundry, or the man tied to an impersonal job, selling is one way to break the routine. Thus, for every pro selling Scott & Fetzer Co.'s Kirby vacuum cleaners, there are probably five women "amateurs" who earn under $1,500 a year selling lipstick and bath oils to members of their bridge club. Howard W. Bonnell, training director of Field Enterprises, claims that selling *World Book* encyclopedias gives many people a sense of contributing to the cultural life of the community. "We don't hire salesmen," says Bonnel. "We hire people and teach them to sell."

Avon and others in cosmetics impress on recruits that they are not employees of a large company but independent businesswomen who purchase their requirements at a discount and sell them to their own customers. So appetizing has this idea proved that the in-home movement could emerge as the first wedge in opening the selling profession to women. In addition to those with cosmetics companies, rather significant numbers of women peddle education for Encyclopaedia Britanica and Grolier; in household goods, the proportion runs as high as 70% at Fuller Brush and 95% at Stanley Home Products.

Even with the great stress put on good management in recent years, turnover remains the industry's biggest problem. Avon reportedly has a rate of about 100%, meaning that, while 80% of the force sticks with the company year after year, some positions are filled three or four times a year. Other companies say they have chopped attrition sharply by spending more time and money on recruitment and training. Viviane Woodard claims the turnover rate for its force of 60,000 is under 20%.

To give the multitudes of salespeople a sense of belonging, most companies employ a heady blend of propaganda, powwows, and payola. Avon ladies get regular mailings of a company magazine with current promotional plans and selling tips. Vanda last fall arranged to have representatives meet once a week with branch distributors so they can discuss sales techniques at the same time they order merchandise. To encourage its distributors to multiply their numbers, Viviane Woodard promises them 5% of the first $25,000 sold by each distributor they recruit. To qualify, however, a distributor must continue her own sales activities at a substantial level.

Unlike other consumer goods companies, direct-selling organizations aim most of their promotion primarily at salespeople rather than consumers. Sarah Coventry donates prizes to such TV shows as "To Tell the Truth" and gets soap opera stars to endorse jewelry. These events are played back to field representatives in a weekly brochure crammed with pictures of tearful sales contest winners receiving bouquets of roses "from President Rex (Wood)." A typical brochure topic is "How My Husband Recruited Me."

President Rex also manages to get himself photographed with such luminaries as Shirley Temple Black, Lawrence Welk, and Leslie Uggams by the simple expedient of presenting them with an award. This year's recipient will be John Wayne. Asked where the presentation will take place, one Coventry representative replied: "Wherever the photographer happens to be."

Many in-home companies manage to survive without advertising, but larger ones usually find it necessary, first, to aid recruitment; second, as a door opener; and third, to build brand awareness. "At a certain point in your growth, TV seems to make sense," says Joseph Hines, new president of Vanda Beauty Counselor. He should know. During the critical postwar expansion years, Beauty Counselor field representatives labored without a door-opening commercial comparable to "Avon Calling," with the result that Vanda has a lot of catching up to do. So far, the company has confined most of its advertising to women's magazines, but it has tested TV often.

Not all direct-selling ventures turn into successes overnight. E. J. Korvette reportedly lost over $1 million before giving up on Eve Nelson cosmetics a few years ago. Despite massive reorganization at the hands of Dart Industries, Vanda Beauty Counselor has yet to turn a profit. Electrolux is generally regarded as Consolidated Foods' most profitable operation, but CF has had a trying time dusting off Fuller Brush.

Still, the lure of low ad budgets and potentially high profit margins is irresistible. Impressed with the record of Dart's Tupperware subsidiary, arch rival Rubbermaid, Inc., is putting together its own direct sales operation. In cosmetics, Bristol Myers continues to build up Luzier Co., and, more recently, Faberge, Inc., agreed to buy Barbizon International, Inc., which plans to introduce both in-home and mail-order marketing.

Each has its own approach to the market, but most adhere to the advice of one veteran: "You'd understand women as best you can."

QUESTIONS FOR DISCUSSION

1. a. Why is this form of selling being accepted so readily by consumers?
   b. Why do manufacturers appear to be showing great interest in direct selling?

2. Do you believe that direct selling is a fad? Why or why not?

3. Assuming the trend to direct selling increases, what ramifications will this have on:
   a. consumers?
   b. existing competitors?

4. What operating problems, if any, do the direct sales firms experience?

11.3 ECONOMIC AND MARKETING ASPECTS OF THE DIRECT SELLING INDUSTRY

Michael Granfield and Alfred Nicols

> "... The Fuller Brush salesman who can earn a
> rent on his own efforts as well as those who historically
> preceded him and thus enable him to earn between
> $8.00 and $10 an hour, often double that which his
> peers earn."

Although representing the oldest and most colorful form of retail selling in the United States, the direct selling industry is one which most businessmen as well as consumers know very little about. Yet a careful analysis of this industry can yield some interesting insights into the competitive and organizational adaptions the firm must undergo as it survives and grows within a changing environment. Essentially a direct selling firm is one which both produces and sells its final product directly to the consumer on a personalized basis in the home (or close to it). Thus the direct selling firm performs the functions of manufacturer, wholesaler, and retail distributor.

Historically, the final sale has most often been made by a salesman acting as an independent contractor who makes his contacts on a door-to-door basis. Recently, this type of contact has been replaced by such devices as salesman-sponsored "parties" in which small groups of potential customers gather in a person's home,[1] customer referrals, and prior phone contacts followed up by a home visit.[2] Despite these modi-

---

Reprinted by permission from the authors and publisher. Michael Granfield and Alfred Nicols, "Economic and Marketing Aspects of the Direct Selling Industry," *Journal of Retailing* (Spring, 1975), pp. 33–50ff.

1. The "parties" seem to lead to a higher level of sales per customer than door-to-door selling due to the psychology of group buying pressure (one doesn't want to be the only one who doesn't buy) and as a guide-pro-quo return by the customer to the person having the party who supplies the location, food, and refreshment (and gets a gift in return).

2. These changes have most likely occurred as a result of a lowered sales per home-contracted rate which in turn is a result of: (1) increased mobility of the potential customer (housewife) lessening the probability she will be home at any given time; (2) greater antipathy which many direct salesmen meet because of the bad image created and fostered by the illegitimate door-to-door salesman; and (3) reluctance of housewives, particularly, to allow strangers to enter their home.

fications, the essential ingredient of the direct in-home customer relationship has been preserved.

Although the selling task performed by the typical direct selling firm may appear simplistic, closer examination reveals that the firm (industry) displays the combined characteristics of: (1) retail trade with its emphasis on the marketing and distribution of the product; (2) professional service organizations with their concern for quality of labor; and (3) franchising with its attendant concerns for initial growth and organizational control. Hence, our examination of the direct selling industry via its product, management, and distributional characteristics will indicate how this industry has adapted to solve problems normally regarded as pervading three distinct industries which seemingly have little in common.

A brief outline of the topics covered is: (1) nature of products sold; (2) competitive advantages of direct selling; (3) nature of competition in the industry; and (4) type and timing of vertical integration.

NATURE OF PRODUCTS SOLD

The products sold by direct selling firms vary from cosmetics to encyclopedias, from vacuum cleaners to vitamins. However, the essential characteristics of most products sold by these firms are:

1. Dependable quality
2. Unconditional guarantee
3. Subject to effective demonstration
4. Potential for frequent repeat sales of the original product or some aspect of it

The first two characteristics help to remove consumer uncertainty concerning the nature of the product and their expenditures on it since consumers may be initially more skeptical of a product sold door-to-door. The latter two characteristics enable the firm to capture the quasi-rents (unique features) that are attributable to direct selling. That is, for certain products, the consumer will purchase more of it (quantity or quality or some combination of these) if he gains sufficient information regarding the optimal utilization of the good which effectively shifts his demand for the product to the right.[3] Examples of this are: (1) in cosmetics where the woman may well purchase more or a better line if she is simultaneously shown how to effectively use the product, the reason why such firms as Avon and Viviane Woodward train their salesmen as fashion consultants; (2) encyclopedias in which the salesman is often a teacher, college student, or college graduate who can demon-

3. In this sense, the demonstration is a joint or complementary input.

strate the usefulness and necessity for the product; (3) kitchenware where lessons in cooking are given. In general, the higher the price of the product, the more critical and hence the more sophisticated is the demonstration. In marketing or economic terms, the education service provided by the salesman becomes an integral part of the good sold and is a way of differentiating one's product.[4]

Given the emphasis on demonstrating as well as exposing the product to the consumer, the major component of selling costs to the salesmen becomes the opportunity cost of the time spent in initially demonstrating the good and in making consumer contacts. In order to spread this overhead over as many units (goods) as possible and hence earn a higher rate of return on fixed costs or quasi-rents, repeat sales become critical since no new demonstration is required and contact costs are kept to a minimum by establishing a set time when he will make delivery.[5] An extreme example of how high the rate of return on these quasi-rents can be is the case of the Fuller Brush salesman who can earn a rent on his own efforts as well as those who historically preceded him and thus enable him to earn between $8 and $10 an hour, often double that which his peers earn.[6]

ADVANTAGES OF DIRECT SELLING

There are several distinct, interdependent advantages that accrue to a firm which decides to sell it's product via the method of direct selling. Briefly these are:

1. Securing distribution and sales quickly at a relatively low level of fixed cost.

2. Gaining consumer acceptance for a new product particularly when this involves a new entrant in that product industry.[7]

3. Gaining entrance to a market while avoiding excessive promotional and advertising expenses as well as potential price wars.

4. Earning a potentially higher rate of return on sales by eliminating large outlays for media advertising.

4. In accordance with this form of product differentiation, certain direct selling firms candidly admit that their products sell for more than their retail counterparts which are not as effectively demonstrated.

5. Such products as cosmetics and soap products are good examples. In the case of less divisible items as encyclopedias and vacuum cleaners, the repeat sales occur via such devices as yearly supplements (yearbooks) or new attachments or cleaning bags respectively.

6. Conversation with Mr. Edward Walsh, President of Fuller Brush.

7. This can be particularly effective at the local or regional vs. national level.

Although these four points are neither exhaustive nor mutually exclusive, an elaboration of their implications explains most of the advantages of direct selling. In terms of factor one, the firm can save a great deal on direct out-of-pocket costs (cash flow) by adopting a multiple-level[8] distribution system in which individuals buy in at whatever hierarchical level they desire to operate, sometimes all the way from salesmen to general supervisor. The higher the managerial level desired, the more capital that must be put forward and hence the more wholesale merchandise that is obtained meaning more immediate sales for the parent firm. For example, if a person wishes to sell the product on a part-time basis only, he will normally buy a demonstrator's kit that costs on the average of $8.50 and begin selling the product on a 30 to 40 percent commission basis. If he desires to come in on a full-time basis (and the opportunity is available), he will put up anywhere from $1,500 to $3,500 and acquire from $3,750 to $8,750 (60 percent commission)[9] in merchandise which will qualify him as a district supervisor.[10] As a district supervisor, he will usually have from five to ten subordinates under him who in turn will have from five to ten part-time salesmen under them. With a multiple-level distribution system, the direct selling firm is very similar to a franchising operation as it is the district supervisors and their subordinates who put up much of the working capital for the firm. Securing financial capital in this manner enables the firm to expand as rapidly as its recruiting efforts allow since capital costs are transferred from fixed to variable, thus lowering the minimal size firm needed for survival.[11]

The second major advantage (other than reducing fixed capital costs) for the new multiple-level firm is a result of the institutional or legal form of the employment contract as it exists *per se* and as it has been expanded and interpreted by state and federal laws. Namely, the firm saves the fixed costs of paying contract salaries, social security, unemployment compensation as well as the costs of administering federal and state withholding taxes. These fixed employee costs are essentially

8. Although the term multiple-level is used here because of its descriptive content, the legal implications of this term are such that to be found guilty of employing such a system may be tantamount to running a lottery or chain letter. Hence, most new firms do not use this descriptive term since their distribution system is not a lottery.

9. Out of this 60 percent commission he will pay the 40 percent retail sales commission plus an average of 10 percent commission to the part-time salesmen's direct supervisor.

10. For further discussion of this topic, see page 510.

11. This particular form of distribution is normally a characteristic of new direct selling firms who face the dual problems of sales expansion as well as insufficient capital. Established firms will usually have only one independent level—the part-time salesmen. All supervisory personnel will be contracted company employees.

transformed into variable commission costs which factor further reduces the optimal, minimum size firm. For the established firms, the fixed cost savings are relegated to the latter three items for its independent contractors.

The second and third points that involve market penetration imply that the firm can avoid the burdensome promotional and advertising expenses as well as price discounts that often accompany the introduction of a new product by having initial exposure and demonstration accomplished by the independent salesmen. The soap industry provides an illustrative example of this point since the introduction of a new product usually involves massive advertising, large mailings of free samples, direct price discounts to the consumer, elaborate market pretesting procedures as well as wholesale discounts to the grocer in order to acquire the more desirable shelf space locations.[12] Hence, unless a firm has a unique new product (e.g., Lestoil) or capital accessibility based on other successful operations (e.g., Armour's Dial soap and Monsanto's All) to launch its entry (or some combination of both), it may be deterred from offering a new product through conventional channels.[13] Despite these apparent or conventional entry barriers or handicaps, the 1960s saw the entry of two new successful direct selling soap firms, Amway and Bestline, which by 1971 accounted for approximately $230 million in retail sales.[14]

The fourth point refers to the fact that direct selling firms offer approximately the same "retail discount" as their conventional product competitors (namely 30 to 40 percent) but spend very little of their gross revenues on direct media advertising expenditures. For example, in cosmetics, both Viviane Woodard and Avon earned a gross profit margin in excess of 24 percent in 1971 whereas Revlon, the major retailer in cosmetics, earned only 15 percent. The net figures are equally impressive with Avon and Viviane Woodard earning 13 percent and Revlon 8 percent.[15]

Given these substantial profit rate differentials between conventional and direct selling firms, why haven't we observed additional entry into the direct selling industry? The answer seems to lie in the unique entrepreneurial ability associated with comprehending, surviving, and pros-

12. This does not imply that there are not opportunity costs involved in such tactics. Clearly, the firm must earn sufficient returns on such promotional activities based on the quasi-rents from the successful introduction of a new product. The problem for a new firm is that it often cannot raise the same level of capital at a competitive rate due to uncertainty about themselves and their product.

13. Even after the successful entry of the product, the firm may have difficulty in preserving its market position when the "big three" emulate the product and enter the market vigorously. Witness the fate of Lestoil's declining market share in home cleaners and profits; or "All" which was ultimately sold to Lever Brothers.

14. 1971 Annual Reports for Amway and Bestline.

15. Source: Annual Reports for the respective firms.

pering in the direct selling field. That is, there appears to be a high level of quasi-rents earned by direct selling firms that reflects a risky situation in which most firms fail but where the successful ones earn significantly higher than normal returns.[16] For example, certain retail chains have attempted to enter the field (E. J. Korvette, Kresges) in a particular product line but have failed since they apparently could not transfer their conventional retailing expertise to the direct selling industry.

COMPETITION IN THE DIRECT SELLING INDUSTRY

The most obvious form of competition is that which occurs in the product field. Avon, Viviane Woodard, Cosgot, and Holiday Magic must compete with Revlon, Max Factor, and Helena Rubinstein in developing new cosmetics products at competitive prices. Electrolux faces formidable competition from Hoover, G. E., and Sears. Amway and Bestline are confronted with the "Big Three" in soap and hence must overcome the American consumer's (housewife's) reluctance to buy a new firm's product in the sensitive area of "cleanliness." Tupperware and Stanley Home Products must deal with larger competitors such as Revereware and Discoware. In fact, only in the encyclopedia market are the major product competitors all direct selling firms (i.e., World Book, Britannica, and Colliers). However, despite the significance, then, of this type of product competition, it is by no means the most obvious significant area of competition for this industry; this fact is implicitly indicated by the existence of so many different kinds of products within the industry boundary.

The major area of competition between the direct selling firms occurs in the factor or labor market. That is, the direct selling firms vigorously compete against each other to attract full- and part-time (usually housewives or students) salesmen. The various direct selling firms indicate that their total level of sales is most critically affected by the *number* and to a lesser extent, the *quality* of people they are able to attract into their labor market as independent salesmen. Further, they feel that success in direct selling at the retail level is more a function of hard work (hours) than it is of skill or luck. They feel that anyone can become a successful direct salesman if he puts forth enough effort to learn the techniques and then gains sufficient experience in employing these rudimentary techniques. These contentions concerning the role of the number of salesmen are partially confirmed in Table 1 which is a regression equation relating total retail sales volume (dependent variable) to number of salesmen, and value of typical sale. The "best" fit was a linear one in which number of salesmen was the dominant variable.

16. In this sense, the industry appears similar to returns earned by performers in the theatre or movie or by professional athletes.

TABLE 1   Factors Affecting Total Sales Volume for Direct Selling Firm

Annual Dollar Sales $= 40{,}016.$ $+1512.$ Number of Salesmen
$$(4.3)^{\circ} \qquad (18.5)$$
$$+1478. \text{ Average Dollar Value of Sale} \quad R^2 = .78$$
$$(2.1)$$

$^{\circ}$ Numbers in parentheses are "T" statistics.

Source: Aggregate data on the following firms: Avon, Fuller Brush, Electrolux, Colliers, World Book, Bestline, Amway, Vivianne Woodward, Beeline Fashions, Britannica, Tupperware.

Indirect confirmation of this contention is indicated by the phenomenal turnover rates experienced by these firms which run from 50 percent to 200 percent per annum with the mean being approximately 100 percent. For example, Avon with 425,000 part-time Avon "Lady's" in the field must recruit that number of new salesmen per year just to hold sales constant.[17] Thus, in order to significantly expand sales, this force must be enlarged which implies that, to expand, the direct selling firm must recruit in excess of 100 percent of its current sales force to achieve its higher sales goals. Recruiting, training, and motivating salesmen become the significant areas of competition between the firms. In other words, the firms feel that even if they develop a "superior" product (per dollar of expenditure), the consumer will remain ignorant of it and unable to purchase it unless sufficient salesmen are recruited to promote and expose the product to him.

Although all the firms use the same basic tools of blind newspaper ads, salesmen referral, phone contracts, etc., they do have differing philosophies concerning the relative importance of raw recruiting versus training and motivating. Obviously, each firm is seeking to equate the marginal returns from each type of effort, but the exact allocation of resources for each task within a given firm will depend critically on the nature of the product, with the more complex products requiring more salesmen training. Yet even within product groups (e.g., cosmetics, encyclopedias, kitchenware), the firms will differ in their allocational strategies in an attempt to seek that combination which will simultaneously lead to higher sales per recruitee and long tenure of employment (which often do coincide). Both factors imply some amount of training and motivating, with the higher the price of the good within the product class, the more training that will occur because such training becomes a part of differentiating the product sold and thus transforms it into a joint or complementary input. For example, a Britannica sales-

17. This does not imply that all are "new" salesmen who never previously worked for Avon. They may be salesmen who retired temporarily and are returning. Nonetheless, most will be new and thus indicate the massive recruiting effort that must be continually undertaken.

man may need to be more knowledgeable about his product than a Colliers' man, since his product is a more comprehensive and encompassing work which necessitates a higher price. This higher price will not be viable, though, if the salesman cannot convince the potential customer of the inherent superiority of his product. Colliers, on the other hand, does not spend as much on training per salesman since its product is more geared to the mass market and is written on an entirely different level than is Britannica. Hence, for Britannica and Colliers to earn the same rate of return on sales dictates that Britannica spend more per salesman on training which, as stated before, becomes part of the product when the product's effectiveness is exhibited.[18]

Although all direct selling firms are potentially in the same general labor market for salesmen, this market is segmented to a certain extent. That is, women tend to sell cosmetics, fashions, and kitchenware rather than vacuum cleaners and encyclopedias. This segmentation occurs not so much as a result of the recruiting efforts of the firms since they try to discourage such preconceived selling notions; but rather, because of where the salesperson feels he or she can be most effective, i.e., earn the highest rate of return. In this sense, the product and factor markets interact as the product can have an effect on the behavior (level) of the labor supply function for the firm.[19] Therefore, the direct selling firms attempt to break down any preconceived segmentation on the part of potential salesmen based on factors other than inherent comparative advantage (e.g., women selling cosmetics and fashions). Their objective is to lower their firm factor supply function (acquire same amount of labor at a lower cost) by shifting a competitor's function upward (i.e., convince the potential salesmen to examine as many alternatives as possible).

COMPETITION FOR MANAGERS

The unique form of managerial expertise that is needed to survive in this industry has already been indicated. Given its existence and the

18. A parallel example in cosmetics is the smaller amount of fashion training Avon gives its salesmen as compared to Viviane Woodward (higher priced line) which gives its salesmen more extensive fashion training as well as requiring them to take more refresher courses.

19. Fuller Brush found this to be the case when they began recruiting women to sell their products on a part-time basis. Accordingly, they added cosmetics to their line of products to enhance the palatability of their product line to women as well as giving their female salesmen an opportunity to exploit any comparative advantages they would have in selling cosmetics. Fuller Brush also entitled these women as "Fullerette's" rather than "Fuller Brush Women." Hence, Avon now regards their major competitor as Fuller Brush since both are in the same direct labor market and to a lesser extent the product market.

knowledge of its importance by the member firms, one might expect that a salary-bidding war would evolve as a result of each firm attempting to capture the most productive managers. However, for the firms themselves, this would be in the short run (before new managerial resources could be bid into the industry and sufficiently trained) self-defeating since the end result would be higher wages for the managers (as a result of their capturing more than their quasirents) and lower profits for the firm.[20] Hence, those managerial moves that do occur are a result of: (1) an employee who can earn a higher marginal product elsewhere because he is being more effectively utilized (which usually means a move from a larger to a smaller firm); (2) the salary offered (marginal product paid) is the same, but the opportunity for upward mobility is greater, thus enhancing the discounted lifetime expectation of earnings; (3) there are personality conflicts within the firm which may impede the salesman's upward mobility or his earning his true marginal product (similar to (1) but is different in that (1) results from the organization of the firm and (3) is a result of irrational factors).

TYPE OF DISTRIBUTION SYSTEM AND FACTOR COMPETITION

The difference in the distribution system adopted by a firm, as well as the level of salaries and their composition, reveals further insights into the nature of factor competition within the industry as well as the adaptive role the firm follows as it evolves from a new entrant to an established firm. New firms in the industry have four major requirements that they must satisfy: (1) raising of venture financial capital; (2) recruiting of managers and supervisory personnel; (3) recruiting of independent salesmen; (4) rapid expansion of sales.

The first requirement could be met by conventional financing arrangements such as commercial loans, corporate bonds, or common stock. However, due to the existent high risks and potential market ignorance (of financial intermediaries) involved with a new direct-selling venture, the explicit (high interest rates paid on loans and bonds) and implicit (excessive dilution of equity via stocks) costs involved with such devices may make them unattractive. The firms choose instead to have the capital advanced by those who will be the equivalent of district managers or supervisors (similar to franchising). Thus the costs of capital are transformed from fixed to variable costs with the interest paid on the money being paid via the discount on acquired merchandise.[21]

---

20. Based on discussions with leading executives of top ten (by sales) direct selling firms.

21. Interestingly enough, the new firm seems to be able to convince investors

Simultaneously, the new firms also satisfy the second requirement for managerial personnel. The most important and crucial role (and the one which is most lucrative) in the short run, particularly, for these managers is to recruit others to come in at their investment level or below. Their commission schedule reflects this by giving them an overwrite (2–4 percent) on all sales generated by those who come in at their level which also means the biggest investors.

To the extent that these firms are successful at recruiting, needs three and four are met by the rapid influx of salesmen as the newly recruited district managers enlist subordinates who, in turn, recruit the ultimate salesmen. The incentive for this recruiting activity lies in the fact that district managers need to unload their large store of product if they are to have a continuing operation. It should be emphasized, however, that the recruiting of salesmen is a more long-run phenomenon and not as critical as the recruiting of peers (district sales managers) for short-run financial gain. This point is demonstrated by an examination of the commission schedules which follows.

COMMISSION SCHEDULES FOR NEW
AND ESTABLISHED FIRMS

Table 2 shows the commissions paid by five established direct selling firms and three new direct selling firms. Of the five established firms, two reward their managers with a salary plus commission (which is converted into a straight commission using average retail sales data) whereas the remaining three use a commission-only basis. These five firms represent four distinct product lines and have been in the direct selling industry for at least fifty years. The prices of the goods sold range from $3 to $350. Unfortunately due to reasons of discretion and disclosure (information was confidentially given) which might affect the firms' competitive position,[22] their actual names cannot be revealed.

Of the three new firms, two sell soap products (Amway and Bestline), and the third sells cosmetics. Their names and schedules can be revealed

---

through information and education about the firm and its product to advance its capital at the opportunity cost of 10 percent. Note the difference between total commissions paid at supervisory levels (see Table 2, levels II and III) between established firms and new firms where the capital is advanced. The 10 percent figure is quite close to approximations of the "average" return to capital. See L. Fisher and J. H. Lorie, "Rates of Return on Investments in Common Stocks," *The Journal of Business* (January 1964), p. 1–21.

22. Probably equally as important or perhaps more so, would be the internal effect of such disclosures if someone in the organization felt he were not being accurately or equitably rewarded. Also, the salesmen at the lowest level are not told how their superiors are compensated.

TABLE 2 Commission Schedules for Established and New Firms in the Direct Selling Industry

	Salary + Commission*		Established Firms Commission Only			New Firms Commission Only		
	A	B	C	D	E	Viviane Woodward	Amway	Bestline
I† Regional supervisor	2.5%†‡	2.5%	3.5% +2.5% overwrite	2% +2% overwrite	25%	1.5%	1.5%	1.5%
II District supervisor	5.0%	4.5%	4%	3.5%	7%	10% + 1% overwrite		8% + 2% overwrite
III Area supervisor	7.0%	5.5%	4.5%	3.5%	7%	10% + 1% overwrite	15% + 3% overwrite	12% + 2% overwrite
IV (Retailer)	25% / 40%	25% Inactive¶ / 40% Active	20%	25% (P-T) 2.5% I / 40% A	(F-T)§ 25% / 45% A	30% Inactive / 40% Active	30% Inactive / 40% Active	30% Inactive / 40% Active

* Salaries converted to commissions assuming $500 sales per week at retail (level IV) and each supervisor managing ten subordinates.
† Refers to highest level in hierarchy or regional supervisor.
‡ Refers to commission on gross sales.
¶ Active means selling a minimum amount of product per month usually $100.
§ P-T refers to part-time which is twenty hours a week or less, but is also defined in dollar volume which would be at least $300 per week.

since it is readily available to any potential investor as well as the general public.

At level IV, which is that of the independent sales representative (e.g., Avon Lady, Fullerette, etc.), all of the "actives" for established firms B and E and for all the new firms earn a 40 percent commission per retail dollar sold whereas their inactive counterparts earn between 25 and 30 percent. The incentive here is to initially accustom the part-time salesman to selling a certain minimum amount each week so that he retains his interest and incentive, thus reducing the probability of his dropping out and necessitating replacement by a new recruit.

Indirect evidence of the cost of recruiting to these firms can be found with firm E which has full-time salesmen at level IV and pays them an average of 45 percent commission (20 percent higher than an inactive, part-time salesman). Since this firm indicated that it would prefer all full-time salesmen (implying they earn a higher rate of return on them) their differential recruiting costs may be as much as 20 percent of the retail price of their products.

Firms A, C, and D offer a 20-25 percent commission to their full-time salesmen, about half of what firm E offers its equivalent salesmen. There are three potential interdependent explanations for this differential: (1) The goods A, C, and D are relatively high priced (in excess of $200) which means their salesmen earn a high commission per sale implying a higher return on those fixed costs common to all direct selling salesmen. Hence if all such salesmen earn the same rate of return (or if the system approaches equilibrium) on sales, a lower commission would be dictated. (2) Higher priced goods may have higher costs of production per dollar of retail price which would allow the firm less leverage in setting commissions. (3) Higher priced goods require more extensive training per retail dollar sold which raises overhead costs (similar to two) thus necessitating a lower commission if these firms are to earn the same rate of return as other types of direct selling firms.

Therefore the compensation differences between level IV salesmen can be attributed to either their status as active or inactive or to their selling an expensive or inexpensive item. Nonetheless, it is at levels II and III particularly that the compensation differences occur, thus emphasizing the different goals of the new versus established firms.

For levels II and III, the new firms pay anywhere from 50 percent to 250 percent more in commissions per level as well as in total or combination (i.e., II plus III). We can analyze the sources and motivations for this differential if we compare firms B and E with the new firms that sell goods that are comparably priced.[23] Firm E offers a total of a 14

23. Firms B and E and the new firms all sell comparably priced goods with average customer sales around $10.

percent commission (level II plus III) which is 4 percent above that of firm B which can be explained by three factors:

1. There is greater certainty of sales with established firm B.

2. Although there are more people to supervise per manager with B, there is greater sales per salesman (relates to one) leading to a higher average volume and higher wages.

3. A larger portion of earned income is guaranteed a fixed salary with B and thus reduces the risk of earning any given minimum level of income. Therefore, the 4 percent differential seems to be a combination of a risk premium plus productive compensation due to average lower sales generation.

For these reasons firm E will be directly compared with the new firms with 2 percent per sales dollars commission being assumed as the differential risk premium between firms B and E.

NEW FIRMS COMPARED WITH FIRM E

Firm E, which pays a total of 14 percent commission on sales for levels II and III, is anywhere from 1 percent to 6 percent below the total commissions paid by the new firms at these levels. For example, for Amway, the figures are essentially identical (55 percent straight commission for Amway versus 54 percent for firm E) with Amway giving the greatest emphasis to its 3 percent overwrite at level II; or in other words, the overwrite reflects the importance of recruiting of peers who will make substantial investments in terms of secured inventory. This overwrite can also be viewed as a risk premium between firm E and Amway. The remaining 1 percent differential between Amway and firm E can potentially be explained in terms of a return on invested capital. That is, an Amway manager at levels II and III must put up $3,000 (for $6,500 worth of product) which, assuming a two-year depletion time has an opportunity cost of $495 which is approximately the 1 percent commission on gross retail sales at level II.[24]

The remaining 5 percent differential between Amway (or firm E) and Bestline and Viviane Woodard can be attributed partly to risk (since they are newer firms than Amway) but more exactly to a differing overall corporate strategy that emphasizes sales generation versus pure recruiting which more lucratively rewards selling by its supervisors. That

24. Include terms:
    3,000 × 9 percent for one year = 270
    3,000 × 7.5 percent (discounted) in second year = $225.
For explanation of 9 percent and 7.5 figures, see L. Fisher and J. H. Lorie, "Rates of Return on Investments."

is, if a supervisor at levels II and III for Bestline or Viviane Woodard is to earn the same rate of return as one with Amway or firm E, he must not only generate sales within his own organization via recruiting, promoting, and training those under him; he must also sell the product himself. In other words, in equating the marginal returns[25] from recruiting, training, promoting and selling, supervisors with Bestline and Viviane Woodward are giving considerably more weight to selling because of the different kind of environment in which their firm operates. More specifically, these firms are the least known and the most risky. This situation implies that diminishing returns probably set in sooner for such activities as recruiting and training than would be the case with a better known firm.

OVERWRITE

Despite the straight percentage differences between firm E and the new firms which are meant to be attractive or competitive in their own right, the major differentiating factor between these firms is the overwrite. The overwrite itself is a straight percentage payment on gross sales generated by a recruitee who is brought in at levels II or III. For example, for a distributor at level II who makes no direct sales, the gross remuneration would be (e.g., using Bestline's figures) 8 percent of all sales generated by his own organization which is directly analogous to firm E whose figure is 7 percent. In addition, one would earn a 2 percent commission (Bestline's overwrite) on all gross sales generated by the organizations of all those individuals recruited by him. Hence, his salary is based on sales generated by his particular organization as well as by organizations administered by others. This overwrite provides a powerful incentive not only to recruit salesmen and supervisors for his own organization but also to recruit peers at levels II and III.[26] Another reenforcing recruiting incentive often employed by new firms on top of the overwrite is the release fee which is a cash payment (from $150 to $300) that is paid to a recruiter by the parent firm for bringing a recruitee in at the managerial level further emphasizing the new firms dual need of rapid sales and financial capital.

25. The economic profit would be equal to gross commissions less selling expenses, inventory costs, promotional expenses, etc. and the opportunity cost of invested time.

26. The allocational goal would be to equate marginal returns from administering one's own organization and from recruiting. Due to potentially high returns from recruiting, supervisors for new firms have often been guilty of excessive recruiting efforts with subsequent diminishing returns which has often led to a rather high failure rate on their part with disastrous consequences for the parent firm since few successful sales organizations were established.

THE EVOLUTION OF THE ORGANIZATION

The combination of the overwrite and the release fee dictate that the manager at levels II and III should spend the majority of his time recruiting which is what the parent firm desires since financial capital and immediate sales volume[27] are its primary goals. However, as the firm matures and becomes more concerned with establishing a viable sales organization, it changes its incentive schema accordingly to direct more resources into the administering of current organizations and less on pure recruiting.

The first incentive to be abandoned is the release fee. This encourages the recruiter to not only bring people in but to ensure that those recruited develop viable sales organizations because if they do not, the overwrite becomes a single period payment and hence loses much of its attractiveness.

After several years of recruiting and growing, the parent firm usually begins granting exclusive territorial rights for selling and recruiting.[28] This forces the local supervisor to further adjust his efforts toward developing a viable and thriving sales organization since the returns from recruiting are sharply limited by the relatively fixed numbers of potential recruits within any given territory. In terms of ultimate sales growth, the organization is compelled to more adequately serve current customers in addition to intensifying promotional activities within the area since they cannot rely on generating sales via new customers who are spread over several current territories.

Due to the parent firm's (as well as the supervisors') dependence on current customers and their continued patronage for reorders, reputation, and goodwill (which effect potential new customers), the parent firm finds it necessary to exercise ever-increasing control over the organization. This control is necessary to ensure such factors as simultaneous introduction of new products in all areas, consistent product

27. By sales volume for the parent firm is meant the disposition of the product from their inventories to the inventories of its independent contractors or supervisors. In other words, sales volume does not necessitate a sale to the ultimate consumer.

28. By so doing, the parent firm becomes involved in a legal paradox via antitrust laws. The granting of exclusive territorial rights could be construed as a per se violation of the Sherman Act since, in essence, it involves the creation of an exclusive monopoly within that territory for the given product. However, by not granting such territorial rights, the firm risks prosecution under the "chain letter" provisions of certain antilottery statutes in which the firm's distribution system is compared with the pyramid structure of a chain letter in which one's rate of return is essentially determined by chance or luck rather than skill. Thus, there is no valid legal structure for them except to grant territories which had been granted immunity (similar to franchising) by local and federal legislators but there is no guarantee of permanent immunity except, perhaps, that of legal precedent.

promotion via pricing and marketing techniques (which among other purposes can serve to even out inventories through price discounting of slow moving items), manpower policies with regard to hiring, training, and motivating personnel. These kinds of controls become virtually impossible to exercise if the firm consists mainly of independent contractors since no punitive or incentive devices can be uniformly enforced.[29]

The solution to the control problem that is adopted by many firms is the gradual vertical integration of the firm, proceeding from the top down. That is, the firm takes its most successful managers (those with the largest organizations) and converts them into District Managers (level I) who work on a salary plus commission basis. This procedure is then followed for levels II and III which, when completed, leaves level IV as the only one made up exclusively of independent contractors. This evolutionary, vertical integration development is one which several of the successful, ongoing firms have adopted. In other words, many direct selling firms begin with a multilevel distribution system since all face the same constraints of inadequate capital and a small operating base and evolve to an integrated form as the first two problems are superseded by those of constrained sales viability and growth as well as internal control.[30]

There are other reasons why a firm would want to vertically integrate in addition to that of increased control. For example: (1) the firm's executives may feel they can perform the roles of recruiters and administer more efficiently than the independent contractor and hence by buying him out can save money. (2) After buying the manager out, it can reduce the level of commissions paid as well as eliminate the bonus overwrite and capture a greater return for the parent firm.

There are also costs involved with vertical integration—since the firm loses a source of capital funds but such a source becomes less important as the firm develops if continued sales growth does not follow.[31] Further-

29. For example, price discounting may not be passed on to the ultimate consumer as it may be absorbed by the contractor thus depriving the discount of its full effect on ultimate sales.

30. It should be noted that some established firms (e.g., Avon, World Book Encyclopedia) use multilevel distribution systems even now in the initial stages of their foreign operations.

31. As stated previously, one might be tempted to view the funds received by the parent firm from recruitees as cost-free as no interest is paid on it. But this is clearly not so as the interest paid is reflected in the higher commissions paid by them. Nonetheless the firm can gain some advantage by securing the funds at a lower cost than a financial intermediary would charge since the firm in essence can offer a higher commission with an implied interest rate which is lower than that explicitly charged by a financial intermediary thus either through ignorance on the part of suppliers (district supervisors) or better knowledge on their part they pay a more competitive (vis-a-vis established firms) interest charge.

more, the availability of new recruits becomes more limited as the firm
expands, reducing the probability of growing via this method and hence
reducing the rate of return from recruiting as costs per recruit begin
to rise due to diminishing returns with the fixed factor being the potential number of investors in any given population.[32] Alternatively,
contact costs (costs of making contact with potential recruits and gaining their confidence) begin rising significantly as one exhausts one's
close relationships with fellow workers, friends, relatives, etc. That is,
the limiting factor in one's social circle which provides low cost access
to potential recruit. After exhausting these contacts and those contacts
made indirectly from them, the cost of gaining exposure to and the confidence of another disparate group begins to rise significantly in terms
of invested time that reduces the return from recruiting which in turn
dictates turning to training and promoting as well as direct sales activities at the expense of pure recruitment.

SUMMARY AND CONCLUSIONS

The most salient points and insights discovered about the direct selling
industry are:

1. Traditional barriers to entry such as economies of scale, capital
requirements, and large advertising outlays are circumvented or
minimized by direct selling firms by successful recruiting and organizational structures that minimize fixed costs;

2. Factor markets and their successful exploitation are more
critical for success than product market developments;

3. Product and factor markets interact in the recruiting of
salesmen;

4. High quasi-rents are earned by managers with the expertise to
run a successful direct selling firm where expertise is significantly
different from that acquired in typical retail merchandising;

5. As the direct selling firm or organization evolves, it has many
parallels with franchising since problems of raising venture capital
and sales are replaced by demands for greater organizational control through increased vertical integration.

QUESTIONS FOR DISCUSSION

1. Identify the factors that explain the rapid growth of the direct
selling industry.

32. P. T. Barnum might disagree with this contention. The continued proliferation
of new direct selling firms confirms this view to a degree.

2. Discuss the characteristics of products typically sold via the direct selling industry. Why are these products generally sold door-to-door?

3. Discuss fully the advantages of direct selling to a manufacturing firm.

4. Is competition increasing or decreasing in the direct selling industry? Explain your answer.

5. Is there a shortage of professional managers in the direct selling industry? Discuss.

6. Explain the commission schedule used for new and established firms in the door-to-door selling industry.

7. The authors state, "This overwrite provides a powerful incentive not only to recruit salesmen and supervisors for his own organization but also to recruit peers at levels II and III." Discuss this statement fully.

8. Discuss the evolutionary trends that have taken place in the direct selling industry.

11.4 MILLIONS BY MAIL

Forbes

*"All in all, mail order is still the entrepreneur's
paradise—perhaps the last such paradise."*

When Aaron Montgomery Ward sent his first catalog to a group of
midwestern Grange farmers in 1872, he spawned a merchandising
method that has become a major industry.

Today his invention accounts for $4.7 billion worth of solicitations
and 17 billion pieces of third-class mail yearly, the selling edge of a
$50-billion industry of over 3,000 firms peddling almost everything by
mail. Over a third of U.S. adults make at least one mail-order purchase
a year, and not just for odds and ends. For example, over half the general hardback books published in the U.S. are sold by mail.

For the customer, shopping with a catalog is often a convenient way
to avoid hassles "downtown." But for the companies doing the selling,
mail order has a special appeal: In contrast with TV advertising, every
direct-mail sales pitch can be aimed at a specific audience. Every customer becomes a name on a list, of which there are now 17,000. The
best include not just the well-to-do, but habitual buyers by mail. The
trick is to find those who are mail-order prone.

The lists are built on names of those responding to solicitations. By
using someone else's names you can build your own list. Renting a competitor's list is the best way to start, says Len Carlson, the founder of
Los Angeles' Sunset House.

Using these lists, it is possible to turn a specialty business into a big
business. For example, how many bass anglers are there in the U.S.?
Certainly not enough to support a large store anywhere. But using
specialized lists, Helen Sevier in five years built the Bass Anglers Sports-
men's Society from 10,000 to 250,000 members, to whom she sells over
$1.5 million worth of fishing gear yearly.

Alexander Lewyt, a onetime vacuum cleaner tycoon, used rented lists
to raise 238,000 contributions nationally, so his tiny North Shore Animal
League of Long Island could find homes for secondhand pets (including Ahab, a three-legged cat). Once he mailed out 43,000 dollar bills

Reprinted by permission of *Forbes* Magazine from the March 15, 1976 issue, pp. 82ff.

and reaped a 93% harvest of donations. (Depending on the product, 9% is considered excellent; 5% is good.)

The list of mail-order hits is a hodgepodge. It includes Ambassador Leather Goods' credit-card wallet, L. L. Bean's camp moccasins, Dr. Rueben's *Everything You Always Wanted to Know About Sex* and a personalized rubber printing stamp that Sunset House, now a division of Carter Hawley Hale, has carried for 25 years.

Then there are the ones that bomb: a "revolutionary" water purifier, a home hobbyist paint sprayer and the Columbia House (formerly the Columbia Record Club) travel program.

The wide use of credit by mailers has made price less crucial: The Admiral Byrd Polar Center sold out its mail-order round-the-world transpolar jet flight in 1968 charging $10,000 per man (Antarctica was then off-limits to women).

But one-shot promotions aren't enough. The way to grow big in mail order is to corral repeat business. Halbert's of Bath, Ohio started in 1970 peddling $2 family histories to name buffs, then sold them wall plaques with coats of arms, and now offers them collections of original famous artists' graphics.

Sears, the biggest of the catalog firms, does some $1.3 billion, or 10% of its gross business, by mail and sends out 300 million catalogs a year. But size has drawbacks. Firms as big as Fingerhut (sales: $244 million) have highly automated fulfillment, whose cost adds to overhead. In a recession, the squeeze on margins put the company in the red.

All in all, mail order is still the entrepreneur's paradise—perhaps the last such paradise. The biggest mail-order firms have started as a single entrepreneur with an idea: Manny Fingerhut with his auto seat covers, Len Carlson with his pocket printer. Today, starting out takes more than a list and a few stamps, but not much more. Most of the starters fail. But the profiles that follow prove there's always room for one more.

STRONG-ARM SALES

In the lobby of the smart new California headquarters of Weider International is a small sign that reads: "Salesmen, visitors and muscle builders please check in with switchboard operator." On the walls are paintings of larger-than-life muscle men. Kids cluster at the front door, hoping for a glimpse of "the legendary Joe."

That would be Joe Weider, trainer of he-men and godfather to the sport of muscle-building, who has built a multimillion-dollar business out of selling fitness (and fantasies) by mail.

Over 3.5 million sometime weaklings have taken Weider's basic body building course ($58.50, with 120 pounds of weights), lured by magazine ads that promise "the body you want in place of your puny weakness." Weider claims to have made skinny hopefuls into rippling champions. Says "Mr. Universe" and "Mr. Olympia," Arnold Schwartzenegger, the Muhammad Ali of body-building, "I wouldn't have made it without Joe."

Weider's business really took off when he diversified from building biceps to developing fitness aids for the overweight. His newest and hottest item is the "Five-Minute Body Shaper," a set of ropes and pulleys you attach to a doorknob and tug on for exercise. So far, he has sold over 3 million by mail.

In 1935, with $7 pocket money, one-time weakling Weider began selling weights and mimeographed instruction booklets from the shed behind his home in his native Montreal. The booklets grew into a magazine, *Your Physique*, and the subscribers became his mailing list.

Weider soon discovered that selling paper was more profitable than selling barbells. With every set of weights, he could tack on a multitude of manuals and training books while using his muscle magazines to lure more prospects. "We'd sell them our course and then convert them to our catalog," he explains. The repeat business came from the converts who lapped up protein pills, diet drinks—anything with the Weider name and seal of approval.

Then in 1958 his magazine distributor, American News Inc., went bust owing Weider $2.2 million, and his business hit the floor like a lead medicine ball. He gave up all his 14 publications except his first love, *Muscle Builder/Power* and began developing more diet supplements for his subculture. He sponsored stars like Schwartzenegger to promote his "proteinizers" and "Kambered Kurling Bars" to the faithful, both in the U.S. and overseas, where muscle-building has greater recognition.

Then, suddenly, like a bully kicking sand in his face, the California state authorities cracked down on Weider's ads for the Five-Minute Shaper. They charged him with stage-managing his "before" and "after" promotional shots.

Weider agreed to offer a special refund supplement that is common practice in mail-order—a moneyback guarantee. Now 100,000 Californians have the opportunity to cash in their shapers if they feel deceived. So far, very few have.

Undismayed, Weider has more fitness aids on the drawing boards, and he still has the most precious thing in any mail-order business: a list of recent purchasers, known as a "live" list. It is this list—not his products or trademark—that is the true capital of Weider's body-building business.

GROW YOUR OWN

Why settle for fruit through the mail when with a little help from Tom Kyle Jr. you can grow your own? For $5.98 he'll mail you a tree.

Kyle, 43, is president of Spring Hill Nurseries of Tipp City, Ohio—an outfit that sprouts plants and seedlings and distributes them to over 1 million gardeners and amateur farmers nationwide. Some 85% of the family's $8-million business is by mail.

Kyle's great-great-grandfather established the company in 1849, but the mail-order operation was not launched until 1936, when Kyle's father was stuck with a surplus of nursery stock. He printed 200,000 catalogs and sold enough plants to carry him through the Depression.

Spring Hill sells 800-odd varieties of stock, including trees, hedges, shrubs and bulbs. Kyle's best seller is a pink flowered ground cover, Crownvetch, that covers "difficult" areas (like brown lawns). Next in sales are dwarf fruit trees, then house plants, which the company intends to catalog separately for indoor gardeners.

Like most mail-order merchants, Kyle tends to pass by necessities in favor of things that people, on impulse, can't resist. He promotes the business with a "Dear Gardening Friend" letter that makes the point that four generations of Kyles have been nurserymen. Then he boosts the response by adding a cash sweepstakes to the order form.

Spring Hill's square mile of growing beds is carefully manicured, and the company's packaging plant looks more like a factory than a farm. Kyle, who studied horticulture at Ohio State University and flew jets in the Air Force, even checks for weeds by helicopter. But his biggest cause for worry these days is not weeds, but the rising cost of growing plants and delivering them by post. Last year, he complains, fertilizer, paper and ink all increased more than 40% in price, while mailing costs went up 30%. And he is often stuck with outdated prices, because he must print his catalog four months in advance.

Kyle keys his mailings to identify which of several mailing lists draws best; he has calculated how much each square inch of catalog space should return ($300) to cover his merchandising and advertising expenses. One of the beauties of mail order, he says, is that "everything is measurable." Culling his list with a computer helped enough last year so that Spring Hill stayed in the black when it could have gone to seed.

The unscientific side of the business is picking new plants for the catalogs. That's a fashion business dealing in hybrids, not hemlines.

For example, how does Spring Hill make mini fruit trees look appetizing? It catalogs six of them together and markets the package as a "postage stamp orchard." Sounds better than "dwarf trees," doesn't it?

MOM, THEN POP

Like veterans fighting the last war, mail-order millionaires tell novices it's too tough to start up and make it in their specialized business these days: The field is too crowded and beginners can't turn profits.

Susan Edmondson of Atlanta didn't believe it. Tired of her job as an adolescent counselor, she set out to go into business for herself, and picked up the basics of mail order by going around the country asking questions of successful entrepreneurs. Most of the people she talked to suggested Edmondson would probably fall on her attractive 30-year-old face.

Armed with $5,000, a degree in art history and a lot of moxie, she formed Kaleidoscope two years ago and put together her first catalog. It was chock full of chic apparel, expensive trinkets and attractive gifts for the woman who has everything. From her backyard carriage house she launched the business with a mailing to a list including names rented from Dallas' Horchow Collection, an upper-crust mail-order house.

The response bowled her over. Instead of a bust, she had a bonanza. Since then, her company has done $9 million in sales, and moved three times to larger quarters. Now Edmondson is turning a profit. She is also working 18-hour days seven days a week.

Horchow now pays her the compliment of refusing to sell her more names. Instead, Edmondson sells Kaleidoscope's list for $50 a thousand to other users, netting $3,700 for each sale of the roster of her nearly 100,000 customers.

Thanks to credit-card buying and the pioneering merchandising of five-figure collectibles merchandised by the Franklin Mint, the big-ticket barrier in mail order has been broken. Edmondson can offer a carousel music box for $1,000 and sell 30 of them. To insure profits, she says she shoots for a generous average order ($50) on a response rate of 5%. She also tries to avoid mailing too many catalogs, because then she has to dig into marginal lists. Some of her best returns up to now have been from a list of subscribers to *Architectural Digest* magazine.

Edmondson now mails 1.5 million catalogs six times per year, and her biggest headache is keeping up with the orders. Her husband came aboard to handle fulfillment, but as a former printing salesman had no inventory experience to guide him. As with most mail-order firms, business for the Edmondsons is seasonal: Summer is slow, and business picks up in the fall. Surprisingly, January is a good month. Why? Possibly because people seem to start the new year by spending what's left over from Christmas.

Kaleidoscope doesn't have a merchandising secret; Susan Edmondson says she just pretends she's buying for herself. Some of her choices have bombed, like the abstract Orrefors crystal vases that are stacked in her warehouse. But she had no trouble moving $550 Japanese screens or $15 Botswana baskets.

Now Edmondson has the satisfaction of knowing she's getting rich in a business the experts warned her had a 90% chance of being a flop.

MAKING PEOPLE SALIVATE

"Satisfy your gouamba!"

The promotion-minded people at Omaha Steaks International have a keen interest in this rare tropical syndrome. In central Africa (wrote storyteller A. J. Liebling), "gouamba" is an insatiable craving for red meat. That's just what the three Simon brothers, Alan, Stephen and Fred, who own and operate this heartland family company, seek to exploit by mail. You pick your steak out of a catalog instead of a meat counter, and it is delivered to you packed in dry ice.

What the Simons don't tell you is that their prime, aged beef costs about three times what you'd pay at a supermarket, and twice the price even at a gourmet grocery. At $12 a pound, Omaha Steak's filet mignon is hardly a bargain.

But the mystique of Nebraska's corn-fed and spring-watered cattle keeps the orders pouring in. With 250 items and half a million catalogs mailed eight times a year, the company is the largest mail-order meat merchandiser in the world. Say the Simons, "We never talk about price; it's our flavor that's special."

Patriarch Benjamin Franklin Simon established the company in 1917, buying an Omaha building that once housed a manufacturer of tables and chairs. It was just another hotel and restaurant supply operation until Benjamin's son Lester, a man who reputedly looked at a carcass of beef the way a lecher focuses on a nude, backed into the mail-order business. He was getting so many calls from holiday gift-givers that he began pitching ads to barbecue nuts and far-flung gourmets. If Oregon's Harry & David could sell a fruit of the month, why not a seasonal sirloin?

The venture got off to a shaky start. Executive Vice President Fred Simon, the promoter in the family, was sent to a mail-order industry seminar in Chicago to learn the ropes. "It was like group therapy," he recalls. "Guys were selling model airplanes and handbags by mail. I picked up 13 ideas and only 11 worked!"

What he picked up were tips on mail-order basics: letter-writing and brochure design. The longer the solicitation letter, advised the experts, the better the response. Now Simon concurs: "Four pages about steaks work better than two pages." People want to know as much as possible about a product they haven't seen.

Simon also brought home a few order-form gimmicks to hook his readers, like miniature steak tokens to be punched out and slipped into a slot. These "action devices" pull 25% more replies, says Simon: "If you give people something to play with, they order more." By such techniques, Simon repeatedly doubled his volume.

Shooting for two orders for each 100 letters mailed and an average of $25 per order, Simon does more than just refine his lists. "You can't operate without the right lists," he says, "but the best list in the world won't make the operation profitable." To protect his margins, a computer keeps track of how many cuts he needs, how many staples and polystyrene bags, then divides his customers into frequent buyers and laggards, so he can mail more often to the faithful.

Steaks are a perfect luxury item, boasts Simon, because they are a repeat business—the key to success in mail order. "We try to create the concept of the good life," he adds. "To us that means making people salivate."

QUESTIONS FOR DISCUSSION

1. Discuss the general characteristics of the $50 *billion* per year mail order business.

2. Why do customers like mail order shopping?

3. The article examines four firms that are very successful in selling via mail. What common factors are present in each firm?

11.5 CO-OP'S SPIRIT OF '76

Martin Everett

"No celebration is complete these days without a government investigation, and co-op is no exception."

Perhaps it's the Bicentennial's pervasive influence, but there is a hint of pageantry as cooperative advertising emerges in 1976 as one of the vital forms of promotion on the U.S. marketing scene. All of a sudden, there seems to be a parade of advertisers marching with co-op plans in hand to rally retailers around the flag of equal rights. Brass bands from the major media are thumping out irresistible rhythms in the hope of getting everyone to dance to their tune. And back behind the grandstands, a few unscrupulous operators are still picking the pockets of the crowd.

Spurred by the increasing regionalization of marketing and by broadcasters' yen for a bigger chunk of the business, co-op is growing rapidly. What's more, its low cost and grass-roots appeal are expected to win it new friends as the economy turns upward and marketers begin to negotiate the cliffs and crags that seem likely to dominate their landscape for the next few years.

Gauging the trend precisely is impossible, of course, because co-op is far from being a measured medium. Manufacturers traditionally are said to have $3–$4 billion "available" for spending, but no one has come up with a reliable figure of how much they do spend and where it all goes. In the past few months, however, the momentum of co-op has picked up discernibly as many companies expanded their budgets and others jumped into the fray for the first time. Says Frank W. Hennessey, vice president for cooperative advertising sales at the Newspaper Advertising Bureau: "There's a real thirst for new ideas on how to move products, and in many cases people are deciding that co-op is the answer."

No celebration is complete these days without a government investigation, and co-op is no exception. For the first time in three years, the Federal Trade Commission (FTC) is beginning to crack down on abuses by both manufacturers and retailers, and there are indications

Reprinted by permission from the publisher. "Co-op's Spirit of '76," *Sales and Marketing Management* (March 8, 1976), pp. 33ff.

that this is just the beginning. Even some influential industry groups are known to be as concerned as the FTC about legal violations and in certain cases have brought pressure on the agency to get on with its work.

But co-op has always had a way of making strange bedfellows. At the moment, there are rumors that the airlines may lie down with the travel agents; that AT&T is interested in expanding the amount of co-op advertising done in the Yellow Pages; that major advertising agencies are out for a larger portion of the co-op pie. None of this should appear unusual, however, because the medium owes its very existence to the overlapping interests of those traditional adversaries, the manufacturer and the retailer (or, in some cases, the distributor).

A typical manufacturer's co-op plan is designed to provide the retailer with an incentive to promote the company's product. The store must buy a specified volume of goods and thereby accrue points that determine how much the manufacturer will pay toward advertising that is placed by the retailer. Most of the hassles occur over how large a stake each party has in the ad and who's going to pay for it, an issue that gets especially hot when it comes to sharing a 30-second TV spot.

"It reminds me of the joke about the 3,000 pound gorilla," says Roger D. Rice, president of the Television Bureau of Advertising. "Where does he sleep? Anywhere he wants. Sometimes it's the advertiser that weighs 3,000 pounds; sometimes it's the retailer. That's likely to decide who gets the best of a co-op deal."

Some companies manage to succeed without co-op, even in the hotly competitive packaged goods field, but two of the most notable holdouts offer stores something that every good co-op plan should: a chance to earn more money. Campbell Soup shuns the medium but provides its own warehousing, which is enough incentive for any grocer. Hanes's L'Eggs supports its hoisery line with extensive in-store services and, more important, provides the goods on consignment so that the retailer is billed only for what was sold the previous week.

Just because it's big doesn't mean that co-op is always used as effectively as it might be, however. "The massive dollars that go into co-op budgets get nowhere near the attention paid to national advertising, which is always preceded by market research and much soul searching about how to address your particular public," Sheldon B. Sosna, marketing vice president of Food Fair Stores, observed recently. He told Sales & Marketing Management's Conference on Promotional Allowances and Co-op Advertising that "the methodology of co-op is frozen somewhere back in the mid-1950s. This includes tombstone newspaper drop-ins, which contribute greatly to ad clutter, and radio and TV commercials that feature the kind of 'store listing' closings that would set any sophisticated retailer's teeth on edge."

Sometimes the incredible kinkiness of co-op plans is traceable not to the manufacturer but to his distributor. A distributor for a large appliance manufacturer was flabbergasted when challenged by a group of radio salesmen that he addressed a few weeks ago. Why, the broadcast men asked, did his plan reimburse stores for 75% of the cost of a newspaper ad, 65% for a TV commercial, but only 50% for radio? When pressed, the distributor, who had composed the plan himself some years ago, admitted he didn't know why it was set up that way.

AT Y&R, A REGIONAL APPROACH TO ADVERTISING BREEDS INTEREST IN CO-OP

If you had mentioned cooperative advertising on Madison Avenue a few years ago, most agency vice presidents would have brushed the words off their gray flannel suits. But times are changing. Although most agencies still subsist largely on lofting campaigns for national advertisers, an increasing number are being drawn into co-op by two factors: (1) growing demands by clients for a more localized marketing strategy and (2) greater interest from retailers in getting into TV and radio advertising.

Needham, Harper & Steers handles an ambitious co-op campaign for GM's Frigidaire subsidiary, and Compton Advertising is getting more heavily involved with the medium. Perhaps most significantly, Young & Rubicam, the nation's largest agency, with domestic billings of $476.6 million, is becoming increasingly committed to co-op, mainly because of assignments from such clients as Cluett, Peabody (Arrow shirts), GE (major appliances), and a number of Chrysler/Plymouth dealer associations.

"Our expanded interest is due to greater use of broadcast in cooperative advertising," says Joseph W. Ostrow, senior vice president and director of communications services at Y&R. "It's clear that the barriers are down and that co-op funds are being diverted to other media besides newspapers." Thus far, Y&R does not have a special co-op department but handles assignments in this area for eight or so national accounts when the need arises.

The need is arising frequently these days. "As co-op moves into broadcast, you have a new set of ground rules," says Ostrow. "There are no tearsheets in TV and radio. When a retailer proposes a buy, we can review it for our client to make sure he's getting the best rate and the kind of audience he wants to achieve his marketing objective." Y&R's broadcast buyers are organized by region, so that the person responsible for, say, Boston is thoroughly familiar with all aspects of the media business in that market, including the daily fluctuation of broadcast rates. In some cases, that function is performed by Y&R National, a group of wholly owned agencies in 10 cities, whose members also advise the home office on other co-op developments as they work with local retailers.

George W. Sharpe, II, vice president for communications services, observes that because of the volume of its media purchases, Y&R often can make a better broadcast buy than the retailer. "We started to buy TV time under Arrow's co-op program last May, and it has gone so well that the company now gives retailers in some markets an incentive to let us do the buying," says Sharpe. Under this plan, which will be extended to all its major markets this spring, Arrow pays 75% of the media costs when Y&R does the buying, and the retailer pays 25%. That compares with the usual 50%–50% arrangement that applies when the retailer makes its own media buy.

From Arrow's standpoint, the program is an important element in trying to gain more control over its co-op efforts and in broadening a media strategy that has been oriented heavily toward newspapers. "We are trying to increase our advertising on TV because it is an effective medium," says Elina Smith, the company's cooperative advertising manager. For example, although newspapers still accounted for about 65% of Arrow's co-op expenditures last fall, over 10% went into TV, compared with an insignificant amount a year earlier.

At this point, Y&R is buying a small but growing portion of the TV time for Arrow's co-op ventures. In addition, it makes available to Arrow a retail version of each national commercial produced, which the company then gives to stores for their co-op use. Y&R also plays a major role in syndication, where an advertiser will produce an entire program and offer it to stations in return for commercial time. Arrow currently is syndicating "Norman Rockwell's World," a tribute to the well-known artist that was shown in some markets two years ago. Under the present arrangement, Arrow takes one or two "national minutes" during the broadcast, and it is up to the company's sales force to recruit local retailers to buy (via Y&R) another two minutes for commercials in their own markets.

Does all this mean that Y&R is on the point of establishing a department to handle nothing but co-op business? Ostrow is reluctant to comment but admits that "the opportunities certainly would make it worth taking a look at carefully." Is the agency considering acquiring one of the many new shops that have done well by specializing in co-op? "Who knows?" he says, gazing at the ceiling.

So exercised is the Radio Advertising Bureau about such instances that it is distributing an antidiscrimination kit to its member stations. When station representatives are told that a manufacturer's plan doesn't provide for radio, they urge the retailer to write to the FTC. "We get the feeling that many retailers are being deprived of the full opportunity to be competitive with other stores when a manufacturer restricts the choice of media and excludes radio," says Miles David, president of RAB. "For example, an independent appliance dealer with a couple of locations can't afford to slug it out with the big discount chains in a metropolitan daily newspaper, but he can reach a high percentage of the market at a reasonable cost by using radio spots."

Some broadcasters, especially in radio, feel that they are at a competitive disadvantage with newspapers because some unscrupulous retailers indulge in double billing when using papers. Mindful of their own history of billing shenanigans, broadcasters claim that such violations have all but disappeared in recent years as the Federal Communications Commission vowed that offenders would have their licenses revoked. Working with the Assn. of National Advertisers, the radio and TV people have also come up with a program to control "script switching" by overzealous stores. This calls for the station to stamp both its invoice and the script of a commercial so that when a store submits a claim, the advertiser can see his share of the ad and what it costs.

Even with tighter regulation, the increasing use of radio and TV may be hindered by the ingrained habits of broadcast salesmen. "Over 80% of co-op is probably in papers, and it's broadcasting's fault," says William L. McGee, president of Broadcast Marketing, a San Francisco consulting service. "We haven't done a good job of getting in sync with retailers. They don't call up a station and ask what the availabilities are the way an advertising agency does. You have to get out there and sell them."

Similar warnings were voiced by Chuck Miller, vice president, advertising and sales promotion for Dayton-Hudson's Target Stores Div., at a recent broadcast meeting. "There are problems that keep retailers from moving even faster into TV," he said. "For example, we have the feeling that retail rate negotiations are a *caveat emptor* jungle."

Although newspapers are more entrenched in the co-op business, they come in for their share of criticism. Jim Brady, merchandising manager for GE Major Appliances, told last month's meeting of the Newspaper Advertising Cooperative Network (NACON) that "you are still our No. 1 medium, but too many space salesmen have become order takers. You have got to beware of boilerplate salesmanship." Brady, who noted that his dealers are becoming more adept at TV advertising, said GE has retail sales counsellors in the field to help retailers with all aspects of merchandising and advertising. Gus Cooper, vice president of U.S. Life Insurance, said that his co-op budget had tripled in the last three years. "TV is moving in fast on newspapers," he told the group. "Some newspapers had co-op programs with our independent agents during the past three years but have lost them."

TAILORING STRATEGY TO THE MARKET

At the root of many co-op disputes is the struggle to control the program—its marketing objectives, timing, and the content and quality of the ads themselves. Some manufacturers, such as Brown Shoe and Masonite, fend well for themselves with traditional plans concentrated in newspapers. Others shape their strategy to suit market conditions or fit their distribution system. The Medical Products Div. of 3M makes sure that co-op ads for its line of medical tapes always feature a price reduction. Kodak, which has increased its spending in radio and outdoor advertising, has not moved heavily into TV because the rates are generally too steep for the camera stores and photo finishers that account for a large part of its retail sales.

One advertiser that manages to walk the fine line between manufacturer control and retailer flexibility is Sperry Rand's Sperry Remington Shaver Div. Using what he calls a "modular personalized" TV commercial, Robert J. Stevens, retail advertising and publicity manager, lets stores choose from among nine segments, each featuring a different product. They select three 7-second modules, which form the core of a 30-second spot. At the beginning and the end, they may run "bookends" of 4½ seconds each that convey their store's merchandising image.

Mel Boyd of Lees Carpets, Valley Forge, Pa., structures his program to get greater performance from dealers. Under the basic plan, Lees will share 50% of the co-op advertising cost, up to 3% of the dealer's sales. If the merchant agrees to buy a large floor display and meet other qualifications for a "Look-Alive Dealer," however, the company pays 75% of the co-op expense, up to 4% of sales. Boyd, who spends most of his dollars in TV, has tried to persuade stores that a sale doesn't have to last a week or more to be successful. "Some of our most effective promotions have been two-day TV blitzes," he says.

In any campaign, of course, it's leg-work and a dash of entrepreneurial spirit that usually make co-op pay off. An example is the recent promotion engineered by Jesse Fitch, co-op coordinator for the Houston *Chronicle*, and Edward F. Keller, advertising manager for Art Jones & Co., the RCA distributor for eastern Texas and part of Louisiana. Unusually successful from the standpoint of manufacturer, distributor, and dealers, it illustrates three key points about the role of co-op in todays regionalized marketing:

1. To be most effective, both the content of the ads and the media mix should be tailored to the local market.

2. Make it easy for dealers to participate, and the chances of success are excellent. Wrap your co-op plan in technicalities and it's uphill all the way.

3. Make sure your budget is adequate to do the job. When Fitch and Keller teamed up in a similar venture over a year ago, $40,000 was allocated for media expenditures. Realizing that that was not enough for a market the size of Houston, Keller spent $100,000 this year.

Fitch and Keller began their custom tailoring by signing up members of the Houston Rockets basketball team to be the spokesmen for RCA dealers in the area. Starting with materials provided by RCA headquarters, the two men built their own campaign, featuring the athletes in print ads and using them as spokesmen on TV and radio. As a traffic builder, dealers could offer a Rockets basketball for a low $1.99.

Keystone of the campaign was an eight-page newspaper tabloid insert that each dealer could have imprinted with his name and address on the front. Fitch arranged the plan so that a store could have exclusive use of the tabloid in one of the *Chronicle's* numerous city or state zones. "This gave us the kind of impact you need to rise above the clutter of local advertising," says Keller. "To the reader, it looked as if his local RCA dealer was one of the *Chronicles's* major advertisers." The tabloids could also be inserted in local papers or used as handouts.

Other media played important roles in the promotion. "Houston is similar to Los Angeles in that it's spread out and there are a lot of drivers on the road at any time of year," Keller observes. "We used a lot of radio to take advantage of the drive time." In the end, Keller spent about 40% of his budget in print and 30% each in radio and TV.

To encourage stores to participate, he prepared a simple one-page description of the plan that was on hand when the dealers came to see the new RCA TV models at an open house in late December. Dealers could select the appropriate zone for distribution of the tabloid and sign on by agreeing to pay $15 per thousand inserts. If they also wished to place a 600-line newspaper ad and share in the radio and TV commercials (an advertising package that Keller valued at $2,000), they could do so by agreeing to pay $400. In most cases, this actually meant paying only $200 because half of the outlay was chargeable to their co-op fund. Art Jones & Co. placed all the advertising, and dealers were not charged for production costs.

HELP FOR MOM AND POP

Making things easier for small and medium-sized retailers is also an objective of the leading media associations. Both the Radio Advertising Bureau and the Television Bureau of Advertising have started seminars to train salesmen in that and other aspects of co-op. At the Newspaper Advertising Bureau, Frank Hennessey has put together a Co-Op Action Plan designed to help stores calculate and collect the co-op funds that are due them and also provide tips on how to run more effective ad campaigns. Says Hennessey, "Many smaller merchants find co-op so complicated, legally confusing, and time-consuming that they just throw up their hands and say, 'Forget it!'"

Two New York City media concerns have developed variations on newspaper co-op. Metro Associated Services recently put together a complete editorial package that will be offered to papers running special sections on lawn and garden matters this spring. The project was produced and paid for by Chevron Chemical's Ortho Div., which feels that the package is an ideal co-op vehicle for its line of pesticides and garden chemicals.

At Metropolitan Sunday Newspapers, whose main business is acting as national rep for the Sunday magazines of a number of major dailies around the U.S., there's a new program that lets apparel and home-fashion manufacturers place co-op ads through MSN. All the details are handled by the manufacturer, but the local paper bills the retailer, which may apply the sum against its co-op allowances.

Magazines, though late starters in co-op, are getting into it as regional editions proliferate. Magazine Networks (SMM, Apr. 3, 1972) has built up co-op business in the regional "signatures" that it inserts in national magazines, and individual publishers are beginning to go after their own co-op dollars. *Better Homes and Gardens* has a contract with an outside sales organization that does nothing but solicit retail ads for the magazine. The firm, Local Marketing, Lincroft, N.J., is headed by Richard Timpone, a Magazine Networks alumnus. As an example of his co-op efforts, he cites an ad for a Kitchen Aid trash compactor that ran in three issues of BH&G last fall, with dealer listings on the opposite page. Timpone says that besides soliciting retail ads, his operation eventually may serve as a way of introducing national advertisers to the magazine.

For the time being, some consumer goods marketers may choose to ignore cooperative advertising, but the chances are that they won't do so for long. And once they're committed, the power and the majesty of the medium are likely to take them by surprise. "This thing is absolutely tremendous compared to other parts of the promotional mix," exclaimed a recent convert, coming slightly unhinged. "Why, it's like the cart wagging the dog!" That's *just* what it's like.

REGULATING CO-OP: AT LAST,
THE FTC GETS ON ITS HORSE

The Federal Trade Commission (FTC) is using its authority under the Robinson-Patman Act to crack down on abuses in cooperative advertising. Although the Dept. of Agriculture's Packer and Stockyards Administration has been bringing similar rulings against meat packers for some time (SMM, Feb. 3, 1975), other industries were subject to all sorts of co-op chicanery. The FTC gave co-op and other types of merchandising allowance programs such a low priority that only two cases have surfaced in the past three years.

Suddenly, things are different. Last month, the commission announced that it had accepted a consent order involving Thrifty Drug Stores. The Los Angeles-based chain (450 units) acknowledged that it had induced some $2 million in co-op and other payments from suppliers—$900,000 of which "exceeded the expenses it incurred in operating promotional programs."

Other co-op cases are expected to be filed soon against manufacturers and retailers in the grocery and drug industries.

Why the turnabout? Co-op ad enforcement is bound up in the fate of the Robinson-Patman (R-P) price discrimination law, which is in turn intertwined with Washington's new-found preoccupation with the "deregulation" of business.

Co-op ads fall within Robinson-Patman's proviso that merchandising allowances be granted to all competing customers in a market on a "proportionately equal" basis. The statute had been policed with some degree of regularity until 1974, when Lewis A. Engman left a top post with the President's Domestic Council to head the FTC. Engman, now campaigning in Michigan for a Senate seat, was convinced that R-P embroiled the commission in too many time-consuming but insignificant cases. Under his reign, staff resources were poured into relatively few major antitrust cases (food, oil, etc.) aimed at producing changes in consumer prices that would blunt inflation's impact.

Engman's second pet project was "deregulation." R-P was cited as one of many "clumsy and archaic" statutes impeding business competition. Although he felt that the FTC couldn't work openly for its repeal while being legally responsible for its enforcement, Engman quietly encouraged the White House and Justice Dept. in their efforts to revamp, or possibly repeal, the 40-year-old law.

The result late last year was the drafting of two bills—the Robinson-Patman Reform Statute and the Predatory Practices Act. Neither Engman nor the White House was prepared for the outcry that followed. In the series of "public forums" launched around the country by the Domestic Council last year, small businessmen showed up in every city to protest the proposals. Even before the bills were formally introduced in Congress, an antagonistic House Small Business Committee set up a special Robinson-Patman subcommittee under Rep. Henry Gonzales (D.-Texas) to head off the President's posse at the pass.

The cause of Robinson-Patman has been strengthened—at least temporarily—by changes within the FTC. Last summer, in full command of the five-member commission, Engman had confided that a majority would probably support R-P's repeal if the issue were "aired openly." Today, the departures of Engman and conservative Democrat Mayo Thompson have left two unfilled vacancies and a three-member commission headed (in caretaker capacity) by veteran Paul Rand Dixon.

R-P couldn't have a stronger friend. And with commissioner Stephan Nye as an ally, the tough-talking Dixon is determined to make up for lost time. In the case of Thrifty Drug, for example, the company had actually agreed to the FTC's proposed consent order in May 1975. The consent order sat on Engman's desk until snatched up by his successor.

Hearings by the Gonzales subcommittee gave Dixon a public forum in which to announce that bureau chiefs had been ordered to report directly to commissioners "when a Robinson-Patman case is opened or closed." Accompanying Dixon was FTC Bureau of Competition head Owen Johnson. "The message is clear from this committee and elsewhere that you want the act enforced," he said. "The staff has been given the green light, and you will see the effect."

No one could be more pleased at the news than the broadcast industry. For one thing, radio and TV stations have long claimed that many retailer-manufacturer co-op ad contracts discriminate against broadcast media as an advertising vehicle. A Bureau of Competition attorney acknowledges having met with the National Assn. of Broadcasters and that "we want to help."

But "it may not be a simple matter," he adds. "Enforcing R-P means that we have to show proof that *competing customers* have been discriminated against. You may have a retailer in a rural area who'd rather use radio instead of newspapers, but you have to prove that he's competing against another retailer in an urban area."

Other alleged abuses may be easier to police. Among the practices most likely to be scrutinized:

DOUBLE BILLING

A manufacturer agrees to match a local retailer's outlay for a newspaper advertising campaign. The retailer buys space at the cheaper local rate but gets the newspaper to send the manufacturer a "receipt" showing that the ad has been purchased at the more expensive national rate. Instead of chipping in 50%, the manufacturer may wind up paying 75% or more of the ad's cost.

COST VS. "VALUE"

(This was the basis for the Thrifty Drug complaint.) Retailers who agree to advertise a manufacturer's product are offered, say, $1 off the price of each case purchased. The large chain retailer takes a $200 ad, buys 20,000 cases, and gets $20,000 in "reimbursement." The small retailer pays for the same ad, buys 20 cases, and winds up with only $20 in reimbursement.

EXAGGERATED AD CLAIMS

A manufacturer offers a retailer co-op ad money, then is astonished to read an ad from the retailer claiming benefits for his product that can't possibly be backed up.

MEDIA DISCRIMINATION

A manufacturer offers retailers 5% of his product's purchase price for advertising in a large metropolitan daily, but only 1% to 4% for ads in newspapers with smaller circulations. Retailers serving only suburban or rural markets thus can't take advantage of the highest discount.

FTC officials won't reveal specific cases under investigation, but Competition Bureau director Johnson offered some hints in recent testimony to the House subcommittee. "In general," he said, "it has always been our goal to select cases with the maximum possible industrywide impact. This means that the respondents are usually selected from among the industry leaders." If the agency adopts the same techniques it used against the apparel industry a few years ago, it may be expected to take on large retailers and manufacturers simultaneously on a market-by-market basis.

Just how fast the FTC will churn out co-op ad and other R-P cases will depend on the clock and the White House. Because R-P has been suppressed for so long, the number of "live" investigations is small. But Acting Chairman Dixon also knows that his new-found majority could be short-lived. Rumors at press time were that the next chairman will be Republican Calvin J. Collier, a close Engman ally on R-P issues when he served as the commission's general counsel in 1974–75. Chances are that Dixon will act quickly and count on a sympathetic Congress to help keep the momentum going.

QUESTIONS FOR DISCUSSION

1. What is cooperative advertising? Why do manufacturers like it? Why do retailers like it?

2. What areas of cooperative advertising are currently being investigated by the Federal Trade Commission?

3. Explain the relationship between the Robinson-Patman Act and co-op.

4. What is "double billing." Explain why it has been a problem area in cooperative advertising.

5. Discuss how Young and Rubicam, the nation's largest advertising agency, uses co-op for its clients.

6. Do you think co-op helps or hinders the "Mom and Pop" retailers? Defend your answer.

11.6 IN-STORE SERVICING CATCHES FIRE

Sales Management

*"With the cost of each sales call going up, manufac-
turers can't afford to have highly paid salesmen
straightening shelves and checking inventory at
each store."*

"We spend $3 million advertising this product, another couple of mil-
lion merchandising and promoting it, and God knows how much up and
down the distribution chain to get on shelves," laments the national
sales manager of a food company, "and in the end it all comes to naught
because our shelf space is either out-of-stock or in disarray." Says
another consumer products sales executive, "We're losing sales because
retail shelves have never been shabbier nor stockout gripes more acute.
Why? Because chains are slashing personnel to stay in the discount race.
The people they do have are setting all-time records for turnover. Rack
jobbers ought to be moving in to fill the gap, but they're running in the
other direction."

WHO'S WATCHING THE IN-STORE? EVERYBODY

Everybody seems to be getting into the in-store servicing act, each claiming to offer something just a little different. Some of the these entrants
include:

Market research groups. As specialized in-store servicing companies
like Space Control (see story) begin offering marketing data as a by-
product, traditional market research firms added inventory control services. One of the first is New York-based Audits & Surveys, which created
Distribution Plus (DP) last October. Since then, DP has transferred a
portion of its 5,000 person research field force to the new division as
quickly as it can recruit retailers and manufacturers for retail servicing.

Reprinted by permission from *Sales Management*, The Marketing Magazine (April
17, 1972), pp. 28–30, Copyright 1972.

Says DP general manager Bob Rhoades, "We can also carry out direct selling to introduce new products and provide product demonstrations in department stores."

Lease operators.   Hard Goods Distributors, Inc., Newton, Mass., says it is prepared to perform many services for retailers. In addition to stocking hard goods departments (housewares, gifts, garden supplies), it leases in about 75 large discount stores. "We can do everything from inventory control to managing stores, buying, and providing advertising services," claims president Sheldon Woolf.

Merchandising consultants.   Master Marketing Group (MMG), Westport, Conn., hopes to combine in-store servicing with a plan to supply complete soft-goods departments to discount drug chains. In a recent experiment at Pittsburgh's White Cross and Red Shield chains, MMG supplied and serviced soft goods lines by Nantucket Industries (ladies' underwear), Amos Hoisery (men's socks), Charleston Hoisery (teenage stockings), and Perfect Plus (pantyhose). Of these, only Perfect Plus was marketed under its own name. The others MMG's Today's Life label.

Last year a leading light bulb manufacturer (who prefers to be anonymous) and a 42-unit discount chain agreed to try out a possible solution. Rather than attempting to service each outlet with its own salesmen or distributors, the manufacturer gave a new breed of middleman the job of tidying displays, keeping shelves full, and checking backroom supplies. By the end of the six month test period, sales to the chain had zoomed 128% over the same span the year before.

WHO'S USING IT

Tales of similar success stories explain why four national in-store servicing firms have caught fire in the past three years and why at least a half-dozen others are springing up regionally. The top four, Inventory Control Co., American In-Store Servicing Co., Space Control Corp., and Custom Marketing, Inc. (see box), all claim that sales have doubled within two years. And while none of the closely held firms will divulge earnings, one sales manager estimates their combined fees from manufacturers "in the $2 million to $3 million range."

The number of manufacturers now using in-store servicing firms probably exceeds 200—ranging from giants like Dupont, Colgate-Palmolive, and Admiral to such vertical market leaders as Imperial Knike, Enterprise Aluminum, and Globe-Superior. While many marketers say they haven't tried in-store services long enough for tangible results, there have been reports of sizable sales increases. "We increased sales by 100% in one chain," says Donald Levine, Eastern regional sales manager for the Brearley Co., a bathroom accessory manufacturer. "We used to get about four turnovers a year per product line at each store. Now we're averaging eight to 12." He said Brearley uses in-store servicing in 14 retail chains and promotes its tie-in as a door opener to new chains.

Buoyed by such testimonials, the four largest in-store service companies sound almost too good to be true. "I'd almost guarantee any manufacturer a 50% sales increase wherever we step in," boasts Bob Gould, the president of Space Control Corp. "The only reason I don't is that people tend not to take you seriously when you guarantee something for nothing. It gives them less incentive to cooperate with our service people.

Gould adds that firms like his have as much beneficial impact on a manufacturer's sales force as they do on retail inventories. "With the cost of each sales call going up," he says, "manufacturers can't afford to have highly paid salesmen straightening shelves and checking inventory at each store. Our people free up the salesman so he can concentrate on selling where it counts. Look at Procter and Gamble with something like 2,000 salesmen all involved in rack servicing. Companies like Colgate-Palmolive keep up with P & G with only 200 men. Why? Because they're leaving more and more of the routine shelf service to us."

Although specialized in-store servicing has deep roots in the grocery business, it is relatively new to discounters, department stores, and durable goods merchandisers. The oldest (at 14 years) and largest is Inventory Control Co. (ICC), Paramus, N.J., which claims a nationwide field force of about 1,400. "The basic idea is simple," says president Gus Eben. "By representing several manufacturers, it costs us a fraction of what the individual company would pay to have one of its own salesmen visit any one store."

Much like its three top competitors, ICC relies on a seemingly inexhaustable supply of part-time housewives (buttressed lately by several retired men) backed up by full-time regional supervisors. Each part-timer works from 20 to 25 hours a week and usually has a set schedule of a dozen or so neighborhood stores to visit in a month-long servicing cycle.

In a typical store visit, ICC's service lady checks in with the manager, signs a logbook, and leaves her purse with a security officer. She first straightens the display area for her client's products, arranging each according to a plan dictated by chain headquarters. "This explains why we can serve competing manufacturers," says Eben. "We simply carry out whatever arrangement the chain and its supplier salesman have agreed on. If her order says Brand X gets three facings in the top shelf, thats what it gets."

Next step: a trip to the back room to count each client's inventory and pricing out replenishments for the front display. After that, all inventory on hand is matched against the optimum amount set in advance by the chain headquarters. The difference is written up as a purchase order and sent direct to the manufacturer or chain headquarters.

"Again, we have nothing to do with selling or setting the amount of the reorder," says Eben. "There's no conflict with the store manager because our people have no reason to sell him something he doesn't need."

Whether that's always true is considered debatable by some retailers and even among the in-store servicers. While the top four companies receive flat fees for individual store visits, all but ICC have some kind of percentage-of-sale commission arrangements with manufacturers. "Too much of that has already put one company (Products Services Co.) out of business," says one sales manager. "They had a bunch of men working on commission, and their manufacturers soon found that the men were servicing the big volume retailers and forgetting all about the little guys."

But Space Control's Bob Gould sees it differently. "We're willing to take the risk because we believe so much in what we can do," he says. "We'll go in and calculate the chain's gross business with our client in the previous year. We'll start from there and take a commission (usually 5%) on anything above that."

Conflict of interest is also a debating point whenever manufacturer's reps and wholesalers get involved in store servicing. ICC, Space Control, and American In-Store contend that rep organizations can't cover all stores in a national chain, seldom follow a manufacturer's servicing schedule, and give low-volume (low-commission) outlets short-shrift. "And no rep," says one, "would dream of giving another rep a competing line to service. Who wants to have the other guy look at his sales records—or worse yet, to run the risk of having his product crammed somewhere on the top shelf?

Actually, such talk aims not so much at service-minded local reps as at Custom Marketing, Inc. (CMI), the newest competitor in the in-store servicing field. CMI's founder-president is Stan Clark, a Cincinnati-based manufacturer's rep. Three years ago, Clark found himself hastily forming a servicing subsidiary after two regional retail chains suggested that he supply total inventory control if he wanted to keep their business. Although the new subsidiary plugged the gap, Clark soon found his chain store customers expanding far beyond his traditional selling area. "The stores wanted chain-wide servicing, and it was obvious that I needed national coverage," he told *Sales Management.*

NO CONFLICTS

His brainchild: a network of rep-controlled servicing subsidiaries covering every major U.S. market. Eight months ago Clark made a deal with 15 regional manufacturer's reps (some of whom already had inventory control subsidiaries) to develop 15 franchised inventory control companies—each capitalized by a regional rep but clustered under the CMI umbrella. Today, CMI claims a field force of 200 and projects a total of 500 by year-end.

"That talk about conflict of interest is propaganda," says Ed Bobrow, of Bobrow/Lewell Associates, CMI's franchisee in the New York City market. "Our subsidiary, for example, is run totally apart from our sales business and services many lines we don't sell. And there's certainly nothing wrong with getting a contract to service one of your own sales lines. Retailers like to see us doing both sales and inventory control because they can really get on our backs if we mess up."

Obviously, as Space Control's Gould says, "in-store servicing still hasn't found its final form." His own company has begun one-shot servicing on test marketed and seasonal products. Example: putting up a Wilkinson Sword shaving display last Christmas at 5,000 outlets in 30 markets. In September 1970, Space Control sparked an even more significant trend when it became the "authorized service agency" in the housewares sections of 70 Topps department stores. Technically, it meant only that by recommending Space Control to manufacturers, Topps could avoid having dozens of shelf servicers scurrying about. That, however, seemed to be all the nudging needed for 30 of the chain's 33 houseware suppliers to sign up with Space Control. ICC has taken a slightly different step in the same direction. It has just signed a pact to provide all in-store servicing for J. C. Penney stores, with the chain—not manufacturers—paying the fee.

Just how far and fast independent servicing firms will penetrate the retail market touches off another sharp debate. On one side, some marketing experts argue that when any one retailer can lay off thousands of inventory control dollars on an outside source, others will have to follow.

Less inclined to join any stampede are men like Gilbert Fox, vice president of Kuhn's Big K Stores in Nashville. "We'd never go to outside 'detailing' completely," he says. "I see it useful mainly where the manufacturer has a product involving lots of sizes, colors, and SKUs (stock keeping units) to contend with."

"We're not running after service organizations," adds Larry Cane, national sales manager of the Lustra Tile Corp., Elmsford, N.Y. While acknowledging a "marked sales improvement" when they've been employed, Cane does so "only when pressured by an individual retail account." One reason: "Many established chains like Sears already have very good stockkeeping. It's primarily the discounters and their personnel problems that have given rise to the service organizations," he says.

But Space Control's Gould thinks the idea is just too strong for most retailers to resist. "Special promotions and loss leaders account for too much of the sales dollar," he says. "One reason is that the high profit, basic items aren't available when the customer walks in. Store managers are under such pressure to cut costs that there aren't enough people to reorder properly. Companies like ours are a way out of the dilemma. And once we've had enough time for the concept to be fully understood, you'll see very few retailers without it."

PONDERING SOME QUESTIONS

If so, retailers and manufacturers could find themselves with some nagging questions to ponder. Examples:

If chains insist on a manufacturer's use of outside servicing, what will be the impact on smaller sellers? Can they absorb the added cost of inventory control? Or will the "bigs" absorb it—and them.

Who will ultimately pay for the cost of servicing and how will it alter the consumer demand for various products? "There is just so much money available for this thing," observes Lustra Tile's Larry Crane. "After awhile you get increased pressures for higher servicing fees. Pretty soon you have to raise prices to the consumer. Yet, every product has its maximum price beyond which you get sluggish movement, Manufacturers will have their breaking point, and beyond that something has to give."

If retail chains do indeed flock to outside servicing, how soon will it be before they'll take it over? Says one sales manager: "One chain has already begun insisting that all manufacturers route their payments to us through its headquarters.

Interstate Department Stores is going one better by creating Store Services, Inc., a subsidiary that will in a spokesman's words, "bid competitively for inventory control business—whether it's in our own stores or others." One of it's first moves was to take over most of the servicing at Interstate's own White Front stores on the West Coast.

Through these clouds, the inventory servicers see patches of blue. Says Brearley's Don Levine: "This may not be the end-all. But until something better comes along, this is the hottest thing going in retailing."

QUESTIONS FOR DISCUSSION

1. Why would a manufacturer prefer to have detailing done by a company specializing in this work as opposed to having company salespersons perform this function?

2. Why might some retailers not like either the manufacturer or their agent performing the detailing activities?

3. Which type of retailers probably are most anxious to have their stores detailed by someone other than their own employees?

4. Do you believe this concept will be long-lived? Defend your answer.

11.7 BIGGER SLICE OF THE PIE: INDEPENDENT GROCERS (AND THEIR SUPPLIERS) CARVE ONE

Carol Kurtis

". . . Retailers have become increasingly reluctant to shell out the $3 million to $10 million needed to build or upgrade warehouses, capital for which might otherwise go to finance the new 'super' stores now in vogue."

Last year, the giant A&P supermarket chain decided to phase out some of its own supply operations and hand over to a quartet of voluntary food wholesalers the job of stocking the shelves at about 400 of its 2,200 stores. Reason, says A&P, is simple: The four can supply its supermarkets "cheaper than we can ourselves." Among the chosen jobbers: Super Valu Stores, Super Food Services, S.M. Flickinger and Fleming Cos.

Nor is this opening-up of the retail chain market to the voluntary wholesaler—which in the past mainly supplied independents and institutions—an isolated A&P phenomenon. On a number of counts other supermarket chains also are finding it cheaper to buy than to stock and distribute. For one thing, the expense of operating a warehouse distribution system in areas where a chain has closed down a number of stores is burdensome; the remaining outlets are too far from each other and typically generate too low a volume to justify such a system. Also, retailers have become increasingly reluctant to shell out the $3 million to $10 million needed to build or up-grade warehouses, capital for which might otherwise go to finance the new "super" stores now in vogue.

OPPORTUNITIES KNOCK

The voluntary wholesalers also are cashing in on a related trend. Many large chains, once the nemesis of the independent grocers, have been

Reprinted by permission from Carol Kurtis, "Bigger Slice of the Pie: Independent Grocers (and Their Suppliers) Carve One," *Barron's* (March 29, 1976), pp. 11ff.

closing their smaller and marginal operations nation-wide, particularly in rural areas. (A&P, for one, has shuttered 1,400 stores.) And a number of these units are being picked up by independent owners—the voluntary wholesalers' traditional customers. Outlets supplied by Fleming, for example, took over leases on 23 stores formerly operated by chains last year. Joseph R. Hyde, president of Malone & Hyde, third largest of the publicly-held "voluntaries," sees opportunities "for a whole new generation of store owners who do not have the capital to build a new unit." And he forecasts that many rural towns will soon be free of chain competition. A larger number of independent stores doing a bigger volume means more money in the till for the wholesalers.

Not only do the "voluntaries" supply their customers (as noted, primarily independents and institutions) with food products (and to a lesser degree non-food items) but they also offer a wide range of sophisticated services. These include computerized accounting and bookkeeping, financing, site selection and acquisition, store engineering, management training and field supervision. Too, many wholesalers prepare and place ads, provide private label lines and offer common logos which endow independents with the aura usually associated with a larger chain. Aided by these imaginative and aggressive jobbers, the independent food stores have been able to compete successfully with their giant rivals.

Indeed, the nation's 12,740 independents have done so well, according to *Progressive Grocer* magazine, that in 1975 they rang up greater volume than the 18,980 chain outlets. In 1975 total sales of the independents reached $70.3 billion, compared to the $66.75 billion worth of food and non-food items checked out of chain stores. And while the latter closed 710 markets last year, the independents added 990.

BIGGER PIE

Comments Edgar B. Walzer, president of *Progressive Grocer*: "It is clear that fast-moving owner-managers coped very well with the economic ups and downs last year. In a broad sense you might say that the boxers outpointed the sluggers."

As the independents have grown and prospered, so have their suppliers. The world's largest food wholesaler, Super Valu, to illustrate, rang up sales of $1.64 billion in fiscal '75. But its "family" of affiliated stores generated a volume of $2.85 billion, making them the fourth largest retail food group in the U.S. behind such goliaths as Safeway, A&P and Kroger. Super Valu, itself, has enjoyed rapid growth. Compounded annually, sales have climbed 15% and per-share profits 18% a year over the past half decade. By 1977, the wholesaler says it will be a $2 billion company.

Another consequence of the swift rise of independent grocers has been a move toward consolidation in the wholesale sector of the field. For the large independent retailer requires a greater variety of services which the smaller wholesalers are increasingly hard pressed to provide in competition with their larger counterparts. Today, roughly 330 voluntary wholesalers in the U.S. compare to 410 in operation three years ago. All signs point to continued decline in the number of wholesalers. (It goes without saying that the survivors will share larger slices of a bigger pie.)

The current roster of voluntaries also includes Scot Lad Foods, Wetterau, Pacific Gamble Robinson, Serivner, Godfrey Co., Schultz Sav-O-Stores and Bozzuto's. Because of their unique position in the long food delivery chain, wholesalers fared relatively well in the recent inflationary environment, thanks largely to an ability to pass on higher costs to their customers. In 1975, when the Consumer Price Index for food at home rose by 8.2%, 87% of the wholesalers registered higher sales, but 78% improved their margins and 64% boosted profits.

Fleming, Pacific Gamble, Godfrey and Schultz Sav-O-Stores all scored strong earnings gains in 1975. Fleming netted $1.90 a share vs. $1.65; Pacific Gamble, $3.94 vs. $3.09; Godfrey $3.05 vs. $2.71 and Schultz, $$1.70 a share vs. 55 cents. Similarly, Super Valu enjoyed a 23.3% jump in fiscal '76 ending February 28, to $3.55 from $2.88 in fiscal 1975. Malone & Hyde earned 90 cents a share in its first half (December), compared to 81 cents in the like year-earlier span. Scrivner nearly doubled its profits in the same stretch, earning $1.35 a share vs. 74 cents.

Meanwhile, at Flickinger, profits rose to 96 cents a share in the first half ended January, from 80 cents in the same six months the previous year, to $1.37 a share from $1.22, and Bozzuto's earned 30 cents in its first quarter (December) vs. 28 cents in the first '74 quarter.

The exceptions that proved the rule among the jobbers: Scot Lad and Super Food. The former suffered a sharp drop in its September quarter, to 20 cents from 40 cents in the year-earlier quarter. And even worse, in its December quarter, to 16 cents a share, from 57 cents. Scot Lad blames a profit squeeze in some of its retail store operations (mainly in the form of a supermarket price war in the Chicago area) and a poor performance by its food processing division. Unlike the other wholesalers mentioned here, Scot Lad derives a significant portion of its earnings from food processing—an industry currently in an oversupply cycle. Says President Walter R. Schaub: "There is a tremendous oversupply of canned vegetables." He worries about what to do with "several million cans of corn," but sees excessive inventories easing in '77.

Super Food's net also softened in the first six months of fiscal 1976 ended February 15—to 65 cents, from 77 cents. And a spokesman says that the comparisons reflect the fact that fiscal '75 profits were unusually high due to inflation in food prices.

For most food wholesalers, though, the trend is unmistakably up. Real gains in unit sales are in the making this year as tonnage is running about 6% ahead of last year. In 1975, roughly half of the gain in volume came from higher unit sales. All told, industry revenues last year, according to Progressive Grocer, rose 15% to $24 billion. This year looks 10%-13% higher.

Besides greater tonnage, margins in the trade are benefitting from a tougher attitude toward slow-moving items. Super Valu's Joseph Slovick explains: "There must be 48 different varieties of pizza, for example, and some just don't move fast. When you have too many lines you also have losers." Weeding out the "losers"—both food and non-food items —should help improve the profits this year. So, too, will a greater stress on faster turnover.

For the year as a whole most of the jobbers are apt to show record profits. Fleming could earn $2.20 a share this year vs. $1.90; Super Valu, about $3.50 vs. $2.88; Malone & Hyde, $2.10 vs. $1.83; Wetterau, $1.70 vs. $1.58.

Although they've had their whirl in the past, the wholesale grocers— despite the rosy forecasts—are not setting any worlds afire in the Street. One drawback (particularly for institutions) is that few companies have floats much above the one million mark. Too, the industry is not a board-room word, and the companies suffer by being lumped in with the food retailers. Sentiment also was chilled by some ill-fated diversification moves in the late 'Sixties.

On the last score, though, a few wholesalers have branched out successfully; Super Valu, for example, into a chain of 80 County Seat Stores Inc., chock full of Levi Strauss casual apparel and Adidas sport shoes. About 60 more County Seat outlets are scheduled to open this year. At the same time, the company is divesting itself of its Deytex retail fabric stores; this division lost about $12 million last year.

Malone & Hyde also has a successful new, non-food operation: Super D Drugs, a chain of 36 company-owned and 25 franchised discount drug stores. The current blueprint is to stabilize the number of company stores but expand the franchised group.

While reassessing non-food operations and phasing out some retail stores, the jobbers are expanding their customer networks and ware-housing facilities. Watterau expects to add 25 new stores as customers this year; Malone & Hyde, 120 new outlets; Scrivner, 12 new super-markets. Fleming, which launched a new warehouse distribution center in San Antonio last year, is opening two more this year—one in Philadelphia, the other in Oklahoma City. Super Food has targeted a new facility in Florida and, with Skaggs and Albertson, will build super retail centers in the Sunshine State.

THE WHOLESALERS' FINANCES

	Period	*Sales in millions* 1975	1974	*Earned Per Share* 1975	1974	*Annual Divid.*	*Approximate Price*
Bozzuto's	3 mos. Dec.	$ 26.5	$ 20.8	$0.30	$0.28	$0.40	6¾
Fleming Cos.	Year Dec.	1,566.0	1,293.0	1.90	1.65	0.80	15¼
Flickinger	6 mos. Jan. (a)	302.6	251.4	0.96	0.80	0.40	13¼
Godfrey Co.	Year Dec.	236.6	207.8	3.05	2.71	0.90	16¾
Malone & Hyde	6 mos. Dec.	459.0	401.7	0.90	0.81	0.56	24¾
Pacific Gamble Robinson	Year Dec.	518.3	481.5	3.94	3.09	1.36	25¾
Schultz Sav-O-Stores	Year Dec.	153.9	130.5	1.70	0.55	0.40	7½
Scot Lad Foods	6 mos. Dec.	377.2	387.2	0.37	0.99	0.36	6½
Scrivner	6 mos. Dec.	193.2	168.9	1.35	0.74	0.50	14¾
Super Food Services	6 mos. Feb. (a)	215.9	185.2	0.65	0.77	0.32	9⅛
Super Valu Stores	Year Feb. (a)	1,820.0	1,642.0	E3.55	2.88	1.10	29½
Wetterau	9 mos. Dec.	601.8	539.1	1.37	1.22	0.60	15¾

a–Of the following years. E–Estimated.

QUESTIONS FOR DISCUSSION

1. Explain the chief reasons for the growth record of the grocery voluntary wholesalers.

2. What services do the voluntary wholesalers often supply to their customers?

3. Do you believe the recent high rates of growth for the grocery voluntary chains can be sustained? Defend your answer.

Bibliography

BOOKS

ADDISON, WILLIAM. *English Fairs and Markets*. B. T. Batsford Ltd., 1953.

ALDERSON, WROE. *Dynamic Marketing Behavior*. Richard D. Irwin, 1965.

ALDERSON, WROE. *Marketing Behavior and Executive Action*. Richard D. Irwin, 1957.

ANDERSON, R. CLIFTON, and William P. Dommermuth, eds. *Distribution Systems: Firms, Functions and Efficiencies*. Appleton-Century-Crofts, 1972.

BALIGH, HEMLY H., and Leon E. Richartz. *Vertical Market Structures*. Allyn and Bacon, Inc., 1967.

BARGER, HAROLD. *Distribution's Place in the American Economy Since 1869*. Princeton University Press, 1955.

BARTELS, ROBERT, ed. *Comparative Marketing: Wholesaling in Fifteen Countries*. Richard D. Irwin, 1963.

BOHANNAN, PAUL, ed. *Markets in Africa*. Northwestern University Press, 1962.

BREYER, RALPH F. *Commodity Marketing*. McGraw-Hill Book Company, 1931.

BRION, JOHN M. *Marketing through the Wholesaler/Distributor Channel*. American Marketing Association, 1965.

BUCKLIN, LOUIS P. *A Theory of Distribution Channel Structure*. Graduate School of Business Administration, University of California, Berkeley, 1966.

BUCKLIN, LOUIS P. *Competition and Evolution in the Distributive Trades*. Prentice-Hall, Inc., 1972.

BUCKLIN, LOUIS P., ed. *Vertical Marketing Systems*. Scott, Foresman, and Co., 1970.

BUZZELL, ROBERT D. *Value Added by Industrial Distributors*. Bureau of Business Research, Ohio State University, Columbus, 1959.

CAPLOVITZ, DAVID. *The Poor Pay More*. The Free Press of Glencoe, 1963.

CARPENTER, HORACE. *Shopping Center Management*. International Council of Shopping Centers, 1974.

CASSADY, RALPH, JR., and Wylie L. Jones. *The Changing Competitive Structure in the Wholesale Grocery Trade*. University of California Press, Berkeley, 1949.

CLEWETT, RICHARD M., ed. *Marketing Channels for Manufactured Products*. Richard D. Irwin, 1954.

COLE, ROBERT. *Vertical Integration in Marketing*. College of Commerce and Business Administration, University of Illinois, Urbana, 1952.

COX, REAVIS, Charles Goodman, and Thomas Fichandler. *Distribution in a High-level Economy.* Prentice-Hall, Inc., 1965.

DALRYMPLE, DOUGLAS J., and Donald L. Thompson. *Retailing: An Economic View.* The Free Press, 1969.

DAVIDSON, WILLIAM R., and Alton F. Doody. *Retailing Management,* 3rd ed. The Ronald Press Co., 1966.

DIAMOND, WILLIAM M. *Distribution Channels for Industrial Goods.* Bureau of Business Research, Ohio State University, Columbus, 1964.

DICKINSON, ROGER A. *Retail Management: A Channels Approach.* Wadsworth Company, Inc., 1974.

DUDDY, EDWARD A., and David A. Revzan. *Marketing: An Institutional Approach.* McGraw-Hill Book Company, 1953.

DUNCAN, DELBERT J., Charles F. Phillips, and Stanley C. Hollander. *Modern Retailing Management: Basic Concepts and Practices,* 8th ed. Richard D. Irwin, Inc., 1972.

FISK, GEORGE. *Marketing Systems: An Introductory Analysis.* Harper & Row, 1967.

GIST, RONALD R., ed. *Management Perspectives in Retailing,* 2nd ed. John Wiley and Sons, Inc., 1971.

GIST, RONALD R. *Retailing: Concepts and Decisions.* John Wiley and Sons, Inc., 1968.

GOLDMAN, MARSHALL I. *Soviet Marketing: Distribution in a Controlled Economy.* The Free Press, The Macmillan Company, 1963.

HALL, MARGARET, John Knapp, and Christopher Winston. *Distribution in Great Britain and North America.* Oxford University Press, 1962.

HARTLEY, ROBERT F. *Retailing: Challenge and Opportunity.* Houghton Mifflin Company, 1975.

HAWKINS, H. C. G. *Wholesale and Retail Trade in Tanganyika.* F. A. Praeger, 1965.

HILL, RICHARD M. *Wholesaling Management: Text and Cases.* Richard D. Irwin, 1963.

HOLDREN, BOB R. *The Structure of a Retail Market and the Market Behavior of Retail Units.* Prentice-Hall, Inc., 1960.

HOLLANDER, STANLEY. *Explorations in Retailing.* Bureau of Business and Economic Research, Michigan State University, East Lansing, 1959.

JAMES, DON L., Bruce J. Walker, and Michael J. Etzel. *Retailing Today.* Harcourt Brace Jovanovich, Inc., 1975.

JEFFERYS, JAMES B. *The Distribution of Consumer Goods.* Cambridge University Press, 1950.

LARSON, CARL M., Robert E. Weigand, and John S. Wright. *Basic Retailing.* Prentice-Hall, Inc., 1976.

LEBHAR, GODFREY M. *Chain Stores in America, 1859–1950.* Chain Store Publishing Corporation, 1952.

LEWIS, EDWIN H. *Marketing Channels: Structure and Strategy.* McGraw-Hill Book Company, 1968.

LEWIS, EDWIN H., and Robert S. Hancock. *The Franchise System of Distribution.* University of Minnesota, Minneapolis, 1963.

McNAIR, MALCOLM, and Mira Berman, eds. *Marketing Through Retailers.* American Management Association, 1967.

McNAIR, MALCOLM P., and Eleanor G. May. *The American Department Store*

(*1920–1960*). Graduate School of Business Administration, Harvard University, 1963.

MAGEE, JOHN F. *Physical Distribution Systems.* McGraw-Hill Book Company, 1967.

MALLEN, BRUCE, ed. *The Marketing Channel: A Conceptual Viewpoint.* John Wiley & Sons, Inc., 1967.

MARKIN, ROM J., JR., ed. *Retailing: Concepts, Institutions, and Management.* The Macmillan Co., 1971.

MARQUARDT, RAYMOND A., James C. Makens, and Robert G. Roe. *Retail Management: Satisfaction of Consumer Needs.* The Dryden Press, 1975.

MICHMAN, RONALD D. *Marketing Channels.* Grid, Inc., 1974.

MOLLER, WILLIAM G., JR., and David L. Wilemon, eds. *Marketing Channels: A Systems Viewpoint.* Richard D. Irwin, Inc., 1971.

PALAMOUNTAIN, JOSEPH CORNWALL, JR. *The Politics of Distribution.* Harvard University Press, 1955.

PINTEL, GERALD, and Jay Diamond. *Retailing.* Prentice-Hall, Inc., 1971.

RACHMAN, DAVID J. *Retail Strategy and Structure: A Management Approach.* Prentice-Hall, Inc., 1969.

RACHMAN, DAVID J., ed. *Retailing Management Strategy: Selected Readings.* Prentice-Hall, Inc., 1970.

REVZAN, DAVID S. *Wholesaling in Marketing Organization.* John Wiley & Sons, Inc., 1961.

RYANS, JOHN K., JR., James H. Donnelly, Jr., and John M. Ivancevich, eds. *New Dimensions in Retailing: A Decision Oriented Approach,* Wadsworth Publishing Co., 1970.

SOMMERS, MONTROSE S. and Jerome B. Kernan. *Comparative Marketing Systems.* Appleton-Century-Crofts, 1960.

STERN, LOUIS W., ed. *Distribution Channels: Behavioral Dimensions.* Houghton Mifflin Co., 1969.

STURDIVANT, FREDERICK S., ed. *The Ghetto Marketplace.* The Free Press of Glencoe, 1963.

THORPE, DAVID. *Research into Retailing and Distribution.* D. C. Heath, 1974.

VAUGHN, CHARLES L. *Franchising: Its Nature, Scope, Advantages, and Development.* D. C. Heath, 1974.

WALKER, BRUCE J. and Joel B. Haynes, eds. *Marketing Channels and Institutions: Readings in Distribution Concepts and Practices.* Grid, Inc., 1973.

WALTERS, C. GLENN. *Marketing Channels.* The Ronald Press Co., 1974.

WARSHAW, MARTIN R. *Effective Selling through Wholesalers.* Bureau of Business Research, University of Michigan, Ann Arbor, 1961.

ARTICLES

"A Changing Pattern for the Franchise Boom." *U.S. News and World Report,* April 24, 1972, pp. 88–89.

ADAMS, KENDALL A. "Achieving Market Organization Through Voluntary and Cooperative Groups." *Journal of Retailing,* Summer 1966, pp. 19–28.

ALDERSON, WROE. "Administered Prices and Retail Grocery Advertising." *Journal of Advertising Research,* March 1963, pp. 2–6.

ALDERSON, WROE. "Factors Governing the Development of Marketing Channels." Richard M. Clewett, ed. *Marketing Channels for Manufactured Products*, Richard D. Irwin, Inc., 1954.

ALDERSON, WROE. "Scope and Place of Wholesaling in the United States." *Journal of Marketing*, September 1949, pp. 149–155.

ALDERSON, WROE, and Miles W. Martin. "Towards a Formal Theory of Transactions and Transvections." *Journal of Marketing Research*, May 1965, pp. 117–127.

ALLVINE, FRED C. "The Supermarket Challenged." *Business Horizons*, October 1968, pp. 61–72.

ANDERSON, R. CLIFTON. "Gasoline Retailing: Self-Service Holdout." *Journal of Retailing*, Fall 1965, pp. 42–45, 56.

ANDERSON, W. THOMAS, JR., and Louis K. Sharpe. "The New Marketplace: Life Style in Revolution." *Business Horizons*, August 1971, pp. 43–50.

APPEL, DAVID L. "Market Segmentation—A Response to Retail Innovation." *Journal of Marketing*, April 1970, pp. 64–67.

APPEL, DAVID. "The Supermarket: Early Development of an Institutional Innovation." *Journal of Retailing*, Spring 1972, pp. 39–53.

APPLEBAUM, WILLIAM. "Management Responsibilities Facing the Wholesale Grocer." *Journal of Marketing*, July 1964, pp. 68–73.

APPLEBAUM, WILLIAM. "Methods of Determining Store Areas, Market Penetration and Potential Sales." *Journal of Marketing Research*, May 1966, pp. 127–141.

ARNDT, JOHAN. "Temporal Lags in Comparative Retailing." *Journal of Marketing*, October 1972, pp. 40–45.

BALIGH, HELMY W., and Leon E. Richartz. "An Analysis of Vertical Marketing Structures." *Management Science*, July 1964, pp. 667–689.

BECKMAN, THEODORE N. "Changes in Wholesaling Structure and Performance." Peter D. Bennett, ed. *Marketing and Economic Development*. Proceedings of the Fall Conference of the American Marketing Association, September 1965.

BEEN, EUGENE R. "Retailing in the 1980's." *Marketing Instights*, November 18, 1968, pp. 10–12.

BENDER, WESLEY C. "Consumer Purchase Costs—Do Retailers Recognize Them?" *Journal of Retailing*, Spring 1964, pp. 1–8ff.

BENNETT, PETER D. "Retailing Evolution or Revolution in Chile?" *Journal of Marketing*, July 1966, pp. 38–41.

BERENS, JOHN S. "A Decision Matrix Approach to Supplier Selection." *Journal of Retailing*, Winter 1971–72, pp. 47–53.

BERG, THOMAS L. "Designing the Distribution System," William D. Stevens, ed. *The Social Responsibilitities of Marketing*. American Marketing Association, 1962.

BERRY, LEONARD L. "Is It Time to Be Wary About Franchising?" *Arizona Business Bulletin*, October 1970, pp. 3–9.

BESSOM, RICHARD M., and Donald W. Jackson, Jr. "Service Retailing: A Strategic Marketing Approach." *Journal of Retailing*, Summer 1975, pp. 75–84.

BINGHAM, WHEELOCK H., and David L. Yunich. "Retail Reorganization." *Harvard Business Review*, July–August 1965, pp. 136ff.

BIRD, MONROE MURPHY. "Reverse Reciprocity: A New Twist to Industrial Buying Behavior." *Atlanta Economic Review*, January–February 1976.

BIRD, MONROE M., Edward R. Clayton, and Laurence J. Moore. "Industrial

Buying: A Method of Planning for Contract Negotiations." *Journal of Economics and Business*, Spring 1974, pp. 209–213.

BISHOP, WILLARD R., JR. "New Approaches to Improving Social Productivity in Food Distribution." In *1974 Combined Proceedings*. American Marketing Association, 1975, pp. 299–303.

BLOCK, CARL E., Robert Schooler, and David Erickson. "Consumer Reaction to Unit Pricing: An Empirical Study." *Mississippi Valley Journal of Business and Economics*, Winter 1971–72, pp. 36–46.

BOGART, LEO. "The Future of Retailing." *Harvard Business Review*, November–December 1973, pp. 16–32.

BOONE, LOUIS E., David L. Kurtz, James C. Johnson, and John A. Bonno. "'City Shoppers and Urban Identification' Revisited." *Journal of Marketing*, July 1974, pp. 67–69.

BOYD, HARPER W., JR., and Ivan Piercy. "Retailing in Great Britain." *Journal of Marketing*, January 1963, pp. 29–35.

BRANCH, BEN S. "Returnable vs. Nonreturnable Beverage Containers: An Evaluation in the Light of Recent Experience." *Atlanta Economic Review*, May–June 1976, pp. 28–34.

BREITENBACH, ROBERT B., and B. Curtis Hamm, "The Implications of Consumer Expectations on Logistical Costs and Channel Conflicts." *Southern Journal of Business*, April 1969, pp. 211–216.

BRIDGES, S. POWELL. "The Schwinn Case: A Landmark Decision." *Business Horizons*, August 1968, pp. 77–85.

BROWN, F. E., and A. R. Oxenfeldt. "Should Prices Depend on Costs?" *MSU Business* Topics, Autumn 1968, pp. 73–77.

BRUCE, GRADY D. "The Ecological Structure of Retail Institutions." *Journal of Marketing Research*, February 1969, pp. 48–53.

BUCKLIN, LOUIS P. "A Theory of Channel Control." *Journal of Marketing*, January 1973, pp. 39–47.

BUCKLIN, LOUIS P. "Competitive Impact of a New Supermarket." *Journal of Marketing Research*, November 1967, pp. 356–361.

BUCKLIN, LOUIS P. "Marketing Channels and Structures: A Macro View." *Proceedings of the 1972 Fall Conference of the American Marketing Association*. American Marketing Association, 1973.

BUCKLIN, LOUIS P. "Merchandising in Department Store Chains." *California Management Review*, Summer 1964, pp. 41–46.

BUCKLIN, LOUIS P. "Postponement, Speculation, and the Structure of Distribution Channels." *Journal of Marketing Research*, February 1965, pp. 26–31.

BUCKLIN, LOUIS P. "Retail Strategy and the Classification of Consumer Goods." *Journal of Marketing*, January 1963, pp. 50–58.

BUSH, RONALD F., Ronald L. Tatham, and Joseph F. Hair, Jr. "Community Location Decisions by Franchisors: A Comparative Analysis." *Journal of Retailing*, Fall 1974, pp. 13–22, 75.

CADY, JOHN F. "Restrictions on Advertising and the Retail Price of Drugs." *Arizona Review*, November 1975, pp. 1–4.

CAIRNS, JAMES P. "Suppliers, Retailers, and Shelf Space." *Journal of Marketing*, July 1962, pp. 34–36.

CARSON, DAVID. "Marketing in Italy Today." *Journal of Marketing*, January 1966, pp. 10–16.

CARUSONE, PETER S. "Institutional Change and Adaptive Behavior in Small-City Retailing." *Marquette Business Review*, Summer 1974, pp. 49–60.

CARUSONE, PETER S. "The Growing Strength of Small-City Retailing." *Journal of Retailing*, Winter 1970–71, pp. 50–57, 76.

CASSADY, RALPH, JR. "The Price Skirmish—A Distinctive Pattern of Competitive Behavior." *California Management Review*, Winter 1964, pp. 11–16.

"Cheaper Ways to Reach the Customer." *Business Week*, September 9, 1972, pp. 120–124.

CHEVALIER, MICHEL, and Ronald C. Curhan, "Temporary Promotions as a Function of Trade Deals: A Descriptive Analysis." *Marketing Science Institute Working Paper*, May 1975.

CHRISTIAN, RICHARD C. "Industrial Marketing: Three Step Method to Better Distribution Channel Analysis." *Journal of Marketing*, October 1958, pp. 191–192.

CLAWSON, C. JOSEPH. "Fitting Branch Locations, Performance Standards, and Marketing Strategies to Local Conditions." *Journal of Marketing*, January 1974, pp. 8–14.

CONVERSE, PAUL D. "Twenty-five Years of Wholesaling: A Revolution in Food Wholesaling." *Journal of Marketing*, July 1957, pp. 40–53.

COOPER, M. BIXBY. "Shopping Center Lease Agreements: Participants and Perceptions of Selected Operating Policies." Henry W. Nash and Donald P. Robin, eds. *Proceedings of the Southern Marketing Association*, Mississippi State University, 1976, pp. 117–119.

COOPER, PHILIP D. "Will Success Produce Problems For the Convenience Store? *MSU Business Topics*, Winter 1972, pp. 39–43.

COPELAND, MELVIN T. "Relation of Consumers' Buying Habits to Marketing Methods." *Harvard Business Review*, April 1923, pp. 282–289.

COURTNEY, PAUL L. "The Wholesaler as a Link in the Distribution Channel." *Business Horizons*, February 1961, pp. 90–95.

COX, ELI P. "The Decline of Metropolitan Retailing." *MSU Business Topics*, Spring 1961, pp. 34–43.

COX, KEITH K. "The Role of Experimentation in the Information System of a Retailer." L. George Smith, ed. *Reflections on Progress in Marketing*, American Marketing Association 1965.

COX, KEITH K., James E. Stafford, James B. Higginbotham. "Negro Retail Shopping and Credit Behavior." *Journal of Retailing*, Spring 1972, pp. 54–66.

COX, REAVIS, and C. W. Goodman. "Marketing of Housebuilding Materials." *Journal of Marketing*, July 1956.

COX, REAVIS, and Thomas F. Schutte. "A Look at Channel Management." Philip R. McDonald, ed. *Marketing Involvement in Society and the Economy*, American Marketing Association, 1970.

COYLE, "Inside the World's Largest Wholesaler." *Progressive Grocer*, September 1975, pp. 62–67ff.

"Critics Rail, But Supermarkets Ask: Why Us?" *Business Week*, April 22, 1972, pp. 97–98.

CUNDIFF, EDWARD W. "Concepts in Comparative Retailing." *Journal of Marketing*, Januray 1965, pp. 59–63.

CUNNINGHAM, ISABELLA C. M., William H. Cunningham, and Russell M. Moore. "Food Retailing in Sao Paulo, Brazil." Henry W. Nash and Donald

P. Robin, eds. *Proceedings of the Southern Marketing Association*, Mississippi State University, 1976, pp. 133–135.

CURHAN, RONALD C. "The Relationship Between Shelf Space and Unit Sales in Supermarkets." *Journal of Marketing Research*, November 1972, pp. 406–412.

DALRYMPLE, DOUGLAS J. "Controlling Retail Inventories." *Journal of Retailing*, Spring 1964, pp. 9–14, 51–52.

DALRYMPLE, DOUGLAS J. "Will Automatic Vending Topple Retail Precedents?" *Journal of Retailing*, Spring 1963, pp. 36–39.

DARLING, JOHN R. "Capital Investment in the Retail Industry and Cyclical Business Fluctuations, 1948 to 1968." *The Southern Journal of Business*, July 1971, pp. 49–57.

DAVIDSON, WILLIAM R. "Changes in Distributive Institutions: A Reexamination." *The Canadian Marketer*, Winter 1975, pp. 7–13.

DAVIDSON, WILLIAM R., and Alton F. Doody. "The Future of Discounting." *Journal of Marketing*, January 1963, pp. 36–39.

DAVIDSON, WILLIAM R., Alton F. Doody, and James R. Lowry. "Leased Departments as a Major Force in the Growth of Discount Store Retailing." *Journal of Marketing*, January 1970, pp. 39–46.

DICKINSON, ROGER. "Channel Management by Large Retailers." Robert L. King, ed. *Marketing and the New Science of Planning*, American Marketing Association, 1968.

DICKINSON, ROGER. "Markup in Department Store Management." *Journal of Marketing*, January 1967, pp. 32–34.

DICKINSON, ROGER. "The Retail Buyer and the Robinson-Patman Act." *California Management Review*, Spring 1967, pp. 47–54.

"Dividing What's Left of Grant's." *Business Week*, March 1, 1976, p. 21.

DIXON, DONALD F. "Demand Relationships in Marketing Channels." *Mississippi Valley Journal*, Spring 1971, pp. 15–31.

DIXON, DONALD F. "The Impact of Recent Antitrust Decisions upon Franchise Marketing." *MSU Business Topics*, Spring 1969, pp. 68ff.

DIXON, DONALD F. and Daniel J. McLaughlin, Jr. "Low Income Consumers and the Issue of Exploitation: A Study of Chain Supermarkets." *Social Science Quarterly*, September 1970, pp. 320–328.

DOMMERMUTH, WILLIAM P. and R. D. Andersen. "Distribution Systems—Firms, Functions, and Efficiencies." *MSU Business Topics*, Spring 1969, pp. 51ff.

DOODY, ALTON F., JR., and William R. Davidson. "Growing Strength in Small Retailing." *Harvard Business Review*, July–August 1964, pp. 69–79.

DOODY, ALTON F., JR., and W. R. Davidson. "Next Revolution in Retailing." *Harvard Business Review*, June 1967, pp. 4–21.

DORNOFF, RONALD J., and Guy R. Banville. "Attitudes of U.S. Retailers Toward Retailing Opportunities Abroad." *Akron Business and Economic Review*, Summer 1971, pp. 21–26.

DOUGLAS, EDNA. "Size of Firm and Structure of Costs in Retailing." *Journal of Business*, April 1962, pp. 158–190.

DOUGLAS, SUSAN P. "Patterns and Parallels of Marketing Structures in Several Countries." *MSU Business Topics*, Spring 1971, pp. 38–48.

DOWD, LAURENCE P. "Wholesale Marketing in Japan." *Journal of Marketing*, January 1959, pp. 257–262.

DREESMAN, A. C. R. "Patterns of Evolution in Retailing." *Journal of Retailing*, Spring 1968, pp. 64–81.

DUNN, S. WATSON. "French Retailing and the Common Market." *Journal of Marketing*, January 1962, pp. 19–22.

EGAN, DOUGLAS M. "Evaluative Bias, Consumer Attitudes and Department Store Image." *The Southern Journal of Business*, November 1971, pp. 73–81.

EL-ANSARY, ADEL. "A Model for Power-Dependence Relations in the Distribution Channel." Fred C. Allvine, ed. *Combined Proceedings: 1971 Spring and Fall Conferences*, American Marketing Association, 1972.

EL-ANSARY, ADEL I. "A Model for the Interorganization Management of Distribution Channel Systems." *Proceedings of the Southern Marketing Association*, 1973, pp. 368–374.

EL-ANSARY, ADEL I. "Determinants of Power-Dependence in the Distribution Channel." *Journal of Retailing*, Summer 1975, pp. 59–74ff.

EL-ANSARY, ADEL I., and Robert A. Robicheaux. "A Theory of Channel Control Revisited." *Journal of Marketing*, January 1974, pp. 2–7.

ENTENBERG, ROBERT D. "Implications of Interfirm Competition at the Retail Level." *Journal of Retailing*, Summer 1967, pp. 1–8.

ENTENBERG, ROBERT D. "Suggested Changes in Census Classifications of Retail Trade." *Journal of Marketing*, January 1960, pp. 39–43.

"Equal Pay for Women Hits Retailers." *Business Week*, January 29, 1972, pp. 76–78.

"Ethan Allen Breaks With Tradition." *Business Week*, June 10, 1972, pp. 22–23.

ETZEL, MICHAEL J. "How Much Does Credit Cost the Small Merchant?" *Journal of Retailing*, Summer 1971, pp. 52–59.

ETZEL, MICHAEL J., and Don L. James. "Can Government Regulation Replace Marketing Orientation?" *Journal of Retailing*, Winter 1970–71, pp. 14–23.

EWING, JOHN S. "Discount Houses in Australia and Mexico." *Journal of Marketing*, July 1962, pp. 37–41.

EWING, JOHN S., and James Murphy. "Impact of Automation on United States Retail Food Distribution." *Journal of Retailing*, Spring 1965, pp. 38–47.

"Facing the New Future of Retailing." *Chain Store Age Executive*, September 1975, pp. 23–98.

"Fast Food Companies Are Hot Again." *Business Week*, September 30, 1972, pp. 54–55.

FIRAT, FUAT A., Alice M. Tybout, and Louis W. Stern. "A Perspective on Conflict and Power in Distribution," *1974 Combined Proceedings*, American Marketing Association, 1975, pp. 435–439.

FOSTER, J. ROBERT, and F. Kelly Shuptrine. "Using Retailers' Perceptions of Channel Performance to Detect Potential Conflict." Thomas V. Greer, ed. *Increasing Marketing Productivity/Conceptual & Methodological Foundations of Marketing*. American Marketing Association, 1974, pp. 118–123.

FOX, HAROLD W. "Food Retailing Needs a Systems Approach." *Management Adviser*, July–August 1972, pp. 24–32.

FRAM, EUGENE H. "Application of the Marketing Concept to Retailing." *Journal of Retailing*, Summer 1965, pp. 19–26.

"Franchising: Too Much, Too Soon." *Business Week*, June 27, 1970, pp. 54–59.

GAINES, GEORGE H., JR., Leonard S. Simon, and Marcus Alexis. "Maximum Likelihood Estimation of Central-City Food Trading Areas." *Journal of Marketing Research*, May 1972, pp. 154–159.

GANNON, DONALD A. "A Critique of Marketing Planning from the Viewpoint of the Retailer." Frederick E. Webster, Jr., ed. *New Directions in Marketing*. American Marketing Association, 1965.

GIGES, NANCY. "Swiss Bell Ringers No Match for U.S. Direct Marketers." *Advertising Age*, January 11, 1971, pp. 1, 79.

GILLESPIE, KAREN P. "The Role of Espionage in Retailing." *Journal of Retailing*, Spring 1963, pp. 7–12, 48.

GOLDMAN, ARIEH. "Outreach of Consumers and the Modernization of Urban Food Retailing in Developing Countries." *Journal of Marketing*, October 1974, pp. 8–16.

GOLDMAN, ARIEH. "Stages in the Development of the Supermarket." *Journal of Retailing*, Winter 1975–76, pp. 49–64.

GOLDMAN, ARIEH. "The Role of Trading-Up in the Development of the Retailing System." *Journal of Marketing*, January 1975, pp. 54–62.

GOLDMAN, MARSHALL I. "Retailing in the Soviet Union." *Journal of Marketing*, April 1960, pp. 9–15.

GOLDMAN, MARSHALL I. "The Marketing Structure in the Soviet Union." *Journal of Marketing*, July 1961, pp. 7–14.

GOLDSTUCKER, JAC L. "A Systems Framework for Retail Location." Raymond M. Haas, ed. *Science, Technology, and Marketing*. American Marketing Association, 1966.

GOLDSTUCKER, JAC L. "The Influence of Culture on Channels of Distribution." Robert L. King, ed. *Marketing and the New Science of Planning*. American Marketing Association, 1968.

GRANBOIS, DONALD H. "Patterns of Conflicting Perceptions Among Channel Members." L. George Smith, ed. *Reflections on Progress in Marketing*. American Marketing Association, 1965.

GRANZIN, KENT L. "Two-Way Communication in the Marketing Channel: The Case of the Consumer Complaint Letter." Henry W. Nash and Donald P. Robin, eds. *Proceedings of the Southern Marketing Association*. Mississippi State University, 1976, pp. 222–224.

GROSS, ALFRED. "Meeting the Competition of Giants." *Harvard Business Review*, May–June, 1967, pp. 172–184.

GROSS, WALTER. "Profitable Listening for Manufacturers and Dealers." *Business Horizons*, December 1968, pp. 35–44.

GROSSMAN, LOUIS H. "Merchandising Strategies of a Department Store Facing Change." *MSU Business Topics*, Winter 1970, pp. 31–42.

GUERIN, JOSEPH R. "Limitations of Supermarkets in Spain." *Journal of Marketing*, October 1964, pp. 22–26.

GUILTINAN, JAMES, and Nonyelu Nwokoye. "Reverse Channels for Recycling: An Analysis of Alternatives and Public Policy Implications." *1974 Combined Proceedings*. American Marketing Association, 1975, pp. 341–346.

GUNN, BRUCE. "An Operational Model of the Marketing System." *The Southern Journal of Business*, July 1970, pp. 188–197.

HAAS, ROBERT W., and Leonard L. Berry. "Systems Selling of Retail Services." *Bankers Monthly Magazine*, July 15, 1972, pp. 23–27.

HALL, WILLIAM P. "Franchising—New Scope for an Old Technique." *Harvard Business Review*, January–February 1964, pp. 60–72.

HANSEN, RICHARD W. "The Growth and Development of Cooperative Retail Chains and Their Marketing Significance." L. George Smith, ed. *Reflections on Progress in Marketing*. American Marketing Association, 1965.

"Hard Times Hit the Discount Stores." *Business Week*, February 10, 1973, pp. 87–90.

HENSEL, JAMES S. "Environmental Change and the Future Structure of Retailing." *Arizona Business*, February 1973, pp. 14–20.

HILL, W. CLAYTON. "Reorganizing Distribution for Higher Profits." *Industrial Marketing*, February 1963, pp. 77–84.

HISE, RICHARD T., and Myron Gable. "An Exploratory Study of the Effort of Large Variety Chains to Segment Their Market for Different Types of Outlets." Barnett A. Greenberg, ed. *Proceedings of the Southern Marketing Association*. Georgia State University, 1975, pp. 57–59.

HISRICH, ROBERT D., Ronald J. Dornoff, and Jerome B. Kernon. "Perceived Risk in Store Selection." *Journal of Marketing Research*, November 1972, pp. 435–439.

HOLLANDER, STANLEY C. "Measuring the Cost and Value of Marketing." *MSU Business Topics*, Summer 1961, pp. 17–27.

HOLLANDER, STANLEY C. "Notes on the Retail Accordion." *Journal of Retailing*, Summer 1966, pp. 29ff.

HOLLANDER, STANLEY C. "Who Does the Work of Retailing?" *Journal of Marketing*, July 1964, pp. 18–22.

HOLMES, JOHN H. "Leverage: A Key Factor in Marketing Channel Negotiations." *Pittsburgh Business Review*, May–June 1974, pp. 1–5.

HOUSTON, MICHAEL J. "The Effect of Unit-Pricing on Choices of Brand and Size in Economic Shopping." *Journal of Marketing*, July 1972, pp. 51–69.

"How Nestle Revives its Money-Losers." *Business Week*, January 27, 1973, pp. 44–47.

"How W. T. Grant Lost $175 Million Last Year." *Business Week*, February 24, 1975, pp. 74–76.

HOWARD, MARSHALL C. "Fair Trade Revisited." *California Management Review*, Summer 1967, pp. 1–7.

HUDSON, J. L., JR. "The Market Place of the Future." *Michigan Business Review*, March 1968, pp. 1–7.

HUNT, SHELBY D. "The Socioeconomic Consequences of the Franchise System of Distribution." *Journal of Marketing*, July 1972, pp. 32–38.

HUNT, SHELBY D., and John R. Nevin, "Power in a Channel of Distribution: Sources and Consequences." *Journal of Marketing Research*, May 1974, pp. 186–195.

KANE, JAMES F. "Marketing Behavior and the Environment: An Ecological Study of the Adaptive Behavior of Marketing Agencies." L. George Smith, ed. *Reflections on Progress in Marketing*. American Marketing Association, 1965.

KARMIN, MONROE W. "Businessmen, Politicians Seek to Renew a City and Help Suburbs, Too." *Wall Street Journal*, July 26, 1972, pp. 1, 19.

KENDERDINE, JAMES M., and Bert C. McCammon, Jr. "Structure and Strategy in Retailing." Henry W. Nash and Donald P. Robin, eds. *Proceedings of the Southern Marketing Association.* Mississippi State University, 1976, pp. 117–119.

KERNAN, JEROME B. "Major Household Appliances—A Lesson in Distribution." *California Management Review*, Spring 1966, pp. 83–92.

KESSLER, RONALD. "Crime Strike Force Begins Investigation Into Garfinkle News-Distributing Firms." *The Wall Street Journal*, August 6, 1969, p. 30.

KINNEY, WILLIAM R., JR. "Separating Environmental Factor Effects for Location and Facility Decisions." *Journal of Retailing*, Spring 1972, pp. 67–75.

KIZILBASH, A. H., and E. T. Garman. "Grocery Retailing in Spanish Neighborhoods." *Journal of Retailing*, Winter 1975–76, pp. 15–21ff.

KONOPA, LEONARD J. "What Is Meant by Franchise Selling?" *Journal of Marketing*, April 1963, pp. 35–37.

KRIESBERG, LOUIS. "Occupational Controls Among Steel Distributors." *American Journal of Sociology*, November 1955, pp. 203–213.

LaGARCE, RAYMOND. "Inner-Urban Poor: An Analysis of Grocery Shopping Scope." *Mississippi Valley Journal of Business and Economics*, Spring 1974, pp. 59–68.

LaLONDE, BERNARD J., and Jerome Herniter. "The Effect of a Trading Stamp Discontinuance on Supermarket Performance: A Panel Approach." *Journal of Marketing Research*, May 1970, pp. 205–209.

LANGEARD, ERIC, and Robert A. Peterson. "Diffusion of Large-Scale Food Retailing in France: Supermarche et Hypermarche." *Journal of Retailing*, Fall 1975, pp. 43–63, 80.

LAZARUS, CHARLES Y. "The Retailer as a Link in the Distribution Channel." *Business Horizons*, February 1961, pp. 95–98.

LeKASHMAN, RAYMOND, and John F. Stolle. "The Total Cost Approach to Distribution." *Business Horizons*, Winter 1965, pp. 33–46.

LEONARD, MYRON, and Walter Gross. "The Implications of Food Chain Involvement in Low-Income Areas." Barnett A. Greenberg, ed. *Proceedings of the Southern Marketing Association.* Georgia State University, 1975, pp. 153–154.

"Lethargic Food Giant Has Glamorous History—And Balance Sheet." *The Wall Street Journal*, February 14, 1973, pp. 1, 9.

LEWIS, EDWIN H. "Comeback of the Wholesaler." *Harvard Business Review*, November–December 1955, pp. 115–125.

LOUDON, DAVID L. "Reversing the Flow of Retailing Technology: The Hypermarket Example." Henry W. Nash and Donald P. Robin, eds. *Proceedings of the Southern Marketing Association.* Mississippi State University, 1976, p. 120.

LOVING, RUSH, JR., "W. T. Grant's Last Days—As Seen from Store 1192." *Fortune*, April 1976, pp. 108–112ff.

LUDERS, ROLF J., and Allen F. Jund. "Retail Competition." *Journal of Marketing*, April 1964, pp. 22–24.

LUSCH, ROBERT F. "Channel Conflict: Its Impact on Retailer Operating Performance." *Journal of Retailing*, Summer 1976.

McCAMMON, BERT C., JR. "Alternative Explanations of Institutional Change and Channel Evolution." Stephen A. Greyser, ed. *Toward Scientific Marketing.* Proceedings of the Winter Conference of the American Marketing Association, December 1963.

McCammon, Bert C., Jr. "The Changing Economics of Wholesaling: A Strategic Analysis." Barnett A. Greenberg, ed. *Proceedings of the Southern Marketing Association.* Georgia State University, 1975, pp. 90–94.

McCammon, Bert C., Jr., and William L. Hammer. "A Frame of Reference for Improving Productivity in Distribution." *Atlanta Economic Review,* September–October 1974, pp. 9–13.

McCarthy, E. Jerome, and R. J. Williams. "Simulation of Production-Marketing Channels." Raymond M. Haas, ed. *Science, Technology, and Marketing.* American Marketing Association 1966.

McClaren, Richard W. "Marketing Limitations on Independent Distributors and Dealers—Prices, Territories, Customers, and Handling of Competitive Products." *The Antitrust Bulletin,* Spring 1968, pp. 161–175.

McDonald, A. L., Jr. "Do Your Distribution Channels Need Reshaping?" *Business Horizons,* Summer 1964, pp. 29–38.

McDonald, John. "The Strategy that Saved Montgomery Ward." *Fortune,* May 1970, pp. 168–171ff.

McGarry, Edmund D. "The Contractual Function in Marketing." *Journal of Business,* April 1953, pp. 96–113.

McLaughlin, Daniel J. "Consumer Reaction to Retail Food Newspaper Advertising in High and Low Income Areas." *Business Ideas and Facts,* Fall 1974, pp. 21–24.

McVey, Phillip P. "Are Channels of Distribution What the Textbooks Say?" *Journal of Marketing,* January 1960, pp. 61–65.

MacKay, David B. "A Microanalytic Approach to Store Location Analysis." *Journal of Marketing Research,* May 1972, pp. 134–140.

"Making Sure the Goods Get on the Shelves." *Business Week,* July 22, 1972, pp. 46–47.

Mallen, Bruce. "A Theory of Retailer-Supplier Conflict, Control, and Cooperation." *Journal of Retailing,* Summer 1963, pp. 24–32, 51.

Mallen, Bruce E. and Stephen D. Silver. "Modern Marketing and the Accountant." *Cost Accounting and Management,* February 1964.

Marcus, Mildred R. "Merchandise Distribution in Tropical Africa." *Journal of Retailing,* Winter 1960, pp. 197ff.

Margulies, Walter. "Fast-Food Chains Push Revamp to Stand Out from the Crowd." *Advertising Age,* September 15, 1975, pp. 33–34.

Markin, Rom J. "The Retailer in the Vertical Marketing Network." *University of Washington Business Review,* Autumn 1971, pp. 39–44.

Markin, Rom J. "The Superette Opportunity for the Independent Owner." *Journal of Retailing,* Spring 1963, pp. 18–26.

Markin, Rom J. "The Supermarket Today and Tomorrow." *Atlanta Economic Review,* October 1972, pp. 20–24.

Markwalder, Don. "The Changing Status of Wholesaling." *Business and Economic Dimensions,* September–October 1972, pp. 15–18.

Maronick, Thomas J., and Bruce J. Walker. "The Dialectic Evolution of Retailing." Barnett A. Greenberg, ed. *Proceedings of the Southern Marketing Association.* Georgia State University, 1975, pp. 147–151.

Martineau, Pierre. "The Personality of the Retail Store." *Harvard Business Review,* January–February 1958, pp. 47–55.

Mason, Joseph Barry. "Threshold Analysis as a Tool in Economic Potential

Studies and Retail Site Location: An Illustrative Application." *The Southern Journal of Business*, August 1972, pp. 43–53.

MATHUR, IQBAL, and Subhash Jain. "Inequity in the Ghetto Distribution Structure and Opportunity Equalization for the Ghetto Dweller." *1974 Combined Proceedings*. American Marketing Association, 1975, pp. 280–283.

MAYER, LAWRENCE A. "How Confusion Caught Up with Korvette." *Fortune*, February 1966, pp. 232ff.

MAYER, MORRIS L., Joseph Barry Mason, and Morris Gee. "A Reconceptualization of Store Classification as Related to Retail Strategy Formulation." *Journal of Retailing*, Fall 1971, pp. 27–36.

MEARS, PETER M. "An Interactive Data Base for Marketing Channels." Henry W. Nash and Donald P. Robin, eds. *Proceedings of the Southern Marketing Association*. Mississippi State University, 1976, pp. 117–119.

MELOAN, TAYLOR W. "The Old and New of Franchise Marketing." Raymond M. Haas, ed. *Science, Technology and Marketing*. American Marketing Association, 1966.

MERTES, JOHN E. "Retailer's Use of Historical Sites." *Journal of Retailing*, Winter 1971–72, pp. 54–64.

MEYER, HERBERT E. "What It's Like To Do Business With the Russians." *Fortune*, May 1972, pp. 167–169, 234–238.

MICHEL, DAVID. "Developments in the Structure of Distribution in France: A Moderate Degree of Concentration." *Journal of Retailing*, Summer 1965, pp. 34ff.

MICHMAN, RONALD D. "Channel Development and Innovation." *Marquette Business Review*, Spring 1971, pp. 45–9.

MICHMAN, RONALD D. "Foundations for a Theory of Marketing Channels." *The Southern Journal of Business*, November 1971, pp. 17–26.

MOCKLER, R. J., and H. E. Easop. "The Art of Managing a Franchise." *Business Horizons*, August 1968, pp. 27ff.

MOGULL, ROBERT G. "Where Do We Stand On Inner City Prices?" *The Southern Journal of Business*, July 1971, pp. 32–40.

MONROE, KENT B., and Peter J. LaPlaca. "What Are the Benefits of Unit Pricing?" *Journal of Marketing*, July 1972, pp. 16–22.

MOORE, CHARLES T., and Joseph Barry Mason. "A Research Note on Major Retail Center Patronage." *Journal of Marketing*, July 1969, pp. 61–64.

MOORE, JAMES R. "A Comparative Analysis of Decision Criteria Used in Channel Formation by Fifteen Industry Groups." *1974 Combined Proceedings*. American Marketing Association, 1975, pp. 440–443.

MOORE, JAMES R., and Kendall A. Adams. "Functional Wholesaler Sales Trends and Analysis." Edward M. Mazze, ed. *Combined Proceedings* American Marketing Association, 1976, pp. 402–405.

MOYER, M. S. "Management Science in Retailing." *Journal of Marketing*, January 1972, pp. 3–9.

MOYER, M. S. "Market Intelligence for Modern Merchants." *California Management Review*, Summer 1972, pp. 63–69.

MOYER, M. S. "The Roots of Large Scale Retailing." *Journal of Marketing*, October 1962, pp. 55–59.

MOYER, REED. "The Structure of Markets in Developing Economies." *MSU Business Topics*, August 1964, pp. 43–60.

MURPHY, PAT. "A Cost/Benefit Analysis of the Oregon 'Bottle Bill'." *1974 Combined Proceedings*. American Marketing Association, 1975, pp. 347–352.

NORBY, JOHN C. "Consumers' Cooperatives in Norway." *Journal of Marketing*, April 1952, pp. 423–434.

PARKET, I. ROBERT, and Manus Rabinowitz. "The Influence of Product Class Perception on Industrial Buyers' Channel Source Choice." *Journal of Economics and Business*, Spring 1974, pp. 203–208.

PARSONS, LEONARD J., and W. Bailey Price. "Adaptive Pricing by a Retailer." *Journal of Marketing Research*, May 1972, pp. 127–133.

PENNINGTON, ALAN L. "Emergence of Marketing Systems." *Tennessee Survey of Business*, February 1971, p. 13.

PETERSON, ESTHER. "Consumerism as a Retailer's Asset." *Harvard Business Review*, May–June 1974, pp. 91ff.

PETROF, JOHN V. "Customer Strategy for Negro Retailers." *Journal of Retailing*, Fall 1967, pp. 30–38.

PORT, RICHARD B. "Changing Impact of Brand Name Promotion on Marketing Channels." John S. Wright and Jac L. Goldstucker, eds. *New Ideas for Successful Marketing*. American Marketing Association, 1966.

PRESTON, LEE, and T. Hertford. "The Anatomy of Retail Price Competition." *California Management Review*, Spring 1962, pp. 13–20.

PRESTON, LEE, and Arthur E. Schramm, Jr. "Dual Distribution and Its Impact on Marketing Organization." *California Management Review*, Winter 1965, pp. 59–70.

PRUDEN, HENRY O. "The Outside Salesman: Interorganizational Link." *California Management Review*, Winter 1969, pp. 57–66.

REYNOLDS, FRED. "An Analysis of Catalog Buying Behavior." *Journal of Marketing*, July 1974, pp. 47–51.

RICHARD, LAWRENCE, M. "A Framework for the Measurement of Control in Distribution Channels." Barnett A. Greenberg, ed. *Proceedings of the Southern Marketing Association*. Georgia State University, 1975, pp. 87–89.

RIDGEWAY, VALENTINE F. "Administration of Manufacturer-Dealer Systems." *Administrative Science Quarterly*, March 1957, pp. 464–483.

ROBBINS, GEORGE W. "Notions about the Origins of Trading." *Journal of Marketing*, January 1947, pp. 228–236.

ROBERTSON, WYNDHAM. "Merchants Fight It Out in A Less Affluent Society." *Fortune*, December 1974, pp. 128ff.

ROERING, KENNETH J. "A Laboratory Study of Bargaining in Distribution Channels." Henry W. Nash and Donald P. Robin, eds. *Proceedings of the Southern Marketing Association*. Mississippi State University, 1976, pp. 178–180.

ROSENBERG, LARRY J. "A New Approach to Distribution Conflict Management." *Business Horizons*, October 1974, pp. 67–74.

ROSENBERG, LARRY J. "Retailers' Responses to Consumerism." *Business Horizons*, October 1975, pp. 37–44.

ROSENBERG, LARRY J., and Louis W. Stern. "Conflict in Distribution: A New Viewpoint." *Bulletin of Business Research*, May 1971, pp. 4–7.

ROSENBERG, LARRY J., and Louis W. Stern. "Conflict Measurement in the Distribution Channel." *Journal of Marketing Research*, November 1971, pp. 437–442.

ROSENBERG, LARRY J., and Louis W. Stern. "Toward the Analysis of Conflict in Distribution Channels: A Descriptive Model." *Journal of Marketing*, October 1970, pp. 40–46.

ROTHBERG, ROBERT. "Consumer-Retailer Loyalty." *Journal of Retailing*, Winter 1971–72, pp. 72–82.

ROTHENBERG, AARON M. "A Fresh Look at Franchising." *Journal of Marketing*, July 1967, pp. 52–54.

RUCKS, CONWAY. "Power Analysis in Distribution Channels." Henry W. Nash and Donald P. Robin, eds. *Proceedings of the Southern Marketing Association*. Mississippi State University, 1976, pp. 189–191.

RYANS, JOHN K., JR. "A Suggested Behavioral Model for Retail Decision Making." *Journal of Retailing*, Spring 1967, pp. 45–57.

SALKIN, E. LAWRENCE. "Linear Programming for Merchandising Decisions." *Journal of Retailing*, Winter 1964–65, pp. 37–41ff.

SALMON, WALTER J., Robert D. Buzzell, and Stanton G. Cort. "Today the Shopping Center, Tomorrow the Superstore." *Harvard Business Review*, January–February 1974, pp. 89–98.

SAMLI, A. COSKUN. "Wholesaling in an Economy of Scarcity: Turkey." *Journal of Marketing*, July 1964, pp. 55–58.

SAUNDERS, C. B., and J. D. Logsdon. "Retailing—What's That?" *Journal of Retailing*, Fall 1969, pp. 46–54.

SAUTER, RICHARD F., and Orville C. Walker, Jr. "Retailers' Reactions to Interest Limitation Laws—Additional Evidence." *Journal of Marketing*, April 1972, pp. 58–61.

SAWITS, MURRAY. "Model for Branch Store Planning." *Harvard Business Review*, July–August 1967, pp. 140–143.

SCHAFFER, WALTER L. "The Catalog Showroom: An Old Game with New Players." Thomas V. Greer, ed. *Increasing Marketing Productivity/Conceptual & Methodological Foundations of Marketing*. American Marketing Association, 1974, pp. 128–130.

SCHARY, PHILIP B., and Boris W. Becker. "Distribution as a Decision System." Boris W. Becker and Helmut Becker, eds. *Marketing Education and the Real World/Dynamic Marketing in a Changing World*. American Marketing Association, 1973, pp. 310–314.

SCHNEIDER, J. B. "Retail Competition Patterns in a Metropolitan Area." *Journal of Retailing*, Winter 1969–70, pp. 67–74.

"Sears' Identity Crisis." *Business Week*, December 8, 1975, pp. 52ff.

SEGALL, MORRIS S. "Some Characteristics of Retail Competition in Canada." *Journal of Marketing*, July 1955, pp. 67–74.

SEXTON, DONALD E., JR. "Black Buyer Behavior." *Journal of Marketing*, October 1972, pp. 36–39.

SEXTON, DONALD E., JR. "Do Blacks Pay More?" *Journal of Marketing Research*, November 1971, pp. 420–426.

SHANKLIN, WILLIAM L. "Dual Distribution as a Source of Channel Conflict." *Proceedings of the Southern Marketing Association*. Virginia Polytechnic Institute and State University, 1974, pp. 357–361.

SHEPPARD, E. J. "Marketing Integration in Early Ohio," *Journal of Marketing*, October 1954, pp. 166–168.

"Shopping Center Trends." *Chain Store Age Executive*, May 1976, pp. 21–49.

SHUPTRINE, F. KELLY. "The Distribution/Retailing Institution of Tomorrow." *Journal of Retailing*, Spring 1975, pp. 20–32ff.

SHUPTRINE, F. KELLY, and J. Robert Foster. "Monitoring Channel Conflict with Evaluations from the Retail Level." *Journal of Retailing*, Spring 1976, pp. 55–74.

SHYCON, HARVEY N., and Richard B. Maffei. "Simulation—Tool for Better Distribution." *Harvard Business Review*, November–December 1960, pp. 66–75.

SHYCON, HARVEY N., and Christopher R. Sprague. "Put a Price Tag on Your Customer Servicing Levels." *Harvard Business Review*, July–August 1975, pp. 71–78.

SKURSKI, ROGER. "Wholesaling of Consumer Goods in the USSR." *The Quarterly Review of Economics and Business*, Spring 1972, pp. 53–67.

SLOM, STANLEY H. "While Retail Sales Have Ups & Downs, Catalog Shopping Gains in Popularity." *The Wall Street Journal*, June 6, 1975, p. 24.

SMITH, BERNARD W. "The Continuity of Retail Problems." *Journal of Retailing*, Summer 1970, pp. 48–59.

SMITH, BROOKS E., and Danny Bellenger. "In Shopping Centers, Tenant Mix is the Key to Success.' *Atlanta Economic Review*, July–August 1972, pp. 13–15.

SMITH, PAUL E., and Eugene J. Kelley. "Competing Retail Systems: The Shopping Center and the Central Business District." *Journal of Retailing*, Spring 1960, pp. 11–18.

SOLDNER, HELMUT. "Conceptual Models for Retail Strategy Formulation." *Journal of Retailing*, Summer 1976.

SPEH, THOMAS W. "Recent Research Developments in Retailing." *Journal of Retailing*, Spring 1976, pp. 75–84, 95.

SPENCE, HOMER E., James F. Engel, and Roger D. Blackwell. "Perceived Risk in Main-Order and Retail Store Buying." *Journal of Marketing Research*, August 1970, pp. 364–369.

STARLING, JACK M. "Franchising." *Business Studies*, Fall 1970, pp. 10–16.

STASCH, STANLEY F. "The Stability of Channel Systems: Two Dynamic Models." R. M. Haas, ed. *Science Technology, and Marketing*. American Marketing Association, 1967.

STEPHENSON, P. RONALD, and Robert G. House. "A Perspective on Franchising: The Design of an Effective Relationship." *Business Horizons*, August 1971, pp. 35–42.

STERN, LOUIS W. "The Concept of Channel Control." *Journal of Retailing*, Summer 1967, pp. 14–20ff.

STERN, LOUIS W. "The New World of Private Brands." *California Management Review*, Spring 1966, pp. 43–50.

STERN, LOUIS W., Brian Sternthal, and C. Samuel Craig. "Managing Conflict in Distribution Channels: A Laboratory Study." *Journal of Marketing Research*, May 1973, pp. 169–179.

STIGLER, GEORGE J. "The Division of Labor is Limited by the Extent of the Market." *The Journal of Political Economy*, June 1951, pp. 185–193.

STURDIVANT, FREDERICK D. "Determinants of Vertical Integration in Channel Systems." Raymond M. Haas, ed. *Science, Technology, and Marketing*. American Marketing Association, 1966.

SUTHERLAND, DENNIS J. "Managing by Objectives in Retailing." *Journal of Retailing*, Fall 1971, pp. 15–26.

SWAN, JOHN E. "Parsons and Smelser's Model of Social Change Applied to the Emergence of Contractually Integrated Chains in the Grocery Trade." *The Southern Journal of Business*, October 1970, pp. 167–174.

SWAN, JOHN E. "Patterns of Competition for Differential Advantage in Two Types of Retail Institutions." *Journal of Retailing*, Spring 1971, pp. 25–35, 96.

SWAN, JOHN E. "Price–Product Performance Competition between Retailer and Manufacturer Brands." *Journal of Marketing*, July 1974, pp. 52–59.

SWEENEY, DANIEL J. "Improving the Profitability of Retail Merchandising Decisions." *Journal of Marketing*, January 1973, pp. 60–68.

SWEENEY, DANIEL J. "The Application of Computer Simulation Techniques to Retail Merchandise Management: A Feasibility Study." Fred C. Allvine, ed., *Combined Proceedings 1971 Spring and Fall Conferences*. American Marketing Association, 1972.

TALLMAN, GERALD B., and Bruce Blomstrom. "Retail Innovations Challenge Manufacturers." *Harvard Business Review*, September–October 1962, pp. 130–141.

TARPEY, LAWRENCE X., SR. "Buyer Liability Under the Robinson-Patman Act: A Current Appraisal." *Journal of Marketing*, January 1972, pp. 38–42.

TATHAM, RONALD L., Ronald F. Bush, and Robert Douglass. "An Analysis of Decision Criteria in Franchisor/Franchisee Selection Processes." *Journal of Retailing*, Spring 1972, pp. 16–29.

TAYLOR, DONALD A. "Retailing in Brazil." *Journal of Marketing*, July 1959, pp. 54–58.

"Telephone Selling." *Sales and Marketing Management*, June 14, 1976, pp. 18, 21.

"The Coming Battle at the Supermarket Counter." *Fortune*, September 1975, pp. 105ff.

THOMPSON, DONALD N. "Franchise Operations and Anti-trust Law." *Journal of Retailing*, Winter 1968–69, pp. 39–53.

TOWER, C. BURK. "Microeconomic Analysis of the Impact of Alternative Royalty Methods on the Franchisor, the Franchisee, and the Franchisor-Franchisee System." Henry W. Nash and Donald P. Robin, eds., *Proceedings of the Southern Marketing Association*. Mississippi State University, 1967, pp. 192–194.

UTTAL, BRO. "Gillette Swings a Mighty Blade Abroad." *Fortune*, November 1974, pp. 172ff.

VARBLE, DALE L., and Jim L. Grimm. "Image Assessment Can Be Administered by a Small Retailer." *Business Ideas and Facts*, Summer 1972, pp. 15–21.

VORZIMER, LOUIS H. "Rx Small Retailer Survival: Community Demand Analysis." *Journal of the Academy of Marketing Science*, Fall 1973, pp. 180–187.

VORZIMER, LOUIS H. "Social and Economic Perspectives for Black Small Retailer Development." *University of Washington Business Review*, Summer 1971, pp. 51–54.

WALKER, BRUCE J., and Michael J. Etzel. "The Internationalization of U.S.

Franchise Systems: Progress and Procedures." *Journal of Marketing*, April 1973, pp. 38–46.

WALKER, ORVILLE C., JR. "The Effects of Learning on Bargaining Behavior." Fred C. Allvine, ed., *Combined Proceedings: 1971 Spring and Fall Conferences.* American Marketing Association, 1972.

WALTERS, J. HART, JR. "Retailing in Poland: A First-hand Report." *Journal of Marketing*, April 1964, pp. 16–21.

WARSHAW, MARTIN R. "Pricing to Gain Wholesalers' Selling Support." *Journal of Marketing*, July 1962, pp. 50–54.

WEBSTER, FREDERICK A. "Model of Vertical Integration Strategy." *California Management Review*, Winter 1967, pp. 49–59.

WEIGAND, ROBERT E. "Department Stores in Japan." *Journal of Retailing*, Fall 1963, pp. 31ff.

WEIGAND, ROBERT E. "Selling Soviet Buyers." *MSU Business Topics*, Spring 1976, pp. 15–21.

WEIGAND, ROBERT E. "The Marketing Organization, Channels, and Firm Size." *The Journal of Business*, April 1963, pp. 228–236.

WEISS, E. B. "Electronic Store is Next Step in Today's Low-Cost Retailing." *Advertising Age*, June 12, 1972, p. 51.

WEISS, E. B. "The Hypermarche Marches into U.S. Mass Retailing." *Advertising Age*, December 30, 1974, p. 20.

WESTFALL, RALPH, and Harper W. Boyd, Jr. "Marketing in India." *Journal of Marketing*, October 1960, pp. 11–17.

WHIPPLE, THOMAS W., and Lester A. Neidell. "Black and White Perceptions of Competing Stores." *Journal of Retailing*, Winter 1971–72, pp. 5–20.

WIEK, JAMES L. "Discrepant Perceptions in Vertical Marketing Systems." Fred C. Allvine, ed., *Combined Proceedings: 1971 Spring and Fall Conferences.* American Marketing Association, 1972, pp. 181–188.

WIEK, JAMES L., E. Jerome McCarthy, and Donald G. Frederick. "Attitude Analysis in Marketing Channels: Two Complementary Multivariate Approaches." Thomas V. Greer, ed., *Increasing Marketing Productivity/Conceptual & Methodological Foundations of Marketing.* American Marketing Association, 1974, pp. 319–323.

WILEMON, DAVID L. "Power and Negotiation Strategies in Marketing Channels." *Southern Journal of Business*, February 1972, pp. 71–81.

WOODSIDE, ARCH G., and J. Patrick Bovino. "Consumer Images of Retail Store Personalities." *Marquette Business Review*, Winter 1971, pp. 173–178.

WOODSIDE, ARCH G., and J. Taylor Sims. "Retail Sales Transactions and Customer 'Purchase Pal' Effects on Buying Behavior." *Journal of Retailing*, Summer 1976.

WUNDERMAN, LESTER. "Direct Marketing: Its Ten Worst Problems, Ten Best Innovations." *Advertising Age*, May 3, 1976, pp. 59–60.

YOUNG, JOHN R. "The Growing Strength of Department Stores." *Journal of Retailing*, Fall 1966, pp. 41–51.

YOSHINO, MICHAEL Y. "International Opportunities for American Retailers." *Journal of Retailing*, Fall 1966, pp. 1–10ff.

Name Index

Subject Index